THE OSLO ACCORDS

THE OSLO ACCORDS

International Law and the Israeli–Palestinian Peace Agreements

GEOFFREY R. WATSON

OXFORD
UNIVERSITY PRESS

OXFORD
UNIVERSITY PRESS
Great Clarendon Street, Oxford OX2 6DP
Oxford University Press is a department of the University of Oxford.
It furthers the University's objective of excellence in research, scholarship,
and education by publishing worldwide in
Oxford New York
Athens Auckland Bangkok Bogotá Buenos Aires Calcutta
Cape Town Chennai Dar es Salaam Delhi Florence Hong Kong Istanbul
Karachi Kuala Lumpur Madrid Melbourne Mexico City Mumbai
Nairobi Paris São Paulo Singapore Taipei Tokyo Toronto Warsaw
with associated companies in Berlin Ibadan
Oxford is a registered trade mark of Oxford University Press
in the UK and in certain other countries
Published in the United States
by Oxford University Press Inc., New York

First published 2000

British Library Cataloguing in Publication Data
Data available
Library of Congress Cataloging in Publication Data
Watson, Geoffrey R.
The Oslo Accords: international law and the Israeli-Palestinian agreements/
Geoffrey R. Watson.
p. cm.
Includes bibliographical references and index.
1. Israel. Treaties, etc. Munaòòamat al-Taòrâr al-Filasòânâyah, 1993 Sept. 13. 2. Israel.
Treaties, etc. Munaòòamat al-Taòrâr al-Filasòânâyah, 1994 April 29. 3. Israel.
Treaties, etc. Munaòòamat al-Taòrâr al-Filasòânâyah, 1994 May 4. 4. Israel,
Treaties, etc. Munaòòamat al-Taòrâr al-Filasòânâyah, 1995 Sept. 28. 5. Arab-Israeli
conflict—1993—Peace. 6. Peace treaties. 7. International law. I. Title
KMM707.W38 2000
341.5′2′026—dc21 00–035611
ISBN 0–19–829891–9
1 3 5 7 9 10 8 6 4 2
Typeset in Palatino
by Cambrian Typesetters, Frimley, Surrey
Printed in Great Britain
on acid-free paper by
Biddles Ltd., Guildford and King's Lynn

To my parents

Edward J. Watson and Elizabeth R. Watson

Preface

This book presents a comprehensive legal analysis of the Israeli–Palestinian peace agreements, better known as the Oslo Accords. The book seeks to answer four major legal questions about the Oslo process: (1) Are the Oslo Accords legally binding agreements governed by treaty law, or are they non-binding political undertakings? (2) To what extent has each side complied with its obligations under the Accords? (3) Insofar as there have been violations of the Accords, what effect (if any) do those violations have on each of the parties' outstanding obligations? (4) How can international law help shape a final settlement of the Israeli–Palestinian conflict?

These questions are all complex. The first question—whether the Accords are legally binding—is difficult because the Accords do not fit the traditional definition of a treaty, which is an agreement between nation-states. The book none the less argues that the Accords are legally binding as agreements between subjects of international law. The issue is important for a variety of reasons. States tend to regard legal obligations more seriously than non-legal ones, and if the Accords are legally binding, they may affect the internal law of both Israel and the Palestinians.

The second question—whether the parties have complied with the Accords—raises knotty issues of law and fact. After extensive analysis, the book concludes that each party has a mixed record of compliance and non-compliance with the Accords. A running theme of this analysis is that each party has tended to interpret its own obligations too narrowly. In particular, neither party has fully acknowledged that its express obligations under the Accords are subject to an implied obligation of performance in good faith.

The answer to the third question—whether this mixed record of compliance terminates either party's obligations—is that the parties remain bound by the Oslo Accords. None of the parties' obligations have been terminated automatically, and while some of the Oslo violations might qualify as 'material breach' of the agreements, neither party has invoked material breach as a basis for formally terminating the Accords. A running theme of this analysis is that each party has been too quick to suspend its own obligations in response to a breach by the other. Each party has occasionally disregarded the principle that countermeasures should be proportionate to the original breach.

The book answers the final question—whether international law can help shape a final settlement—by suggesting that the Oslo Accords and general international law require both parties to negotiate in good faith. This obligation will necessitate significant compromises by both sides.

This part of the book also offers some general suggestions on how international law might shape a final status agreement.

Other books have analysed the history and politics of the Arab–Israeli conflict, but few have ventured a comprehensive, dispassionate legal analysis of the Oslo Accords. In this connection, it is worth mentioning what this book is not. It is not a history of the negotiation of the Accords. Participants on each side and journalists have already published interesting and detailed books and articles on that subject.[1] Nor is this book a legal brief for one side or the other. Anyone looking for an exclusively pro-Israel or pro-Palestinian legal argument will be disappointed. Indeed, the book will doubtless provoke protests from both sides that it is biased in one way or the other. Inevitably the book does side with one party or the other on any given issue, but its overall goal is to provide an impartial legal analysis of the Accords, not to take sides.

A word on methodology is also in order. One theme of this work is that the Oslo Accords are legally binding agreements that are governed by public international law, not by Israeli or Palestinian domestic contract law. Thus this is a book on public international law, and as such it relies primarily on the traditional sources of public international law: international agreements, customary international law, general principles of law, judicial opinions, and the writings of leading scholars. On occasion it does make reference to internal Israeli and Palestinian legal sources, since these sometimes have a bearing on interpretation of the Accords or on the content of 'general principles' of law, but in general the book relies on the traditional sources of public international law. Thus the legal argument in the book will be most familiar to those with some background in international law.

It should be emphasized, however, that the book is intended for lawyers and non-lawyers alike. Anyone who has an interest in the Middle East should be able to follow the legal arguments presented. By the same token, this work is not aimed solely at scholars of Middle East law and politics. The book assumes that the reader has some basic familiarity with the history and politics of the Arab–Israeli conflict, but it also provides (in Part I) a legal history of the conflict. Inevitably, parts of it are somewhat technical and will be of interest mainly to international lawyers and legal scholars. For the most part, though, the book should be accessible to all readers.

Some readers may wonder whether it is pointless to read a book on the

[1] See, e.g., Shimon Peres, *Battling for Peace: A Memoir*, edited by David Landau (New York: Random House, 1995); Mahmoud Abbas [Abu Mazen], *Through Secret Channels* (Reading: Garnet Publishing, 1995). For a leading account by a journalist, see David Makovsky, *Making Peace with the PLO: The Rabin Government's Road to the Oslo Accord* (Boulder, Co: Westview Press, 1996).

Oslo Accords, on the theory that the Accords will either die of neglect or be replaced by a final status agreement. During the Netanyahu era, commentators frequently suggested that the Oslo process was dead, that the Oslo Accords were a dead letter.[2] Since the creation of the Barak government, predictions of the demise of the Accords have become less common. None the less, it is reasonable to ask whether a final status agreement might not wipe away the Oslo Accords, making them irrelevant.

The answer is that the Oslo Accords will remain highly relevant whether or not the parties reach a final status agreement. The Oslo Accords have irreversibly altered the legal and political landscape in the Middle East. Even if the peace process remains stalled for the next decade, the Accords will continue to furnish the basis for Israeli–Palestinian relations, to serve as a sort of 'Basic Law' or Constitution for an unhappy polity. Alternatively, if the peace process finally does produce a comprehensive settlement, the Oslo Accords will still be at the heart of it. The Accords contain detailed, working arrangements on a wide variety of issues, ranging from security to civil aviation to extradition to human rights. The parties are not likely to throw these out and start over. Instead, any final status agreement will build on the Accords by addressing the thorny issues left untouched by the Accords: Jerusalem, settlements, borders, refugees, water, and so on.

It is therefore quite likely that the Oslo Accords are here to stay. Whether or not the flower of peace blooms or withers, the soil in which that flower is planted, the Oslo Accords, will remain.

The plan of the book is straightforward. Part I (Chapters 1–2) presents a legal history of the Arab–Israeli conflict and the peace process. Part II (Chapters 3–5) analyses whether the Oslo Accords are legally binding and, if so, on what theory. Part III (Chapters 6–9) assesses the extent of Israeli compliance with the Accords, and Part IV (Chapters 10–13) assesses the extent of Palestinian compliance. Parts III and IV also address the extent to which one party's non-compliance might relieve the other of its own obligations. Finally, Part V (Chapters 14–15) considers how international law might influence resolution of the 'final status' issues.

I would like to take this opportunity to acknowledge all of those who have helped make this book possible. I thank The Catholic University of America for its generous support in the form of research grants, and in particular Dean Bernard Dobranski, Interim Dean Robert Destro, and

[2] See, e.g., Amos Perlmutter, 'A Land Settlement First', *Wash. Post*, 17 July 1998; Steve Rodan and Mohammed Najib, 'The deferral of bright Palestinian dreams', *Jerusalem Post*, 11 Sept. 1998 (reporting that many Palestinian officials 'have declared Oslo dead').

Associate Dean Veryl Miles for helping make those grants possible. My thanks to Larry Bowring for preparing the maps. I also thank Professors Margaret Barry, Marshall J. Breger, Stacy Brustin, Susanna Fischer, William Fox, Alice Kaswan, Kathryn Kelly, Sandy Ogilvy, Antonio F. Perez, Heidi Mandanis Schooner, Ellen Scully, and Lucia Ann Silecchia for their valuable comments and suggestions. I am also grateful for the helpful comments of the anonymous reviewers retained by Oxford University Press. My thanks also to my editors at OUP, Michael Belson and John Louth, and copy-editor Cyril Cox. I am especially indebted to the thoughtful comments and criticisms of Jonathan B. Schwartz, Deputy Legal Adviser at the US Department of State.

I would also like to acknowledge the outstanding work of my research assistants Teresa Boyle, Chuck Feezor, Pete Frenquelle, Marcie Frum, Matt Hans, Mike Kaibni, Roxana Wizorek, and Erica Zuba. I would particularly like to thank Matt Hans for his substantive contributions to the work, especially his extensive research on Chapters 3 to 5. Finally, I would like to thank my wife, Anne Korbel Albright, for her incisive comments and unwavering support.

Peace in the Middle East, an almost unimaginable prospect just a decade ago, is now a live possibility. It is the thesis of this book that international law can help bring about the dream of peace.

G.R.W.

January 2000

Contents

List of Maps

PART I

Historical Background

The Israeli–Palestinian conflict has always had a legal dimension. The conflict has been waged primarily on political and military battlegrounds, but a legal war has also raged on paper, and it has been as hard-fought as any of the Arab–Israeli wars. A full understanding of the Oslo Accords requires some familiarity with the legal history of the Arab–Israeli dispute.

In a sense, the Oslo Accords comprise not just the agreements entered into since 1993, but also legal materials that are decades old. The Accords explicitly invoke a number of older legal instruments, most notably Security Council Resolutions 242 and 338. They also acknowledge the existence of a relevant body of general international law, such as human rights law. To be sure, the parties to the Accords do not agree on precisely what early instruments are still relevant, or how. For example, the Palestinians have recently asserted that the 1948 General Assembly Partition Resolution is highly relevant to interpretation of the Accords, while Israel takes a different view. Likewise, some scholars believe the British Mandate (and perhaps the Balfour Declaration, which is cited by the Mandate) never terminated and thus still has some legal force; others believe the Mandate terminated decades ago. But whatever the merits of these particular debates, it is clear that some historical materials are, in a very real sense, a part of the Oslo Accords.

Accordingly, this part of the book presents a brief legal history of the Palestinian–Israeli conflict. This chapter considers the evolution of the conflict up to 1993. Chapter 2 takes up the history of the peace process since the signing of the Declaration of Principles in September 1993.

1

Before Oslo: A Brief Legal History of the Arab–Israeli Conflict

Origins of the conflict

Jews and Palestinians both assert that their peoples have inhabited Palestine continuously for thousands of years. Each side claims further that this continuous occupation validates its claim to Palestine. Palestinians, for example, have traditionally asserted that 'they had been immemorially settled in the land where they constituted the majority', and that this longstanding occupation gave them the strongest claim to Palestine.[1] Likewise, supporters of Israel emphasize (in the words of the Israeli Proclamation of Independence) that 'the Land of Israel was the birthplace of the Jewish people', the place in which their 'spiritual, religious and national identity was formed', the place in which 'they wrote and gave the Bible to the world' thousands of years ago.[2]

These competing historical narratives are thought to have legal relevance because one traditional means of acquiring territorial sovereignty is occupation.[3] But the principle of occupation does not clearly vindicate either side's claim. To begin with, modern notions of territorial sovereignty

[1] Elie Kedourie, *In the Anglo-Arab Labyrinth: The McMahon–Husayn Correspondence and its Interpreters 1914–1939* (Cambridge: Cambridge University Press, 1976), 244 (describing the arguments of early 20th-century Palestinian Arab leaders against Britain's pro-Zionist policy). See also John Quigley, 'Sovereignty in Jerusalem', 47 *Catholic U.L. Rev.* 765, 768 (1996) (citing Henry Cattan, *Palestine and International Law: The Legal Aspects of the Arab–Israeli Conflict* (London: Longman, 1973), 65–8) (asserting that the Palestinians have the best claim because of their 'longtime status as the majority population of Palestine'). Cf. David McDowall, *The Palestinians: The Road to Nationhood*, 3 (London: Minority Rights Group, 1994) ('Today's Palestinians are almost certainly descended from the earliest recorded inhabitants').

[2] State of Israel, Declaration of Independence, 14 May 1948, 1 L.S.I. 3, ¶ 1. Indeed, it has been said that the Jews are 'the only people in the world today who possess a historical record, however obscure in places, which allows them to trace their origins back into very remote times'. Paul Johnson, *A History of the Jews* (New York: Harper & Row, 1987), 7. See also Louis Rene Beres, *Response to John Quigley*, 12 *Am. U.J. Int'l L. & Pol'y* 509, 510 (1997) ('a substantial and continuous Jewish presence has existed in the land for 3000 years').

[3] See Sir Robert Jennings and Sir Arthur Watts (eds.), *Oppenheim's International Law*, 9th edn (Harlow, Essex: Longman, 1993), §243, at 679, and §§250–5, at 686–92. Since the 19th century the doctrine has apparently been narrowed to require *effective* occupation. See, e.g., *Island of Palmas Case* (US v. Neth.), 2 *U.N. Rep. Int'l Arb. Awards* 829 (Perm. Ct. Arb. 1928); *Legal Status of Eastern Greenland* (Den. v. Nor.), P.C.I.J., Ser. A/B, No. 53, 3 Hudson, *World Ct. Rep.* 148 (requiring 'some actual exercise or display of [sovereign] authority'). But the validity of ancient Jewish and Palestinian claims must be tested by the law prevailing at the time of occupation. See *Island of Palmas Case*; Philip Jessup, 'The Palmas Island Arbitration', 22 *Am. J. Int'l L.* 735, 740 (1928).

(and its acquisition) were not familiar to the ancient world. 'When Grotius laid the foundations of modern international law [in the seventeenth century], state territory was still, as in the Middle Ages, more or less identified with the private property of the monarch of the state.'[4] Nor is it possible to apply modern notions of 'effective occupation by a state' to the ancient world; under the doctrine of inter-temporal law, 'a juridical fact must be appreciated in the light of the law contemporary with it, and not of the law in force at the time when a dispute in regard to it arises . . .'.[5] Even if we sought to apply modern notions of territorial sovereignty to an era with utterly different sensibilities, it would not be easy to determine which party had the better claim to Palestine. The Palestinians never seem to have established a kingdom or state of their own, and while the Israelites did establish great kingdoms beginning in the eleventh century BC, these did not endure.[6] The Assyrians conquered the northern kingdom of Israel in the eighth century BC, and the Babylonian Empire took control of the southern kingdom of Judah in the sixth century BC.[7]

Palestine fell under Roman rule in 63 BC and was governed by the Romans more or less continuously until the decline of the Roman Empire.[8] In AD 629 the Moslem prophet Mohammed conquered Mecca,

[4] *Oppenheim's International Law*, vol. 2, §242, at 678–9. See also F. H. Hinsley, *Sovereignty*, 2nd edn (Cambridge: Cambridge University Press, 1986), 27–44 (arguing that no real concept of sovereignty emerged until Roman times, and that it waned again after the decline of the Roman Empire).

Scholarship on sovereignty has flourished in the past few years. For some interesting examples, see, e.g., Abram Chayes and Antonia H. Chayes, *The New Sovereignty: Compliance with International Regulatory Agreements* (Cambridge, MA: Harvard University Press, 1995); Harold Hongju Koh, Review of Chayes and Chayes, *The New Sovereignty*, 91 *Am. J. Int'l L.* 389 (1997); Antonio F. Perez, 'Who Killed Sovereignty? Or: Changing Norms Concerning Sovereignty in International Law', 14 *Wis. Int'l L.J.* 463 (1996); Peter J. Spiro, 'New Players on the International Stage', 2 *Hofstra L. & Pol'y Symp.* 19 (1997); Hurst Hannum, *Autonomy, Sovereignty, and Self-Determination: The Accommodation of Conflicting Rights* (Philadelphia, PA: University of Pennsylvania Press, 1990); Jurgen Habermas, 'The European State: Its Achievements and Its Limitations: On the Past and Future of Sovereignty and Citizenship', 9 *Ratio Juris* 125 (1996); Anne F. Bayefsky, 'Cultural Sovereignty, Relativism, and International Human Rights: New Excuses for Old Strategies', ibid. 42 (1996).

[5] *Island of Palmas Case* (US v. Neth.), 2 *U.N. Rep. Int'l Arb. Awards* 829 (Perm. Ct. Arb. 1928). See generally T. O. Elias, 'The Doctrine of Intertemporal Law', 74 *Am. J. Int'l L.* 285 (1980).

[6] See generally John Bright, *A History of Israel* (Philadelphia, PA: Westminster Press, 1959), 184–266 (describing the rise of the monarchies); ibid. 269–339 (describing their fall). See also Max L. Margolis and Alexander Marx, *A History of the Jewish People*, 35–74 (New York: Atheneum, 1969) (reprint of Philadelphia, PA: Jewish Publication Society of America, 1927). For an interesting social and religious history of the period, including a description of early Israelite law, see generally Salo W. Baron, *A Social and Religious History of the Jews*, 2nd edn (New York: Columbia University Press, 1952), 1:63–101.

[7] See Bright, *A History of Israel*, 269–76 (on the fall of Israel); ibid. 326–39 (on the fall of Judah).

[8] See Johnson, *A History of the Jews*, 109 (on the beginning of Roman rule); ibid. 109–68 (on the duration of Roman rule).

and within twenty years the Moslems had occupied all of Palestine as well.[9] Palestine remained under Moslem rule, in one form or another, for more than 1200 years. In 1516 the Ottoman Turks took control of Palestine and governed it until they were driven out by British troops at the end of World War I.[10] During that war, European countries (and especially the British) conducted their policies towards Palestine on the assumption that some European state or states would replace the Turks in the governance of Palestine after the war.[11] As we shall see in a moment, European (and especially British) decisions during the war and immediate post-war period proved decisive in the political and legal development of the modern Middle East.

As with almost every other aspect of the Arab–Israeli conflict, there is intense disagreement over the demographic make-up of Palestine during Ottoman rule. There is also disagreement about the extent and cause of Jewish and Arab immigration into Palestine in the mid- to late-nineteenth century.[12] Whatever the make-up of Palestine during the early centuries of Ottoman rule, it is generally agreed that there was a large Arab majority and a much smaller Jewish population in Palestine by the end of World War I, when British troops seized Palestine as part of the Allied war against the Central Powers. Most writers put the population figures at somewhere

[9] Barbara W. Tuchman, *Bible and Sword: England and Palestine from the Bronze Age to Balfour* (New York: Funk & Wagnalls, 1956), 24–5; Johnson, *A History of the Jews*, 166; Guy LeStrange, *Palestine Under the Moslems: A Description of Syria and the Holy Land from AD 650 to 1500* (London: 1890; Beirut: 1975).

[10] For more on Ottoman administration of Palestine, see David Kushner (ed.), *Palestine in the Late Ottoman Period: Political, Social, and Economic Transformation* (Oxford: Oxford University Press, 1986; Jerusalem: Yad Izhak Ben-Zvi, 1986); Donna Robinson Divine, *Politics and Society in Ottoman Palestine: The Arab Struggle for Survival and Power* (Boulder, CO; London: Lynne Rienner Publishers, 1994).

For more on the Ottoman empire generally, see Karen Barkey, *Bandits and Bureaucrats: The Ottoman Route to State Centralization* (Ithaca, NY: Cornell University Press, 1997); Cemal Kafadar, *Between Two Worlds: The Construction of the Ottoman State* (Berkeley, CA: University of California Press, 1995); Stanford Shaw, *History of the Ottoman Empire and Modern Turkey* (Cambridge: Cambridge University Press, 1976).

[11] This is one of the recurring themes of David Fromkin's marvellous book on British policy towards Palestine during and after the World War I. See generally David Fromkin, *A Peace to End All Peace: The Fall of the Ottoman Empire and the Creation of the Modern Middle East* (New York: Henry Holt, 1989). There is a rich scholarly literature on the period, including most notably the work of Elie Kedourie. See, e.g., Elie Kedourie, *England and the Middle East: The Destruction of the Ottoman Empire 1914–1921* (London: Bowes & Bowes, 1956; reprint, Hassocks, Sussex: The Harvester Press, 1978); Kedourie, *In the Anglo-Arab Labyrinth*.

[12] For the view that Jewish settlement improved the economy and drew Arab immigrants to Palestine in the late nineteenth and early twentieth century, see, e.g., 'The Influence of Jewish Colonization on Arab Development in Palestine', 3 *Palestine Y.B.* 185, 190 (1947–8) (reprinting memorandum by Jewish Agency presented in March 1946, to Anglo-American Committee of Inquiry); see also Fred M. Gottheil, 'Arab Immigration into Pre-state Israel', in *Palestine and Israel in the 19th and 20th Centuries*, edited by Elie Kedourie and Sylvia C. Haim (London, Totowa, NJ: Frank Cass, 1982), 147–50.

around 500,000 Arabs and 100,000 or fewer Jews.[13] Those numbers are significant because they underscore the significance of Britain's decision in 1917 to endorse a 'national home' for the Jewish people in Palestine. That decision, of course, was embodied in the Balfour Declaration.

The Balfour Declaration

The Balfour Declaration was contained in a letter dated 2 November 1917 from British Foreign Secretary A. J. Balfour to Lord Rothschild, the purported leader of Britain's Jewish community.[14] There were a variety of motives for the Declaration, including Britain's desire to exert its influence in post-war Palestine, the view that Palestine was a critical overland bridge to British possessions in the East, the genuine belief that Zionist aspirations were not inconsistent with Arab and British aspirations in Palestine, and even the belief that the support of Russian Jews would help keep Russia allied with Britain in the war.[15] Although the Declaration was cast as a letter, its text had been negotiated between Balfour and Rothschild—and among various officers of the British government—well in advance. An earlier draft had endorsed making *all* of Palestine a Jewish homeland and guaranteeing an open-ended right of

For the view that Arab immigration accounted for only a small percentage of the Arab population in Palestine in the early twentieth century, see Roberto Bacchi, *The Population of Israel* (Jerusalem: Scientific Translations International, 1974), 388–9; see also Justin McCarthy, *The Population of Palestine: Population History and Statistics of the Late Ottoman Period and the Mandate* (New York: Columbia University Press, 1990), 33–4.

[13] See Martin Gilbert, *Sir Horace Rumbold: Portrait of a Diplomat 1869–1941* (London: Heinemann, 1973), 398 ('In 1918 there had been less than 100,000 Jews in Palestine, and over a half a million Arabs'); Erich W. Bethmann (ed.), *Decisive Years in Palestine, 1918–1948* (New York: American Friends of the Middle East, Inc., 1957), 19 ('In 1919 the total estimated population of Palestine was 590,000. The Jewish population of Palestine was 55,000 or nine per cent'); Johnson, *A History of the Jews*, 430 (85,000–100,000 Jews out of a total population of 600,000).

[14] For a facsimile of the letter, see Leonard Stein, *The Balfour Declaration* (New York: Simon and Schuster, 1961), frontispiece.

In Johnson's view, Walter the Second Lord Rothschild was a 'curious choice to take part in one of the most decisive events in Jewish history'. Lord Rothschild had devoted his life not to public affairs or foreign policy but to 'the silent amassing of the greatest man-made collection ever assembled', one that included more than two million moths and butterflies and 300,000 bird-skins. 'Unknown to anyone . . . he was also being steadily stripped of his fortune by an unscrupulous peeress and her husband, who blackmailed him for over forty years.' Johnson, *A History of the Jews*, 429.

[15] See Howard M. Sachar, *A History of Israel: From the Rise of Zionism to Our Time* (New York: Alfred A. Knopf, 1981), 111, 828 (describing British hopes that the Declaration might mobilize Jewish support for the Allied cause); Fromkin, *A Peace to End All Peace*, 283 (on British views on the compatibility of Zionist, Arab, and British aims in Palestine); ibid. 293–6 (on British imperial interests in Palestine); ibid. 296 (on British views on the influence of Russian Jews).

Jewish immigration, but the British balked at this broad a guarantee.[16] The final text, which was approved by the British War Cabinet, read in pertinent part:

> His Majesty's Government view with favour the establishment in Palestine of a national home for the Jewish people, and will use their best endeavours to facilitate the achievement of this object, it being clearly understood that nothing shall be done which may prejudice the civil and religious rights of existing non-Jewish communities in Palestine, or the rights and political status enjoyed by Jews in any other country.[17]

The political consequence of the Declaration was enormous: it 'electrified Jews all over the world'[18]—though not all Jews[19]—just as surely as it angered Arabs in and out of Palestine.[20] The Declaration's legal consequence, however, is harder to assess.

First there is the question of whether the Declaration was legally binding at all. At first blush it would appear to have had no legal effect, since it was neither a treaty nor an agreement between states, but the International Court of Justice has held that unilateral declarations can be legally binding on the international plane on the basis of good faith, if made with intent to be bound.[21] The formality of the Balfour Declaration,

[16] See Johnson, *A History of the Jews*, 429–30.

[17] The Balfour Declaration, 2 Nov. 1917, reprinted in Ruth Lapidoth and Moshe Hirsch (eds.), *The Arab–Israel Conflict and Its Resolution: Selected Documents* (Dordrecht, Boston: Martinus Nijhoff Publishers, 1992), 20, and in Stein, *The Balfour Declaration*, frontispiece.

[18] Martin Gilbert, *Israel: A History* (New York: William Morrow, 1998), 34; see also Sachar, *A History of Israel*, at 111 (describing the 'exhilarated' reactions of Jews in America and elsewhere).

[19] For example, Edwin Montagu, a Jewish member of the British Cabinet, regarded Zionism as a 'threat to the position in British society that he and his family had so recently, and with so much exertion, attained'. Fromkin, *A Peace to End All Peace*, 294; see also Stein, *The Balfour Declaration*, 496–501; Sachar, *A History of Israel*, 107. Fromkin asserts further that 'in his non-Zionism, Montagu was speaking for a majority of Jews'. Ibid. and 587 n. 31 (citing Stein, *The Balfour Declaration*, 66) (describing low rates of payment of the 'shekel' that indicated 'adherence' to Zionism). Cf. also Stein, *The Balfour Declaration*, 67 (stating that Zionism was 'the faith of a comparatively small minority of Jews' at the beginning of the war). But see Sachar, *A History of Israel*, 111 ('There was nothing equivocal about the reaction of American Jewry,' whose 'members hardly were less exhilarated by news of the declaration than were the Jews of Britain and Russia').

[20] Charles D. Smith, *Palestine and the Arab–Israeli Conflict*, 3rd edn (New York: St Martin's Press, 1996), 55; Bernard Wasserstein, *The British in Palestine: The Mandatory Government and the Arab–Jewish Conflict 1917–1929*, 2nd edn (Oxford: Basil Blackwell, 1991), 31–2, 97 (describing Arab protests against the Declaration in 1918 and later). For more on early Arab reactions to Zionism, and on the development of Palestinian nationalism, see generally Muhammad Y. Muslih, *The Origins of Palestinian Nationalism* (New York: Columbia University Press, 1988); Yehoshua Porath, *The Emergence of the Palestinian–Arab National Movement, 1918–1929* (London: Frank Cass, 1974); Yehoshua Porath, *The Palestinian Arab National Movement: From Riots to Rebellion* (London: Frank Cass, 1977).

[21] *Nuclear Tests* (Aus. v. Fr.), 1974 I.C.J. Rep. 253; 1974 I.C.J. Rep. 668 (NZ v. Fr.); cf. also *Legal Status of Eastern Greenland* (Den. v. Nor.), 1933 P.C.I.J. (ser. A/B) No. 53 (April 5).

and its endorsement by the War Cabinet, suggests intent to be bound—certainly more so than the comparatively informal statements of French officials in *Nuclear Tests*, in which the International Court of Justice found statements to the press to have legal consequence.

In addition, the Balfour Declaration may have been binding on the theory that it was incorporated into the 1923 League of Nations Mandate for Palestine, which clearly was legally binding.[22] Indeed, the Mandate does mention the Declaration specifically, and it paraphrases its terms almost verbatim, though this paraphrasing appears only in the Preamble of the Mandate, not in its operative text.[23] For that matter, the operative text of the Mandate expands on the undertakings in the Declaration. Thus Article 2 of the Mandate provides: 'The Mandatory shall be responsible for placing the country under such political, administrative and economic conditions as will secure the establishment of the Jewish national home . . .' The Mandate may have gone further in recognizing Jewish rights than the Declaration was intended to do. None the less, it seems fair to conclude, as most scholars have, that the Balfour Declaration was generally incorporated into the Mandate.[24] Whether the

[22] For the text of the Mandate, see League of Nations Doc. C. 529. M. 314. 1922. VI., reprinted in 44 Stat. 2184; see also Lapidoth and Hirsch, *Selected Documents*, 25. As to its binding nature, see Manley O. Hudson, *World Court Reports: A Collection of the Judgments, Orders, and Opinions of the Permanent Court of International Justice* (Washington: Carnegie Endowment for International Peace, 1934–43) 1:362 n. 1 (noting that the Mandate 'came into force' on 29 Sept. 1993).

[23] 'Whereas the Principle Allied Powers have also agreed that the Mandatory should be responsible for putting into effect the declaration originally made on the 2nd November, 1917, by the Government of His Britannic Majesty, and adopted by the said Powers, *in favour of the establishment in Palestine of a national home for the Jewish people, it being clearly understood that nothing should be done which might prejudice the civil and religious rights of existing non-Jewish communities in Palestine, or the rights and political status enjoyed by Jews in any other country*; . . .'

British Mandate for Palestine, confirmed by the Council of the League of Nations on 24 July 1922, League of Nations Official Journal, Aug. 1922, at 1007, reprinted in 44 Stat. 2184, Preamble, ¶2 (italics added). The italicized language is identical to that of the Balfour Declaration—except that it does not include Britain's undertaking to 'use their best endeavours to facilitate the achievement of this object', instead providing that the Balfour Declaration has been 'adopted by' the Allied Powers and that the Mandatory 'should be responsible for putting into effect the declaration'.

It might be argued that the Mandate's preamble imposed a broader obligation than the original Balfour Declaration, since the Mandate spoke flatly of 'putting into effect' the Declaration, whereas the Declaration itself merely obliged Britain to use its 'best endeavours to facilitate the achievement' of its 'object'. A more reasonable interpretation, however, is that the two provisions were intended to be read together. Thus the Mandate obliges Britain to 'put into effect' its earlier undertaking to use its 'best endeavours to facilitate the achievement' of the Declaration's 'object'.

[24] See George E. Bisharat, 'Land, Law, and Legitimacy in Israel and the Occupied Territories', 43 *Am. U. L. Rev.* 467, 473 (1994) (asserting that the Declaration was incorporated into the Mandate); Samira Shah, 'On the Road to Apartheid: The Bypass Road Network in the West Bank', 29 *Colum. Human Rights L. Rev.* 221, 228 (1997) (similar) (citing United Nations, *The Origins and Evolution of the Palestine Problem: 1917–1988*, at 8 (New York: United

Mandate is entirely consistent with the Declaration is a separate question, to be dealt with shortly.[25]

Arab critics of the Balfour Declaration also argued that it was invalid because it conflicted with prior British promises of Arab independence in the Middle East. In 1915 Sir Henry McMahon, the British High Commissioner at Cairo, and Hussein ibn Ali, Sherif and Emir of Mecca, had exchanged correspondence in which McMahon seemingly promised British support for Arab 'independence' in vaguely defined portions of the Middle East in return for Arab military cooperation against the Ottomans.[26] Obviously, if McMahon's promise of Arab independence included Palestine, it might be inconsistent with the Balfour Declaration, with its promise of a 'national home' for the Jews 'in Palestine'.

It is not clear, however, whether McMahon's promise of 'Arab independence' included any of Palestine. McMahon's promise excluded 'portions of Syria lying to the west of the districts of Damascus, Homs, Hama and Aleppo . . .'.[27] McMahon and other British officials later interpreted this language broadly, as excluding all of Palestine west of the River Jordan.[28] One leading historian, Professor Elie Kedourie, argues that the language 'could, in logic, equally include and exclude "Palestine" '—and therefore

Nations, 1990)); Allan Gerson, *Israel, the West Bank and International Law*, 43 (London; Totowa, NJ: Frank Cass 1978); cf. The Mavromattis Palestine Concessions, P.C.I.J. Ser. A, No. 2, at 69 (1924) (opinion of Judge Moore). Cf. also Yoav Tadmor, 'The Palestinian Refugees of 1948: The Right to Compensation and Return', 8 *Temp. Int'l & Comp. L.J.* 403, 405 (1994) (asserting that the Balfour Declaration was 'included' in the Mandate).

25 Cf. Rosalyn Higgins, Review of Gerson, *Israel, the West Bank and International Law*, 74 *Am. J. Int'l L.* 704, 705 (1980) (asserting that the 'compatibility of the Balfour Declaration with the terms of the mandate is of genuine legal interest').

26 See Great Britain, *Correspondence*, Cmd. No. 5957 (1939), reprinted in Lapidoth and Hirsch, *Selected Documents*, 3–12, and in Walter Laqueur (ed.), *The Israel–Arab Reader: A Documentary History of the Middle East Conflict* (New York: Bantam, 1970), 15. For an in-depth treatment of the McMahon–Hussein correspondence, see generally Kedourie, *In the Anglo-Arab Labyrinth.*

27 See letter of 24 Oct. 1915 from Sir Henry McMahon to the Sherif of Mecca, reprinted in Lapidoth and Hirsch, *Selected Documents*, 7, and in Kedourie, *In the Anglo-Arab Labyrinth*, 97. An earlier version of the phrase excluded '*the* portions of Syria lying to the west of the districts of Damascus, Homs, Hama and Aleppo . . .'. Lapidoth and Hirsch, *Selected Documents*, 8 n. 9 (italics added). It might be argued that the deletion of the definite article 'the' from the final text implies that some 'portions of Syria' (such as Palestine) were covered by McMahon's assurances of independence.

28 See letter of McMahon to *The Times*, 23 July 1937, reprinted in Lapidoth and Hirsch, *Selected Documents*, 19 ('I feel it my duty to state, and I do so definitely and emphatically, that it was not intended by me in giving this pledge to King Hussein to include Palestine in the area in which Arab independence was promised'); Kedourie, *In the Anglo-Arab Labyrinth*, 247 (describing McMahon's letter of 12 Mar. 1922 to the colonial office, asserting 'that his intention had been to exclude Palestine . . .'); ibid. 245 (quoting a colonial office memorandum of 3 June 1922 concluding that the 'whole of Palestine' was 'excluded' from McMahon's 'pledge').

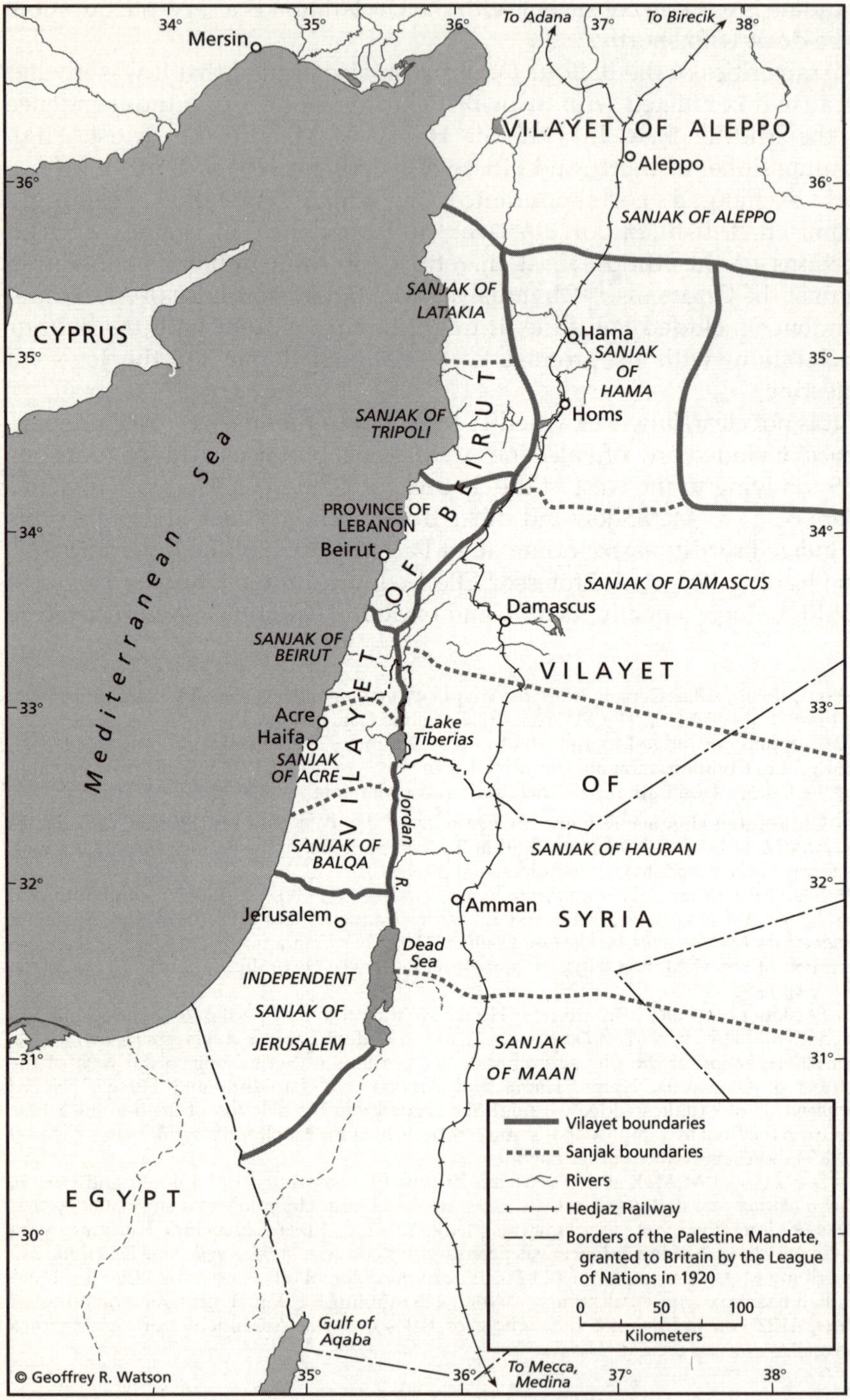

Map 1. Ottoman Administration of Palestine

'what the British government declared the phrase to mean had an authority at least equal to that of any other interpretation'.[29] Likewise, it might be argued that either reading is consistent with the underlying purpose of the exclusion of 'western' lands—to acknowledge French claims to parts of the Levant.[30] None the less, as Professor David Fromkin has observed, the letter's exclusion of 'portions of Syria west' of Damascus and three other towns in a rough north–south line should most naturally be read to exclude only areas *west* of the districts—the Syrian coastal plain—not large tracts of Palestine south-west and south-south-west of the towns.[31]

In any event, this famous interpretive debate misses the broader point: whether the McMahon–Hussein understandings had any legal effect at all. It is not that an exchange of letters lacked the requisite formality; then, as now, treaties could take a variety of forms.[32] Indeed, according to Kedourie, British officials persistently assumed that the understandings were 'embodied in a strict, contractual, treaty-like obligation', instead of pursuing arguments that they were not intended to be binding, that Hussein lacked treaty-making capacity, or that Arab promises had themselves gone 'unfulfilled'.[33] Rather, the problem is that even if the British undertakings were intended to be binding, they were made in such cautious, crabbed terms as to constitute no commitment at all. In particular, Britain made assurances only insofar as 'she can act without detriment to the interest of her ally France'—and yet, as British officials knew, France at the time claimed Palestine *and* Syria, strongly implying that

[29] Kedourie, *In the Anglo-Arab Labyrinth*, 247. At the same time, Kedourie is critical of the 'lame argument' the British government used to arrive at its interpretation—namely, the argument that the 'district' of Damascus meant the Ottoman *vilayet* of Damascus, whose western boundary ran down the River Jordan to the Gulf of Aqaba. Ibid. 246. In Kedourie's (and Hussein's) view, McMahon cannot possibly have meant the *vilayet* of Damascus, since he used the word 'district' to describe Homs and Hama, as to which there had never been a *vilayet*. Ibid. 236–7.

[30] This purpose is evident in the text of McMahon's famous letter of 24 Oct. 1915, which gave Hussein assurances only 'in regard to those portions of the territories wherein Great Britain is free to act without detriment to her Ally, France . . .'. See Kedourie, *In the Anglo-Arab Labyrinth*, 97. Even a ranking British official who was opposed to French ambitions in the interior of Syria 'recognized that France could not be excluded from the coast of Syria–Lebanon, where Christians under French patronage resided'. Fromkin, *A Peace to End All Peace*, 178–9 (describing the views of Gilbert Clayton, then the head of British Intelligence in Cairo).

[31] See ibid. 183 ('McMahon's language can be read [as referring to Palestine], but on a more natural reading he was referring only to Syria–Lebanon here, not Palestine').

[32] Cf. Lassa Francis Lawrence Oppenheim, *International Law*, 3rd edn, edited by Ronald F. Roxburgh (London: Longmans, Green and Co., 1920), §507, 663–4 (providing that there is 'no necessary form' of treaties, and that an exchange of 'personal letters' between heads of state can suffice) with Vienna Convention on the Law of Treaties, 22 May 1969, UN Doc. A/CONF. 39/27, 8 I.L.M. 679 (1969), Art. 2(1)(a) (providing that a treaty is binding, 'whatever its particular designation', even if it is embodied 'in two or more related instruments').

[33] See Kedourie, *In the Anglo-Arab Labyrinth*, 246, 249.

'Britain could not pledge support for Arab claims' there.[34] Moreover, McMahon's promise of Arab 'independence' was qualified by the assertion that 'Great Britain will give to the Arabs her advice and will assist them to establish what may appear to be the most suitable forms of government in those various territories'.[35] McMahon went on to make clear that any such 'advice' would have to come from the British exclusively. These provisions strongly imply that 'independence' really meant some form of British protectorate.[36] It is thus no surprise that some commentators have concluded that the McMahon pledges have little if any binding legal effect.[37]

Arabs also protested that the Balfour Declaration was inconsistent with the secret Sykes–Picot–Sazanov Agreement of 1916 among Britain, France, and Russia, which provided for some form of international supervision of Palestine after the end of the war.[38] The British government responded that the Sykes–Picot–Sazanov Agreement was no longer in force because Russia no longer existed, having been succeeded by the Soviet Union.[39] This theory of invalidity might be open to question,[40] but there might be

[34] Fromkin, *A Peace to End All Peace*, 183. Indeed, Fromkin argues that Britain's promises in respect of other portions of the Middle East were equally empty. As he puts it, 'Britain did not bind herself to support Hussein's claims anywhere at all.' Ibid.

[35] McMahon, Letter of 24 Oct. 1915, in Kedourie, *In the Anglo-Arab Labyrinth*, 97.

[36] See Fromkin, *A Peace to End All Peace*, 183 (interpreting these phrases to mean that any 'independent' Arab kingdom 'would have to be a British protectorate').

[37] See, e.g., Richard Wilner, Comment, 'Nationalist Movements And The Middle East Peace Process: Exercises In Self-Determination', 1 *U.C. Davis J. Int'l L. & Pol'y* 297, 313 n. 74 (1995), citing Helen C. Metz, *Israel: A Country Study*, 3rd edn (Washington: Library of Congress, 1990), 33.

[38] Exchange of Letters between France and Great Britain respecting the Recognition and Protection of an Arab State in Syria (Sykes–Picot Agreement), 9–16 May 1916, Gr. Brit.–Fr., De Martens 3, X, 350; 222 Consol. T.S. 323; Exchange of Notes between Great Britain and Russia relative to the Sykes–Picot Agreement of 9/16 May 1916, 23 May–1 Sept.–23 Oct. 1916, Gr. Brit.–Russ., 222 Consol. T.S. 336.

For an illuminating account of the secret negotiations culminating in the Sykes–Picot Agreement, and especially of the bureaucratic in-fighting surrounding it, see Fromkin, *A Peace to End All Peace*, 188–99. Many British officials felt that Mark Sykes MP—a relative novice to diplomacy—gave away too much to the French, and that Sykes failed to safeguard British interests in the Middle East. Consider this reaction, from one of Sykes' old friends:

> 'I am afraid that swine Monsieur P[icot] has let M.S. [Mark Sykes] badly down. . . . [I]t is an awful pity both for the thing itself, and for M. and also because it is one up to the old early Victorians who are in a position to say "We told you so. This is what comes of disregarding the ABC of Diplomacy, and letting Amateurs have a shy at delicate and important negotiations." '

Aubrey Herbert, quoted in Margaret FitzHerbert, *The Man Who Was Greenmantle: A Biography of Aubrey Herbert* (London: John Murray, 1983), 173, and in Fromkin, *A Peace to End All Peace*, 195.

[39] See Gerson, *Israel, the West Bank, and International Law*, 83 n. 6.

[40] Modern treaty law is distinctly sceptical about claims of changed circumstance. See Vienna Convention on the Law of Treaties, Art. 62. Similarly, modern law on state succession evinces a distinct preference for continuity in treaty relations, not a 'clean slate' rule. See

other grounds to question the validity of the Sykes–Picot–Sazanov Agreement. It might be argued, for example, that the agreement violated the emerging rights of self-determination of the inhabitants of Palestine. There is also some question about whether the Sykes–Picot–Sazanov Agreement was intended to establish enforceable rights among the inhabitants of Palestine.

In the decades since the Balfour Declaration, Palestinian critics of the Declaration have attacked its validity on broader legal grounds. In the 1960s, for example, the Palestinian National Charter asserted that the Balfour Declaration, the Mandate that later incorporated it, and 'everything that has been based upon them' were 'null and void'. The Charter also declared that any 'historical or religious ties of Jews with Palestine are incompatible with the facts of history and the true conception of what constitutes statehood'.[41] In particular, the Charter asserted that the Balfour Declaration and later instruments recognizing Jewish rights in Palestine violated Palestinian rights of self-determination.[42]

There is no question that modern international law recognizes a right of 'peoples' to self-determination. That right was recognized in some form by the international community after World War I,[43] and it was explicitly enshrined in the United Nations Charter after World War II and in the Covenants on human rights in 1966.[44] But the precise scope of that right, and in particular which communities qualify as 'peoples' entitled to exercise that right, remains uncertain. As one Secretary-General of the United Nations has put it, 'if every ethnic, religious or linguistic group claimed statehood, there would be no limit to fragmentation and peace, security

Vienna Convention on Succession of States in Respect of Treaties, opened for signature 23 Aug. 1978, Art. 2(1)(b), 17 I.L.M. 1488 (1978); see generally Geoffrey R. Watson, 'The Law of State Succession', in *Contemporary Practice of Public International Law* (Dobbs Ferry, New York: Oceana, 1997), 117–21.

41 Palestinian National Charter, Art. 20 (July 1968). The Oslo Accords obliged the Palestinians to amend the Charter to delete references calling for the destruction of the State of Israel. Palestinian compliance with this obligation is taken up in Ch. 10.

42 Ibid., Art. 19.

43 See *Oppenheim's International Law*, 9th edn, §274, 1:712 (asserting that the 'concept' of self-determination 'goes back at least to President Wilson, the post-First World War settlement, and the League of Nations'); cf. Covenant of the League of Nations, Art. 22 (establishing the system of mandates as a 'sacred trust of civilisation'); ibid., Art. 23(b) (obliging members of the League to 'undertake to secure just treatment of the native inhabitants of territories under their control'); Michla Pomerance, 'The United States and Self-Determination: Perspectives on the Wilsonian Conception', 70 *Am. J. Int'l L.* 1 (1976).

44 UN Charter, 26 June 1945, T.S. No. 993, Art. 1(2) (providing that one of the purposes of the United Nations is to develop friendly relations among nations based on respect for 'self-determination of peoples'); ibid., Art. 55 (similar); International Covenant on Civil and Political Rights, 16 Dec. 1966, 999 U.N.T.S. 171, Art. 1(1) ('All peoples have the right of self-determination. By virtue of that right they freely determine their political status . . .'); International Covenant on Economic, Social and Cultural Rights, 16 Dec. 1966, 993 U.N.T.S. 3, Art. 1(1) (similar).

and economic well-being for all would become even more difficult to achieve'.[45] Indeed, the same UN Charter that endorses self-determination also reaffirms a state's right to territorial integrity.[46] One respected scholar has gone so far as to suggest that 'the notion of a legal right of self-determination is nonsense, for how can an as yet judicially non-existent entity be the possessor of a legal right?'.[47]

Assuming that there is some meaningful right of self-determination, the question still remains why international law at the time of the Balfour Declaration should have protected Arab but not Jewish rights of self-determination in Palestine, given that there is reasonable evidence that both peoples have a long history of inhabiting Palestine, and that there was a sizeable (albeit distinct minority) Jewish population in Palestine at the time of the Balfour Declaration. In fact, the Declaration did purport to protect the interests of both peoples by respecting the rights of 'existing non-Jewish communities'—although admittedly it tilts in favour of Jewish self-determination, since there is no promise of a 'national home' for Arabs in Palestine. In so far as the document appears to protect Jewish self-determination more explicitly than Arab self-determination, it should be construed as being consistent with international law, and thus as protecting the rights of *both* peoples to self-determination.[48] Indeed, in so far as the Declaration might have purported to *disclaim* any right of Arab self-determination, it might well have run afoul of what was then an emerging *jus cogens* rule of self-determination.[49] Thus the traditional Palestinian charge that the Declaration is entirely 'null and void' appears to go too far, but there is merit to the suggestion that any such document must be construed as protecting Arab as well as Jewish rights of self-determination.

Assuming that the Balfour Declaration was valid and, further, that it had some legally binding character, the Declaration still raises some interesting questions of interpretation. One might ask, for example, whether the Declaration envisioned a single Jewish state in all of Palestine. It appears not: the plain text of the Declaration speaks of a Jewish national

[45] Boutros Boutros-Ghali, 'An Agenda for Peace', UN Doc. S/24111, ¶17 (1992), 31 I.L.M. 953 (1992).

[46] See UN Charter, Art. 2(4). See also Thomas M. Franck, *The Power of Legitimacy Among Nations* (New York: Oxford University Press, 1990), 166.

[47] Sir Gerald Fitzmaurice, 'The Future of Public International Law', in *Livre du Centenaire, Ann. Inst. de Droit Int'l* (1973), 233 n. 85.

[48] It is a maxim of treaty law that treaties should be interpreted in light of 'any relevant rules of international law applicable in the relations between the parties'. Vienna Convention on the Law of Treaties, Art. 31(3)(c). Of course, the Balfour Declaration was not a treaty, but in so far as it might have some legal effect, the rules of treaty interpretation might apply by analogy.

[49] See *Oppenheim's International Law*, 9th edn, §2, 1:7–8 (noting that the International Law Commission has suggested that self-determination is a *jus cogens* norm).

homeland '*in* Palestine', not in *all* of Palestine, leaving room for a separate Arab homeland in Palestine.[50] In fact, a 1922 Winston Churchill White Paper adopted precisely this interpretation.[51] There is also ambiguity in the Declaration's reference to a 'national home' for the Jewish people; it is noteworthy that the Declaration stopped short of an explicit reference to a 'state'. Similarly, the British commitment to this national home was less than complete; instead of flatly promising the Jews a state, the British government said it viewed such a prospect 'with favour' and undertook to 'use their best endeavours to facilitate the achievement of this object'. Finally, the Declaration promised not to 'prejudice' the 'civil and religious rights' of non-Jewish communities in Palestine, and yet made an arguably broader promise not to prejudice 'the rights *and political status*' of Jews in other countries. The reference to the 'political status' of Jews is conspicuously absent from the reference to the rights of non-Jews. Still, it may be that the drafters understood the 'civil and religious rights' of non-Jews to include 'political status'. Of course, the term 'political status' is itself undefined.

These uncertainties about the Declaration were in some ways resolved and in some ways carried forward by the League of Nations Mandate for Palestine.

The League of Nations Mandate for Palestine

Article 22 of the Covenant of the League of Nations established the system of Mandates to provide 'tutelage' to peoples 'not yet able to stand by themselves under the strenuous conditions of the modern world'.[52] Article 22 envisioned that different peoples might progress towards independence at different rates, and it was relatively optimistic about '[c]ertain communities belonging to the Turkish Empire', providing that their 'existence as independent nations' could be 'provisionally recognised' until 'such time

[50] See Gerson, *Israel, the West Bank and International Law*, 43–4; Sachar, *A History of Israel*, 109.

[51] '[T]he terms of the Declaration referred to do not contemplate that Palestine as a whole should be converted into a Jewish National Home, but that such a Home should be founded *in Palestine*. . . . When it is asked what is meant by the development of the Jewish National Home in Palestine, it may be answered that it is not the imposition of a Jewish Nationality upon the inhabitants of Palestine as a whole, but the further development of the existing Jewish community. . . .' Winston Churchill, White Paper, 23 June 1922. See also Gerson, *Israel, the West Bank and International Law*, 43–4 and n. 22.

[52] Covenant of the League of Nations, 28 June 1919, Art. 22(2) ('tutelage') and Art. 22(1) ('stand by themselves'), reprinted in Hudson, *International Legislation*, vol. 1, at 1. The Covenant forms Part I of the Treaty of Versailles of 28 June 1919, reprinted in 112 *British and Foreign State Papers* 1; Georg Friedrich de Martens, *Nouveau Recueil Général de Traités et Autres Actes Relatifs aux Rapports de Droit International*, 3 sér., 11: 323.

as they are able to stand alone'. In such cases, the 'wishes of these communities must be a principal consideration in the selection of the Mandatory'.[53] Great Britain was chosen as the Mandatory for Palestine.[54] The League Council confirmed the Mandate on 24 July 1922, and it entered into force more than a year later on 29 September 1923.[55]

In many ways the Mandate appeared to endorse a Jewish 'national home' more vigorously than the Balfour Declaration.[56] As has already been noted, the Preamble of the Mandate repeated much of the Declaration verbatim, and it also spoke of 'putting into effect' the Declaration, not just using 'best endeavours' to do so. But the operative provisions of the Mandate went further. Article 2 provided that the Mandatory 'shall be responsible for placing the country under such political, administrative and economic conditions as will secure the establishment of the Jewish national home . . .'. Article 4 provided that an 'appropriate Jewish agency shall be recognised as a public body' to advise and cooperate with the Administration of Palestine, and that the Zionist organization 'shall be recognised as such agency'. Article 6 obliged the Administration of Palestine to 'facilitate Jewish immigration' and to 'encourage . . . close settlement by Jews on the land'—a provision later invoked to defend Jewish settlement in the West Bank and Gaza Strip. Article 7 provided for citizenship for Jews who took up permanent residence in Palestine. Article 11 vested the Administration of Palestine with power to provide for 'public ownership or control' of natural resources and public works,[57] and to 'introduce a land system appropriate to the needs of the country' with a view towards 'close settlement and intense cultivation of the land'. That Article also authorized the Administration to 'arrange with the Jewish agency' the construction or operation of public works. Taken as a whole, these provisions of the Mandate elaborate considerably on the Declaration's favourable attitude towards a Jewish national home in Palestine.

On the other hand, the Mandate also elaborated on the Balfour

[53] League Covenant, Art. 22(4).

[54] On the establishment of the Mandate, see Sachar, *A History of Israel*, 116–37.

[55] Quincy Wright, *Mandates Under the League of Nations* (Chicago, IL: University of Chicago Press, 1930), 607 n. 9.

[56] Allan Gerson has said that analysis of the inconsistencies between the Balfour Declaration and the Mandate is 'pointless'. Gerson, *Israel, the West Bank and International Law*, at 43 (citing The Mavrommatis Palestine Concessions, Judgment No. 2 (Jurisdiction), 30 Aug. 1924, P.C.I.J. Ser. A, No. 2, at 6, 54 (dissenting opinion of Judge Moore)). For criticism of Gerson's view, see Higgins, review of Gerson, *Israel, . . . International Law*, 705.

[57] This provision was at the heart of a later World Court dispute between Britain and Greece over allegations that Britain had refused to recognize the full extent of a Greek national's concessionary rights in Palestine. See generally *The Mavrommatis Palestine Concessions*, Judgment No. 2 (Jurisdiction), at 6–93; *The Mavrommatis Palestine Concessions*, Judgment No. 5 (Merits), 26 Mar. 1925, P.C.I.J. Ser. A, No. 5, at 6–51.

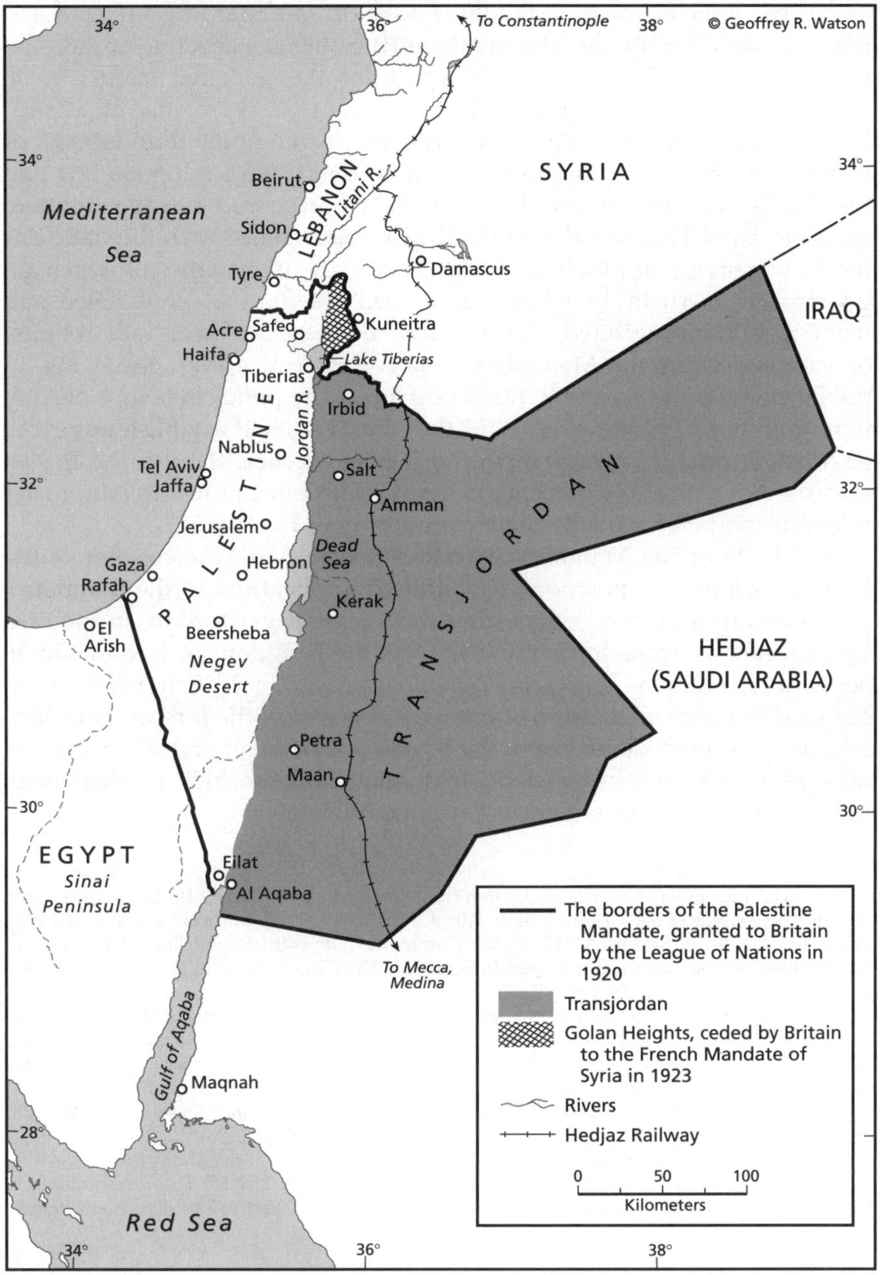

Map 2. The British Mandate for Palestine

Declaration's proviso that the rights of non-Jewish communities be respected. Article 2 of the Mandate spoke of 'safeguarding the civil and religious rights of all the inhabitants of Palestine, irrespective of race and religion'. Article 9 mandated '[r]espect for the personal status' of all people in Palestine, guaranteed their 'religious interests', and in particular provided that the *Wakfs*—charitable or religious foundations or trusts[58]—should be administered 'in accordance with religious law and the dispositions of the founders'. Article 13 preserved existing rights of access to Holy Places and forbade British interference with the 'fabric or the management' of Muslim 'sacred shrines, the immunities of which are guaranteed'. Article 15 again guaranteed freedom of conscience and worship, and it prohibited discrimination on the grounds of 'race, religion or language'. But the Mandate did not give Arabs any special role in public works projects, and it did not establish any policy in favour of Arab immigration to Palestine. Nor did the Mandate itself establish any Arab or Moslem organization akin to the Jewish Agency, though the British government did later establish a Supreme Moslem Council to administer religious matters for the Moslem community of Palestine.[59]

Article 25 of the Mandate permitted Britain, with the consent of the League Council, to 'postpone or withhold application' of the Mandate's provisions to that part of Palestine east of the River Jordan, in the area known then as Trans-Jordan and now as the Kingdom of Jordan. On 16 September 1922 the League Council approved a British proposal to suspend the implementation of Jewish rights east of the Jordan. This decision disappointed Zionists, but the British government argued that it was necessary to give effect to the McMahon pledge, which implied Arab independence in at least part of Palestine.[60]

[58] For definitions of the term *wakf*, often transliterated as *waqf*, see John L. Esposito (ed.), *Oxford Encyclopedia of the Modern Islamic World*, 14, s.v. *'waqf'* (New York: Oxford University Press, 1995), 312–16; Monica M. Gaudiosi, Comment, 'The Influence of The Islamic Law of Waqf on the Development of the Trust in England: The Case of Merton College', 136 *U. Pa. L. Rev.* 1231, 1231 n. 1 (1988) ('charitable trust').

For more on *waqfs* generally, see Michael Dumper, *Islam and Israel: Muslim Religious Endowments and the Jewish State* (Washington, DC: Institute for Palestine Studies, 1994); Majid Khadduri and Herbert J. Liebesny (eds.), *Law in the Middle East*, vol. 1, *Origin and Development of Islamic Law* (Washington, DC: Middle East Institute, 1955), 203–22.

[59] Sachar, *A History of Israel*, 170–1; Kenneth W. Stein, *The Land Question in Palestine, 1917–1939* (Chapel Hill, NC: University of North Carolina Press, 1984), 12, 29–30. For more on the Supreme Moslem Council, see generally Yitzhak Reiter, *Islamic Endowments in Jerusalem under British Mandate* (London: Frank Cass, 1996); Uri M. Kupferschmidt, *The Supreme Muslim Council: Islam under the British Mandate for Palestine* (Leiden, Netherlands: E. J. Brill, 1987).

[60] See Gerson, *Israel, the West Bank and International Law*, 44–5. As Gerson notes, the Churchill White Paper of June 1922—issued just a few months before the decision on Trans-Jordan—strongly hinted that Britain would suspend Jewish national rights east of the Jordan. See ibid.

In any event, the British government did implement the Mandate's most significant pro-Zionist feature, the provision encouraging Jewish immigration into Palestine. To be sure, British policy on Jewish immigration wobbled during the inter-war years. Indeed, Jewish immigration was rather slow in the 1920s, when times were relatively good for Jews elsewhere, but even so the Jewish population in Palestine roughly doubled to about 160,000 in that decade.[61] Jewish immigration provoked increasingly angry and violent anti-Zionist protests from the Arab population of Palestine, including bloody riots in 1929.[62] None the less, the pace of Jewish immigration grew dramatically in the 1930s, as Nazism took root in Germany and anti-Semitism spread across Europe, and as depression gripped the world economy.[63] By 1939 there were a half million Jews in Palestine. While this number still constituted a minority of the population of all of Palestine, Arab–Jewish conflict was threatening to veer out of control, and the British government felt increasing pressure to do something to mollify Arab concerns.[64]

Accordingly, in 1939 Britain issued a White Paper proposing sharp limits on Jewish immigration and calling for a single state in Palestine. The White Paper envisioned that this new state would be composed of Jews and Arabs alike, and that its Jewish population would be no more than one-third of the total population. Both sides rejected the White Paper. The Zionists, pointing to an increasingly Nazified Europe, objected to the limits on Jewish immigration, while the Palestinian Arab leadership objected to the absence of a sufficiently firm commitment to an independent Palestine.[65]

World War II brought the Nazi Holocaust, which killed at least

[61] See Johnson, *A History of the Jews*, 444.

[62] See ibid. (asserting that over 150 Jews died); Marshall J. Breger and Thomas A. Idinopulos, *Jerusalem's Holy Places and the Peace Process* (Washington, DC: Washington Institute for Near East Policy, Policy Papers Ser. No. 46, 1998), 9 (describing a massacre of 116 Arabs and 232 Jews); Gilbert, *Israel: A History*, 60 (asserting that there were 133 Jewish deaths and 87 Arab deaths, and that 4,000 Jews were forced to leave their homes); Porath, *The Emergence of the Palestinian–Arab National Movement*. Another Arab revolt against Jewish immigration took place in 1936. See generally Porath, *From Riots to Rebellion*, 140–216; Benny Morris, *The Birth of the Palestinian Refugee Problem 1947–49* (New York: Cambridge University Press, 1987), 5.

[63] Sachar, *A History of Israel*, 189.

[64] In 1937 the Peel Commission, appointed by the British government to recommend a solution to the Palestine problem, proposed partition of Palestine into a Jewish and an Arab state. Arab leaders rejected the recommendation, while Zionists were divided on it, and the plan was dropped. See Morris, *Birth of the Refugee Problem*, 5; Sachar, *A History of Israel*, 201–8, 217–19. For a map depicting the Peel plan, see Gilbert, *Israel: A History*, 626.

[65] See Sachar, *A History of Israel*, 222–6; Mark Tessler, *A History of the Israeli–Palestinian Conflict* (Bloomington, IN: Indiana University Press, 1994), 241–2; J. C. Hurewitz, *The Struggle for Palestine* (New York: Norton, 1950), 94–111.

six million Jews—two-thirds of the Jewish population of Europe.[66] Meanwhile conflict between Jews and Arabs in Palestine intensified. After the war, all efforts to mediate this conflict failed, and Jewish leaders repeatedly called for a new Jewish state in Palestine. In early 1947 Britain declared its intention to terminate its Mandate for Palestine and to refer the matter to the new United Nations for resolution.[67] In June 1947 a UN Special Commission on Palestine met for the first time in Jerusalem, and it eventually recommended partition of Palestine into a Jewish State and an Arab State.[68] Shortly thereafter, the UN General Assembly put this recommendation on its agenda.

The Partition Resolution and the founding of the State of Israel

On 29 November 1947 the UN General Assembly adopted Resolution 181 (II), which called for the partition of Palestine into a Jewish State and an Arab State, with Jerusalem to be a *corpus separatum*, an international city.[69] The vote was 33 in favour, 13 against, with 10 abstentions. Under the terms of the Resolution, the Jewish State would comprise 57 per cent of Palestine, or 14,500 square kilometres, while the Arab State would comprise 43 per cent of Palestine, or 11,800 square kilometres. The Jewish State would include about 500,000 Jews and 400,000 Arabs, while the Arab State would include more than 700,000 Arabs but only 10,000 Jews.[70] The Resolution called for the British Mandate to end on 1 August 1948.

The Zionists accepted the Partition Resolution as the 'ultimate minimum acceptable'.[71] The Arab states rejected it, arguing that they were not bound by the Resolution and that the General Assembly lacked the authority to act on the issue, and asserting that the Balfour Declaration

[66] For one breakdown of the numbers of Jews killed by nationality, see Sachar, *A History of Israel*, 249. For a sampling of the overwhelming volume of literature on the history of the Holocaust, see Saul Friedlander, *Nazi Germany and the Jews* (New York: HarperCollins 1997); Saul Friedlander, *Memory, History, and the Extermination of the Jews of Europe* (Bloomington: Indiana University Press, 1993); Raul Hilberg, *The Destruction of the European Jews* (New York: Holmes and Meier, 1985); Yehuda Bauer with Nili Keren, *A History of the Holocaust* (New York: F. Watts, 1982); Yehuda Bauer, *The Holocaust in Historical Perspective* (Seattle: University of Washington Press, 1978); Lucy S. Dawidowicz, *The War Against the Jews, 1933–1945* (New York: Holt, Rinehart, and Winston, 1975).

[67] S. Ettinger, 'The Modern Period', in *A History of the Jewish People*, ed. H. H. Ben-Sasson (Cambridge, MA: Harvard University Press, 1976), 1044.

[68] Ibid. 1052; Morris, *Birth of the Refugee Problem*, 6.

[69] Palestine Partition Plan, G.A. Res. 181(II), UN Doc. A/519, at 131 (1947), reprinted in Lapidoth and Hirsch, *Selected Documents*, 33.

[70] See Gilbert, *Israel: A History*, 149.

[71] The Acceptance of the Above Resolution by the Representatives of the Jewish Community in Palestine, UN GAOR, 2nd Sess., Ad hoc Comm. on Palestine Question, UN Doc. A/364, at 12–19 (1947); Gerson, *Israel, the West Bank and International Law*, 47.

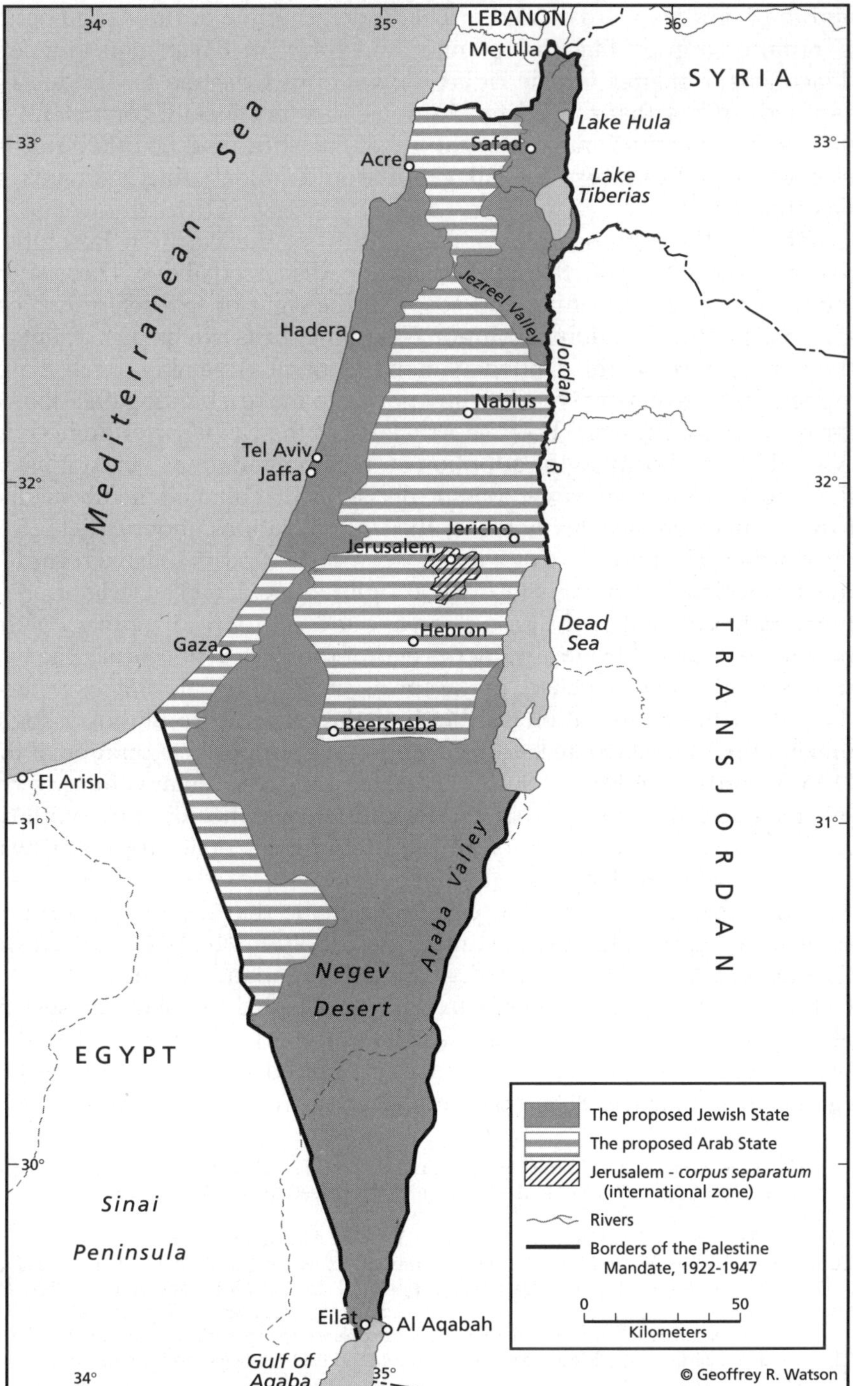

Map 3. The 1947 UN Partition Plan for Palestine

and the Mandate were invalid.[72] The Representative of the Arab Higher Committee argued that the 'manner and form' of Palestinian independence was 'a matter for the rightful owners of Palestine to decide'. He asserted further that the United Nations was 'not legally competent' to decide the 'constitutional organization' of Palestine, and he called for the election of a legislature by 'all genuine and law-abiding nationals of Palestine'.[73]

Some of the arguments over the validity of the Partition Resolution resemble those over the Balfour Declaration, discussed above. These arguments turn on the meaning and scope of the right of self-determination. But whether the Partition Resolution is binding turns to a greater extent on the competence of the United Nations General Assembly. Arab states argued that the Assembly lacked any power to make a binding decision on the question of Palestine because Article 10 of the UN Charter limited the Assembly's authority to the adoption of 'recommendations', in contrast to the Security Council's power to issue decisions that bind all members (and to a certain extent non-members) of the United Nations under Article 25 of the Charter. The new State of Israel, by contrast, appears to have regarded the Resolution as a document of legal significance; Israel's Declaration of Independence invoked the Resolution as one basis for the legitimacy of the new Jewish state.[74] Ironically, by the end of the twentieth century the two sides seem to have switched. In the spring of 1999 the Palestinians argued that the Partition Resolution was binding; they saw the Resolution as legitimizing their threats to declare a state upon the supposed expiration of the Oslo Accords on 4 May 1999. At the same time, the Netanyahu government argued strenuously that the Resolution was not binding, without explaining why Israel once found the Resolution so relevant that it was cited in Israel's Proclamation of Independence.

In any event, there is a fair case to be made that the Resolution had some legal effect, at least at the time of its adoption. The UN Charter gave the General Assembly an important role in the management of the new UN trusteeship system, which effectively succeeded the Mandate system of the League of Nations. Article 77(1) of the Charter provided that Mandate territories 'may' (not 'must') be placed under UN trusteeship agreements,[75] Article 83 vested the Security Council with power over

[72] The Rejection of the Above Resolution by the Arab States and the Higher Arab Committee, UN GAOR, 2nd Sess., Ad hoc Comm. on Palestine Question, UN Doc. A/364, at 5–11 (1947).

[73] The Rejection of the Above Resolution by the Arab States and the Higher Arab Committee, UN GAOR, 2nd Sess., Ad hoc Comm. on Palestine Question, UN Doc. A/364, at 5–11 (1947) (statement of Mr Husseini), reprinted in Lapidoth and Hirsch, *Selected Documents*, 57.

[74] Israel, Declaration of Independence, ¶9.

[75] The International Court of Justice has interpreted the permissive language of the Charter as not requiring a Mandatory to place a mandated territory under trusteeship. See

'strategic' trust territories, and Article 85(1) vested the General Assembly with authority over all other non-strategic trusts. Moreover, Article 80(1) provided that the Charter did not 'alter in any manner' the terms of existing arrangements, and the International Court of Justice subsequently indicated that the General Assembly would assume the supervisory functions formerly carried out by the League.[76] To be sure, the International Court has equivocated on the scope of the Assembly's power to make binding decisions in respect of former Mandates,[77] and the Partition Resolution itself called on the Security Council to implement its terms, implying that the authors of the Partition Resolution did not believe it to be binding in and of itself.[78] Moreover, the Security Council, already beginning to suffer from the Cold War paralysis that would grip it for the next forty years, took no action on the Partition plan. Still, the better view would seem to be that the plain text of Article 85 of the Charter does give the Assembly power (including 'alteration or amendment') over trusteeships, including a Mandate that the Mandatory has referred to the United Nations for disposition.

But even if the Partition Resolution was binding at the time of its adoption, it is unlikely that it is still binding today. Unlike Security Council Resolution 242, which was accepted by most of the relevant parties, General Assembly Resolution 181(II) was vigorously rejected by the Arab states. After 1948, no state in the region behaved as if the Resolution was binding, leading some to conclude that the Resolution simply lapsed.[79] It has been argued, however, that this state practice alone can not abrogate a binding obligation under the UN Charter.[80] Article 103 of the Charter

International Status of South-West Africa, 1950 I.C.J. 128 (Advisory Opinion of 11 July 1950) (8–6 decision on this issue).

[76] Ibid. 130. See also *Legal Consequences for States of the Continued Presence of South Africa in Namibia Notwithstanding Security Council Resolution 276*, 1971 I.C.J. 70.

[77] A majority in the *Namibia* case held that Assembly resolutions might have binding effect but stopped short of such a holding on the facts of that case. See 1971 I.C.J. at 49–50 (suggesting that the Assembly is not 'disbarred from adopting . . . resolutions which make determinations or have operative design'). A number of the various concurring opinions expressed the view that the Assembly's resolution in the Namibia case was binding. See, e.g., 1971 I.C.J. at 61 (opinion of Judge Kahn); ibid. 146–7 (opinion of Judge Onyeama). See generally Gerson, *Israel, the West Bank, and International Law*, 48–9 and nn.

[78] See U.N.G.A. Res. 181 (II), ¶7 (requesting the Council to take 'necessary measures' to implement the resolution), reprinted in Lapidoth and Hirsch, *Selected Documents*, 33; 10 UN SCOR, 263rd mtg. (1974).

[79] See Shlomo Slonim, 'The United States and the Status of Jerusalem 1947–1984', 19 *Isr. L. Rev.* 179, 229 (1984) ('Even if it is accepted that the Partition Resolution was binding when it was adopted, it lapsed after May 15 when the United Nations and the other parties concerned failed to implement the resolution').

[80] See Henry Cattan, *Jerusalem* (New York: St Martin's Press, 1981), 105–6 ('The non-implementation or even the violation of a UN resolution does not entail its lapse or abrogation').

does, of course, provide that Charter norms override obligations 'under any other international agreement'. Strikingly, however, Article 103 says nothing about conflicting obligations under customary law, or about new norms of customary law that post-date the Charter norm in question. Indeed, Article 103 might not stamp out all conflicting obligations under customary law; for example, it might not apply to peremptory norms (*jus cogens*) that are superior even to Charter norms.[81] But even assuming that Article 103 requires fidelity to Charter norms over conflicting customary norms, Article 103 does not rule out the possibility that customary law might itself create new Charter norms—i.e. that subsequent practice of states or the United Nations or both might result in 'a new interpretation of Charter provisions'.[82]

Indeed, the practice of the United Nations suggests that it acquiesced in—or even implicitly endorsed—the demise of the Partition Resolution. In the years after the establishment of the State of Israel, resolutions of the General Assembly and Security Council generally avoided mention of the Partition Resolution.[83] Immediately after its adoption, there were some half-hearted attempts to delimit the new frontier and take other steps in preparation for partition,[84] but the partition plan obviously was not implemented after the 1948 War. After 1948, UN resolutions did not generally rely on the Partition Resolution. Instead, they more typically pointed to legal instruments reflective of the actual situation on the ground, such as the 1949 Armistice Agreements. This neglect of the Partition Resolution might suggest acquiescence in its death.[85] Moreover, Security Council Resolution 242—which is, as we shall see in a moment, binding—implicitly superseded the territorial formula in the Partition Resolution, since it called only for Israeli withdrawal from territories occupied in the 1967 War, not withdrawal to the borders envisioned by the Partition Resolution. The Oslo Accords themselves invoke Resolution 242 (and Resolution 338), not the Partition Resolution; this is further evidence that the relevant framework begins with Resolution 242, not the Partition Resolution.

In any event, the Partition Resolution was never put into effect, and in 1948 Palestine slid towards war. In early 1948 Arab states threatened

[81] See Geoffrey R. Watson, 'Constitutionalism, Judicial Review, and the World Court', 34 *Harv. Int'l L. J.* 1, 36–7 (1993).

[82] Bruno Simma (ed.), *The Charter of the United Nations: A Commentary* (New York: Oxford University Press, 1994), 1121.

[83] See Michael Eisner, 'Jerusalem: An Analysis of Legal Claims and Political Realities', 12 *Wis. Int'l L.J.* 221, 255–6 (1994).

[84] See generally UN Palestine Commission, *1st Monthly Report to the Security Council*, S/663, 29 Jan. 1948.

[85] Cf. Elihu Lauterpacht, *Jerusalem and the Holy Places* (London: Anglo-Israel Association, 1968), 36 (arguing that the UN acquiesced in the 'demise' of an internationalized Jerusalem).

forcible 'defence' of Palestine, and Arab guerrillas infiltrated Palestine in order to frustrate partition.[86] In the spring of 1948, the Zionists adopted their 'Plan Dalet' (i.e. 'Plan D'), whose announced goal was to 'gain control of the territory of the Hebrew State and defend its borders' and to gain control of 'areas of Jewish settlement and population' outside the area designated for the Jewish State.[87] Palestinians charge that this Plan was implemented by a large-scale campaign of forced expulsions of Arabs, while Israel denies that there was any policy of forced expulsion. The truth probably lies somewhere between: the Plan did not endorse ethnic cleansing of all Arabs from the future Israel, but it did give military commanders discretion on how to secure their objectives, and in some cases commanders did expel Arab inhabitants who resisted.[88]

In the meantime, the British were taking steps to withdraw from Palestine, both militarily and legally. In late 1947, as violence broke out between Arabs and Jews, the British found themselves increasingly unable to impose order in Palestine. On 11 December 1947 the British colonial secretary announced that Britain would terminate its Mandate for Palestine on 15 May 1948.[89] By the spring of 1948 there was an exodus of British troops from Palestine.[90] By 15 May most British troops and administrators had departed, and the Mandate terminated on that day. It has been argued that Britain lacked the authority unilaterally to terminate a League of Nations Mandate, and that termination required the approval of the League's successor—the United Nations.[91] If true, this argument might suggest that the Mandate is still a source of legal obligations for the parties to the Oslo Accords. But the 1947 UN Partition Resolution had explicitly provided: 'The Mandate for Palestine shall terminate as soon as possible but in any case no later than 1 August 1948,' which would seem to remove any doubt about Britain's authority to terminate the Mandate.[92]

[86] UN Palestine Commission, *1st Special Report*, 16 Feb. 1948, S/676, ¶¶8–9; Gerson, *Israel, the West Bank and International Law*, 49–50.

[87] Gilbert, *Israel: A History*, 166.

[88] For a relatively balanced look at the 'Plan Dalet' and the larger refugee issue, see generally Morris, *Birth of the Refugee Problem*.

[89] See Rosalyn Higgins, *United Nations Peacekeeping 1946–1967: Documents and Commentary* (London, New York: Oxford University Press, 1969–81), 1:8–11.

[90] Gilbert, *Israel: A History*, 154–5 (late 1947); ibid. 171 (spring of 1948).

[91] See Eugene V. Rostow, ' "Palestinian Self-Determination": Possible Futures for the Unallocated Territories of the Palestine Mandate', 5 *Yale Stud. in World Pub. Order* 147, 159 (1979).

[92] Partition Resolution, Part III.D., in Lapidoth and Hirsch, 52. Other commentators have concluded that the Mandate did terminate on 15 May 1948. See, e.g., Richard A. Falk and Burns H. Weston, 'The Relevance of International Law to Palestinian Rights in the West Bank and Gaza: In Legal Defense of the Intifada', 32 *Harv. Int'l L.J.* 129, 140 (1991); Higgins, *United Nations Peacekeeping*, 1:14; Eisner, 'Jerusalem', 249–50; Slonim, 'The United States and the Status of Jerusalem', 228 n. 165.

On 14 May 1948, the date before the Mandate terminated, David Ben-Gurion proclaimed the establishment of the State of Israel.[93] The next day, armies of five Arab states invaded Israel.[94] The Arab forces were outmatched and, to some extent, divided among themselves, and Israel eventually prevailed. The Partition Resolution had envisioned that Israel would control 57 per cent of Palestine; by 1949, when Israel concluded armistice agreements with its Arab neighbours, it controlled 73 per cent of Palestine.[95] Trans-Jordan controlled the West Bank and the eastern part of Jerusalem, including the Old City; Egypt controlled the Gaza Strip. The war resulted in hundreds of thousands of Arab refugees. To this day, there is intense debate over how many refugees voluntarily left Palestine and how many were driven out.[96]

Some scholars also continue to debate whether the founding of the State of Israel was legal. It has been suggested, for example, that Israel could not base its claim to statehood on the Partition Resolution because it was non-binding and invalid, and that Israel had no historic claim to statehood.[97] As we have seen, however, the Charter did empower the General Assembly to act on questions relating to trusteeships, and Britain's abdication in favour of UN disposition of the Mandate for Palestine plainly gave the United Nations authority to act. In any event, the Partition Resolution certainly gave a certain political and moral validity to Israel's claim to statehood.[98] As for the historical argument, it is difficult to see why Arabs but not Jews should be entitled to invoke their

[93] Declaration, 1 L.S.I. 3 (1948) (Isr.). Because the Mandate was set to expire during the Jewish Sabbath on 15 May, Ben-Gurion chose to declare independence on Friday, 14 May. See Gilbert, *Israel: A History*, 186.

[94] Ibid. 191.

[95] Gerson, *Israel, the West Bank and International Law*, 63–4. For the text of the Armistice Agreements, see Hashemite Jordan Kingdom–Israel: General Armistice Agreement, 3 Apr. 1949, Jordan–Isr., 42 U.N.T.S. 303; Israeli–Syrian General Armistice Agreement, 20 July 1949, Isr.–Syria, 42 U.N.T.S. 327; Egyptian–Israeli General Armistice Agreement, 24 Feb. 1949, Egypt–Isr., 42 U.N.T.S. 251; Israeli–Lebanese General Armistice Agreement, 23 Mar. 1949, Isr.–Leb., 42 U.N.T.S. 287.

[96] See Morris, *Birth of the Refugee Problem*. For one of many examples of the competing narratives of the parties, see David Shipler's account of how the two sides have characterized the massacre by Jewish radicals of civilian Arabs in the village of Deir Yassin. David Shipler, *Arab and Jew: Wounded Spirits in a Promised Land* (New York: Times Books, 1986), 37–41, 201–2, 206. Cf. also ibid. 33–4 (reporting that Israeli censors prohibited former Prime Minister Yitzhak Rabin from publishing an account of his involvement in 'driving out' the civilian populations of Lod and Ramle during the 1948 War).

[97] John Quigley, *Politics, Law, and Society: Palestine and Israel: A Challenge to Justice* (Durham, NC: Duke University Press, 1990), 47–53.

[98] Cf. James E. Hopenfeld, Review of Quigley, *A Challenge to Justice*, 89 *Mich. L. Rev.* 1800, 1806 (1991) (asserting that the Partition Resolution created a 'moral basis' for statehood).

Professor Schachter has also argued that General Assembly resolutions might serve as 'evidence' of customary law, and in that sense play some role in the formation of international law. See Oscar Schachter, 'International Law in Theory and Practice', 178 *Rec. des Cours* 111–21 (1982–V). Be that as it may, it is difficult to make the case that customary law had recognized a partition of Palestine by late 1947, when no partition had ever been achieved.

historical connection to the land as a basis for self-determination in Palestine.[99] In any event, Israel's statehood is now long past dispute. Dozens of states recognize Israel. Its longtime nemesis, the PLO, has done so itself.[100] Israel meets the traditional objective test of statehood, including territory, population, government, and foreign relations.[101] Israel's membership in the United Nations is further evidence of its valid claim to statehood.[102]

The next two decades did not bring any improvement in Arab–Israeli relations. Nor did it bring about any significant change in the position of the parties as a matter of international law. Jordan purported to annex the West Bank, but this act was recognized by only two states, Britain and Pakistan; it would be another forty years before Jordan would finally surrender its claim to the West Bank. The Suez crisis of 1956 worsened Arab–Israeli relations but again did not appreciably change the legal situation: Israel, France, and Britain jointly invaded Egypt, only to be forced to retreat in the face of determined opposition from the United States and the international community.[103] Israel's relations with its neighbours remained tense through the next decade.

The 1967 War and Resolution 242

The next major development from the standpoint of international law was the Six-Day War of June 1967. The principal legal issue surrounding the war itself was whether Israel's pre-emptive strike on Egyptian airfields on 5 June 1967 was an unlawful use of force or a permissible instance of 'anticipatory self-defence' against an imminent attack. The answer to this question bears on the legality of Jordan's attack on Israel, which took place shortly after Israel's strike on Jordan's ally Egypt. If Israel's strike was an act of aggression, then Jordan's attack was a permissible instance of collective self-defence; if Israel's strike was a justifiable exercise of self-defence, then Jordan's attack was an act of aggression. As usual, there are both factual and legal components to the debate.

[99] See Hopenfeld, Book Review, 1806 and n. 15.

[100] Letter of 9 Sept. 1993 from Yasser Arafat to Yitzhak Rabin, reprinted in David Makovsky, *Making Peace with the PLO: The Rabin Government's Road to the Oslo Accord* (Boulder, CO: Westview Press, 1996), 201.

[101] Montevideo Convention on Rights and Duties of States, 26 Dec. 1933, art. 1, 165 L.N.T.S. 19, 25. See Geoffrey R. Watson, 'Progress for Pilgrims? An Analysis of the Holy See–Israel Fundamental Agreement', 47 *Catholic U. L. Rev.* 497, 500 (1998) (arguing that Israel is 'unquestionably' a state).

[102] Cf. UN Charter Art. 4(1) (making UN membership available to all peace-loving 'states'); Watson, 'Progress for Pilgrims?', 502.

[103] See Gerson, *Israel, the West Bank and International Law*, 65–70.

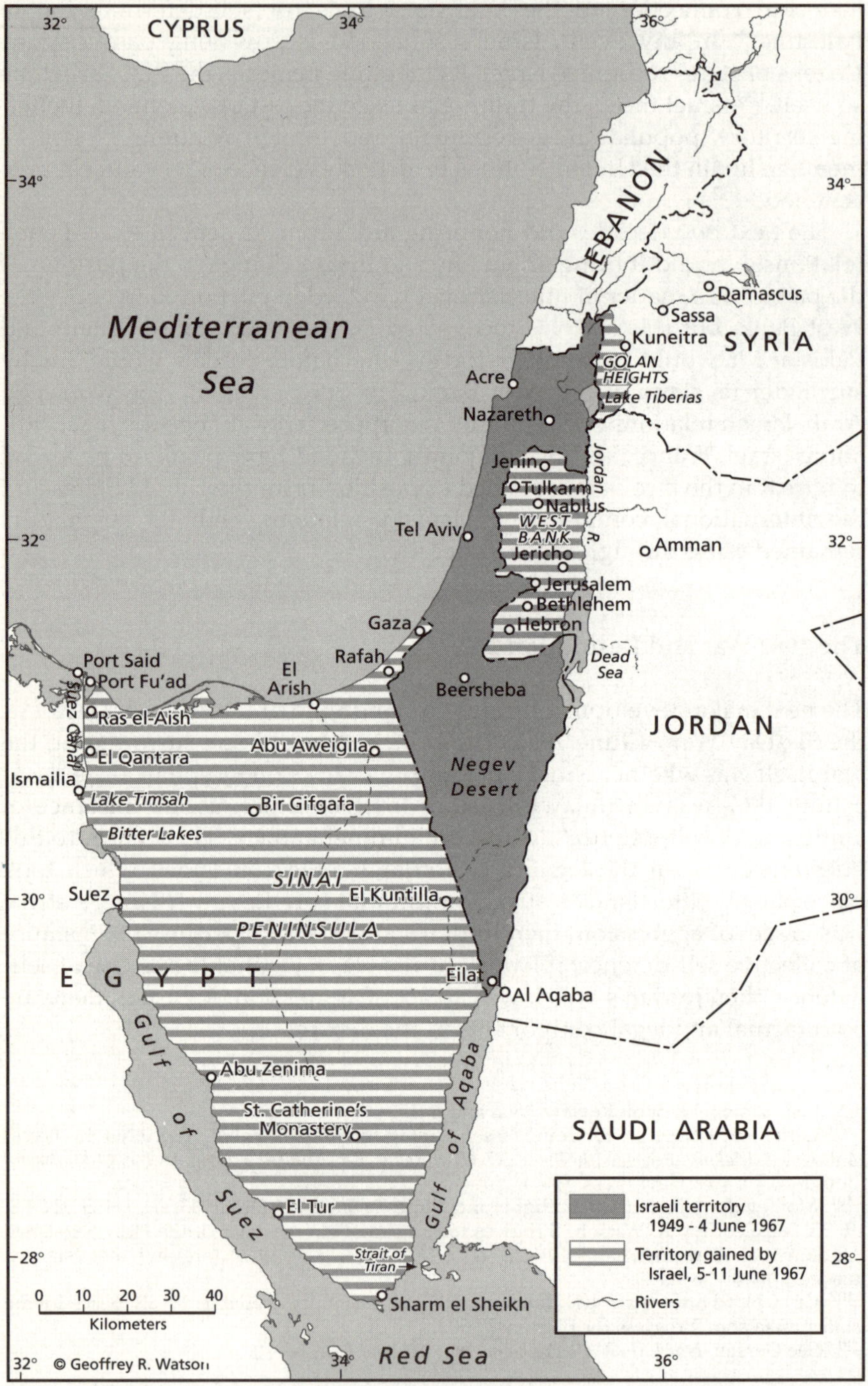

Map 4. Territory Gained by Israel in 1967

As to facts, Israel asserts that Egypt and other Arab states were facilitating guerrilla attacks against Israel in the months and years leading up to the 1967 War; that Egypt had closed the Straits of Tiran, strangling Israel's shipping; and that Egypt and other Arab states had amassed troops on Israel's border and threatened Israel with imminent invasion.[104] Arabs assert that Israel used *fedayeen* attacks as a pretext for harassing its neighbours, as a 'policy of border belligerence', that Israel acted 'increasingly as an instrument of Western domination', and that the closure of the Straits of Tiran 'provided Israel with the pretext for attack'.[105] The common theme to these narratives is that there were guerrilla attacks on Israel; that Israel engaged in reprisals against them; and that Egypt closed the Straits of Tiran to Israeli ships.

The relevant law is also in dispute. Scholars have long disagreed over whether there is any doctrine of 'anticipatory self-defence' at all, given that Article 51 of the Charter permits self-defence only in response to an 'armed attack'.[106] Still, most scholars, particularly in recent decades, have endorsed the notion that a state may defend itself from an attack that is clearly imminent.[107] That view is eminently sensible. It certainly comports with the overwhelming position of states in their domestic criminal and tort law[108]—a body of law that can have some bearing on the rules of international law.[109]

[104] See ibid. 70–3. See also Randolph S. Churchill and Winston S. Churchill, *The Six-Day War* (Boston, MA: Houghton Mifflin, 1967), 53–5; Walter Laqueur, *The Road to War, 1967: The Origins of the Arab–Israeli Conflict*, 2nd edn (London: Weidenfeld & Nicolson, 1969).

[105] McDowall, *The Palestinians*, 38. For similar views, see Henry Cattan, *Palestine, The Arabs and Israel: The Search for Justice* (London: Longmans, 1969).

[106] Cf. Phillip Jessup, *A Modern Law of Nations: An Introduction* (New York: Macmillan, 1948), 166–7 (arguing that 'alarming military preparations by a neighboring state would justify a resort to the Security Council, but would not justify resort to anticipatory force') with Louis Henkin, *How Nations Behave: Law and Foreign Policy*, 2nd edn (New York: published for the Council on Foreign Relations by Columbia University Press, 1979), 143–5 (endorsing a limited concept of anticipatory self-defence on the grounds that 'the only meaningful defense for the potential victim might indeed be the pre-emptive attack').

[107] See, e.g., Richard Gardner, 'Commentary on the Law of Self-Defense', in Laurie Fisler Damrosch and David J. Scheffer (eds.), *Law and Force in the New International Order* (Boulder: Westview Press, 1991), 51–2; Oscar Schachter, 'The Right of States to Use Armed Force', 82 *Mich L. Rev.* 1620, 1633–5 (1982); Brunson MacChesney, 'Some Comments on the "Quarantine" of Cuba', 57 *Am. J. Int'l L.* 592, 596 (1963) (arguing that the 'quarantine' of Cuba was an example of permissible 'anticipatory' self-defence).

[108] See Timothy L. H. McCormack, *Self-Defense in International Law: The Israeli Raid on the Iraqi Nuclear Reactor* (New York: St Martin's Press; Jerusalem: The Magnes Press, The Hebrew University, 1996), 271; George K. Walker, 'Anticipatory Collective Self-Defense in the Charter Era: What the Treaties Have Said', 31 *Cornell Int'l L.J.* 321, 358 n. 248 (1998) ('Most municipal legal systems recognize a right of anticipatory self-defense') (citing McCormack). For a recent example from US law, see *State v. Janes*, 121 Wash. 2d 220, 850 P.2d 495 (1993) ('Imminence does not require an actual physical assault. A threat, or its equivalent, can support self-defense when there is a reasonable belief that the threat will be carried out').

[109] See Statute of the International Court of Justice, Art. 38(1)(c) (providing that 'general principles' of law can be sources of international law).

Applying the law of anticipatory self-defence to the 1967 War, most (though not all) commentators have come to the conclusion that Israel's first strike was justifiable on self-defence grounds.[110] This conclusion is well-founded. The closing of the Straits of Tiran, together with the massing of troops on Israel's borders and vows to destroy Israel,[111] suggest that an attack on Israel was indeed imminent. Even a large majority of the United Nations General Assembly—a body not noted for being particularly pro-Israel—refused to condemn Israel's first strike as a violation of international law.[112] The Security Council likewise refused to condemn Israel's strike.[113]

The United Nations did, however, take a position on the aftermath of the Six-Day War, which left Israel in control of the Gaza Strip, the Sinai Peninsula, the Golan Heights, and the West Bank, including all of Jerusalem. On 22 November 1967 the Security Council adopted Resolution 242, the resolution that still provides the framework for Arab–Israeli peace. It provides:

The Security Council,

Emphasizing the inadmissibility of the acquisition of territory by war and the need to work for a just and lasting peace in which every State in the area can live in security,

1. *Affirms* that the fulfillment of Charter principles requires the establishment of a just and lasting peace in the Middle East which should include the application of both the following principles:
   - (i) Withdrawal of Israel armed forces from territories occupied in the recent conflict;
   - (ii) Termination of all claims or states of belligerency and respect for and acknowledgement of the sovereignty, territorial integrity and political independence of every State in the area and their right to live in peace within secure and recognized boundaries free from threats or acts of force;

[110] See, e.g., Gardner, 'Commentary', 51–2 ('I think most people felt that was justified self-defense'); Gerson, *Israel, the West Bank and International Law*, 70–4; Thomas M. Franck, 'Who Killed Article 2:4?', 64 *Am. J. Int'l L.* 804 (1970); Eugene V. Rostow, 'Legal Aspects of the Search for Peace in the Middle East', 64 *Proc. of the Am. Soc. of Int'l L.* 64, 67 (1970); Yoram Dinstein, 'The Legal Issues of "Para-War" and Peace in the Middle East', 44 *St John's L. Rev.* 466, 469–70 (1970).

For the opposing view, see, e.g., Quigley, *A Challenge to Justice*, 161–7. See also Ch. 5 of Istvan S. Pogany, *The Security Council and the Arab–Israeli Conflict* (New York: St Martin's Press, 1984).

[111] See, e.g., Smith, *Palestine and the Arab–Israeli Conflict*, 199 ('For most of the Israeli public, the strident Arab propaganda and increasingly specific threats of destruction established an atmosphere of encirclement that became increasingly oppressive as the crisis wore on').

[112] See UN Docs. A/L519, A/L52, A/2524, A/L525, rejected by votes of 88–32, 98–22, 81–36, and 80–36 respectively, cited in Gerson, *Israel, the West Bank and International Law*, 103 n. 169.

[113] See UN Docs. S/7951, S/7951/Rev. 1, S/7951/Rev. 2, S/PV 1360 (1967), cited in Gerson, *Israel, the West Bank, and International Law*, 103 n. 170.

2. *Affirms further* the necessity
   (a) For guaranteeing freedom of navigation through international waterways in the area;
   (b) For achieving a just settlement of the refugee problem;
   (c) For guaranteeing the territorial inviolability and political independence of every State in the area.[114]

Like the Balfour Declaration and the Mandate, Resolution 242 points in different directions at once. On the one hand, its preamble speaks of the 'inadmissibility of the acquisition of territory by war', implying that Israel should return all the territories obtained in the 1967 War. On the other hand, the English text of the resolution provides that peace 'should' (not 'must') include withdrawal of Israeli forces 'from territories occupied in the recent conflict', not 'from *the* territories occupied' in that conflict.[115] The deliberations of the Council suggest that this wording was no accident, and that many of the drafters intended that withdrawal 'is required from some but not all of the territories'.[116]

However it is interpreted, there is little doubt that Resolution 242 is legally binding—and thus an important part of the legal landscape occupied

[114] UN Doc. S/242 (1967), reprinted in Lapidoth and Hirsch, *Selected Documents*, 134. For a useful collection of Council resolutions and statements relating to the Middle East, see Karel C. Wellens (ed.), *Resolutions and Statements of the United Nations Security Council (1946–1992)*, 2nd edn (Dordrecht; Boston; London: Martinus Nijhoff, 1993), 625–60 (Palestine); ibid. 661–821 (Middle East generally); ibid. 669 (text of Resolution 242).

[115] The French and Spanish texts could be read as endorsing withdrawal from all 'the' territories. The French text calls for 'Retrait des forces armées israéliennes *des* territoires occupés lors du récent conflit'. It has been suggested that this phrase should be translated as 'from *the* territories', not 'from territories'. See Bernard Reich, *Quest for Peace: United States–Israel Relations and the Arab–Israeli Conflict* (New Brunswick, NJ: Transaction Books (Rutgers University), 1977), 131 and n. 33. Likewise, the Spanish text provides for 'Retiro . . . *de los* territorios'. The Russian and Chinese texts do not use a definite article, but no definite article is used in those languages.

It has nevertheless been suggested that the French text is in fact an accurate translation of the final English text, which omits a definite article. See Sydney D. Bailey, *The Making of Resolution 242* (Dordrecht: Martinus Nijhoff, 1985), 152–3; Shabtai Rosenne, 'On multilingual interpretation', 6 *Israel L. Rev.* 360, 363 (1971). In any event, the negotiations surrounding the text were 'based on the English text', not the French or Spanish texts, suggesting that the English text is more authoritative. Bailey, *The Making of Resolution 242*, 153; see also Pogany, *The Security Council*, 107.

[116] Gerson, *Israel, the West Bank and International Law*, 76. As Gerson points out, the Council rebuffed efforts to require 'withdrawal from all the territories' occupied in the 1967 War. Ibid. 104 n. 179.

Likewise, the text of Resolution 242 speaks of every state's right to 'secure and recognized boundaries free from threats or acts of force', a phrase that might be interpreted to permit some adjustment of territorial boundaries for security reasons. Cf. ibid. 76 (asserting that Resolution 242 requires that boundaries be negotiated in a peace treaty, and that the extent of 'territorial concessions' that may be bargained for is limited to 'territorial adjustments mandated by "security considerations" ') (citing Abba Eban's discussion of an analogous issue raised by the 1949 Armistice Agreements in Abba Eban, *Voice of Israel*, 108 (New York, Horizon Press, 1957)).

by the Oslo Accords. Unlike the Partition Resolution, Resolution 242 was a resolution of the Security Council, whose 'decisions' bind all Members of the United Nations under Article 25 of the UN Charter. It is true that Resolution 242 does not invoke Chapter VII of the Charter, the section of the Charter that most clearly confers on the Council the power to make decisions binding on member states. For this reason, many commentators have argued that Resolution 242 is not binding on the grounds that it was adopted pursuant to Chapter VI (on peaceful settlement of disputes), and that Chapter VI empowers the Council to make only recommendations, not binding 'decisions'.[117]

This argument is not as airtight as it might appear. To begin with, it is not clear that Resolution 242 is founded on Chapter VI rather than Chapter VII. The text of the Resolution does not invoke either chapter of the Charter, though the substance of the Resolution admittedly is more focused on peaceful resolution of disputes (the stuff of Chapter VI) than enforcement measures (the stuff of Chapter VII). In the (admittedly controversial) *Advisory Opinion on Namibia*, the International Court of Justice held that a similarly ambiguous Council resolution was legally binding. The Court did not maintain that silence in a Council resolution implies that the Council has invoked Chapter VII; instead, the Court suggested that 'decisions' of the Council are not confined to enforcement actions under Chapter VII.[118] It is true that the Court's broad interpretation of the term 'decisions' has been criticized as inconsistent with the text and as jeopardizing 'acceptance of decisions of the UN by its members'.[119] But there is also a respectable body of scholarly opinion maintaining that

117 See UN Charter Art. 36(1) (providing that the Council may 'recommend' procedures for settlement of disputes); ibid., Art. 37(2) (providing that the Council may 'recommend' terms of settlement).

For the view that Resolution 242 was not, in itself, binding, see Pogany, *The Security Council*, 108 (Because Resolution 242 'was adopted in accordance with Chapter VI of the Charter' it 'does not impose binding obligations on the combatants'); Gidon Gottlieb, 'Legal Theory for a Relational Society', 50 *U. Chi. L. Rev.* 567, 578 (1983); Mohamed ElBaradei, 'The Egyptian–Israeli Peace Treaty and Access to the Gulf of Aqaba: A New Legal Regime', 76 *Am. J. Int'l L.* 532, 546 (1982).

Gerson brushes aside this issue on the grounds that it has no 'measurable political significance'. See Allan Gerson, Review of Pogany, *The Security Council*, 79 *Am. J. Int'l L.* 801, 801 (1985). The issue would, however, seem highly relevant to the legal rights and obligations of the parties to the Oslo Accords, especially since the Accords refer explicitly to Resolution 242.

118 *Advisory Opinion on South West Africa/Namibia*, 1971 I.C.J. Rep. 16, 52–3.

119 Thomas Bruha, 'Security Council', in Rüdiger Wolfrum (ed.), *United Nations: Law, Policies and Practice* (Dordrecht: Martinus Nijhoff, 1995), 2:1151. For pre-*Namibia* analysis in the same vein, see Hans Kelsen, *The Law of the United Nations: A Critical Analysis of Its Fundamental Problems* (London: Stevens & Sons, 1954), 95–6; Leland M. Goodrich and Edvard Hambro, *Charter of the United Nations: Commentary and Documents* (Boston: World Peace Foundation, 1946), 122 ('The word "decisions" ... does not include recommendations' under Chapter VI).

the term 'decisions' can embrace at least some components of Chapter VI such as Article 33, which empowers the Council to 'call upon' states to settle disputes—language that echoes the mandatory use of the term 'call' in Article 43 and in resolutions enforcing Chapter VII.[120] It is therefore possible to conclude that Resolution 242 was binding in and of itself.[121]

As such, it may not have been necessary that the parties 'accept' the Resolution. In any event, however, the Resolution was eventually 'accepted' by Israel, by most of Israel's immediate Arab neighbours, and by the PLO. These 'acceptances' make clear that the Resolution is binding on those parties 'accepting' it, either on the theory that the acceptances were part of international agreements, or on the theory that they were binding unilateral declarations made in good faith.[122] If that were not enough, there is still more evidence to support the conclusion that 242 is binding. For example, Security Council Resolution 338 'calls upon' the parties to implement Resolution 242; in Security Council practice, the phrase 'calls upon' often indicates a binding obligation.[123] Likewise, Resolution 242 is formally invoked in the Oslo Accords, which (as Part II of this book argues) are themselves binding instruments.[124]

One way or another, then, Resolution 242 is binding. Indeed, it is still binding today. In this respect it may differ from many if not all of the instruments that preceded it. The Balfour Declaration may have been incorporated into the British Mandate, but the Mandate most likely terminated in 1948. The General Assembly's Partition Resolution may or may not have been binding when adopted, on the theory that it was an exercise of the Assembly's supervisory power over trusteeships, but (in contrast to 242) it was rejected by all the Arab states. As a political matter, the 'land-for-peace' scheme of Resolution 242 remains the cornerstone of

[120] See, e.g., Simma, *The Charter of the United Nations*, 410–13; see also Helmut Freudenschuss, 'Article 39 of the UN Charter Revisited: Threats to the Peace and the Recent Practice of the UN Security Council', 46 *Austrian J. Pub. & Int'l L.* 33–4 (1993) ('neither Article 25 nor Chapter VII as such but the will or the intention of the Security Council to take a binding decision is the decisive yardstick . . .'). But cf. Kelsen, *The Law of the United Nations*, 96 (asserting that the term 'call' in Article 33(2) means a 'recommendation', whereas the same term in Article 43 is 'binding').

[121] The Soviet Union took this view shortly after the adoption of Resolution 242. See Sydney D. Bailey and Sam Daws, *The Procedure of the UN Security Council* (Oxford: Clarendon Press, 1998), 270–1. See also John Norton Moore, 'The Regime of Straits and the Third United Nations Conference on the Law of the Sea', 74 *Am. J. Int'l L.* 77, 113 (1980).

[122] See ElBaradei, 'The Egyptian–Israeli Peace Treaty', 546; Gottlieb, 'Legal Theory for a Relational Society', 578. Unilateral declarations can be binding. See *Nuclear Tests* (Austl. v. Fr.), 1974 I.C.J. 253, 267–70 (20 Dec.).

[123] Cf. S.C. Res. 338, 22 Oct. 1973, ¶2 ('calls upon' parties to implement S.C. Res. 242) with S.C. Res. 661, 6 Aug. 1990, ¶5 ('calls upon' states to abide by resolution imposing sanctions on Iraq).

[124] See, e.g., Declaration of Principles, Isr.–PLO, 13 Sept. 1993, Art. I, ¶1 (envisioning a 'permanent settlement based on Security Council Resolution 242 and 338'); ibid., ¶2 (envisioning 'implementation of Security Council Resolutions 242 and 338').

peace plans for the Middle East. As a legal matter, it is the most significant plank of the legal framework underlying the Oslo Accords.

After 1967: The Yom Kippur War, Camp David, and Madrid

The 1967 War had international legal consequences other than Security Resolution 242. The war also ushered in a whole new set of legal issues relating to Israel's administration of the territories it gained in the war. To this day, there is disagreement about whether Israel's administration of the territories is governed by the law of belligerent occupation, which gives the occupant special rights and responsibilities and restricts controversial practices such as settlements and demolitions.[125] The law of occupation is a subset of the larger field of humanitarian law, the law that protects individuals in time of war. Israel's position is that the law of occupation is generally inapplicable to the West Bank and other territories gained in 1967 because there is no 'legitimate ousted sovereign' whose territory is being 'occupied' by Israel.[126] Israel none the less applies some provisions of humanitarian law to the territories as a *de facto* matter, on a voluntary basis. The opposing view, which reflects the view of the Palestinians and the majority of the international community, is that the law of occupation applies to the Israeli presence whether or not there is a 'legitimate ousted sovereign'.[127] In addition, there is disagreement over whether occupation law continues to apply in those areas that the Palestinian Authority now controls as a result of the Oslo Accords. Finally, the parties disagree about the extent to which occupation law restricts or forbids Israeli settlements in the territories, the deportation of suspected terrorists, the demolition of houses of suspected terrorists, and other Israeli activities affecting the territories. These issues are still relevant to interpretation of the Oslo Accords, and they will be discussed in detail as they arise in various parts of this book.

[125] It has also been suggested that Israel's position is best described as that of a 'trustee-occupant', not restricted by the full panoply of humanitarian law, but still required to treat the territory as a trust for its inhabitants. See Allan Gerson, 'Trustee-Occupant: the Legal Status of Israel's Presence in the West Bank', 14 *Harv. Int'l L. J.* 1 (1973). Even the proponent of this view, however, readily admits that it has not been accepted by any of the parties to the conflict. See Gerson, *Israel, the West Bank and International Law*, 82.

[126] See Yehuda Blum, 'The Missing Reversioner: Reflections on the Status of Judea and Samaria', 3 *Israel L. Rev.* 279 (1968); Meir Shamgar, 'The Observance of International Law in the Administered Territories', 1 *Isr. Yb. Hum. Rts.* 262, 263 (1971); Nathan Lorch, 'The Applicability of the Fourth Geneva Convention to the Territories Administered by Israel', 1 *Isr. Yb. Hum. Rts.* 366, 366 (1971).

[127] See, e.g., Esther R. Cohen, *Human Rights in the Israeli-Occupied Territories 1967–1982* (Manchester: Manchester University Press 1985), 52–6; Eyal Benvenisti, *The International Law of Occupation*, 109–10 (Princeton, NJ: Princeton University Press, 1993).

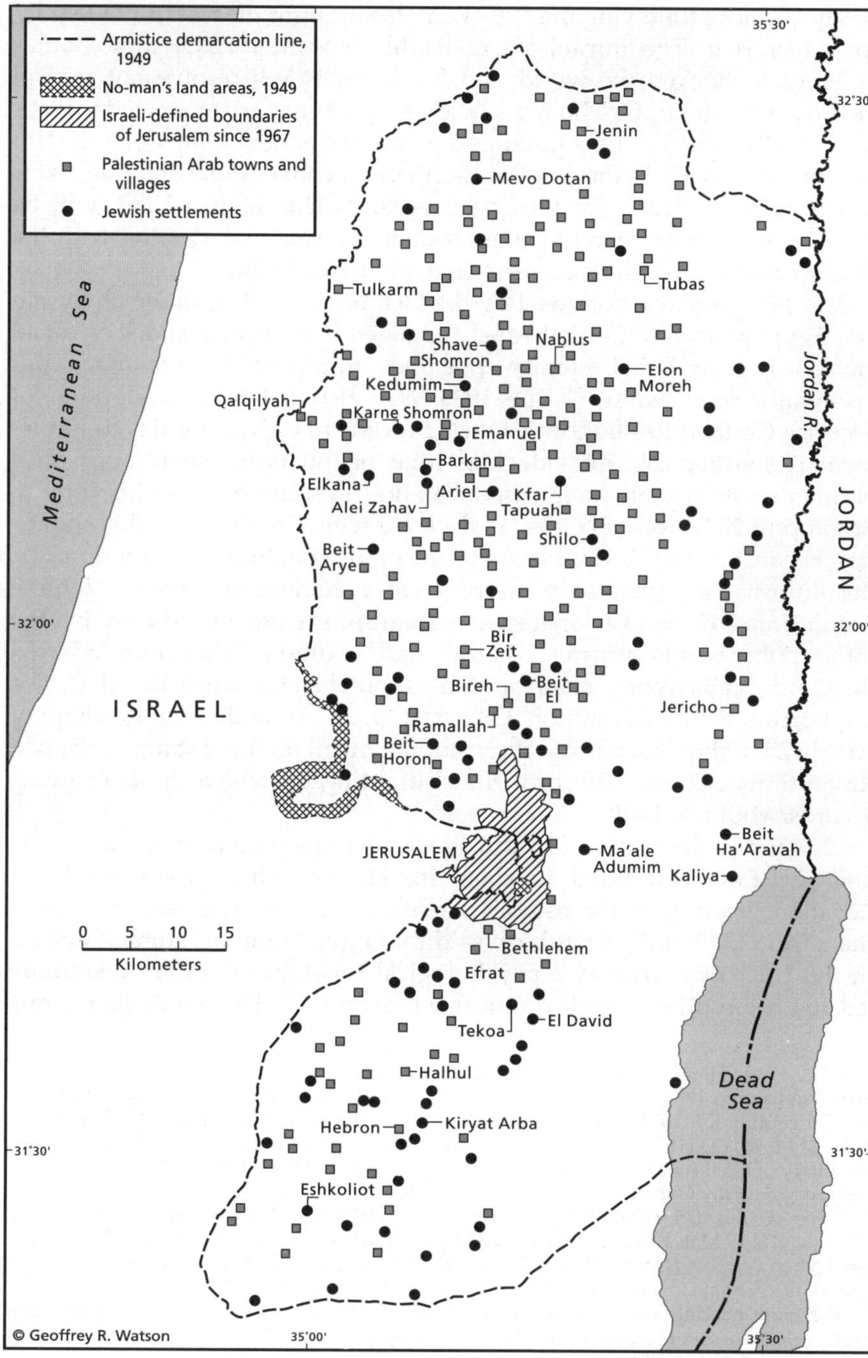

Map 5. The West Bank since 1967

The decades following the 1967 War also brought the rise of PLO-sponsored terrorism. The murder of Israeli athletes at the 1972 Olympic Games in Munich shocked the world and hardened Israeli resolve not to deal directly with the PLO. The worldwide surge in terrorism since the 1960s has contributed to a concomitant surge in international law dealing with the subject, mostly in the form of multilateral conventions obliging states to extradite or prosecute terror suspects.[128] This body of law will be considered in more detail in those sections of the book dealing with the Oslo Accords' provisions on terrorism and extradition.

The 1967 War was followed by the October 1973 War, in which Syrian and Egyptian forces simultaneously engaged in a surprise attack on Israel on Yom Kippur. Israel initially appeared unprepared for the attack, but eventually repulsed it.[129] The 1973 War also led to the adoption of Security Council Resolution 338, which 'calls upon' the parties to implement Resolution 242 and 'decides' that negotiations 'shall' start on a permanent peace settlement. In substance, Resolution 338 adds little to Resolution 242. None the less, as we have seen, Resolution 338 is significant because it dispels doubts about the binding nature of Resolution 242. Resolution 338 speaks in more clearly mandatory terms. Unlike Resolution 242, whose operative paragraphs were introduced by the rather polite words 'affirms', 'should', and 'requests', Resolution 338 used the words 'calls upon', 'shall', and, most notably, the word 'decides'. The implication is that Resolution 338 was a 'decision' within the meaning of Article 25 of the Charter, and thus binding on all member states. Together, Resolutions 242 and 338 form the scaffolding on which the later peace accords would be built.

Of course, Resolution 338 did not lead immediately to peace. Israel and the PLO continued to clash in, among other places, southern Lebanon, leading to the establishment of a UN peacekeeping mission there in 1978.[130] Still, it has been said that Egypt's initial military success in the 1973 War 'created a psychological breakthrough that eventually led to an Egyptian–Israeli political settlement'.[131] That settlement came

128 See Louis Henkin, *et al.*, *International Law: Cases and Materials*, 3rd edn (St Paul, MN: West Publishing, 1993), 391–4. Examples of the multilateral terrorism conventions include the Convention for the Suppression of Unlawful Seizure of Aircraft, 16 Dec. 1970, 22 U.S.T. 1641, 10 I.L.M. 133 (1971) and the Convention for the Suppression of Unlawful Acts Against the Safety of Civil Aviation, 23 Sept. 1971, 24 U.S.T. 564, 10 I.L.M. 1151 (1971).

129 See generally Gilbert, *Israel: A History*, 426–61.

130 See S.C. Res. 425, 19 Mar. 1978, ¶3 (deciding to establish a UN interim force for Lebanon); S.C. Res. 426, 19 Mar. 1978, ¶2 (establishing the UN Interim force in Lebanon, or UNIFIL). See also Gilbert, *Israel: A History*, 490. UNIFIL is still in place today. The Security Council routinely renews its mandate for six-month periods. See, e.g., S.C. Res. 1254, 2 Aug. 1999.

For more on UN peacekeeping in the Middle East and elsewhere, see the magisterial multi-volume work, Higgins, *United Nations Peacekeeping*.

131 Gilbert, *Israel: A History*, 460.

in the Camp David Accords of 1978 and the Egypt–Israel peace treaty of 1979.

The road to peace at Camp David began with Egyptian President Anwar el-Sadat's sudden and dramatic visit to Jerusalem in late 1977. 'No more war,' he told Israeli Prime Minister Menachem Begin. 'Let us make peace.'[132] And, indeed, they did. On 18 September 1978 Begin and Sadat signed a 'Framework for Peace in the Middle East Agreed at Camp David' and a 'Framework for the Conclusion of a Peace Treaty Between Egypt and Israel'.[133] US President Jimmy Carter signed the Accords as a 'witness', and the Accords were accompanied by a series of side letters among the parties providing assurances on various points.[134] Among other things, the Framework for Peace in the Middle East called for an 'elected self-governing authority in the West Bank and Gaza'.[135] The Framework for Egypt–Israel peace called for negotiation of a peace treaty within three months.[136] And, indeed, Egypt and Israel did sign a peace treaty on 26 March 1979; among other things, it provided for the withdrawal of Israeli troops from the Sinai.[137]

But other Arab states and the Palestinians refused to participate in the Camp David Accords, and it soon became clear that Begin took a narrow view of the Palestinian autonomy envisioned by the Accords. For these and other reasons, the Camp David process foundered. In 1981 Sadat was assassinated by Moslem fundamentalists who viewed his peace treaty with Israel as a criminal act of betrayal. The prospects for peace grew even dimmer in June 1982, when Israel invaded Lebanon. The invasion immediately followed a PLO attempt to assassinate the Israeli Ambassador to Great Britain, but its fundamental purpose was to stamp out PLO bases in southern Lebanon, which had been used to shell Israeli settlements and other targets in northern Israel.[138] As the death count mounted, and as news of the massacre at the Sabra/Shatila camp emerged, the war tarnished Israel's reputation even among its allies.[139] Still, Israel

[132] Ibid. 489. See also William B. Quandt, *Camp David: Peacemaking and Politics*, 147 (Washington: Brookings Institution, 1986). For the text of President Sadat's remarks to the Israeli Knesset, see ibid. 345–55 and *N.Y. Times*, 21 Nov. 1977.

[133] See Quandt, *Camp David*, 376–81 (reprinting the Framework for Peace in the Middle East); ibid. 381–3 (reprinting the Framework for Egypt–Israel peace).

[134] For the text of the side letters, see ibid. 383–7.

[135] Framework for Peace in the Middle East, ¶A(1)(b).

[136] Framework for Egypt–Israel Peace, Preamble.

[137] Treaty of Peace Between the Arab Republic of Egypt and the State of Israel, 26 Mar. 1979, Art. I(2), reprinted in Quandt, *Camp David*, 397. Again, the treaty was 'witnessed' by President Carter, and again it was accompanied by a variety of agreed minutes and side letters, the text of which are reprinted in ibid. 401–6.

[138] Gilbert, *Israel: A History*, 503–4.

[139] See Kahan Commission Report, in *Jerus. Post*, 9 Feb. 1983; Thomas Friedman, *From Beirut to Jerusalem* (New York: Farrar, Straus & Giroux, 1989); Gilbert, *Israel: A History*, 509.

succeeded in chasing the PLO leadership from Beirut to Tunis and in destroying much of the PLO presence in southern Lebanon. Israel eventually withdrew from most (though not all) of southern Lebanon.[140]

Once installed in Tunis, the PLO gradually shifted away from a strategy of military confrontation towards one of diplomacy. But as the 1980s wore on without visible progress towards peace, Palestinians in the occupied territories became increasingly restive, and in 1987 began an uprising against Israel—the *intifada*—that put further pressure on the parties to reach some agreement. In the summer of 1988 Jordan formally relinquished its claims to the West Bank,[141] undermining those (including US President Ronald Reagan) who sought to resolve the Palestinian problem through some confederation involving Jordan.[142] In late 1988 the PLO renounced terrorism and recognized the state of Israel; shortly thereafter, in December, the United States government announced it would begin discussions with the PLO. The end of the Cold War spurred the PLO and Arab states to support some sort of peace talks, since the breakup of the Soviet Union deprived the Arab world of a traditional military and political ally—just as the Bush Administration's threats to curtail some US financial support for Israel put pressure on Israel to come to the table as well. Israel insisted, however, that any Palestinian representatives at peace talks be part of a joint Jordanian–Palestinian delegation. Under these and other conditions, Palestinian representatives agreed to meet face-to-face with their Israeli counterparts at a US- and Soviet-sponsored conference in Madrid in October 1991.

The Madrid conference established a framework for peace negotiations on a variety of fronts. There would be bilateral discussions between Israel and each of its neighbours on a variety of topics, as well as multilateral discussions involving all of the parties. These talks were to take place in Washington, DC, under the sponsorship of the United States. But little progress was made in these relatively public discussions in Washington. By the summer of 1993, the Washington negotiations had dragged on through eleven rounds, with no real progress in sight.[143]

[140] See Rashid Khalidi, *Under Siege: PLO Decision-making During the 1982 War* (New York: Columbia University Press, 1986).

[141] See King Hussein's Statement Concerning Disengagement from the West Bank, 31 July 1988, reprinted and translated in 28 I.L.M. 1637 (1988) and in Lapidoth and Hirsch, *Selected Documents*, 339. See also *N.Y. Times*, 1 Aug. 1988.

[142] For the text of President Reagan's peace initiative, see President Reagan's Address of 1 Sept. 1982, reprinted in 21 I.L.M. 1199 (1982) and in Lapidoth and Hirsch, *Selected Documents*, 287, 291 ('self-government by the Palestinians of the West Bank and Gaza in association with Jordan offers the best chance for a durable, just and lasting peace').

[143] For a useful account of the Washington talks from the point of view of a Palestinian lawyer who advised the Palestinian delegation, see Raja Shehadeh, *From Occupation to Interim Accords: Israel and the Palestinian Territories* (London: Kluwer Law International, 1997), 104–21.

From Madrid to Oslo

In August 1998 Israel and the PLO surprised the world by announcing that their representatives had been meeting in secret for months in Oslo, Norway, and that they were preparing to sign an agreement involving mutual recognition and gradual transition towards some form of autonomy for the Palestinians. On 13 September 1993 PLO Chairman Yasser Arafat and Israeli Prime Minister Yitzhak Rabin met on the White House lawn and, under a bright Washington sky, as the world watched on television and US President Bill Clinton stood by, they signed the historic Declaration of Principles. Tears welled in the eyes of some of the onlookers on the South Lawn as Rabin and Arafat each took the podium to speak. First Rabin, speaking in heavily accented English:

> This signing of the Israeli–Palestinian declaration of principles here today is not so easy, neither for myself as a soldier in Israel's wars, nor for the people of Israel, nor for the Jewish people in the *diaspora* who are watching us now with great hope mixed with apprehension. It is certainly not easy for the families of the victims of the wars, violence, terror, whose pain will not heal, for the many thousands who defended our lives with their own and have even sacrificed their lives for our own. For them, this ceremony has come too late.
>
> . . . We have come from Jerusalem, the ancient and eternal capital of the Jewish people. We have come from an anguished and grieving land. We have come from a people, a home, a family that has not known a single year, not a single month, in which mothers have not wept for their sons. We have come to try and put an end to the hostilities so that our children, and our children's children, will no longer experience the painful cost of war, violence and terror. . . .
>
> Let me say to you, the Palestinians—we are destined to live together on the same soil in the same land. We, the soldiers who have returned from battles stained with blood; we, who have seen our relatives and friends killed before our eyes; we, who have attended their funerals and cannot look into the eyes of their parents; we who have come from a land where parents bury their children; we, who have fought against you, the Palestinians, we say to you today in a loud and clear voice—enough of blood and tears. Enough!

Then Arafat, speaking in Arabic:

> Now as we stand on the threshold of this new historic era, let me address the people of Israel and their leaders, with whom we are meeting today for the first time, and let me assure them that the difficult decision we reached together was one that required great and exceptional courage.
>
> We will need more courage and determination to continue the course of building coexistence and peace between us. . . .
>
> Ladies and gentlemen, the battle for peace is the most difficult battle of our

lives. It deserves our utmost efforts because the land of peace, the land of peace yearns for a just and comprehensive peace. Thank you.[144]

As Clinton gently pushed the two men together, the two longtime adversaries sealed their agreement with a handshake—one of the most widely watched handshakes in human history. The first Oslo Accord was complete.

[144] 'Statements by Leaders at the Signing of the Middle East Pact', *N.Y. Times*, 14 Sept. 1993. The speeches are also reprinted in Makovsky, *Making Peace with the PLO*, 223, 225.

2

An Overview of the Oslo Accords

The first Oslo Accord was the 1993 Declaration of Principles on Interim Self-Government Arrangements, better known as the Declaration of Principles or simply 'Oslo I'.[1] The Declaration began with a Preamble that was itself striking, for it provided that the parties 'recognize their mutual legitimate and political rights'. This mutual recognition had first been agreed to in an exchange of letters signed four days earlier.[2] The Preamble also recited the ultimate goal of the instrument: to 'achieve a just, lasting and comprehensive peace settlement and historic reconciliation through the agreed political process'.

The main text of the Declaration called for a gradual transfer of power from Israel to Palestinians in the West Bank and the Gaza Strip, with 'permanent status' negotiations on the most difficult issues—Jerusalem, final borders, settlements, refugees, security arrangements, etc.—to begin two years after Israel's initial withdrawal from Jericho and the Gaza Strip.[3] In particular, the Declaration of Principles envisioned that this transfer of authority take place in four stages. The first stage would involve Israeli withdrawal from the Gaza Strip and Jericho; the second, a transfer of some civil authority and responsibility to the Palestinians

[1] Declaration of Principles on Interim Self-Government Arrangements, Israel–Palestine Liberation Organization, 13 Sept. 1993, 32 I.L.M. 1525 (1993), reprinted in Appendix B. Several useful accounts of negotiation of the Declaration have been published. See, e.g., Mahmoud Abbas [Abu Mazen], *Through Secret Channels* (Reading: Garnet Publishing Ltd., 1995); David Makovsky, *Making Peace with the PLO* (Boulder, CO: Westview Press, 1996); Samuel Segev, *Crossing the Jordan* (New York: St Martin's Press, 1998); Shimon Peres, *Battling for Peace: A Memoir*, edited by David Landau (New York: Random House, 1995). See also Raja Shehadeh, *From Occupation to Interim Accords: Israel and the Palestinian Territories* (The Hague: Kluwer Law International, 1997), 104–31, 259–72 (providing insights into the parallel, and more public, talks in Washington).

For press accounts of the signing of the Declaration, see, e.g., Thomas L. Friedman, 'Rabin and Arafat Seal Their Accord as Clinton Applauds "Brave Gamble" ', *N.Y. Times*, 14 Sept. 1993; David Makovsky, 'Israel, PLO sign accords; Rabin and Arafat shake hands', *Jerus. Post*, 14 Sept. 1993.

[2] See letter of 9 Sept. 1993, from Yitzhak Rabin to Yasser Arafat; letter of 9 Sept. 1993 from Yasser Arafat to Yitzhak Rabin. The letters are reprinted in Appendix A. In his letter to Rabin, Arafat also declared 'inoperative' and 'no longer valid' those provisions of the Palestinian Covenant that 'deny Israel's right to exist', and he promised to 'submit to the Palestinian National Council for formal approval the necessary changes in regard to the Palestinian Covenant'.

[3] Declaration of Principles, Art. V(1) (providing that a five-year 'transitional period' will begin upon withdrawal from Gaza and Jericho); ibid., Art. V(2) (providing that permanent status negotiations will begin 'not later than the beginning of the third year of the interim period').

throughout the West Bank; the third, an Interim Agreement on implementation of the Declaration of Principles; and the final and most difficult stage, agreement on 'permanent status arrangements'—a final settlement of questions such as Jerusalem, settlements, water, and refugees.

Implementation of the first phase of the Declaration—withdrawal from Gaza and Jericho—took somewhat longer than the early 1994 timetable envisioned by the Declaration.[4] Both parties obtained legislative approval of the agreement fairly quickly, albeit after contentious debate: the Israeli Knesset ratified the Accord on 23 September 1993 by a vote of 61–50 with 8 abstentions, while the PLO Central Council in Tunis approved the Accord on 11 October 1993, by a vote of 63–8 with 9 abstentions.[5] But talks between the parties to implement the Declaration dragged on for months.

The Gaza–Jericho Agreement

The parties haggled through the winter of 1993/4 over how to implement Israel's promise to withdraw from the Gaza Strip and Jericho. At last, in the spring of 1994, they came to an agreement. On 4 April 1994 the Israeli Defence Forces began the process of evacuating from their headquarters in Jericho and the Gaza Strip.[6] On 29 April Israel and the PLO signed the 'Paris Protocol', the Protocol on Economic Relations that today still forms the basis for economic relations between the parties.[7] Finally, on 4 May 1994, the parties met in Cairo and signed the Agreement on the Gaza Strip and the Jericho Area, which called on Israel to withdraw from the Gaza Strip and Jericho within three weeks.[8] Significantly, the Gaza–Jericho

[4] As to the timetable, see Declaration of Principles, Annex II: Protocol on Withdrawal of Israeli Forces from the Gaza Strip and Jericho Area, Art. 1 (providing that the parties sign an agreement on withdrawal from Gaza and Jericho within two months of the signing of the Declaration); ibid., Art. 2 (providing that Israel begin withdrawal upon signature of the Jericho Agreement and complete its withdrawal within four months of that time).

[5] See Dan Izenberg, 'Knesset okays accord with PLO, 61–50; Vote gives Rabin "freedom of action" ', *Jerus. Post*, 24 Sept. 1993; Nora Boustany, 'PLO Council Ratifies Pact; Accord With Israel Accepted After Heated Debate', *Wash. Post*, 12 Oct. 1993. See also Shehadeh, *From Occupation to Interim Accords*, 11–12. According to Shehadeh, twenty-five PLO Council delegates did not attend the meeting at which the Council approved the Declaration. Ibid. 12.

[6] See Shehadeh, *From Occupation to Interim Accords.*

[7] See Hillel Kuttler, 'Investors get call after peace deal signed', *Jerus. Post*, 1 May 1994 (reporting on the signing of the Protocol). The Paris Protocol was incorporated by reference into the 1994 Gaza–Jericho Agreement, which was later superseded by the 1995 Interim Agreement. See Agreement on the Gaza Strip and the Jericho Area, 4 May 1994, Isr.–PLO, 33 I.L.M. 622 (1994), Art. II(1), Art. XIII & Annexe IV; Interim Agreement, Art. XXIV & Annexe V. Ch. 8 takes up the Paris Protocol in more detail.

[8] Agreement on the Gaza Strip and the Jericho Area, 4 May 1994, Isr.–PLO, 33 I.L.M. 622 (1994), Art. II(1). The main text of the Agreement is reprinted in Appendix C. See also David Makovsky, 'Rabin, Arafat sign Gaza/Jericho pact; PLO asks Israel to delay implementation by four weeks', *Jerus. Post*, 5 May 1995 (reporting on the signing of the Agreement).

Agreement also established a Palestinian self-governing entity called the 'Palestinian Authority', and it obliged Israel to transfer some civil authority to the Authority.[9]

Shortly thereafter, Israel did indeed complete the withdrawal of its forces from most of the Gaza Strip and Jericho, as called for in the agreement of 4 May. On 10 May Palestinian police entered the Gaza Strip from Egypt, and the next day began taking up their new posts in Dayr al-Balah and other towns in the Gaza Strip.[10] Shortly thereafter Palestinian officials began taking up their posts in the Jericho area as well.[11] On 15 May 1994 Israel issued Military Proclamation Number 4, calling for implementation of the Gaza–Jericho Accord, and three days later the last IDF troops left the Palestinian areas of the Gaza Strip.[12] On 17 May the *New York Times* ran a Reuters photograph of a Palestinian dancing in the street as a truck carried away the last Israeli soldiers from an army prison in Gaza.[13] Meanwhile, the new Palestinian Police force arrived to replace outgoing Israeli soldiers. On 1 July 1994, after twenty-seven years of exile, Yasser Arafat triumphantly entered Gaza City, where he received a hero's welcome.[14]

Thereafter the parties moved to implement their agreement to transfer further civil authority to the Palestinian Authority. On 29 August 1994 Israel and the PLO signed an agreement providing for the transfer of six 'spheres' of civil authority to the Palestinian Authority: education and culture, health, social welfare, tourism, direct taxation, and Value Added Tax on local production.[15] Under this agreement, the Palestinian Authority's power over these spheres extended beyond Gaza and Jericho; it encompassed the entire West Bank, except that it did not extend to

[9] Gaza–Jericho Agreement, Art. III(1), IV, V.

[10] See Jon Immanuel and Alon Pinkas, 'First group of Palestinian police arrives in Gaza', *Jerus. Post*, 11 May 1994; 'IDF out of Deir el-Balah', ibid.; David Makovsky and Jon Immanuel, 'Gaza/Jericho pullout may be finished by next Friday; Cabinet approves accord; more police enter areas', ibid. 12 May 1994; Jon Immanuel, 'Deir el-Balah becomes first Gazan town "free" of IDF', ibid.

[11] See Joel Greenberg, 'First 20 Palestinian Policemen Arrive in Jericho', *N.Y. Times*, 13 May 1994; Clyde Haberman, 'Occupation Ends as Israeli Troops Evacuate Jericho', ibid. 14 May 1994.

[12] See Jon Immanuel, Alon Pinkas, and Lamia Lahoud, 'IDF Completes Gaza Withdrawal', *Jerus. Post*, 19 May 1994; Shehadeh, *From Occupation to Interim Accords*, 134.

[13] See Reuters photograph, in Clyde Haberman, 'Israeli Troops in Gaza Fold Their Tents Quietly', *N.Y. Times*, 17 May 1994.

[14] See 'Arafat triumphant as he returns to Gaza Strip', *Deutsche Presse-Agentur*, 1 July 1994; Joel Greenberg, 'Arafat in Gaza: the Israelis', *N.Y. Times*, 2 July 1994; Bruce W. Nelan, 'The Walls Came Tumbling Down', *Time*, 11 July 1994, 30 (US edition); Shehadeh, *From Occupation to Interim Accords*, 12.

[15] Agreement on Preparatory Transfer of Powers and Responsibilities, 29 Aug. 1994, Isr.–PLO, 34 I.L.M. 455 (1994), excerpted in Appendix D. See also Jon Immanuel, 'Early empowerment pact signed by Israeli, Palestinian negotiators', *Jerus. Post*, 30 Aug. 1994 (reporting on the signing of the Agreement).

'Jerusalem, settlements, military locations and, unless otherwise provided in this Agreement, Israelis'.[16] Still, as Israeli negotiator Joel Singer has said, the provision was designed to apply 'throughout' the West Bank, to avoid 'an unbalanced situation in which self-government arrangements were in effect in the Gaza Strip and Jericho Area, while the rest of the West Bank continued to be placed under the military government in its fullest scope . . .'.[17] On 27 August 1995 the parties signed a protocol transferring responsibility to the Palestinian Authority in several other civilian 'spheres', namely 'Labour, Commerce and Industry, Gas and Petroleum, Insurance, Postal Services, Local Government and Agriculture'.[18]

The Interim Agreement

The next major step in implementing Oslo I came on 28 September 1995, when the parties met in Washington to sign the Interim Agreement on Implementation of the Declaration of Principles, better known as 'Oslo II' or the 'Interim Agreement'.[19] Again, there was great fanfare on the White House lawn as the parties signed the Interim Agreement, but this time some of the novelty seemed to have worn off. Still, while the Declaration of Principles may have been a more stunning political achievement, from a legal standpoint the Interim Agreement is the most important of the Oslo Accords. The relationship of the Declaration to the Interim Agreement in some ways mirrors that of the US Declaration of Independence to the US Constitution: in each case the earlier document announcing a dramatic shift in policy was more dramatic, but the later, more detailed, instrument—the one that detailed how the new polity will be governed—was more important legally.

First, the Interim Agreement established important organs of Palestinian self-government. It provided for the creation of an elected 82-person Palestinian Council to supersede the Palestinian Authority established by the Gaza–Jericho agreement.[20] It also provided that a *Ra'ees* (Arabic for either 'President' or 'Chairman') would be elected to serve as head of a 24-person Executive Authority, most of whose members would

[16] Agreement on Preparatory Transfer, Art. III(2).

[17] Joel Singer, 'The West Bank and Gaza Strip: Phase Two', in *Justice*, Dec. 1995, No. 7, 2.

[18] Protocol on Further Transfer of Powers and Responsibilities, 27 Aug. 1995, Isr.–PLO, Art. I. See also David Makovsky, 'Peres–Arafat Talks Next Week', *Jerus. Post*, 28 Aug. 1995 (reporting on the signing of the Protocol).

[19] The Israeli–Palestinian Interim Agreement on the West Bank and the Gaza Strip, Israel–PLO, 28 Sept. 1995, 36 I.L.M. 551 (1997), reprinted (without annexes) in Appendix E. See also Alison Mitchell, 'Arafat and Rabin Sign Pact to Expand Arab Self-Rule', *N.Y. Times*, 29 Sept. 1995 (reporting on the signing of the Accord).

[20] Interim Agreement, Arts. I–IX.

come from the Council, and all of whom would be appointed by the *Ra'ees* subject to approval by the Council.[21] Although the official language of the Oslo Accords has always been English,[22] the Arabic word *Ra'ees* was chosen as a compromise between the Palestinian preference for 'President' and the Israeli preference for 'Chairman', a term that would not so clearly connote a head of state.[23]

In addition, the Interim Agreement established new and more detailed arrangements for the 'redeployment' of Israeli forces from areas of the West Bank. The Agreement contemplated four phases of Israeli redeployments in the West Bank. The first phase was to be Israeli redeployment from 'populated areas' of the West Bank; this phase was to be completed before the elections for the Palestinian Council.[24] The remaining three phases would involve gradual redeployment to 'specified military locations' over the next eighteen months, to take place at six-month intervals.[25]

The Interim Agreement imposed a wide variety of other obligations on the parties. Israel was obliged to permit some form of 'safe passage' by Palestinians between the Gaza Strip and the West Bank, to permit the Palestinians to construct and operate sea and airports in the Gaza Strip, to cooperate with the Palestinians on security matters and border control, to cooperate with the Palestinians on economic issues, and to share tax and tariff revenue with the Palestinian Authority.[26] In addition, the Interim Agreement required Israel to pay 'due regard' to 'internationally-accepted

[21] Ibid., Art. V. Up to 20 per cent of the *Ra'ees*'s appointments to the Executive Authority may consist of people who are not members of the Council. These people may participate as full members of the Executive Authority but may not vote in meetings of the Council. Ibid., Art. V(4)(c).

[22] 'To date there is no official version in Arabic of [the Declaration or Interim Agreement], although a standard translation of both by a local non-governmental organization exists.' Shehadeh, *From Occupation to Interim Accords*, 14 (citing an Arabic translation published by the Jerusalem Media Center in East Jerusalem). The working language of negotiations has generally been English as well. Ibid.

[23] See Serge Schmemann, 'With Placards and Slogans, Palestinians Face the Unknown: An Election', *N.Y. Times*, 4 Jan. 1994 ('During the Palestinian–Israeli talks, neither side could agree on whether the Palestinian chief executive would be known as the President, Mr Arafat's choice, or Chairman, the Israeli choice. So they settled on 'Ra'ees,' an Arabic word that can be translated either way.').

[24] Interim Agreement, Art. X(1), Art. XI(2)(a); ibid., Annexe I, Art. I(1).

[25] Interim Agreement, Art. X(2) ('Further redeployments of Israeli military forces to specified military locations will commence after the inauguration of the Council . . ., to be completed within 18 months from the date of the inauguration of the Council. . . .'); ibid., Art. XI(2)(d); ibid., Annex I, Art. I(9); Appendix I to Annexe I, ¶ B.

[26] As to safe passage, see, e.g., Interim Agreement, Annexe I, Art. X(1)(b); ibid., Art. X(1)(a) ('There shall be a safe passage connecting the West Bank with the Gaza Strip . . .'); ibid., Art. X(1)(d) ('Israel shall make such passage available through the route indicated on attached map No. 6'). As to the airport, see, e.g., ibid., Art. XIII(13) ¶1. As to the Gaza seaport, see, e.g., ibid., Art. XIV(4)(a). As to security cooperation, see, e.g., Interim Agreement, Art. XII(1). As to tax and economic questions, see generally the Protocol on Economic Relations.

norms . . . of human rights'.[27] The Palestinians were obliged to amend the Palestinian National Charter to remove anti-Semitic and anti-Israel clauses, particularly those calling for the destruction of the state of Israel.[28] The Interim Agreement also obliged the Palestinians to combat terrorism, to extradite terror suspects to Israel, to cooperate with Israel on security matters, and to meet regularly with the Israeli side on security matters.[29] Finally, the Interim Agreement required the Palestinians (like Israel) to pay 'due regard' to human rights.[30]

The Interim Agreement is a comprehensive document that today still governs virtually all aspects of the relations between Israel and the Palestinian Authority. Its basic text is only a few pages long, but it is accompanied by hundreds of pages of annexes detailing everything from aviation to water rights, from carefully crafted rules on sharing of tax revenue to deliberately vague obligations on Israeli military withdrawals. The Interim Agreement superseded the Gaza–Jericho Agreement and the agreements on transfer of civilian responsibility, though most provisions of those agreements were incorporated into the text or annexes of the Interim Agreement. The Interim Agreement did not, of course, supersede the 1993 Declaration of Principles, which still provides the overall framework for peace. And the Interim Agreement has since been modified and elaborated by the 1997 Hebron Protocol, discussed below. Still, for all practical purposes, the Interim Agreement is now the centrepiece of the Oslo Accords. It is the 'Basic Law' that governs the Israeli–Palestinian relationship.

The parties did move forward to implement some important provisions of the Interim Agreement. The Palestinian elections envisioned by the Agreement took place, albeit belatedly, in January 1996.[31] To no one's surprise, PLO Chairman Yasser Arafat was elected *Ra'ees* of the new Palestinian Executive Authority, and a majority of the new Palestinian Council was composed of members of Arafat's *Fatah* faction of the PLO. Although there were some charges of corruption and other irregularities in the election, international observers certified that the elections were generally free and fair. Israel, for its part, made good on its obligations to carry out an initial phase of redeployments. By the end of

[27] Interim Agreement, Art. XIX.

[28] Ibid., Art. XXXI(9).

[29] As to terrorism, see ibid., Art. XV(1) and Annexe I. As to extradition, see ibid., Annexe IV. As to security cooperation, see ibid., Arts. XII–XV and Annexe I.

[30] Ibid., Art. XIX.

[31] Some of the delay was attributable to a dispute over whether Palestinians in Jerusalem would be required to vote outside the confines of Jerusalem, as the Israelis insisted. The Israelis were opposed to any electoral arrangement that implied that East Jerusalem was part of the jurisdiction of the new Palestinian Council. The Interim Agreement fashioned a compromise under which Palestinians in Jerusalem were permitted to vote at five different post offices in Jerusalem. Interim Agreement, Annexe II, Art. VI(2).

1995, Israel had withdrawn its forces from six urban areas—Jenin, Nablus, Tulkarem, Kalkilya, Ramallah, and Bethlehem.[32] Together with the earlier withdrawal from Jericho, this development meant that Israel had withdrawn from seven of the eight major populated areas of the West Bank.

But Israeli redeployment from Hebron, which was supposed to be completed within six months after the signing of the Interim Agreement,[33] was postponed for almost a year. A number of factors contributed to the delay: political turmoil brought on by the assassination of Prime Minister Rabin in November 1995;[34] a spate of suicide bombings in Israel in the spring of 1996; and charges that the Palestinians had still failed to amend their National Covenant to remove anti-Israel clauses.[35] In March 1996, just before the scheduled withdrawal, the commander of Israeli forces in Hebron announced that plans to redeploy had been 'suspended' because of recent terrorist attacks against Israelis.[36]

Moreover, the three 'further redeployments' of Israeli troops from other parts of the West Bank did not take place as scheduled. At the end of May 1996 Benjamin Netanyahu was elected Prime Minister of Israel, the first directly elected Prime Minister in the country's history.[37] Netanyahu's campaign for Prime Minister had stressed his considerable scepticism about the Oslo process. Under the Interim Agreement, the first of three 'further redeployments' from the West Bank was to take place by September 1996,[38] but the redeployment was not carried out. As the parties continued to haggle over the terms of the Hebron redeployment, Palestinians accused Israel of attempting to reopen the Oslo Accords, and Israel charged the Palestinians with failing to honour their pledge to combat terrorism.[39]

[32] Shehadeh, *From Occupation to Interim Accords*, 135.

[33] Interim Agreement, Annexe I, Appendix I, ¶ A (as amended).

[34] Raine Markus, Sarah Honig, and Alon Pinkas, 'Rabin Assassinated', *Jerus. Post*, 5 Nov. 1995.

[35] See Arieh O'Sullivan, 'IDF likely to leave Hebron later than sooner', ibid. 29 Mar. 1996; Arieh O'Sullivan, 'IDF redeployment in Hebron likely only after elections', ibid. 28 Mar. 1996.

[36] 'Hebron Redeployment Plans Suspended', ibid. 11 Mar. 1996 (quoting commander of the Hebron area brigade).

[37] Serge Schmemann, 'Netanyahu Narrow Victor; Sets Out to Form a Cabinet and Assure Arab Neighbors', *N.Y. Times*, 1 June 1996.

[38] Interim Agreement, Arts. X(2) and XI(2)(d).

[39] See Jon Immanuel and David Makovsky, 'Hebron talks to resume in Eilat tomorrow', *Jerus. Post*, 20 Oct. 1996 (quoting Ahmed Abdel Rahman, secretary of the PA cabinet) ('It is very clear that day by day, the Israeli government tried to reopen the agreement and renegotiate it. We completely reject this.').

The Hebron Protocol and its Aftermath

The deadlock over Hebron was at last broken on 15 January 1997, when Israel and the PLO signed the Protocol Concerning the Redeployment in Hebron.[40] The Protocol called for redeployment of Israeli forces in Hebron within ten days of signing of the instrument.[41] It provided that Israeli forces would retain control of the section of the city populated by Jewish settlers as well as the area containing the Tomb of the Patriarchs. This division of the city was similar though not identical to that envisioned by the Interim Agreement.[42] The Israeli forces would thus control about one-fifth of the city's area, generally in the eastern and south-eastern reaches of the city, and Palestinian Police would take control of the remaining areas of the city. Shortly after the agreement was signed, Israel redeployed its forces accordingly.[43]

A 'Note for the Record' accompanying the Hebron Protocol revisited previous understandings not directly related to Hebron. The 'Note' is a short document prepared by US negotiator Dennis Ross 'at the request' of Arafat and Netanyahu. Although the Note is not in the form of a traditional international agreement, it is nevertheless an authoritative restatement of the parties' undertakings under the Declaration of Principles and the Interim Agreement. In the Note, Israel reaffirmed its commitment to begin the 'first phase of further redeployments'—in other words, the second of the four redeployments contemplated by Oslo II—'during the first week of March'.[44] Israel also reaffirmed its commitment to release certain prisoners, and to negotiate certain 'outstanding issues' from the Interim Agreement.[45] For its part, the PLO promised to '[c]omplete the process of revising the Palestinian National Charter', to fight terrorism and violence, to regulate the size of the Palestinian police force, and to exercise its governmental functions in the manner and place specified in the Interim Agreement.[46]

[40] Protocol Concerning the Redeployment in Hebron, Isr.–PLO, 15 Jan. 1997, 36 I.L.M. 650 (1997), reprinted in Appendix F. See also Serge Schmemann, 'Accord on Hebron Gets Endorsement of Israeli Cabinet', *N.Y. Times*, 16 Jan. 1997. For an interesting Palestinian view on the process of negotiation of the Hebron Protocol, see Shehadeh, *From Occupation to Interim Accords*, 159 (criticizing the Palestinian side for failing to include an attorney in its delegation).

[41] Hebron Protocol, Art. 1.

[42] Cf. ibid., Art. 2(a) with Interim Agreement, Annexe I, Article VII.

[43] Douglas Jehl, 'After 30 Years, the Palestinians Take Over in Hebron', *N.Y. Times*, 18 Jan. 1997. See also Joel Greenberg, 'In Hebron, the Unthinkable Is in Place', ibid. 28 Jan. 1997.

[44] Note for the Record, Isr.–PLO, 15 Jan. 1997, 'Israeli Responsibilities', ¶1. The Note is reprinted in Appendix G.

[45] These were safe passage, a Gaza airport, a Gaza port, passages, economic, financial, civilian and security issues, and 'people-to-people' questions. Ibid., 'Israeli Responsibilities', ¶3.

[46] Ibid., 'Palestinian Responsibilities', ¶¶1–4.

The Protocol was apparently accompanied by other, undisclosed, side letters as well. The text of one has surfaced. Shortly after the Protocol was signed, the Israeli Ministry of Foreign Affairs released the unsigned text of a letter from US Secretary of State Warren Christopher to Prime Minister Netanyahu in which Christopher told Netanyahu that he had 'conveyed our belief' to Arafat 'that all three phases of the further redeployments should be completed . . . not later than mid-1998'.[47] The letter also suggested that the United States had a view on the process of redeployment—and, crucially, on whether Israel had the right to 'specify' unilaterally the scope of Israeli withdrawals. According to this unsigned text, Secretary Christopher wrote: 'I have advised Chairman Arafat of U.S. views on Israel's process of redeploying its forces, designating specified military locations and transferring additional powers and responsibilities to the Palestinian Authority.'[48]

The day after the Hebron Protocol was signed, Israel released a 'Cabinet Communiqué' that shed further light on Israeli interpretation of the Oslo Accords. Among other things, this document asserted that '[d]etails of the further stages of the redeployment in Judea and Samaria will be determined by the Government of Israel'.[49] Thus Israel reaffirmed its position that the term 'specified military locations' meant that Israel alone would 'specify' which locations would be the target of redeployments.

In fact, the next development after Hebron was to be the 'further redeployment' of Israeli forces, now rescheduled for the first week in March 1997. In late February, however, Israel announced that it would construct Jewish housing in East Jerusalem,[50] in an area known to Jews as Har Homa and to Arabs as Jabal Abu-Ghuneim.[51] Israel's announcement triggered angry reactions among Palestinians and their leaders, and it provoked criticism from other states and commentators around the world.[52] Palestinian leaders argued that Israel was prejudging the status

[47] Letter to be provided by US Secretary of State Christopher to Benjamin Netanyahu at the time of the signing of the Hebron Protocol, ¶4 (undated) (avail. at http://www.israel-mfa.gov.il/peace/hebltr.html).

[48] Ibid., ¶4.

[49] Cabinet Communiqué, 16 Jan. 1997, ¶3.

[50] As to the argument that Har Homa is not inside East Jerusalem, see Ch. 6.

[51] Ministerial Committee on Jerusalem Affairs Communiqué, 26 Feb. 1997, ¶1 (reporting that the Committee 'decided today, unanimously, to approve construction of the Har Homa neighborhood, and also decided to approve construction for the Arab population of Jerusalem . . .'); Serge Schmemann, 'Jewish Housing for East Jerusalem Approved', *N.Y. Times*, 27 Feb. 1997. The Har Homa neighbourhood was to include 6,500 housing units; construction for the Arab population was to amount to 3,000 units in 'ten different Jerusalem neighborhoods'. Ministerial Communiqué, ¶2.

[52] See, e.g., Serge Schmemann, 'King Hussein Rebukes Netanyahu for "Intent to Destroy" Peace Plan', *N.Y. Times*, 12 Mar. 1997. Even the United States took issue with the Israeli decision. See, e.g., 'Clinton to Send Envoy to Middle East', ibid. 26 Mar. 1997. None the less, the

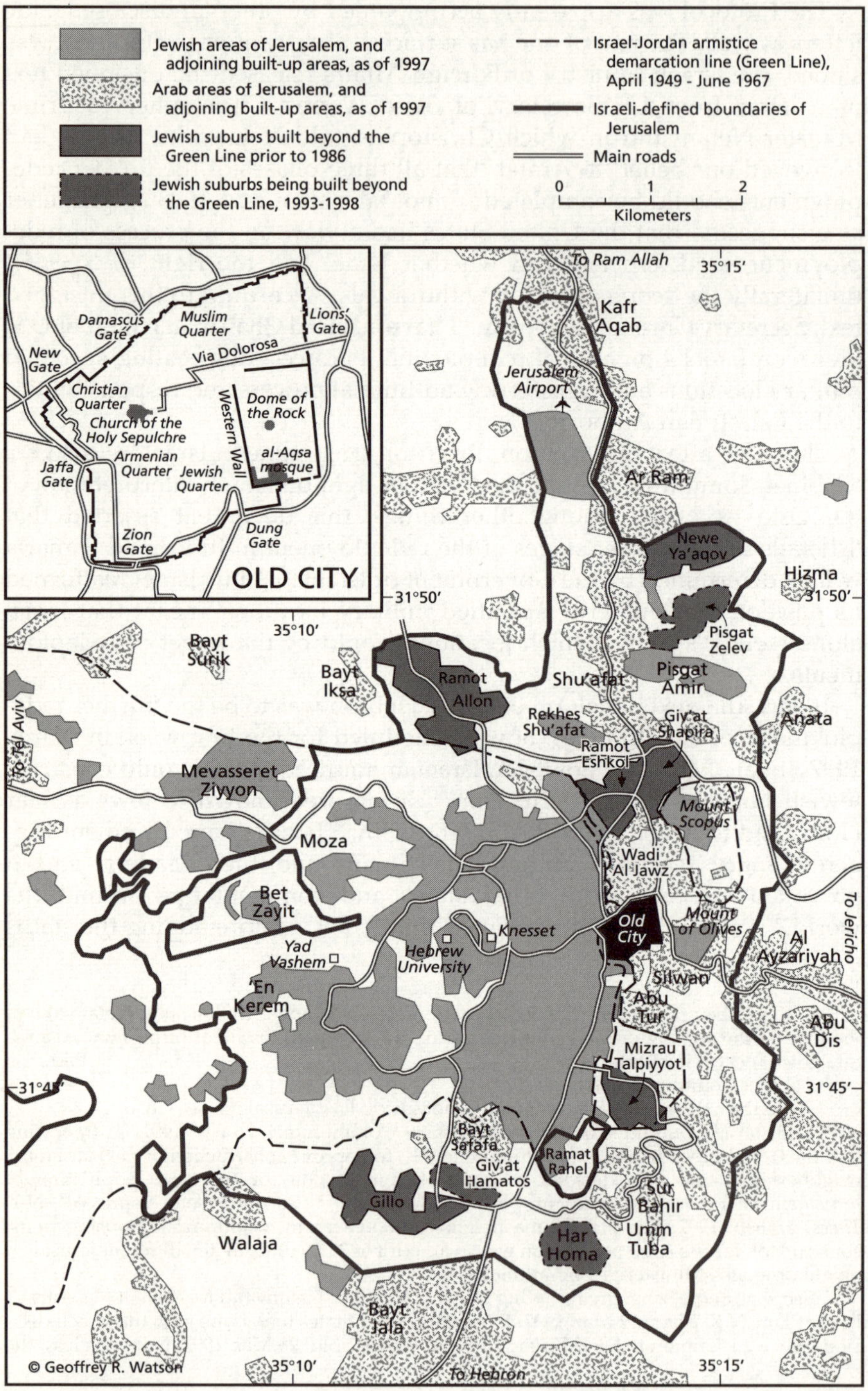

Map 6. Jerusalem and the Old City

of East Jerusalem, an issue reserved for the final status talks. Prime Minister Netanyahu responded that nothing in the Oslo Accords precluded Israel from taking steps to ensure that Jerusalem continued to function as a working metropolis.

For eighteen months after the Har Homa announcement, the peace process was more or less stalled. Around the time of the announcement, the Israeli Cabinet did approve Netanyahu's plan to carry out the second of the four redeployments called for by the Interim Agreement. Under the plan, Israel would have transferred to the Palestinians jurisdiction over as much as 9 per cent of the West Bank.[53] But PLO Chairman Arafat condemned the proposed pullback as too limited, again reflecting the Palestinian view that Palestinians should have a say in defining 'specified' military locations.[54] For its part, the United States expressed cautious support for Netanyahu's move, arguing that it meant the peace process was still on track.[55] But as 1997 turned into 1998, there was little tangible evidence of progress. In the meantime, important deadlines came and went: the permanent status talks were supposed to have begun in earnest in March 1997, and the final two 'further redeployments' were to have been completed by mid-1998.

Through much of 1998 the United States reportedly attempted to convince Israel to agree to a larger redeployment than the 9 per cent Netanyahu had proposed in March 1997. There were also persistent reports that Israel was interested in dispensing with the final redeployments in exchange for an immediate jump to 'permanent status' negotiations. Meanwhile, Arafat indicated that he intended to declare a Palestinian state on 4 May 1999—the supposed end of the interim period envisioned by the Declaration of Principles.[56] Israel emphatically denounced these statements. There was speculation that Israel would respond to a Palestinian declaration of statehood by annexing some of the West Bank or using force to take back land under PA jurisdiction.

In the autumn of 1998, however, the peace process lurched forward

United States vetoed a proposed UN Security Council Resolution that would have condemned the Israeli plan. See James Bennet, 'Mideast Veto Was Justified, Clinton Says', ibid. 11 Mar. 1997.

[53] David Makovsky and Arieh O'Sullivan, 'US pledged support for 9 percent pullback', *Jerus. Post*, 9 Mar. 1997 (reporting that the Cabinet voted 10–7 to approve a withdrawal from 9.1% of the West Bank).

[54] Serge Schmemann, 'Arabs Assail Israeli Move', *N.Y. Times*, 8 Mar. 1997 (quoting Yasser Arafat) ('This is a big deceit operation. . . . It came from one party, without consultation from us.').

[55] Marilyn Henry and Hillel Kuttler, 'Arabs press for Har Homa debate in UN General Assembly', *Jerus. Post*, 9 Mar. 1997 (reporting on the 'mixed' reaction from the Clinton Administration to the 9 per cent proposal).

[56] See Serge Schmemann, 'Arafat Likely to Declare Statehood in '99', *N.Y. Times*, 8 July 1998.

once more. On 15 October 1998 Arafat, Netanyahu, Clinton, and their top aides met at the Wye River resort in eastern Maryland to attempt to break the deadlock. Although the meeting was originally intended to last only four days, it stretched on for more than a week. On Monday, 20 October, an ailing King Hussein arrived and, by all accounts, took an active role in urging the parties to come to an agreement. Finally, on 23 October 1998, the parties signed the Wye River Memorandum.[57]

The Wye River Memorandum did not abrogate the existing Oslo Accords or impose radically new obligations on the parties. None the less, it significantly clarified and amplified existing obligations under the Accords, and it set forth an elaborate timetable for fulfilment of those obligations. The most striking example involved Israel's most significant obligation, its undertaking to carry out three 'redeployments' from the West Bank. The original incarnation of that obligation, set forth in the Interim Agreement, was deliberately vague; it merely called on Israel to redeploy to 'specified military locations'. The Wye River Memorandum concretized that obligation by defining the precise size of the first two of the three redeployments. Likewise, the PA was obliged to take concrete steps to outlaw and combat terrorist organizations, to prohibit illegal weapons, to prevent incitement of violence, to cooperate in security and law enforcement matters, and to amend its Charter.[58]

The parties did implement some features of the Wye Memorandum in fairly timely fashion. Most significantly, Israel made good on its obligation to carry out the first stage of the redeployments outlined in the Memorandum,[59] and the Palestine National Council formally amended its Charter to delete provisions calling for the destruction of Israel and other anti-Israel references.[60] But shortly thereafter the peace process ground to a halt once more. The Netanyahu government charged that the Palestinians had failed to make good on their obligations on terrorism and security, and Israel indicated that it would not make further redeployments until it was satisfied that the PA was complying with its obligations under Wye and the Oslo Accords. This deadlock continued through the summer of 1999.

In the meantime, the political landscape of the Middle East shifted in two significant ways. First, in February 1999, Jordan's King Hussein

57 For an account of the opening of the Wye summit, see Steven Erlanger, 'Clinton Urges Netanyahu and Arafat to Take Risks', ibid. 16 Oct. 1998. For the text of the Wye River Memorandum, see 37 I.L.M. 1251 (1998) and Appendix H.

58 Wye River Memorandum, ¶I(A), ¶II.

59 See Lee Hockstader, 'Israel Withdraws from 200 Square Miles', *Wash. Post*, 21 Nov. 1998; Arieh O'Sullivan with Mohammed Najib, 'IDF wraps up Wye's first stage today', *Jerus. Post*, 22 Nov. 1998.

60 See Deborah Sontag, 'Clinton Watches as Palestinians Drop Call for Israel's Destruction', *N.Y. Times*, 15 Dec. 1998.

passed away and was succeeded by his son Abdullah, who moved quickly to reassure the world that he would continue his father's foreign policy, including his support for the peace process.[61] Second, in May 1999, Ehud Barak decisively defeated Benjamin Netanyahu in the Israeli election for Prime Minister, and Barak indicated that he would attempt to reinvigorate the peace process.[62]

Barak formed a new government in the summer of 1999. Upon taking office, he suggested that Israel and the Palestinians attempt to reach a final agreement by the autumn of 2000. He also indicated that he would like to modify the timetable for further redeployments set forth in the Wye River Memorandum. Barak has advocated renewal of negotiations with Syria, whose aging leader, Hafez al-Assad, is reportedly anxious to reach some sort of agreement before he leaves power. The Palestinian leadership welcomed Barak with cautious optimism.

On 4 September 1999 the Barak government concluded a new agreement with the PLO at the Egyptian resort of Sharm el-Sheikh.[63] The Sharm el-Sheikh Memorandum established new timetables for Israeli withdrawals, and it codified Barak's goal of reaching a final status agreement by the autumn of 2000. It also called for a framework agreement on final status issues by February 2000. It remains to be seen whether these deadlines are unduly optimistic. None the less, as the new millennium dawns, there is renewed hope for peace in the Middle East.

[61] See Douglas Jehl, 'Hussein of Jordan, Voice for Peace, Dies', *N.Y. Times*, 8 Feb. 1999.

[62] See Lee Hockstader, 'Barak Wins Israeli Vote; Rabin's Protege Gains Landslide Victory Over Netanyahu', *Wash. Post*, 18 May 1999.

[63] The Sharm el-Sheikh Memorandum on Implementation Timeline of Outstanding Commitments of Agreements Signed and the Resumption of Permanent Status Negotiations, 4 Sept. 1999, Isr.–PLO, reprinted in Appendix I.

PART II

Are the Oslo Accords Legally Binding?

It might well be asked why it matters whether the Oslo Accords are legally binding. Several answers suggest themselves. One is that states and individuals—even those who are sceptical about the existence of international law—appear to take legally binding instruments more seriously than purely political, non-binding undertakings. If Israel and the Palestinians have indeed signed binding commitments, then the international community as well as the parties themselves may expect a higher degree of fidelity to the agreements than if they are non-binding policy papers.

A related reason is that the parties themselves seem to attach some importance to the question. Indeed, it has frequently been suggested that the Oslo Accords are not legally binding, thus implying that one or both parties might bolt at any time. *Ra'ees* Arafat himself has reportedly hinted that the Oslo Accords are something less than binding commitments; he has invoked the supposed precedent of the Prophet Mohammed's abrogation of unfavourable treaties. (In fact, Islamic law adheres to the doctrine *pacta sunt servanda*—i.e. that treaties must be observed.[1]) In Israel, too, critics of the Oslo Accords have denounced the Accords as meaningless pieces of paper that fall short of full-fledged treaties. Some legal scholars have recently argued that the Accords were never binding in the first place, either because they violated Palestinian rights of self-determination or because they violated Israeli rights to peace and security.

There is yet another reason that the binding nature of the Accords is important. If the Accords are binding, they clearly have implications for the internal law of both parties. Israel has already changed its military regulations to comply with the Accords, and of course the Israeli Knesset gave its assent to the Accords by a formal vote. Likewise, the Palestinians have adopted internal rules designed to give effect to various provisions of the Accords. Moreover, if the Accords constitute some form of conventional or customary law, then it is possible that they have been received in full or in part into the law of one or both parties. In Israel, for example, customary law is part of Israeli domestic law, and treaty law can be made part of Israeli domestic law. It is even conceivable that Israel's international

[1] See M. Cherif Bassiouni, 'Protection of Diplomats Under Islamic Law', 74 *Am. J. Int'l L.* 609, 614–15 (1980) (quoting relevant passages from the Koran).

obligations to the Palestinians might some day give rise to domestic Israeli legal obligations that could be enforceable in Israeli courts.

The Oslo Accords themselves certainly indicate that the parties thought they were legally binding. Without exception, each Accord asserts that it has some sort of binding and lasting effect. All of them speak of 'entering into force' on a particular date.[2] Moreover, the 1995 Interim Agreement confidently declared that the Oslo peace process was 'irreversible'.[3] As the peace process has run into repeated obstacles, that optimism has often seemed misplaced, but it is true that the Oslo Accords have created facts that would be politically difficult to reverse. It is hard to imagine that the Palestinians will ever be stripped of the partial autonomy they have achieved in Gaza and in parts of the West Bank.

Is there a legal basis for the assertion that the Oslo process is 'irreversible'? Put another way, is it true that the Accords have 'entered into force' as a legal matter? There is in fact considerable doubt about whether the Accords are binding. This Part takes up the question in detail.

Chapter 3 begins the analysis by asking whether the Oslo Accords are binding as traditional treaties. As this chapter demonstrates, the Accords do not easily fit within the traditional, rather narrow definition of a treaty. Chapter 4 examines whether the Accords might be binding as unilateral declarations, as customary international law, or as some quasi-binding form of 'soft law'. I reject these suggestions as incompatible with the nature of the Accords and the intent of their drafters. I also reject the suggestion that the Accords have no legal effect at all. Finally, Chapter 5 argues that the Accords are binding as formal agreements between subjects of international law.

[2] See, e.g., Declaration of Principles, Art. XVII(1) ('This Declaration of Principles will enter into force one month after its signing'); Interim Agreement, Art. XXXI(1) ('This Agreement shall enter into force on the date of its signing').

[3] See Interim Agreement, Preamble ¶4. Commentators have also suggested that the Oslo process is irreversible. See, e.g., Aharon Klieman, *Approaching the Finish Line: The United States in Post-Oslo Peace Making*, 40 (Ramat Gan, Israel: Begin–Sadat Center of Bar-Ilan University, 1995) ('[T]he process is already essentially irreversible . . .'); Eyal Benvenisti, 'The Israeli–Palestinian Declaration of Principles: A Framework for Future Settlement', 4 *Eur. J. Int'l L.* 542, 546 (1993) (arguing that the Declaration of Principles establishes an 'irreversible step towards the settlement of the conflict'); Graham Usher, *Palestine in Crisis: The Struggle for Peace and Political Independence after Oslo* (London; East Haven, CT: Pluto Press, 1995), 28 ('From the moment Arafat shook Rabin's hand, most Islamists understood that Oslo was politically irreversible').

3

Are the Oslo Accords Treaties?

Are the Oslo Accords binding treaties? The leading definition of a treaty is contained in the 1969 Vienna Convention on the Law of Treaties, which is generally regarded as 'the principal authoritative source of the law of treaties'.[1] Although neither Israel nor the PLO is a party to the Vienna Convention, many regard the Convention as an authoritative codification of customary law, making it an indispensable starting point for analysis.[2] Under the Vienna Convention, a treaty is defined as 'an international agreement concluded between States in written form and governed by international law . . .'.[3] This formula comports with that of traditional treaty law, which maintained that only states and some international organizations[4] possessed treaty-making capacity.[5]

Early drafts of the Vienna Convention also covered agreements

[1] Louis Henkin, *et al.*, *International Law: Cases and Materials*, 3rd edn (St Paul, MN: West Publishing Co., 1993), 416.

[2] See, e.g., S. Exec. Doc. L., 92d Cong., 1st Sess. 1 (1971) (statement of the US Department of State) (asserting that the Convention 'is already recognized as the authoritative guide to treaty law and practice').

[3] Vienna Convention on the Law of Treaties, 23 May 1969, UN Doc. A/CONF. 39/27, Art. 2(1)(a).

[4] The term 'international organization' is 'generally used to refer to organizations composed entirely or mainly of states and usually established by treaty'. Henkin, *International Law*, 344. The PLO would not qualify as an international organization because it is not composed of 'states'.

[5] See, e.g., Lord McNair, *The Law of Treaties* (Oxford: Clarendon Press, 1961), 52–3 (asserting that an agreement between a state and a 'native chief or tribe' is not a treaty because 'native chiefs and tribes are neither States nor International Organizations; and thus possess no treaty-making capacity'). It is true that McNair acknowledged that a state might make a treaty with an 'insurgent community which it has recognized as belligerents'. Ibid. 680 (citing relations between the British government and the Confederate States of America during the American Civil War). McNair added, however, that there exists '[v]ery little authority' pertaining to treaties made by an insurgent community. Ibid. 676.

In any event, McNair's acknowledgement of treaties by insurgents was limited to those communities 'recognized as belligerents'. In the traditional view, a belligerent possesses at least some attributes of statehood. See Gerhard von Glahn, *Law Among Nations: An Introduction to Public International Law*, 2nd edn (New York: Macmillan, 1970), 85 (noting that recognition of belligerency requires 'treatment of the [belligerent] community as a state engaged in war'); R. J. Vincent, *Nonintervention and International Order* (Princeton: Princeton University Press, 1974), 286 (asserting that recognition of belligerency 'admits the insurgent into membership, though not full membership, in the international club'); cf. Sir Hersch Lauterpacht, *Recognition in International Law* (Cambridge: Cambridge University Press, 1948), 176, 270 (describing the salient characteristics of belligerency and asserting that belligerency gives rise to 'definite rights and obligations'). In so far as belligerency resembles statehood, it is not surprising that McNair concludes that belligerents might have some treaty-making capacity.

between states and 'other subjects of international law'—defined in commentary as international organizations, the Holy See, and perhaps some 'insurgent' movements like the PLO—but this language was struck out of the final draft.[6] Even so, the final text of the Convention does still recognize that agreements involving 'other subjects of international law' might be binding. Article 3 provides: 'The fact that the present Convention does not apply to international agreements concluded between States and other subjects of international law . . . shall not affect . . . the legal force of such agreements. . . .' In other words, agreements involving 'other subjects of international law' may be binding under the customary law of treaties, even if they are not binding under the Vienna Convention itself. It is quite likely that the Oslo Accords fall into this category; that possibility is discussed in detail in Chapter 5.

For now, our focus is on the more traditional (and narrow) definition of a treaty in Article 2 of the Vienna Convention. It has been argued that the Oslo Accords fit even that narrow definition, on the grounds that both parties to the Accords are 'States'.[7] As Palestinian institutions have acquired more of the attributes of statehood, this suggestion has grown increasingly plausible, and thus it merits thorough analysis.

The view of the parties

Israel and the PLO have not made their views on the juridical nature of the Accords entirely clear. Before the 1993 Declaration of Principles, the PLO argued vigorously that 'Palestine' was a state, implying that any agreement it made with another state would be a 'treaty'. Since the adoption of the Declaration, however, the Palestinian side has retreated from claims of statehood,[8] and it has not often addressed whether the Oslo

[6] See 2 Yb. I.L.C. 161 (1962) (draft Article 1) (defining a treaty as an agreement between 'two or more States or other subjects of international law'); ibid. 162 (commentary on draft Article 1) (¶ 8) (describing 'other subjects of international law' as international organizations, the Holy See, and 'other international entities, such as insurgents, which may in some circumstances enter into treaties').

Similarly, draft Article 3 provided that treaty-making capacity 'is possessed by States and by other subjects of international law'. Ibid. 164. Again, 'other subjects of international law' included international organizations, the Holy See, and 'more special cases such as an insurgent community to which a measure of recognition has been accorded'. Ibid. (Comment 2).

[7] See John Quigley, 'The Israel–PLO Interim Agreements: Are They Treaties?', 30 *Cornell Int'l L. J.* 717, 739 (1997) (arguing that the agreements are 'treaties' because the PLO is either a state or a subject of international law).

[8] See Mahmoud Abbas [Abu Mazen], *Through Secret Channels* (Reading: Garnet Publishing Ltd., 1995), 218 ('We do not claim that we signed an agreement that created an independent Palestinian State; none of the provisions in the Declaration of Principles make such a claim').

Accords are treaties between states. There have, however, been accusations that Yasser Arafat has compared the Oslo Accords to treaties made and thereafter abrogated by the Prophet Mohammed.[9] The theme of these accusations is that Arafat regards treaties as non-binding instruments. For its part, Israel has denied the PLO's claim to statehood but has avoided discussion of whether the Oslo Accords are treaties. The United States seems to have adopted a similar posture.

Interestingly, neither Israel nor the PLO has attempted to register the Oslo Accords with the United Nations.[10] Of course, the PLO's failure to do so is not surprising; only Members of the United Nations are required to register, and only states can be Members.[11] Still, Israel's failure to do so might suggest that Israel does not believe the instruments are treaties or international agreements.[12] None the less, failure to register is far from dispositive.[13] Not all treaties are registered with the United Nations,[14]

[9] See, e.g., Esther Wachsman, 'Too much in return for nothing', *Jerus. Post*, 13 Dec. 1996 ('Arafat constantly refers to the covenant the prophet Mohammed made with the tribe of Kureish, a treaty he broke when the time was right, when that tribe became weak. He then proceeded to slaughter them').

[10] See Facsimile dated 19 Mar. 1997 from Ines Price, Treaty Section, Office of Legal Affairs, United Nations, to Geoffrey R. Watson, The Catholic University of America (on file with author) ('I regret to inform you that these agreements [i.e. the Oslo and Hebron Accords] have not been submitted to the Secretariat for registration').

[11] See Charter of the United Nations, 26 June 1945, T.S. 993, Art. 102(1) (registration), Art. 4(1) (membership).

[12] Sir Robert Jennings and Sir Arthur Watts (eds.), *Oppenheim's International Law*, 9th edn (Harlow, Essex: Longman, 1993), § 663, 2:1317 n. 7 ('[I]ntentional non-registration may be evidence of an intention that the instrument should not constitute a treaty or international agreement'). See also Michael Brandon, 'Analysis of the Terms "Treaty" and "International Agreement" for Purposes of Registration Under Article 102 of the United Nations Charter', 47 *Am. J. Int'l L.* 49, 63 (1953) ('the term "treaty" in international law has not been applied to any instrument recording an agreement between a state and an entity possessing none of the qualities of statehood') (footnotes omitted).

[13] As the UN Secretariat has put it:

> Registration of an instrument submitted by a Member State . . . does not imply a judgment by the Secretariat on the nature of the instrument, the status of a party, or any similar question. It is the understanding of the Secretariat that its action does not confer on the instrument the status of a treaty or an international agreement if it does not already have that status and does not confer on a party a status which it would not otherwise have.

'Statement of Treaties and International Agreements Registered or Filed and Recorded with the Secretariat during November, 1955', UN Doc. ST/LEG/SER.A/105, Nov. 1955 (prefatory note), quoted in Leland M. Goodrich, *et al.*, *Charter of the United Nations: Commentary and Documents*, 3rd edn (New York: Columbia University Press, 1969), 612. See also *Oppenheim's International Law*, §663, 2:1317 ('[T]he nature of the instrument depends upon its own characteristics, and registration . . . is an ancillary matter only').

[14] For example, treaties and agreements between non-Member states do not have to be registered, although non-Member states do have the option to 'file and record' such instruments. See G.A. Res. 97 (I), 14 Dec. 1946 (regulations implementing Article 102), Art. 10(c) (providing that non-Members may file and record treaties and international agreements); 13 *Docs. of the San Francisco Conf.* 706; Goodrich, *Charter of the United Nations*, 612–13.

and, conversely, not all instruments registered with the United Nations are treaties.[15]

The popular press sometimes takes its cues on nomenclature from governments, but in this case the press too has equivocated on the precise nature of the Accords. A number of journalists have used the term 'treaty' to describe one or more of the Oslo Accords, but usually without any close attention to the definition of a treaty in international law.[16] More often journalists, following the lead of most governments, use more ambiguous terms like 'agreements' to refer to the Oslo Accords.[17]

Of course, the nomenclature adopted by the parties (or the press) is no more dispositive than the parties' failure to register the Accords with the United Nations. In the end, whether the Accords fall within the narrow definition of a 'treaty' in the Vienna Convention turns on a relatively objective question: whether both parties are 'states'. As the PLO has acknowledged, Israel is without question a state,[18] but it is doubtful that there is a 'State of Palestine'. The traditional test of statehood, endorsed by most of the international community, holds that a state must consist of four elements: a defined territory, a permanent population, a government in control of the territory, and the capacity to engage in foreign relations.[19] Application of this four-part test to the PLO and the Palestinian side

[15] The Charter itself provides that instruments other than treaties can be registered; Article 102(1) calls for registration of '[e]very treaty *and international agreement*' (emphasis added). The Secretariat has interpreted the term 'agreement' broadly to include even '*unilateral* engagements of an international character which have been accepted'. 1 U.N.T.S. xvi (1948) (emphasis added).

[16] See, e.g., Georgie Anne Geyer, '2 Weak Leaders Erase Hope for Peace In Middle East', *Chi. Tribune*, 28 Mar. 1997 (asserting that the Oslo Accords 'have the status of a treaty'); David Pryce-Jones, 'Israel and the Arabs must go back to basics', *The Times*, 28 Sept. 1996 (referring to the Accords as 'treaties'); Martin Sherman, 'When treaties do not bind', *Jerus. Post*, 20 Aug. 1996 (arguing that the Netanyahu government is not bound by the Oslo 'treaties').

[17] Cf. Moshe Zak, 'Cairo: Land for threats', *Jerus. Post*, 26 June 1996 (deriding Israeli politicians for using the term 'treaty' to describe the Oslo Accords).

[18] Letter of Arafat to Rabin, 9 Sept. 1993 ('The PLO recognizes the right of the State of Israel to exist in peace and security').

Some states apparently still dispute Israel's statehood. But Israel clearly meets the traditional four-prong test of statehood: it has a sufficiently defined territory, a permanent population, a government, and the capacity to engage in foreign relations. See Montevideo Convention on Rights and Duties of States, 26 Dec. 1933, 165 L.N.T.S. 19, T.S. 881, Art. I. Nor is it relevant that a number of states have not recognized the State of Israel. Under the prevailing 'declaratory' view of statehood, recognition is not a requirement of statehood. See American Law Institute, *Restatement (3rd) of Foreign Relations Law of the United States*, §202, Reporter's Note 1 (1987). Israel's membership in the United Nations is also strongly suggestive of its statehood. Cf. UN Charter, Art. 4(1) (providing that membership may be extended to peace-loving 'states' that accept Charter obligations); Hermann Mosler, 'The International Society As a Legal Community', 140 *Rec. des Cours* 1, 60 (1974–IV). See also 3 UN SCOR, 383 Mtg., 2 Dec. 1948, No. 128, pp. 9–12 (remarks of US delegate Philip C. Jessup) (arguing that Israel is a state).

[19] Montevideo Convention, Art. I.

varies depending on the instrument in question, since the Palestinian claim to statehood has grown stronger with time.

Application of this four-part test to the Palestinian party to the Oslo Accords is complicated by another consideration. The party that has signed all of the Accords is the Palestine Liberation Organization, not the Palestinian Council or Palestinian Authority. The 1994 Gaza–Jericho Agreement did establish a Palestinian self-governing entity, the Palestinian Authority, but that Agreement—and all subsequent Oslo Accords—was still signed by the PLO. The parties apparently chose this arrangement to assuage Israeli concerns that neither the PLO nor the new PA could be regarded as states. On this view, the PLO may be a subject of international law with capacity to make treaties, but it does not have actual control over territory or population; those functions are delegated to the PA. Conversely, the PA has control over territory and population, but it lacks the authority to make international agreements or otherwise conduct foreign relations; those functions reside in the PLO. Under this formal allocation of power, the PLO today is supposedly no more state-like than it was in 1993, when the first Oslo Accord was signed.

There might none the less be some argument that the Palestinian party to the Accords, whatever its designation, has a stronger claim to statehood today than it did in the early 1990s. If the Palestinian party is more state-like, then it is more likely that the later Oslo Accords are agreements 'between states', and thus qualify as formal treaties. Accordingly, we now turn to the central question: was the Palestinian signatory a 'state' at the time of the adoption of any of the Oslo Accords?

The Declaration of Principles

When the Declaration of Principles was signed in 1993, the PLO was clearly not a state. To be sure, it may have satisfied one requirement of statehood, that of a 'permanent population'. Israel itself acknowledged that the PLO was the 'representative of the Palestinian people'.[20] The Palestinian population is certainly large enough to meet any quantitative requirement of statehood, and its ethnic and religious composition is at least as uniform as that of many states.

It is far less clear, however, that the ostensible Palestinian state had a 'defined territory'—a second requirement of statehood. It is true that the existence of a border dispute is not in itself inconsistent with the requirement of a 'defined territory'; many states (including Israel) have

[20] Letter from Rabin to Arafat, 9 Sept. 1993.

border disputes. But in this case, the territory 'defined' by the PLO—territory including the West Bank, the Gaza Strip, and its capital in East Jerusalem[21]—was entirely in dispute by Israel.

In any event, even if for the sake of argument one accepts the claim that the Palestinian state had a 'defined territory' and a 'permanent population' before the adoption of the Declaration of Principles, it is very difficult to argue that the Palestinian 'state' satisfied the third requirement of statehood: a PLO 'government' in control of that territory. The reality then was that Israel, not the PLO, governed the day-to-day lives of Palestinian people in the West Bank, Gaza Strip, Golan Heights, and Israel itself. A Palestinian in the West Bank would have been surprised to hear that he or she lived in a 'state' with a PLO government. More likely he or she would have complained of living under Israeli occupation.

The PLO did have a plausible claim on the fourth element of statehood—the requirement that it have the 'capacity to engage in foreign relations'. In the late 1980s the PLO did undertake an effort to demonstrate that its 'State of Palestine' had such a capacity. The PLO established 'embassies' around the world, maintained some form of diplomatic relations with over a hundred states, and purported to receive diplomatic officials in East Jerusalem and elsewhere in the territory of the 'State of Palestine'.[22] The PLO also obtained observer status at the United Nations,[23] and it attempted to accede to multilateral conventions to which only states may be party.[24]

This diplomatic offensive may have achieved some political goals, but it did not clearly establish a capacity to engage in foreign relations. The PLO was not granted membership in the United Nations, one of the best modern indicia of statehood.[25] Its effort to accede to the four Geneva Conventions on the law of war was unsuccessful; in 1989 Switzerland, the depository for the

[21] Political Communiqué and Declaration of Independence by Palestinian National Council, 15 Nov. 1988, 27 I.L.M. 1660 (1988).

[22] See Eyal Benvenisti, 'The Israeli–Palestinian Declaration of Principles: A Framework For Future Settlement', 4 *Eur. J. Int'l L.* 542, 544 (1993).

[23] Observer Status for the Palestine Liberation Organization, G.A. Res. 3237, UN GAOR, 29th Sess., 2296th plen. Mtg., Supp. No. 31, at 4, UN Doc. A/9631 (1974).

[24] See, e.g., International Committee of the Red Cross, 'Geneva Conventions of 12 August 1949 and Additional Protocols of 8 June 1977: Ratifications, accessions and successions as at 31 December 1994', 304 *Int'l Rev. Red Cross* 111–19 (1995), ¶6 (noting that in 1989 the PLO attempted to adhere to the four Geneva Conventions on humanitarian law).

[25] See Mosler, 'The International Society As a Legal Community', 60.

After more than 100 states recognized the 'State of Palestine', the United Nations did change the name of the PLO's observer delegation to 'Palestine'. Question of Palestine, G.A. Res. 43/177, UN GAOR, 43rd Sess., 82nd plen. mtg, Supp. No. 49, at 62, UN Doc. A/43/49 (1988); Francis A. Boyle, 'The Creation of the State of Palestine', 1 *Eur. J. Int'l L.* 301, 302 (1990) (noting that the General Assembly adopted the 'Question of Palestine' resolution by 104–2, with only Israel and the United States voting No). But this resolution 'did not recognize a Palestinian state. . . . Instead, it acknowledged that the Palestine National Council had

Conventions, announced that it was 'not in a position to decide whether the PLO's letter [purporting to adhere to the Conventions] constituted an instrument of accession, due to the uncertainty within the international community as to the existence or non-existence of a State of Palestine'.[26] It is true that 'Palestine' was recognized by dozens of states, but recognition is generally not thought to be an independent element of statehood. Under the prevailing 'declaratory' view of recognition, recognition is not a necessary or sufficient component of statehood; at most, it is some evidence of a state's capacity to engage in diplomatic relations.[27]

At a minimum, moreover, capacity to engage in foreign relations requires 'the political, technical and financial capabilities' to do so.[28] The PLO may have had the political and financial wherewithal to establish and maintain its 'embassies' abroad, but it lacked the capability to carry out any of the actual objects of diplomatic relations—say, to regulate the terms of its trade with other states, or to make its armed forces available to aid an ally, or even to maintain and police its borders with neighbouring states. On the whole, it seems doubtful that the PLO had the 'capacity to engage in foreign relations' at the time of the 1993 Declaration of Principles.

Thus it seems unlikely that the PLO was a 'state' at the time of the Declaration because it lacked a government truly in control of its territory, and because it probably lacked a true capacity to engage in foreign relations. This conclusion is buttressed by the language of the Declaration itself, which describes Israel as a 'state' but the PLO as merely 'representing' the Palestinian people. Even one of the PLO's principal negotiators, Arafat's deputy Abu Mazen, concedes that the Declaration did not create a Palestinian state,[29] which again implies that the Declaration was not an agreement 'between states'.

Therefore it seems unlikely that the Declaration was a 'treaty' in the narrow sense of the Vienna Convention, since it was not an agreement 'between states'. Many commentators have reached the same conclusion.[30] That is not to say that the Declaration is not binding under the customary law of treaties, which does recognize that 'subjects of international law' have the capacity to make treaties. On the contrary: as Chapter 5 will

proclaimed the State of Palestine. . . .' Frederic L. Kirgis, Jr., 'Admission of "Palestine" as a Member of a Specialized Agency and Withholding the Payment of Assessments in Response', 84 *Am. J. Int'l L.* 218, 219–20 (1990).

[26] See ICRC, 'Geneva Conventions', ¶6.

[27] See *Oppenheim's International Law*, §39, 1:128–30.

[28] *Restatement*, §201, Comment e.

[29] Abu Mazen, *Through Secret Channels*, 218.

[30] See, e.g., Ruth Lapidoth and N. K. Calvo-Goller, 'Les Elements Constitutifs de L'Etat et la Declaration du Conseil National Palestinien du 15 Novembre 1988', 96 *Revue Generale de Droit Int'l Public* 777 (1992); James Crawford, 'The Creation of the State of Palestine: Too Much Too Soon?', 1 *Eur. J. Int'l L.* 307 (1990); Note, 'The Israel–PLO Declaration of Principles: Prelude to a Peace?', 34 *Va. J. Int'l L.* 435, 451 (1994). But see Maurice Flory, 'Naissance d'un Etat Palestinien', 93 *Revue Generale de Droit Int'l Public* 385 (1989).

demonstrate, that is the most compelling explanation of the juridical nature of the Declaration (and of most if not all of the Oslo Accords). For now, though, it does seem fair to conclude that the Declaration is not a 'treaty' within the strict, traditional definition set forth by the Vienna Convention.

Even if the Declaration were an agreement 'between states', a sceptic might still argue that the terms of the Declaration were not sufficiently definite to make it legally binding. After all, the Vienna Convention defines a treaty as an agreement between states that is 'governed by international law', perhaps implying that an instrument that speaks in hortatory rather than 'legal' terms is non-binding. Some aspects of the Declaration could understandably give rise to this sort of scepticism.

For example, the title of the instrument—a 'Declaration of Principles,' not 'Treaty' or even 'Agreement'—might suggest that the Declaration was a political document, not a legal one. It is clear, however, that the title of an instrument is never 'determinant'.[31] Indeed, while the term 'declaration' sometimes denotes a non-binding instrument, such as the Universal Declaration of Human Rights,[32] it has also been used to denote a binding treaty.[33] The better view would seem to be that the title 'Declaration' does not rule out binding effect.[34]

31 *South-West Africa Cases* (Preliminary Objections), 1961 I.C.J. 31 (Judgment of 21 Dec.). See Vienna Convention on the Law of Treaties, Art. 2(1)(a) (providing that a treaty is a treaty 'whatever its particular designation').

32 G.A. Res. 217A(III), UN Doc. A/810, at 71 (1948). Moreover, even General Assembly 'declarations' may have some legal consequence. See Oscar Schachter, 'International Law in Theory and Practice', 178 *Rec. des Cours* 111–21 (1982–V) (arguing that such declarations may constitute 'evidence' of the law rather than a treaty or other formal 'source' of law). See also Joseph Gold, 'Strengthening the Soft International Law of Exchange Arrangements', 77 *Am. J. Int'l L.* 443, 443 (1983).

For other examples of 'declarations' that are not treaties, see, e.g., *NV de Bataafasche Petroleum Maatschappij v. War Damage Comm'n*, 23 I.L.R. 810, 826–7 (1953) (declining to hold a World War II multilateral 'declaration' was a treaty); *Iran v. United States (Case A/1)*, 68 I.L.R. 523, 525, 545 (1982) (holding that the Algiers Declarations ending the 'hostage crisis' are not treaties).

33 See, e.g., Joint Declaration of China and the United Kingdom on the Question of Hong Kong, cited in *Oppenheim's International Law*, §577, 1:1189 n. 2 (noting that China and the United Kingdom jointly registered the Declaration with the United Nations as a treaty); Declaration of St Petersburg 1868, cited in ibid. 1:1188 n. 1; Declaration of Paris 1856, cited in ibid.; *Restatement* §301, Comment ('The terminology used for international agreements is varied. Among the terms used are . . . declaration'); *Werner v. Widow Rothschild*, 20 I.L.R. 406 (1953) (holding a 'Declaration' of 17 states to be a treaty); *De Rothschild v. Teuscher and Soc. d'Encouragement pour l'Amélioration des Races de Chevaux en France*, 20 I.L.R. 655 (1953). Declarations accompanying treaties have also been found to be legally binding. See, e.g., *Ambatielos Case* (Greece v. UK) (Preliminary Objection), 1952 I.C.J. 28, 40 (1 July) (treating as binding a 'Declaration' associated with a treaty of commerce and navigation). Cf. also *South-West Africa Cases* (Preliminary Objections), 1962 I.C.J. at 331 (Judgment of 21 Dec.) (finding 'no legal significance' in the fact that the Mandate for South-West Africa was 'described in its last paragraph as a Declaration').

34 See Note, 'The Israel–PLO Declaration of Principles', 450 ('the Declaration assumes, to a considerable degree, the character of a hard law instrument').

The operative provisions of the Declaration are also consistent with intent to be legally bound, even if they sometimes do smack more of an agreement to agree than of a specific commitment to action. By its terms the Declaration is a 'framework'[35] for future arrangements—a general statement of intention rather than a specific commitment to action. For example: 'The Israeli and Palestinian delegations will negotiate an agreement on the interim period.'[36] 'Agreements to agree' are not always enforceable in municipal contract law. But in treaty law, there is little doubt that parties can enter into legally binding 'agreements to agree'.[37]

Nor is the Declaration's frequent use of the passive voice inconsistent with intent to be bound. It is true that the Declaration often fails to identify precisely which party must do what, creating a sometimes deliberate ambiguity that would raise problems of definiteness in municipal contract law. For example, the Declaration provides simply that 'free and general political elections will be held'[38] without identifying who will be responsible for holding them. Indeed, the passive voice pervades this document.[39] But in many cases it seems apparent that the parties were

35 'The agreed framework for the interim period is set forth in this Declaration of Principles.' Declaration of Principles, Art. II.

36 Ibid., Art. VII(1). And: 'The two parties will invite the Governments of Jordan and Egypt to participate in establishing further liaison and cooperation arrangements. . . .' Ibid., Art. XII. See also Joel Singer, 'The Declaration of Principles on Interim Self-Government Arrangements', in *Justice*, Feb. 1994, No. 1, at 4, 5 ('As its title suggests, the DOP is not a comprehensive agreement, but rather a statement of agreed principles. In other words, it is not a self-executing document which purports to set out practical arrangements, but rather an "agreement to reach agreement" . . .'); Antonio Cassese, 'The Israel–PLO Agreement and Self-Determination', 4 *Eur. J. Int'l L.* 564, 565–6 (1993) (noting that the Declaration contains both *pacta de contrahendo*—obligations to conclude agreements—and *pacta de negotiando*—obligations to negotiate agreements).

37 Cf. E. Allan Farnsworth, *Contracts*, 2nd edn (Boston: Little Brown & Co., 1990) §3.29, 218–22 (noting that American courts may find 'agreements to agree' too indefinite to enforce) with Cassese, 'The Israel–PLO Agreement', 566–7 (arguing that the Declaration's agreements to agree impose legal obligations) and Prosper Weil, 'Towards Relative Normativity in International Law', 77 *Am. J. Int'l L.* 413 (1983) (noting that a 'soft' norm such as an agreement to agree 'does not thereby cease to be a legal norm'). Cf. also Gidon Gottlieb, 'Global Bargaining: The Legal and Diplomatic Framework', in Nicholas G. Onuf (ed.), *Lawmaking in the Global Community* (Durham, NC: Carolina Academic Press, 1982), 109, 120–3 (noting that the 'legal character of international agreements . . . can itself become the object of negotiations'); *Railway Traffic Between Lithuania and Poland*, P.C.I.J., Series A/B, No. 42, at 116 (Advisory Opinion of 15 Oct. 1931) (observing that an agreement to negotiate imposed a legal obligation to negotiate).

38 Declaration of Principles, Art. III(1).

39 Other examples include these: 'Jurisdiction of the [Palestinian] Council will cover West Bank and Gaza Strip territory, except for issues that will be negotiated in the permanent status negotiations.' Ibid., Art. IV. '[A]uthority will be transferred to the Palestinians on the following spheres.' Ibid., Art. VI(2). 'After the inauguration of the Council, the Civil Administration will be dissolved, and the Israeli military government will be withdrawn.' Ibid., Art. VII(5). 'The Council will be empowered to legislate, in accordance with the Interim Agreement. . . .' Ibid., Art. IX(1). '[A] Joint Israeli–Palestinian Liaison Committee will be established. . . .' Ibid., Art. X. '[A]n Israeli–Palestinian Economic Cooperation Committee will be established. . . .' Ibid., Art. XI.

seeking the ambiguity the passive voice provides, in order to hold disagreements over for another day's negotiations. The presence of lawyers in the negotiations, particularly on the Israeli side, is further evidence that the parties were seeking to draft a legally binding document, not just a political one.[40] Indeed, one theme of Palestinian critique of the Accords is that the Palestinian negotiating team did not include Palestinian lawyers.[41]

Any doubts about the parties' intent to be legally bound should be resolved by the 'final clauses' of the Declaration of Principles. One such clause provides: 'This Declaration of Principles will enter into force one month after its signing.'[42] This formulation is quite typical of treaties. It makes no reference to any state's domestic law, suggesting that it will 'enter into force' under international rather than domestic law. In other words, the language suggests that the instrument is 'governed by international law', as is required of a treaty, rather than domestic law.[43] Indeed, there is practice to suggest that states and other actors draft such clauses carefully to distinguish between instruments creating international obligations and those with only domestic legal consequences.[44]

[40] This is not to say that lawyers participated in every phase of the Oslo negotiations. At the seventh round of negotiations, on 13 June 1993—precisely three months before the Declaration was signed—the Israeli delegation was expanded to include Joel Singer, who had served as a legal adviser to the Israeli government in the 1970s and 1980s. See Abu Mazen, *Through Secret Channels*, 151–5. According to Abu Mazen, 'the Israeli delegation regarded Singer's involvement in the Oslo channel as representing full participation on the part of the Israeli decision-making centre'. Ibid. 152. See also David Makovsky, *Making Peace with the PLO: The Rabin Government's Road to the Oslo Accords* (Boulder, CO: Westview Press, 1996), 49 (noting that Singer was added to the team to enhance its legal expertise); ibid. 52 (reporting the Palestinian negotiators' impression that during negotiations Singer 'often acted like a prosecuting attorney conducting cross-examination').

Lawyers seem to have played a less prominent role on the Palestinian side in the early stages of negotiations. According to Abu Mazen:

> 'I must admit that throughout the Oslo negotiations we did not review the texts with a legal consultant for fear of leaks. We had therefore to depend on our own experience and handling of texts. I tried to make use of the remnants of the legal knowledge I had acquired while studying law at the Damascus University, but I could not draw much comfort from them. I must mention, however, that the DOP documents were reviewed by our legal consultant, Taher Shash, whom we had sent to Oslo for this purpose just before they were initialed on 20 August 1993.'

Abu Mazen, *Through Secret Channels*, 162.

[41] See generally Raja Shehadeh, *From Occupation to Interim Accords: Israel and the Palestinian Territories* (London: Kluwer Law International, 1997).

[42] Declaration of Principles, Art. XVII(1).

[43] Vienna Convention on the Law of Treaties, Art. 2(1)(a).

[44] Cf. General Framework Agreement for Peace in Bosnia and Herzegovina, 21 Nov. 1995, Bos.–Croa.–Yugo., Art. XI, reprinted in 7 *U.S. Dept. of State Dispatch Supp.* 1 (Mar. 1996) (providing that '[t]his Agreement shall enter into force upon signature') with Constitution of Bosnia and Herzegovina, Art. XII(1), reprinted in ibid. 25, 31 ('This Constitution shall enter into force upon signature of the General Framework Agreement *as a constitutional act amend-*

In sum, the Declaration of Principles does evince most of the characteristics of a binding treaty under the Vienna Convention. Its overall formality, its operative provisions, and especially its final clauses all suggest an 'agreement' that is 'governed by international law', and it is in writing, as is required by the Vienna Convention. But it is not an agreement 'between States', and thus falls short of the Vienna Convention standard, with its narrow definition of treaty-making capacity. None the less, as we shall see in Chapter 5, the Declaration probably does qualify as a binding international agreement under customary international law, whose rules on treaty-making capacity are somewhat more liberal.

The Gaza–Jericho Agreement

The 1994 Agreement on the Gaza Strip and the Jericho Area is probably not a 'treaty' under the Vienna Convention either. The PLO's legal status had not changed appreciably between September 1993, when the Declaration of Principles was signed, and 4 May 1994, when the Gaza–Jericho Agreement was signed. The PLO had not acquired any further control over its purported 'territory', and it still lacked the capacity to police its boundaries or carry out other basic functions of international relations. Like the Declaration, the Preamble of the Gaza–Jericho Agreement refers only to Israel as a 'state'; the PLO is again described as the 'representative of the Palestinian people'.

The Gaza–Jericho Agreement does speak in a more 'legal' voice than the Declaration. The title 'Agreement' connotes more of a legal obligation than a 'Declaration'; the term 'agreement' is more commonly used to denote a treaty or other international agreement than the term 'Declaration'. Like the Declaration, the Gaza–Jericho Agreement provides that it will 'enter into force', but the Gaza–Jericho Agreement also contains more specific language of commitment than the Declaration. It speaks in the active voice more often than the Declaration. Thus, for example, the Gaza–Jericho Agreement provides that Israel 'shall implement an accelerated and scheduled withdrawal',[45] and that the Palestinian Authority 'shall establish a strong police force'.[46]

The Gaza–Jericho Agreement is also more detailed than the Declaration, as one might expect of an instrument that implements a framework. Thus the agreement is accompanied by six maps and four detailed Annexes on withdrawal and security arrangements, civil affairs,

ing and superseding the Constitution of the Republic of Bosnia and Herzegovina') (emphasis added).

45 Gaza–Jericho Agreement, Art. II(1).

46 Ibid., Art. VIII.

legal matters, and economic questions. It might be fair to say, then, that the Gaza–Jericho Agreement is more formal than the Declaration of Principles, and that formality is a characteristic of many treaties.[47] But added formality alone does not make the agreement a treaty within the traditional definition of the Vienna Convention. It does not supply the missing ingredient: an agreement between states.

The Interim Agreement

There is a somewhat stronger argument that the agreements following the Gaza–Jericho Agreement—in particular, the Interim Agreement of September 1995 and the Hebron Protocol of January 1997—are treaties within the meaning of the Vienna Convention. Shortly after the signing of the Gaza–Jericho Agreement, Israel withdrew its forces from much of the Gaza Strip and from the Jericho Area, and it transferred many (though not all) responsibilities for governance of those areas to the Palestinian Authority. It might be argued that these developments at last did create a Palestinian state, at least in Gaza and Jericho, since some crucial missing elements of statehood—a 'government in control' of a 'defined territory'—had been supplied.

If the Palestinian self-governing entity is a state, then the PLO's subsequent agreements with Israel are probably treaties within the meaning of the Vienna Convention. The only counter-argument rests on the fact that the PLO, not the PA, signed the Interim Agreement and later accords. But if the PLO is merely the foreign-policy arm of the PA, and the PA otherwise meets the requirements of statehood, then the real 'party in interest' to the Accords might be said to be the PA. In any event, however, it seems that neither the PLO nor the PA has yet acquired statehood.

By the time of the Interim Agreement, there was a stronger argument that the Palestinian Authority possessed the attributes of a state. One requirement of statehood—that of a permanent population—now seemed clearly satisfied, if there ever was doubt. The second element of statehood also seemed to have been satisfied: the Palestinian Authority had a 'defined territory', comprising much of the Gaza Strip and the Jericho Area. It could no longer be argued that the territory of the Palestinian state was territory only on paper; the Palestinian Authority now had some degree of control over that territory. Indeed, that control implied progress towards the third element of statehood, a government in control of the territory. For the first time in history, a Palestinian self-governing authority was responsible for

[47] See generally Charles Lipson, 'Why Are Some International Agreements Informal?', 45 *Int'l Org*. 495, 495–513 (1991).

some—though not all—of the governance of Palestinians in the territory of former Mandate Palestine.[48] The Gaza–Jericho Agreement had even accorded the Palestinians some progress on the fourth and final prong of statehood, the capacity to engage in foreign relations. The Agreement permitted some PA dealings with foreign governments, but only for limited purposes, such as the disposition of economic aid and the conclusion of cultural agreements, not the establishment or receipt of embassies or the conduct of 'foreign relations'.[49]

Thus, at the time of the Interim Agreement, the Palestinian Authority was closer to statehood—but it was still not quite there. It was still not clear, for example, that the PA satisfied the third prong of statehood—the requirement of a government in 'control' of its territory. It is true that the PA did at last exercise a range of governmental and quasi-governmental functions in the West Bank and Gaza Strip, but then again so did Israel. Even after the Interim Agreement, Israel retained 'residual' powers not exercised by the PA; in the words of the Agreement, 'Israel shall continue to exercise powers and responsibilities not . . . transferred' to the Palestinian Legislative Council.[50] Likewise, the Interim Agreement and other Oslo Accords assert that the 'status' of the territories 'will be preserved during the interim period'.[51]

In more concrete ways, the Gaza–Jericho Agreement and Interim Agreement ensured a continuing and important role for Israel in the 'control' of PA-administered areas. One striking example is law enforcement. The PA lacks criminal jurisdiction over offences committed in the PA's territory by Israelis.[52] Israel retained criminal and, in many cases, civil jurisdiction over Israelis in the PA's territories; indeed, Palestinian authorities even lack the authority to 'arrest Israelis or place them in

[48] For an argument that the PLO was a 'government in control' of part of the occupied territories even before the Oslo process, see Boyle, 'The Creation of the State of Palestine', 302.

Most commentators have rejected this argument. Before Oslo, the reality was that Israel, not the PLO, was in 'control' of the territories for most purposes. See, e.g., Kirgis, 'Admission of "Palestine" ', 219; Crawford, 'The Creation of the State of Palestine', 308 (disputing PLO claims of actual 'control' over the territories); Lapidoth and Colvo-Goller, 'Les elements constitutifs', 792–6. See also *Klinghoffer v. Achille Lauro*, 937 F.2d 44, 47–8 (2nd Cir. 1991) (finding that the PLO did not 'control' territory).

[49] Gaza–Jericho Agreement, Art. VI(2)(a); Interim Agreement, Art. IX(5)(a).

[50] Interim Agreement, Art. 1(1). Advocates for both sides agree on this interpretation. See Joel Singer, 'The West Bank and Gaza Strip: Phase Two', in *Justice*, Dec. 1995, at 3 (arguing that Israel retains 'residual' powers of government in the territories); Shehadeh, *From Occupation to Interim Accords*, 35 ('all residual powers and responsibilities shall continue to be exercised by Israel').

[51] Interim Agreement, Art. XXXI(8).

[52] Ibid., Annexe IV, Art. I(2)(b) ('Israel has sole criminal jurisdiction over . . . offenses committed in the Territory by Israelis'). The 'Territory' refers to Areas A and B. Ibid., Art. I(1)(a).

custody', though PA police may 'detain' Israeli suspects 'in place' until Israeli police arrive.[53] As a leading Palestinian lawyer has observed, 'the security arrangements agreed upon substantially limit the jurisdiction of the Palestinian Council in all respects including in Area A', the area of maximal Palestinian authority.[54] These examples can be multiplied to include Israeli authority over PA airspace and sea-lanes, Israeli regulation of safe passage between the West Bank and the Gaza Strip, and other Israeli authority over internal matters that no true state would cede to another. These examples raise continued doubts about any claim that the PA satisfies the requirement that a state be in 'control' of its territory.

It has been argued that the traditional requirement of 'control' has been 'relaxed' where 'the putative state was seen to have a right to statehood and where there was not a competing entity seeking statehood in the same territory'.[55] Thus the Congo and Guinea-Bissau obtained UN membership before Belgium and Portugal, respectively, had ceded them actual control over territory.[56] But in both those cases Belgium and Portugal had already agreed to recognize the new states before withdrawing their troops. That is not the case here. Israel has repeatedly made clear that it does not recognize any Palestinian state, at least not yet.[57] As we have seen, Israel's view on this point is reflected in the Oslo Accords, which pointedly stop short of referring to a Palestinian state.

There is one last difficulty with the claim that the PA had 'control' of territory at the time of the Interim Agreement, and that difficulty also

[53] Interim Agreement, Annex IV, Art. II(2)(c) (restricting PA powers of arrest).

[54] Shehadeh, *From Occupation to Interim Accords*, 63.

[55] Quigley, 'The Israel–PLO Interim Agreements', 725, citing Malcolm N. Shaw, *International Law* (Cambridge: Grotius Publications, 1991), 142 and James Crawford, *The Creation of States in International Law* (Oxford: Clarendon Press, 1979), 46.

[56] G.A. Res. 3205, UN GAOR, 29th Sess., Supp. No. 31, at 2, UN Doc. A/9631 (1975); Joint Declaration (Guinea-Bissau–Portugal), 26 Aug. 1974, reprinted in 78 *Revue Gen. de Droit Int'l Public* 1252–3 (1974); Crawford, *Creation of States*, 43; Quigley, 'The Israel–PLO Interim Agreements', 724–5.

[57] Professor Quigley suggests that Israel's 'insistence that the PLO recognize it' somehow implies 'Israel's acknowledgment that the PLO represents a state, even though Israel officially maintains the contrary'. Quigley, 'The Israel–PLO Interim Agreements', 725. Quigley's argument rests on the traditional assumption that only *states* may recognize other states. See Lauterpacht, *Recognition in International Law*, 6. There is nothing, however, to prevent non-state entities from purporting to recognize states, as the PA has done here, and indeed national courts and international organizations now routinely assess whether to treat entities as states.

More to the point, it seems inappropriate to suggest that Israel has impliedly recognized the PLO simply because Israel seeks the PLO to recognize it, given that Israel has *explicitly* refused to recognize any Palestinian state. Implied recognition is increasingly common in international practice, but 'recognition is a matter of intention and . . . care must be taken not to imply recognition from acts which, although amounting to a limited measure of intercourse, do not necessarily reveal an intention to recognise'. *Oppenheim's International Law*, §50, 1:169–70. Israel's 'intention' could not be more plain: it does not recognize a Palestinian state.

relates to the final element of statehood, the capacity to engage in foreign relations. A government in 'control' of its territory presumably has the right to exclusive control over the borders of that territory; that was not the case with the Palestinian Authority at the time of the Interim Agreement, or today. Israel retained (and still retains) that power.[58] That suggests not only that the PA lacks ultimate 'control' over its territory, but also that it lacks the final element of statehood, the capacity to engage in foreign relations. Such capacity presumes the most fundamental aspect of sovereignty—the ability to control one's own borders.

It is true, as some proponents of PA statehood argue, that states can delegate responsibility for foreign relations to other states.[59] Morocco, for example, was treated as a state even after it agreed to permit France to handle its foreign relations.[60] More recently, Monaco was admitted to the United Nations even though it has effectively delegated many responsibilities for external relations to France. But it is more difficult to characterize the Palestinian–Israel relationship as a 'delegation' of pre-existing Palestinian rights to Israel. Before the Oslo Accords, it was even more clear that there was no State of Palestine, and thus no power of foreign relations to delegate. The Interim Agreement starkly forbids the PA to engage in even the most fundamental aspect of foreign relations, the establishment of diplomatic relations via embassies and consulates. This type of limitation is obviously inconsistent with the suggestion that the PA now has the 'capacity to engage in foreign relations'.[61]

It thus appears that there was no Palestinian state at the time of the signing of the Interim Agreement, and thus that the Interim Agreement is not an agreement 'between states', as is required of treaties under the Vienna Convention. There is an increasingly plausible argument that the PA meets some or most of the elements of statehood, but it remains doubtful that it satisfies all of them, in particular the requirements of control and foreign relations.

To be sure, the Interim Agreement is by far the most 'legal' of the Oslo Accords in tone and appearance. Unlike the Declaration of Principles, it

58 Interim Agreement, Art. XII(1) (Israel has 'all the powers to take the steps necessary to meet' its 'responsibility' for external security). Again, advocates for each side agree on this point. See Singer, 'The West Bank and Gaza Strip', 9; Shehadeh, *From Occupation to Interim Accords*, 63 (Israel 'has taken no chances and left overall responsibility for security in its hands').

59 See Quigley, 'The Israel–PLO Interim Agreements', 725 ('An entity does not lack the quality of statehood . . . if it agrees to let another state handle its external relations').

60 Ibid., citing Oliver Lissitzyn, 'Territorial Entities Other Than States in the Law of Treaties', 125 *Recueil des Cours* 5, 53 (1983–III) and *Case Concerning Rights of Nationals of the United States of America in Morocco* (Fr. v. US), 1952 I.C.J. 176, 185, 188, 193–4.

61 See Justus R. Weiner, 'Hard Facts Meet Soft Law—The Israel–PLO Declaration of Principles and the Prospects for Peace: A Response to Katherine W. Meighan', 35 *Va. J. Int'l L.* 931, 942–3 (1995); Note, 'The Israel–PLO Declaration of Principles', 452.

creates immediate and specific obligations for both parties, not just agreements to agree. Unlike the Declaration, it is detailed and lengthy, including a number of Annexes comprising hundreds of pages of specific rules. Although it occasionally lapses into the constructive ambiguity that plagues all of the Accords, the Interim Agreement often speaks quite clearly, and often in the active voice. The title of the Agreement leaves no doubt about the parties' intent to be bound, and the final clauses again speak of entry into force, implying legal obligation.

In sum, the Interim Agreement is a treaty in almost every sense of the Vienna Convention—except that it is not an agreement between states. As we shall see in Chapter 5, however, there is an especially strong case to be made that the Interim Agreement is binding in customary law as an agreement between a state and a subject of international law.

The Hebron Protocol

Most of the foregoing conclusions about the Interim Agreement apply with equal force to the Hebron Protocol, with two qualifications. The first is that by the time of the Hebron Protocol, the Palestinian Authority had acquired even more of the incidents of statehood than had been the case at the timing of the Interim Agreement, since that Agreement further expanded the scope of the PA's authority in civil matters. But the fundamental obstacles to a claim of Palestinian statehood remained: the Interim Agreement continued to impose significant restrictions on PA 'control' of its territories and on the PA's conduct of foreign relations.

The second qualification is that the Hebron Protocol's most wide-ranging obligations are set forth in a document that is not signed by either party, the famous 'Note for the Record' prepared by US Ambassador Dennis Ross 'at the request' of the parties. Even if the Hebron Protocol is binding as an agreement involving a 'subject of international law', it might be argued that the Note for the Record is not binding because it was not signed by the parties, and signature is a traditional means of expressing assent to treaties. But signature is not the *only* means of expressing assent; the Vienna Convention on the Law of Treaties provides that consent of a state can be expressed 'by any other means if so agreed'.[62] The parties plainly did indicate to Ambassador Ross their assent to the Note.

In any event, the context of the Note does suggest that the parties intended the Note to have some legal consequence, even though it was not actually signed by the parties. The Note was issued as part of a whole

62 Vienna Convention on the Law of Treaties, Art. 11.

package of agreements on Hebron, and it is cast in mandatory rather than hortatory terms. Moreover, as we shall see in Parts III and IV, it has been invoked by both sides (especially Israel) as a source of obligations. As a practical matter, the legal status of the Note is not crucial, since the Note mainly restates the most important obligations of the Interim Agreement. On occasion the Note does alter the obligations of the Interim Agreement, mostly by setting new deadlines, but it does not fundamentally contradict the earlier Accords. In any event, it would seem that the Note has no less binding character than the Hebron Protocol to which it is attached. And while the Hebron Protocol and the other Oslo Accords are not formal treaties, they are none the less binding (as we shall see in Chapter 5) as agreements between subjects of international law.

The Wye River Memorandum

For the same reasons, the Wye River Memorandum does not qualify as a formal treaty either, though again (as we shall see in Chapter 5) it probably *does* qualify as a binding agreement between subjects of international law. It is worth noting, though, that the Wye River Memorandum is rather less formal than most of the earlier agreements. It is styled a 'memorandum' rather than an 'agreement' or 'protocol'; its preamble describes its provisions as 'steps to facilitate implementation' of earlier agreements; and it is structured as an outline rather than a series of traditional treaty 'Articles', and in that sense resembles the Note for the Record more than the Hebron Protocol or Interim Agreement. Unlike the Note, however, the Wye Memorandum was signed by both parties (and witnessed by the United States), and it specifically provided that it would 'enter into force' ten days after signature. Taken as a whole, the Memorandum does possess the formal attributes necessary to qualify as a binding agreement between subjects of international law. None the less, because the PLO still did not constitute a state at the time of the signing of the Wye Memorandum, it is not a formal treaty.

The Sharm el-Sheikh Memorandum

The Sharm el-Sheikh Memorandum of 4 September 1999 is similar in structure and style to the Wye River Memorandum, and many of the same considerations apply to it. Both instruments bear the rather informal title 'memorandum', but both contain mandatory language that is often cast in quite specific terms. Again, the Sharm el-Sheikh Memorandum is not a traditional treaty because one party is not a state. The PLO is no more a state now than it was in the autumn of 1998. *Ra'ees* Arafat did not declare an independent Palestinian state on 4 May 1999, and even if he had, it is doubtful that the Palestinian entity would have qualified as a state, which must have a government in actual control of its own territory.

In sum, the Oslo Accords are probably not treaties under traditional treaty law, as embodied in the Vienna Convention on the Law of Treaties. That counter-intuitive conclusion says something about the narrow scope of the Vienna Convention and, more generally, about the formalism that pervades international law. As we shall see, the modern customary law of international agreements is broader than the Vienna Convention; under customary law, the Oslo Accords probably are legally binding international agreements between subjects of international law. But first we turn to some more exotic theories about the juridical nature of the Accords.

4

Other Theories of Obligation

Having determined that the Oslo Accords are not probably binding as traditional treaties, we now turn to a variety of other, less traditional theories about their juridical nature. These include suggestions that the Accords are an exchange of binding unilateral declarations, that they are binding codifications of customary international law, that they are only loosely binding as 'soft law', and that the Accords have no binding effect whatsoever. Chapter 5 will return to a treaty-like theory of obligation: that the Accords are binding as agreements between subjects of international law.

The Accords as an exchange of binding declarations

The World Court has suggested that unilateral promises made in the context of international negotiations may be binding if they are made in good faith. In *Legal Status of Eastern Greenland*,[1] the Permanent Court of International Justice held that Norway was bound by its promise[2] to acquiesce in Danish claims to Greenland. The Court stressed, however, that Norway's promise was given in response to an enquiry from Denmark, in which Denmark promised not to challenge Norwegian sovereignty over Spitzbergen.[3] In other words, the Court believed it was crucial that the 'unilateral' promise was made during negotiations.

The holding in *Eastern Greenland* arguably implies that Israel's promises to the Palestinians are binding as 'unilateral declarations made in the context of negotiations', and vice-versa, even though the promises did not form treaties within the traditional meaning of the term. But the promises in the Oslo Accords differ from those in *Eastern Greenland* in that only one of the two promisors—Israel—is a state. Should the decision in *Eastern Greenland* be applied in such circumstances?

As we shall see in Chapter 5, non-state actors like the PLO can constitute 'subjects of international law' that possess the capacity to make

[1] (Den. v. Nor.), 1933 P.C.I.J. (ser. A/B) No. 53 (5 Apr.).

[2] Elsewhere I have expressed doubt over whether Norway ever made a 'promise' in the *Eastern Greenland* case. See Geoffrey R. Watson, 'The Death of Treaty', 55 *Ohio St. L.J.* 781, 800 (1994).

[3] See Thomas Franck, Editorial Comment, 'Word Made Law: The Decision of the ICJ in the Nuclear Test Cases', 69 *Am. J. Int'l L.* 612, 615 (1975).

treaties. Treaty-making capacity might imply a capacity to make binding unilateral promises as well. If that is the case, then of course the Oslo Accords can be seen as an exchange of binding unilateral declarations made in the context of negotiations. But it would be simpler to conclude that the Accords are binding as full-fledged agreements between subjects of international law.

If, on the other hand, *Eastern Greenland* applies only to declarations by states, and if states are bound by their promises to non-state actors, then the Oslo Accords are a one-way street: only Israel is bound, since the Palestinian promises were not made by a state. It is highly unlikely that Israel intended to enter into such a one-sided bargain. Indeed, the texts of the Oslo Accords suggest that both parties thought they were making binding pledges. As we have already seen, the agreements provide that they shall 'enter into force' at a certain date; they do not say they shall enter into force only for Israel. Similarly, Article XXXI of the Interim Agreement requires both parties to 'pass all necessary legislation to implement' the agreement—language normally associated with a mutually binding treaty obligation. Subsequent practice of the parties also suggests that both sides regard themselves as bound at least to some extent. The two sides have traded accusations of breach, but neither has contended that non-performance is justified on the grounds that the Accords are non-binding. Thus, if *Eastern Greenland* applies only to the unilateral promises of states (and not those of non-state actors), it seems inappropriate to extend that precedent to the Oslo Accords.

The World Court expanded on *Eastern Greenland* in the *Nuclear Tests* cases, in which the Court held that France's unilateral promises not to undertake nuclear testing were legally binding.[4] The Court explicitly rejected the implication in *Eastern Greenland* that a promise was binding only if made in the context of negotiations. The Court said that a state's promise, 'if given publicly, and with an intent to be bound, even though not made in the context of international negotiations, is binding'. No 'quid pro quo' or 'reply or reaction' is required for such a declaration to 'take effect'.[5] Thus the Court unambiguously adopted a theory of obligation for unilateral promises.

As in *Eastern Greenland*, the Court in *Nuclear Tests* said nothing to indicate whether a state's promise to a sub-state entity should be binding as well. If Israel's promises to the PLO are binding on this theory, then any state's public promise to any sub-state entity presumably should be binding on the international plane. A state would be bound by all its public promises to political subdivisions, corporations, and individuals, and it would be responsible in international law for any breach of those promises.

[4] (Austl. v. Fr.), 1974 I.C.J. 253, 267–70 (20 Dec.). [5] Ibid. 267.

It is unlikely that the Court intended to go that far. The rule in the case is itself *dictum*, it has not been codified in the conventional law of treaties, and it has rarely if ever been applied since it was announced more than twenty years ago. Extending the rule to cover promises to sub-state entities would seem premature given that we are not sure how broadly the rule covers promises made to states. Nor is such an extension required by 'general principles of law' recognized by 'civilized nations'. It is true that municipal legal systems do sometimes impose liability on states and other actors for their unilateral promises, and while this liability often depends on reliance by the promisee, on occasion liability may be possible without reliance.[6] But such rules presuppose that the promise is made to a promisee with capacity to contract. By analogy, Israel's gratuitous promises to the Palestinians would seem to lack an essential ingredient to make them binding as unilateral promises: a promisee with capacity to make treaties.

A related theory of obligation might rest on estoppel. It might be argued that the promises of Israel and the Palestinians are binding because the promises induced justifiable reliance. Israel has relied on Palestinian promises by withdrawing from the Gaza Strip and portions of the West Bank, by recognizing the PLO as the representative of the Palestinian people, and by ceding certain governmental functions to the Palestinian Authority. The PLO has relied on Israeli promises by recognizing Israel, by undertaking to amend the Palestinian National Covenant, and by accepting some responsibility to govern in cooperation with Israel. In many municipal systems, this sort of reliance on a promise may make the promise legally binding. Moreover, this theory of promissory estoppel was endorsed by the International Court of Justice in *North Sea Continental Shelf*.[7] In that case the Court declined to enforce a promise by West Germany but suggested that the promise might be binding if there were evidence of reliance on the part of the promisees.[8]

As with *Nuclear Tests*, the scope of the decision in the *North Sea Continental Shelf* case is uncertain, and this alone may be reason to hesitate about applying it to a politically complex situation like the Middle East peace negotiations. Would the estoppel doctrine apply only to the written promises in the Oslo Accords, or also to any oral undertakings made in the course of negotiations? Would estoppel doctrine apply only to statements of Arafat and Netanyahu, or also to high-ranking aides and negotiators? Could statements to third parties (such as the United States) or the

[6] See, e.g., American Law Institute, *Restatement (2nd) of the Law, Contracts*, §90(2).
[7] (FRG v. Den., FRG v. Neth.), 1969 I.C.J. 3, 26 (20 Feb.).
[8] Ibid. 25. See also *Temple of Preah Vihear* (Camb. v. Thai.), 1962 I.C.J. 6 (15 June) (applying a doctrine of estoppel to the one state's acquiescence in another's maps depicting sovereignty over territory).

press be binding? Introducing these uncertainties into the Oslo Accords would needlessly complicate an already complex process.

Another problem with applying the estoppel rule to the Oslo process is remedial. If the PA is to be 'responsible' for promises that induce justifiable reliance, how will that responsibility be enforced? Not being a state, the PA cannot be sued in the International Court of Justice, and it is presumably not subject to liability as a state under the doctrine of state responsibility. For that matter, why should a non-state actor be liable at all under a doctrine of international promissory estoppel? There are few instances in municipal estoppel law in which a party lacking capacity to contract is held liable for its promises, even if those promises induce reliance. And if estoppel doctrine applies only to Israel's promise, not the PA's, then again we are left with a one-sided obligation that was plainly not intended by either party.

In sum, the World Court's jurisprudence on unilateral declarations and estoppel is an unlikely basis for enforcing the Oslo Accords. The Court's decisions concern promises made between states, not promises between a state and a non-state actor like the PLO. If, on the one hand, the Court's jurisprudence on unilateral promises did not cover the promises of non-state actors, then it would mean that only Israel is bound by the Oslo Accords—a result not intended by the parties. If, on the other hand, the Palestinians can be bound by their promises, then the Accords should simply be enforced as binding agreements between subjects of international law, as discussed in Chapter 5. Either way, the Court's jurisprudence on unilateral promises does not appear to be controlling.

The Accords as Binding Customary Law

A second possibility is that the Oslo Accords have codified or created customary international law. Customary law consists of two components: (1) general and consistent state practice that is (2) followed out of a sense of legal obligation, or *opinio juris*.[9] The Accords might have legal consequences in the same way that certain General Assembly declarations may have legal consequences—perhaps as 'evidence' or 'codification' of existing customary international law,[10] or perhaps as the source of new customary international law.

One difficulty with this theory is that the Accords themselves do not

[9] Cf. Statute of the International Court of Justice, 26 June 1945, T.S. 993, Art. 38(1)(b) (referring to custom as 'evidence of a general practice accepted as law').

[10] Cf. Oscar Schachter, 'International Law in Theory and Practice', 178 *Rec. des Cours* 111–21 (1982–V) (arguing that General Assembly resolutions may be 'evidence' of international law).

explicitly purport to codify or create customary law. The parties speak of the Accords entering into force as if they are treaties, not as if they ratify pre-existing custom. Even if the Accords did announce that they codified or created customary law, that declaration would be evidence of customary law but would not be 'conclusive' on the parties.[11]

Still, it might be argued that some of the later Accords impliedly 'codify' or provide 'evidence' of the first component of customary law, state practice. It is difficult to maintain that the 1993 Declaration of Principles, the first of the Oslo Accords, constituted 'evidence' or a 'codification' of existing customary law, if only because there was no pre-existing state practice to codify. But it may have some value as a source of new state practice: even the signing of the Declaration itself might be an example of 'practice'. In any event, the 1995 Interim Agreement and the 1997 Hebron Protocol could be regarded as sources of new custom and codifications of pre-existing practice. The later agreements not only establish detailed new rules that still govern the conduct of the parties, they also incorporate by reference practice under the earlier Accords, such as the Israeli withdrawal from Gaza and Jericho in 1994 and the parties' mutual recognition in 1993. By the same token, the Note for the Record and the Wye and Sharm el-Sheikh Memoranda restate many of the major obligations of the Interim Agreement.

The Oslo Accords also contain evidence that the parties have engaged in this 'practice' out of a 'sense of legal obligation' (*opinio juris*), which is the second requirement of customary law. As we have already seen, the Oslo Accords are cast in legal terms; they all provide for 'entry into force', and the parties repeatedly declare that the process is 'irreversible'. Few if any states have objected to these assertions. Does this evidence of *opinio juris*, together with the state practice described in the Accords, add up to the conclusion that the Accords have memorialized customary international law?

On the whole, it seems unlikely that the Accords are customary law. One problem is that the Accords offer evidence of only one state's practice—Israel's. State practice does not require a large number of states; customary international law can include 'special' or 'regional' customs involving just a few states, even just two.[12] But how can one state alone make customary international law? There are two possible responses to this objection, neither of which is convincing.

First, it might be said that the Accords actually concretize the practice of a variety of states, not just Israel. For example, other states signed

[11] American Law Institute, *Restatement (3rd) of the Foreign Relations Law of the United States*, §102, Reporter's Note 5, at 33 (1987).

[12] See, e.g., *Asylum Case* (Col. v. Peru), 1950 I.C.J. 266; *Case Concerning Right of Passage Over Indian Territory* (Merits) (Port. v. India), 1960 I.C.J. 6.

various Accords as 'witnesses'; their signatures might be regarded as 'state practice' in the same way that a vote for a General Assembly resolution is sometimes said to be an instance of 'state practice'. Likewise, some states in the region have relied on the Accords politically and legally. The most prominent example is Jordan, which concluded a peace treaty with Israel after the Oslo process began.[13] States outside the region, most notably the United States, have made the Oslo Accords the centrepiece of their foreign policy in the Middle East. These states may all regard the Oslo Accords as binding evidence of state practice and *opinio juris*.

The problem with this theory is that third states have generally refrained from overt expressions of opinion on whether the Accords are legally binding, and there have been few opportunities for third states to engage in 'practice' that demonstrates the binding nature of the Accords. Even the United States, one of the principal facilitators of the peace process, has stepped lightly around the question of the legal status of the Oslo Accords. For example, in January 1997 US Secretary of State Warren Christopher prepared a draft letter to Prime Minister Netanyahu congratulating him on signing the Hebron Protocol and referring to the undertakings in Oslo II as 'commitments'.[14] Christopher's letter said nothing about legal obligations. Other states have been similarly circumspect.

Second, it might be argued that the Palestinian Authority or PLO counts as a second 'state' for the purposes of 'state practice'. As we have seen, the better view is that there is not, as yet, a Palestinian state. Still, modern international law now regards some of the practice of non-state actors as relevant to 'state' practice. In particular, customary law sometimes may bind individuals, implying that individuals might conversely help create customary law. For example, the Statute of the International Criminal Tribunal for the Former Yugoslavia criminalizes individual violations of the 'laws or customs of war'.[15] If non-state actors can be bound by customary international law, perhaps they can also contribute to its creation.

In reality, however, the direct application of customary law to individuals or other sub-state entities is unusual. Many of the 'customary law' norms in the Statute for the Yugoslavia war crimes tribunal were already

[13] For a useful account of the politics behind the Israel–Jordan peace treaty, see Samuel Segev, *Crossing the Jordan* (New York: St Martin's Press, 1998), 297–348.

[14] See letter to be provided by US Secretary of State Christopher to Benjamin Netanyahu at the time of the signing of the Hebron Protocol, undated manuscript, available at the website of the Israeli Ministry of Foreign Affairs, http://www.israel-mfa.gov.il/peace/heblttr.html.

[15] Statute of the International Tribunal, Art. 3, in Annex to the Report of the Secretary General Pursuant to Paragraph 2 of Security Council Resolution 808 (1993), UN Doc. S/25704, 3 May 1993, 32 I.L.M. 1192 (1993).

embedded in treaties and in the municipal law of states, including Yugoslavia. And in any event international war crimes prosecutions have been rare to say the least; the Bosnia tribunal is the first such international tribunal since Nuremberg and Tokyo. Given that customary law has not often been applied directly to individuals, it would seem somewhat novel to apply it directly to a sub-state entity like the PLO. If the PLO is not bound by customary law, it seems unlikely that it can play a role in creating it.

If the PLO cannot create 'state' practice, then it might follow that the PLO cannot be bound by it either. This conclusion leads to another familiar objection: that only Israel, not the Palestinians, would be bound by the Accords. As we have already seen, it is inconceivable that Israel intended to make binding promises in exchange for non-binding promises. Either Israel expected both parties to be bound by international law, or it expected neither party to be bound.

There is yet another objection to the notion that the Oslo Accords have codified or created customary international law. Normally customary law requires a general and consistent practice, and 'consistency' implies the passage of some time. How much 'custom' can take hold in the space of five years? Some commentators have derided the notion that the signing of international instruments can give rise to brand-new 'customary' law. They refer to this notion as 'instant custom' or 'custom on demand'.[16] They note that emphasizing legal instruments in effect elevates *opinio juris* over actual state practice.[17] To be fair, there has been at least some state practice in the case of the Oslo process, but it is worth pausing to remember that customary international law does presuppose actual custom.

That observation leads to the ultimate point about customary law and the Oslo Accords: in the end, the actual implementation of the Accords is a much more reliable indicator of state practice than the signatures on them. And, as we shall see in Parts III and IV, implementation of the Accords has been uneven at best, on both sides. The actual 'custom' in the Oslo process has been as much characterized by inaction and obstruction as by 'practice' and *opinio juris*. Put another way, the actual 'practice'

[16] See Louis Henkin, *et al.*, *International Law: Cases and Materials*, 3rd edn (St Paul, MN: West Publishing, 1993), 82; Louis Henkin, 'International Law: Politics, Values and Functions', 216 *Rec. des Cours* 58 (1989–IV). But cf. Oscar Schachter, 'International Law in Theory and Practice', 178 *Rec. des Cours* 114–21 (1982–V) (describing the term 'instant custom' as 'misleading' and adding that 'several [UN General Assembly] resolutions have asserted rules or principles of general international law when practice was negligible or inconclusive and these resolutions have been regarded as sufficient evidence of the legal character of the norm asserted').

[17] See Henkin, *International Law*, 82 n. 3. Cf. also Sir Robert Jennings, 'The Identification of International Law', in Bin Cheng (ed.), *International Law, Teaching and Practice* (London: Stevens, 1982), 5 (asserting that some supposed customary law 'is not only not custom; it does not faintly resemble a customary law').

under the Accords varies considerably from their text, and the parties' conduct raises questions about whether either feels a true 'sense of legal obligation'. The Oslo Accords probably are binding as agreements between subjects of international law, but it seems doubtful that they reflect actual (as opposed to hoped-for) practice.

In sum, it seems doubtful that the Oslo Accords codify or create customary international law. It is far from clear that the parties thought they were codifying or creating norms of customary law; the Accords themselves make no such claim. Even if the Accords did purport to codify or create customary law, it is not clear that there is enough relevant state practice from which to infer the existence of binding customary norms. And even if there is some such state practice, it does not completely comport with the norms set forth in the Accords themselves. On the whole, the Accords are best understood simply as agreements, not as the encapsulation of customs.

The Accords as quasi-binding 'soft law'

It has been suggested that another theory of obligation is relevant to the Oslo Accords: 'soft law.'[18] Soft law supposedly consists of non-binding norms that for political, social, or economic reasons exert a 'pull toward compliance'.[19] Some commentators have justifiably questioned whether this kind of norm should be called 'law' at all.[20] Others have argued that the Oslo Accords have little if any force as soft law, and in any event that the Declaration of Principles and the Gaza–Jericho Agreement are the softest of soft-law instruments.[21] If one accepts that non-legal norms may have law-like consequences, then of course the Oslo Accords represent a species of soft law, and some of the Accords are softer than others. The Declaration of Principles is the softest of the instruments, and the Interim Agreement is among the hardest.

The notion of soft law may have some theoretical appeal. It suggests that the binding force of law may vary from one norm to the next, that the force of law is a continuum rather than an on–off switch. But this notion

[18] See, e.g., Note, 'The Israel–PLO Declaration of Principles: Prelude to a Peace?', 34 *Va. J. Int'l L.* 435 (1994).

[19] Thomas M. Franck, *The Power of Legitimacy Among Nations* (New York: Oxford University Press, 1990), 24.

[20] See, e.g., Jonathan Carlson, 'Hunger, Agricultural Trade Liberalization, and Soft International Law: Addressing the Legal Dimensions of a Political Problem', 70 *Iowa L. Rev.* 1187, 1200–1 (1985).

[21] See, e.g., Justus R. Weiner, 'Hard Facts Meet Soft Law—The Israel–PLO Declaration of Principles and the Prospects for Peace: A Response to Katherine W. Meighan', 35 *Va. J. Int'l L.* 931 (1995).

of law does not comport with everyday understanding of law on the international plane or in municipal legal systems. In the real world, people and states do tend to act as if law is an on–off switch. There is a continuum of compliance with law, but it is probably more directly related to lack of clarity in the norm, or lack of enforcement of the norm, than to some notion that the norm is only 'partly binding'. Indeed, the phrase 'partly binding', like the metaphor 'soft law' itself, seems a contradiction in terms.

More to the point, the notion of soft law does not describe what Israel and the PLO thought they were creating on the White House lawn and at Wye River and Sharm el-Sheikh. The parties wrote that their agreements would 'enter into force', not into partial force or into soft force or into any other lesser state of 'force'. The parties intended to be legally bound. They were attempting to create hard law. To suggest that they have created half a law, or law that is not really law, is to set aside their intentions. Even if one does recognize the possibility of soft law, the suggestion that the Accords are merely 'soft' seems to diminish them in a way that is not consistent with the intent of the parties.

Again, an analogy to municipal law is instructive. Parties to an instrument may mistakenly believe they have entered into a legal relationship, as when parties to a contract forget to include some formality. But in these cases municipal law does not equivocate by suggesting that there is a 'soft contract'; it either enforces the agreement or it does not. International law, like municipal law, is and should be hard law. States already concoct enough excuses to bend or break international law; splintering that law into lesser law and greater law will only compound the problem of non-compliance.

The Accords as non-binding instruments

Finally, it has been suggested that the Oslo Accords are utterly non-binding instruments that have no legal consequence whatsoever. A variety of legal grounds have been advanced to support this claim. These include the suggestion that the Accords violate one or more peremptory norms (*jus cogens*) of international law, that a *jus cogens* norm of 'self-preservation' requires Israel to terminate the Accords, that the doctrine of changed circumstances (the *clausula rebus sic stantibus*) invalidates the agreements, and that the Accords are partly or wholly invalid because they oblige Israel to release prisoners, including convicted terrorists, thus amounting to a 'denial of justice'.[22] These arguments all miss the mark.

[22] See Louis Rene Beres, 'Why the Oslo Accords Should Be Abrogated by Israel', 12 *Am. U. J. Int'l L. & Pol'y* 267, 267 n. 2 (1997) (on *jus cogens*); ibid. 273 (on self-preservation); ibid.

The first of these arguments, that the Oslo Accords violate some *jus cogens* norm, has been advanced both by pro-Israel and pro-Palestinian critics of the Accords. These commentators argue that the Accords violate peremptory norms such as the Palestinian right of self-determination or the Israeli right of self-preservation. Assessment of this argument requires some familiarity with peremptory norms of international law, or *jus cogens*.

The notion of *jus cogens* has its roots in natural law, but it now finds expression in positive law, in particular in the Vienna Convention on the Law of Treaties.[23] Article 53 of the Vienna Convention describes *jus cogens* as 'a peremptory norm of general international law' that is 'accepted and recognized by the international community of States as a whole as a norm from which no derogation is permitted and which can be modified only by a subsequent norm of general international law having the same character'. The requirement that such a norm be 'accepted and recognized' by the international community 'as a whole' is a strenuous one; a *jus cogens* norm must reflect 'a genuine consensus among all essential components of the modern international community' without any dissent from any 'one important element' of that community.[24] Once a *jus cogens* norm has been firmly established, it can never be overridden by an international agreement—only by emergence of a new *jus cogens* norm.[25] The Vienna Convention does not specify just what norms qualify as *jus cogens*. Commentators have identified a range of leading candidates, including

272 (on *rebus sic stantibus* and release of prisoners). Related arguments can be found in Louis Rene Beres and Zalman Shoval, 'On Demilitarizing a Palestinian "Entity" and the Golan Heights: An International Law Perspective', 28 *Vand. J. Transnat'l L.* 959 (1995); Louis Rene Beres and Zalman Shoval, 'Why a Demilitarized Palestinian State Would Not Remain Demilitarized: A View Under International Law', 11 *Temp. Int'l & Comp. L. J.* 347 (1997); Louis Rene Beres, 'Opposing the "Peace Process": Israel, Civil Disobedience and the Principle of a Higher Law', 13 *Ariz. J. Int'l & Comp. Law* 117 (1996).

For a response to Professor Beres, see John Quigley, 'The Oslo Accords: More than Israel Deserves', 12 *Am. U. Int'l L. & Pol'y* 285 (1997). For Professor Beres' reply, see Louis Rene Beres, 'Response to John Quigley', ibid. 509 (1997).

[23] For a useful survey of the International Law Commission's view of *jus cogens*, see Egon Schwelb, 'Some Aspects of International Jus Cogens as Formulated by the International Law Commission', 61 *Am. J. Int'l L.* 946 (1967). See also Edward McWhinney, *United Nations Law Making: Cultural and Ideological Relativism and International Law Making for an Era of Transition*, 73–5 (New York: Holmes & Meier Publishers, 1984) (asserting that the Vienna Convention's concept of *jus cogens* 'represented a compromise, in legal theory terms, between positivism and natural law'); Christos L. Rozakis, *The Concept of* Jus Cogens *in the Law of Treaties* (Amsterdam; New York: North-Holland Pub. Co., 1976); Jerzy Sztucki, Jus Cogens *and the Vienna Convention on the Law of Treaties* (Vienna, New York: Springer-Verlag, 1974).

[24] Gennady M. Danilenko, 'International Jus Cogens', 2 *Eur. J. Int'l L.* 42, 65 (1991).

[25] Article 64 of the Vienna Convention provides: 'If a new peremptory norm of general international law emerges, any existing treaty which is in conflict with that norm becomes void and terminates.' It has not been seriously suggested that any 'new' norms of *jus cogens* have emerged in the seven years since the adoption of the first Oslo Accord.

the prohibition of genocide, slavery, apartheid, murder, torture, prolonged arbitrary detention, and certain other 'international' crimes.[26] It is also generally agreed that the list includes the UN Charter's prohibition on the use of force except in self-defence.[27]

It has also been suggested that *jus cogens* includes the right of peoples to self-determination.[28] There is no doubt that there is a right of peoples to self-determination; that right is enshrined in the UN Charter and in the major multilateral covenants on human rights.[29] There is, unfortunately, some reason to doubt that this right has evolved into *jus cogens*, which requires that a norm be 'accepted and recognized' by the international community 'as a whole'. Many states continue to disregard the right of self-determination in practice, and even the Human Rights Committee seems reluctant to enforce it.[30] But assuming there is a *jus cogens* norm of self-determination, it is fair to ask whether the Oslo Accords respect it.

As we saw in Chapter 1, Palestinian Arabs have long denounced the Balfour Declaration, the Mandate, and the 1948 UN Partition Resolution as violations of a *jus cogens* norm of self-determination. The Palestinian leadership that negotiated the Oslo Accords obviously has refrained from making similar claims about the Accords, but pro-Palestinian commentators have hinted that the Accords are subject to a higher law of self-determination.[31] Assuming there is such a higher law, the Accords so far appear to comply with it. The Accords establish a reasonable measure of interim self-government for the Palestinians and, more importantly, they pave the way to fuller self-determination in the future.

Concern about self-determination is not limited to Palestinians. Some pro-Israel writers have denounced the Accords as violating an Israeli right of 'self-preservation', which would seem to be a mélange of a people's right of self-determination and a state's right to self-defence.[32]

[26] See Report of the International Law Commission, [1966] 2 *Y.B. Int'l L. Comm'n* 95, 121; Richard B. Lillich, 'Remarks', 1985 *Proc. Am. Soc. Int'l L.* 84, 84–6; *Restatement (3rd)*, §102 n. 6, at 34 and §702 n. 11, at 174–5.

[27] See UN Charter, 26 June 1945, T.S. 993, Art. 2(4); Alfred Verdross and Bruno Simma, *Universelles Völkerrecht*, 83–7 (Berlin: Duncker und Humblot, 1976).

[28] See [1966] 2 *Y.B. Int'l L. Comm'n* 247–9.

[29] See UN Charter, Art. 55; International Covenant on Civil and Political Rights, 16 Dec. 1966, 999 U.N.T.S. 171, Art. 1(1) ('All peoples have the right of self-determination'); International Covenant on Economic, Social and Cultural Rights, 16 Dec. 1966, 993 U.N.T.S. 3, Art. 1(1) (similar).

[30] See Richard B. Lillich and Hurst Hannum, *International Human Rights*, 3rd edn (Boston: Little, Brown & Co., 1995), 335 (noting that the Committee has 'refus[ed] to consider [self-determination] arguments raised in several communications').

[31] See Quigley, 'The Oslo Accords', 297 ('The question is whether the Oslo agreements and, more importantly, the agreement that emerges from the final status negotiations, protect the rights of the Palestinians. This is what the international community must ensure, given the preponderance of power on the Israeli side.').

[32] See Beres, 'Why the Oslo Accords Should Be Abrogated by Israel', 273.

An Israeli right to terminate the Accords is also said to be found in Thomas Jefferson's doctrine of necessity, which holds that 'the law of self-preservation overrules the laws of obligation to others'.[33] Again, this line of argument assumes there is a *jus cogens* norm of self-determination, not to mention a similar norm of self-defence. Article 51 of the UN Charter does, of course, recognize a state's right of self-defence, and as we have seen the Charter's prohibition on the use of force may be a *jus cogens* norm. Although the Charter could be read as limiting the right of self-defence in certain circumstances,[34] in general a *jus cogens* right of self-defence would seem to follow from a *jus cogens* prohibition on the use of force. Assuming that self-defence, self-preservation, and self-determination are all *jus cogens* norms, it would again appear that the Oslo Accords comply with these norms. It is hardly clear that the Oslo Accords threaten Israel's existence or right of self-preservation; on the contrary, it has been suggested that the Accords enhance Israel's security by improving its relations with its Arab neighbours like Jordan, with whom Israel now has a peace treaty, and perhaps by lessening the threat of terrorism.[35]

One commentator has gone so far as to suggest that the Accords violate a *jus cogens* norm that requires Israel to prosecute terrorists.[36] On this view, for Israel to 'honor agreements with terrorists' is to 'dishonor the very meaning of international law', in particular 'the peremptory expectation known in law as *Nullum crimen sine poena*' ('No crime without a punishment'). In other words, Israel has violated international law by signing the Oslo Accords because it is ignoring its duty to extradite or prosecute terrorists. 'By freeing terrorists,' it is claimed, 'Israel is guilty of participating in a "denial of justice".'[37]

This argument has little basis in international law. To begin with, it is not clear that there is a *jus cogens* norm requiring states to extradite or prosecute terrorists. The traditional rule is that there is no general duty to extradite or prosecute for ordinary crimes in general international law.[38]

[33] Thomas Jefferson, 'Opinion on the French Treaties', in Merrill D. Peterson (ed.), *Thomas Jefferson: Writings* (New York, NY: Viking Press, 1984), 423.

[34] Article 51 of the Charter provides that nothing shall impair 'the inherent right of individual or collective self-defense if an armed attack occurs against a Member of the United Nations, *until the Security Council has taken the measures necessary to maintain international peace and security*' (emphasis added). The italicized language could be read to imply that the right of self-defence disappears once the Council begins to take 'measures necessary' to maintain peace, even if peace has not yet been achieved. The better reading, however, is that the right of self-defence persists 'until' the Council has in fact ensured the restoration of peace—at which point self-defence is presumably unnecessary.

[35] See John V. Whitbeck, 'Israeli security requires a Palestinian state', *Middle East Int'l*, 25 Oct. 1996, cited in Quigley, 'The Oslo Accords', 296 n. 70.

[36] See Beres, 'Why the Oslo Accords Should Be Abrogated by Israel', 268–72.

[37] Ibid. 269 and n. 8, 272.

[38] Jordan J. Paust, *et al.*, *International Criminal Law: Cases and Materials* (Durham, North

In the past three decades, however, the multilateral terrorism conventions have imposed broad duties to extradite or prosecute terrorists,[39] and likewise the law of war requires states to prosecute 'grave breaches' of the Geneva Conventions.[40] These obligations may have become part of customary international law, but it seems unlikely that they have also become *jus cogens*. Many states routinely flout their obligation to extradite or initiate prosecution of terrorists.[41] A few states actively support terrorism.[42] This practice hardly amounts to evidence of a *jus cogens* norm—one accepted and recognized by the international community 'as a whole'.

Even if there were a *jus cogens* norm requiring punishment of terrorists, it would not invalidate the Oslo Accords. The Accords reflect an effort to prevent and punish terrorism, not to reward it. As we shall see in Part IV, one of the most important Palestinian obligations under the Accords is the obligation to cooperate with Israel in combating terrorism and in extraditing

Carolina: Carolina Academic Press, 1996), 298 ('there is no duty under customary international law to extradite'). But see M. Cherif Bassiouni, *International Criminal Law—A Draft International Criminal Code* (Dordrecht; Boston: Martinus Nijhoff, 1980), 110, 152 ('It is now recognized as a general principle of international law to "prosecute or extradite" ') (citing Hugo Grotius, *De Jure Belli ac Pacis* (1624)).

39 More precisely, the terrorism conventions require a state to 'submit the case to its competent authorities for the purpose of prosecution'—not simply to 'prosecute'. This phrasing presumably leaves some room for prosecutorial discretion, and of course for judicial independence. See, e.g., Convention for the Suppression of Unlawful Seizure of Aircraft, opened for signature 16 Dec. 1970, 22 U.S.T. 1641, Art. 7; Convention for the Suppression of Unlawful Acts against the Safety of Civil Aviation, 23 Sept. 1971, 24 U.S.T. 564, Art. 7; see also Convention on the Prevention and Punishment of the Crime of Genocide, 9 Dec. 1948, 78 U.N.T.S. 277, Arts. VI and VII.

As to the difficulty in defining 'terrorism', see Alex P. Schmidt, *Political Terrorism: A Research Guide to Concepts, Theories, Data Bases and Literature* (New Brunswick, NJ: Transaction Press, 1994), 103–4 (finding more than 100 different definitions of terrorism).

40 Geneva Convention Relative to the Treatment of Civilian Persons in Time of War, 12 Aug. 1949, Art. 146, 75 U.N.T.S. 287, 386.

41 See Elizabeth A. Faulkner, 'The Right to Habeas Corpus: Only in the Other Americas', 9 *Am. U. J. Int'l L. & Pol'y* 653, 677 n. 161 (1994) (deriding European states' failure to punish terrorism and their 'craven surrender to terrorists' threats'). See generally David E. Long, *The Anatomy of Terrorism* (New York: Free Press; Toronto: Collier Macmillan Canada; New York: Maxwell Macmillan International, 1990); John F. Murphy, *Punishing International Terrorists: The Legal Framework for Policy Initiatives* (Totowa, NJ: Rowman & Allanheld, 1985); Andrew Selth, *Against Every Human Law: the Terrorist Threat to Diplomacy* (Rushcutters Bay, NSW, Australia; Elmsford, NY: Australian National University Press, 1988); Adrian Guelke, *The Age of Terrorism and the International Political System* (London: Tauris Academic Studies, I.B. Tauris Publishers, 1995); Michael F. Noone and Yonah Alexander (eds.), *Cases and Materials on Terrorism: Three Nations' Response* (The Hague: Kluwer Law International, 1997). Cf. also *Case Concerning Questions of Interpretation and Application of the 1971 Montreal Convention Arising From the Aerial Incident at Lockerbie* (Libya v. US), 1992 I.C.J. 114 (Request for Provisional Measures).

42 See generally Raymond Tanter, *Rogue Regimes: Terrorism and Proliferation* (New York: St Martin's Press, 1998); Rosemary H. T. O'Kane, *Terror, Force, and States: The Path from Modernity* (Cheltenham, UK; Brookfield, US: Edward Elgar, 1996); Henry H. Han (ed.), *Terrorism & Political Violence: Limits & Possibilities of Legal Control* (New York: Oceana, 1993).

terrorists. Moreover, many states have peacefully resolved disputes with enemy states or former colonies even when leaders of those states or colonies had engaged in arguably criminal conduct. To outlaw such agreements would discourage peaceful resolution of such disputes.[43]

It is true that the Accords also require Israel to release some prisoners, but, as we shall see in Part III, Israel retains a great deal of discretion in deciding who to release and when. Even a *jus cogens* norm requiring punishment of terrorism would permit states to commute sentences. Indeed, the terrorism conventions arguably permit prosecutorial discretion not to prosecute at all. They typically oblige a state either to extradite or to 'submit the case to its competent authorities for the purpose of prosecution'.[44] This formulation leaves open the possibility that 'competent authorities' in a state's executive branch will exercise prosecutorial discretion not to prosecute, that the state's judicial branch might exercise judicial independence and acquit, or that the state's head of state might later commute a sentence.

In sum, customary law may oblige states to extradite or initiate prosecution of terrorists, but that rule probably is not a *jus cogens* norm because it is not in fact accepted by the international community 'as a whole'. Even if such a rule were a *jus cogens* norm, it still would not invalidate the Oslo Accords, one main purpose of which is the reduction and punishment of terrorism. Moreover, any such norm would surely leave room for prosecutorial discretion or executive clemency.

One or two commentators have advanced a final argument against the validity of the Oslo Accords: the claim that changed circumstances have undermined their original premises, and thus that one or the other party is entitled to terminate them.[45] This claim is unfounded. Treaty law does recognize a doctrine of changed circumstances (sometimes described as the *clausula rebus sic stantibus*), but it applies only in the most unusual circumstances. Article 62 of the Vienna Convention on the Law of Treaties provides: 'A fundamental change of circumstances' that 'was not foreseen by the parties' may 'not be invoked as a grounds for terminating or withdrawing from the treaty unless: (a) the existence of those circumstances constituted an essential basis of the consent of the parties to be bound by the treaty; and (b) the effect of the change is radically to transform the extent of the obligations still to be performed under the treaty'. Thus the

43 Cf. Quigley, 'The Oslo Accords', 291 (citing the peace treaties with Germany and Japan ending World War II). Cf. also Agreement on the Normalization of Relations, 23 Aug. 1996 (Croatia-FRY), 35 I.L.M. 1219 (1996).

44 See, e.g., Hague Convention for the Suppression of Unlawful Seizure of Aircraft, Art. 7; Convention for the Suppression of Unlawful Acts against the Safety of Civil Aviation, Art. 7.

45 See Beres, 'Why the Oslo Accords Should Be Abrogated by Israel', 272; Jeffrey Weiss, 'Terminating the Israel–PLO Declaration of Principles: Is It Legal Under International Law?', 18 *Loy. L.A. Int'l & Comp. L.J.* 109, 140 (1995).

provision starts from the presumption that changed circumstances ordinarily may not be invoked as a basis for termination—a presumption that reflects how rarely the doctrine has in fact been invoked in actual practice.

In this case, neither of the two required conditions in Article 62 have been met: there has been no fundamental change of circumstances that were an 'essential basis' of the consent of the parties, and the parties' obligations have not been 'radically' transformed. As to the first condition, the only real 'change' cited is that 'the PLO no longer serves as de facto representative of the Palestinians'.[46] It might indeed be said that the PLO has changed since 1993, in that it has effectively ceded some Palestinian decision-making authority to the PA. But it is hard to see how this development has altered the 'essential basis' of the parties' obligations. In fact, the rise of a Palestinian self-governing entity—the PA—is precisely what the parties had in mind when they concluded the Accords. It has also been suggested that some 'changes' have taken the form of Palestinian breaches.[47] But that basis for termination is covered by a different provision of the Vienna Convention, Article 60, which covers material breach; it is discussed in detail in Parts III and IV of this book. Article 62, on changed circumstances, deals with a much narrower type of 'change'—a change in the underlying factual premises of the agreement, akin to a doctrine of frustration, impracticability, or perhaps mistake in municipal contract law.[48] There has been no fundamental change in the underlying factual circumstances since 1993.

The second condition for a viable claim of changed circumstances, the requirement of a 'radical' transformation in obligations, is entirely inapplicable in this case. The parties' obligations remain more or less identical to what they were when the Accords were signed. There has been no fundamental change in circumstances, no radical transformation of the parties' obligations, and thus no basis for either party to terminate the Accords under Article 62 of the Vienna Convention.

In sum, none of the foregoing theories about the juridical nature of the Oslo Accords is entirely plausible. The notion that the Accords are a binding exchange of unilateral declarations seems inconsistent with the intention of the parties, which was to bind each other by mutual agreement. The suggestion that the Accords codify or create customary law is unsatisfactory because actual state practice under the Accords does not comport with their text. The argument that the Accords are semi-binding

[46] Weiss, 'Terminating the Declaration of Principles', 140.

[47] See Beres, 'Why the Oslo Accords Should Be Abrogated by Israel', 272.

[48] See Sir Ian Sinclair, *The Vienna Convention on the Law of Treaties*, 2nd edn (Manchester; Dover, NH: Manchester University Press, 1984), 2:15–17; Edwin M. Smith, 'Understanding Dynamic Obligations: Arms Control Agreements', 64 *S. Cal. L. Rev.* 1549, 1606 (1991).

as 'soft law' finds no support in the traditional sources of international law, which do not recognize an intermediate category of 'quasi-law'. And the suggestion that the Accords are invalid because they violate higher norms of law has little basis in international law.

We have already seen that traditional treaty law, embodied in the Vienna Convention, does not give effect to the parties' intention that the Accords be binding in and of themselves. The next Chapter returns to treaty-based theories of obligation. It considers whether the Accords might none the less be regarded as a different form of binding international agreement—agreement between subjects of international law.

5

The Oslo Accords as Binding Agreements Between Subjects of International Law

As we saw in Chapter 3, the Oslo Accords are not traditional 'treaties' under the Vienna Convention on the Law of Treaties, but Article 3 of the Convention also provides that it does not affect the 'legal force' of agreements between states and 'other subjects of international law'. The deliberations of the International Law Commission indicate that the phrase 'other subjects of international law' was intended to cover international organizations, the Holy See, and 'other international entities, such as insurgents, which may in some circumstances enter into treaties'.[1] Some scholars have argued that the PLO is a 'subject of international law', and thus that most or all of the Oslo Accords are treaties under customary international law.[2] Similar arguments have been made on behalf of other agreements involving national liberation movements.[3]

There are compelling reasons to conclude that the Accords are indeed

[1] 2 Yb. I.L.C. 162 (1962) (Commentary on draft Article I) (¶ 8). The ILC proceedings also indicate that the phrase 'other subjects of international law' was not intended to include 'individuals or corporations created under national law, for they do not possess capacity to enter into treaties nor to enter into agreements governed by public international law'. Ibid. (footnote omitted).

The ILC later produced a separate convention on the law of treaties as it applies to international organizations. The convention makes clear that international organizations may have the capacity to enter into treaties, if their organic instruments permit them to do so. See UN Convention on the Law of Treaties Concluded Between States and International Organizations or Between Two or More International Organizations, 25 I.L.M. 543 (1986), Art. 6. This development reflects state practice indicating that international organizations can enter into treaties. Cf., e.g., Sir Robert Jennings and Sir Arthur Watts (eds.), *Oppenheim's International Law*, 9th edn (Harlow, Essex: Longman, 1993), 1:1219–20.

[2] See, e.g., Eyal Benvenisti, 'The Israeli–Palestinian Declaration of Principles: A Framework for Future Settlement', 4 *Eur. J. Int'l L.* 542, 544–5 (1993) (arguing that the 1993 Declaration of Principles is an 'agreement between two equal subjects of international law' and that such agreements are governed by treaty law). Cf. also Jiménez de Aréchaga, 'International Law in the Past Third of a Century', 159 *Rec. des Cours* 35–7 (1978–I) (asserting that a treaty is an agreement between 'two or more subjects of international law', including not just states but also international organizations); Julio A. Barberis, 'Nouvelles questions concernant la personalité juridique internationale', 179 *Rec. des Cours* 145, 239–68 (1983–I) (arguing for a broader definition of international personality). See also Malcolm N. Shaw, *International Law*, 4th edn (Cambridge: Grotius Publications, 1997), 174–5 (discussing changes in the position of the PLO since 1993).

[3] See, e.g., Barberis, 'Nouvelles questions', 259–64 (describing the treaty relations of various national liberation movements). Cf. James Crawford, *The Creation of States in International Law* (Oxford: Clarendon Press, 1979), 310 (comparing the independence movement in Guinea-Bissau to the PLO).

agreements between a state and a 'subject of international law'. As we saw in Chapter 4, the parties to the Oslo Accords most likely intended either that both sides be legally bound or that neither be bound. The text of the Accords, moreover, strongly suggests that the parties had in mind a legally binding arrangement. Each of the Accords provides for entry into force, and after the admittedly general Declaration of Principles, the Accords have taken on increasing complexity and detail, again consistent with a binding character.

Thus the paradox of the Accords is that the parties seem to have intended both sides to be bound, and yet under traditional international law only one side—Israel—can be bound. Has modern international law evolved to the point at which a state might make a binding international agreement with a sub-state entity?

Such a rule certainly would make sense. As a logical matter, there should be some device by which states can make binding agreements with sub-state entities that are aspiring for self-determination or autonomy. Otherwise existing states would have less incentive to bargain with sub-state entities, since existing states would have no assurance of return performance. There must be an 'international constitutional moment'[4] at which a sub-state entity can begin to bind itself on the international plane even though it does not yet qualify as a state.[5] International law should recognize a new species of binding international agreement, perhaps styled a 'compact'—an agreement between a state and a sub-state entity, made with intent to be legally bound on the international plane.[6] One might expect, but not necessarily require, that such compacts have as their purpose the attainment of self-determination by the sub-state entity.

In fact, there is precedent for a binding international agreement between states and sub-state entities. From the seventeenth century on, European states made agreements with indigenous peoples that were binding, at least in theory. Still, these agreements may have limited relevance to the Oslo Accords because the indigenous parties, unlike the PLO, were then regarded as states under contemporary international law.

[4] Cf. Bruce A. Ackerman, *We The People: Foundations* (Cambridge, MA: Belknap Press of Harvard University Press, 1991).

[5] See Sanford R. Silverberg, 'Diplomatic Recognition of States in Status Nascendi: The Case of Palestine', 6 *Tulsa J. Comp. & Int'l L.* 21 (1998).

[6] There is some precedent for the use of the term 'compact'. See, e.g., Agreement for the Implementation of the Compact of Free Association between the Government of the United States and the Government of the Federated States of Micronesia, 24 Oct. 1986, P.L. 99–239; Compact of Free Association between the Government of the United States and the Government of Palau, 12 Dec. 1989, P.L. 101–219; cf. also US Constitution, Art. I, §10, cl. 3 ('No State shall, without the Consent of Congress . . . enter into Any Agreement or Compact with another State'). The Holy See's practice furnishes another possibility: the term 'concordat'. For more on concordats, see, e.g., Ehler, *The Recent Concordats*, 104 *Rec. des Cours* 7–63 (1961–III).

Vitoria, for example, rejected Spanish claims to Native American lands on the grounds that Native Americans had 'dominion in both public and private matters' in their lands.[7] Grotius held that all peoples had the capacity to enter into treaties.[8] Vattel denied that the peoples who 'roamed' [*parcourroient*]) over North America constituted states, but even he argued that the 'civilized [*policés*] Empires of Peru and Mexico' were states.[9]

Early colonial practice adhered to the view that indigenous peoples could constitute 'states' with treaty-making capacity. Some of the early European and US agreements with Native American peoples explicitly recognized the sovereignty of the indigenous state party. The 1840 Treaty of Waitangi between Great Britain and the Maori people of New Zealand was later held by the Privy Council to be a treaty on the international plane, even though it was non-justiciable for purposes of municipal law.[10] The British government seems to have regarded the Maori as possessing treaty-making capacity, even though there was some uncertainty about which Maori chiefs were the proper representatives of the Maori people.

During the nineteenth century, however, European states and the United States gradually moved away from the view that indigenous peoples were states, even as Europeans and the United States continued to make 'treaties' with indigenous peoples. This practice does establish a precedent for treaties between states and entities regarded (rightly or wrongly) as less than fully sovereign. Some of the most prominent examples involve the treaties between the United States and Native American tribes. As early as 1831 the US Supreme Court rejected the argument that Indian tribes were 'foreign states' for the purposes of federal subject-matter jurisdiction.[11] This holding would seem to imply that Indian tribes were less than fully sover-

[7] Francisco de Vitoria, *De Indis et de Ivre Belli Relectiones* (1532), translated by John Pawley Bate (Washington: Carnegie Institution, 1917), 128.

[8] Hugo Grotius, *De Jure Belli ac Pacis* (1624), 397.

[9] Emmerich de Vattel, *Le Droit des Gens, ou Principes de la Loi Naturelle* (1758), Bk. I, Ch. VII, 79.

[10] See *Hoani Te Heuheu Tukino v. Aotea District Maori Land Board*, [1941] AC 308. According to Ian Brownlie, doubts about the treaty-making capacity of the Maori did not arise until after conclusion of the agreement:

> There can be no doubt . . . that the Treaty of Waitangi presupposed the legal and political capacity of the chiefs of New Zealand to make an agreement which was valid on the international plane. Moreover, there is evidence that, in the decade prior to conclusion of the Treaty, the British Government conducted itself on the basis that relations with the Maori tribes were governed by the rules of international law. . . . Moreover, the fact that *subsequent* developments in international law doctrine denied treaty-making capacity to [the Maori] is irrelevant. Facts have to be appreciated according to the principles of international law prevailing at the time.

Ian Brownlie, *Treaties and Indigenous Peoples* (Oxford: Clarendon Press; New York: Oxford University Press, 1992), 8–9 (footnotes omitted) (emphasis in original).

[11] See *Cherokee Nation v. Georgia*, 30 U.S. (5 Pet.) 1 (1831) (Marshall, C.J.); cf. also *Johnson v.*

eign. A year later, however, the Supreme Court held that Indian tribes possessed the capacity to make treaties, and that they had not surrendered their 'independence' by associating with a stronger state and 'taking its protection'.[12] Read together, these holdings suggest that states can conclude binding agreements with less-than-sovereign entities.

Later US practice reinforces that conclusion. As the nineteenth century wore on, US policy towards Indians hardly resembled that of a state dealing with co-equal states: Indians were run off their land, pushed west, and sometimes exterminated altogether. None the less, the US government continued to describe its agreements with American Indians as 'treaties', and American courts interpreted the agreements as treaties. Although the United States violated many of those treaty obligations with impunity in the nineteenth century, in the late twentieth century US courts have belatedly given effect to some of them.[13] There are similar examples in Canadian and British practice from the period.[14] Taken as a whole, this practice suggests that Native American tribes of the nineteenth century had treaty-making capacity, even though the United States did not treat them as states, implying that states can make binding agreements with sub-state entities.[15]

M'Intosh, 21 U.S. (8 Wheat.) 543 (1823) (Marshall, C.J.) (enunciating a doctrine of limited 'Indian title' to land).

By the end of the nineteenth century, commentators were also expressing scepticism over whether Indian nations constituted states. See, e.g., John Westlake, *Chapters on the Principles of International Law* (Cambridge: Cambridge University Press, 1894), 143 ('international law has to treat such natives as uncivilised'). By the early twentieth century this scepticism had hardened into received doctrine. See, e.g., William Edward Hall, *A Treatise on International Law*, 8th edn, edited by A. Pearce Higgins (Oxford: Clarendon Press, 1924), 47.

12 *Worcester v. Georgia*, 31 U.S. (6 Pet.) 515 (1832) (Marshall, C.J.).

13 See, e.g., *United States v. Sioux Nation of Indians*, 448 U.S. 371 (1980). Many of the most successful Indian land claims, however, have been brought for violations of statutes such as the federal Nonintercourse Act of 1790, which prohibited sale of Indian land without congressional consent. See, e.g., *County of Oneida v. Oneida Nation*, 105 S. Ct. 1245, 1249 (1985); *Joint Tribal Council of the Passamaquoddy Tribe v. Morton*, 388 F. Supp. 649 (D. Me.), aff'd, 528 F.2d 370 (1st Cir. 1975).

For a useful historical account of the relationship between international law and indigenous peoples, see generally S. James Anaya, 'The Rights of Indigenous Peoples and International Law and Contemporary Perspective', in *1989 Harvard Indian Law Symposium* 191 (1990).

14 See, e.g., *Reg. v. George*, 55 D.L.R. (2d) 386, 53 I.L.R. 575, 585 (1966) (Martland, J.) (recognizing an 1827 Canada–Chippewa agreement as a treaty but holding that the treaty was subordinate to an Act of Parliament); cf. ibid. 584 (Cartwright, J., dissenting) (arguing that the Act of Parliament is subordinate to the 1827 treaty).

For a thorough treatment of treaties involving indigenous peoples, see generally UN Commission on Human Rights, Sub-Commission on Prevention of Discrimination and Protection of Minorities, 'Discrimination Against Indigenous Peoples: Study on treaties, agreements and other constructive arrangements between States and indigenous populations', UN Doc. E/CN.4/Sub.2/1996/23, 15 Aug. 1996 (3rd progress report).

15 US policy shifted in 1871, when the Congress enacted a statute providing that 'no Indian nation or tribe within the territory of the United States shall be acknowledged or recognized as an independent nation, tribe, or power with whom the United States may

Twentieth-century state practice also supports the proposition that states can make binding agreements with certain non-state actors. The most salient involve decolonization agreements between states and sub-state entities aspiring for autonomy or independence—agreements roughly analogous to the Israeli–Palestinian Accords. British practice furnishes several examples. In 1921 Great Britain and a delegation of Irish leaders entered into a 'Treaty',[16] providing that Ireland would henceforth have the same 'constitutional status' in the British Commonwealth as dominions such as Canada, which themselves were less than fully independent states at the time.[17] Although the British apparently did not regard the Irish Free State as a subject of international law, Ireland later registered the instrument with the League of Nations as a treaty, provoking objections from the British.[18]

Later British practice even more clearly suggests that Britain has recognized treaty-making capacity in national liberation movements. In 1967 the United Kingdom and the National Front for the Liberation of Occupied South Yemen entered into a 'Memorandum of Agreed Points Relating to Independence for South Arabia', which provided for the termination of British sovereignty over South Arabia and the establishment of the new state of the People's Republic of South Yemen.[19] Unlike the Oslo Accords, the Memorandum did not provide for its entry into 'force', but it none the less contained clear promises by both parties, and it did not deny that it had legal effect. The Memorandum did not specify any governing law, but its most important provisions—those calling for transfer of sovereignty, mutual recognition, establishment of diplomatic relations, and so forth—strongly suggest that it was an agreement governed by international law, not a contract governed by municipal (i.e. domestic) law. Thus the Memorandum was an agreement between a state and a national liberation movement, governed by international law—an international agreement. The same can be said of the 1979 Lancaster House accords between Britain, the African National Council, and the Patriotic Front comprised of the Zimbabwe African National Union and the Zimbabwe African National People's Union.[20]

contract by treaty'. R.S. §2079, 16 Stat. 566, 3 Mar. 1871, c. 120, §1. Thereafter the United States stopped making 'treaties' with Indian tribes.

[16] Treaty Between Great Britain and Ireland, 6 Dec. 1921, 26 L.N.T.S. 10. The Treaty is also known as the 'Anglo-Irish Articles of Agreement'. See *Oppenheim's International Law*, §595, 1:1218–19 n. 10.

[17] See ibid., §78, at 257–60 (describing the gradual progress from self-governing dominions to independence).

[18] 26 L.N.T.S. 449–50.

[19] Memorandum of Agreed Points Relating to Independence for South Arabia (The People's Republic of Southern Yemen), with Financial Note and Final Communiqué, Cmnd. 3504 (29 Nov. 1967).

[20] See Barberis, 'Nouvelles questions', 261. See also *State v. Eliasov*, 52 I.L.R. 408 (1967) (treating South Africa's 1963 agreement with the entity that became Southern Rhodesia as an international agreement).

Portuguese practice also provides examples of binding agreements between a state and non-state actors. In August 1974 Portugal entered into a decolonization agreement with the African Party for the Independence of Guinea-Bissau and the Cape Verde Islands.[21] The parties appear to have regarded this instrument as a binding international agreement even though only one party was a state. A month later Portugal entered into an agreement with the Mozambique Liberation Front providing for the 'progressive transfer' of Portuguese power to a new independent government.[22] Again, the agreement dealt with subjects traditionally governed by international law, and again it did not purport to deny that it had legal effect. Later that year Portugal entered into yet another such agreement, this time with the Liberation Movement of Sao Tomé and Principe.[23] The final clause of this agreement implied quite strongly that it had legal effect. It provided that the accord 'depends on its confirmation by the President of the Republic of Portugal and by the Secretary-General of the Liberation Movement of Sao Tomé and Principe, to become formally valid'.[24] In 1975 Portugal signed a similar agreement with UNITA and other national liberation movements seeking independence for Angola.[25]

France's exit from Algeria is another instance of an international agreement between a state and a national liberation movement. In March 1962 France and the Front de Libération Nationale Algérien entered into an agreement providing for a cessation of hostilities, a referendum on Algerian independence, and a mechanism for the establishment of a new Algerian state.[26] Although the Algerian liberation movement may not have then constituted a state, French jurisprudence later recognized the accord as 'une convention internationale'.[27]

Decolonization through mandate or trusteeship has also produced

[21] 26 Aug. 1974, 13 I.L.M. 1244 (1974).

[22] Agreement between the Portuguese State and the Mozambique Liberation Front, 7 Sept. 1974, Art. 1, attached as Annex I to 'Implementation of the Declaration on the Granting of Independence to Colonial Countries and Peoples: Question of Territories Under Portuguese Domination', UN Doc. A/9769 (24 Sept. 1974), 13 I.L.M. 1467 (1974).

[23] Protocol of the Accord between the Portuguese Government and the Liberation Movement of Sao Tomé and Principe, 26 Nov. 1974, annexed to UN Doc. A/9953 (17 Dec. 1974), 14 I.L.M. 39 (1975).

[24] Ibid., Art. 17.

[25] Agreement of 15 Jan. 1975, cited in Barberis, 'Nouvelles questions', 261 and n. 317. Yet another example is the instrument that led to the independence of the Republic of Guinea-Bissau. See Agreement Granting Independence of Portuguese Guinea, Portugal–African Party for the Independence of Guinea, 26 Aug. 1974, reprinted in *Le Monde*, 27 Aug. 1974 (French text), and in 13 I.L.M. 1244 (1974) (English translation). See also G.A. Res. 355 (1974), 13 I.L.M. 225 (1974) (relating to UN membership for Guinea-Bissau).

[26] 1962 *Journal Officiel de la République Française* 3019, cited in Barberis, 'Nouvelles Questions', 84 n. 313.

[27] 'La jurisprudence française a reconnu que les accords d'Evian sont une convention internationale.' Barberis, 'Nouvelles questions', 284 n. 313.

some relevant precedents. The International Court of Justice has held that a mandate or trusteeship can have the 'character' of a 'treaty or convention'.[28] More to the point, agreements between the mandatory power and the mandated territory, and even agreements between mandated territories, have been characterized as treaties. The Compact of Free Association between the United States and the Federated States of Micronesia was apparently regarded as a binding international agreement, even though Micronesia was not yet a full-fledged state.[29] The US Compact of Free Association with Palau was intended to have binding character as well; like the Compact with Micronesia, it was forwarded to Congress for approval and implementation.[30] Significantly, US courts did not treat Palau as a 'foreign state' for purposes of sovereign immunity until after adoption of the Compact.[31] In other words, when the parties agreed to the Compact, Palau was not a 'state' in the eyes of the US courts, implying that the Compact was a binding international agreement between a state and something other than a 'foreign state'.

Many recent precedents involve the regularization of relations between national liberation movements and their neighbours. In 1979, for example, Mauritania and the POLISARIO, a 'liberation movement' seeking self-determination in the Western Sahara, entered into an agreement in which Mauritania renounced any claim to territories in the Western Sahara, and the POLISARIO in return pledged to respect Mauritanian territory. That agreement has been reported to the United Nations as if it were a legally binding instrument.[32] There have even been agreements between national liberation movements. Consider, for example, the 1975 agreement between two Angolan movements, the MPLA and the FNLA, providing that the parties would not interfere in each other's internal

[28] *South West Africa Cases*, 1962 I.C.J. Rep. 330. See also *Namibia* (Legal Consequences), 1971 I.C.J. 46–7 (Advisory Opinion).

[29] Compact of Free Association between the Government of the United States and the Government of the Federated States of Micronesia, 1 Oct. 1982, entered into force 24 Oct. 1986, P.L. 99–239, 99 Stat. 1770 (1986); 81 *Am. J. Int'l L.* 405 (1987).

[30] See Compact of Free Association between the Government of the United States and the Government of Palau, 10 Jan. 1986, P.L. 101–219, 100 Stat. 3673, 3678, 48 U.S.C. §1681 note; Presidential Proclamation No. 6726, 27 Sept. 1994, §2 (proclaiming the Compact to be 'in full force and effect'), reprinted in 89 *Am. J. Int'l L.* 96, 97 (1995) and in S. Rep. No. 403, 99th Cong., 2nd Sess. (1986). See also 59 Fed. Reg. 49,777–8 (1994) (describing Palau's approval of the Compact).

[31] Cf. *Bowoon Sangsa Co., Ltd. v. Micronesian Indus. Corp.*, 720 F.2d 595, 602 (9th Cir. 1983) (holding that Palau was not a 'foreign state' for the purposes of sovereign immunity because it had not completed its transition to independence) with *Morgan Guaranty Trust Co. v. Republic of Palau*, 639 F.Supp.706 (S.D.N.Y. 1986) (holding that Palau was a 'foreign state' for purposes of sovereign immunity). See generally Monroe Leigh, Comment, 81 *Am. J. Int'l L.* 220 (1987).

[32] Mauritano–Sahraoui Agreement, 10 Aug. 1979, reprinted as Annex I to 'Letter Dated 18 August 1979 From the Permanent Representative of Mauritania to the United Nations Addressed to the Secretary-General', UN Doc. A/34/427 (1979).

affairs.[33] It has been suggested that this agreement is binding on the international plane. This type of agreement is apparently governed by treaty law, not contract law.

There is also precedent involving the Palestinians themselves. Before the Oslo process, the PLO was especially active in making international agreements. As we have seen, it has tried (and generally failed) to accede to a number of multilateral conventions, most notably the four Geneva Conventions on humanitarian law, though it has entered into agreements with the Arab League.[34] But the PLO has also entered into a number of bilateral international agreements. Before Oslo I, for instance, the PLO entered into a variety of agreements with Arab states. The 1969 Cairo accord with Lebanon established rights for Palestinian inhabitants in Lebanon, and it set forth rules on PLO movements across the Lebanese border.[35] Later unpublished agreements with Lebanon regulated Palestinian refugee camps in Lebanon and the location and operation of PLO terrorist cells.[36] In 1970 the PLO entered into agreements with Jordan designed to end the fighting between PLO operatives in Jordan and the Jordanian armed forces.[37] In the autumn of 1970, for example, the PLO and Jordan entered into a series of five agreements regulating Palestinian forces in Jordan and, in one writer's view, conferring on those forces 'un statut international' ('an international status').[38] Since the signing of the Declaration of Principles, the PLO has even entered into international agreements with Western powers like the United States. A US–PLO 'Agreement on Encouragement of Investment' by its own terms entered into 'force' on 12 September 1994—almost exactly a year after the signing of Oslo I—strongly suggesting that both

33 Mombasa Accord, 4 Jan. 1975, FNLA–MPLA, described in Barberis, 'Nouvelles questions', 264.

34 See Decision of Council of Ministers, League of Arab States, 6 Sept. 1976, reported in *Le Monde*, 8 Sept. 1976 (cited in Barberis, 'Nouvelles Questions', 265 and n. 333) (describing admission of PLO into Arab League); Arab League Res. 2485/51 (Mar. 1969) (accepting Arafat as representative of Palestine). See generally Boutros Boutros-Ghali, 'La Ligue des Etats arabes', 137 *Rec. des Cours* 37 (1972–III).

35 PLO–Lebanon Agreement of 3 Nov. 1969, described in *Le Monde*, 22 Apr. 1970.

36 See *Le Monde*, 10 Jan. 1970; ibid. 17 Sept. 1970. The 1969 and 1970 accords are described briefly in Barberis, 'Nouvelles Questions', 262. According to Barberis, the full texts of the 1970 agreements have not been published. Ibid. 285 n. 323.

37 PLO–Jordan Agreement of 8 Sept. 1970, reported in *Le Monde*, 10 Sept. 1970; PLO–Lebanon Agreement of 15 Sept. 1970, reported in ibid. 17 Sept. 1970.

For more on the PLO's early agreements with Jordan and Lebanon, see generally Feuer, 'Les accords passés par les Gouvernements de Jordanie et du Liban avec les organisations palestiniennes', 1970 *Ann. Français de Droit Int'l* 177.

38 Barberis, 'Nouvelles Questions', 262. The first of these accords was signed in Amman on 10 July 1970; it is described in ibid. 262–3. The next was signed in Cairo on 27 Sept. 1970; it is described in ibid. 263. A third accord was signed in Amman on 13 Oct. 1970; it is described in ibid. Two 'complementary' accords were signed on 22 Oct. and 13 Dec. 1970. Ibid. 285 n. 327.

parties believed the Agreement was a legally binding international agreement.[39]

There are also relevant, if less compelling, precedents involving delegation of authority to colonies or subdivisions of federal states. On occasion a colonial or mandatory power has delegated treaty-making capacity to its dependent territories. With Britain's acquiescence, Palestine entered into a postal agreement with the United States in 1944.[40] In 1959 the British Crown Colony of Hong Kong made a binding international trade agreement with Burma; like Palestine, Hong Kong had the implied consent of Great Britain to do so.[41] Similarly, Britain ceded extensive treaty-making capacity to Singapore in 1961.[42] Sometimes a political unit within a federal state will make an international agreement with a foreign state, again with the express or implied consent of the federal government. In the United States, individual states may, with congressional consent, enter into an 'Agreement or Compact'—but not 'a Treaty, Alliance, or Confederation'—with one another or with foreign governments.[43] A number of American states have in fact done so.[44]

None the less, it is probably inappropriate to describe the Oslo Accords as a case of delegation by Israel to the PLO of treaty-making power. The parties sought to avoid any suggestion that Israel was delegating power to a puppet regime. Such an arrangement is looked on with disfavour by the law of belligerent occupation, which (as we shall see in Part III) is probably applicable.[45] Instead, the parties established a buffer between Israel and the PA—namely, the PLO itself. The PA may be subordinate to Israel, but the PLO is not, and it is the PLO that has negotiated 'for the benefit of' the PA. This arrangement is designed to 'avoid the presumption that the PA is merely a puppet of the Government of Israel'.[46] Thus

[39] Agreement on Encouragement of Investment Between the United States of America and the Palestine Liberation Organization for the Benefit of the Palestinian Authority Pursuant to the Agreement on the Gaza Strip and the Jericho Area, 11 Aug. and 12 Sept. 1994, State Dept. No. 94–233, KAV 4032, available at 1994 WL 621519 (Treaty). Article 6 provides: 'This Agreement shall enter into force when signed by both Parties.'

[40] Parcel Post Agreement, 10 May 1943 and 6 Sept. 1944, EAS 439, 10 Bevans 651, 58 Stat. 1522. Bevans describes the accord as 'obsolete', noting that the UK relinquished its Mandate over Palestine on 15 May 1948 and that the State of Israel was founded effective that same date. 10 Bevans 651 n. 2. See also US Dept. of State, *Treaties in Force* (1996) (omitting any mention of the agreement).

[41] See TS No. 37 (1959).

[42] See Elihu Lauterpacht, 'The Contemporary Practice of the United Kingdom in the Field of International Law—Survey and Comment, IX', 10 *Int'l & Comp. L. Q.* 548, 576–7 (1961).

[43] US Constitution, Art. I, §10, cls. 1 and 3.

[44] See Laurence H. Tribe, *American Constitutional Law*, 2nd edn (Mineola, NY: Foundation Press, 1988), §6-33, pp. 521–4.

[45] See Convention Relative to the Protection of Civilian Persons in Time of War, 12 Aug. 1949, 75 U.N.T.S. 287, Art. 47.

[46] Omar M. Dajani, 'Stalled Between Seasons: The International Legal Status of Palestine During the Interim Period', 26 *Denv. J. Int'l L. & Pol'y* 27, 90 (1997).

the Oslo Accords are not so much a delegation from Israel to the Palestinians as an agreement between two subjects of international law, each already endowed with capacity to enter into agreements.

A final, more exotic possibility is that the Oslo Accords are simply contracts, governed by Israeli civil law. The texts of the Accords, however, say nothing about what law applies, and the absence of a choice-of-law clause can imply that the agreement is governed by international law rather than domestic contract law.[47] Moreover, Israeli law does not appear to favour treating political agreements as simple contracts. Agreements between Israeli political parties, for example, are more likely to be governed by public administrative law than private contract law. In *Geregewski v. Prime Minister*,[48] the Israeli High Court of Justice considered whether 'general contract law' applied to a coalition agreement between the conservative Likud party and a small group of liberal members of the Knesset. Citing commentary to the French Civil Code, Justice Barak answered with a tentative no: 'The answer of French law is negative. . . . I am inclined to accept the idea that the same law applies here . . . the reason being that the political agreement deals with the exercise of governmental power which in turn, by its very nature, is exclusively subject to the rules of public law.'[49] By analogy, this dictum might suggest that the Oslo Accords should be 'subject to the rules of public law', not private contract law. In the context of the Oslo Accords, the governing 'public law' would presumably be public international law.[50]

47 Cf. Vienna Convention on the Law of Treaties, Art. 2(1)(a) (providing that a treaty must be 'governed by international law'). See Aréchaga, 'International Law', 35–7 (noting that an agreement that purports to be governed by municipal contract law may not be a treaty, since treaties must be governed by international law).

48 45(1) P.D. 749 (1990).

49 Ibid. 838 §3. Justice Barak also questioned whether any form of law applied to political agreements. 'Some promises . . . are of a kind falling outside the area of legal ordering, for example, invitation to lunch . . .' Ibid. (citing commentary to the *Bürgerliches Gesetzbuch* (German Civil Code, or *BGB*)). This dictum does not necessarily imply that Israeli law would deny legal effect to the Oslo Accords. A formal, written agreement with the recognized 'representative' of the Palestinian people is more likely to be governed by law than an oral bargain among politicos inside Israel.

For more on political agreements in Israeli law, see, e.g., Nili Cohen, 'Political Agreements', 26 *Israel L. Rev.* 499 (1992); Gabriela Shalev, 'Political Agreements', 16 *Iyunei Mishpat* 215 (1991) (in Hebrew); Claude Klein, 'French Administrative Law as a Paradigm: Some Remarks Concerning Its Use by the Supreme Court of Israel', 11 *Tel Aviv Univ. Studies in Law* 111, 119–21 (1992).

For overviews of Israeli contract law, see, e.g., Ariel Bin-Nun, *The Law of the State of Israel: An Introduction*, 2nd edn (translated from the German by Menachem Eichelberg; edited by Daniel C. Furman) (Jerusalem: Rubin Mass, 1992), 166–81; Gabriela Shalev, 'Contract Law', in Itzhak Zamir and Sylvanie Colombo (eds.), *The Law of Israel: General Surveys* (Jerusalem: Sacher Institute, 1995), 198–229; Nili Cohen, 'Good Faith in Bargaining and Principles of Contract Law', 9 *Tel Aviv Univ. Studies in Law* 249 (1989); Nili Cohen, 'Status, Freedom and Contract', 10 *Tel Aviv Univ. Studies in Law* 213 (1990).

50 It is perhaps possible that the governing 'public law' for the Oslo Accords might be

In sum, there appears to be ample precedent for the proposition that a national liberation movement has the capacity to enter into binding international agreements with states and even with other national liberation movements. A common purpose for such agreements is to facilitate the achievement of self-determination by the non-state entity, but it is not the exclusive purpose; some of the agreements regulate existing relations rather than establish new ones. In other words, not all of the precedents were simple boot-strapping treaties between old and new states. Some of the precedents, like the Oslo Accords, were agreements between existing states and entities that would not immediately become states after signing of the agreements. As we have seen, these agreements have sometimes been treated as if they have legal consequences on the international plane. Some commentators have also concluded that the Palestinian Authority and other sub-state entities might constitute 'subjects of international law' even if they have not yet achieved statehood.[51] And the Vienna Convention on the Law of Treaties itself endorses the notion that certain non-state actors are 'subjects of international law' with the capacity to conclude binding international agreements.

Of course, agreements between two subjects of international law can still be non-binding, if for example the parties choose to describe them that way. But the Oslo Accords clearly evince an intent to impose mutual legal obligations. As we saw in Chapter 3, virtually every one of the Accords speaks of 'entry into force'. The only real exception, the Note for the Record accompanying the Hebron Protocol, is probably binding anyway because it was part of the Hebron package and because it plainly reflects the mutual assent of the parties. Most of the Accords have the formal attributes of binding instruments; they are styled 'agreements' and 'protocols', they are structured like treaties, and they contain mandatory rather than permissive language. Even the somewhat less formal instruments—the Note for the Record and Wye River Memorandum—still clearly reflect an intent to be legally bound.

It appears, then, that the Oslo Accords are legally binding international agreements. Thus there is a legal basis for the assertion that the Oslo process is 'irreversible'. Whether there is a practical basis for that assertion

public administrative law rather than public international law. But the texts of the Accords fail to mention Israeli administrative law, and few if any Israeli commentators or jurists have argued that administrative law governs the Oslo Accords.

For an excellent explication of the relationship between Israeli municipal law and international law, see Ruth Lapidoth, 'International Law', in Zamir and Colombo, *The Law of Israel*, 86. A shorter version of the article is reprinted in 24 *Isr. L. Rev.* 451 (1990).

51 See, e.g., Benvenisti, 'The Israeli–Palestinian Declaration of Principles', 545 (describing Oslo I as 'an agreement between two subjects of international law'); cf. Barberis, 'Nouvelles Questions', 259 ('La personalité internationale des movements de libération nationale se traduit . . . dans la pratique conventionnelle dans des domaines très différents').

is more a question of political will. Conversely, there is no basis for the claim that the Accords are non-binding 'political' documents.

Having determined that the parties are legally (and not just politically) bound by the Oslo Accords, we next consider whether the parties have in fact complied with their legal obligations under the Accords. The following two Parts take up that question.

PART III

Israeli Compliance with the Oslo Accords

Israel and the PA have repeatedly accused one another of violating the Oslo Accords. Palestinians have accused Israel of violating the Accords by, among other things, failing to withdraw from enough of the West Bank in a timely fashion, constructing Jewish housing in East Jerusalem, and withholding funds from the Palestinian Authority. Israel has accused the PA of violating the Accords by, among other things, failing to suppress terrorism or punish terrorists, delaying the process of deleting objectionable provisions from the Palestinian National Charter, and exceeding the limits on Palestinian self-government. Each side also charges the other with human rights violations.

This Part of the book assesses Israeli compliance with the Accords; Part IV will examine Palestinian compliance. This Part consists of four chapters. Chapter 6 examines Israel's compliance with its obligations to redeploy Israeli troops from the West Bank. Chapter 7 asks whether the Har Homa project and other Israeli settlements violate either the Oslo Accords or any other source of international law. Chapter 8 analyses Israeli compliance with its obligations on safe passage for Palestinians between the Gaza Strip and the West Bank, on the establishment and operation of a seaport and airport in the Gaza Strip, on economic questions, and on other related questions of infrastructure and civil affairs. Chapter 9 examines Israel's compliance with its human rights obligations under the Oslo Accords.

6

Redeployment from the West Bank

Israel's most significant obligation under the Oslo Accords was its undertaking to 'redeploy' its military forces from portions of the West Bank and Gaza Strip. This was obviously a crucial concession: it gave the Palestinians some land over which to exercise a degree of self-government, and it represented an important confidence-building measure, a show of good faith that would point the way to permanent status negotiations. To many Israelis, however, the promise to 'redeploy' was a far more weighty undertaking than anything promised by the Palestinian side, because giving up land was more tangible and more irreversible than amending the text of the Palestinian National Charter or clamping down on terrorism. But without Israel's promise to redeploy, there would have been no Oslo Accords. Israeli redeployment was the *sine qua non* of the Accords.

And yet the first of the Oslo Accords did not delineate precisely the scope of this, the most significant of all the obligations in the Accords. Indeed, the Israeli obligation to redeploy was one of the most striking examples of 'constructive ambiguity' in the entire set of agreements. The parties have agreed on some of the details of redeployment, and in fact Israel has withdrawn from a significant amount of territory in the Gaza Strip and the West Bank. Indeed, as of this writing, Israel has substantially complied with all its redeployment obligations under the latest accord, the Sharm el-Sheikh Memorandum. But the scope of the final redeployment was left vague by the Memorandum, and the parties have very different ideas about how large that redeployment should be.

This Chapter takes up the precise scope of Israel's remaining obligations to redeploy from the West Bank. It begins by analysing the relevant provisions of the Accords. It then turns to Israel's argument that Palestinian violations of the Accords justify Israel's suspension of its obligations to withdraw. The Chapter concludes by analysing the parties' disagreement over the meaning of 'specified military locations'.

The relevant texts

The first Oslo Accord, the Declaration of Principles of September 1993, was, among other things, an agreement to trade land for peace. The extent of land in question, however, was left deliberately ambiguous. Article XIII of the Declaration called first for redeployment from the Gaza Strip and the Jericho Area and, second, for a 'redeployment of Israeli military forces in the West Bank and the Gaza Strip' to 'specified locations' that would be 'outside population areas'. Implementation of the second of these two obligations proved considerably more difficult than implementation of the first. After a fair amount of haggling, the parties were able to agree in 1994 on the precise contours of Israel's initial withdrawal from Gaza and the Jericho area, and Israel withdrew from those areas in May 1994. But negotiations on the second, more ambiguous, obligation—the obligation to redeploy to 'specified locations'—stretched into 1995.

The Interim Agreement of 28 September 1995 clarified some but by no means all of this ambiguity. The Interim Agreement envisioned that the remaining redeployment would take place in four phases over a period of less than two years. The first phase was described in concrete terms. In this phase, Israel would withdraw from certain 'populated areas in the West Bank' by the end of 1995.[1] This boiled down to an obligation to withdraw from seven West Bank towns: Jenin, Nablus, Tulkarm, Qalqilyah, Ramallah, Bethlehem, and four-fifths of Hebron.[2] Because of disagreements over security, the Hebron redeployment was delayed until early 1997, but withdrawal from the remaining six towns took place by the end of 1995, just before the first set of Palestinian elections.[3]

The remaining three redeployments were not defined anywhere near as precisely. There was a reasonably precise time frame. The redeployments were to be 'gradually implemented' in three 'phases' over a period of eighteen months in six-month intervals—i.e. from January 1996 to mid-1997. But the Interim Agreement described the territorial scope of these redeployments in only the most vague terms, calling for 'further redeployments of Israeli military forces to specified military locations'.[4] Nowhere did the Agreement define 'specified military locations'. Nor did the Agreement state explicitly *who* would 'specify' the relevant locations. (As we shall see in a moment, Israel argues that the language gives Israel the unilateral authority to designate the 'specified military locations'.) Even the term 'redeployment' was seemingly ambiguous, since it

[1] Interim Agreement, Art. X(1) and Map No. 1.

[2] Ibid., Art. XI(3)(a) and Map No. 1. The Hebron Protocol, implemented in January 1997, provided for Israeli withdrawal from about four-fifths of Hebron. See Hebron Protocol, Art. 1 (providing for redeployment in Hebron); ibid., Art. 2(a)(1) (providing that Palestinian police will assume 'responsibilities' in most of Hebron 'similar to those in other cities in the West Bank'); ibid., Appendix I (providing a map of the division of Israeli and Palestinian responsibilities in Hebron).

[3] See Raja Shehadeh, *From Occupation to Interim Accords: Israel and the Palestinian Territories*, 135 (The Hague: Kluwer Law International, 1997); Joel Singer, 'The West Bank and Gaza Strip: Phase Two', *Justice* (Dec. 1995), 10.

[4] Interim Agreement, Art. XI(2)(d) and Art. X(2).

might be taken to mean a mere reshuffling of forces rather than a withdrawal.

Still, the Agreement did contain *some* clues on the scope of the three 'further redeployments'. Article XI(2) provided in part: 'The two sides agree that West Bank and Gaza Strip territory, except for issues that will be negotiated in the permanent status negotiations, will come under the jurisdiction' of the Palestinians over the course of the three further redeployments.[5] This provision is a classic example of Middle East-speak: like Resolution 242, it calls for withdrawal from 'territory' without defining how much, and it contains a grammatically incoherent exception for 'issues'. None the less, the provision adds a bit of meat to the bones of the redeployment obligation. It clearly obliges Israel to transfer some territory to Palestinian jurisdiction, and there is just as clearly some limit to that obligation—the limit being 'issues' such as the boundaries of settlements. Indeed, the exception for 'issues' has prompted Palestinian arguments that 'what should be left in Israeli hands after phase three is an "issue", like military locations, Jerusalem and settlements, rather than a great expanse of territory'.[6] In any event, one thing about the exception for 'issues' is reasonably clear: the redeployments would not include withdrawal from Israeli settlements or other areas that raised questions reserved for final status negotiations.[7]

The Interim Agreement fleshed out the redeployment obligation in another important way. It provided that during the three further phases of redeployment, 'powers and responsibilities relating to territory will be transferred gradually to Palestinian jurisdiction'.[8] In other words, the Agreement envisioned a functional transfer as well as a territorial one. To facilitate the transfer of authority to the Palestinians, the Agreement divided the West Bank into three Areas—Areas 'A', 'B', and 'C'—and provided that the parties would have varying degrees of authority in each.

In Area A, the Palestinians have full authority over internal security and civil affairs, while Israel retains responsibility for external security.[9]

[5] Ibid., Art. XI(2).

[6] Jon Immanuel, 'A Different View of Oslo', *Jerus. Post*, 14 Mar. 1997 (describing the views of Palestinian negotiator Saeb Erekat).

[7] Indeed, the Interim Agreement emphasizes that the redeployments are not intended to change the status of the West Bank pending final status negotiations. Thus Article XXXI(7) provides: 'Neither side shall initiate or take any step that will change the status of the West Bank and the Gaza Strip pending the outcome of the permanent status negotiations.' See also ibid., Art. XXXI(8): 'The two Parties view the West Bank and the Gaza Strip as a single territorial unit, the territorial integrity and status of which will be preserved during the interim period'; Declaration of Principles, Art. V(4) ('the outcome of permanent status negotiations should not be prejudiced or preempted by agreements reached for the interim period').

[8] Ibid., Art. XI(2)(e).

[9] See ibid., Art. XIII(1) (providing that the Palestinian Council will 'assume the powers

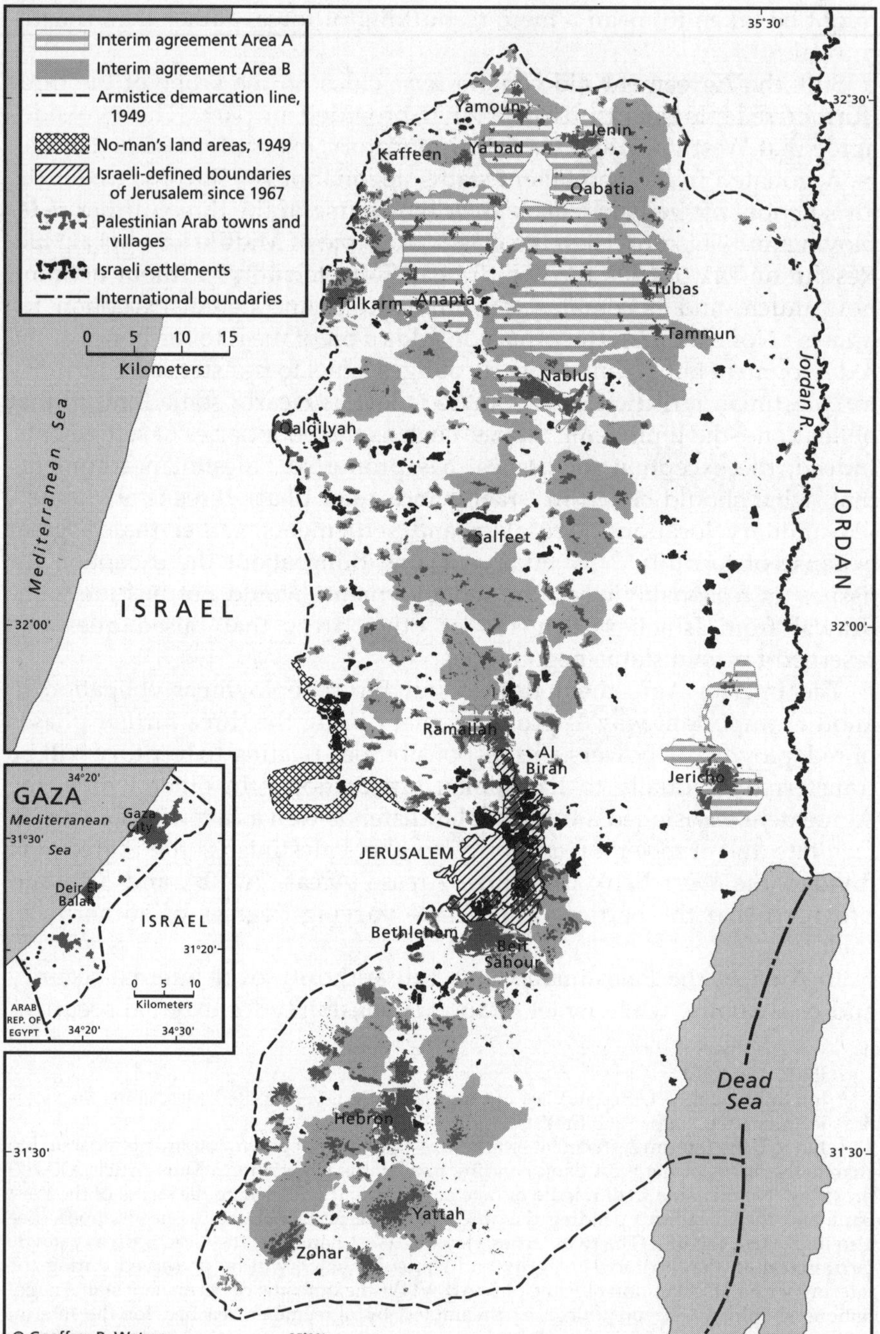

Map 7. West Bank and the Gaza Strip after the 1995 Interim Agreement

After implementation of the initial phase of redeployments under the Interim Agreement, Area A consisted of the Jericho Area and six other Palestinian cities on the West Bank: Jenin, Nablus, Tulkarem, Qalqilyah, Ramallah, and Bethlehem.[10] The Palestinian Authority immediately began to exercise full civil and security authority in these areas. The Agreement had intended that Area A would also include four-fifths of Hebron, but redeployment from Hebron was delayed until the signing and implementation of the Hebron Protocol in January 1997. After Israel's withdrawal from Hebron, Area A comprised about 3 per cent of the total area of the West Bank.[11]

In Area B, the Palestinian Authority exercises civil authority and maintains a police force to protect the 'public order for Palestinians',[12] while Israel retains 'overriding responsibility for security for the purpose of protecting Israelis and confronting the threat of terrorism'.[13] According to one Israeli negotiator, this phrase was intended to make clear that in Area B, 'Israeli responsibility shall take precedence over the Palestinian responsibility for public order'.[14] Under the Interim Agreement, Area B consisted of all areas of the West Bank (other than those in Area A) that are populated by Palestinians—a total of about 450 towns, villages, refugee camps, and hamlets.[15] As with Area A, the Interim Agreement mandated a 'complete redeployment of Israeli military forces from Area B';[16] this redeployment was more or less carried out by the beginning of 1996. After this redeployment, Area B amounted to about one-quarter of the land area of the West Bank.[17] The intent of the negotiators was that parts of Area B might eventually be transferred to Area A as part of the 'further redeployments'.[18]

and responsibilities for internal security' in Area A); ibid., Art. XI(2)(b) (providing that the Council will also assume all 'civil powers and responsibilities' in Area A); ibid., Art. XII(1) ('Israel shall continue to carry the responsibility for defense against external threats . . .').

10 See ibid., Art. XI(3)(a).

11 See David Makovsky, 'ABCs of Redeployment', *Jerus. Post*, 7 Mar. 1997; Ilene R. Prusher, 'What the Oslo Deal Left Out Hinders Mideast Peace Process', *Christian Science Monitor*, 13 Mar. 1997.

12 Ibid., Art. XIII(2)(b). As to the Palestinian police force, see ibid., Art. XIV and Art. IV of Annex I to the Interim Agreement.

13 Interim Agreement, Art. XIII(2)(a). Again, Israel also retained responsibility for external security. See ibid., Art. XII(1).

14 Singer, 'The West Bank and Gaza Strip', 10.

15 See Interim Agreement, Art. XI(3)(b) and attached map; Appendix 6 to Annex I to the Interim Agreement (listing hamlets included in Area B). See also Singer, 'The West Bank and Gaza Strip,' 9 (describing Area B).

16 Interim Agreement, Art. XIII(2)(a); ibid., Art. XI(2)(a) (making clear that the first phase of redeployment would include redeployment from Areas A and B).

17 See Prusher, 'What the Oslo Deal Left Out'; Makovsky, 'ABCs of Redeployment'.

18 See Singer, 'The West Bank and Gaza Strip', 10 (asserting that 'parts of Area "B" may become Area "A" ').

In Area C, Israel retains complete territorial jurisdiction, though the Interim Agreement did provide that the Palestinian Council would have 'functional jurisdiction' in Area C, but only over Palestinians, and only in matters 'not related to territory'.[19] Area C consists of the remainder of the West Bank, including areas populated by Jewish settlements. As of early 1997 (after the redeployment from Hebron), this area comprised about 70 per cent of the land area of the West Bank.[20] Israel is obligated to make 'further redeployments' from this Area to 'specified military locations'.[21] In particular, the Interim Agreement provides that Area C 'means areas of the West Bank outside Areas A and B, which, except for the issues that will be negotiated in the permanent status negotiations, will be gradually transferred to Palestinian jurisdiction'.[22] The Agreement also provides explicitly for '[f]urther redeployments from Area C'[23] as part of the three-stage 'further redeployments' to 'specified military locations'.

One implication of these provisions is that parts of Area C were supposed to become either Area A or Area B. In other words, parts of Area C were to be transferred from complete Israeli control to partial or complete Palestinian control.[24] Another implication is that not *all* of Area C—i.e. not all of the West Bank—would be transferred to Palestinian control as part of the three 'further redeployments'. The Agreement envisions transfer of Area C 'except for the issues' to be negotiated in final status talks.

Thus, while the terms 'further redeployments' to 'specified military locations' are not defined explicitly, other provisions of the Interim Agreement do lend some meaning to them. The plain intent of the drafters was that 'redeployment' would involve more than a mere reshuffling of Israeli military forces in existing locations. The Agreement contemplates complete 'redeployment' from Areas A and B, and it speaks of redeployments 'from' Area C, not 'in' Area C. The Agreement clearly obligates Israel to withdraw from at least some—though not all—parts of Area C in three phases of withdrawals over a period of eighteen months. But the Agreement said nothing more specific about just how much of Area C must be transferred to Palestinian control. Nor did the Agreement

[19] Interim Agreement, Art. XVII(2)(d); ibid., Annexe III, Art. IV and Appendix I. 'As of late November 1996, even this limited jurisdiction has not yet been transferred.' Omar M. Dajani, 'Stalled Between Seasons: The International Legal Status of Palestine During the Interim Period', 26 *Den. J. Int'l L. & Pol'y* 27, 63 n. 209 (1997).

[20] See Makovsky, 'ABCs of Redeployment'.

[21] Interim Agreement, Art. X(2); ibid., Art. XI(2)(f).

[22] Ibid., Art. XI(3)(c).

[23] Ibid., Art. XIII(2)(b)(8) ('Further redeployments from Area C and transfer of internal security responsibility to the Palestinian Police in Areas B and C will be carried out in three phases . . . except for the issues of permanent status negotiations and of Israel's overall responsibility for Israelis and borders').

[24] See Singer, 'The West Bank and Gaza Strip', 10.

say anything about what is a 'specified' military location—or about *who* 'specifies' the appropriate locations.

Treaty law provides that the subsequent practice of the parties to an agreement can be relevant to its interpretation.[25] Unfortunately, the practice of the parties following the Interim Agreement sheds little light on its meaning. Israel did not make the first scheduled 'redeployment', which was due in July 1996, until six months after the inauguration of the Palestinian Council, which took place in January 1996. Israel justified its failure to redeploy by charging that the Palestinian side had failed to live up to its own obligations under the Accords, including its obligation to combat terrorism and its obligation to change the Palestine National Charter to remove references calling for the destruction of Israel. Other developments also contributed to Israel's refusal to redeploy: the assassination of Prime Minister Yitzhak Rabin in November 1995; the election of Likud Prime Minister Benjamin Netanyahu, who had made known his scepticism about the Oslo Accords, in the spring of 1996; a series of deadly suicide bombings by Hamas members in Israel in February and March 1996, which led to arrests of Islamic militants and the sealing off of the occupied territories;[26] and the bombing of northern Israel by Hezbollah guerrillas in the spring of 1996.

In January 1997 the parties finally reached an agreement on the withdrawal of Israeli forces from most of the city of Hebron, which was supposed to take place in early 1996.[27] Prime Minister Netanyahu and Chairman Arafat signed the Hebron Protocol[28] on 15 January 1997, and Israeli forces withdrew from most of Hebron the next day. The Hebron Protocol was accompanied by a two-page 'Note for the Record', prepared by US negotiator Dennis Ross, in which each side 'reaffirm[ed]' some of its central obligations under the Interim Agreement.[29] Among other things, Israel pledged itself to a new timetable for further redeployment: 'The first phase of further redeployments will be carried out during the first week of March' of 1997.[30]

And in March Israel did in fact propose the first of the three mandated 'further redeployments'—but only involving a transfer of 9 per cent of the

[25] See Vienna Convention on the Law of Treaties, 23 May 1969, UN Doc. A/CONF. 39/27, Art. 31(3) and (3)(b).

[26] Hamas claimed responsibility for the bombings, saying that they were in retaliation for Israel's assassination of Yahya Ayyash, 'the Engineer,' in January 1996. See Glenn E. Robinson, *Building a Palestinian State* (Bloomington, IN: Indiana University Press, 1997), 190.

[27] See Art. VII(1)(b) of Annexe I to the Interim Agreement (providing that redeployment from Hebron 'will be completed not later than six months after the signing [in September 1995] of this Agreement').

[28] Protocol Concerning the Redeployment in Hebron, 15 Jan. 1997.

[29] See Note for the Record, 15 Jan. 1997, reprinted in Appendix G.

[30] Ibid., 'Israeli Responsibilities', ¶1.

West Bank, including 7 per cent from Area B (presumably leading to its transfer to Area A), and 2 per cent from Area C (leading to its transfer to either Areas A or B).[31] In fact, as Palestinians have since pointed out, only the proposal to withdraw from 2 per cent of Area C involved a true redeployment; the remaining 7 per cent would simply be transferred from shared jurisdiction to exclusive Palestinian jurisdiction.[32] Still, the Israeli proposal was not radically different from the first stage of redeployment agreed to in the Wye River Memorandum of late 1998, under which only 2 per cent of Area C became Area B.

At any rate, Arafat—already angered by Israel's announcements of plans to construct Jewish housing at Har Homa in East Jerusalem—rejected the Israeli redeployment proposal as far short of that required by the Interim Agreement. One poll of 500 Palestinians in the Bethlehem, Hebron, and Jerusalem areas indicated that 95 per cent of them believed the Israeli redeployment proposal was unsatisfactory.[33] Some reports suggested that the Palestinian side had in mind a first redeployment of around 25 to 30 per cent.[34] Others suggested that some Palestinian negotiators acknowledged that hoping for a 30 per cent redeployment was not 'realistic', but argued that 'at least it should not be 2 per cent'.[35] Israeli negotiators responded that the Accords did not set any particular percentage; they merely obliged Israel to withdraw to 'specified military locations'. Because Arafat had rejected Israel's proposal, Israel did not go forward with it. Thus the parties found themselves locked in a bitter disagreement over the scope of the next redeployment.

This deadlock persisted for another year and a half. In 1998 Israel hinted that it might support moving directly to final status talks after a single redeployment, but the Palestinians apparently preferred to stick to the Interim Agreement's blueprint of a series of redeployments. The United States proposed that Israel make one redeployment from about 13 per cent of the West Bank and that final status talks begin immediately thereafter. The Palestinian side apparently accepted this proposal in principle, but the Israeli side maintained that 13 per cent was too much, since

[31] See Serge Schmemann, 'Israel to Yield 9% More of West Bank; A Victory for Netanyahu', *N.Y. Times*, 7 Mar. 1997.

[32] See, e.g., 'Why Israeli Plan Upsets Palestinians', *San Francisco Chronicle*, 13 Mar. 1997 (quoting Palestinian negotiator Saeb Erekat's view that the Israeli forces redeployed from the 7% in December 1995, and that '[w]e don't need them to redeploy from there again. We need them to redeploy from Area C . . .').

[33] See Jon Immanuel, 'Arafat: Peace process near breakdown; Gaza forum uneventful', *Jerus. Post*, 16 Mar. 1997.

[34] See, e.g., David Makovsky and Jon Immanuel, 'Cabinet debates up to 10% pullback', ibid. 7 Mar. 1997 (noting that the PA 'is expecting about 25% of Areas C and B to be turned over to Area A, far more than is being contemplated by the government or the US').

[35] Jon Immanuel, 'A different view of Oslo', ibid. 14 Mar. 1997 (paraphrasing and quoting Palestinian negotiator Saeb Erekat).

it would inevitably require Israel to cede land around settlements, making them isolated islands in Palestinian-controlled territory. Israel hinted that 11 per cent might be acceptable, but neither the Palestinians nor the United States were willing to accept that figure. The American insistence on 13 per cent rather than 11 per cent had a psychological component: since the Palestinians already had some control over roughly 27 per cent of the West Bank, an additional 13 per cent would give them 40 per cent, which 'sounded' much more substantial than 36 per cent or even 38 per cent.

Ultimately the parties did agree to a modified version of the American plan. That agreement was embodied in the Wye River Memorandum, signed at the White House on 23 October 1998 after more than a week of hard bargaining. The Memorandum put a precise number on two of the three remaining redeployments required by the Interim Agreement. At the time of the adoption of the Memorandum, 3 per cent of the West Bank was Area A, 24 per cent was Area B, and 73 per cent was Area C. The Memorandum provided that after the first two redeployments, the West Bank would be reconfigured so that 17.2 per cent was Area A, 21.8 per cent Area B, and 60 per cent Area C—thus codifying the American plan to give the Palestinians some control over 40 per cent of the West Bank. To complicate matters further, the Memorandum provided that the first two redeployments would be carried out in three stages, each with its own numerical requirements.[36]

The parties did not, however, agree on numerical targets for the third and final further redeployment. Instead, they agreed to establish a committee on the question. Thus the parties put numbers on the first two redeployments but left intact the Interim Agreement formula for the final redeployment—namely, that Israeli forces would be obliged to redeploy to 'specified military locations'. Wye therefore eliminated some but not all of the ambiguity in the Interim Agreement. Not surprisingly, the parties later found themselves disagreeing once more about the extent of this third and final obligation.

In November 1998 Israel did carry out the first of the three stages of redeployments called for by the Wye Memorandum by withdrawing from

[36] In stage 1, which was in fact implemented shortly after the Memorandum was signed, 2% of the West Bank would be transferred from Area C to Area B, and 7.1% from Area B to Area A. In stage 2, which was supposed to take place a few weeks later but never was carried out, 5% of Area C would become Area B. In stage 3, also not carried out, 5% of Area C would become B, 1% of Area C would become Area A, and 7.1% of Area B would become Area A. Wye River Memorandum, Time Line, ¶¶2–4. The net effect of all this was 13% of Area C would be transferred, of which 1% would become Area A and 12% Area B, and another 14.2% of Area B would become Area A. Wye River Memorandum, ¶I.A. The agreement also provided that the Palestinians would treat 3% of Area B as 'Green Areas and/or Nature Preserves'. Ibid. ¶I.A.1.

7 per cent more of the West Bank.[37] Soon thereafter, President Clinton visited Gaza and watched as the Palestine National Council finally amended its Charter to remove anti-Israel clauses.[38] But shortly thereafter the Netanyahu government charged that the Palestinians had violated their obligations under Wye and the earlier Accords, and it soon became clear that neither party would take any further steps to implement the Wye River Memorandum. As of the summer of 1999, Israel still had not carried out the further redeployments called for by the Memorandum.

The Sharm el-Sheikh Memorandum resolved some but not all of the deadlock over Wye. It called for Israel to carry out the first two 'phases' of redeployment in three steps. First, on 5 September 1999 Israel would transfer 7 per cent from Area C to Area B. Second, on 15 November 1999 Israel would transfer 2 per cent from Area B to Area A and 3 per cent from Area C to Area B. Finally, on 20 January 2000 Israel would transfer 1 per cent from Area C to Area A, and 5.1 per cent from Area B to Area A.[39] Unfortunately, the Memorandum did not resolve the question left open by the Wye River Memorandum and the earlier Accords—namely, the size of the final redeployment.

Israel has thus far complied with the redeployment requirements of the Sharm el-Sheikh Memorandum. The first withdrawal took place in September 1999, only a few days behind schedule. Interestingly, the Israeli Prime Minister's office released a statement asserting that once Arafat signed maps describing the withdrawal, those maps would 'become binding'.[40] This statement is odd because it might imply that Israel needed Arafat's signature to make its decision to withdraw 'binding'. In other words, the statement might be read to vindicate the PA's traditional view that it must approve the precise contours of each withdrawal. Israel would doubtless argue that the statement was merely intended to estop Arafat from complaining about Israel's decision in the future. In other words, Israel's view is that it gave Arafat the maps as a courtesy, and that he bound only himself by signing them. Arafat's view is that he is entitled to approve or disapprove particular redeployments, and that the sharing of the maps reflects this reality.

This disagreement surfaced again in November 1999, the date of the second scheduled redeployment under Sharm el-Sheikh. As Israel

[37] See Lee Hockstader, 'Israel Withdraws from 200 Square Miles', *Wash. Post*, 21 Nov. 1998; Arieh O'Sullivan (with Mohammed Najib), 'IDF wraps up Wye's first stage today', *Jerus. Post*, 22 Nov. 1998.

[38] See Deborah Sontag, 'Clinton Watches as Palestinians Drop Call for Israel's Destruction', *N.Y. Times*, 15 Dec. 1998.

[39] Sharm el-Sheikh Memorandum, ¶2.

[40] Lamia Lahoud and Arieh O'Sullivan, 'First Sharm pullback set for today', *Jerus. Post*, 10 Sept. 1999.

prepared to withdraw, Arafat objected to Israel's choice of land. Arafat asserted that Israel was required to seek his approval on what particular areas of Areas B and C would be transferred.[41]

Thus the parties continue to disagree over redeployments, as they have for the past five years. These disagreements reflect underlying disagreements about two major legal issues: (1) Do Palestinian violations justify Israel's suspension of its own undertakings to redeploy? (2) Does the PA have any say over what particular land is transferred, and in particular over the size and scope of the third and final redeployment to 'specified military locations'? Even after the Sharm el-Sheikh Memorandum, both of these issues are still relevant. The Memorandum does not define the scope of the third and final redeployment, and it leaves open the possibility that the parties will quarrel about reciprocity in the future. Accordingly, the next two sections take up each of these questions in turn.

Palestinian violations as justifying Israeli suspension

Israel argues vigorously that it is not obliged to redeploy so long as the Palestinians fail to live up to their own obligations under the Oslo Accords, including the Wye River Memorandum. Israel has invoked reciprocity in other circumstances as well, for example when it suspended certain financial obligations to the Palestinians in 1997. In Israel's view, and in the view of its supporters, reciprocity is the cornerstone of the Oslo Accords. Nowhere does reciprocity have more resonance than in the context of the redeployment question. As Israel has pointed out, surrendering land is a concrete, perhaps irreversible decision, one that no state undertakes lightly, and Israel did not undertake it without assurances that it would receive something important—security—in return.

International law embraces the principle that international agreements are, in general, reciprocal. We have already seen in Part II that the Oslo Accords, including the Wye River Memorandum, are binding international agreements even if they are not technically treaties within the traditional meaning of the term. As binding international agreements, they are subject to interpretation in accordance with the rules of the customary law of treaties.[42] As we have already seen in Part II, the Vienna Convention on the Law of Treaties mostly codifies the customary law of treaties, including the law relating to performance and breach.

Article 60 of the Vienna Convention permits a party to suspend or

[41] See Danna Harman and Lamia Lahoud, 'Barak, Arafat meet on pullback dispute', ibid. 15 Nov. 1999.

[42] Cf. Vienna Convention on the Law of Treaties, Art. 3(b).

terminate its performance 'in whole or in part' in response to a 'material breach' by the other.[43] A 'material breach' is defined as a repudiation of the treaty or a 'violation of a provision essential to the accomplishment of the object or purpose of the treaty'.[44] Incidentally, this standard is hardly unique to international law. Municipal contract law in both civil- and common-law systems routinely holds that non-performance by one party justifies suspension or termination by the other.[45] Indeed, this aspect of contract law is sufficiently widespread that it might itself qualify as a rule of international law—a 'general principle of law' recognized by 'civilized nations'.[46]

Curiously, the Vienna Convention fails to specify the rights of the parties in the event of a minor breach—i.e. non-performance that is not serious enough to qualify as a material breach within the meaning of Article 60. Interpretation of this gap in the Convention is crucial because the parties to the Oslo Accords have frequently taken countermeasures against one another without explicitly charging a material breach. It is possible, in other words, that the parties have felt free to suspend their own obligations even in response to non-performance that does not amount to material breach by the other side. In suspending its redeployments, for example, Israel has typically not charged the Palestinians with 'material breach' of the Accords. Must Israel identify a material breach by the Palestinians before it can take any retaliatory action, or can it respond to minor breaches as well? The plain text of Article 60 seems silent on this question.

One possible interpretation of this silence is that an aggrieved party has *no* right to respond at all to a minor breach by the other. The explicit mention of a remedy for material breach, read together with the provision's silence on minor breach, might imply no remedy for lesser breaches. While this might be a natural reading of the text of the Vienna Convention, it appears to be inconsistent with state practice; countermeasures taken in response to minor breaches seem at least as common as countermeasures to material breaches. Indeed, customary international law has long recognized rights of reprisal and retorsion (now often

[43] Vienna Convention on the Law of Treaties, Art. 60(1).

[44] Ibid., Art. 60(3)(a) (repudiation); ibid., Art. 60(3)(b) (object or purpose).

[45] See, e.g., German Civil Code (*Bürgerliches Gesetzbuch*) §320 ('A person who is bound by a two-sided contract may refuse to perform his part until the other party has performed his part, unless the former is bound to perform his part first), translated in Arthur T. von Mehren and James Russell Gordley, *The Civil Law System*, 2nd edn (Boston: Little, Brown & Co., 1977); French Civil Code (*Code Civil*), Art. 1184, cl. 1 (providing that constructive conditions of exchange are always implied in bilateral contracts); American Law Institute, *Restatement of the Law (2nd), Contracts*, §237 (providing that each party's performance is conditioned on performance by the other party).

[46] See Statute of the International Court of Justice, 26 June 1945, T.S. 993, Art. 38(1)(c).

lumped together as 'countermeasures') in response to even minor breaches of international agreements. Reprisal is a countermeasure by the aggrieved party that would violate the treaty but for the first party's minor breach; retorsion is a countermeasure (such as an adjustment in the level of diplomatic relations) that would be lawful even absent the first party's breach.[47] It seems unlikely that Article 60 was intended to alter this pre-existing regime of reprisal and retorsion in response to minor breaches. There is some arbitral practice, as well as a fair amount of scholarly opinion, that supports this conclusion.[48]

At the same time, it is generally agreed that if there is some right to take non-forcible countermeasures in response to a minor breach, those countermeasures must be proportionate to the breach.[49] This view is consistent with the text of Article 60, which plainly was intended to prevent states from seizing on pretexts to suspend or terminate their treaty obligations. There may be other limitations on reprisals and retorsion as well. It has been suggested, for example, that countermeasures must be 'appropriate' as well as proportionate.[50] It might, indeed, be inappropriate to counter a human rights violation with a 'proportionate' human rights violation. There may also be some requirement to exhaust reasonable remedies, most notably those provided by the Oslo Accords themselves, before resorting to countermeasures. We will take up this point shortly.

For now, it is fair to conclude that the Oslo Accords are indeed premised on reciprocity; that each party is entitled (though not required) to suspend or terminate its own performance in response to material breaches by the other party; that each party is probably entitled to undertake countermeasures in response to lesser breaches by the other; and that those countermeasures must be proportionate to the original breach, and

[47] See Oscar Schachter, 'United Nations Law', 88 *Am. J. Int'l L.* 1, 15 (1994).

[48] See *Case Concerning the Air Services Agreement of 27 Mar. 1946*, Arbitral Award of 9 Dec. 1978, 54 I.L.R. 304 (US v. Fr.) (1979); Lori Fisler Damrosch, 'Retaliation or Arbitration—or Both? The 1978 United States–France Aviation Dispute', 74 *Am. J. Int'l L.* 785, 790 (1980) ('By reading between the lines of the International Law Commission's commentary [to the draft Vienna Convention], it is fortunately possible to conclude that the Commission did not intend to foreclose appropriate responses to breaches not covered by Articles 60's materiality standard'); Omer Yousif Elagab, *The Legality of Non-Forcible Counter-Measures in International Law*, 163–4 (1988); cf. also John K. Setear, 'Responses to Breach of a Treaty and Rationalist International Relations Theory: The Rules of Release and Remediation in the Law of Treaties and the law of State Responsibility', 83 *Va. L. Rev.* 1, 20 n. 21 (1997). But cf. Frederic L. Kirgis, Jr., 'Some Lingering Questions about Article 60 of the Vienna Convention on the Law of Treaties', 22 *Cornell Int'l L.J.* 549, 572 (1989).

[49] See *Case Concerning the Air Services Agreement*, *supra* n. 46, ¶83; Damrosch, *supra* n. 46, at 791–2; D. W. Greig, 'Reciprocity, Proportionality, and the Law of Treaties', 34 *Va. J. Int'l L.* 295, 360 (1994). In Greig's view, proportionality is an 'overriding principle of customary law, a principle that must be applied both to the interpretation of the Vienna Convention's specific provisions and to matters not covered by the Convention'. Ibid.

[50] Dennis Bower, Note, 'An Evaluation of the Proposed Fair Trade in Financial Services Act', 27 *Case W. Res. J. Int'l L.* 407, 414, and n. 63 (1995).

probably must be 'appropriate' as well; and that there may be some duty to exhaust remedies under the Accords before pursuing countermeasures.

If there was any doubt about whether the Oslo Accords are premised on reciprocity, it was removed by the Wye River Memorandum. The Memorandum set forth a detailed, week-by-week timeline for completion of each party's obligations. In Week 2, for example, the parties listed five obligations, the first four of which were primarily Palestinian duties, and the last of which—the first stage of redeployment—was Israeli. Likewise, in Weeks 2–6, the parties first listed seven obligations, five of which were primarily Palestinian duties, and the last of which—the second stage of redeployment—was Israeli. Plainly the obligations in Week 2 were to be carried out before those in Weeks 2–6, and material breach of Palestinian obligations in Week 2 would presumably entitle Israel to suspend Israeli obligations in Weeks 2–6.

The Palestinians do not dispute that the Wye River Memorandum establishes reciprocal obligations, but they do assert that the Memorandum obliges the parties to perform each set of obligations simultaneously. In other words, the Palestinians argue that Israel must carry out the redeployment in Weeks 2–6 at the same time that Palestinians undertake their obligations (for example, on weapons collection). Israel argues that the Palestinians are obliged to perform first. Israel points out that the Israeli obligation to redeploy is always the final item on the lists of obligations for a given week or set of weeks. Israel also stresses that the Memorandum obliges the Palestinians to carry out their obligations 'during' the relevant time periods, implying that Palestinian obligations are continuous, whereas the most significant Israeli obligation (redeployment) is a one-time only undertaking. Obviously Israel's argument would be stronger if the Memorandum explicitly indicated the order in which obligations were to be performed. Still, its reading seems more plausible. The Vienna Convention on the Law of Treaties does not speak to the question of simultaneity, but municipal contract law furnishes support for Israel's position. The traditional common-law view is that if one party's performance will take a period of time, that party is obliged to go first unless the agreement provides otherwise.[51]

Given that the Accords establish reciprocal (if not simultaneous) obligations, have Palestinian violations been sufficiently serious to justify Israel's suspension of its own obligations to redeploy? Part IV takes up the question of Palestinian compliance in detail, but a few general points can be made now. First, for the Israelis, no provisions in the Oslo Accords are more 'material' or 'essential' to their 'object or purpose' than the

[51] See, e.g., *Restatement (2nd) of Contracts*, §234(2).

provisions on security and terrorism. If the Palestinians have indeed failed to carry out these obligations, that failure would be a material breach. As we shall see in Part IV, the PA's record of compliance with the Accords is at best mixed. There is evidence that the PA has at various points violated its obligations on security cooperation and incitement, but it is unclear to what extent the PA has violated its counter-terrorism obligations. The PA has complied, albeit belatedly, with its obligation to amend the Palestine National Charter to remove anti-Israel clauses.

Second, even assuming that the PA has materially breached the Accords, treaty law does not *require* Israel to suspend its obligations in response to a material breach by the other party. The Vienna Convention merely provides that the innocent party is 'entitled' to suspend (or terminate) its own duties, not that it is obliged to do so. Thus suspension (or termination) of a breached treaty is not automatic; the innocent party must take the affirmative step of suspending (or terminating) its obligations. Moreover, once Israel decided to take such a step, it has had the further choice of deciding whether to suspend its obligations or terminate them altogether, and it has invariably chosen the lesser remedy of suspension. Having made that choice, Israel was further entitled to choose between suspending some or all of its obligations; Article 60 of the Vienna Convention permits the innocent party to suspend its obligations 'in whole or in part'.[52] Israel was not required to respond with a mirror-image of the asserted violation by the PA, for example by suspending Israeli security obligations under the Accords. The Vienna Convention permits the innocent party to choose which if any provisions it would like to suspend—within certain limits.

One of those limits is found in Article 60(5), which provides that the innocent party may not suspend 'provisions relating to the protection of the human person contained in treaties of a humanitarian character, in particular to provisions prohibiting any form of reprisals against persons protected by such treaties'. But it is hard to argue that Israel's redeployment obligations fall within this exception. For one thing, Article 60(5) applies, oddly, only to treaties 'of a humanitarian character', and the Oslo Accords might or might not fit this description. (One would have thought that states would be prohibited from suspending *all* human rights obligations, even those that do not appear in treaties that are predominantly 'humanitarian', especially given the difficulties in classifying complex

[52] Another provision of the Convention maintains that treaty obligations are generally *not* separable—except in a case of material breach, the type of case at issue here. See Vienna Convention on the Law of Treaties, Art. 44(2) ('A ground for . . . suspending the operation of a treaty . . . may be invoked only with respect to the whole treaty except as provided in the following paragraphs [on certain types of severable clauses] or in article 60 [on material breach]').

agreements like the Oslo Accords.[53]) But even assuming that the Oslo Accords are sufficiently 'humanitarian' to fall within Article 60(5), it seems unlikely that a promise to deliver up land to a political entity like the PA rises to the level of a provision on the 'protection of the human person'. Plainly the drafters of Article 60 had in mind more traditional human rights provisions, such as those obliging the PA and Israel to respect internationally accepted norms of human rights.

Third, the Netanyahu government's decision to suspend redeployment is more vulnerable to criticism if one concludes that the Palestinians have not materially breached the Accords. In this event, Israel probably would have some right of retorsion or reprisal, but such countermeasures would have to be proportionate and appropriate. The Netanyahu government certainly accepted the principle that it had a right of reprisal, but it did not explicitly acknowledge that this right must be exercised in a proportionate and appropriate manner.

Palestinians might argue that the Netanyahu government retaliated in a disproportionate fashion. In the Palestinian view, Israel repeatedly suspended its most important obligation, redeployment, in response to a variety of lesser breaches by the Palestinians, such as their delay in amending the Charter. The Palestinians might contend that Israel should have chosen to suspend a less central obligation, such as its obligations relating to ports or safe passage.

Israel could respond that it has suspended its redeployment obligations because they depend most critically on the security provisions breached by the Palestinians, and that the Palestinian security obligations are just as central as Israeli redeployment obligations. In Israel's view, delays in redeployment are undoubtedly a proportionate and appropriate response to delays in Palestinian security cooperation. Given that Israel's obligation to redeploy is more concrete and irreversible than any corresponding Palestinian obligation, there is considerable merit to this argument.

Fourth, even if Israel's suspension was an appropriate and proportionate reprisal, it might still be objectionable because Israel did not use the dispute-resolution mechanisms set forth in the Vienna Convention on the Law of Treaties or, especially, in the Oslo Accords themselves. (As we shall see in Part IV, the PA has also failed to use these mechanisms when it has complained of Israeli violations of the Accords.) The Vienna

[53] Treaty taxonomy is a notoriously hazardous exercise. See Shabtai Rosenne, *Breach of Treaty* (Cambridge: Grotius Publications, 1985), 103. None the less, states and international organizations routinely classify international agreements, even the most complex ones. See, e.g., UN Secretariat, *Multilateral Treaties Deposited with the Secretary-General*, ST/LEG/SER. E/—(dividing treaties into 28 categories); US Dept. of State, *Treaties in Force* (1997) (classifying both bilateral and multilateral treaties by subject-matter).

Convention provides that parties may only suspend their own obligations after giving the other party three months' notice, 'except in cases of special urgency'.[54] This procedural requirement, however, is rarely honoured in actual practice.[55] In any event, the Vienna Convention adds that it is 'without prejudice to any provision in the treaty applicable in the event of breach'.[56]

The Oslo Accords have several such provisions. The Declaration of Principles established a Joint Israeli–Palestinian Liaison Committee, and the Interim Agreement provided that the Committee 'shall deal with issues requiring coordination, other issues of common interest *and disputes*'.[57] The Declaration of Principles also provides that disputes 'may be resolved' by a conciliation method to be agreed upon by the parties.[58] Under the law of international agreements, the parties must abide by these dispute–resolution provisions in good faith. Israel says it has made repeated but futile efforts to resolve its differences with the PA by negotiation. Even if Israel has not had recourse to the formal mechanisms established by the Accords (and the Vienna Convention), a good-faith effort at reconciliation might satisfy the spirit of the dispute–resolution provisions. Whether either party has made such an effort remains doubtful.

In sum, the lawfulness of the Netanyahu government's decision to suspend its redeployments depends largely on whether and to what extent the Palestinians have materially breached the Accords, including the Wye River Memorandum. Assessment of Palestinian compliance is considerably more complex than assessment of Israeli compliance, since the Palestinian obligations are not as easily quantifiable. But even if the PA has materially breached the Memorandum and other Oslo Accords, Israel is required to make good-faith recourse to the dispute–resolution mechanisms in the Accords. The obligation to negotiate continues to this day.

[54] Vienna Convention on the Law of Treaties, Art. 65(2). The Convention also provides that aggrieved parties may, in certain circumstances, avail themselves of conciliation procedures set forth in the Convention. Ibid., Art. 66(b). These procedures are rarely used in practice.

[55] Cf. Rosenne, *Breach of Treaty*, 36 (asserting that the Vienna Convention's procedure on dispute–resolution constitutes an 'over-emphasis on a legal approach not really compatible with general diplomatic experience or the diplomatic temperament').

[56] Vienna Convention on the Law of Treaties, Art. 60(4). See also ibid., Art. 65(4) ('Nothing in the foregoing paragraphs shall affect the rights or obligations of the parties under any provision in force binding the parties with regard to the settlement of disputes').

[57] Declaration of Principles, Art. X (emphasis added); Interim Agreement, Art. XXVI(1). See also Gaza–Jericho Agreement, Art. XV.

[58] Declaration of Principles, Art. XV(2). See also Gaza–Jericho Agreement, Art. XVII(2) (similar language); Interim Agreement, Art. XXI(2) (similar).

The scope of the obligation to redeploy to 'specified military locations'

Assuming that Israel is still obliged to redeploy from the West Bank, then there remains the question of precisely how much redeployment is required. The Wye River and Sharm el-Sheik Memoranda have removed much doubt about the size of the first and second redeployments called for by the Interim Agreement: the Memoranda describe them in percentage terms. But the Memoranda fail to specify *which* portions of Area C should become Area B, which portions of Area B should become Area A, and so forth. More ominously, the Memoranda did not alter the vague prescription of the Interim Agreement on the final redeployment, which must be to 'specified military locations'. This issue continues to generate intense disagreement between the parties.

According to Israeli negotiator Joel Singer, the term 'specified' locations means that 'the number, extent and location of these areas is not a subject for negotiations between the parties, but rather will be decided unilaterally by Israel'.[59] Indeed, Singer says that everyone involved in the negotiations understood this to be the case.[60] According to Singer, the Israeli negotiators specifically rejected the term 'agreed' military locations, which was apparently proposed by the Palestinian side, in favour of the term 'specified' military locations.[61] Indeed, there have been press reports suggesting that both Palestinian and American officials have 'accepted' that the decision is exclusively Israel's.[62] Israel takes the same position with respect to the size of the smaller redeployments described in the Sharm el-Sheikh Memorandum: that Israel alone decides which land to cede, and that Israel's practice of sharing maps with Arafat is (as Barak himself put it) a 'sign of good will, not an obligation'.[63]

The counter-argument for the Palestinian side is that the Accords simply do not indicate *who* 'specifies' the 'specified' military locations for redeployment. As the PA points out, the text does not say 'military locations specified solely by Israel'.[64] In the absence of clear language to the contrary, this argument runs, the text should reasonably be interpreted to mean that the two sides will negotiate on 'specifying' the appropriate

[59] Singer, 'The West Bank and Gaza Strip', 10.

[60] See Immanuel, 'A Different View of Oslo' (reporting on Singer's recollection that 'a unilateral decision was intended and that it was understood by everyone involved').

[61] See Singer, 'The West Bank and Gaza Strip', 10.

[62] See, e.g., Serge Schmemann, 'Arabs Assail Israeli Move', *N.Y. Times*, 8 Mar. 1997.

[63] Harman and Lahoud, 'Barak, Arafat meet'.

[64] See, e.g., Immanuel, 'A Different View of Oslo' (reporting the view of Saeb Erekat, the Palestinian chief negotiator, that Oslo 'simply does not permit unilateral decisions' and that Oslo II does not 'mention a unilateral decision').

locations. Indeed, this view is consistent with the elaborate mechanisms for consultation and coordination built into the Interim Agreement,[65] and with the notion of 'constructive ambiguity' itself—i.e. the notion that the parties simply agreed to agree on the thorniest issues. Even if the Interim Agreement permits a unilateral Israeli decision, Palestinians point out that the Accord does not *prevent* Israel from consulting or negotiating first. Finally, Palestinians and Jordan's King Hussein have argued that whatever the text of Oslo II says, the spirit of Oslo calls for consultation.[66]

Does international law require that the final redeployment be of any particular size? As we have seen, the texts of the Interim Agreement and Hebron Protocol say little on this question, except that there must be redeployment—that is, withdrawal—from some but not necessarily all of Area C, the portion of the West Bank currently under sole Israeli control. General international law, however, furnishes more guidance. In particular, the law of treaties would appear to be applicable.

As we saw in Chapter 3, the Oslo Accords may not be traditional treaties between states, but they are none the less binding international agreements between a state and a sub-state entity, and such agreements have in the past been interpreted and performed like treaties. By its terms, the Vienna Convention on the Law of Treaties would not apply to interpretation or performance of the Oslo Accords, since the Vienna Convention applies only to 'an international agreement concluded between States in written form and governed by international law . . .'.[67] Moreover, Israel is not party to the Vienna Convention, and the Palestinian Authority is presumably not eligible to accede because it is not a state.[68] None the less, it is generally agreed that the Vienna Convention is declaratory of the customary international law of treaties and international agreements, and in particular that the Convention's provisions on interpretation and performance of agreements reflect customary law.[69] As

65 See ibid. ('a unilateral decision is an anomaly considering that almost everything else in the Oslo agreement emphasizes cooperation and coordination').

66 See ibid. ('The argument over making unilateral decisions without consultation comes down to the spirit of the Oslo accord, which if King Hussein is right, Netanyahu has seriously violated').

67 Vienna Convention on the Law of Treaties, Art. 2(1)(a).

68 Cf. ibid., Art. 83 (providing that the Convention is open only for accession by 'any State' that is a member of the United Nations or certain other organizations).

69 See, e.g., Michel Virally, 'Good Faith in Public International Law', 77 *Am. J. Int'l L.* 130, 130 (1983) ('Articles 26 and 31(1) of the Vienna Convention are declaratory of customary rules'). Cf. also UN Charter, 26 June 1945, T.S. 993, Art. 2(2) (providing that all Members of the United Nations 'shall fulfill in good faith' their obligations under the Charter); Convention on Contracts for the International Sale of Goods, 1980, Art. 7(1) (providing that interpretation of the Convention should be made with regard to 'good faith in international trade').

The Sales Convention, however, 'rejects "good faith" as a general requirement' and limits its application to interpretation. John O. Honnold, *Uniform Law for International Sales under the 1980 United Nations Convention* (Deventer; Boston: Kluwer, 1982), 123–4.

such, the Convention's rules are relevant to the international agreements of non-parties.[70]

A fundamental principle of treaty law is that agreements are to be interpreted and performed in good faith. As to interpretation, Article 31(1) of the Vienna Convention on the Law of Treaties provides: 'A treaty shall be interpreted in good faith in accordance with the ordinary meaning to be given to the terms of the treaty in their context and in the light of its object and purpose.' As to performance, Article 26 of the Convention sets forth the traditional rule *pacta sunt servanda*: 'Every treaty in force is binding upon the parties to it and must be performed by them in good faith.' Interestingly, the Oslo Accords generally avoid the term 'good faith', even when the Accords establish obligations to negotiate issues of the greatest importance.[71] By contrast, one of the side letters to the Camp David Accords made explicit reference to an obligation to negotiate in good faith.[72] In any event, however, the Oslo Accords do not expressly *disclaim* good faith, even if they could lawfully do so.[73]

Again, these particular provisions on good faith, like most of the Vienna Convention, are declaratory of customary international law.[74]

[70] Cf. Vienna Convention on the Law of Treaties, Art. 3(a) (providing the Convention shall not affect the 'legal force' of agreements not covered by the Convention); ibid., Art. 3(b) (providing that agreements not covered by the Convention can still be governed by other rules 'independently of the Convention'); ibid., Preamble (providing that customary international law will continue to govern 'questions not regulated by the provisions' of the Convention).

[71] See, e.g., Declaration of Principles, Art. V(3) (providing that permanent status negotiations 'shall cover remaining issues, including: Jerusalem, refugees, settlements, [etc.]', but containing no obligation to bargain in good faith); Interim Agreement, Art. XXXI(5) (containing similar language).

[72] See letter of 20 Mar. 1979, accompanying the Israel–Egypt Peace Treaty. See also Allan Gerson, Book Review, 77 *Am. J. Int'l L.* 918, 922 (1983) (citing the letter accompanying the Israel–Egypt treaty).

[73] It is not clear that Articles 26 and 31 of the Vienna Convention are *jus cogens* norms. The Preamble to the Vienna Convention does suggest that the obligation of good faith is 'universally recognized', which might satisfy the requirement that a *jus cogens* norm be 'accepted and recognized by the international community of States as a whole' as non-derogable. See ibid., Art. 53. But the doctrine of good faith is not in fact quite so universal; some common-law countries have been slow to embrace it. See E. Allen Farnsworth, 'The Eason–Weinmann Colloquium on International and Comparative Law: Duties of Good Faith and Fair Dealing under the UNIDROIT Principles, Relevant International Conventions, and National Laws', 3 *Tul. J. Int'l & Comp. L.* 47, 54 (1995).

That good faith is often non-disclaimable might imply that it has some *jus cogens* character. The non-binding UNIDROIT principles expressly prohibit disclaimer of good faith. See UNIDROIT Principles, Art. 1.7(2) (forbidding parties to 'exclude or limit' the duty of good faith). Likewise, many domestic legal systems forbid such disclaimers. See, e.g., U.C.C. §1-102(3); but cf. ibid., §1-102(3) (permitting parties to *define* good faith for the purposes of a particular agreement). Roman law similarly held that the obligation of good faith is non-derogable. Justinian, *Digest*, II.XIV.27.3.

[74] See, e.g., American Law Institute, *Restatement (3rd) of the Foreign Relations Law of the United States*, §102, Reporter's Note 7, at 35 (asserting that ' "Good faith" . . . is now accepted

Indeed, the provisions on good faith also appear to constitute 'general principles of law recognized by civilized nations',[75] which can be a subsidiary source of international law under Article 38 of the Statute of the International Court of Justice. The Preamble to the Vienna Convention asserts that the principles of good faith and the *pacta sunt servanda* rule are 'universally recognized', suggesting that they are 'general principles'. In fact, the principle of good faith may not be quite as 'universal' as the Convention suggests, at least not in the common law world.[76] But it is true that the municipal law of many states, particularly civil law states, provides that agreements are to be interpreted and performed in good faith.[77] Israeli contract law, for example, imposes an implied obligation of good faith not only in the performance of private agreements, but also in the negotiation of agreements.[78] In Israel, it has even been suggested that

as a principle of customary law'); Virally, 'Good Faith', 130 (asserting that Articles 26 and 31(1) of the Vienna Convention reflect customary law).

[75] See Bin Cheng, *General Principles of Law as Applied by International Courts and Tribunals* (London: Stevens, 1953), 105 (suggesting that good faith is a 'general principle' of law, but adding that the term is 'perhaps difficult to define'); J. F. O'Connor, *Good Faith in International Law* (Aldershot, Hants; Brookfield, VT: Dartmouth, 1991), 1 ('Good faith is a general principle of law recognized by civilized nations, and as such is a formal source of international law').

[76] See Farnsworth, 'Duties of Good Faith and Fair Dealing', 54 (noting that England lacks a doctrine of good faith, and that the United States is a 'leader among common-law countries' in development of such a doctrine). As Professor Farnsworth notes, several common-law countries are eyeing with interest the relatively new doctrines of good faith in US law. See ibid. 52–4 (citing Australia, Canada, and England).

[77] The notion of an implied obligation of good faith is a familiar one in the civil-law world. See, e.g., *BGB* §242, translated in von Mehren and Gordley, *The Civil Law System*, 1190 ('The debtor is bound to perform according to the requirements of good faith [*Treu und Glauben*], ordinary usage being taken into consideration'); *Code Civil* [French Civil Code] Art. 1134 translated in ibid. 1169 ('[Agreements] must be performed in good faith'); Civil Code of Japan, Bk. I, ch. I, §I, Art. 1.2, translated in John Henry Merryman *et al.*, *The Civil Law Tradition: Europe, Latin America, and East Asia* (Charlottesville: Michie, 1994), 1230 ('The exercise of rights and the performance of duties shall be carried out in conformity with the principles of good faith and trust'); Shoji Kawakami, 'Precontractual Liability: Japan', reprinted in Merryman, *The Civil Law Tradition*, 1227–30; cf. Spanish Civil Code, Art. 3(1), translated in ibid. at 980 (providing that norms should be interpreted by 'closely paying attention to their spirit and purpose').

An implied obligation of good faith is, by comparison, a 'novel' notion in the common-law world, E. Allen Farnsworth and William F. Young, *Contracts: Cases and Materials*, 5th edn (Westbury, NY: Foundation Press, 1995), 616, but there too it has begun to take hold. See, e.g., U.C.C. §1-203; *Restatement (2nd), Contracts*, §205. As to Canada, Australia, and England, see Farnsworth, 'Duties of Good Faith and Fair Dealing', 52–4.

[78] Section 39 of the Contracts (General Part) Law, 1973, 27 L.S.I. 117, provides that 'an obligation or right arising out of a contract shall be fulfilled or exercised in customary manner and good faith'. Section 12(a) of the Contracts (General Part) Law provides: 'in negotiating a contract, a person shall act in customary manner and in good faith.' Section 12 is regarded as the 'more innovative and impressive' of the two, in part because it applies a 'new substantive principle' of good faith in negotiation, not just interpretation or performance. Gabriela Shalev, 'Contract Law', in Itzhak Zamir and Sylvanie Colombo (eds.), *The Law of Israel: General Surveys* (Jerusalem: Sacher Institute, 1995), 213–14. See also Ariel Bin-Nun, *The Law of the State of Israel:*

political agreements between different political parties (or within a particular party) are legally binding[79] and that such agreements include an implied obligation of reasonableness—arguably a higher standard than good faith.[80]

What is the content of 'good faith'? There is general (though perhaps not universal) agreement that the phrase is not intended to *weaken* treaty obligations. In other words, an implied obligation of good faith does not mean that a party's obligations to perform a treaty are merely ethical obligations rather than legal ones.[81] Instead, the term is meant

An Introduction, 2nd edn (translated from the German by Menachem Eichelberg; edited by Daniel C. Furman) (Jerusalem: Rubin Mass, 1992), 170 (describing the new provision on good faith negotiation as 'the most far-reaching innovation in the law'); Nili Cohen, 'Good Faith in Bargaining and Principles of Contract Law', 9 *Tel Aviv Studies in Law* 249, 249 (1989) (noting that Section 12 has been 'crowned as the most revolutionary' part of the 1973 Contracts Law).

The emphasis on good faith in Israel's 1973 contract law reflects the influence of section 242 of the German Civil Code. See Yoel Sussman, 'A Forecast of Problems in the Law of Contracts', 2 *Tel Aviv Studies in Law* 17 (1976). Section 242 provides: 'The debtor is bound to perform according to the requirements of good faith, ordinary usage being taken into consideration.' *BGB* §242, translated in von Mehren and Gordley, *The Civil Law System*, 1190. Section 39 of the Israeli contract law is 'almost verbatim a translation of the *BGB*, Section 242'. Sussman, 'A Forecast of Problems', 18. For more on the enormous influence of *BGB* §242, and for a slightly different translation of §242, see generally John P. Dawson, 'Unconscionable Coercion: The German Version', 89 *Harv. L. Rev.* 1041 (1976).

As one Israeli judge has put it, the principle of good faith 'has cast its net . . . over the whole legal system in Israel'. *Paz v. Paz*, (1981) 38(ii) *P.D.* 736, 742 (Elon, J.). Under the doctrine of good faith, 'the parties to a contract are not angels in respect of each other, but neither should they be wolves'. *Public Transport Service Beer Sheva v. National Labour Court* (1980) 35(I) *P.D.* 828, 834 (Barak, J.). It has even been suggested that as between 'good faith and writing—good faith prevails'. *Zonnenstein v. Gabasso*, (1983) 42(ii) *P.D.* 278, 289 (Barak, J.). For a useful discussion of these and other precedents, see generally Shalev, *Contract Law*, 212–13.

[79] See, e.g., Gabriela Shalev, 'Political Agreements', 26 *Israel L. Rev.* 442, 449–54 (1992) (arguing that political agreements can and should be treated as binding contracts); Itzhak Zamir, 'Political Contracts', ibid. 466–72 (1992) (arguing that political agreements can be legally binding, but that the law should presume the parties do not intend to be legally bound unless they clearly express such intent). But see David Kretzmer, 'Political Agreements—A Critical Introduction', ibid. 407, 414 (1992) (arguing that political agreements 'are neither contracts nor agreements that are binding according to alternative theories'); Nili Cohen, 'Political Agreements', ibid. 499, 524 (1992) ('I do not believe that obligatory legal force should be attributed to political agreements, either in contract law or in public law').

[80] The most prominent exponent of this view is Justice Barak. See *Zerzevsky v. The Prime Minister*, (1991) 34(I) *P.D.* 749, 858 (Barak, J.) ('Why does a judge have the ability to judge the reasonableness of a medical specialist, an expert pilot or an expert governmental authority, but not the ability to judge the reasonableness of a political party's conduct?'). Justice Elon has taken the opposite view. See ibid. 788 ('we have yet to hear of a legal criterion for a *reasonable* political party or a *reasonable* political commitment, and it [is] only proper that generally we should not hear of it').

[81] See 'Research in International Law Under the Auspices of the Faculty of the Harvard Law School, Part III', 29 *Supp. Am. J. Int'l L.* 981 (1935) ('The phrase "carry out in good faith" . . . is not intended to suggest that the obligation of a State to fulfill its treaty engagements is

to imply that parties should abide by the 'spirit' as well as the 'letter' of a treaty.[82]

There is less agreement, however, on whether good faith is to be judged by a purely subjective standard, or whether it contains an objective component. In other words, is it enough for a party to believe honestly (even if unreasonably) that the party is complying with its treaty obligations? Or is the standard one of 'reasonable good faith'—good faith in the eyes of a reasonable person? Unfortunately, the term 'good faith' is not defined in the Vienna Convention on the Law of Treaties or in other treaties using the term,[83] and commentators differ on whether international law defines it as a subjective or objective standard.[84]

Decisions of the International Court of Justice arguably provide support for both the objective and subjective definitions. In some cases, the Court seems to define good faith in terms of reasonableness, which is a relatively objective standard. In the *Fisheries Jurisdiction Cases*, for example, the Court held that the obligation to negotiate in good faith obliges the parties not just to conduct themselves honestly, but also to 'pay reasonable regard to each other's rights'.[85] In Judge Alfaro's separate declaration in the *Case Concerning the Temple of Preah Vihear*, he likewise propounded a fairly objective definition of good faith; in his view, 'inconsistency of conduct or opinion on the part of a State to the prejudice of another is incompatible with good faith'.[86] On the other hand, the Court

merely one of good faith rather than legal obligation'); Virally, 'Good Faith', 33. But cf. Elisabeth Zoller, *La Bonne Foi en Droit International Public* (Paris: A. Pedone, 1977) (suggesting that good faith is little more than an ethical principle).

[82] See 'Harvard Research', 981 (asserting that good faith requires treaties to be 'observed in their spirit as well as according to their letter').

[83] See, e.g., Treaty on the Non-Proliferation of Nuclear Weapons, 1 July 1968, 729 U.N.T.S. 161, 7 I.L.M. 811 (1968), Art. VI (obliging parties to 'pursue negotiations in good faith' on nuclear disarmament, but providing no definition of good faith); Convention on Contracts for the International Sale of Goods, 1980, Art. 7(1) (providing that interpretation of the Convention should be informed by 'good faith in international trade', but providing no definition of good faith). Apparently the Sales Convention was not intended to establish as broad a standard as that set forth in, say, U.C.C. §1-203, which provides a mixed objective and subjective definition of good faith. See Honnold, *Uniform Law*, 114–15, 123–4.

[84] Compare, e.g., Virally, 'Good Faith' (suggesting that good faith requires 'resort to more precise criteria' such as 'the concept of reasonableness') with Zoller, *La Bonne Foi*, xix, 202–5 (suggesting that good faith may be either a subjective or objective concept) and Antonio F. Perez, 'Survival of Rights Under the Nuclear Non-Proliferation Treaty: Withdrawal and the Continuing Right of International Atomic Energy Agency Safeguards', 34 *Va. J. Int'l L.* 749, 780 (1994) (arguing that theories on the meaning of good faith 'seem too indeterminate to be of much use in constructing objective criteria that could facilitate resolution of concrete cases').

[85] *Fisheries Jurisdiction* (FRG v. Iceland), 1974 I.C.J. at 202. Cf. also *Fisheries Jurisdiction* (UK v. Iceland), 1974 I.C.J. at 33 (holding that the parties 'must in good faith pay reasonable regard to the legal rights of the other'); *North Sea Continental Shelf Case*, 1969 I.C.J. 18, 60.

[86] *Case Concerning the Temple of Preah Vihear* (Camb. v. Thai.), 1962 I.C.J. at 39 (declaration of Judge Afaro).

has sometimes linked good faith with reasonableness, perhaps implying that the two concepts are not one and the same, and that good faith imports a more subjective test of 'honesty' while reasonableness applies to more objective, external measures of conduct. In *Admission of a State to the United Nations*, for example, the Court said parties should interpret Article 4 of the UN Charter 'reasonably and in good faith'.[87] The jurisprudence of other international tribunals resembles that of the International Court: it has established no single objective or subjective definition of good faith.[88]

In municipal law, too, good faith is sometimes defined in both objective *and* subjective terms. In the United States, for example, the Uniform Commercial Code defines 'good faith' in the case of a merchant as 'honesty in fact'—a subjective standard—*and* the 'observance of reasonable commercial standards of fair dealing in the trade'—an objective standard.[89] On the other hand, the same UCC also applies a purely subjective standard of good faith—'honesty in fact'—to non-merchants.[90] German law appears to attach somewhat more objective standards to 'good faith',[91] but then again good faith has been stretched to cover a broad variety of topics in German law, not just interpretation or performance of agreements.[92] Sometimes municipal laws define good faith in apparently subjective terms, but then consistently link this subjective concept with more objective terms.[93] Israeli contract law seems to follow this approach. It holds that parties should negotiate and perform contracts 'in customary manner *and* in good faith'.[94]

As is the case with international tribunals, no single definition of good

[87] *Admission of a State to the United Nations (Charter, Art. 4)*, Advisory Opinion, 1948 I.C.J. 57, 63. The Court has since used the same or similar formulations in other contexts. See, e.g., *Rights of Nationals of the United States of America in Morocco*, 1952 I.C.J. 176, 212 (describing the obligations of customs authorities in Morocco to act 'reasonably and in good faith').

[88] See generally O'Connor, *Good Faith*, 98–102 (describing arbitral practice); ibid. 99 (describing one arbitral tribunal's definition as 'one of objective good faith, judged by the minimum standards of the international community') (citing the Neer Claim, US v. Mexico, 4 U.N.R.I.A.A. 60 (1926)).

[89] U.C.C. §2-103(b). As to the definition of a 'merchant', see U.C.C. §2-104(1).

[90] See U.C.C. §1-201(19) (' "Good faith" means honesty in fact in the conduct or transaction concerned'). As to good faith in other areas of US law, such as labour and human rights law, see generally David A. Koplow, 'Parsing Good Faith: Has the United States Violated Article VI of the Nuclear Non-Proliferation Treaty?', 1993 *Wisc. L. Rev.* 301, 371–4.

[91] German law appears to link good faith to an objective standard: 'Obligations shall be performed *in the manner required* by good faith, *with regard to commercial usage.*' *BGB* Art. 242 (emphasis added).

[92] See generally Dawson, 'Unconscionable Coercion'.

[93] See, e.g., Arthur S. Hartkamp, 'Judicial Discretion Under the New Civil Code of the Netherlands', 40 *Am. J. Comp. L.* 554–5 and n. 6 (1992) (noting that Dutch law defines good faith subjectively as honest dealing, but that good faith is also invoked to invalidate rules that would be 'unacceptable according to criteria of reasonableness and equity').

[94] Section 39 of the Contracts (General Part) Law, 1973, 27 L.S.I. 117 (on performance); ibid., §12(a) (on negotiation).

faith emerges from the municipal law of states. It seems fair to conclude, however, that good faith is often associated with both an objective and a subjective meaning in municipal contract law. The objective component often refers to custom or commercial usage.[95] The subjective component typically seems to refer to honesty or sincerity,[96] though this component is often undefined.[97] If there is a 'general principle' of municipal law on good faith, it would appear to be that good faith is not usually applied in an exclusively subjective fashion. Good faith is either defined in partly objective terms, or it is defined in subjective terms but invariably linked to (and applied with) more objective terms. In this light, it seems inappropriate to conclude that public international law recognizes only a subjective component of good faith. More likely the drafters of the Vienna Convention on the Law of Treaties understood good faith in the same sense that municipal contract law does: as a term embracing both subjective notions of honesty and sincerity and objective notions of custom and reasonableness.[98]

Even assuming for the moment that international law recognizes only a subjective component of good faith, that definition of good faith would still hold Israel to honest and sincere interpretation and performance of its obligation to 'redeploy' to 'specified military locations'. Even this relatively weak subjective standard of good faith would constrain Israel's reading of the 'redeployment' obligation. It would be difficult for Israel to argue with sincerity that the term 'redeployment' contemplates only a reshuffling of Israeli troops in place rather than a withdrawal. One premise of the Oslo Accords was that some land would be transferred to Palestinian control on an interim basis, and the text of the Interim Agreement says explicitly that parts of Area C 'will be gradually transferred to Palestinian jurisdiction'.[99] On the other hand, under a subjective standard of good faith, Israel's reading of the term 'specified military locations' to mean 'Israeli-specified military locations' might pass muster, since the available evidence suggests this has always been Israel's sincere reading of the clause.[100]

[95] See, e.g., U.C.C. §2-103(b) (defining good faith for merchants in terms of 'reasonable commercial standards'); *BGB* §242 (referring to 'commercial usage'); Hartkamp, 'Judicial Discretion', 554–5 (noting that Dutch law links good faith with reasonable commercial standards); Section 39 of the Contracts (General Part) Law, 1973, 27 L.S.I. 117 (linking good faith in performance with the 'customary manner').

[96] See, e.g., U.C.C. §1-201(19) (' "Good faith" means honesty in fact in the conduct or transaction concerned').

[97] See, e.g., *Code Civil* [French Civil Code], Art. 1134 (requiring performance in good faith).

[98] See Zoller, *La Bonne Foi*, xix.

[99] Interim Agreement, Art. XI(3)(c).

[100] See, e.g., Singer, 'The West Bank and Gaza Strip', 10 (asserting that Israel successfully resisted Palestinian efforts to change the phrase to 'agreed' military locations, and therefore that Israel can unilaterally 'specify' the locations).

In any event, the better view seems to be that good faith embraces an objective component as well as a subjective one. From this standpoint, the question is not simply whether Israel sincerely believes its interpretation of the redeployment obligation, but whether that belief is reasonable or otherwise supported by custom or other objective evidence.

From this perspective, the Netanyahu government's interpretation of the 'redeployment' clause is open to question. (The Barak government's interpretation remains unclear.) Netanyahu's position seemed to be that Israel had unfettered discretion to determine the scope and shape of the final redeployment, leaving open the possibility that it might be a token movement of forces. The objective evidence, however, supports the conclusion that 'redeployment' reasonably means withdrawal, not just rearrangement, of Israeli military forces. Beyond that, an objective interpretation of the term 'specified' military locations is that both Israel and the Palestinians have a say in 'specifying' the locations to which Israeli forces withdraw. Similarly, an objective standard would imply that the final redeployment under the Wye River Memorandum should be more than just a token withdrawal from, say, 1 per cent of Area C.

On the other hand, the Palestinians also read too much into the 'further redeployment' clause when they suggest that the Oslo Accords require as much as 90 per cent of the West Bank to be returned to them before the start of final status negotiations. A reasonable construction of the Wye River Memorandum is that the final redeployment should not be radically different from the first two redeployments. If the final redeployment were roughly the same size as either of the first two, then the Palestinians would end up with jurisdiction over roughly half the West Bank at the start of final status negotiations. This result would give both parties some room to manoeuvre as permanent status talks begin in earnest.

In sum, both parties are right about some aspects of the debate over further redeployments. Israel is right that significant breaches by the Palestinians do justify Israel in suspending its own redeployment obligations, but Israel has not clearly abided by the restrictions on such suspension, including most notably the requirement that countermeasures be proportionate to the original breach. The Palestinians are right that the Accords contain an implied obligation of good faith, and that good faith requires that the final redeployment under the Wye River and Sharm el-Sheikh Memoranda be more than a token reshuffling of forces. But neither Wye nor the earlier Accords can be read to vindicate Palestinian hopes that as much as 90 per cent of the West Bank would be transferred to Palestinian control before the beginning of final status negotiations.

It can only be hoped that the parties will build on the progress they made at Wye, where for the first time they put concrete figures on the redeployment obligation. The Sharm el-Sheikh Memorandum, which revised the percentages set forth at Wye, certainly suggests that the parties have committed themselves to drafting more specific agreements in the mould of Wye. Such agreements are more difficult to reach in the short run, but they are more effective in the long run. The more precisely drafted the legal instrument, the less room for creative lawyering later.

The next Chapter considers whether Israeli settlement policy comports with the Oslo Accords.

7

Settlements

The Netanyahu government set off a firestorm of protest when it announced in early 1997 that it would construct housing for Jews in a neighbourhood in East Jerusalem called Har Homa (known to Palestinians as Jabal Abu-Ghuneim), as well as housing for Arabs in ten different Jerusalem neighbourhoods.[1] (See map 6, p. 50.) Palestinian leaders immediately denounced the construction plan as an effort to prejudge the final status negotiations on Jerusalem. Palestinian protesters took to the streets to protest the plan, and Arab states weighed in with angry condemnations of the Netanyahu government.[2] Fourteen members of the UN Security Council voted for a resolution condemning the Har Homa plan; only a US veto prevented adoption of the resolution. But even US President Bill Clinton took pains to explain that its veto did not constitute 'approval of the decision made by the Israeli Government'.[3] Indeed, the United States has repeatedly said that it wishes Israel had not decided to go ahead with the Har Homa project.[4]

The settlement dispute worsened after the Wye River Memorandum. Ariel Sharon urged Israelis to establish hilltop encampments in the West Bank before implementation of the Memorandum, and indeed about forty such encampments were established, many without formal permits from Israel. In the autumn of 1999 the Barak government announced a plan to remove only about a dozen of these settlements, angering Palestinians and settlers alike.[5] In general, the Barak government remains committed to improving existing settlements and, to some extent, constructing new ones. It has, for now, put a stop to plans for Jewish housing at Ras El Amud, in East Jerusalem, but it apparently intends to proceed with the Har Homa project.[6]

[1] Ministerial Committee on Jerusalem Affairs Communiqué, 26 Feb. 1997, available at http://www.israel-mfa.gov.il/new/hhoma.html.

[2] See, e.g., Serge Schmemann, 'King Hussein Rebukes Netanyahu for "Intent to Destroy" Peace Plan', *N.Y. Times*, 12 Mar. 1997.

[3] See James Bennet, 'Mideast Veto Was Justified, Clinton Says', ibid. 11 Mar. 1997.

[4] See, e.g., 'Clinton to Send Envoy to Middle East', ibid. 26 Mar. 1997: '[S]enior American officials are also upset about Mr. Netanyahu's actions, suggesting the Israeli leader has not thought through the consequences of his decision—against clear American advice, public and private—not to break ground for the new housing in East Jerusalem.'

[5] See Nina Gilbert, 'Coalition unites against no-confidence over encampments', *Jerus. Post*, 19 Oct. 1999; Ben Lynfield, Lamia Lahoud, and Margot Dudkevitch, 'PA denounces Barak's deal with settlers: Safe passage opening delayed', ibid. 17 Oct. 1999.

[6] See Jacob Lefkowits Dallal, 'Olmert–Ramon Meet', ibid. 23 July 1999.

The Palestinians have traditionally cast many of their arguments against Israeli settlements in legal terms. Until the Oslo Accords, these arguments rested primarily on the international law of belligerent occupation. Since 1993, however, Arafat and his aides have occasionally charged that expansion of existing settlements violate the Oslo Accords, not just general international law.[7]

The Palestinian legal position on Har Homa is particularly unclear, possibly because the Har Homa issue threatens to compromise the Palestinian position on Jerusalem. Palestinians (and many states and the UN) have traditionally taken the view that Israel's expansion of Jerusalem's boundaries in 1967 was invalid.[8] It might undermine this view for the Palestinians to acknowledge that Har Homa is in Jerusalem rather than the West Bank.

Thus the question of settlements continues to haunt the peace process. Accordingly, this chapter asks whether Israeli settlement policy is consistent with the Oslo Accords and general international law. The first section asks whether the text of the Oslo Accords outlaws new or existing settlements. This section concludes that the Accords do not outlaw existing settlements but do limit new settlements in the West Bank and the Gaza Strip and perhaps impose some good-faith restriction on new settlements in East Jerusalem. The second section of the chapter asks whether the settlements are inconsistent with any other source of law. This section concludes that the law of belligerent occupation is applicable to territories occupied by Israel in 1967, and that aspects of Israeli settlement policy are inconsistent with occupation law.

The text of the Oslo Accords

The Palestinian leadership has denounced the Har Homa project as 'illegal'. Chairman Arafat has said that 'the agreement between me and Mr. Rabin and, after that, Mr. Peres . . . [provides that] not one single house [may] be added in any settlement'.[9] The vetoed Security Council resolution also condemned the Har Homa plan as a violation of international law.

These accusations generally do not, however, cite a particular provision of the Oslo Accords. As Israel has pointed out, even the PLO has sometimes refrained from calling the Har Homa plan a violation of the

[7] See, e.g., Steven Erlanger, 'Christopher Is Sending Envoy to Spur the Mideast Peace Effort', *N.Y. Times*, 20 Dec. 1996.

[8] See, e.g., GA Res. 2254 (ES-V), 14 July 1967; SC Res. 252, 21 May 1968.

[9] Remarks of Yasser Arafat, Press Conference, National Press Club, Washington, DC, 4 Mar. 1997.

Accords.[10] The PLO's letters to the President of the Security Council charge that the Har Homa plan constitutes a 'threat to the integrity' of the agreements, but not a violation of the agreements.[11]

Israel, on the other hand, argues that the Oslo Accords do not prohibit the construction of new Jewish housing in East Jerusalem.[12] Israel points to the text of the agreements. According to Israel, the Oslo Accords and the related agreements 'contain no commitment to refrain from the construction of settlements, neighbourhoods, houses, roads, or any other such building project'.[13] Indeed, Israel argues that the agreements permit construction 'in those areas under [the parties'] respective jurisdictions . . .'. In addition, Israel has emphasized the negotiating history of the Interim Agreement. According to Israel, 'the Palestinian side sought to include in this agreement restrictions on the building of settlements. This issue was discussed but was not agreed upon, and no ban on building—either in the territories or in Jerusalem—is contained anywhere in the agreement.'[14]

It is true that the Oslo Accords do not outlaw existing settlements. Had the parties intended for Israel to dismantle existing settlements, they would have said so explicitly, as was done in the Camp David Accords. The Declaration of Principles and the later Oslo Accords repeatedly intone that settlements will be discussed in permanent status negotiations.[15] Plainly the Palestinians were expected to live with existing settlements during the interim period leading to final status talks. (For a map of settlements in the West Bank, see Map 5, p. 35.)

Some Arab writers also seem persuaded that the Accords permit *new* settlements as well. Arab critics of the Oslo Accords have lamented their

[10] See 'Har Homa—Legal Aspects', ¶9, 3 Mar. 1997, available at http://www.israel-mfa.gov.il/news/hhomaleg/html (noting that the PLO's letters complain only of a 'threat to the integrity of the agreements', not a violation, 'because there has in fact been no violation'). Similarly, a Palestinian press release accused Israel of violating the Accords by refusing to withdraw from a sufficiently large portion of the West Bank, but the same document avoided accusations of illegality when criticizing the Har Homa plan. See Press Statement, Palestinian Authority Ministry of Information, 10 Mar. 1997.

[11] See letter from the Palestine Liberation Organization to the President of the Security Council, UN Doc. S/1997/149, 21 Feb. 1997; letter from the Palestine Liberation Organization to the President of the Security Council, UN Doc S/1997/165, 27 Feb. 1997.

[12] See, e.g., Statement by the Spokesman of the Ministry of Foreign Affairs, 27 Feb. 1997, available at http://www.israel-mfa.gov.il/news/hhomamfa.html ('The decision to commence the construction of the Har Homa neighborhood in Jerusalem does not in any way contradict the various agreements which have been signed between Israel and the Palestinians. A careful reading of the agreements bears this out'). The Barak government has apparently adopted the legal reasoning of its predecessor. Among other things, the Barak Ministry of Foreign Affairs has continued to maintain Web pages arguing that the Oslo Accords do not outlaw new or existing settlements.

[13] 'Har Homa—Legal Aspects', ¶1.

[14] Ibid., ¶¶2–3.

[15] Declaration of Principles, Art. V(3).

failure to outlaw settlements, whether in East Jerusalem or the West Bank.[16] The better view, however, is that the Accords *do* prohibit significant new settlements, at least in the West Bank and Gaza Strip.

Article XXXI(7) of the Interim Agreement provides: 'Neither side shall initiate or take any step that will change the status of the West Bank and the Gaza Strip pending the outcome of the permanent status negotiations.' Surely this provision outlaws any significant new settlement construction in the West Bank and Gaza Strip, since the expansion of Jewish housing there tends to change the 'status' of the area by making it more likely to remain in Israeli hands. Much of the *point* of settlements is to increase the likelihood that the settled area will enjoy the 'status' of Israeli territory. Only an exceedingly formalistic reading of the word 'status' would permit Israel to construct vast new settlements under the pretence that they were prompting no change in 'status' of the territories. Not every enhancement of existing settlements changes the 'status' of the territories, but expansion of existing settlements on to new land does tend to change the 'status' of that land.

Israel points out that this 'status' provision covers only the West Bank and Gaza Strip, implying that Israel has greater latitude in East Jerusalem. It is indeed striking that the drafters of this provision omitted Jerusalem. Israel may be right, then, that it has a more explicit duty to refrain from altering the 'status' of the West Bank and Gaza Strip than of East Jerusalem. But even in East Jerusalem, the Accords place an implicit duty on Israel to avoid steps that prejudge the 'permanent status' of the city. After all, the Accords call for 'permanent status' talks on Jerusalem, and for Israel to engage in such talks in good faith, it can hardly take steps designed to alter the 'permanent status' in advance.

None the less, the Netanyahu government took a narrow view of its implicit duty to avoid prejudging the final status talks on Jerusalem. It argued that the 'permanent status' provisions merely meant that 'life in Jerusalem . . . continues, with the status of the city remaining unchanged so long as no decision to the contrary is taken in the permanent status negotiations'. On this view, construction within Jerusalem 'does not constitute a change in the status of Jerusalem, [nor] does it create a situation which can adversely affect or influence the permanent status negotiations'.[17] This again seems like an excessively formalistic reading of the

[16] See, e.g., Raja Shehadeh, *From Occupation to Interim Accords: Israel and the Palestinian Territories* (The Hague: Kluwer Law International, 1997), 27 (asserting that the Declaration of Principles 'did not limit Israel's ability to expand the settlements and create more facts on the ground'); ibid. 167 (asserting that the Accords 'retained the possibility during the interim period to continue to create facts'); Raja Shihadeh, 'Can the Declaration of Principles Bring About a "Just and Lasting Peace?" ', 4 *Eur. J. Int'l L.* 555, 556 (1993) (asserting that settlements have been left '[u]ntouched' by the Declaration of Principles).

[17] 'Har Homa—Legal Aspects', ¶¶4–5.

term 'status'. By this logic, the Oslo Accords also permit Israel to construct housing earmarked exclusively for hundreds of thousands of Jewish immigrants in East Jerusalem. Construction surely can prejudge the 'status' of Jerusalem, just as new settlements can prejudge the 'status' of the West Bank and Gaza Strip. On the other hand, not every construction project has implications for territorial sovereignty over Jerusalem; the Har Homa project itself also includes housing for Arabs. The guiding principle, as is true of all international agreements, is one of good faith. Israel can pursue construction whose good-faith purpose and effect is not to prejudge the final status of East Jerusalem.

There are other, structural, arguments that the Oslo Accords limit settlement activity. The redeployment process, for example, implies that Israel will stop building new settlements in the West Bank. The purpose of those provisions is to shrink, not expand, the Israeli presence in the West Bank. Likewise, the Interim Agreement makes reference to existing settlements; to add new settlements, or expand existing ones, is to alter the factual foundations of the parties' agreement. If nothing else, the structure of the Accords certainly forbids Israeli settlements in the Palestinian self-governing areas—i.e. in Areas A and B.

In sum, the Oslo Accords do not outlaw existing settlements, but they do impose some restrictions on new settlements, especially in the West Bank and Gaza Strip. In particular, the Accords restrict Israel from taking steps that would alter the 'status' of the West Bank and Gaza Strip, and they impliedly forbid Israel from taking steps that would effectively moot the 'final status' issue of Jerusalem.

The next section considers whether general international law, apart from the Oslo Accords, imposes restrictions on Israeli settlements. This entails analysis of the law of belligerent occupation. A full treatment of occupation law would take up half this book, but some attention to the question is indispensable.

The law of belligerent occupation

The first question about occupation law is whether it applies to either East Jerusalem or to the West Bank and Gaza Strip. Much of that law is embodied in two multilateral conventions on occupation in time of war: the 1907 Hague Convention IV on Land Warfare[18] and the Fourth Geneva Convention on the Protection of Civilian Persons in Time of War.[19] Israel

[18] Convention Respecting the Laws and Customs of War on Land, with Annex of Regulations, 18 Oct. 1907, TS 539.

[19] Convention (No. IV) Relative to the Protection of Civilian Persons in Time of War, 12 Aug. 1949, 75 U.N.T.S. 287.

is party to the Fourth Geneva Convention, and it regards the Hague Convention as an authoritative codification of customary international law. As we shall see, it is the Fourth Geneva Convention that contains the most specific restrictions on settlements. Israeli courts do apply the Hague Regulations *de jure* to the West Bank and the Gaza Strip,[20] but Israel and its courts do not consider the Fourth Geneva Convention applicable there—though Israel says it applies the humanitarian provisions of the Geneva Convention to those territories on a *de facto* basis anyway. Israel takes the view that occupation law is generally inapplicable to East Jerusalem.

Israel has been roundly condemned for its view that the Fourth Geneva Convention does not apply to the territories occupied in 1967, but Israel's arguments on this score are hardly frivolous. The debate begins with the text of Article 2 of the Convention, which sets forth the scope of applicability of the Convention. The relevant portions of Article 2 are paragraphs 1 and 2, which provide:

> In addition to the provisions which shall be implemented in peacetime, the present Convention shall apply to all cases of declared war or of any other armed conflict which may arise between two or more of the High Contracting Parties even if the state of war is not recognized by one of them.
>
> The Convention shall also apply to all cases of partial or total occupation of the territory of a High Contracting Party, even if the said occupation meets with no armed resistance.

Israel stresses the second paragraph, which is limited to 'cases of partial or total occupation of *the territory of a High Contracting Party*'.[21] The traditional view of Israeli governments is that the reference to the 'territory' of a party implies that the Convention applies only when there is a 'legitimate ousted sovereign', and Jordan's claim to sovereignty over the West Bank was illegitimate, having been recognized by only two states and having since been abandoned by Jordan itself.[22]

[20] See *Jama'iat Iscan v. Commander of the IDF in Judea and Samaria*, 37 (4) PD 785, 792 (1983) ('Judea and Samaria are administered by Israel by way of "belligerent occupation" '); Esther R. Cohen, *Human Rights in the Israeli-Occupied Territories 1967–1982* (Manchester: Manchester University Press 1985), 51; Eyal Benvenisti, *The International Law of Occupation* (Princeton, NJ: Princeton University Press 1993), 111.

[21] Fourth Geneva Convention, Art. 2(2) (emphasis added).

[22] See Yehuda Blum, 'The Missing Reversioner: Reflections on the Status of Judea and Samaria', 3 *Is.L. Rev.* 279 (1968); Meir Shamgar, 'The Observance of International Law in the Administered Territories', 1 *Isr. Yb. Hum. Rts.* 262, 263 (1971); Nathan Lorch, 'The applicability of the Fourth Geneva Convention to the territories administered by Israel', 1 *Isr. Yb. Hum. Rts.* 366, 366 (1971) ('The Fourth Geneva Convention uses a very important term of art, namely, "territory of a High Contracting Party"—in other words, territory which presumably, until the outbreak of conflict, was under the sovereignty of one of the High Contracting

This interpretation of the second paragraph of Article 2 does have a plausible textual basis, but a number of commentators take issue with it,[23] and indeed textual and structural arguments can be arrayed against it. To begin with, Article 2 does not speak of 'territory to which a state party has a lawful claim'; it merely speaks of 'territory' of a state party. The absence of any reference to 'clear title' is not surprising; many states possess territory that is claimed by other states. Article 4 of the Convention also raises questions about the Israeli view. It provides: 'Persons protected by the Convention are those who, at a given moment and in any manner whatsoever, find themselves, in case of a conflict or occupation, in the hands of a Party to the conflict or Occupying Power of which they are not nationals.' This provision supports the view of those commentators who argue that the Convention is 'people-oriented', not 'territory-oriented'.[24] Israel's argument also seems inconsistent with the structure and purpose of the Convention. By Israel's logic, a party to the Convention could invade and occupy a state that is not party to the Convention, or a populated area that is *terra nullius*, and conduct the occupation without regard to the Fourth Geneva Convention, since (on Israel's reading) the Convention applies only to occupation of another party's territory. All these arguments—textual and structural—raise real doubts about Israel's 'missing reversioner' theory.

Another objection to the 'missing reversioner' interpretation of paragraph two of Article 2 is that it overlooks paragraph *one* of Article 2, which applies to '*all* cases of . . . armed conflict which may arise between two or more of the High Contracting Parties', without regard to any 'missing reversioner'.[25] In response, Israel has suggested that the first paragraph applies only during the conduct of the 'armed conflict'. This reading draws some support from Article 6(2) of the Convention, which provides that the Convention's applicability 'shall cease on the general close of military operations'. Israel's interpretation would mean that the

Parties'). See also Rubinstein, 'The Changing Status of the "Territories" (West Bank and Gaza): From Escrow to Legal Mongrel', 8 *Tel-Aviv U. Studies in Law* 59 (1988).

As to Jordan's renunciation of its claim to the West Bank, see *N.Y. Times*, 1 Aug. 1988; 28 I.L.M. 1637 (1988).

[23] See, e.g., Yoram Dinstein, 'The International Law of Belligerent Occupation and Human Rights', 8 *Isr. Yb. Hum. Rts.* 104, 107 (1978); Cohen, *Human Rights*, 52–6.

[24] Cohen, *Human Rights*, 53, citing S. M. Boyd, Symposium, 'The applicability of international law to the occupied territories', 1 *Isr. Yb. Hum. Rts.* 367–8 (1971).

As Cohen points out, Pictet's authoritative commentary on Article 2 also raises questions about Israel's reading of paragraph 2. Ibid. 52–3. Among other things, Pictet says that paragraph 2 'does not refer to cases in which territory is occupied during hostilities; in such cases the Convention will have been in force since the outbreak of hostilities' in accordance with paragraph 1. Jean S. Pictet (ed.), *The Geneva Conventions of 12 August 1949* (Geneva: International Committee of the Red Cross, 1958), 4 volumes, translated from the French, quoted in ibid. 52.

[25] Fourth Geneva Convention, Art. 2(1) (emphasis added). See Benvenisti, *The International Law of Occupation*, 109–10.

Fourth Geneva Convention did apply during the six days of the 1967 War but suddenly ceased to apply after the guns fell silent. This reading is inconsistent with the humanitarian purpose of the Convention, and it is arguably inconsistent with Pictet's authoritative commentary on Article 2, which states: 'In case of war being declared or of armed conflict, the Convention enters into force; the fact that the territory of one or other of the belligerents is later occupied in the course of hostilities does not in any way affect this; the inhabitants of the occupied territory simply become protected persons as they fall into the hands of the Occupying Power.'[26] If the West Bank and Gaza Strip are occupied territory, as seems likely, then most of the relevant provisions on occupation (including the crucial provision on settlements) are still applicable, since Article 6 of the Convention provides that these provisions continue to apply 'for the duration of the occupation'.[27]

To its credit, Israel has voluntarily chosen to apply *de facto* the humanitarian provisions of the Convention to the West Bank and Gaza Strip, regardless of whether the Convention applies *de jure*. This makes Israel the only state ever to apply the Convention's provisions on even a voluntary basis.[28] It is conceivable that this policy could expose Israel to international responsibility for violation of the Convention, perhaps on an estoppel theory, or on the theory that Israel's unilateral commitment is a binding promise made in good faith, like that in the *Nuclear Tests Cases*.[29] It seems doubtful, though, that any other state is entitled to 'rely' on an undertaking that was not made with intention to become legally bound.[30] Nor is it likely that Israel's voluntary compliance can itself evolve into any form of customary law, since *opinio juris* is lacking.

It appears, then, that the Fourth Geneva Convention probably does apply *de jure* to the territories occupied in 1967. Is there any reason to exclude East Jerusalem from the ambit of the Convention? Israel may well have a stronger

26 Pictet, *The Geneva Conventions*, 4:21–2. See also ibid. 22 (indicating that paragraph 2 of Article 2 was not intended to diminish the scope of paragraph 1, but rather 'was intended to fill the gaps left by paragraph 1'). For further review of Pictet's explanation of Article 2, see Cohen, *Human Rights*, 52–3.

27 This is the conclusion of the International Committee on the Red Cross (ICRC), the body charged with implementing the Convention as a Protecting Power. See, e.g., 'Report of the ICRC', No. 113, 429–30 (Aug. 1970). This is also the traditional Palestinian view. See, e.g., R. Kosirnik, 'Étude sur les problèmes de fond: Applicabilité de la IVème Convention' (Tel Aviv: ICRC internal document, 9 Feb. 1977), cited in Cohen, *Human Rights*, 59 n. 56.

28 See Benvenisti, *The International Law of Occupation*, 149 ('With the exception of the Israeli occupation after the 1967 war, all other occupants after World War II refrained from resorting to the Hague Conventions or the Fourth Geneva Conventions as the source of their authority or as a guide to their actions').

29 *Nuclear Tests* (Aus. v. Fr.; NZ v. Fr.), 1974 I.C.J. 253.

30 Cf. ibid., ¶43 ('When it is the intention of the State making the declaration that it should become bound according to its terms, that intention confers on the declaration the character of a legal undertaking . . .').

claim of territorial sovereignty to East Jerusalem than it does to the West Bank or Gaza Strip. That is an interesting and difficult question—one discussed in more detail in Chapter 14, on 'final status' issues like Jerusalem. As we have seen, however, the applicability of occupation law does not necessarily depend on the strength of the occupier's claim to the occupied territory. Even if Israel has the best claim to East Jerusalem, it is still likely that occupation law applies on an interim basis there, until the parties reach a final settlement regularizing the question of territorial sovereignty.

Thus the Fourth Geneva Convention does appear applicable *de jure* as well as *de facto* to the territories occupied by Israel in 1967. That conclusion leads to the central substantive question: whether the Convention prohibits new or existing Israeli settlements in any of those territories.

Article 49(6) of the Fourth Geneva Convention provides: 'The Occupying Power shall not deport or transfer parts of its own civilian population into the territory it occupies.' Israel's settlement policy does not seem consistent with this obligation. Israel has had a deliberate policy of 'creating facts' in the territories by encouraging, facilitating, and subsidizing settlement there.[31] Israel has argued that 'drop-by-drop' voluntary migration by individual settlers is not what is contemplated by Article 49, which was drafted in response to the Nazis' policy of forced relocation of civilian populations.[32] This argument has two components: first, that Article 49(6) deals only with *involuntary* transfer of civilian population, not voluntary migration; and second, that Article 49(6) contains a state action component that is not present in the case of voluntary Israeli settlements.

Eyal Benvenisti criticizes the first of these arguments on the grounds that Article 49(6) is designed to 'protect the interests of the occupied population, rather than the population of the occupant'.[33] Benvenisti's point is well-taken. Article 49(6) on its face prohibits any transfer of civilian population, whether voluntary or involuntary.[34] Indeed, the voluntary transfer of enthusiastic settlers might well be *more* threatening to the inhabitants of the occupied territory than the involuntary transfer of recalcitrant deportees. In a similar vein, Israel also contends that settlements are consistent with Article 49(6) because they do not 'displace' Palestinian inhabitants. Article 49(6), however, does not mention displacement of inhabitants; it prohibits transfer of civilian population into the occupied territory, whether or not the particular point of transfer is inhabited.[35]

[31] See, e.g., Benvenisti, *The International Law of Occupation*, 140.

[32] Ibid.

[33] Ibid.

[34] See Herbert J. Hansell, letter of 21 Apr. 1978, Dept. of State File No. P78 0065–0030, in 72 *Am. J. Int'l L.* 908, 910 (1978), 17 I.L.M. 777 (1978).

[35] See ibid. ('Displacement of protected persons is dealt with separately in the Convention and paragraph 6 would be redundant if limited to cases of displacement'); ibid. ('[T]he paragraph appears applicable whether or not harm is done by a particular transfer').

Israel's second main argument, on state action, has more force; there is unquestionably a 'private action' component to settlements. In Yoram Dinstein's famous phrase, 'There is nothing wrong with Jewish settlement undirected from above, drop by drop, on land purchased on the open market from local inhabitants on the West Bank.'[36] Indeed, a flat prohibition on voluntary, individual relocation to the West Bank would raise novel questions of human rights law, which protects the right to 'leave' one's own country and the right to own property—but not necessarily the right to 'enter' a foreign state or territory.[37] Still, the settlements are the result of substantial state action—namely, in the form of Israel's policy of facilitating, subsidizing, and encouraging settlements and their underlying infrastructure.[38] This level of state action is more than mere failure to prevent private migration to occupied territory, an omission that might not be cognizable under Article 49(6); Israel's affirmative policy of promoting settlement in occupied territory is probably enough to trigger the protections of Article 49(6). To that extent, Israeli settlement policy does appear inconsistent with the Fourth Geneva Convention.

In sum, Israel's arguments against the applicability of the Fourth Geneva Convention are hardly frivolous, as has sometimes been suggested, but the better view is that the Convention is applicable to all the territories occupied in 1967. Israel is right that some voluntary, purely private settlement in the West Bank might be permissible under Article 49 of the Convention. But state-sponsored and -subsidized settlement does begin to look like an impermissible 'transfer' of civilians to occupied territory, a violation of Article 49.

The Oslo Accords themselves place additional constraints on settlement in the West Bank and Gaza Strip. The Interim Agreement forbids either party to take any step that might 'alter' the 'status' of those areas.[39] At the very least, this provision would seem to bar the construction of any

[36] Yoram Dinstein, 'Settlements and deportations in the occupied territories', 7 *Tel Aviv Univ. L. Rev.* 188, 189 (1979) (Hebrew), quoted in Cohen, *Human Rights*, 162. See also Allan Gerson, *Israel, the West Bank and International Law* (London; Totowa, NJ: Frank Cass, 1978), 173–4 ('Israel's land acquisition and settlement policy was not unlawful as it neither aimed for, nor neared, a state involving displacement of the existing population as a prelude to future annexation').

[37] See International Covenant on Civil and Political Rights, 16 Dec. 1966, 999 U.N.T.S. 171, Art. 12(2) (right to leave); Universal Declaration of Human Rights, 10 Dec. 1948, G.A. Res. 217 (III 1948), Art. 17(1) (right to own property); ibid., Art. 17(2) (right not to be 'arbitrarily deprived' of property).

[38] See, e.g., Hansell, letter, 910; UN General Assembly, Special Committee to Investigate Israeli Practices Affecting the Human Rights of the Population of the Occupied Territories, A/8389 (1971), at 27–41. See also Dinstein, 'Settlements', 189.

[39] Interim Agreement, Art. XXXI(7).

new settlements in the territories, and it would also raise questions about significant enlargement of existing settlements.

Chapter 14 returns to the question of settlements in the context of the 'final status' issues. For now, we turn to another major set of Israeli obligations under the Oslo Accords, those relating to commerce, infrastructure, and economics.

8

Passages, Ports, and Economic Issues

The 1995 Interim Agreement obliged Israel to permit 'safe passage' between the West Bank and the Gaza Strip under certain conditions, to allow the Palestinians to open and operate airports and seaports in Gaza, to cooperate with the PA on certain economic issues, and to participate in 'people-to-people' contacts with the Palestinians. In the Note for the Record accompanying the 1997 Hebron Protocol, Israel reaffirmed its commitment to negotiate over these questions of passages and economics. The Wye River and Sharm el-Sheikh Memoranda reaffirmed these undertakings, but only in general terms.

Thus the Interim Agreement, as summarized in the Note for the Record, continues to govern issues relating to ports, passages, and economics. Although these issues necessarily require the cooperation of both parties, the Note for the Record listed them under the broad heading of 'Israeli responsibilities'. The Note enumerated six such issues: (1) 'Safe Passage', (2) the Gaza Airport, (3) the Gaza Port, (4) 'Passages', (5) 'Economic, financial, civilian and security issues', and (6) 'People-to-People'.

It is fair to ask whether these undertakings should be considered in this Part of the book (on Israeli obligations) rather than in Part IV (on Palestinian obligations) or in a separate Part on joint obligations. Most of these issues involve joint obligations—most commonly, joint obligations to negotiate. None the less, the book follows the parties' division of responsibilities set forth in the Note for the Record. The parties appear to have concluded that most of these joint obligations really require more concessions by Israel than the Palestinians. Accordingly, this Chapter takes up each of the six issues in turn.

Safe passage

Many Palestinians regard a 'safe passage' between the West Bank and Gaza Strip as a matter of enormous importance. In their view, the free flow of goods and people is essential to the improvement of the Palestinian economy and, more generally, to the realization of Palestinian self-determination. Without free interchange between the Gaza Strip and West Bank, some Palestinians fear that the Gaza Strip might be marginalized from the dominant West Bank in much the same way that East

Pakistan (now Bangladesh) was marginalized from Pakistan.[1] Israel has recognized this concern by agreeing to permit Palestinian passage between the West Bank and Gaza, provided that this passage does not jeopardize Israeli security.

The first Oslo Accord, the 1993 Declaration of Principles, called on the parties to negotiate arrangements for safe passage for Palestinians who wished to travel between the Jericho Area and the Gaza Strip.[2] In accordance with this general mandate, Annexe I to the 1994 Gaza–Jericho Agreement contained detailed provisions on safe passage. Among other things, these provisions obliged Israel to ensure safe passage during daylight hours; designated appropriate routes for safe passage; required persons using safe passage to carry a safe-passage card or a permit for entering Israel; provided that persons denied entry to Israel 'may' be permitted safe passage in accordance with special arrangements made through the parties' joint committee on security; authorized special arrangements for passage of Palestinian leaders and 'distinguished personalities'; provided that people making safe passage would travel non-stop and that they would not carry firearms; and allowed Israel 'for security or safety reasons' to 'temporarily modify' these arrangements, provided that at least one route for safe passage remains open.[3]

When the Palestinian autonomous area expanded beyond Jericho to the other cities of the West Bank, revised arrangements for safe passage were necessary. Annexe I to the 1995 Interim Agreement, which superseded the Gaza–Jericho Agreement,[4] set forth the new arrangements. They carried forward the basic structure of the safe passage regime of the Gaza–Jericho Agreement, but they also added new crossing points and routes, authorized Israel to deny safe passage to anyone who has 'seriously or repeatedly' violated the safe-passage rules, provided that persons denied entry into Israel would be escorted across Israel in shuttle buses escorted by Israeli police, and clarified that Israel's right to 'modify' the safe-passage regime for security reasons included a right to interrupt a safe-passage route temporarily so long as at least one route remained open.[5] Finally, a new provision cautioned that these arrangements would

[1] Sharif S. Elmusa and Mahmud El-Jaafari, 'Power and Trade: The Israeli–Palestinian Economic Protocol', in Eugene Cotran *et al.* (eds.), *The Arab–Israeli Accords: Legal Perspectives* (London: Kluwer Law International, 1996), 173, 184.

[2] Declaration of Principles, Annexe II, ¶3(g).

[3] Gaza–Jericho Agreement, Annexe I, Art. IX(1)(b) (daylight hours); ibid., Art. IX(1)(c)–(d) (designating crossing points and routes); ibid., Art. IX(2)(a)–(c) (describing documents for safe passage); ibid., Art. IX(2)(d) (on those who are denied entry into Israel); ibid., Art. IX(2)(e) (Palestinian leaders); ibid., Art. IX(3) (prohibiting firearms and requiring non-stop travel); ibid., Art. IX(4)(c) (temporary modifications for security reasons).

[4] Interim Agreement, Art. XXXI(2).

[5] Interim Agreement, Annexe I, Art. X(1)(c)–(d) (new crossing points and routes); ibid.,

not prejudice final status talks.[6] This last addition probably reflected concern that the new crossing points might establish the *de facto* borders of a new Palestinian state.[7] This provision (and others) help ensure that safe passage will never lead to a Palestinian claim to territorial sovereignty by prescription.

The parties haggled over implementation of these provisions for four years. The major sticking point was the extent of Israeli control over Palestinians making the passage. Palestinian civilians wanted more freedom to visit other parts of PA-controlled territory, and Palestinian security forces said that more freedom of movement would help them fight crime and terrorism. Israel was concerned that free movement of Palestinians through Israeli territory posed a security threat.[8] At one point, the Netanyahu government even proposed that safe passage be confined to air travel[9]—a proposal that Germany's Gerhard Schroeder 'laughed . . . off' as an 'interesting arabesque',[10] and one that is inconsistent with the Interim Agreement, which plainly envisioned a land crossing.[11] Shortly after taking office, Prime Minister Barak proposed erecting an elevated bridge to connect the Gaza Strip to the West Bank, but the PA replied that while such a bridge might be an appropriate topic for final status talks, the Interim Agreement called for a more immediate solution.[12]

At last, on 5 October 1999, the parties concluded a written Protocol Concerning Safe Passage.[13] Israel agreed to permit Palestinians to travel by an agreed 28-mile route between the Erez crossing at the Gaza Strip and the southern West Bank town of Tarkumiya. Under the agreement, Palestinians are expected to make the trip in less than ninety minutes; if they take longer, or if they switch vehicles en route, they will be questioned on arrival.[14]

Art. X(2)(d) (on serious or repeated violations of safe-passage rules); ibid., Art. X(2)(e) (shuttle buses); ibid., Art. X(4)(c) (temporary halts).

The Interim Agreement, like the Gaza–Jericho Agreement, also provides that safe passage will not be available on Yom Kippur, Israel's Memorial Day and Israel's Independence Day. Ibid., Art. X(4)(b).

6 Ibid., Art. X(1)(e).

7 Cf. Jay Bushinsky and Margot Dudkevitch, Hillel Kuttler and Mohammed Najib, ' "Safe passage" talks stall', *Jerus. Post*, 4 Mar. 1998 ('To pinpoint [the location of the northernmost checkpoint] now would be tantamount to demarcating the border between Israel and the PA, something Israel prefers to postpone until negotiations on a final agreement').

8 See James Howard Gibbons, 'Best model for Mideast peace? An amicable divorce', *Houston Chronicle*, 13 Mar. 1998.

9 Julian Borger, 'Israel floats "flyover" road for Palestinians', *Guardian* (London), 26 Mar. 1998.

10 Jay Bushinsky, 'Schroeder dismisses "overland" safe passage', *Jerus. Post*, 26 Mar. 1998.

11 Cf. Interim Agreement, Annexe I, Art. X(1)(d) and attached map No. 6.

12 Ben Lynfield, 'PA cool to Barak's bridge idea', *Jerus. Post*, 20 June 1999.

13 Protocol Concerning Safe Passage between the West Bank and the Gaza Strip, 5 Oct. 1999, available at www.-israel-mfa.gov.il.

14 Margot Dudkevitch and Lamia Lahoud, 'Safe-passage link opens today', *Jerus. Post*, 25 Oct. 1999.

Israel will issue and check safe-passage permits, and it will retain the right to interrupt some passages for security reasons and to prohibit the carrying of firearms. It is expected that most traffic will flow from Gaza to the West Bank rather than the other direction, since there are more employment opportunities in the West Bank than in the Gaza Strip. On 25 October 1999 the parties inaugurated the new arrangement, and busloads of Palestinians made the passage without incident.[15]

None the less, the parties' agreement on safe passage has deferred at least two issues. The first is whether Israel may deny passage to some Palestinians altogether.[16] Israel has posted what Palestinians call a 'blacklist' of people to whom Israel will not issue the magnetized cards authorizing safe passage.[17] Israel's position is that these Palestinians are security risks who are not permitted to enter Israel and, indeed, should be arrested by the Palestinians. Israel stresses that Annex I to the Interim Agreement provides that those in transit are 'subject to Israeli law' and that Israel has the right to deny passage to those who have 'violated the safe passage provisions' in the past.[18] Palestinians point out that Annex I also provides: 'Persons who are denied entry into Israel will use safe passage by means of shuttle buses which will be escorted by the Israel Police' and will operate twice a week.[19] Israel has indicated that it plans to operate such buses twice a week, but it insists that it is not required to grant this form of passage to every applicant.

If the only governing law were the Interim Agreement, the Palestinian position would seem more persuasive. The Interim Agreement provides categorically: 'Israel will ensure safe passage for persons and transportation during daylight hours . . .'[20] The shuttle-bus provision also appears to be mandatory: persons denied entry 'will' use buses for safe passage, and buses 'will' operate twice a week. The only provision entitling Israel to deny safe passage is limited to those who have 'violated the safe passage provisions'—not those who have violated other provisions of Israeli law. True, the Interim Agreement provides that persons 'using the safe passage through Israel shall be subject to Israeli law', but this provision seems more aimed at regulating conduct during passage than authorizing denial of passage altogether. Israel's strongest argument is that the

[15] Deborah Sontag, 'Link Opens West Bank to Gaza's Job Hunters', *N.Y. Times*, 26 Oct. 1999.

[16] See Protocol Concerning Safe Passage, Art. 6(c).

[17] Lamia Lahoud, 'Israel said [*sic*] "blacklisting" Palestinians on safe passage', *Jerus. Post*, 22 Oct. 1999.

[18] Interim Agreement, Annexe I, Art. X(2)(d), X(3)(b).

[19] Ibid., Art. X(2)(e). See Daoud Kattab, 'Not fit to pass?', *Jerus. Post*, 21 Oct. 1999.

[20] Interim Agreement, Annexe I, Art. X(1)(b). See also ibid. Art. X(1)(a) ('There shall be a safe passage . . .'); ibid., Art. X(1)(d) ('Israel shall make such passage available through the route indicated on attached map No. 6').

power to issue permits presumably includes the power to deny them, but given the categorical obligation to permit passage, the permitting provisions might simply be understood as a means of tracking who makes passage, not a means of denying it altogether.

But even if the Interim Agreement requires Israel to permit all travellers to pass, the 1999 Safe Passage Protocol explicitly acknowledges that Israel might foreclose passage to some applicants. Article 6(c) provides: 'Cases of persons denied entry into Israel whose applications to use safe passage are not agreed upon shall be discussed in the agreed channels.' The 'agreed channels' would be the existing mechanisms for consultation and dispute resolution. So long as Israel makes good-faith use of these channels, and so long as it normally does make safe passage available, its position is defensible. Palestinians might argue that the 'agreed channels' compromise does not clearly authorize Israel to deny passage, and that it must be construed as consistent with the Interim Agreement, which the Protocol implements. But the 'agreed channels' provision (and the Interim Agreement itself) must also be read against the background of general international law, which traditionally affords states wide discretion to deny entry to non-nationals.[21]

The second unresolved issue is the location of the crossing point into the northern part of the West Bank. The Interim Agreement provides for safe passage in and out of two crossing points on the West Bank: one at Tarkumiya, in the southern half of the West Bank, and the other to be 'around Mevo Horon', which is located in the northern half of the West Bank, north of Jerusalem.[22] The Protocol repeats this language.[23] The agreements' use of the vague term 'around' is no accident. Israel would prefer that crossing point to be further inside PA-controlled territory, perhaps near Beit Horon; the Palestinian Authority wants it at Mevo Horon, which is near the Green Line—the 1967 border. As one PA official has said, 'The location of the checkpoint is important, because it will in some way influence the location of the future borders in the final status talks.'[24] As a legal matter, however, the location of the checkpoint has no bearing on final status talks; a provision of the Interim Agreement says explicitly that the safe-passage arrangements 'are without prejudice to the permanent status negotiations'.[25]

[21] See, e.g., Detlev F. Vagts, 'The Proposed Expatriation Tax—A Human Rights Violation?', 89 *Am. J. Int'l L.* 578, 579 n. 13 (1995). But cf. James A. R. Nafziger, 'The General Admission of Aliens Under International Law', 77 *Am. J. Int'l L.* 804, 804–7 (1983).

[22] Interim Agreement, Annexe I, Art. X(1)(c)(3)–(4).

[23] Protocol Concerning Safe Passage, Art. 2(C)(2)(iv).

[24] Lamia Lahoud, 'PA, Israel to set timetable for implementing security issues', *Jerus. Post*, 16 Feb. 1997 (quoting Maj.-Gen. Abdul Razak Yahya, head of the PA delegation to the security talks).

[25] Interim Agreement, Annexe I, Art. X(1)(e).

In sum, Israel has mostly satisfied its obligations on safe passage. Even its refusal to permit safe passage to all Palestinians is probably permissible, so long as Israel discusses such refusals in good faith in the 'agreed channels'. The parties still need to agree on a northern crossing point, but the selection of such a point will not prejudice any final status issue, at least not as a legal matter.

Gaza airport

The Note for the Record next called on the parties to negotiate an agreement on the opening and operation of a Palestinian airport in the Gaza Strip. In late 1998, after three years of dickering, the parties implemented this obligation by concluding a 'Protocol Regarding the Establishment and Operation of the International Airport in the Gaza Strip During the Interim Period'.[26] On 24 November 1998 the PA proudly opened the new Gaza International Airport, in the southern part of the Gaza Strip. Shortly after the airport opened, flights touched down from Egypt, Morocco, Jordan, Spain, and Europe.[27] Many Palestinians regard the airport not only as an important link to the rest of the world but also as a symbol of Palestinian self-determination. The PA is now talking about building a second airport in the vicinity of Bethlehem.[28]

The negotiations over the Gaza airport were not free of turbulence. Much disagreement centred around the size and location of the airport. The early Oslo Accords called for the parties to discuss and agree upon airports in the Gaza Strip and the West Bank, but they did not establish a timetable for their construction, and they supplied few details on the size or location of the airports.[29] When the Palestinians began arranging financing for a large airport complex at Dahaniya, near Rafah, in the southernmost portion of the Gaza Strip,[30] the Israelis complained that the size and location of the airport had not been 'agreed upon by the two sides' as required by the Gaza–Jericho Agreement.[31] It turned out that the

[26] The Protocol is cited in the Wye River Memorandum, ¶III.2, but the text is not yet available on either party's website, and apparently it has not yet been translated into English.

[27] Ben Lynfield, 'PA gets lift from airport opening', *Jerus. Post*, 25 Nov. 1998.

[28] Danna Harman, 'PA plans to build Bethlehem airport', ibid. 22 Jan. 1999.

[29] Gaza–Jericho Agreement, Annexe I, Art. XII(8) ¶1; Interim Agreement, Annexe I, Art. XIII(13), ¶1. Cf. also Declaration of Principles, Annexe III, Art. 5 (on establishing 'transport and communications lines').

[30] According to one report, the Palestinians 'borrowed $18 million from Egypt and put up $12 million more for construction. They received donations of $35 million in equipment for navigation, airport control and baggage handling from Spain and Germany.' Doug Struck, 'Disputes Clipping Airport's Opening; Israelis, Palestinians Work on Compromise', *Wash. Post*, 28 Mar. 1998 (citing figures supplied by Palestinian negotiator Fayez Zaidan).

[31] Gaza–Jericho Agreement, Annexe I, Art. XII(8) ¶1.

two parties had in mind two very different conceptions of 'airports and air terminals'—the terms used in the Oslo Accords. The Israelis imagined a relatively small airfield to permit commuting and regional travel. To their chagrin, the Palestinians began building a large terminal complex and a runway almost 3 kilometres long, large enough to accept Boeing 747s and Airbuses.[32] 'It's twice as big as they need,' complained one of Netanyahu's aides. The Palestinians saw the airport as an important symbol of Palestinian autonomy and an important opportunity to develop tourism and trade. 'This airport is one of the most important symbols of the coming Palestinian state,' said the director general of the Palestinian Civil Aviation Authority. Or, as one Palestinian-American businessman involved in the construction of the airport said, 'This airport will open the gate for the Palestinians, it will make us feel like we are part of the world'.[33]

The most vexing issue was (and continues to be) security at the airport. Israel has sought the right to inspect cargo and to regulate who flies in and out of the airport. Otherwise, the Israelis argued, the Palestinians 'could bring 20,000 volunteers trained in Libya. They could bring 50 tanks, heavy arms, mortars, armoured cars.'[34] The PA has sought greater freedom to operate the airport. On the whole, the Oslo Accords support Israel's position. The Interim Agreement does not envision a wholly independent Palestinian airport. All aviation activity is subject to the 'prior approval of Israel'. Air crews must be licensed in Israel or other states members of the International Civil Aviation Organization (ICAO), and even then such licences must also be 'validated by Israel'. Air services may be conducted by operators 'approved by both sides', and arrangements for such services 'will be discussed and agreed upon by the two sides' in a joint aviation committee.[35] The Palestinians have grudgingly acknowledged that these provisions give Israel a role in security arrangements at the airport. The parties have tentatively agreed to allow Israel to station inspectors at the airport, though they may operate behind the scenes, for example by watching travellers through one-way windows and having Palestinian officials hand them travel documents instead of dealing with travellers directly.

32 See Neil MacFarquhar, 'As Gaza Airport Expands, Israel's Alarm Grows', *N.Y. Times*, 16 Aug. 1996 (reporting that the Israelis expected a 'commuter field' and that they were 'dismayed' to see the construction of a 3-km runway); Struck, 'Disputes Clipping Airport's Opening' (reporting that the Israelis 'envisioned a small strip for light planes').

33 Struck, 'Disputes Clipping Airport's Opening' (quoting David Bar-Illan, Fayez Zaidan, and Mahmoud El-Farra).

34 Ibid. (quoting David Bar-Illan).

35 Interim Agreement, Annexe I, Art. XIII(4) (prior approval of Israel); ibid., Art. XIII(5) (Israeli validation of licences); ibid., Art. XIII(12) ¶1 (approval of operators and joint agreement on 'arrangements' for operating airports).

As one Palestinian involved in the construction put it, Oslo II 'is an agreement, and we will respect it'.[36]

Disagreements even extended to the name of the airport. The Oslo Accords themselves are silent on this question. The Israelis wanted a name with a local or regional flavour, such as 'Dahaniya Air Strip' or 'Rafah Airport'; the Palestinians wanted a name with a more international ring. The parties settled on 'Gaza International Airport,' which would seem to be a victory for the Palestinians. On the other hand, the Palestinians agreed not to call their new airline 'Air Palestine' in deference to Israeli concern that such a name implied statehood; the name is now *al-Falasteeniya*, or 'Palestinian Airways'. Even the call-sign of the airport—again not covered in the Oslo agreements—provoked disagreement. The Israelis preferred a designation beginning with LL, which would be consistent with the symbols used at other Israeli airports, but the parties settled on LFG, implying a measure of Palestinian independence.[37]

In any event, Palestinian Airlines is up and running. The recent agreement on safe passage augurs well for the airport, since it means residents of the West Bank will have access to it. Indeed, Palestinians have high hopes for their airport. As one PA official put it, 'I hope we will receive any American airlines that want to fly direct from New York to Gaza and they will be very welcome'.[38]

Gaza port

The West Bank may hold more economic opportunities for Palestinians than the impoverished Gaza Strip, but the Gaza Strip does have one economic advantage: its access to the sea.[39] Accordingly, the Oslo Accords envision that the Palestinians will construct and operate a seaport on the Mediterranean. In the Sharm el-Sheikh Memorandum of September 1999, Israel agreed that the Palestinians should begin constructing the port as of 1 October 1999,[40] and indeed construction has begun at a site south of Gaza City. Like the airport, a seaport would have both economic and symbolic importance to Palestinians.

Until the Sharm el-Sheikh Memorandum, the parties had repeatedly 'agreed to agree' on a seaport. The 1993 Declaration of Principles envisioned a programme that would 'define guidelines for the establishment

[36] Struck, 'Disputes Clipping Airport's Opening' (quoting Sayeed Basheer).
[37] Sakher Abu El Oun, 'Palestinian Airport', *Agence France Presse*, 29 Oct. 1998.
[38] MacFarquhar, 'As Gaza Airport Expands'.
[39] See David Newman, 'The politics of a transit route', *Jerus. Post*, 6 Oct. 1999.
[40] Sharm el-Sheikh Memorandum, ¶6(a).

of a Gaza Sea Port Area'.[41] The 1995 Interim Agreement provided: 'Plans for the establishment of a port in the Gaza Strip . . ., its location, and related matters of mutual interest and concern . . . will be discussed and agreed upon.'[42] The 1997 Note for the Record listed the 'Gaza port' as an 'Israeli responsibility', but this responsibility boiled down to a joint obligation to negotiate.[43] The 1998 Wye River Memorandum reiterated that the parties 'commit themselves to proceeding without delay to conclude an agreement' on construction and operation of the port.[44]

The Sharm el-Sheikh Memorandum finally did authorize construction of a seaport, but like its predecessors the Memorandum left almost all other issues for further negotiation. In particular, the Memorandum provided that a Gaza port 'will not be operated in any way before reaching a joint Sea Port protocol on all aspects of operating the Port, including security'.[45] As with the airport, security has been the leading source of disagreement between the parties. The parties have repeatedly locked horns over whether and to what extent Israel should be empowered to inspect incoming and outgoing cargo.[46] Israel's chief concern about the port is that it might be used to import military equipment or supplies or otherwise to support terrorism.[47] It is no accident that the Interim Agreement's provisions on the port are part of a larger article on 'Security along the Coastline to the Sea of Gaza'. Resolution of the security question is of course primarily a political matter; the principal legal consideration is that the parties are both obliged to negotiate on this issue in good faith. As we saw in Chapter 6, that means at least that the parties cannot hold up agreement unless they have an 'honest' belief that their positions are warranted, and it may mean that the parties are held to a higher 'reasonable good faith' standard.

In the absence of a complete agreement on the main seaport, the Palestinians began reconstructing and expanding a former Israeli port in Gaza. Israel charged that this second port violates the Interim Agreement, which authorizes only 'a port'—a single port—in the Gaza Strip.[48] The

41 Declaration of Principles, Annexe III, Art. 5.

42 Interim Agreement, Annexe I, Art. XIV(4)(a), 4(c).

43 Note for the Record, 'Israeli responsibilities', Issues for Negotiation, ¶3(c).

44 Wye River Memorandum, ¶III(4).

45 Sharm el-Sheikh Memorandum, ¶6(b).

46 See Jay Bushinsky, 'PA: Israel trying to block Gaza port', *Jerus. Post*, 11 July 1997; Steve Rodan and Mohammed Najib, 'PA, Israeli committees resume talks on Gaza ports', ibid. 13 Oct. 1997 (reporting on disagreements over whether imports should first traverse Israeli ports);

47 'We want to make sure that the Palestinians bring neither an army nor military equipment into Gaza through the port.' Lamia Lahoud, 'Economic link or security risk?', ibid. 26 Sept. 1997 (quoting an aide to Netanyahu).

48 Ibid. See Interim Agreement, Annexe I, Art. XIV(4)(a) ('Plans for the establishment of *a port* in the Gaza Strip . . . will be discussed and agreed upon . . .') (emphasis added).

Palestinians respond that this second port is merely a 'fishing port' for 'local use', not the kind of deep-water commercial port envisioned by the Interim Agreement, which speaks of 'international voyages', 'entry and exit of vessels, passengers and goods by sea', and otherwise implies a port for exports and imports.[49] The Israelis say that the second port is larger than necessary for a fishing port, and in any event they stress that the Accords call for joint discussions and agreement on a port. The Israeli view would seem to have more support in the Accords, which do speak of mutual agreement on one 'port'. None the less, the fishing port is mostly complete, and Israel has grudgingly acquiesced in it, all the while urging greater coordination on future projects.[50]

There have also been disagreements about Palestinian fishing. On its face, the Interim Agreement grants the Palestinians broad fishing and boating rights. The Interim Agreement, like the Gaza–Jericho Agreement before it, divided the Gaza seacoast into three areas, Zones K, L, and M, each of which extends 20 nautical miles into the sea. Zone L, by far the widest zone, consists of most of the coast of the Gaza Strip; it is sandwiched between Zone K, a 1.5 nautical-mile-wide sliver at the northernmost part of the Strip, and Zone M, a one nautical-mile-wide sliver at the southernmost part of the Strip.[51] Zones K and M—the 'borders' of the Gaza maritime area—are closed to all navigation except that of the Israel Navy.[52] Zone L is open to Palestinian 'fishing, recreation and economic activities'.[53]

There are nevertheless some restrictions on Palestinian fishing and boating. Palestinian fishermen are limited to boats of 25 horsepower for outboard motors and speeds up to 18 knots for inboard motors.[54] Fishing boats are not permitted to exit Zone L for the open ocean, but otherwise the Interim Agreement appears to permit free access for boats within the entire area of Zone L. Yachts and recreational boats, by contrast, are limited to a distance of 6 nautical miles from the coast in Zone L. All boat operators must be licensed, and boats must bear appropriate markings.[55] Foreign vessels are permitted to enter Zone L but only up to 12 nautical miles from the coast, except when visiting the new Gaza port.[56] The Oslo

[49] See, e.g., Interim Agreement, Annexe I, Art. XIV(4)(c) (entry and exit by sea); ibid., Art. XIV(4)(a) ('international voyages'); Lahoud, 'Economic link or security risk?' (reporting PA's view that the facility is a fishing port for 'local use' only).

[50] See Ethan Bronner, 'Israeli Cabinet Member Visits Gaza to Clear the Air', *N.Y. Times*, 4 Aug. 1999.

[51] Interim Agreement, Annexe I, Art. XIV(1)(a)(1)–(2)(a).

[52] Ibid., Art. XIV(1)(a)(1)(c).

[53] Ibid., Art. XIV(1)(a)(2)(b).

[54] Ibid., Art. XIV(1)(a)(2)(b)(i). By contrast, the Gaza–Jericho Agreement established a 15-knot limit. Gaza–Jericho Agreement, Annexe I, Art. XI(1)(a)(2)(b)(i).

[55] Interim Agreement, Annexe I, Art. XIV(1)(b)(1)–(2).

[56] Ibid., Art. XIV(1)(a)(2)(b)(iv).

Accords thereby envision a 12 nautical-mile territorial sea, in accordance with the modern law of the sea.[57] The Interim Agreement also authorizes a small, ten-boat Palestinian Coastal Police (PCP) to patrol Palestinian fishing for up to 6 nautical miles from the coast, and upon joint agreement up to 12 nautical miles.[58] Israeli officials have occasionally complained that the PCP has operated well inland, in violation of the terms of reference in the Interim Agreement, which envision only coastal patrols.

The Palestinians have on occasion asserted that Israel does not permit fishermen to operate more than 6 nautical miles from the coast, even though the Interim Agreement appears to permit Palestinian fishing throughout Zone L.[59] This is a 'clear violation' of the agreement, a PA official has charged.[60] In response, Israel can point to the security exception to the free-boating regime, which provides that 'Israel Navy vessels may sail throughout [Zones K, L, and M], as necessary and without limitations, and may take any measures necessary against vessels suspected of being used for terrorist activities or for smuggling arms, ammunition, drugs, goods, or for any other illegal activity'.[61] Israel justifies its limits on fishing beyond 6 nautical miles as a security precaution taken in response to terrorist attacks in Israel. But a broad-brush prohibition on fishing past

[57] See UN Convention on the Law of the Sea, UN Doc. A/CONF. 62/122, 21 I.L.M. 1261 (1982), Art. 3 ('Every State has the right to establish the breadth of its territorial sea up to a limit not exceeding 12 nautical miles . . .'); Louis Henkin, *et al.*, *International Law: Cases and Materials*, 3rd edn (St Paul, MN: West Publishing, 1993), 1245 ('The 1982 Convention probably states the present customary law, and claims beyond 12 miles will doubtless be challenged').

The Interim Agreement's 20 nautical-mile limit for fishing is also consistent with the law of the sea. International law permits states to establish an Exclusive Economic Zone (EEZ) in which they can exercise 'sovereign rights' to exploit the ocean's natural resources. Convention on the Law of the Sea, Art. 56(1)(a). The EEZ can extend up to 200 nautical miles from the state's coast. Ibid., Art. 57.

It is less clear, however, whether the Interim Agreement's categorical prohibition on all foreign vessels (other than those visiting the Gaza port) is consistent with international law. The Law of the Sea Convention recognizes a broad right of innocent passage for 'ships of all States', even warships, through the territorial sea of other states subject to certain conditions. See Convention on the Law of the Sea, Art. 17-19.

[58] Interim Agreement, Annexe I, Art. XIV(2)(a). The PCP 'shall have up to 10 boats with a displacement of up to 50 tons and a maximum speed of up to 25 knots'. Ibid., Art. XIV(2)(b). PCP boats 'shall' fly the Palestinian flag. Ibid., Art. XIV(2)(d). The two sides 'shall cooperate on all sea matters, including mutual help at sea, and pollution and environmental issues'. Ibid., Art. XIV(2)(e). Israeli boats are subject to exclusive Israeli jurisdiction. Ibid., Art. XIV(2)(g).

By contrast, the Gaza–Jericho Agreement envisioned a PCP with eight boats, not ten, and somewhat smaller displacements and lower speeds. Gaza–Jericho Agreement, Annex I, Art. XI(2)(b). In addition, the Gaza–Jericho Agreement provided that PCP boats 'may' fly the Palestinian flag; the Interim Agreement replaced 'may' with 'shall'.

[59] See Interim Agreement, Annexe I, Art. XIV(1)(a)(2)(b)(b(i), Art. XIV(2)(a).

[60] Lahoud, 'Economic link or security risk?' (quoting Gen. Abdel Razak Yahiya, co-chair of the joint committee on security).

[61] Interim Agreement, Annexe I, Art. XIV(1)(b)(4).

6 nautical miles seems inconsistent with the rather narrow wording of the security exception, which speaks of 'vessels suspected' of involvement in terrorism or illegal activity. This provision seems to envision a particularized suspicion of foul play, not a generalized sense that all Palestinian fishing boats are suspect.

In sum, the parties have a shared obligation to come to some understanding on security at the Gaza port. Both are obliged to carry out this obligation in good faith; delay for political reasons would not constitute good faith. The PA was obliged to refrain from opening an alternative commercial port without Israeli agreement, but the PA is permitted to facilitate local fishing from the docks at that port. Finally, Israel is obliged to permit fishing up to the 20 nautical-mile limit in Zone L unless it has reason to believe that a particular fishing boat is engaged in illegal activity.

Passages

The next 'Israeli responsibility' listed in the Note for the Record is, on its face, rather cryptic: it calls for the negotiation of an agreement on 'passages'. This is a reference to the parties' agreement to permit some Palestinian participation in regulating the passage of people travelling between the West Bank and Jordan and between the Gaza Strip and Egypt.[62] The 1993 Declaration of Principles set forth a general obligation to establish coordination between the parties on passages.[63] The 1994 Gaza–Jericho Agreement established an elaborate system of joint management of the Allenby Bridge border crossing (from the West Bank into Jordan) and the Rafah crossing (from the Gaza Strip into Egypt).[64] The 1995 Interim Agreement, which supplanted the Gaza–Jericho Accord, created even more complex mechanisms for control of the border crossings.[65]

The Interim Agreement begins by reaffirming that Israel has responsibility for external security during the 5-year interim period envisioned by

[62] Technically speaking, the term 'passages' is defined as 'the area from the crossing barrier at the Egyptian border or the Allenby Bridge, passing through and including the terminal'. In the case of the Allenby Bridge crossing, this includes the area from the terminal to the Jericho Area; in the case of the Rafah crossing, this includes the area from the terminal up to the 'outer limit of the Israel military location along the Egyptian border'. Interim Agreement, Annexe I, Art. VIII(2)(a).

[63] Declaration of Principles, Annexe II, Art. 4.

[64] See Gaza–Jericho Agreement, Annexe I, Art. X.

[65] See Interim Agreement, Art. XXX ('Arrangements for coordination between Israel and the Council regarding passage to and from Egypt and Jordan, as well as any other agreed international crossings, are set out in Annexe I'); ibid., Annexe I, Art. VIII (setting forth detailed arrangements).

the Declaration of Principles. The Agreement then states a general goal of 'creating a mechanism that facilitates the entry and exit of people and goods, reflecting the new reality created by the DOP [Declaration of Principles], while providing full security for both sides'.[66]

A central feature of this mechanism is the division of the crossing terminals at the Allenby Bridge and Rafah into two wings, a 'Palestinian Wing' to process 'Palestinian residents of the West Bank and Gaza Strip and visitors to those areas', and an 'Israeli Wing' to process Israelis and others.[67] Israel retains 'exclusive' control over management of the Israeli Wing, as well as overall responsibility for overall security in the terminal and along the passage routes between the terminal and the relevant borders.[68] In the Palestinian Wing, however, the parties exercise shared responsibility for many operations at the border crossings, including checking identification and travel documents, detaining suspicious travellers, conducting searches when appropriate, and approving and denying entry and exit in certain circumstances.[69]

The most notable consequence of this bifurcation is that Palestinian residents of the West Bank and Gaza Strip are normally processed by a Palestinian control officer. Their documents are checked by an Israeli officer as well, but only 'in an invisible manner'.[70] In practice, this means that Israeli officers are stationed behind two-way mirrors or otherwise out of sight of Palestinian travellers; Palestinian officers pass travel documents through a drawer back to their Israeli counterparts, who examine the documents and then pass them back to the Palestinian officers.[71] Once travellers leave the document-control area of the Palestinian Wing, they proceed to a Palestinian customs lane in which inspection and duty-collection is carried out by Palestinian officials, with Israeli customs officials 'invisibly present'.[72] Palestinian VIPs and their guests are entitled to expedited passage through the border terminals.[73] The provisions on 'invisible' Israeli supervision were an important concession for the Palestinians, who have long chafed at what they regard as degrading treatment at the crossing points. The concession on document-control was

66 Interim Agreement, Annexe I, Art. VIII(a).

67 Ibid., Art. VIII(1)(g).

68 Ibid., Art. VIII(2)(b)(3)(a), Art. VIII(2)(b)(1).

69 See generally ibid., Art. VIII(3)–(4).

70 Ibid., Art. VIII(3)(d)(1).

71 See Christopher Walker, 'Israel eases ordeal of West Bank crossing', *The Times*, 21 June 1994.

72 Interim Agreement, Annexe V, Art. III(14)(b). See also Interim Agreement, Annexe I, Art. 3(g).

73 There are elaborate provisions on VIPs, who are divided into three categories of importance. The most important VIPs include senior members of the Palestinian Legislative Council and Palestinian Police with the rank of Major-General. See Interim Agreement, Annexe I, Appendix 5, §F, Art. 1(b)(1). They are subject only to a 'brief visual inspection of their vehicle by an Israeli official', and they are accommodated in a VIP lounge while their documents are presented to Palestinian and Israeli border officials. Ibid., Art. 3(a).

limited, however, to Palestinian residents of the West Bank and Gaza Strip. Visitors to those areas have their documents checked directly by both Israeli and Palestinian border officials.[74]

The Interim Agreement also includes provisions on interrogation, detention, arrest, and denial of entry. In the Palestinian Wing, both parties are authorized to 'deny the entry of persons who are not residents of the West Bank and the Gaza Strip'.[75] This provision is consistent with international human rights law, which recognizes some right to *leave* a state but not necessarily a right to *enter* a foreign state or territory.[76] Some Palestinian officers at the terminal are permitted to be armed with handguns.[77] The Interim Agreement provides that either side may interrogate a traveller who has a record of terrorism, who conceals weapons or explosives, who holds forged or invalid travel documents, or who acts 'in an obviously suspicious behaviour during the passage via the terminal'.[78] Such a traveller may be 'apprehended' if the 'suspicion has not been removed' by interrogation.[79] It might well be asked whether a mere unarticulated 'suspicion' is a sufficient basis for arrest under international human rights law, which forbids 'arbitrary' arrest and holds that 'No one shall be deprived of his liberty except on such grounds and in accordance with such procedure as are established by law'.[80]

As might be expected, the Interim Agreement's provisions on passages

[74] Interim Agreement, Annexe I, Art. VIII(3)(d)(2).

[75] Ibid., Art. VIII(3)(f).

[76] See International Covenant on Civil and Political Rights, 16 Dec. 1966, 999 U.N.T.S. 171, Art. 12(2) (providing that everyone 'shall be free to leave any country, including his own', but failing to provide a correlative right to enter a foreign country); ibid., Art. 12(4) (providing that no one shall be 'arbitrarily deprived' of the right to enter his own country, but failing to provide a correlative right to enter a foreign country). Israel is a party to the Covenant. See also Universal Declaration of Human Rights, 10 Dec. 1948, G.A. Res. 217 A(III), UN GAOR, 3rd Sess., UN Doc. A/810, at 74 (1948), Art. 13(2) (recognizing a right to leave one's own country but not necessarily a correlative right to enter a foreign country); Hurst Hannum, *The Right to Leave and Return in International Law and Practice* (Dordrecht; Boston: Martinus Nijhoff, 1987), 20; Geoffrey R. Watson, 'Progress for Pilgrims? An Analysis of the Holy See–Israel Fundamental Agreement', 47 *Catholic U. L. Rev.* 497, 506–27 (1998) (arguing that there is no general right to enter a foreign country for pilgrimage or other purposes); Patrice Jean, 'Le Contenu de la Liberté de Circulation', in Maurice Flory, *et al.* (eds.), *Liberté de Circulation des Personnes en Droit International* (Paris: Economica, 1988), 21, 33 (arguing that there is no 'liberté fondementale d'entrée'). See also Rainer Hofman, *Die Ausreisefreiheit nach Volkerrecht und staatlichem Recht* (Berlin; New York: Springer, 1988).

The international law of travel is taking on increased importance for Israel. Pope John Paul II has declared the year 2000 a Jubilee Year and has urged Catholics to make pilgrimages to the Holy Land. Accordingly, Israel expects unprecedented millions of tourists and Christian pilgrims to visit during the year 2000. See Sue Fishkoff, 'Apocalypse Soon?', *Jerus. Post*, 4 Apr. 1997.

[77] Interim Agreement, Annexe I, Art. VIII(2)(b)(8); ibid., Appendix V, §D.

[78] Ibid., Annexe I, Art. VIII(3)(e) ¶1, §§ (1)–(4).

[79] Ibid., Art. VIII(3)(e) ¶2.

[80] International Covenant on Civil and Political Rights, Art. 9(1); Universal Declaration of Human Rights, Art. 9 (forbidding arbitrary arrest or detention).

have not all been implemented smoothly. There have been disputes about the location of armed Palestinian police officers at and around the terminal, about the timeliness of Israel's renovation of the terminals at the Allenby Bridge and Rafah, and even about the hours of operation of the Allenby terminal. The parties also accuse each other of dragging their feet on pursuing negotiations over other details about the passages. Again, this is more a joint obligation than a sole Israeli obligation; both parties are bound to fulfil it in good faith.

Economic and financial issues

The next 'Israeli responsibility' listed in the Note for the Record is again really a joint obligation to negotiate over a set of issues—in this case, economic, financial, civilian, and security questions. The economic provisions in particular reflect the hope that trade and other economic cooperation between the parties might strengthen the Palestinian economy and lead to cooperation in other spheres.[81] Unfortunately, the Palestinian economy has in some ways lost ground since 1993, and the economic provisions of the Accords have not always prompted cooperation. The most controversial economic issues have been Israel's 1997 decision to withhold funds due to the PA and Israel's repeated 'closures' of the West Bank and the Gaza Strip for security reasons.[82] Before turning to these issues, this section first presents an overview of the unique legal regime established by the economic provisions of the Oslo Accords.

The parties first addressed economic questions in the 1993 Declaration of Principles. The Declaration established a joint economic committee to promote cooperation on trade, industry, finance, labour relations, social welfare, transport and communications, energy, electricity, and other fields, and it envisioned a regional development programme involving the G-7 and other interested states and international organizations.[83] The

[81] See, e.g., Amir H. Khoury, 'International Trade and Commerce: A Bridge for the Israeli–Palestinian Peace', 7 *Cardozo J. Int'l & Comp. L.* 11 (1999); Jack I. Garvey, 'Regional Free Trade Dispute Resolution as Means for Securing the Middle East Peace Process', 47 *Am. J. Comp. L.* 147 (1999).

[82] There is also an ongoing dispute between Israel and the European Union over the tariff treatment of goods from Israeli settlements in the occupied territories and, more generally, over trade between the EU and the PA. See, e.g., 'Israel 1, European Union 0', *Foreign Report*, 1 Apr. 1999 (Jane's Info. Group, available on LEXIS/NEWS); 'Israel says alleged EU blacklist of settlement goods violation of accords', *Yediot Aharonot*, 23 Apr. 1998 (in Hebrew), translated and reported in *BBC Summary of World Broadcasts*, 25 Apr. 1998.

There are also questions of PA compliance, many relating to allegations that the PA has mismanaged its finances. See, e.g., Judy Dempsey, 'Use of pension fund puts Palestinian openness in doubt', *Financial Times*, 2 Dec. 1998. PA governance is considered in more detail in Part IV.

[83] See Declaration of Principles, Art. XI and Annexes III and IV.

1994 Gaza–Jericho Agreement and the 1995 Interim Agreement helped create the legal framework necessary for economic relations between Israel and the PA, for example by providing for mutual enforcement of civil judgments[84] and by affirming that the PA had the capacity to conclude contracts and to sue and to be sued.[85] These provisions on capacity do not constitute 'recognition of a Palestinian state or sovereign' but do give the PA 'a formal legal identity' that makes it possible for it to 'function as a trading partner'.[86]

The main provisions on economics are contained in the Protocol on Economic Relations, signed in Paris on 9 April 1994 and incorporated by reference into the Gaza–Jericho Agreement and the Interim Agreement.[87] Before considering the extent of the parties' compliance with the Paris Protocol, it is important to consider its overall structure and purpose.

It is not clear whether the purpose of the Protocol is to establish economic union or to pave the way for economic separation. The Preamble of the Paris Protocol declares that economics is 'the cornerstone in their mutual relations', and it speaks of 'strengthening the economic base for the Palestinian side', but it stops short of declaring any free-trade area or common market. Similarly, Article II of the Protocol establishes a Joint Economic Committee to pursue the economic 'cooperation' first outlined in the Declaration of Principles,[88] but it stops short of establishing joint institutions that one would expect of a common market. For example, the Protocol contains no mechanisms to formulate a common agricultural or industrial policy, to deal with anti-competitive practices, or to harmonize commercial law or contract law—though it does harmonize road-accident law by requiring the PA to adopt Israel's system of no-fault liability, compulsory automobile insurance, and a Victims Compensation Fund.[89]

[84] Gaza–Jericho Agreement, Annexe III, Art. IV(4); Interim Agreement, Annexe IV, Art. IV(3).

[85] Gaza–Jericho Agreement, Art. VI(1)(c); Interim Agreement, Art. IX(2).

[86] Celia Wasserstein Fassberg, 'Legal Aspects of Israeli–Palestinian Economic Relations', in Cotran, *The Arab–Israeli Accords*, 157–9.

[87] Gaza–Jericho Agreement, Art. XIII and Annex IV; Interim Agreement, Art. XXIV and Annexe V.

[88] Interim Agreement, Annexe V, Art. II.

[89] See Fassberg, 'Legal Aspects', 161; Interim Agreement, Annexe V, Art. XI (setting forth rules on road accidents). The Protocol Concerning Legal Affairs not only fails to harmonize law as between Israel and the PA, it also fails to harmonize law as between the West Bank (whose law has Jordanian roots) and the Gaza Strip (whose law stems from British Mandatory law). The Protocol provides only that Israelis conducting commercial activity in PA territory 'are subject to the prevailing civil law in the Territory relating to that activity'. Interim Agreement, Annexe IV, Art. III(4). See Fassberg, 'Legal Aspects', 166. For a survey of these and other legal 'hurdles', see Keith C. Molkner, 'Legal and Structural Hurdles to Achieving Political Stability and Economic Development in the Palestinian Territories', 19 *Fordham Int'l L.J.* 1419, 1429–49 (1996).

The Protocol does appear to establish a customs union between Israel and the PA,[90] but it is less than complete. As defined in the General Agreement on Tariffs and Trade (GATT), a customs union means that (1) tariffs and other trade barriers 'are eliminated with respect to substantially all the trade' between members of the union, and (2) 'substantially the same duties' are applied by all members of the union to non-members.[91] The Paris Protocol pursues both these goals. Article IX(1) provides that 'there will be free movement of industrial goods free of any restrictions including customs and import taxes between the two sides subject to each side's legislation'. And Article III(5)(a) provides that, for most goods, 'the Israeli rates of customs, purchase tax, levies, excises and other charges, prevailing at the date of signing of the Agreement, shall serve as the minimum basis for the Palestinian Authority'. Still, the PA customs rate need not be identical to the Israeli rate, which serves only as the 'minimum basis' for the PA rate. And the PA does have authority to set its own, independent customs tariffs and other charges for some goods, including some food and agricultural products, construction materials, and certain household appliances.[92] On the whole, however, the parties' customs rates are sufficiently similar that the arrangement does resemble a customs union, albeit a limited one. It certainly resembles a customs union more than a free trade area, in which member states eliminate trade barriers between them but are free to maintain different tariff rates for different foreign states.[93]

[90] See Talia Einhorn, 'The Customs Union Between Israel and the Palestinian Authority: A Critical Analysis', Prepared Statement Before the Joint Economic Committee, in Fed. News Service, 21 Oct. 1997 (available on LEXIS/NEWS), n. 3.

[91] Text of the General Agreement on Tariffs and Trade, 30 Oct. 1947, Art. XXIV(8)(a)(i)–(ii), 55 U.N.T.S. 194, IV GATT B.I.S.D. 1 (1969). This and other provisions of the original GATT 1947 have been carried forward by the new World Trade Organization in the form of a new GATT 1994. See General Agreement on Tariffs and Trade 1994, Marrakesh Agreement Establishing the World Trade Organization, Annexe 1B, *The Results of the Uruguay Round of Multilateral Trade Negotiations—The Legal Texts* 325 (1994), 33 I.L.M. 1154; Antonio F. Perez, 'WTO and U.N. Law: Institutional Comity in National Security', 23 *Yale J. Int'l L.* 301, 305 n. 16 (1998).

GATT 1994 also includes an Understanding on Article XXIV of GATT 1994, the article on customs unions and free trade areas. See GATT 1994, Art. 1(c)(iv). The Understanding clarifies the circumstances under which a customs union or free-trade area comply with the GATT. See Understanding on the Interpretation of Article XXIV of the General Agreement on Tariffs and Trade 1994, 33 I.L.M. 1161 (1994).

[92] Interim Agreement, Annex V, Art. III(2)(a) and (b). See Elmusa and El-Jaafari, 'Power and Trade', 178–81 (describing the import regime in detail). Cf. also David P. Fidler, 'Foreign Private Investment in Palestine: An Analysis of the Law on the Encouragement of Investment in Palestine', 19 *Fordham Int'l L.J.* 529 (1995).

[93] See GATT 1994, Art. XXIV(8)(b) ('A free-trade area shall be understood to mean a group of two or more customs territories in which the duties and other restrictive regulations of commerce ... are eliminated on substantially all the trade between the constituent territories on products originating in such territories'); Einhorn, 'The Customs Union', nn. 143–6.

Some Palestinian commentators have argued that Palestinians would be better off with

The Protocol's provisions on monetary and currency policy also reflect only a limited commitment to economic union. There is a common currency, the New Israeli Shekel, but the Protocol merely provides that it will be 'one of the circulating currencies' in the PA's areas, not the exclusive currency[94]—though in practice it is used in most Palestinian transactions.[95] Moreover, the shekel is the currency of one of the parties rather than a new common currency along the lines of the Euro. Most significantly, the Paris Protocol contemplates that there might someday be a separate Palestinian currency: the parties agreed to discuss the 'possibility of introducing mutually agreed Palestinian currency'.[96] The head of the Palestinian Monetary Authority—the PA monetary board authorized by the Paris Protocol[97]—has called the establishment of a Palestinian currency 'one of the most important national aims', an 'expression of Palestinian sovereignty' and a step that 'represents an essential factor for achieving monetary independence'.[98] It does not appear that the parties intend to use a single currency for the long term.

a free-trade area than a customs union, for political if not economic reasons, since the ability to set its own tariffs would give it more control over its trade policy. See Samir Huleileh, 'Palestinian Israeli Trade Relations (2): Trade Policy Options for the West Bank and Gaza Strip', MAS Policy Notes, Issue No. 2, Sept. 1996, and Nu'man Kanafani, 'Palestinian–Israeli Trade Relations (1): Free Trade Area or Customs Union?', MAS Policy Notes, Issue No. 1, Aug. 1996, both cited in Einhorn, 'The Customs Union', n. 143. Einhorn argues that the framers of the Oslo Accords were 'wise' to reject this solution because it is 'practically impossible to establish customs borders between Israel and the West Bank due to the "leakiness" of such borders'. Ibid., n. 145. None the less, if a final settlement does lead to Palestinian statehood, the borders will presumably become less porous, and the notion of a separate Palestinian tariff policy (and of a free-trade area) will perhaps have greater appeal than it does now. For more on developments in Palestinian trade law and policy, see David P. Fidler, 'Peace Through Trade? Developments in Palestinian Trade Law During the Peace Process', 38 *Va. J. Int'l L.* 155 (1998).

94 See Interim Agreement, Annexe V, Art. IV(10)(a). Thus the Protocol permits continued use of the Jordanian dinar and the US dollar in PA territories. Elmusa and El-Jaafari, 'Power and Trade', 177.

95 The PA economy is in fact so tied to the shekel that an Israeli devaluation of the currency can have direct effects on the Palestinian economy. Cf. 'PNA–NIS Devaluation Hurts Local Income', in *Middle East News Items*, 28 Apr. 1998 (Info-Prod Research, available on LEXIS/NEWS) (reporting a PA official's view that a recent devaluation of the shekel 'negatively impacted the Palestinian economy' by decreasing Palestinian purchasing power).

96 Gaza–Jericho Agreement, Annexe IV, Art. IV(10)(b).

97 Ibid., Art. IV(1).

98 Interview with Dr Fu'ad Busaysu, governor of the PMA, by Hasan al-Nurani, in *Al-Dustur* (Amman), 16 Apr. 1998 (in Arabic), translated and reprinted in BBC Summary of World Broadcasts, 'PNA official discusses Palestinian monetary policy', 21 Apr. 1998, ME/W0534/WME. Dr Busaysu added, however, that 'we still need to guarantee certain conditions' before moving to a Palestinian currency. Other experts have similarly asserted that 'the Palestinian economy is probably not in a position to support a convertible currency at present'. Elmusa and El-Jaafari, 'Power and Trade', 177.

For an interesting discussion of banking in Palestinian territory, see Amir H. Khoury, 'An American Bank in the Palestinian Authority: Investing in the Peace', 24 *Brooklyn J. Int'l L.* 739 (1999).

The provisions on revenue-sharing similarly point towards independent economies rather than economic union. There is to be no single treasury; instead, the parties split up revenues from taxes, tariffs, and the like. For example, the Protocol provides for the collection and sharing of direct and indirect tax revenue. As to direct taxation, the PA is free to set its own policies on income tax, property taxes, and municipal taxes and fees.[99] Interestingly, Israel transfers to the PA 75 per cent of income taxes collected from Palestinians employed in Israel and the full amount of income taxes collected from Palestinians employed in Israeli settlements.[100] As to indirect taxation, the PA and Israel are both authorized to levy and collect value-added taxes (VAT) and purchase taxes on local production in their respective territories; the Israeli VAT rate is 17 per cent, and the PA VAT rate 'shall not be lower than 2 per cent below the Israeli VAT rate'—i.e. no lower than 15 per cent.[101]

Import taxes are split up in a similar fashion, depending on the destination of the imported good.[102] This regime has been criticized because it creates a 'zero-sum game' in which the parties compete with each other for import taxes.[103] Indeed, each party has incentive to determine that imported goods are destined for its own territory, thus justifying that party to claim the import tax on the good, even if the goods in fact end up somewhere else. By contrast, the European Union transfers all such revenues to the central EU budget,[104] as do federal states such as the United States.[105] Not surprisingly, there have been allegations that the Palestinians have overstated their imports in order to clear more revenues

[99] Interim Agreement, Annexe V, Appendix 1, Art. V(1).

[100] Ibid., Art. V(4)(a) and (b). This provision is at odds with international practice because income tax usually 'accrues to the treasury of the territory in which a person works'. Einhorn, 'The Customs Union', 39 n. 5. Still, states do generally accord non-resident commuters some tax benefits. In the United States, for example, a person who commutes from Mexico or Canada to the United States is treated as a non-resident for tax purposes, meaning that he or she is liable for taxes on income 'originating' in the United States but not for worldwide income. See Internal Revenue Code, §7701(b)(7)(B); Prop. Reg. §301.7701(b)–3(e) (defining 'commute'); Boris I. Bittker and Lawrence Lokken, *Fundamentals of International Taxation*, ¶65.2.3, at 65–10 (Boston; New York: Warren, Gorham & Lamont, 1991).

[101] Interim Agreement, Annexe V, Appendix 2, Arts. VI(1) and VI(3). An earlier version of this provision obliged the PA to set its VAT between 15% and 16%. See Interim Agreement, Annex V, Art. VI(3).

[102] Interim Agreement, Annexe V, Art. III(15) ('The clearance of revenues from all import taxes and levies, between Israel and the Palestinian Authority, will be based on the principle of the place of final destination').

[103] Einhorn, 'The Customs Union', nn. 5–6.

[104] 'Customs duties and agricultural levies . . . were designated as a source of [European] Community revenue.' Ibid., n. 6.

[105] Cf. US Constitution. Art. I, §8, cl. 1 ('The Congress shall have Power to lay and collect Taxes, Duties, Imposts and Excises . . .'); ibid. ('all Duties, Imposts and Excises shall be uniform throughout the United States').

from import taxes, and indeed the PA's own figures showed a rise in imports in 1996 even as closure of the territories and other factors continued to depress the Palestinian economy.[106] Whatever the merits of the import-destination dispute, it is another example of the ambivalence of the Paris Protocol, which speaks of cooperation on the one hand but points towards disunity and competition on the other.

All told, the Paris Protocol requires Israel to transfer to the PA, on a monthly basis, proceeds from at least five different sources: direct (income) taxation; indirect (VAT) taxation; import taxes; fuel excise taxes; and taxes for social benefits and health services.[107] These revenues are important to the PA: they constitute more than 60 per cent of the PA budget, amounting to $436 million in 1996, $540 million in 1997, and $182 million in the first third of 1998.[108] Israel's obligation to share these tax revenues forms the basis of the first of the PA's two major complaints about Israeli compliance with the Paris Protocol.

In August 1997 a suicide bombing at Mahaneh Yehuda, a Jerusalem market, killed many Israeli civilians. Outraged, Prime Minister Netanyahu and his security cabinet agreed to withhold the transfer of all tax revenues to the PA. This announcement was condemned by the PA as 'effectively a cancellation of the Paris protocol'.[109] A spokesman for Netanyahu replied that agreements 'must be respected by both sides', while another Israeli official acknowledged that Israel's refusal to pay was a 'serious breach' but added 'so was the terror attack'.[110] Initial reports suggested that the transfers would resume within a week, after the seven-day mourning period for the victims of the attack at Mahaneh Yehuda, but Israel withheld the funds for a number of weeks, citing the PA's failure to cooperate in preventing terrorism.[111] In the autumn of 1997 Israel

[106] See Einhorn, 'The Customs Union', nn. 9–10.

[107] Interim Agreement, Annexe V, Appendix 1, Art. V(4) (income tax); ibid., Annexe V, Appendix 2, Art. VI (VAT); ibid., Annexe V, Art. III(15) (import taxes and levies); ibid., Art. VII(3) (taxes for social benefits and health services).

[108] 'Transfer of Funds to the Palestinian Authority', *Middle East News Items*, 28 May 1998 (Info-Prod Research, available on LEXIS/NEWS). The most widely accepted estimate is that tax revenues comprise about 60% to 65% of the PA's budget. The director-general of the Palestinian Customs Authority has asserted, however, that as much as 75% of PA revenues come from tax revenues. *Al-Hayat*, 10 Jan. 1998, translated and reprinted in BBC Summary of World Broadcasts, 'Officials say customs duties account for 75 per cent of revenue', 20 Jan. 1998.

[109] David Harris, 'Ne'eman to hold back money transfers to PA', *Jerus. Post*, 5 Aug. 1997 (quoting Dr Maher Kurd, economics adviser to Arafat).

[110] Ibid. (quoting Shai Bazak and a 'senior government official').

[111] This was not the first time that the parties had haggled over financial obligations. In early 1997 the parties signed an agreement settling mutual debts, including an Israeli obligation to pay the PA 65 million shekels to cover VAT accrued from May to December 1994. 'Israel and Palestinians Sign Accord on Debts', *Reuters Financial Service*, 15 Feb. 1997 (available on LEXIS/NEWS).

started releasing some of the money to the PA, and released the remainder of the funds in October 1997.[112]

Israel's main legal justification for withholding the funds was the PA's failure to honour its own Oslo obligations, in particular its obligations to combat terror. As Prime Minister Netanyahu's spokesman put it, 'When the PA fulfills its obligations Israel will transfer moneys. Israel will no longer pay with dead lying in the streets and while the PA does not fight terror or prevent it from being committed.'[113]

As we saw in Chapter 6, a party to an international agreement is permitted (but not obliged) to suspend or terminate its own performance 'in whole or in part' in response to a material breach by the other. A 'material breach' is one that goes to the 'object or purpose' of the treaty.[114] And while the Vienna Convention on the Law of Treaties is silent on 'minor' breaches, the better view is that a party may respond to minor breaches with 'proportional' countermeasures. Indeed, it might be said that proportionality is a requirement of any countermeasures, whether in response to a material or a non-material breach.[115]

These standards certainly leave room for Israel to argue that its retaliation was justified, but the matter is not free from doubt. The PA is obliged to 'take all measures necessary in order to prevent acts of terrorism, crime and hostilities' directed at Israel.[116] Violation of this duty of prevention would surely constitute material breach of the Oslo Accords: for Israel, security is a central 'object and purpose' of the Accords. As we shall see in Chapter 11, the PA's cooperation in security matters has sometimes fallen short. Still, it is not entirely clear that the Jerusalem bombing itself was a product of the PA's failure to take 'all necessary steps' to combat terrorism. In so far as there was a factual dispute on this point, the parties should have availed themselves of the dispute-resolution mechanisms under the Accords—mechanisms whose purpose is, in part, to review disputed facts.

Moreover, even Israel conceded that the PA had made some effort to comply with its anti-terror obligations, even during the strife of 1997. The PA's partial breach of a material obligation might not amount to a material breach. Given that the PA has performed at least part of its anti-terror obligations, a more proportional response by Israel would have been to suspend only part of its financial obligations—for example, to reduce

[112] Avi Machlis, 'Israel relents on withheld Palestinian cash', *Financial Times*, 15 Oct. 1997.
[113] Harris, 'Ne'eman to hold back money' (quoting Shai Bazak).
[114] Vienna Convention on the Law of Treaties, 23 May 1969, UN Doc. A/CONF. 39/27, Art. 60(1), 60(3)(b).
[115] Cf. D. W. Greig, 'Reciprocity, Proportionality, and the Law of Treaties', 34 *Va. J. Int'l L.* 295, 360 (1994).
[116] Interim Agreement, Art. XV(1).

rather than eliminating altogether its required payments to the PA. In a way, this is the path Israel eventually chose: it later did resume its payments to the PA.

The funding issue is moot for now, but another important economic issue continues to divide the parties: Israel's practice of sealing off the West Bank and Gaza following terrorist attacks. The PA complains that these closures have suffocated the Palestinian economy. Israel counters that they are necessary security measures.

There is little doubt that closure of the territories hurts the Palestinian economy. Every year since 1967, tens of thousands of Palestinians have commuted from the territories to jobs in Israel, mostly in construction. In 1992 these commuters numbered more than 100,000, but in early 1993, after a series of violent incidents, Prime Minister Rabin sealed off the territories and declared that Israel would rely less heavily on Palestinian workers in the future.[117] Since then the number of Palestinian labourers in Israel has decreased substantially, and the PA has sought to provide substitute employment in the form of short-term public works jobs, while Israel has replaced Palestinian labour with workers from third world countries such as Romania and Thailand. Still, tens of thousands of Palestinians in the West Bank and Gaza still depend on jobs in Israel.[118] By preventing these Palestinians from reaching their jobs, the closures have had a 'severe impact' on the economy of the West Bank and Gaza Strip.[119] Lost wages have led to declining income-tax revenues for the PA, which has struggled to avoid multimillion dollar budget deficits.[120] And the closures have helped discourage private investment in the West Bank and Gaza Strip; uncertainty and delays in the transit of goods do not create a hospitable environment for external trade.[121] Of course, a variety of other factors have hurt the Palestinian economy since the adoption of the Oslo Accords—for example, agricultural exports have been hampered by

[117] See Einhorn, 'The Customs Union', text at nn. 103–6. The Barak government has continued the practice of closing off the territories for security reasons. See, e.g., 'Israel Seals off West Bank Towns', *Toronto Star*, 12 Aug. 1999.

[118] See 'Economic Relations Between Israel and the Palestinian Authority', *Middle East News Items*, 9 Feb. 1998 (Info-Prod Research, available on LEXIS/NEWS) (reporting that 45,000 Palestinians hold permits to work in Israel proper and another 12,000 work in industrial parks and Israeli settlements in the West Bank and Gaza).

[119] Einhorn, 'The Customs Union', text at n. 131.

[120] See, e.g., 'Israel, Palestinians discuss economic plight of territories', *Agence France-Presse*, 27 Aug. 1996 (reporting a UN official's view that the PA might face 'financial collapse' because of Israel's closure of the territories).

[121] See Oussama Kanaan, 'Uncertainty deters private investment in the West Bank and Gaza Strip', *Information Access Co.* (International Monetary Fund Finance and Development, June 1998) (available on LEXIS/NEWS), at 34 (asserting that the closures have 'dampened average demand and driven up production costs while sharply increasing the variability of demand and costs', thereby creating a poor climate for investment); Mel Levine, 'Palestinian Economic Progress Under the Oslo Agreements', 19 *Fordham Int'l L. J.* 1393, 1405 (1996).

adverse agricultural conditions at home and unfavourable market conditions abroad[122]—but there is no denying that the closures have had a significant adverse impact on the Palestinian economy.

As a legal matter, do security considerations justify the closures? On the one hand, the Interim Agreement states that the Agreement 'shall not prejudice Israel's right, for security and safety considerations, to close the crossing points to Israel and to prohibit or limit the entry into Israel of persons and of vehicles from the West Bank and the Gaza Strip'.[123] Similarly, entry into Israel 'shall be subject to Israeli laws and procedures regulating entry into Israel . . .'.[124] Moreover, general international law plainly permits a state to restrict the entry of non-citizens into its territory.[125] On the other hand, general international law also requires Israel to respect the human rights of the Palestinian residents of the West Bank and Gaza Strip, including their 'right to liberty of movement' within their territory and their right to 'leave any country, including their own'.[126]

In any event, states can enter into agreements obliging them to permit entry of non-citizens, and to some extent the Oslo Accords impose such an obligation on Israel. The Interim Agreement provides that regulation of Palestinian travel into Israel shall respect 'the importance of the economic and social life, development programs and projects, and emergency health care services of the Palestinian population'.[127] The Protocol on Economic Relations provides that each side 'will attempt to maintain the normality of movement of labor between them, subject to each side's right to determine from time to time the extent and conditions of the labor movement into its area'.[128] The same provision provides for discussion in the joint Economic Committee if 'the normal movement is suspended temporarily by either side'—implying that closures cannot be permanent, and that they are the exception rather than the 'normal' order of things. The Protocol also requires 'free movement of industrial goods free of any restrictions including customs and import taxes between the two sides, subject to each side's legislation'.[129] Similarly, '[t]here will be free movement of agricultural produce, free of customs and import taxes', subject to a variety of health and safety restrictions.[130]

122 'Inverted Cornucopia Worsening Performance of Gaza's Agricultural Exports', *International Market Insight Reports*, 6 Mar. 1998 (FT Asia Intelligence Wire, available on LEXIS/NEWS); 'Direct Export of Gazan Tomatoes to US: Update', *International Market Insight Reports*, 20 Mar. 1998.

123 Interim Agreement, Annexe I, Art. IX(1)(d).

124 Ibid., Art. IX(1)(c).

125 See Vagts, 'The Proposed Expatriation Tax', 579 n. 13; Francis A. Gabor, 'Reflections on the Freedom of Movement in Light of the Dismantled "Iron Curtain" ', 65 *Tul. L. Rev.* 849, 851 (1991) (concluding that the right of emigration is only a 'one-way freedom'); Watson, 'Progress for Pilgrims?', 508–9. But cf. Nafziger, 'The General Admission of Aliens', 804–7.

126 International Covenant on Civil and Political Rights, Art. 12(1) and (2).

127 Ibid., Art. IX(2)(b).

128 Gaza–Jericho Agreement, Annexe IV, Art. VII(1).

129 Ibid., Art. IX(1).

130 Ibid., Art. VIII(1).

Taken together, these provisions do suggest that Israel has the right to impose closures 'for security and safety reasons', but that such closures should be considered both temporary and extraordinary rather than permanent and normal. Moreover, Israel's limited right to impose closure must, like all obligations under the Accords, be exercised in good faith.[131] This means, at a minimum, that Israel must have an honest belief that full closure of the territories will prevent terrorist attacks and otherwise enhance Israeli security. It also means that closure cannot be imposed simply as a means of collective economic punishment of all Palestinians for the crimes of a few.

In sum, the economic provisions of the Oslo Accords point as much towards economic separation as economic union, towards competition rather than cooperation. In this respect the Accords merely reflect the reality on the ground. Israel's decision to withhold PA funds was clearly inconsistent with its obligations under the Accords. The decision might have been legally justifiable as a response to the PA's own violations of the Accords, but only if Israel first exhausted its remedies under the Accords and general international law. Israel's closures of its borders are legally permissible so long as they are temporary, extraordinary, and imposed as a good-faith security measure rather than a form of collective punishment.

People-to-people

The Note for the Record also cites an 'Israeli responsibility' to negotiate an agreement with the Palestinians on the 'people-to-people' programme—a plan to facilitate direct contacts between ordinary Israelis and Palestinians in order to enhance mutual understanding and respect. This responsibility grows out of the Interim Agreement, which required the parties to 'establish a mechanism to develop programs of cooperation between them' and created a people-to-people programme designed to enhance 'dialogue and relations' between the two peoples, to 'foster public debate and involvement, to remove barriers to interaction, and to increase the people to people exchange and interaction'.[132] Again, it is not clear why the Note lists this as an 'Israeli responsibility'; the Accords clearly oblige both sides to cooperate in developing people-to-people programmes.

Progress on such programmes has been modest. The parties have sponsored a joint tourism school; it now operates at the Ben-Gurion University of the Negev and at Bethlehem University. In February 1998 the Israeli co-

[131] Cf. Vienna Convention on the Law of Treaties, Art. 26.
[132] Interim Agreement, Art. XXV(1) and Annexe VI, Art. VIII(2)–(3).

chair of the people-to-people committee, Eytan Bentsur, proposed a 'Tolerance Game' that models peaceful coexistence of Muslims and Jews in medieval Spain; the Palestinian Center for Peace is planning to translate the game into Arabic. Bentsur also proposed 'Twinning Schools' to bring Palestinian and Israeli teenagers together, as well as an Internet database on joint Israeli–Palestinian projects. And he suggested a sort of 'sister city' programme to promote understanding between adjacent Palestinian and Israeli cities, which might in turn adopt 'sister cities' abroad.[133]

These proposals may not be earth-shaking, but they would seem to comply with Israel's obligation to negotiate and implement the people-to-people programme in good faith. The PA's willingness to implement at least some of Israel's proposals is likewise an encouraging sign. In any event, either party's failure to honour its obligations under this programme probably would not amount to a 'material' breach of the Oslo Accords, since a material breach must involve violation of a provision 'essential to the accomplishment of the object or purpose of the treaty'.[134] The people-to-people programme is surely a worthy one, but it is not the main object or purpose of the Oslo Accords.

To summarize this Chapter, it would appear that most of the so-called 'Israeli responsibilities' on ports, passages, and economics are really joint obligations of negotiation and implementation. In particular, Israel and the PA are both obliged to negotiate and implement in good faith. If good faith is defined as 'honesty in fact', Israel's negotiating posture on safe passage, international passages, the ports, and the people-to-people programme would generally seem to pass muster. On ports and passages, Israel's main negotiating concern has been security, and the Oslo Accords do call on the parties to make suitable arrangements for security.

But Israel's decision to withhold funding for the PA was plainly inconsistent with its obligations under the Paris Protocol, justifiable only as a response to violations by the PA. Given that the PA had at least partly performed its anti-terror obligations, a partial suspension of payments by Israel would have been a more proportional response. Finally, Israel's closures of PA-controlled areas are justifiable only as security measures, not as punitive ones.

133 See Jay Bushinsky, 'Bentsur touts "Tolerance Game" to boost Israel–PA ties', *Jerus. Post*, 20 Feb. 1998; 'Joint Israeli–Palestinian Projects', *Risk Monitor Briefing*, 22 Feb. 1998 (Info-Prod Research, available on LEXIS/NEWS).

134 Vienna Convention on the Law of Treaties, Art. 60(3)(b).

9

Israeli Human Rights Obligations

There is a striking paucity of human rights provisions in the Oslo Accords. The first Oslo Accord—the 1993 Declaration of Principles—said little about human rights. Its Preamble spoke in general terms of the parties' 'mutual legitimate and political rights', but it did not contain operative provisions dedicated to the protection of human rights. The 1995 Interim Agreement did contain some human-rights provisions, such as those relating to prisoners, as well as a vague mutual obligation to 'exercise their powers and responsibilities . . . with due regard to internationally-accepted norms and principles of human rights and the rule of law'.[1] But, as we shall see in a moment, the parties may read this 'due regard' clause as imposing no particular legal obligation at all. To be sure, the Wye River Memorandum reiterates that Palestinian police must pay 'due regard' to human rights norms, and the Sharm el-Sheikh Memorandum deals again with prisoner release.[2] Taken as a whole, however, the Oslo Accords do not reflect any particular obsession with human rights.

The parties each have their reasons for downplaying human-rights norms in the Accords. The Palestinians have traditionally been sharply critical of Israeli human rights practices in the occupied territories, but now they find themselves obliged to cooperate with Israel on security matters and to police their own people. Israel, for its part, has traditionally argued that the threat of terrorism justifies its policies in the occupied territories, and now Israel also expects the PA to combat terror with vigour.

A comprehensive review of the parties' respective human rights records is beyond the scope of this book, but in so far as the Oslo Accords impose human rights obligations on the parties, some consideration of the issue is indispensable. Accordingly, this Chapter begins by critiquing the parties' apparent belief that the Oslo Accords do not incorporate general norms of human rights law. Next, the Chapter examines precisely what 'norms' must be respected by the parties—the international law of human

[1] Interim Agreement, Art. XIX. Similarly, general human rights obligations appear elsewhere in the Accords. See, e.g., ibid., Annexe I, Art. XI(1) (obliging security personnel to respect 'human rights norms'); ibid., Annexe IV, Art. II(7)(h)(1) (providing that extradition should be carried out in accordance with 'internationally-accepted norms of human rights regarding criminal investigations').

[2] Wye River Memorandum, ¶II.C.4; Sharm el-Sheikh Memorandum, ¶3.

rights, the humanitarian law of war, or both? Thereafter the Chapter applies the relevant norms to the most controversial Israeli practices in the West Bank and the Gaza Strip: extrajudicial killing, torture, arbitrary arrest and detention, denial of a fair trial, deportations, and demolitions. The Chapter concludes by assessing Israeli compliance with the few specific human rights obligations in the Oslo Accords: the release of prisoners, and access to the Holy Places. PA human rights practices are taken up in Part IV.

Human rights in the Oslo Accords

As was mentioned earlier, the Interim Agreement does contain a general statement on human rights: the parties are to 'exercise their powers and responsibilities . . . with due regard to internationally-accepted norms and principles of human rights and the rule of law'. It is possible that one or both the parties believe that this language fails explicitly to incorporate human rights law by reference, and thus creates no legal obligation at all. This interpretation is incompatible with the plain meaning and general usage of the clause.

The question is relevant because the clause, if binding, expands the obligations of both parties, especially the PA. There is as yet no Palestinian state that is party to human rights treaties or subject to customary law. If the provision does incorporate human rights norms, it clearly would enlarge existing Palestinian obligations. As for Israel, it is true that Israel is already bound by many of the 'internationally-accepted norms and principles of human rights' mentioned in the provision, since Israel is a party to a variety of human rights treaties and is further bound by the customary international law of human rights. But the 'due regard' provision refers to more than those norms that already bind Israel; it speaks of *all* 'internationally-accepted norms', not just those to which Israel has consented. In sum, if the clause is binding, then it broadens the human rights obligations of both parties.

Does the 'due regard' clause incorporate human rights norms, or is it merely hortatory? Put another way, what does it mean to pay 'due regard' to a legal norm? There is some state practice to suggest that 'due regard' requires more than just a passing glance. The phrase appears in a variety of legal instruments, ranging from treaties on human rights to the UN Charter to the UN Convention on the Law of the Sea.[3] Sometimes treaty

[3] See, e.g., International Covenant on Economic, Social and Cultural Rights, 16 Dec. 1966, 993 U.N.T.S. 3, Art. 2(3) ('Developing countries, with due regard to human rights and their national economy, may determine to what extent they would guarantee' certain economic

drafters use slightly different words than 'due', such as 'reasonable regard' or simply 'regard', suggesting that there are greater and lesser degrees of 'regard'.[4] More to the point, states seem to attach varying levels of obligation to a requirement of 'due regard', usually depending on the importance of the norm to which 'regard' must be paid.

For example, Article 4 of the Convention on Racial Discrimination obliges states party to adopt measures 'designed to eradicate all incitement to . . . [racial] discrimination', for example by criminalizing hate speech and outlawing racist organizations, 'with due regard to the principles embodied in the Universal Declaration of Human Rights'. The United States interprets these provisions as 'not imposing on a State party the obligation to take any action impairing the right to freedom of speech and freedom of association'.[5] Of course the United States might have taken the position even in the absence of the 'due regard' clause, but one might also conclude that the United States believes that the 'due regard' clause has some legal consequence. Likewise, the British government regards Article 4 as limited by the Universal Declaration.[6] Other governments interpret these provisions as requiring both legislation and respect for freedoms of speech and association.[7] The government of Germany arguably gives less effect to the 'due regard' clause, taking the view that

rights to non-nationals); International Convention on the Elimination of All Forms of Racial Discrimination, 7 Jan. 1966, 5 I.L.M. 352 (1966), Art. 4 (requiring states to eradicate racial incitement 'with due regard to the principles embodied in the Universal Declaration of Human Rights'); European Convention for the Protection of Human Rights and Fundamental Freedoms, 4 Nov. 1950, 312 U.N.T.S. 221, Art. 63(3) ('The provisions of this Convention shall be applied in such territories with due regard, however, to local requirements'); African Charter on Human and Peoples' Rights, 27 June 1981, 21 I.L.M. 59 (1981), Art. 22 (providing that all peoples have the right to economic, social, and cultural development 'with due regard to their freedom and identity'); UN Charter, 26 June 1945, T.S. 993, Art. 23(1) (providing for election of non-permanent members to the Security Council, 'due regard being specially paid' to various factors); Convention on the Law of the Sea, 10 Dec. 1982, UN A/CONF. 62/122, 21 I.L.M. 1261 (1982), Arts. 56(2), 58(3), 87(2) (requiring 'due regard' for the rights, duties, and interests of other states in certain circumstances); Rio Declaration on Environment and Development, 14 June 1992, 31 I.L.M. 874 (1992), Principle 16 (providing for internalization of environmental costs, 'with due regard to the public interest').

[4] See, e.g., Treaty of Extradition, US–UK, 8 June 1972, 28 U.S.T. 227, Art. X (providing that the Requested Party shall decide among competing extradition requests 'having regard to all the circumstances'); Philip Allott, 'Power Sharing in the Law of the Sea', 77 *Am. J. Int'l L.* 1, 11 (1983) (noting that delegates to the UN Conference on the Law of the Sea 'spent countless hours' on a 'number of subtle distinctions', including the distinction between 'due regard' and 'reasonable regard').

[5] UN GAOR 3rd Comm., 20th Sess., 1318th mtg., ¶59, UN Doc. A/C.3/SR.1318 (1965) (statement of the US representative); 1978 *Digest of U.S. Practice in International Law* 443. See generally Stephanie Farrior, 'Molding the Matrix: The Historical and Theoretical Foundations of International Law Concerning Hate Speech', 14 *Berk. J. Int'l L.* 3, 49–50 (1996).

[6] See Theodor Meron, 'The Meaning and Reach of the International Convention on the Elimination of All Forms of Racial Discrimination', 79 *Am. J. Int'l L.* 283, 301 n. 90 (1985).

[7] Ibid. (describing the Belgian view).

'dissemination of opinions of racial superiority should be punishable if it was intended to create racial discrimination or hatred'.[8] The Committee on Racial Discrimination seems to side with the German view, arguing that the 'due regard' clause cannot be read as 'cancelling' the obligations relating to hate speech.[9] Scholarly opinion is as variegated as state practice, with some scholars reading the 'due regard' clause as establishing a 'balancing test',[10] and others arguing that 'due regard' to the Universal Declaration means that the norms of the Declaration control in the event of conflict.[11]

In other contexts, states and scholars have interpreted 'due regard' clauses as imposing some sort of legal obligation, though not necessarily a full legal obligation. The Statute for the International Criminal Tribunal for the Former Yugoslavia (ICTY) provides that trials take place 'with full respect for the rights of the accused and due regard for the protection of victims and witnesses'.[12] According to one commentator, 'due regard' for the protection of witnesses 'may take many forms', including the use of pseudonyms, anonymity, voice and image distortion, and detailed rules for rape victims, including a rape-shield rule excluding evidence of prior sexual history.[13] This practice might suggest that the responsible actors at the Tribunal believe they are bound by the 'due regard' clause. The constitutional law of Ireland furnishes another example. Ireland's Constitution 'acknowledges the right to life of the unborn' and guarantees respect for that life 'with due regard to the equal right to life of the mother'. The Irish High Court of Justice has interpreted this 'due regard' clause as permitting abortion when there is a 'real and substantial risk to the life, as distinct from the health, of the mother'.[14] At the same time, there is some precedent suggesting that a 'due regard' clause imposes no binding obligations at all. Consider an 1889 agreement in which certain American railroads were given the right to operate on Crow Indian lands in exchange for a promise to 'operate trains with due regard for the rights of Indians'.

[8] Ibid.

[9] Professor Meron argues that the Committee has merely 'paid lip service' to the due regard clause, 'while expressing clear preference for the application of the norms stated in Article 4'. Ibid., at 300.

[10] Farrior, 'Molding the Matrix', 49 ('This language incorporates all the rights in the Universal Declaration into a balancing test').

[11] Meron, 'The Meaning and Reach of the International Convention', 300 (asserting that the provisions of Article 4 'do not have the purpose or effect of destroying the rights or freedoms' stated in the Universal Declaration).

[12] Statute of the International Criminal Tribunal, 32 I.L.M. 1163 (1993), Art. 20(1).

[13] See Sean D. Murphy, 'Developments in International Criminal Law: Progress and Jurisprudence of the International Criminal Tribunal for the Former Yugoslavia', 93 *Am. J. Int'l L.* 57, 84 (1999) (citing ICTY Rules 69 and 75).

[14] *Society for the Protection of Unborn Children v. Grogan*, 1989 I.R. 753, 764–5 (Ir. H. Ct. 1992) (interpreting Art. 40.3.3 of the Irish Constitution).

When a Burlington Northern superintendent was asked at a deposition whether the railroad showed 'due regard' for Indians, he replied (among other things) that the railroad showed due regard 'to everyone it ran over everywhere'.[15]

Taken as a whole, the better view is that a 'due regard' clause imposes some legal obligation on parties to comply with the norms to which regard must be paid. The state practice following this view appears to be more extensive, and more persuasive, than the practice that gives it no effect whatsoever. That the parties to the Oslo Accords (and their negotiators) may have intended the clause to be a nullity is not dispositive. Treaties are to be interpreted 'in good faith in accordance with the ordinary meaning' of their terms 'in their context' and in light of the treaty's 'object and purpose'. The 'ordinary meaning' of the phrase 'due regard' to human rights norms suggests that some attention to human rights must be paid. It is true that Article 31(4) of the Vienna Convention provides: 'A special meaning shall be given to a term if it is established that the parties so intended.' As one commentator has observed, 'This provision would appear to place the burden squarely on the proponent of the special meaning.'[16] Neither party appears to have met this burden. The text does not offer any special meaning for the obligation to pay due regard to human rights norms. One should not lightly infer such a meaning in this case, where the human rights of individuals are at stake.

That said, the choice of words 'due regard' does suggest less than a full-scale incorporation of the norms to be 'regarded'. The apparent existence of a hierarchy of 'regard'—ranging from 'regard' to 'due regard' to 'reasonable regard'—further suggests that 'due regard' means something less than punctilious observance of every jot and tittle of the norms to be 'regarded'. But it also means something more than a self-serving announcement that 'due regard' has been extended to those norms. In the context of the Oslo Accords, 'due regard' to human rights norms would mean at least a good faith effort to comply with the most important norms of human rights law. Accordingly, we now consider precisely what norms the parties must respect.

[15] Phillip Allen White, 'The Tribal Exhaustion Doctrine: "Just Stay on the Good Roads, and You've Got Nothing to Worry About" ', 22 *Am. Indian L. Rev.* 65, 166 (1997) (quoting 'Crash History Boosts Plaintiffs' Case in Wrongful Death Trial', *Inside Litigation*, Mar. 1996, at 5).

[16] Martin A. Rogoff, 'Interpretation of International Agreements by Domestic Courts and the Politics of International Treaty Relations: Reflections On Some Recent Decisions Of The United States Supreme Court', 11 *Am. U.J. Int'l L. & Pol'y* 559, 577 (1996). Cf. also Baron Arnold Duncan McNair, *The Law of Treaties* (New York: Columbia University Press, 1938), 175–6 (arguing that the plain meaning creates a 'presumption' that can be rebutted, and that the party seeking to rebut it bears the 'burden of proof').

Humanitarian law, human rights law, or both?

What law governs Israeli conduct in the West Bank and Gaza Strip: the humanitarian law of war, the international law of human rights, or both? As we saw in Chapter 7 (on Israeli settlements), the extent to which the law of belligerent occupation applies to the West Bank and Gaza Strip has been a matter of fierce academic and political debate ever since Israel took those areas in the 1967 War. Chapter 7 concluded that Israeli practices in those territories are generally governed by the law of belligerent occupation, including the Fourth Geneva Convention Relative to the Protection of Civilian Persons in Time of War[17] of 1949 (the 'Fourth Geneva Convention') and the Hague Convention Respecting the Laws and Customs of War on Land of 1907 and its attached Regulations.[18] Chapter 7 did not consider the more general question of whether human rights law might apply (along with humanitarian law) to the territories still under Israeli occupation. Nor did Chapter 7 consider whether humanitarian law applies at all in areas now under the PA's jurisdiction. Both of these questions are taken up here.

As to the first question, the better view is that both humanitarian law and human rights law govern Israeli human rights practices in areas still under Israeli occupation. The major human rights treaties do not expressly limit themselves to time of peace. Some human rights instruments, such as the Genocide Convention and the Torture Convention, explicitly state that they apply in both war and peace.[19] The more 'general' human rights conventions, such as the International Covenant on Civil and Political Rights and the regional human rights treaties, contain provisions permitting some derogation in time of war, but these derogation provisions typically require states to make formal notification of derogation, and they forbid suspension of the most important human rights obligations even in time of war.[20] These explicit exceptions for wartime derogation clearly imply that the major human rights conventions do normally apply in full in time of war.

[17] Convention (No. IV) Relative to the Protection of Civilian Persons in Time of War, 12 Aug. 1949, 75 U.N.T.S. 287.

[18] Convention (No. IV) Respecting the Laws and Customs of War on Land (with Annexe of Regulations), 18 Oct. 1907, 205 C.T.S. 277 (French), 1910 U.K.T.S. 9.

[19] Convention on the Prevention and Punishment of the Crime of Genocide, 9 Dec. 1948, 78 U.N.T.S. 277, Art. I ('genocide, whether committed in time of peace or in time of war, is a crime under international law . . .'); Convention Against Torture and other Cruel, Inhuman, or Degrading Treatment or Punishment, 10 Dec. 1984, 23 I.L.M. 1027 (1984), Art. 2(2) (providing that 'a state of war' may not be invoked to justify torture). Cf. also Statute of the International Criminal Tribunal, Art. 4 (criminalizing genocide in time of war and peace).

[20] See, e.g., International Covenant on Civil and Political Rights, 16 Dec. 1966, 999 U.N.T.S. 171, Art. 4; American Convention on Human Rights, 22 Nov. 1969, 9 I.L.M. 673 (1970), Art. 27; European Convention on Human Rights, Art. 15.

One argument against the applicability of human rights law to Israeli conduct in the territories is that human rights law is concerned only with a state's treatment of its own nationals inside its borders, not its treatment of aliens. That doctrine may have been a feature of human rights law in the past, but modern human rights treaties plainly reject it. The Civil and Political Covenant applies to 'all individuals' within a state's 'territory and subject to its jurisdiction'.[21] This provision makes clear both that aliens are covered by the Covenant and that a state's obligation to protect human rights is not necessarily limited to its 'territory' but also extends to people within its 'jurisdiction'. (The term 'jurisdiction' presumably includes Israel's extraterritorial jurisdiction, which, the Interim Agreement makes clear, can extend to people in the West Bank and Gaza Strip.[22]) The inclusive language of the Civil and Political Covenant is typical of most major human rights treaties.[23] This is not to say that human rights law forbids all distinctions between citizens and aliens; it does permit some such differentiation.[24] But the Civil and Political Covenant and other instruments establish a baseline of human rights to which all people, citizens and aliens, are entitled.

It might also be argued that the application of two sets of norms—humanitarian law and human rights law—might expose Israel to conflicting obligations. It is true that the two bodies of law are conceptually distinct; the military occupier is allowed more leeway in some realms and less in others. For example, humanitarian law restricts the relocation of the occupier's population into the occupied territory, whereas human rights law does not, and humanitarian law restricts deportation more rigorously than human rights law does. By and large, however, the two bodies of law point in the same direction, towards humane treatment of civilians. It is not so much that they conflict with each other, but that one sometimes imposes more restrictive rules than the other. There seems no reason that the two bodies of law cannot coexist, as indeed they do now in the Yugoslavia and Rwanda war crimes tribunals, which expose defendants to prosecution under Hague and Geneva law as well as the law of the Genocide Convention.

[21] International Covenant on Civil and Political Rights, Art. 2(1).

[22] See, e.g., Interim Agreement, Annexe IV, Art. I(7)(a) ('Israel has . . . criminal jurisdiction in accordance with its domestic laws over offenses committed in the [PA-controlled] Territory against Israel or an Israeli').

[23] See, e.g., Torture Convention, Art. 1(1) (defining torture as infliction of severe pain and suffering on 'any person'); European Convention on Human Rights, Art. 1 (providing that parties 'shall secure to everyone within their jurisdiction' the human rights enumerated in the Convention); American Convention on Human Rights, Art. 1(1) (providing that states must respect human rights of 'all persons subject to their jurisdiction'); ibid., Art. 1(2) (defining 'person' as 'every human being').

[24] Cf., e.g., Convention on Racial Discrimination, Art. I(2) (providing that the Convention 'shall not apply to distinctions, exclusions, restrictions or preferences made by a State Party to this Convention between citizens and non-citizens').

Finally, it might be argued that even if the 'due regard' clause in the Interim Agreement incorporates norms of 'human rights', it says nothing about humanitarian law. This argument is well-taken. Israel has traditionally opposed the application of the Fourth Geneva Convention to the territories, and the plain meaning of the 'due regard' clause is consistent with this view. Even so, the 'due regard' clause does not purport to *exclude* humanitarian law, even if it could do so. Put another way, the 'due regard' clause does not expand Israel's existing humanitarian obligations in the same way it expands Israel's human rights obligations, but nor does it derogate from existing humanitarian obligations.

Thus the answer to the first question is that human rights law does supplement humanitarian law in Israeli-occupied territory. The second question is whether any part of the West Bank and Gaza Strip still constitutes 'Israeli-occupied territory'. On one view, Israel's withdrawal means that PA-administered territories are no longer occupied, since they are not under Israel's 'effective control'.[25] This view emphasizes that occupation requires actual and not just hypothetical control of day-to-day life on the ground. A competing view is that Israel's withdrawal was not complete, since Israel retains overall responsibility for external security even as to Area A, and thus that the territories are still occupied and therefore governed by the humanitarian law of belligerent occupation.[26] On this view, the status of Area B is especially problematic, for although the PA has responsibility for 'public order' there, Israel retains 'overriding responsibility for security' for the purpose of 'protecting Israelis and confronting the threat of terrorism'.[27] This overriding authority is not just hypothetical, the argument runs; Israeli forces in fact routinely patrol Area B, and it is therefore still occupied territory.

Occupation law does stress actual rather than theoretical control. Article 6 of the Fourth Geneva Convention provides that most relevant provisions of the Convention continue to bind the Occupying Power 'for the duration of the occupation, to the extent that such Power exercises the functions of government in such territory'. Similarly, Article 42 of the

[25] Eyal Benvenisti, 'The Israeli–Palestinian Declaration of Principles: A Framework for Future Settlement', 4 *Eur. J. Int'l L.* 542, 548 (1993).

[26] Al-Haq, *A Human Rights Assessment of the Declaration of Principles on Interim Self-Government Arrangements for Palestinians* (1993), 9 ('The legal status of the West Bank and Gaza Strip continues to be that of occupied territories, and Israel the Occupying Power because Israel will continue to hold all authority regarding external security, border control' and partial authority in other spheres); John Quigley, 'The Israel–PLO Agreements versus the Geneva Civilians Convention', 7 *Palestine Yb. Int'l L.* 45, 56–62 (1992/4) (arguing that the Declaration of Principles and Gaza–Jericho Agreement did not alter the applicability of the Fourth Geneva Convention).

[27] Interim Agreement, Art. XIII(2)(a). Cf. Joel Singer, 'The West Bank and Gaza Strip: Phase Two', *Justice*, No. 7, Dec. 1995, p. 10 (arguing that this 'overriding' responsibility 'shall take precedence' over the PA's authority for public order).

Hague Convention provides that territory is occupied when it is 'actually placed under the authority of the hostile army', but only 'where such authority has been established and can be exercised'. These two tests are similar in so far as they stress actual rather than hypothetical authority. They differ in that one stresses 'governmental' functions and the other 'army' authority, but plainly both types of control are relevant in deciding whether a power is an occupant.

Applying these standards, it seems fair to conclude that Israel still does occupy Area C, since it has not withdrawn its military forces from that area. That the PA exercises civilian functions there is not dispositive, since Area C is sparsely populated and is not the focus of Palestinian civilian administration, and the PA lacks civil authority over land-related matters there. Area B, however, is probably not 'occupied' territory because Israel has withdrawn from it and because the PA exercises substantial civilian control there. It is true that Israel continues to patrol Area B, and that it maintains responsibility for external security, but it no longer maintains a permanent military presence in that area, nor is it the sole civilian administrator. Likewise, Area A would no longer seem to be occupied territory: Israel has withdrawn from it, and PA authority there is at its maximum. That Israel maintains responsibility for external security is not, in itself, enough to rise to the level of 'occupation', which implies day-to-day control on the ground.

This conclusion does not necessarily imply that the PA is a state. The absence of military occupation does not automatically indicate the presence of an independent state. It is true that occupation law looks with disfavour on 'puppet governments' established by the occupant to do its bidding, but, as we shall see in Part IV, the parties seem to have successfully created a Palestinian entity that is neither state nor puppet.

In sum, humanitarian law has ceased to apply in the areas no longer 'occupied' by Israel—Area A and, most likely, Area B. Only human rights law applies there. In Area C, in which the Israeli military occupation continues, both human rights law and humanitarian law continue to be applicable. Applying both sources of law, we now turn to the Israeli human rights practices most relevant to Israeli–Palestinian relations. For reasons of space, a full consideration of all these issues is not possible here, but some treatment of them is essential.[28]

[28] For more extended analysis of Israeli human rights practice generally, see, e.g., Esther R. Cohen, *Human Rights in the Israeli-Occupied Territories 1967–1982* (Manchester: Manchester University Press 1985); Richard A. Falk and Burns H. Weston, 'The Relevance of International Law to Palestinian Rights in the West Bank and Gaza: In Legal Defense of the Intifada', 32 *Harv. Int'l L.J.* 129 (1991); Yoram Dinstein, 'The International Law of Belligerent Occupation and Human Rights', 8 *Isr. Yb. Hum. Rts.* 104 (1978); John Quigley, 'The Israel–PLO Agreements versus the Geneva Civilians Convention', 7 *Palestine Yb. Int'l L.* 45

Extrajudicial killing

Since the Interim Agreement, dozens of Palestinians have died at the hands of Israeli military and police officials. Many of these deaths have come about during violent clashes between Palestinian demonstrators and Israeli security forces. Others resulted from Israeli undercover operations in Palestinian areas, though the number of deaths related to undercover operations has apparently decreased since the adoption of the Interim Agreement. In a few cases, detainees have been beaten or shaken to death by Israeli prison guards. Still other deaths resulted from confrontations between Israeli security personnel and Palestinians at military checkpoints and roadblocks in the occupied territories. In some cases, Israeli security officials said they had acted in self-defence; in others, they said that the Palestinians in question had refused to stop at a checkpoint.[29]

The murder of Palestinian prisoners is a clear violation of human rights law, as is the reckless killing of prisoners. Article 6(1) of the International Covenant on Civil and Political Rights, to which Israel is a party, provides: 'No one shall be arbitrarily deprived of his life.' Similarly, Article 3 of the Universal Declaration of Human Rights provides: 'Everyone has the right to life, liberty and the security of person.' These provisions do not forbid all state-sponsored killing; in certain circumstances, for example, the Covenant expressly permits the use of the death penalty.[30] The Covenant does not address use of force in self-defence, but other human rights instruments explicitly permit a state's police or military personnel to defend themselves with lethal force when it is absolutely necessary to do so.[31] On the other hand, the Covenant outlaws all 'arbitrary' killings, not just intentional or premeditated homicide, implying that reckless or even negligent homicide can be 'arbitrary'. Thus when Israeli interrogators

(1992/4); Meir Shamgar, 'The Observance of International Law in the Administered Territories', 1 *Isr. Y.B. Hum. Rts.* 262 (1971).

29 See generally Amnesty International, *AI Report 1999* (London: Amnesty International, 1999), and *AI Reports* for earlier years; US Dept. of State, 'Country Report on Human Rights Practices for 1998—The Occupied Territories' (Washington, DC: US Dept. of State, 1999), and 'Country Reports' for earlier years. Other relevant sources for human rights data include the Israeli organization B'Tselem and the Palestinian organization Al-Haq.

30 Under Article 6(2) of the Covenant, the death penalty is permissible only when carried out 'pursuant to a final judgement rendered by a competent court'. Other human rights treaties also permit the death penalty in certain circumstances. See, e.g., American Convention on Human Rights, Art. 4(2); European Convention on Human Rights, Art. 2(1). An optional Protocol to the European Convention provides: 'The death penalty shall be abolished. No one shall be condemned to such penalty or executed.' Protocol No. 6, opened for signature 28 Apr. 1983, E.T.S. 114, 22 I.L.M. 538 (1983) (entered into force 1 Mar. 1985), Art. 1. Most but not all parties to the European Convention have adopted the Protocol.

31 See, e.g., European Convention on Human Rights, Art. 2(2)(a).

beat a prisoner to death—even without intending to kill the prisoner—the interrogators' conduct is surely 'arbitrary' within the meaning of human rights law.[32]

Humanitarian law also prohibits extrajudicial killing of prisoners. Article 46 of the Hague Regulations provides simply that 'the lives of persons ... must be respected'. Article 32 of the Fourth Geneva Convention flatly prohibits parties from 'taking any measure ... to cause ... extermination of protected persons'.[33] This prohibition 'applies not only to murder, torture, corporal punishment, [and] mutilation ... but also to any other measures of brutality whether applied by civilian or military agents'.[34] The death penalty is permitted, but only after a 'final judgment confirming such death sentence'.[35]

The killing of Palestinians at security checkpoints raises more complex questions. There is no question that law-enforcement personnel can pursue and detain people who defy lawful instructions or orders. But can they use lethal force? The Civil and Political Covenant and the Universal Declaration are silent on when and whether the use of lethal force to apprehend a fleeing suspect is 'arbitrary'. The drafters of the Covenant did not enumerate the circumstances in which lethal force is permissible because it 'would convey the impression that the exceptions were more important than the right [to life] itself'.[36] None the less, it has been said that the term 'arbitrary' was intended to provide the 'highest possible level of protection' to the right of life, and that an 'international consensus' has concluded that the term includes deaths 'resulting from excessive use of force by law-enforcement personnel'.[37] Indeed, the Human Rights

[32] See B. G. Ramcharan, 'The Concept and Dimensions of the Right to Life', in B. G. Ramcharan (ed.), *The Right to Life in International Law* (Dordrecht; Boston: Martinus Nijhoff, 1985), 28 (asserting that there is an 'international consensus' that deaths resulting from 'torture or from ill-treatment in prison or detention' are 'arbitrary' within the meaning of the Civil and Political Covenant).

[33] 'Protected persons' are 'those who, at a given moment and in any manner whatsoever, find themselves, in case of a conflict or occupation, in the hands of a Party to the conflict or Occupying Power of which they are not nationals.' Fourth Geneva Convention, Art. 4, ¶1.

[34] Ibid., Art. 32, second sentence.

[35] Ibid., Art. 75, ¶2. Even then, the Occupying Power must give the Protecting Power six months' notice of the proposed execution. Ibid., Art. 75, ¶3. Moreover, the death penalty may be imposed only for the most serious offences. Ibid., Art. 68, ¶2.

[36] Angela K. Carlson-Whitley, Note, 'Dowry Death: A Violation of the Right to Life Under Article Six of the International Covenant on Civil and Political Rights', 17 *U. Puget Sound L. Rev.* 637, 655 (1994), citing B. G. Ramcharan, 'The Drafting History of Treaty Provisions on the Right to Life: The Drafting History of Article 6 of the International Covenant on Civil and Political Rights', in Ramcharan, *The Right to Life*, 42, 54. Some delegates to the drafting committee for the Covenant did favour enumeration, but they were outvoted. See Carlson-Whitley, 'Dowry Death', 655 and n. 139.

[37] See B. G. Ramcharan, 'Concept and Dimensions', 27–8.

Committee has interpreted the Covenant as restricting the use of lethal force by law enforcement officers.[38]

The European Convention does seem to permit deadly force to arrest even when a suspect does not pose an immediate threat to others, but only when 'absolutely necessary'.[39] Of course the European Convention is not applicable to Israel, and in any event its limited endorsement of lethal force may be out of step with trends in municipal law.[40] The better view is that deadly force should be confined to cases in which the fleeing suspect poses an immediate threat to others. Measured by this standard, Israeli practice has sometimes fallen short.

Similar legal questions are raised by the killing of Palestinians at demonstrations and riots. The general prohibition against 'arbitrary' deprivations of life would seem to cover most such killing. True, the European Convention permits lethal force if 'absolutely necessary' when 'lawfully taken' for 'quelling' a riot or demonstration. It is open to question, however, how often deadly force is 'absolutely necessary' to quell a demonstration or riot.

Whether the victim is a Palestinian prisoner, a fleeing suspect, or a demonstrator, lethal force by Israeli security officials is never justified on the grounds that the PA has also killed Palestinians in violation of human rights law. As a legal matter, one party's human rights violations can never justify another party's human rights violations. As we saw in Chapter 6, Article 60(5) of the Vienna Convention on the Law of Treaties forbids a party to a human rights treaty to suspend any 'provisions relating to the protection of the human person'. Likewise, the Civil and Political Covenant and other human rights instruments forbid parties to 'derogate' from (i.e. suspend) the obligation to respect human life, even in a 'time of public emergency'.[41] Indeed, the right to life is probably a peremptory norm of international law—*jus cogens*—from which no derogation is ever permitted.[42] The non-derogation provision of the Covenant

[38] Report of the Human Rights Committee (1982) (Guerrero Case), A/37/40, pp. 146–7. See Ramcharan, 'Concept and Dimensions', 26–7.

[39] See European Convention on Human Rights, Art. 2(2)(a)–(c). See also Code of Conduct for Law Enforcement Officials, U.N.G.A. GAOR (1979), Art. 3 and commentary.

[40] See, e.g., *Tennessee v. Garner*, 471 U.S. 1 (1985) (restricting the use of deadly force to apprehend fleeing felons).

[41] International Covenant on Civil and Political Rights, Art. 4(1); *Silva v. Uruguay*, 1 H.R.C. 65 (1981) (elaborating on the limits to derogation); European Convention on Human Rights, Art. 15(2).

As to derogation generally, see, e.g., Thomas Buergenthal, 'To Respect and to Ensure: State Obligations and Permissible Derogations', in Louis Henkin (ed.), *The International Bill of Rights* (1981), 78–86; Louis Henkin, 'International Human Rights as "Rights" ', 1 *Cardozo L. Rev.* 446 (1979); Rosalyn Higgins, 'Derogations Under Human Rights Treaties', 48 *Brit. Y.B. Int'l L.* 281 (1975–6).

[42] See American Law Institute, *Restatement (3rd) of the Foreign Relations Law of the United*

also casts doubt on any 'security' justification for extrajudicial homicide that is not carried out in self-defence.

In sum, Israel's extrajudicial killings—of prisoners, demonstrators, and Palestinians who refuse to cooperate at checkpoints—all raise serious questions of human rights law. Comparable violations by the PA do not in any way vitiate Israeli responsibility for the unjustified killing of Palestinians. It is true that Israel's record on extrajudicial killing is superior to that of many states around the world, but again that fact does not relieve Israel of the responsibility to ensure that all extrajudicial homicide stops.

Torture

Another of the 'internationally-accepted norms of human rights' to which the parties must pay 'due regard' is the obligation not to commit torture. Until recently, Israel's record on this score was very disturbing, but a recent decision of the Israeli Supreme Court appears to have outlawed interrogation methods that constitute torture.

The relevant norm is adumbrated in the 1984 Convention Against Torture and other Cruel, Inhuman or Degrading Treatment or Punishment,[43] to which Israel is a party. The Convention defines torture as 'any act by which severe pain or suffering, whether physical or mental, is intentionally inflicted on a person' for such purposes as obtaining information or a confession, when inflicted 'by or at the instigation of or with the consent or acquiescence of a public official or other persons acting in an official capacity'.[44] Each state party is obliged to take 'effective' measures to 'prevent acts of torture' in its territory.[45] Superior orders do not excuse torture.[46] Each party is obliged to review its interrogation practices to prevent torture.[47] And, significantly: 'No exceptional circumstances whatsoever, whether a state of war or a threat of war, internal political instability or any other public emergency, may be invoked as a justification of torture.'[48] Other human rights instruments also outlaw torture, usually without defining the term.[49]

Israel has run afoul of these provisions in the past. In 1987 the

States §702, comment n and n. 11 (describing *jus cogens*). *Jus cogens* is described in more detail in Ch. 4.

43 10 Dec. 1984, 23 I.L.M. 1027 (1984), as modified, 24 I.L.M. 535 (1985).

44 Ibid., Art. 1(1).

45 Ibid., Art. 2(1).

46 Ibid., Art. 2(3).

47 Ibid., Art. 11.

48 Ibid., Art. 2(2).

49 See, e.g., International Covenant on Civil and Political Rights, Art. 7 ('No one shall be subjected to torture or to cruel, inhuman or degrading treatment or punishment . . .'); Universal Declaration of Human Rights, Art. 5 (similar).

government-appointed Landau Commission condemned torture but endorsed 'moderate physical and psychological pressure', apparently on the theory that it does not amount to the 'severe pain and suffering' prohibited by the Torture Convention.[50] Until recently, Israel's general security service, Shin Bet, admittedly used such 'pressure' to obtain information and confessions. Interrogation techniques included hooding; forced standing or squatting for long periods of time; prolonged exposure to extreme temperatures; tying or chaining the detainee in contorted and painful positions; blows and beatings with fists, sticks, and other instruments; confinement in small and often filthy spaces; violent (and occasionally fatal) shaking; sleep and food deprivation; and threats against the detainee's life or family.[51]

Many of these acts plainly qualified as the intentional infliction of 'severe pain and suffering' within the meaning of the Torture Convention. Moreover, that Convention covers not just torture but 'other acts of cruel, inhuman or degrading treatment or punishment which do not amount to torture' as defined in the Convention. The main difference between torture and 'cruel, inhuman or degrading treatment' is that Israel is obliged to extradite or prosecute in cases of the former but not the latter.[52] Beatings, chaining, and shakings are surely 'degrading' if nothing else, and probably both 'cruel' and 'inhuman'. Indeed, one would expect most forms of 'physical and psychological pressure' to be at least 'degrading'; tearing down the detainee is part of the point of such pressure.

Israel cannot justify such practices on security grounds. The Torture Convention unequivocally rejects security-related rationales for torture, including 'public emergency' or 'state of war' or 'political instability'.[53] This categorical rule is sensible. A security exception would cut the heart out of the Torture Convention, since security is likely to be a major justification for torture, wherever it occurs. Nor can Israel's past interrogation practices be brushed off as the normal discomfort that is 'incidental to lawful sanctions'—i.e. part of any ordinary prison sentence.[54] The interrogations in question were not part of a prison routine, but rather were designed to coerce the detainee into providing information or confessions.

Until recently, the Israeli Supreme Court had consistently declined to enjoin the application of physical 'pressure', but in September 1999 it

[50] See Orit Shohat, 'Chair and bench', *Ha'aretz*, 22 May 1998.

[51] See, e.g., Amnesty International, *AI Report 1999* and preceding reports; US Dept. of State, 'Country Reports, 1999' and preceding reports. See also 'Israel Defends Use of Force in Interrogation', *N.Y. Times*, 8 May 1997; 'Shin Bet methods criticised', *Financial Times*, 20 May 1998 (describing Israeli interrogation techniques).

[52] Cf. Torture Convention, Arts. 7, 8, and 16(1).

[53] Ibid., Art. 2(b).

[54] Ibid., Art. 1(1).

abruptly changed course. Ruling on seven different applications charging Israel with torture, the Court unanimously held that the government lacked statutory authorization for 'the use of liberty infringing physical means during the interrogation of suspects'.[55] The Court based its opinion primarily on Israeli domestic law, but the Court also cited various sources of international law, including the European Court's landmark decision outlawing five interrogation methods in *Ireland v. United Kingdom*.[56] The Court rejected Israel's argument that the criminal-law doctrine of necessity justified torture, though the Court did acknowledge that if individual members of Shin Bet were prosecuted for torture, they might be able to use a necessity defence in cases in which they believed torture was essential to prevent imminent harm.[57] The Court acknowledged that its ruling might hamper the fight against terror, but observed: 'Although a democracy must often fight with one hand tied behind its back, it none the less has the upper hand.' Still, the Court made clear that the Knesset has the authority to enact specific statutory authorization for the use of 'physical means' in interrogation.[58]

This final aspect of the decision may prove to be the most telling. There will always be some public support in Israel for 'physical means' of interrogation, and thus it is possible that the Knesset will some day authorize those 'means', thereby placing Israel in violation of its international obligations. The unfortunate reality of modern international practice is that the domestic law of most states permits them to enact statutes overriding international law. Municipal law may require a 'clear' legislative intent to violate international law, but such clarity is not difficult to achieve. For now, Israel appears to have brought itself into compliance with the Torture Convention, but who knows what the millennium will bring.

Arbitrary arrest or detention

Another 'internationally-accepted norm' of human rights is the obligation to refrain from 'arbitrary arrest or detention', sometimes formulated as an

[55] *Public Committee Against Torture in Israel v. Israel*, H.C. 5100/94, 6 Sept. 1999, 38 I.L.M. 1471 (1999), ¶38.

[56] 2 E.H.R.R. 25 (1978), cited in ibid., ¶30. See also ibid., ¶23 (invoking human rights treaties).

[57] Ibid., ¶¶33–6. See also Alan M. Dershowitz, 'Is it Necessary to Apply "Physical Pressure" to Terrorists—And to Lie About it?', 23 *Israel L. Rev.* 193 (1989).

The scope of the necessity defence is one of the most commonly discussed problems in criminal law. For a sampling, see George Fletcher, *Basic Concepts of Criminal Law* (New York; Oxford: Oxford University Press, 1998), 138–42; Lon L. Fuller, 'The Case of the Speluncean Explorers', 62 *Harv. L. Rev.* 616 (1949); and of course *Queen v. Dudley & Stephens*, 14 Q.B.D. 273 (1884) (affirming convictions for cannibalism).

[58] Ibid., ¶39.

obligation to refrain from 'arbitrary arrest, detention or exile'.[59] Related to the prohibition on 'arbitrary exile' is a limitation on deportation.[60] This section briefly considers Israel's record on both arbitrary arrest and arbitrary deportation.

Israel often detains Palestinians suspected of security offences for long periods of time without a full and fair trial. Although administrative detainees have a right to counsel, there are persistent complaints of delays in access to an attorney, and interrogations sometimes proceed for weeks before a detainee can consult with counsel. Because Israel often moves detainees from the occupied territories to prisons in Israel, it can be difficult for lawyers and family of detainees to visit, since Israel sometimes restricts or prohibits Palestinian travel from the territories into Israel proper. There are hearings to test the validity of a detention, but often the evidence and even the offences charged remain secret, and the defendant is not always entitled to be present. Detentions are almost always sustained by the courts. There is a right of appeal, but it is usually unavailing.[61]

Many aspects of the administrative detention procedure are inconsistent with human rights law. The Civil and Political Covenant requires that the defendant be informed 'promptly and in detail' of the 'nature and cause of the charge against him'.[62] The defendant is entitled to be 'tried without undue delay'.[63] The trial must take place in the presence of the defendant, and the defendant has the right to confront and examine adverse witnesses.[64] It is true that the press and public may be excluded for reasons of 'national security in a democratic society',[65] and it is understandable that Israel does not wish to publicize intelligence sources and methods used to marshal evidence against the detainee. But the Covenant stops short of permitting the exclusion of the detainee and counsel.

[59] International Covenant on Civil and Political Rights, Art. 9(1) ('No one shall be subjected to arbitrary arrest or detention'); Universal Declaration of Human Rights, Art. 9 ('No one shall be subjected to arbitrary arrest, detention or exile').

[60] International Covenant on Civil and Political Rights, Art. 13 (providing that deportation of aliens must be carried out in accordance with certain minimum standards of due process); ibid., Art. 12(4) ('No one shall be arbitrarily deprived of the right to enter his own country'); Universal Declaration of Human Rights, Art. 9 (prohibiting 'arbitrary . . . exile'); ibid., Art. 13(1) ('Everyone has the right to freedom of movement and residence within the borders of each State'); ibid., Art. 15(2) ('No one shall be arbitrarily deprived of his nationality nor denied the right to change his nationality'); ibid., Art. 15(1) ('Everyone has the right to a nationality'). See also Fourth Geneva Convention, Art. 49 (prohibiting deportations of civilians from occupied territory).

[61] See generally Amnesty International, *AI Report 1999* and previous reports; US Dept. of State, 'Country Reports' for 1998 and previous reports.

[62] International Covenant on Civil and Political Rights, Arts. 14(3)(a), 9(2).

[63] Ibid., Art. 14(3)(c); see also Art. 9(4).

[64] Ibid., Art. 3(e)–(f); see also Universal Declaration of Human Rights, Art. 10.

[65] International Covenant on Civil and Political Rights, Art. 14(1).

Related to the question of arbitrary detention is the question of arbitrary exile or deportation. Israel has from time to time deported Palestinians from the occupied territories to other Arab states such as Jordan and Lebanon. This dispute has faded from view in recent years as Israel has generally put a halt to deportations.[66] This development is a welcome one. Some of Israel's deportations were probably inconsistent with Article 49 of the Fourth Geneva Convention, which forbids 'forcible transfers' of the 'civilian population' out of occupied territory. Even if Article 49 is intended to prohibit only transfers of large 'populations', it probably still covers deportations of large numbers of Palestinians.[67] Moreover, general human rights law also restricts deportations. Article 13 of the Civil and Political Covenant permits a state to expel an 'alien lawfully in [its] territory' only after a decision 'reached in accordance with law', and it gives the alien some due process right to challenge the expulsion 'except where compelling reasons of national security otherwise require'. This provision applies most clearly to Palestinians in Israel proper, but it seems doubtful that it authorizes Israel to deport from Areas A or B, which are not clearly Israeli 'territory'. In any event, it is to be hoped that the legality of deportations remains moot.

Demolitions

One Israeli practice that is not moot is its policy of demolishing homes of Palestinians owned or rented by Palestinians suspected of terrorism. According to the State Department, Israel destroyed one such home in 1998, eight in 1997, eight in 1996, and one in 1995.[68] After a home is destroyed, Israel typically prevents the owner from rebuilding or even removing the rubble. Palestinians and human rights groups see this practice as a form of collective punishment against Palestinians. Israel says this practice is necessary to deter, prevent, and punish terrorism.[69]

[66] See US Dept. of State, 'Country Reports' for 1997 and 1998, ¶1(d).

[67] For more on humanitarian law and Israeli deportations, see, e.g., Dan Simon, 'The Demolition of Homes in the Israeli Occupied Territories', 19 *Yale J. Int'l L.* 1 (1994); Yoram Dinstein, 'The Israel Supreme Court and the Law of Belligerent Occupation: Deportations', 23 *Isr. Yb. Hum. Rts.* 1 (1993); John L. Habib, 'Israeli Deportations of Palestinians Under International Law', 4 *Emory Int'l L. Rev.* 133 (1990); Wendy Olson, 'UN Security Council Resolutions Regarding Deportations From Israeli Administered Territories: The Applicability of the Fourth Geneva Convention Relative to the Protection of Civilian Persons in Time of War', 24 *Stan. J. Int'l L.* 611 (1988).

[68] US Dept. of State, 'Country Reports' from 1995 to 1998.

[69] See generally Uri Shoham, 'The Principle of Legality and the Israeli Military Government in the Territories', 153 *Mil. L. Rev.* 245, 258–64 (1996) (describing Israeli policy on demolitions). As to the domestic legal authority for Israel's demolitions, see Defence (Emergency) Regulations 1945, Regulation 119. For more on the regulation, see Cohen, *Human Rights*, 94.

The Israeli Supreme Court has repeatedly turned aside Palestinian claims that such demolitions violate the Hague Regulations, which as customary law are part of Israeli domestic law.[70] Recently the Court has, however, imposed some restrictions on demolitions, including a requirement of prior notification[71] and a requirement that demolition be limited to the one or two rooms in which the terrorist actually resided with his or her family.[72] Partly as a result of these limitations, and partly as a result of the Oslo process, the rate of demolitions is declining.[73] But the practice continues: a few demolitions still take place every year.

It is doubtful that this practice comports with international law. The Fourth Geneva Convention provides: 'Any destruction by the Occupying Power of real or personal property belonging individually or collectively to private persons . . . is prohibited, except where such destruction is rendered absolutely necessary by military operations.'[74] And: 'Reprisals against protected persons and their property are prohibited.'[75] It is difficult to escape the conclusion that these provisions prohibit the demolition of houses of terror suspects. Demolitions often do seem like 'reprisals' against terror suspects, since their purpose is often punitive. Nor is it easy to see why demolitions are ever 'rendered absolutely necessary by military operations', given that demolition of a private home hardly guarantees that its owners will desist from terrorism, and given that the real purpose of demolitions often appears more retributive than preventative.

Israel's demolition policy finds no more support in human rights law than it does in humanitarian law. Oddly, the Civil and Political Covenant says relatively little about property rights,[76] but the Universal Declaration

[70] See, e.g., *Sachwil v. The Military Commander of the West Bank*, 34(1) P.D. 464 (H.C.J. 434/79); *Mutzlah v. The Minister of Defense*, 36(4) P.D. 610 (H.C.J. 572/82); *Hamed v. The Military Commander of the West Bank*, 35(3) P.D. 223 (H.C.J. 22/81). See generally Shoham, 'The Principle of Legality', 259–60.

[71] *The Association for Civil Rights in Israel v. The O.C. Central Command*, 43(2) P.D. 529 (H.C.J. 358/88).

[72] *Turqeman v. The Minister of Defense*, 48(1) P.D. 271 (H.C.J. 5510/92).

[73] See Shoham, 'The Principle of Legality', 260.

[74] Fourth Geneva Convention, Art. 53.

[75] Fourth Geneva Convention, Art. 33, ¶3. See also Hague Regulations, Art. 46, ¶¶1–2 ('private property . . . must be respected' and private property 'cannot be confiscated'). The Hague Regulations also restrict the taking or destruction of certain public buildings. Ibid., Arts. 55–6; see also Art. 23(g), 25. On the other hand, the Regulations do permit the occupying power to collect taxes and contribution in certain circumstances and to requisition goods and services. Ibid., Art. 48 (taxes); ibid., Art. 51 (contribution); ibid., Art. 52 (requisitions). Israeli tax policy has in the past sparked Palestinian tax revolts, most notably in the West Bank village of Beit Sahour. See, e.g., Jack Rosenthal, 'Costs of the Intifada', *N.Y. Times*, 5 Nov. 1989.

[76] Cf. International Covenant on Civil and Political Rights, Art. 17(1) ('No one shall be subjected to arbitrary or unlawful interference with his privacy, family, home or correspondence . . .'). See American Law Institute, *Restatement (3rd)*, §702, comment k (noting that the 'wide disagreement' about the content of property rights 'weighs against the conclusion that a human right to property generally has become a principle of customary law').

of Human Rights provides that 'Everyone has the right to own property' and that 'No one shall be arbitrarily deprived of his own property'.[77] And while there is intense disagreement about the proper measure of compensation for expropriation, there is no doubt that there is a right to compensation of some sort.[78] Most important, the demolition policy implicates not only property rights but also the right not to be subjected to arbitrary punishment. On this subject, human rights law is quite clear. Everyone is presumed innocent until proven guilty in a court.[79] In general, criminal defendants are not supposed to be punished prior to their conviction.[80] In so far as it is punitive, pretrial demolition is incompatible with these norms.

In sum, Israel's policy of house demolitions is probably inconsistent with both humanitarian law and human rights law. Demolitions that take place prior to a criminal conviction are especially problematic. It does not appear that Israel is paying 'due regard' to the human rights norms implicated by demolition.

Freedom of speech, press, and movement

By pledging to pay 'due regard' to 'internationally-accepted norms of human rights', Israel has committed itself to respect basic civil liberties, including freedom of speech, press, association, religion, and movement. Israel generally has a good record on these issues, but there are some exceptions, most notably in freedom of movement—an issue already considered in Chapter 8, in connection with closures of the territories. Freedom of religion raises special issues relating to the Holy Places; it is considered separately in the next section.

Israel has a good record on freedom of speech, association, and the press. Palestinians enjoy a wide measure of freedom of speech, though they are formally prohibited from expressing support for Hamas and other groups dedicated to violent struggle against Israel. Israel no longer enforces its ban on the display of Palestinian flags and political symbols. Likewise, Israel has relaxed some of its prohibitions on large public gatherings, though it still restricts Palestinian demonstrations on settlements and other land-

[77] Universal Declaration of Human Rights, Arts. 17(1) and 17(2). See also American Convention on Human Rights, Art. 21(1) ('Everyone has the right to the use and enjoyment of his property').

[78] See generally Patrick M. Norton, 'A Law of the Future or a Law of the Past? Modern Tribunals and the International Law of Expropriation', 85 *Am. J. Int'l L.* 474 (1991); Richard B. Lillich and Burns H. Weston, 'Lump Sum Agreements: Their Continuing Contribution to the Law of International Claims', 82 *Am. J. Int'l L.* 69 (1988).

[79] International Covenant on Civil and Political Rights, Art. 14(2); Universal Declaration of Human Rights, Art. 11(1).

[80] See International Covenant on Civil and Political Rights, Art. 9(3).

related issues. There is a lively Arab-language press in Israel and the occupied territories, though Israeli military censors do review Arabic publications for security-related material.[81]

Some limited censorship is permissible under human rights law. The Civil and Political Covenant endorses freedom of speech and press, but it adds that these freedoms may be 'subject to certain restrictions ... provided by law', including restrictions 'necessary' for the 'protection of national security or of public order (*ordre public*), or of public health or morals'.[82] Indeed, the Covenant apparently *requires* some censorship. It provides: 'Any advocacy of national, racial or religious hatred that constitutes incitement to discrimination, hostility or violence shall be prohibited by law.'[83] Moreover, the Oslo Accords themselves oblige Israel and the PA to refrain from and to prevent 'incitement' and 'propaganda'. The Interim Agreement provides that Israel and the PA shall 'abstain from incitement, including hostile propaganda, against each other' and shall 'take legal measures to prevent such incitement by any organizations, groups or individuals within their jurisdiction'.[84]

This provision clearly does oblige the parties to prevent certain forms of expression. Read literally, it seems to oblige Israel to clamp down only on anti-*Palestinian* rhetoric, since the parties are obliged to abstain from incitement 'against each other' and to prevent 'such incitement' by individuals and groups 'within their jurisdiction'. The intent of the provision, in other words, might be to give the PA sole responsibility for stopping anti-Israeli and anti-Semitic rhetoric emanating from Palestinian sources, and to give Israel sole responsibility for anti-Palestinian rhetoric emanating from Israeli sources. Even if the provision must be read this narrowly, it does nothing to undermine Israel's broader authority under the Civil and Political Covenant to suppress 'advocacy' of 'hatred'. In general, then, Israel seems to be in compliance with its free-speech obligations under the Oslo Accords and general international law.

Israel's record on freedom of movement, however, is more mixed. As we have already seen in Chapter 8, Israel's policy of sealing off the territories is inconsistent with international law, at least in so far as its purpose is collective punishment rather than prevention of imminent harm. Other questions of freedom of movement involve religious freedom. These include access to the Holy Places, restrictions on Palestinians who wish to make the pilgrimage (*Hajj*) to Saudi Arabia, and restrictions on tour groups visiting pilgrimage sites in Israel. These and other questions of religious freedom are taken up in the next section.

81 See US Dept. of State, 'Country Reports, 1998'; Amnesty International, *AI Report 1999*.

82 International Covenant on Civil and Political Rights, Art. 19(2) (freedom of expression), Art. (3)(b) (permissible restrictions).

83 Ibid., Art. 20(2).

84 Interim Agreement, Art. XXII(1).

Religious freedom and the Holy Places

Religious freedom is one of the few human rights addressed in any detail by the Oslo Accords. Annex 3 to the Interim Agreement provides that 'Both sides shall respect and protect' the 'religious rights of Jews, Christians, Moslems and Samaritans'.[85] Israel and the PA are charged with 'protection of' and 'free access to' the Holy Sites, as well as an obligation to respect 'freedom of worship and practice' generally.[86] Israel is also obliged to permit Palestinians 'safe passage' to make the periodic pilgrimage to Al-Maghtas 'under the Palestinian flag'.[87] The Accords transfer responsibility for some Holy Sites to the PA, with the expectation that further sites will be transferred to PA jurisdiction in the course of further Israeli redeployments.[88]

More generally, religious freedom is one of the 'internationally-accepted norms of human rights' incorporated by the Interim Agreement. Human rights law and humanitarian law both oblige states to respect religious freedom. Human rights law obliges states to respect religious freedom and worship, including the right to 'adopt a religion or belief', and it permits only such limitations on this freedom as are 'necessary to protect public safety, order, health, or morals or the fundamental rights and freedoms of others'.[89] It also forbids discrimination based on religion.[90] Likewise, humanitarian law requires 'respect' for 'religious convictions and practices'.[91]

[85] Interim Agreement, Annex 3, Art. 32(2).

[86] Ibid., Art. 32(2)(a)–(c).

[87] Ibid., Art. 32(5).

[88] Ibid., Arts. 32(1), 32(3), 32(4). Schedule 4 to the Annex details which Sites are under PA jurisdiction.

[89] International Covenant on Civil and Political Rights, Art. 18(1) and (3); ibid., Art. 4(2) (providing that Art. 18 is non-derogable); Universal Declaration of Human Rights, Art. 18 ('Everyone has the right to freedom of thought, conscience and religion; this right includes freedom to change his religion or belief, and freedom, either alone or in community with others and in public or private, to manifest his religion or belief in teaching, practice, worship and observance').

Article 18 of the Civil and Political Covenant has been described as 'the most important provision on religious freedom in international law'. T. Jeremy Gunn, Book Review, 90 *Am. J. Int'l L.* 707, 708 (1996) (reviewing Bahiyyih G. Tahzib, *Freedom of Religion or Belief: Ensuring Effective International Legal Protection* (The Hague, Boston, London: Martinus Nijhoff, 1996)). The terms 'religion' and 'belief' in Article 18 have been 'broadly construed' by the Human Rights Committee. W. Cole Durham, Jr., *et al.*, 'The Future of Religious Liberty in Russia: Report of the De Burght Conference on Pending Russian Legislation Concerning Religious Liberty', 8 *Emory Int'l L. Rev.* 1, 15 (1994).

[90] International Covenant on Civil and Political Rights, Art. 2(1); UN Charter, Arts. 1(3), 55(c); International Covenant on Economic and Social Rights, 16 Dec. 1966, 993 U.N.T.S. 3, Art. 2(2).

[91] Fourth Geneva Convention, Art. 27. See also Hague Regulations, Art. 46 ('religious convictions and practice' must be 'respected'). The Hague Regulations also forbid all 'seizure of, destruction or wilful damage' to 'institutions dedicated to religion'. Ibid., Art. 56.

In general, Israel has an admirable record of compliance with these obligations. People of all faiths in Israel and the occupied territories enjoy wide freedom to worship, to change their faith, and, as a general matter, to visit the Holy Places. The principle of religious freedom is enshrined in the 1948 Declaration on the Establishment of the State of Israel,[92] in the 1922 Palestine Order in Council,[93] and, it appears, in the general provisions of the 1992 Basic Laws protecting '[f]undamental human rights'.[94] Israel does occasionally draw distinctions based on religion, for example in exempting certain Orthodox Jews from military service, but while this policy rankles some Israelis, it seems defensible from a legal perspective as a reasonable accommodation of religious belief.

It has been said that 'Israel's conduct regarding the holy places, while certainly not perfect, must be considered exemplary'.[95] Indeed, Israel has taken a variety of legal steps to protect the Holy Sites and to ensure access to them. One is the Protection of Holy Places Law of 1967, which prohibits desecration of the Holy Places, guarantees freedom of access to them, and imposes criminal penalties on anyone who 'does anything likely to violate' that 'freedom of access'.[96] Israeli law also incorporates older British mandatory laws protecting the Holy Places.[97]

During sieges and bombardments, belligerents must take 'all necessary steps' to 'spare' religious buildings. Ibid., Art. 27.

[92] Declaration of the Establishment of the State of Israel, 1 L.S.I. 3, 4 (1948) (providing that the State of Israel 'will guarantee freedom of religion, conscience, language, education and culture; it will safeguard the Holy Places of all religions'). The Declaration is not directly binding; it is 'neither a constitution nor a statute'. Ruth Lapidoth, 'Freedom of Religion and of Conscience in Israel', 47 *Cath. L. Rev.* 441, 445 (1998). None the less, the Israeli Supreme Court has made clear that it 'expresses the nation's vision and its credo' and should be considered 'when we attempt to interpret or clarify the laws of the State'. Election Appeal, 1/65, *Yardor v. Chairman of the Central Elections Committee for the Sixth Knesset*, 19(3) P.D. 365, 386 (opinion of J. Agranat); Lapidoth, 'Freedom of Religion', 445.

[93] Palestine Order in Council, 1922, in 3 *Laws of Palestine* 2587, § 83 (Drayton ed., 1934) ('All persons in Palestine shall enjoy full liberty of conscience, and the free exercise of their forms of worship subject only to the maintenance of public order and morals'). The Order in Council is still in force in Israel. Lapidoth, 'Freedom of Religion', 446.

[94] Basic Law: Human Dignity and Liberty, 1993/94, S.H. 90, §1 ('Fundamental human rights in Israel . . . shall be upheld in the spirit of the principles set forth in the Declaration on the Establishment of the State of Israel'); Basic Law: Freedom of Occupation, 1994, S.H. 90, §1 (similar). Thus these Basic Laws make reference to the 1948 Declaration, which explicitly protects religious freedom. According to Professor Lapidoth, these provisions may establish the principle that 'freedom of religion would, to a certain extent, prevail over regular laws'. Lapidoth, 'Freedom of Religion', 446.

[95] Marshall J. Breger and Thomas A. Idinopulos, *Jerusalem's Holy Places & The Peace Process* (Washington, D.C.: Washington Inst. for Near East Policy, 1998), 23.

[96] Protection of the Holy Places Law, 21 L.S.I. 76 (1967), §1. For more on the Law, see generally Walter Zander, *Israel and the Holy Places of Christendom* (New York: Praeger, 1971), 102–10.

[97] See Offences Against Sentiments of Religion and Tradition, Penal Law, 1977, §§170–4, Special Volume L.S.I. 54 (1977); Shmuel Berkovitz, 'The Holy Places in Jerusalem: Legal Aspects (Part One)', 11 *Justice* 4, 7–9 (1996); Lapidoth, 'Freedom of Religion', 450–1. The

More recently, Israel has reaffirmed its commitment to uphold the so-called *Status quo*—the nineteenth-century Ottoman *firman* regulating management of Christian Holy Places—in its 1993 Fundamental Agreement with the Holy See.[98] Israel has also agreed in its peace treaty with Jordan that 'Israel respects the present special role of the Hashemite Kingdom of Jordan in Moslem holy shrines in Jerusalem. When negotiations on the permanent status take place, Israel will give high priority to Jordan's historic roles in these shrines.'[99] (That undertaking has dismayed many Palestinians, who believe that they rather than Jordan should have the highest 'priority'.) Israel has also permitted pilgrims from hostile states such as Libya to come and pray at the Al-Aqsa Mosque in the Old City.[100] Still, Israel's periodic closures of the territories, especially its 'internal closures', obviously interfere with access to Holy Places.[101]

Questions of religious freedom are also raised by Israel's refusal to permit Muslims under the age of 30 to make the pilgrimage—the *Hajj*—to Saudi Arabia. Israel's position is that international pilgrimage is a privilege, not a right.[102] On the one hand, Israel is probably correct that international law does not, as yet, recognize *international* (as opposed to

terms of the British Mandate called on the Mandatory Power to preserve and protect existing rights in the Holy Places. Terms of the British Mandate for Palestine Confirmed by the Council of the League of Nations, 24 July 1922, reprinted in Ruth Lapidoth and Moshe Hirsch (eds.), *The Arab–Israel Conflict and its Resolution: Selected Documents* (Dordrecht, Boston: Martinus Nijhoff, 1992), 25–32. Cf. also The Palestine (Holy Places) Order in Council, 25 July 1924, 3 *Laws of Palestine* 2625 (Drayton ed. 1934) ('no cause or matter in connection with the Holy Places . . . shall be heard or determined by any Court in Palestine'); Lapidoth, 'Freedom of Religion', 450 (noting that the Order in Council implied that the British High Commissioner, now the Minister of Religious Affairs, would handle 'causes' involving the Holy Places).

98 Fundamental Agreement Between the Holy See and the State of Israel, 30 Dec. 1993, 33 I.L.M. 153 (1994), Art. 4(1) ('The State of Israel affirms its continuing commitment to maintain and respect the "Status quo" in the Christian Holy Places to which it applies and the respective rights of the Christian communities thereunder'). For more on the *status quo*, see generally L. G. A. Cust, *The Status Quo in the Holy Places* (Jerusalem: Ariel, 1980); Izhak Englard, 'The Legal Status of the Holy Places in Jerusalem', 28 *Isr. L. Rev.* 589, 591–3 (1994); Zander, *Israel and the Holy Places of Christendom*, 178–80 (providing a translation of the *firman*).

For more on the Fundamental Agreement, see, e.g., Fr. David-Maria A. Jaeger, 'The Fundamental Agreement Between the Holy See and the State of Israel: A New Legal Régime of Church–State Relations', 47 *Cath. L. Rev.* 427 (1998); Moshe Hirsch, 'The Freedom of Proselytism Under the Fundamental Agreement and International Law', ibid. 407 (1998); Silvio Ferrari, 'The Fundamental Agreement Between the Holy See and Israel and the Conventions Between States and the Church Since the Vatican II Council', ibid. 385 (1998); Geoffrey R. Watson, 'Progress for Pilgrims? An Analysis of the Holy See–Israel Fundamental Agreement', ibid. 497, 506–27 (1998).

99 Treaty of Peace, Isr.–Jor., 26 Oct. 1994, 34 I.L.M. 43 (1995).

100 See Breger and Idinopulos, *Jerusalem's Holy Places*, 23 (on pilgrimage); ibid. 37–9 (on Palestinian–Jordanian rivalry).

101 See US Dept. of State, 'Country Reports, 1998', §2.d.

102 Ibid.

domestic) pilgrimage as a human right.[103] That is, there is a right to leave one's own country, but not necessarily a right to *enter* any other country. It is perhaps desirable that international pilgrimage *should* some day be a human right, but for now the major human rights instruments protect only the right to leave and return, not the further right to enter a foreign state except in limited circumstances as a refugee.[104] A 1981 UN Declaration on the Elimination of Religious Intolerance speaks of a freedom to 'assemble in connection with a religion or belief' and, more vaguely, of a right to 'maintain communications' on 'national and international levels',[105] but it is not clear whether this provision is intended to cover international pilgrimage, and in any event the Declaration is not legally binding because it is only a General Assembly resolution.[106] That said, one does have a right to travel and make pilgrimages *within* one's own state, and there may be an emerging customary-law right to make the *Hajj*.[107] There is still, however, no general right to enter a foreign state.

But of course Israel's refusal to allow young Muslims to make the *Hajj* implicates the right to leave and return, not the right to enter. Now, human rights law does permit some limitations on the right to leave. Article 12(3) of the Civil and Political Covenant permits such 'restrictions' on exit as are 'necessary to protect national security, public order (*ordre public*), public health or morals or the rights and freedoms of others . . . '.[108] Moreover, the right to leave and return is derogable under Article

[103] See Watson, 'Progress for Pilgrims?', 506–27 (arguing that there is no general right of international pilgrimage in international human rights law). That said, Israel has recognized a Palestinian 'right' to make a pilgrimage to *local* Holy Sites. See Interim Agreement, Annex 3, Art. 32(5): (on certain occasions, 'Palestinians shall have the right to religious pilgrimage' to Al-Maghtas).

[104] See, e.g., Universal Declaration of Human Rights, Art. 13(2) (providing that everyone has a 'right to leave any country, including his own, and to return to his own country'); Universal Declaration of Human Rights, Art. 14 (recognizing a right of asylum); International Covenant on Civil and Political Rights, Art. 12(4) (providing only that 'No one shall be arbitrarily deprived of the right to enter his *own* country') (emphasis added); Detlev F. Vagts, 'The Proposed Expatriation Tax—A Human Rights Violation?', 89 *Am. J. Int'l L.* 578, 579 n. 13 (1995) ('The right to enter a country does not . . . exist except in certain cases involving asylum seekers and, without that right to enter, the right to leave may be an empty one').

[105] Declaration on the Elimination of All Forms of Intolerance and of Discrimination Based on Religion or Belief, 28 Nov. 1981, G.A. Res. 36/55, UN GAOR, 36th Sess., Supp. No. 51, at 171, UN Doc. A/36/51.

[106] See Roger S. Clark, 'The United Nations and Religious Freedom', 11 *N.Y.U. J. Int'l L. & Pol.* 197, 208 (1978) (asserting that the Declaration would have 'no enforcement procedures' and would not be 'binding on any state'); Watson, 'Progress for Pilgrims?', 514–15.

[107] See Watson, 'Progress for Pilgrims?', 522–4.

[108] The Universal Declaration puts the right of exit in more absolute terms: 'Everyone has the right to leave any country, including his own, and to return to his country.' Universal Declaration of Human Rights, Art. 13(2). But the Declaration has a catch-all derogation provision that permits 'limitations' on rights to meet 'the just requirements of morality, public order and the general welfare'. Ibid., Art. 29(2).

4 of the Covenant, though only in 'time of public emergency which threatens the life of the nation', and only when the derogating state formally notifies other parties to the Covenant.[109] Presumably Israel can justify refusing travel permits to some would-be pilgrims on grounds of 'national security' or 'public order', but denying permission to *all* Muslims under 30 seems overbroad. Surely there are some 29-year-old pilgrims who would pose less of a threat to security than some 31-year-old pilgrims. More particularized regulation would be more consistent with human rights law.

One last issue of religious freedom deserves mention: whether Israel may assign tour guides to visitors seeking to worship at various Holy Sites. Israel once considered requiring pilgrimage groups to accept an Israeli guide while visiting Holy Places, but apparently the government has backed off, leading one Israeli official to comment that 'Israel has abdicated its sovereignty over Christian holy places by allowing Christian groups to visit without Israeli guides'.[110] Whether a state may require religious pilgrims to accept a state-designated guide again depends on the balance between security and freedom embodied in Article 12 and other provisions of the Civil and Political Covenant. Human rights law may well permit states to assign a guide who does not interfere with observance, especially if the guide is of the same religious faith as the pilgrims. But if the presence of a guide would substantially interfere with religious observance, then human rights law would probably insist that Israel find a less-restrictive means of ensuring security at pilgrimage sites.

In sum, Israel has a good record on religious freedom, but its closure policy raises questions about free access to holy sites. Israel is probably entitled to regulate travel to Saudi Arabia for the *Hajj*, but human rights law may require a more narrowly tailored policy than Israel's current flat prohibition of any pilgrimage by Moslems under the age of 30. Whether Israel may assign guides to Christian or Moslem pilgrimage groups depends on the extent to which guides would interfere with religious observance.

Prisoner release

The release of Palestinian prisoners is an especially sensitive issue. For many Palestinians, it is at least as important as Israeli redeployment from the West Bank. For many Israelis, it is just as distressing.

[109] International Covenant on Civil and Political Rights, Art. 4(1) (emergency); ibid., Art. 4(3) (notification).

[110] See Haim Shapiro, 'PM Aide: Sovereignty Over Christian Holy Sites Lost', *Jerus. Post*, 15 Dec. 1994.

The Gaza–Jericho Agreement of May 1994 provided that 'Israel will release, or turn over, to the Palestinian Authority within a period of 5 weeks, about 5,000 Palestinian detainees and prisoners . . .'.[111] Israel substantially performed this obligation, albeit a bit belatedly, by releasing thousands of Palestinian prisoners over the next two months.[112] Palestinians complained that Israel conditioned release on the prisoner's signing a statement renouncing terrorism; they argued that this condition had no basis in the Oslo Accords.[113] But the Gaza–Jericho Agreement did permit Israel to subject release to 'procedures determined by Israeli law'.[114] More to the point, the Israeli condition was consistent with the underlying purpose of the prisoner-release programme, namely 'confidence building'.

The 1995 Interim Agreement provided that Israel would release more Palestinian detainees and prisoners in three stages. The first stage of releases was to take place upon the signing of the Agreement, the second stage before the elections for the Palestinian Council, and the third stage 'during the permanent status negotiations'.[115] Annexe VII to the Interim Agreement established who was eligible for release; the list included older and younger prisoners, as well as prisoners who had committed less serious crimes, and it added that 'all female detainees and prisoners shall be released in the first stage of release'.[116] Apart from the provision on female detainees, however, these provisions on prisoner release were quite vague, conferring on Israel a fair amount of discretion. As with most international obligations, that discretion had to be exercised in good faith.

Israel does seem to have made a good-faith effort to exercise this discretion. In October 1995, shortly after the signing of the Interim Agreement, Israel released hundreds of Palestinian prisoners.[117] In January 1996 Israel released roughly a thousand Palestinian prisoners.[118] Israel at first was reluctant to release some female prisoners. Israeli President Ezer Weizman, who has the power to commute sentences,[119] initially refused to release four Palestinian women in the first stage of

[111] Gaza–Jericho Agreement, Art. XX(1).

[112] See Nahal Oz, 'Israel Releases 170; Hundreds Still Jailed', *N.Y. Times*, 17 June 1994; Clyde Haberman, 'Israel Freeing Palestinians, But Slowly', ibid. 10 June 1994.

[113] See Jon Immanuel, 'Prisoners refusing no-terror pledge stay in jail', *Jerus. Post*, June 1994; 'Hundreds of prisoners freed', ibid. 10 June 1994.

[114] Gaza–Jericho Agreement, Art. XX(3).

[115] Interim Agreement, Art. XVI(1) (setting forth the timing of the first two stages); ibid., Annex VII, Art. 4 (on the timing of the third stage of release).

[116] Ibid., Annexe VII, Arts. 2–3.

[117] Batsheva Tsur and Alon Pinkas, '950 prisoners freed amid confusion', *Jerus. Post*, 11 Oct. 1995. Cf. Amnesty International USA, 'Human Rights in the Middle East', available at http://www.igc.apc.org/amnesty/mideast/isrmsp.html (putting the number at 750).

[118] Amnesty International, *AI Report 1997* (putting the number at 1,155).

[119] Israel Basic Law: President of the State §11(b) (June 1993).

release because they had been found guilty of homicide.[120] Weizman's refusal was later sustained by the Israeli Supreme Court.[121] But other female prisoners declined their own amnesty unless the four homicide convicts were also released, and eventually Israel relented, releasing the four in question along with other Palestinian women in February 1997.[122]

The text of the Wye River Memorandum contains no reference to prisoner release, but it has been widely reported that the parties orally agreed at Wye to the release of 750 Palestinian prisoners.[123] Oral agreements are enforceable in international law.[124] There is no international 'parol evidence rule' that excludes collateral oral understandings made contemporaneously with written agreements, though the Vienna Convention does look with some disfavour on *travaux préparatoires*.[125] The problem with any oral agreement, however, is proving its terms. In the case of the Wye Memorandum, the parties disagreed over whether all or just some of the released prisoners would be 'security' prisoners—that is, prisoners imprisoned for terrorism and other politically motivated crimes.[126] In November 1998 Israel released 250 prisoners, about 150 of whom were common criminals, not security prisoners.[127] Further releases were delayed because of continuing disagreement about who should be released.

The parties resolved only a few of these differences in the Sharm el-Sheikh Memorandum of September 1999. The Memorandum provided that 200 prisoners would be released in September and another 150 in October, and that Israel would release only prisoners whose offences took

120 Barton Gellman, 'Israel Backs off Pact on Inmates: Won't Free 4 Convicted of Homicide', *Sacramento Bee*, 7 Oct. 1995.

121 'Israeli Supreme Court Rejects Freeing Palestinians', *APS Diplomatic Recorder*, 21 Oct. 1995.

122 '30 Palestinian Women Prisoners Freed', *Jerus. Post*, 12 Feb. 1997.

123 See, e.g., Steven Erlanger, 'Arafat and Netanyahu in Pact on Next Steps Toward Peace', *N.Y. Times*, 24 Oct. 1999. The American press has occasionally reported, mistakenly, that the 'text' of Wye requires release of 750 prisoners. See, e.g., Deborah Sontag, 'A Time to Fight, a Time to Agree', ibid. 4 Sept. 1999 ('text of Wye' calls for prisoner release); cf. Jane Perlez, 'Mideast Standoff Remains Unsolved as Albright Visits', ibid. 3 Sept. 1999 ('The [Wye] deal calls for the release of 750 prisoners, but other details . . . were decided in oral agreements . . .').

124 Article 2(1)(a) of the Vienna Convention on the Law of Treaties requires that a treaty be in writing, but Article 3 provides that the Convention does not affect the 'legal force' of unwritten agreements. See also American Law Institute, *Restatement (3rd)*, §301, comment; McNair, *The Law of Treaties*, 47–51.

125 Compare Vienna Convention on the Law of Treaties Art. 31(1) and (2)(a) (providing for interpretation 'in context', including 'any agreement relating to the treaty') with ibid., Art. 32 (providing for resort to *travaux* in more narrow circumstances). Cf. U.C.C. §2-202 (parol evidence rule) (excluding supplementary agreements in certain circumstances).

126 Danna Harman, 'Wye questions, and some answers', *Jerus. Post*, 26 Aug. 1999.

127 Joel Greenberg, 'Israeli Release Of Criminals Elicits Dismay In Palestinians', *N.Y. Times*, 30 Nov. 1998.

place before 13 September 1993 (the date of the signing of Oslo I) and who were arrested before 4 May 1994 (the beginning of the interim period). But the Memorandum did not specify what type of prisoners would be released, leaving the identification of prisoners to a new joint committee. The Memorandum also left open the possibility of further prisoner releases in the future.[128]

Israel substantially complied with these provisions when it released about 200 prisoners in September 1999 and another 150 in October 1999.[129] The Israeli Cabinet agreed to waive the provision requiring that only pre-Oslo offenders be released, allowing for the release of some who had killed Arab 'collaborators' since Oslo.[130] The PA expressed its appreciation for these developments, even as many Israelis fumed that most of those released had been 'security' offenders.[131]

As Israel has emptied its prisons of imprisoned PLO operatives, the legal questions surrounding prisoner release have gradually diminished in importance. Still, the parties may again confront one legal question: whether imprisoned PLO *fedayeen* are prisoners of war, entitled to amnesty and release upon the close of hostilities. This argument has consistently and correctly been rejected by Israel's courts.[132] Under the Third Geneva Convention on the Treatment of Prisoners of War, POWs are entitled to be 'released and repatriated without delay after the cessation of active hostilities'.[133] But even assuming that 'hostilities' have ceased, the Third Geneva Convention makes clear that the *fedayeen* are not POWs. Article 4A(2) of the Convention provides that members of militias and other irregular groups can be considered POWs only if the armed force carries arms 'openly' and conduct their operations 'in accordance with the laws and customs of war', requirements never met by the PLO or other Palestinian terror groups.[134] Protocol I to the Geneva Conventions does expand the definition of POWs to include any

[128] Sharm el-Sheikh Memorandum, ¶3.

[129] Lamia Lahoud, '151 more Arab prisoners released', *Jerus. Post*, 17 Oct. 1999.

[130] Danna Harman *et al.*, 'Cabinet alters criteria for prisoner release', ibid. 7 Oct. 1999.

[131] Compare Evelyn Gordon, 'When terrorists walk', ibid. 19 Oct. 1999 (condemning the releases) with Lahoud, '151 more Arab prisoners released' (reporting PA satisfaction).

[132] See, e.g., *Military Prosecutor v. Ohmar Mahmud Kassem*, 42 I.L.R. 470 (1971) (denying POW status to imprisoned members of the Popular Front for the Liberation of Palestine); *Military Prosecutor v. Abu Kabar*, in 7 *Isr. Y.B. Hum. Rts.* 265 (1977) (refusing to grant POW status to a member of Fatah).

[133] Convention (No. III) Relative to the Treatment of Prisoners of War, 12 Aug. 1949, 75 U.N.T.S. 135, Art. 118.

[134] Ibid., Art. 4A(2)(c) and (d). In addition, irregular units must be 'commanded by a person responsible for his subordinates' and must bear a distinctive insignia—a 'fixed distinctive sign recognizable at a distance'. Ibid., Art. 4A(2)(a) and (b). Interestingly, an Israeli court has found that the PFLP's hats and green clothing did meet the requirement of a distinctive insignia. *Prosecutor v. Kassem*, 478. See also Christopher C. Burris, Comment, 'Re-examining the Prisoner of War Status of the PLO Fedayeen', 22 *N.C. J. Int'l L. & Com. Reg.*

armed forces of a Party, 'even if that Party is represented by a government or an authority not recognized by an adverse Party',[135] but Israel is not a party to Protocol I. Moreover, even if Protocol I has become customary law, Israel has persistently objected to this and other provisions in it.[136] Israel is not required to treat the imprisoned *fedayeen* as prisoners of war who are automatically entitled to release upon the cessation of hostilities.

In any event, Israel is now in compliance with its obligations on prisoner release. The parties will doubtless haggle again over the issue during permanent status negotiations, but for now Israel has made good on its promises.

Women's rights; non-discrimination; other rights

By obliging each party to pay 'due regard' to 'internationally-accepted norms' of human rights, the Oslo Accords presumably refer to the whole panoply of human rights, including economic and social rights. A full review of Israel's treatment of its own citizens is beyond the scope of this study, but a few highlights deserve attention.

Israel's record on women's rights is no worse or better than that of many other industrialized states. On the one hand, women have a full panoply of civil and political rights, and the government has taken a number of laudable steps to combat violence against women and to promote the economic advancement of women. On the other hand, violence against women remains a serious problem in Jewish and Arab communities in Israel, women remain woefully under-represented in high positions in government and in industry, and women sometimes have fewer rights than men in divorce cases. There is also growing

943, 984 (1997) ('there is little question that in the past the PLO did not meet the criteria of Article 4A'). But see W. Thomas Mallison and Sally V. Mallison, 'The Juridical Status of Irregular Combatants under the International Humanitarian Law of Armed Conflict', 9 *Case W. J. Int'l L.* 39, 40–3 (1977).

As to the reception of the Third Geneva Convention and the law of war in Israeli law, see generally Ruth Lapidoth, 'International Law Within the Israeli Legal System', 24 *Isr. L. Rev.* 451 (1990); Benjamin Rubin, 'PLO Violence and Legitimate Combatancy: A Response to Professor Green', 19 *Isr. Y.B. Hum. Rts.* 167, 172–3 (1989).

[135] Protocol Additional (No. I) to the Geneva Conventions of 12 Aug. 1949, and Relating to the Protection of Victims of International Armed Conflicts (without Annexes), 8 June 1977, 1977 U.N.J.Y.B. 95, 16 I.L.M. 1391 (1977), Art. 43(1).

There is disagreement among commentators on the scope of the new POW provisions of Protocol I. Compare Douglas J. Feith, 'Protocol I: Moving Humanitarian Law Backwards', 19 *Akron L. Rev.* 531 (1986) with Howard S. Levie, 'Prisoners of War Under the 1977 Protocol I', 23 ibid. 55 (1989).

[136] See Rubin, 'PLO Violence', 172–3 n.12 (1989); Burris, 'Re-examining POW Status', 992, 1006.

concern about physical attacks by extremist religious Jews on 'immodestly dressed' women, particularly in Jerusalem.[137]

Israel has made commendable efforts on behalf of children. It has a system of compulsory education until age 15 or tenth grade. There is also an impressive health care programme for children. The government has also taken active steps to prevent and punish child abuse.[138]

Discrimination against Israel's Arab minority is a continuing problem. Arabs are under-represented in the top levels of business, education, and government. According to the US State Department, 'government spending is far lower in predominately Arab areas than in Jewish areas', though there has been some effort to 'close the gaps' in spending in recent years. Dozens of Arab villages remain 'unrecognized', meaning that they are ineligible for basic social services such as electricity or water. Arabs assert that Arab land is expropriated for public use more often than Jewish land, and more generally that Israel's policies on real property favour Jewish citizens. Schools for Arab children are not as well funded as those for Jewish children. As the State Department puts it, 'Many schools in Arab communities are dilapidated and overcrowded, lack special education services and counselors, have poor libraries, and have no sports facilities. Arab groups also note that the public school curriculum stresses Israel's Jewish culture and heritage.'[139]

Israel has a good record on workers' rights. There is an active trade union movement in Israel, and workers have the right to bargain collectively and to strike. There are active and independent trade unions, most of which belong to Histadrut, the General Federation of Labour in Israel. There are laws governing the maximum hours of work, and there is a minimum wage.[140]

In sum, Israel has a mixed record of compliance with its general obligation to pay 'due regard' to 'internationally-accepted norms of human rights'. This obligation includes norms of human rights law, such as those embodied in the Civil and Political Covenant, as well as norms of humanitarian law in so far as Israel continues to occupy part of the West Bank and Gaza Strip. Israel's most serious violations of its human rights obligations are extrajudicial killings of prisoners and other Palestinians, torture of Palestinian prisoners, and the arbitrary arrest and detention of Palestinians. Other troubling practices include demolition of Palestinian homes and the closures of the territories, which interfere with Palestinians' right to travel and to worship at religious sites. Israel has a much better record of compliance with human rights norms spelled out

[137] See US Dept. of State, 'Country Reports' for 1997 and 1998, §5.
[138] Ibid. [139] Ibid. [140] Ibid., §6.

more explicitly in the Oslo Accords, such as access to the Holy Places and release of prisoners.

As we shall see in Chapter 13, the PA has committed serious human rights violations of its own. For now, it should be emphasized that one side's human rights violations can never justify the other side in committing similar violations. On this point, treaty law is unequivocal. Article 60(5) of the Vienna Convention on the Law of Treaties provides that a state may not invoke the violations of another party to a treaty to excuse the violation of 'provisions relating to the protection of the human person contained in treaties of a humanitarian character'. Israel cannot justify its own human rights violations on the grounds that the PA's may be worse—any more than the PA can justify its violations by pointing to Israel's.

This concludes Part III, on Israeli compliance with the Oslo Accords. On the whole, Israel's record of compliance has been uneven, but it has steadily improved over the past few years, to the point at which Israel is now in substantial compliance. The Netanyahu government's position on redeployment—that Israel had complete discretion on how and when to redeploy—did not fully account for Israel's obligation to perform in good faith. And while the Netanyahu government was entitled to respond to PA violations with countermeasures, it never acknowledged that countermeasures (such as refusal to redeploy) must be proportionate to the original breach. Fortunately, the Netanyahu and Barak governments both proved willing to quantify Israel's redeployment obligations more precisely in the Wye River and Sharm el-Sheikh Memoranda, and that decision appears to have smoothed some of the disagreements between the parties over redeployment.

Israel's insistence on proceeding with the Har Homa project seems inconsistent with its obligation to participate in good faith in 'final status' talks on Jerusalem and settlements. The Oslo Accords do not outlaw existing settlements, but they do put some good-faith limits on their expansion and on the creation of new settlements. On ports, passages, and economics, Israel was mostly obliged to negotiate solutions in good faith with the Palestinians, and for the most part Israel has done so. But on some questions, such as closure of the territories and the seas off Gaza, Israel has responded to legitimate security concerns with too sweeping a curtailment of freedom of movement. On others, such as the withholding of Palestinian funds, Israel's non-compliance was only partially justified by PA violations; a lawful response must be proportionate, and proportionality called for a partial rather than a total cut-off of funds. Finally, as we have just seen, no amount of PA human rights violations can excuse Israeli violations such as extrajudicial killing and torture. None the less, the Israeli Supreme Court decision on torture is a very promising development, and Israel has largely complied with its most specific human rights obligations under the Accords, namely protection of Holy Sites and release of prisoners.

At this writing, in sum, Israel is in compliance with most (but not all) of its obligations under the Oslo Accords. We now turn to Palestinian obligations under the Accords.

PART IV

Palestinian Compliance with the Oslo Accords

This Part assesses Palestinian compliance with the Oslo Accords. It consists of four chapters. Chapter 10 examines the now-completed Palestinian obligation to amend the Palestinian National Charter. Chapter 11 considers the Palestinian record on counter-terrorism and security matters. Chapter 12 asks whether the Palestinian Authority is complying with the limits on Palestinian self-government imposed by the Accords. Chapter 13 examines the PA's compliance with its human rights obligations under the Accords.

10

Amendment of the Palestinian National Charter

The parties are now in agreement that the Palestinians have amended their National Charter to delete clauses offensive to Israel, including those calling for the destruction of Israel. Precisely *when* this was achieved is a matter of disagreement, however. The Palestinians have maintained that they did so as early as 1996, when the Palestine National Council adopted a resolution endorsing changes in the Charter, or even as early as 1993, when Chairman Arafat wrote to Prime Minister Rabin that the offending provisions were 'no longer valid'. Israel maintains that the Palestinians did not formally amend the Charter, in accordance with their own constitutional requirements, until December 1998, when Palestinians gathered in Gaza and endorsed amendment of the Charter in the presence of US President Bill Clinton and other foreign dignitaries.

In one sense, then, the Charter issue is now moot. Still, if the PLO breached its obligations under Oslo Accords by failing to amend the Charter quickly enough, then that breach might have justified some temporary and proportionate suspension of Israeli obligations—though of course the PLO breach has now been cured, presumably removing any basis for reciprocal countermeasures by Israel. More to the point, the episode generated so much anger on both sides that it may continue to sour relations between the parties in the future. Accordingly, it would still appear useful to provide a brief legal history of the dispute over the Charter, together with some conclusions on precisely when the Palestinians made good on their promise to amend it.

The 1968 Palestinian National Charter, also known as the Palestinian National Covenant, is a revised version of the 1964 Palestinian National Charter.[1] Both documents call repeatedly for the 'liberation' of all of Palestine, the destruction of the state of Israel, and the outlawing of Zionism. Article 22 of the 1968 Covenant, for example, states that 'the liberation of Palestine will destroy the Zionist and imperialist presence'.

[1] Palestinian National Charter of 1964, reprinted in John N. Moore (ed.), *The Arab–Israeli Conflict* 3:699 (Princeton, NJ: Princeton University Press, 1974); Palestinian National Charter of 1968, as amended 17 July 1968, reprinted in ibid. 706. The 1968 Charter is also reprinted in Ruth Lapidoth and Moshe Hirsch (eds.), *The Arab–Israel Conflict and its Resolution: Selected Documents* (Dordrecht, Boston: Martinus Nijhoff, 1992), 136.

Article 21 rejects 'all solutions which are substitutes for the total liberation of Palestine'. Article 9 provides: 'Armed struggle is the only way to liberate Palestine. Thus it is the overall strategy, not merely a tactical phase.' These provisions are obviously inconsistent with the spirit of the land-for-peace formula of the Oslo Accords. Not surprisingly, Israel insisted that the Palestinian side agree to eliminate those portions of the Covenant calling for the destruction of the state of Israel.[2]

The Palestinian side agreed to do so. In his letter of 9 September 1993 to Prime Minister Rabin—part of the exchange of letters accompanying the Declaration of Principles—PLO Chairman Yasser Arafat said:

> The PLO affirms that those articles of the Palestinian Covenant which deny Israel's right to exist, and the provisions of the Covenant which are inconsistent with the commitments of this letter are now inoperative and no longer valid. Consequently, the PLO undertakes to submit to the Palestinian National Council for formal approval the necessary changes in regard to the Palestinian Covenant.[3]

In the next two years, however, little progress was made towards amending the Covenant.

Accordingly, the 1995 Interim Agreement put amendment of the Covenant on a strict timetable. Article XXXI(9) of the Interim Agreement provided: 'The PLO undertakes that, within two months of the date of the inauguration of the Council, the Palestinian National Council will convene and formally approve the necessary changes in regard to the Palestinian Covenant.' The Council was inaugurated in late January 1996. But by then, Arafat was taking the position that the Covenant did not need to be amended because the PNC had already made declarations in 1988 and 1991 recognizing Israel's right to exist and renouncing terrorism. None the less, in March 1996, the Palestinians released a new draft Palestinian National Charter that omitted references to the destruction of Israel, spoke of 'coexistence' between Palestinians and Israelis, and set

[2] According to Abu Mazen, invalidation of the relevant provisions of the Covenant was one of seven Israeli conditions related to mutual recognition. The others were that the PLO recognize Israel, accept Security Council Resolutions 242 and 338, commit to resolve permanent status issues only through negotiations, renounce terrorism, cease acts of violence and terrorism, and assure Israel that Arafat was prepared to 'meet any Israeli official'. Mahmoud Abbas (Abu Mazen), *Through Secret Channels* (Reading: Garnet Publishing, 1995), 207–8. The 'details of mutual recognition' were hammered out in late August and early September 1993, after the Declaration of Principles had already been initialled but before the Declaration was signed. Ibid. 208–9; David Makovsky, *Making Peace with the PLO* (Boulder, CO: Westview Press, 1996), 79–80.

Abu Mazen also reports that Arafat discussed the Covenant with Norwegian Foreign Minister Johan Joergen Holst in July 1993. At that meeting Holst and Arafat apparently discussed having Arafat merely repeat his earlier statement that the Covenant was now 'outdated'. Abbas, *Through Secret Channels*, 107–8.

[3] Letter of Yasser Arafat to Yitzhak Rabin, 9 Sept. 1993, reprinted in Appendix A.

forth some general structural features of a new Palestinian state, including parliamentary democracy and an independent judiciary.[4]

On 22 April 1996 the PNC met for the first time in five years. On 24 April, by a vote of 504–54, with 14 abstentions, the PNC resolved to cancel the anti-Israel clauses from its Covenant and to authorize a drafting committee to draft a new charter within six months. The operative parts of the resolution read:

> The Palestinian National Council, at its 21st session held in the city of Gaza . . . based upon the principles which constituted the foundation of the Madrid Peace conference and the Washington Negotiations, decides:
>
> 1—The Palestinian National Charter is hereby amended by canceling the articles that are contrary to the letters exchanged by the P.L.O. and the Government of Israel 9–10 September 1993.
>
> 2—Assigns its legal committee with the task of redrafting the Palestinian National Charter in order to present it to the first session of the Palestinian central council.[5]

On 4 May Arafat formally transmitted the text of this resolution to Israeli Prime Minister Shimon Peres. Arafat wrote that he wished to convey 'the recent historic resolution' and that the PNC had 'decided that the Palestine National Charter is hereby amended by cancelling the provisions' referred to in the 1993 Arafat–Rabin letters.[6]

Supporters of the peace process greeted these developments with enthusiasm. Prime Minister Peres, who had been worried that the issue might jeopardize his Labour Party's hopes in the impending elections in June, expressed satisfaction with the PNC vote. Indeed, there were suggestions that Israeli officials informally requested that the PNC refer the matter to a committee rather than draft a new document, one that probably would have restated Palestinian aspirations for a state with its capital at Jerusalem. The White House, which had made no secret of its preference for a Labour victory,[7] issued a statement in which President

[4] See 'Palestinian Affairs: "Text" of Draft National Charter Published', FBIS-NES-96-059, 25 Mar. 1996, translation of article by Anwar al-Khatib in *Al-Hadath*, 25 Mar. 1996 (in Arabic). Draft Article 6 of the Charter provided: 'Coexistence between the Palestinians and the Israelis is an irrevocable matter that requires both peoples to observe each other's security, traditions, customs, and conditions.' Draft Article 2 provided for a 'parliamentary' and 'republican' system of government. Draft Article 10 provided for 'the supremacy of law within the framework of the independent judiciary's complete surveillance'.

[5] Official translation, reprinted in 36 I.L.M. 772 (1997). The full text includes references to the Declaration of Principles, the Cairo Agreement, the Interim Agreement, and various UN resolutions. At the time, a somewhat different 'unofficial' translation of the PNC resolution also circulated. The unofficial translation read in part: 'it has been decided upon: Amending the National Charter by canceling', etc., language that was less definitive than the operative text of the official translation, which said simply that the Charter is 'hereby amended'.

[6] Letter of Yasser Arafat to Shimon Peres, 4 May 1996, 36 I.L.M. 772 (1997).

[7] See Terry Atlas, 'U.S., Israel Fortify their "Partnership" to Stop Terrorism', *Chi. Trib.*,

Clinton 'warmly welcome[d]' this vote to 'revoke' the offending provisions, a vote that 'honored' the commitment made in the Interim Agreement and constituted a 'major step' on the road to peace. 'The President applauds this action as a decisive statement, at this difficult moment, that those who champion peace will not be deterred by the murderous acts of those desperate to prevent the people of the Middle East from building a better future.'[8] Some influential members of the US Congress echoed these sentiments.[9]

But sceptics in the Likud party asked why the PNC did not vote on a new charter immediately, and they argued that the offending language might reappear in any new document produced by the PNC drafting committee. The PNC resolution was certainly vague about which (if any) provisions of the Charter had been 'cancelled'. The resolution made reference to the Arafat–Rabin letters, but those letters did not specify exactly which clauses had to be eliminated or amended. After the PNC vote, leading Palestinians offered conflicting interpretations of the resolution, fuelling Israeli suspicions that the vote had changed little.[10]

Unfortunately, the PNC drafting committee's six-month deadline came and went without any evidence that the committee was anywhere near completion of a new text.[11] Accordingly, the new Netanyahu government sought a renewed, more definite Palestinian commitment to amend the Covenant. The Note for the Record accompanying the January 1997 Hebron Protocol contained such a pledge. The Note provided that the Palestinian side 'reaffirms its commitments' to '[c]omplete the process of revising the Palestinian National Charter'.[12] This obligation was to be undertaken 'immediately and in parallel' with other remaining commitments. As 1997 wore on, however, the PNC drafting committee still did not produce a new text of the Palestinian National Covenant. There were reports that Arafat had requested specific guidance from the Israelis on precisely what language needed to be amended, and that Arafat sent letters to President Clinton and British Prime Minister Tony Blair asserting that various provisions of the Charter had been amended, but there was still no published final text of the amended Charter. The Netanyahu government said the PLO was in clear violation of its obligations under

1 May 1996 (reporting that Clinton's 'effusive praise of Peres' had 'raised eyebrows in Israel', creating the perception that Clinton favoured Peres over Netenyahu in the upcoming elections).

[8] 7 *US Dept. of State Dispatch*, no. 17 (statement of Mike McCurry) (24 Apr. 1996).

[9] See, e.g., 142 Cong. Rec. S4187 (daily edn 25 Apr. 1996) (remarks of Senator Pell) ('The vote is further evidence of sea change in Palestinian attitudes and ideology . . .').

[10] Jon Immanuel, 'Begin: Government in conspiracy with PLO on covenant', *Jerus. Post*, 1 May 1996 (reporting conflicting statements by Palestinian officials).

[11] See Editorial, 'Covenant deadline unmet', *Jerus. Post*, 27 Oct. 1996.

[12] Note for the Record, 'Palestinian Responsibilities', ¶1.

the Note for the Record and the earlier Accords. A number of commentators had already reached the same conclusion.[13]

In fact, this dithering by the Palestinians probably did run afoul of the Note for the Record, but it is less clear that it violated the earlier Oslo Accords. The Arafat–Rabin letter of September 1993 merely required Arafat to 'submit' the Covenant to the PNC for revision, an obligation that was probably met by the April 1996 submission to the PNC. The Arafat–Rabin letter carries an implied obligation of good faith, and thus the submission to the PNC had to be an honest effort to change the Covenant, not a sham or a delaying tactic. But the PNC resolution did seem to reflect a genuine effort to move forward. The 1995 Interim Agreement strengthened the obligation to amend, but it was still less than absolute. It provided that the PLO 'undertakes' that within two months the PNC 'will convene and formally approve' the changes 'as undertaken' in the 1993 letters. The PNC did not take this step. Did the PNC's inaction mean the PLO was in breach?

The principal argument for the PLO is that its obligation was only to make a good-faith effort to persuade the PNC to approve the changes, and that it did so. Indeed, there is state practice to support the proposition that an 'executive' is not always held responsible for the failure of a co-ordinate branch of government to act. In extradition law, for example, a state is sometimes required to extradite or 'submit the case to its competent authorities for the purpose of prosecution'.[14] This kind of obligation does not require a successful prosecution, or even a trial of the accused; it is enough if the case is 'considered for prosecution' by the prosecuting authorities, acting in good faith in the context of a judicial system of 'integrity'.[15] The Clinton Administration apparently accepted some argument along these lines, because it repeatedly certified to Congress that the PLO had abided by its commitment to 'submit' the required changes to the PNC for formal approval.[16]

[13] See, e.g., Justus R. Weiner, 'An Analysis of the Oslo II Agreement in Light of the Expectations of Shimon Peres and Mahmoud Abbas', 17 *Mich. J. Int'l L.* 667, 692 (1996) (book review) ('Significantly, the PLO has yet to carry out its commitment to abrogate' the offending provisions); Mortimer B. Zuckerman, 'Ditch the Double Standard', *US News & World Report*, 30 Dec. 1996.

[14] See, e.g., International Convention Against the Taking of Hostages, 17 Dec. 1979, 18 I.L.M. 1456 (1979), Art. 8(1).

[15] See John F. Murphy, 'The Future of Multilateralism and Efforts to Combat International Terrorism', 25 *Colum. J. Trans. L.* 35, 41–53 (1986). See also John F. Murphy, 'Civil Liability for the Commission of International Crimes as an Alternative to Criminal Prosecution', 12 *Harv. Hum. Rts. J.* 1, 3 (1999). The scope of a state's duty to extradite or submit for prosecution is now pending before the International Court. See *Questions of Interpretation and Application of the 1971 Montreal Convention Arising From the Aerial Incident at Lockerbie* (Libya v. UK, Libya v. US), 1992 I.C.J. 3, 114 (Orders of 14 Apr.).

[16] See Presidential Determination No. 96-8, 8 Jan. 1996 ('I hereby . . . certify that the Palestine Liberation Organization continues to abide by the commitments described in

But the PLO's obligation under the Interim Agreement was stronger than merely to 'submit for PNC consideration'. The PLO 'undertook' that the PNC 'will convene and formally approve' the changes within two weeks. The better analogy is not to extradition practice, but to implementation of treaty obligations by national legislatures. A party to a treaty is not excused simply because one of its internal organs fails to implement the treaty unless the treaty explicitly makes that party's obligations contingent on internal implementation.[17] If the PLO did not wish to subject itself to international responsibility for the inaction of its PNC, it could have said so in the text of the Interim Agreement.

In any event, the 1997 Note for the Record explicitly required more than merely 'submitting' the Charter to the PNC for approval. By re-affirming its 'commitment' to '[c]omplete the process of revising the Palestinian National Charter', the PLO seemed to take on direct responsibility for amendment of the Charter. Unfortunately, this language still contained some ambiguity. The reference to 'process' might conceivably be read as focusing on submission to the PNC rather than actual amendment of the Charter. The PLO also floated a variation on this argument: that Arafat had already revised the Charter in his 1993 letter, and all that remained to be done was mechanical implementation—process, if you will. Ultimately, however, these arguments are unpersuasive.

For example, any suggestion that the objectionable sections were automatically revoked by Arafat's 1993 letter or his more recent letters to Clinton and Blair is unavailing. Arafat's 'affirmation' that the offending provisions are 'inoperative' would seem to have had little if any legal effect. Article 33 of the 1968 Covenant provides that it can only be amended by a two-thirds majority of the National Assembly of the PLO.[18] Indeed, the text of Arafat's letter to Rabin contains a promise to submit the matter to the PNC. As Abu Mazen later explained, the PLO was 'careful not to offer the Israelis the kind of recognition that would entail a firm commitment on our part to cancel the relevant article in the Covenant because the authority to make such a commitment rested with the PNC'.[19] Indeed, the new post-Wye Covenant retains the two-thirds requirement,

section 583(b)(4)' of the Middle East Peace Facilitation Act [MEPFA] of 1994). The MEPFA conditions aid to the PLO on a Presidential certification that the PLO has continued to abide by its Oslo commitments, including its promise to submit the Covenant to the PNC for amendment. See MEPFA of 1994, P.L. 103–236, 108 Stat. 488, §583(b)(4)(A)(vi).

[17] Cf. Vienna Convention on the Law of Treaties, Art. 27 (a party 'may not invoke the provisions of its internal law as justification for its failure to perform a treaty').

[18] In fact, the original 1964 Charter was amended in accordance with this process in 1968. See 1968 Charter, reprinted in Lapidoth and Hirsch, *The Arab–Israel Conflict*, 136. The 1968 amendment added provisions condemning the Israeli occupation of territories gained in the 1967 War.

[19] Abbas, *Through Secret Channels*, 208.

and Arafat has not explicitly claimed a power to amend it on his own authority.

The PLO's other arguments about its slow implementation of the 1997 Note were equally unimpressive. For example, it was suggested that the PNC approved, in principle, the amendments embodied in Arafat's letters to Blair and Clinton—that the PNC delegated the task of drafting, and that Arafat's letters derived their authority from that delegation. But the PNC delegated drafting responsibilities to a PNC committee, not to Arafat. Nor is it persuasive to suggest that the Note simply restated the obligations of the Interim Agreement simply because it called for completion of the process 'in accordance with the Interim Agreement'. This language simply makes clear that the Note should be construed, where possible, as consistent with the Interim Agreement—not that the new language in the Note on 'completing the process' was hortatory. Likewise, the fact that the Interim Agreement in turn refers to the 1993 letters does not mean that the Note added nothing to the understandings in the letters.

In sum, it appears that the Palestinian delays in revising the Palestinian National Charter were a violation of Palestinian obligations under the Note for the Record accompanying the Hebron Protocol, and possibly under the Interim Agreement as well. That breach has since been cured; Israel has said that the post-Wye ceremony in Gaza constituted an acceptable, formal amendment of the Charter. But there remains a question of legal history—namely, whether the PLO's breach was serious enough to justify countermeasures by Israel.

It may be that the PLO's vacillation on the Charter did not entirely dismay the government of Israel. Some press reports suggest that the Peres government discouraged the Palestinians from completing the process at the PNC meeting in April 1996 because the Labour officials feared that a new Charter would contain other, politically damaging provisions, such as an insistence on a Palestinian state with its capital at Jerusalem. Moreover, there has been speculation that the present Israeli government did not relish the prospect of a new PNC meeting to approve a new Charter because the PNC might also take the opportunity to declare a Palestinian state.

But assuming that Israel felt damaged by the PLO's breach, was the injury so great as to justify serious countermeasures, such as the suspension of Israel's obligation to redeploy from the West Bank? It will be recalled from Chapter 6 that countermeasures generally must be proportionate to the breach, and that the injured party may also have an obligation to exhaust their legal remedies under the parties' agreement or under general international law.

A fair case can be made that the PLO's obligations on the Charter were as central to Israel as Israel's obligations to redeploy were to the PLO. After all, Israel is giving up land for peace, and the Charter is as tangible evidence of Palestinian commitment to peace as Israel is likely to obtain. Before it was amended, it contained repeated expressions of distinctly unpeaceful sentiments. It may be that Israel did not make full resort to the dispute–resolution mechanisms under the Accords, but neither has the PLO, perhaps suggesting that the parties have tacitly waived or amended the relevant dispute–resolution provisions. Some Israeli countermeasure, accordingly, may have been warranted up until the Charter was indisputably amended in 1998. Still, in so far as the Israeli government was not wholly obsessed with the issue, a proportionate response would have stopped short of suspension of Israel's main obligations.

In any event, the Charter has now been successfully amended, amidst great fanfare, in the presence of many foreign dignitaries. The PLO's cure of its earlier breach means that Israel can no longer invoke it as a basis for suspending reciprocal obligations. We now turn to the central Palestinian obligation under the Oslo Accords: the obligation to prevent terrorism and to cooperate in security matters.

11

The Palestinian Duty to Prevent Terror and Violence

The most important Palestinian obligation under the Oslo Accords is to combat terrorism and to prevent violence. This overarching obligation encompasses a number of significant commitments. The Note for the Record that accompanies the Hebron Protocol lists six: (1) strengthening security cooperation; (2) preventing incitement of violence and 'hostile propaganda'; (3) combating terrorist organizations; (4) arresting and prosecuting terrorists; (5) extraditing criminal suspects to Israel; and (6) confiscating illegal firearms. Again, the Palestinian record of compliance with these obligations is at best mixed, but there are indications that it has improved over the past year.

Security cooperation

Cooperation on security is obviously a joint obligation, not solely a Palestinian one. None the less, Israel has complained about PA non-compliance with this obligation much more frequently than the PA has complained about any Israeli non-compliance. In fact the PA's record of compliance has been uneven, and its legal justifications for non-compliance are not entirely convincing. Still, even Israel has on occasion commended the PA for security cooperation. Ten years ago, the current level of cooperation between Israeli and Palestinian security personnel would have obviously been unthinkable.

The Oslo Accords contain various statements of the obligation to cooperate in law enforcement and security. Article XII of the 1994 Gaza–Jericho Agreement obliged the parties to 'cooperate in combating criminal activity which may affect both sides, including offenses related to trafficking in illegal drugs and psychotropic substances, smuggling, and offenses against property, including offenses related to vehicles'. Article VIII of the Gaza–Jericho Agreement obliged the PA to take steps to 'guarantee public order and internal security'. Article VIII(3) established a joint Coordination and Cooperation Committee for mutual security purposes (known as the 'JSC') as well as three joint District Coordination and Cooperation Offices (known as 'DCOs') for the Gaza district, the Khan Yunis district, and the Jericho district respectively. An annex to the agreement provided for joint patrols, normally to consist of 'two 4-wheel drive vehicles, one Palestinian and one Israeli', to police main roads.[1]

The 1995 Interim Agreement expanded somewhat on these provisions. It added two Joint Regional Security Committees ('RSCs'), one for the West Bank and one for the Gaza Strip, and a number of new Joint District Coordination Offices.[2] It also obliged the JSC to develop a 'comprehensive plan' to ensure coordination between Israeli military forces and the Palestinian police during the interim period. Like the Gaza–Jericho Accord, the Interim Agreement envisioned intelligence-sharing, joint training operations, and joint operations in the field. Moreover, the Oslo Accords were designed to combat not just terrorism but ordinary street crime as well—to 'guarantee public order and internal security' for Palestinians and Israelis alike.[3]

For a period of time after the adoption of the Gaza–Jericho Agreement, the parties did meet regularly as required, and there was some level of cooperation between security forces of both sides. Officials of Israel's internal security service, Shin Bet, have in the past acknowledged that the PA security people 'did their jobs' and helped prevent several suicide bombers after the PA and Israel began working together in 1994. 'It was not a love story,' said one former Shin Bet chief. 'It was an "interest" story on both sides. The Palestinian interest was to move the peace process.'[4] Joint Israeli and Palestinian teams patrolled main roads and cooperated in fighting ordinary crime, such as narcotics trafficking.[5] There were reports that the PA had prevented several attacks against Israelis, including suicide bombings.[6] Although Palestinians complained that the Israelis sometimes operated unilaterally, and Israelis complained that the Palestinians did not do enough to cooperate in fighting terrorism, none the less there were reports that the parties were sharing intelligence, sometimes on a bilateral basis, and sometimes with the mediation and encouragement of the CIA.[7]

[1] Gaza–Jericho Agreement, Annex I, Art. III(3)(b). Normally each vehicle was to be staffed by 'an officer, a signal officer, a driver and a guard'. Ibid. 'In roads under Israeli security responsibility, the Israeli vehicle will be the leading vehicle. In roads under Palestinian security responsibility, the Palestinian vehicle will be the leading vehicle.' Ibid., Art. III(3)(d).

[2] These provisions continued in force, and to some extent expanded, similar committees established by Article VIII(3) of the Gaza–Jericho Agreement, which by its terms applied only to Gaza and Jericho.

[3] Interim Agreement, Art. XII(1). See also Declaration of Principles, Art. VIII.

[4] Marjorie Miller and Rebecca Trounson, 'Intelligence Cooperation Mideast Casualty', *L.A. Times*, 26 Mar. 1997 (quoting former Shin Bet chief Carmi Gillon).

[5] See Mary Curtius, 'Israeli Crackdown Strains Relations with Palestinians', ibid. 11 Mar. 1996.

[6] See, e.g., David Makovsky *et al.*, 'PA foils car-bomb attack; Cabinet to approve plan for easing of closure', *Jerus. Post*, 5 Feb. 1995.

[7] See Tim Weiner, 'C.I.A. will Press Arafat and Israel on Anti-terrorism', *N.Y. Times*,

One high-water mark of cooperation came in the spring of 1996, just six months after the signing of the Interim Agreement. After a series of suicide bombings by Palestinian militants in February and March 1996, Arafat joined with Israel in cracking down on terrorist attacks from PA-controlled areas. The PA arrested hundreds of Palestinian militants.[8] But security cooperation faded after Netanyahu's election in June, and by the autumn 'Arafat was emptying PA prisons'.[9]

If the late spring of 1996 was the zenith of security cooperation, the period from the autumn of 1996 to the spring of 1997 was its nadir. In the autumn of 1996, the Netanyahu government opened a tunnel near the Haram in Jerusalem, provoking riots and demonstrations in the course of which PA security personnel fired on their Israeli counterparts. In March 1997, when Netanyahu announced his plans for the construction of Jewish housing at Har Homa in East Jerusalem and for a withdrawal from only 9 per cent of the West Bank, violent protests erupted in PA-controlled towns on the West Bank. Thereafter the PA announced that it was suspending joint security operations and intelligence sharing.[10] Meanwhile the Netanyahu government accused Arafat of giving the 'green light' to renewed terrorist attacks against Israeli targets.[11]

Still, even in the midst of this crisis, there were some instances of co-operation in the field, if not in intelligence-sharing. In late March 1997, for example, Palestinian police managed to keep an angry crowd of about 5,000 Palestinians from attacking Israeli soldiers at Joseph's Tomb, a Jewish holy site in Nablus.[12] Similarly, some IDF officials publicly commended the Palestinian Police for its efforts to keep Palestinian demonstrations in Hebron from turning violent, and they asserted that security cooperation was continuing, albeit at a 'lower level' than in the

9 Mar. 1996. See also Douglas Jehl, 'Israelis and Palestinians Agree to U.S. Role in Attack Inquiry', ibid. 13 Aug. 1997. Israel and the PA also took part in multilateral meetings on counter-terrorism. See, e.g., Steven Erlanger, 'Intelligence Experts Meet to Combat Mideast Terrorism', ibid. 30 Mar. 1996.

[8] See Steve Rodan, 'Arafat's balancing act with terror', ibid. 12 Sept. 1997; Weiner, 'C.I.A. will Press Arafat' (reporting that 'the Palestinian secret police have arrested hundreds of militants and raided 30 Islamic institutions'); David Horovitz, 'Israeli Arab held as joint crackdown intensifies', ibid. 7 Mar. 1996.

[9] Rodan, 'Arafat's balancing act with terror'.

[10] See Barton Gellman, 'Gap Widens in Mideast Peacemaking; Palestinians, Israel Take Hard Lines, Endangering Oslo Accords', *Wash. Post*, 25 Mar. 1997; Deborah Horan, 'Tensions mounting in Israel', *Houston Chronicle*, 25 Mar. 1997 (quoting a PA official) ('We stopped both security activities and intelligence cooperation as a result of the Israeli violations of the agreement by continuing to establish settlements'); Christopher Walker, 'Palestinians reject Israeli demands', *The Times*, 25 Mar. 1997.

[11] See Judy Dempsey, 'Israel calls on US over impasse', *Financial Times*, 25 Mar. 1997.

[12] See Marjorie Miller, 'Palestinian Police Curb Protests Against Israelis', *L.A. Times*, 31 Mar. 1997 ('Arab police in the Palestinian-ruled city of Nablus fired into the air and formed a human chain to keep about 5,000 demonstrators away from Israeli soldiers at Joseph's Tomb').

past.[13] In April the PA and Israel acted jointly to arrest members of a Hamas terrorist cell, and Prime Minister Netanyahu acknowledged that the PA had provided 'pinpoint assistance' in locating the cell, though he added that full cooperation in counter-terrorism 'is not yet being implemented'.[14] The PA, not anxious to be seen as 'Israel's policemen', played down its own role, but American officials confirmed that the PA had played an 'important role' in the arrests.[15] At about the same time, a Shin Bet official also asserted that PA security had recently helped prevent a suicide attack.[16] But publicly the PA continued to reject Israeli demands to resume formal cooperation, including intelligence-sharing and the meetings required by the Interim Agreement. One PA security official asked, 'How can there be security cooperation at a time when Israel is mocking the peace process?'[17]

None the less, some cooperation gradually resumed, both in the field and at the policy-making level. By May 1997, for example, the parties had resumed the joint road patrols mandated by the Interim Agreement.[18] In August 1997 IDF and PA police conducted a joint training exercise involving a simulated road accident involving a Palestinian and an Israeli vehicle. There were new reports that the PA and Israel were working together to prevent Palestinian demonstrations from turning violent.[19]

Still, Israel complained that the Palestinian side would not share much useful intelligence, which was now much harder for Israel to obtain in areas now under Palestinian control.[20] Meanwhile the Palestinians complained that Israel simply provided the PA with information on fugitives and then demanded that the PA arrest them. The PA also defended its posture on intelligence-sharing by stressing that even close allies like

[13] See Arieh O'Sullivan, 'IDF, Palestinians talking on low level', *Jerus. Post*, 9 Apr. 1997.

[14] Barton Gellman, 'Joint Effort Breaks Up Hamas cell; Israel, Palestinians Arrest Group Members', *Wash. Post*, 11 Apr. 1997.

[15] Ibid. (reporting an American official's view that 'The Israelis won't pump it up, and the Palestinians don't want them to, but the Palestinians played an important role here').

[16] See 'Palestinians Aid in Hamas Arrests', *Newsday*, 11 Apr. 1997 (quoting an anonymous 'senior Shin Bet official').

[17] Ibid. (quoting Gaza security chief Mohammed Dahlan).

[18] See 'Arafat Seeks to Restart Peace Talks', *St.-Louis Post-Dispatch*, 5 May 1997 (noting that patrols had resumed in all West Bank cities except Nablus, and that patrols in Nablus were expected to restart soon).

[19] See Rodan, 'Arafat's balancing act with terror' (reporting that the PA and Israeli commanders 'both will plan ways to ensure that [a] protest doesn't get out of hand').

[20] See Ilene R. Prusher, 'Israel Vows a Reply / Threatens Raids Into Palestinian Areas', *Newsday*, 1 Aug. 1997 (reporting that Israeli officials say they are 'almost totally dependent' on the PA for intelligence in PA-controlled areas); Dore Gold, 'War against terrorism requires intelligence', *Jerus. Post*, 25 Aug. 1995 ('if the war on terror is indeed an intelligence war, Israel's access to that sort of intelligence is likely to continually decline as Palestinians, expecting the imminent control of the PLO, no longer see that it is in their interest to work with the Israel authorities').

the United States and Israel have been historically cagey about sharing intelligence.[21] Still, the PA agreed to meet with Israeli and US intelligence officials following a suicide bombing in August 1997,[22] and there were reports that Arafat had agreed to resume some sharing of intelligence with Israel.[23]

The same pattern of intermittent and strained security cooperation continued in 1998. Israel charged that the Palestinian Authority suspended all cooperation in early 1998 and then only partly resumed security cooperation. On the other hand, there were indications that the PA was cracking down again on Hamas militants, not so much to placate Israel as to reduce a political threat to Arafat.[24] In the spring of 1998, for example, the PA arrested dozens of Hamas activists, perhaps as many as 300, and even interrogated Palestinian journalists who had simply interviewed members of Hamas.[25]

The Wye River Memorandum of 23 October 1998 offered hope that security cooperation would improve. The Memorandum established a 'high-ranking' trilateral US–Palestinian–Israeli committee on security cooperation. Among other things, this committee would report to the parties on the 'status of cooperation'.[26] One controversial implication of this arrangement was that the CIA and other US intelligence agencies would play some role in monitoring security cooperation, particularly Palestinian cooperation. In fact, three-way cooperation seems to have helped diminish the rate of terror bombings.[27] Netanyahu's defence minister, Moshe Arens, praised the PA for cooperation in preventing particular terror attacks.[28] But Arens and Netanyahu himself criticized the PA for not doing more to attack the infrastructure of terror groups. Disagreements over this and other matters derailed the Wye process by early 1999. The Barak government took steps to revive the Wye formula; in August 1999, for example, the parties resurrected the JSC, which had not met regularly for three years.[29] At the same time, however, Barak indicated that he felt

[21] See Rodan, 'Arafat's balancing act with terror'.

[22] Jehl, 'Israelis and Palestinians Agree to U.S. Role'. There is a long history of contacts between American and Palestinian security officials, and there have been reports that the CIA is helping to train Palestinian operatives in order to increase Israeli confidence in the PA's security forces. See Tim Weiner, 'C.I.A. Officers, With Israel's Knowledge, Teach Palestinians the Tricks of the Trade', *N.Y. Times*, 5 Mar. 1998.

[23] See, e.g., Editorial, 'Arafat's move', *South China Morning Post*, 6 Sept. 1997.

[24] See, e.g., David Horovitz, '200 Hamas activists arrested by Palestinian Authority', *Irish Times*, 13 Apr. 1998.

[25] See Patrick Cockburn, 'Arafat's battle with Hamas pushes Palestinians to war', *Independent*, 14 Apr. 1998.

[26] Wye River Memorandum, ¶II.B.3.

[27] See Joel Greenberg, '3-Way Effort Seems to Slow Bombings By Terrorists', *N.Y. Times*, 7 Nov. 1998.

[28] Ben Lynfield *et al.*, 'Security cooperation—mixed record', *Jerus. Post*, 29 Aug. 1999.

[29] Lamia Lahoud, 'Joint Security C'tee resumes active role', ibid. 17 Aug. 1999.

the CIA should play a smaller role in monitoring the accord, even as the PA expressed its hope for a continuing CIA role.[30]

The Sharm el-Sheikh Memorandum of 4 September 1999 reaffirmed the parties' commitment to security cooperation without adding any significant new obligations.[31] There was a terrorist incident right after the adoption of the Memorandum, but the PLO quickly condemned it. The Barak government has called on the Palestinians to do more to combat terrorism, but it has not expressed the same level of dissatisfaction as did its predecessor.

Taken as a whole, the foregoing account suggests that the PA's record on security cooperation has been mixed. The PA's record certainly has improved since 1996–7, when it suspended cooperation altogether. The PA has cooperated with Israeli security personnel in the field, even if that cooperation has been less than complete. In general, the PA has been less than fully forthcoming in intelligence sharing, but there was improvement in this area in 1999. The PA's compliance with its security obligations has fluctuated over time, and the fluctuations correspond roughly to the ups and downs in the peace process. The PA's main legal justification for these deficiencies is to point to asserted Israeli violations of the Oslo Accords. Indeed, there is little doubt that PA suspension of security cooperation would be a 'material breach' of Palestinian obligations under the Oslo Accords; for Israel, nothing is more central to the 'object and purpose' of the Accords than prevention of terrorism. Thus the PA's main legal argument parallels Israeli justifications for Israeli non-compliance in other areas, such as redeployment.

The PA's reciprocity argument is subject to the same vulnerability as Israel's: that international law requires countermeasures to be proportional to the original breach. Even if the PA were right that Israel 'breached first' by announcing its plans for Har Homa and for a relatively small redeployment from the West Bank, these asserted violations did not necessarily justify a wholesale suspension of Palestinian security obligations. As we saw in Part III, the early Accords did not set forth explicit provisions either on settlements or on the scope of redeployments, making it harder for the PA to argue that either event was a 'material breach' that justified PA suspension or termination. If Israel's actions were minor breaches, then the PA was entitled to pursue only proportionate countermeasures that themselves were not material breaches. Even if Israel's actions were 'material' breaches, any PA response should have been proportionate to them.

30 See John M. Broder, 'Syrian Peace His Aim, Barak Tells Clinton', *N.Y. Times*, 16 July 1999; Deborah Sontag, 'How Barak Intends to Deal With Arabs, and Americans', ibid. 14 July 1999. Cf. Lamia Lahoud, 'PA wants continued CIA involvement here', *Jerus. Post*, 25 July 1999.

31 See generally Sharm el-Sheikh Memorandum, ¶8.

For example, Israel's plan for a smaller-than-expected redeployment from the West Bank was not a total repudiation of Israel's obligation to redeploy. It was, at worst, a partial repudiation of an obligation that was not spelled out in any concrete terms. Rather than suspend its security obligations altogether, the PA should have responded with a partial suspension of those obligations, perhaps confined to its extradition or weapons-confinement undertakings, or perhaps consisting of a refusal to engage in some form of bureaucratic 'cooperation' (JSC meetings) while continuing to engage in operational cooperation on the ground. In fact, the PA did resume operational cooperation, impliedly admitting that Israel's actions were not so serious a breach as to require complete termination or suspension of all PA obligations.

Another problem with the PA's suspension of its security obligations is that the PA ignored the dispute–resolution provisions of the Oslo Accords and of general treaty law. As we saw in Part III, Israel has done the same in reverse circumstances. The Vienna Convention on the Law of Treaties requires non-breaching parties to give up to three-months' notice of suspension,[32] and the Oslo Accords provide that the parties 'shall' refer disputes to the 'appropriate coordination and cooperation mechanism' established by the agreements.[33]

In any event, at Wye and Sharm el-Sheikh the PA reaffirmed its obligation to cooperate with Israel in security matters. At this writing, the PA appears to be in substantial (though not perfect) compliance with that obligation. The parties are meeting to discuss security questions, they are cooperating to some extent on the sharing and use of intelligence, and the Palestinians are cooperating in the field with Israeli security teams. Full compliance requires the PA to move beyond preventing particular terrorist incidents and to dismantling the infrastructure of terrorist groups. We will return to the infrastructure question in a few moments. We now turn to PA obligations on incitement.

Preventing incitement and hostile propaganda

The Palestinian side has repeatedly run afoul of its obligation to refrain from incitement and hostile propaganda. Article XXII(1) of the Interim Agreement provides that Israel and the Palestinians

> shall seek to foster mutual understanding and tolerance and shall accordingly abstain from incitement, including hostile propaganda, against each other and,

[32] Vienna Convention on the Law of Treaties, 23 May 1969, UN Doc. A/CONF. 39/27, Arts. 65(1), 67(1).

[33] Interim Agreement, Art. XXI.

without derogating from the principle of freedom of expression, shall take legal measures to prevent such incitement by any organizations, groups or individuals within their jurisdiction.

This provision has two main prongs: it prohibits the PA itself from engaging in 'incitement', and it obliges the PA to take 'legal measures' to prevent incitement by private parties. Interestingly, Article XXII(2) also obliges the parties to ensure that their educational systems 'contribute to the peace' between them and that they will 'refrain from the introduction of any motifs' that might harm the peace process.

PA officials have repeatedly made statements that are inconsistent with the PA's obligation to 'abstain from incitement, including hostile propaganda', against Israel. One recurring theme has been the baseless charge that Israel purposely poisons Palestinians. In 1997 a Palestinian representative asserted at a session of the UN Human Rights Commission in Geneva that 'Israeli authorities' had 'infected by injection 300 Palestinian children with the HIV virus during the years of the intifada'.[34] This charge echoed Arafat's 1983 assertion that Israel had been 'poisoning Palestinian schoolgirls'.[35] More recently, Suha Arafat, wife of Yasser Arafat, embarrassed a visiting Hillary Clinton by renewing the charge of Israeli poisoning as Mrs Clinton listened: 'Our people have been subjected to the daily intensive use of poisonous gas by the Israeli forces, which have led to an increase in cancer cases among women and children.'[36] The PA's Deputy Ministry of Supplies has also accused Israel of deliberately distributing spoiled or carcinogenic food in the PA's territories. This indictment has included the curious (and unfounded) charge that Israel distributes chewing gum laced with an aphrodisiac.[37]

The PA has also likened Israel's policies to those of Nazi Germany. In 1997 the PA Information Ministry asserted that Israeli practices are 'equal with, if not more brutal than, those practiced by occupying Nazi soldiers' in Europe during World War II.[38] One member of the PA's Legislative Council has compared Netanyahu's book *A Place Among the Nations* to

[34] Uriel Heilman, 'PA official: Israel infected Palestinians with AIDS', *Jerus. Post*, 17 Mar. 1997 (quoting Nabil Ramlawi). This and other examples are collected at Israel's website.

[35] Ibid. See '2 Americans Study Schoolgirl Illness in West Bank', *N.Y. Times*, 5 Apr. 1983. The *New York Times* reported the poison charges and then later ran this 'correction': 'The [*Times'*] coverage gave more weight to the Arab charges than to the American and Israeli explanations. There was no journalistic justification for the disparity.' Correction: Editor's Note, ibid. 18 June 1983. See also Moshe Kohn, 'The Palestinian "Protocols" ', *Jerus. Post*, 2 May 1997.

[36] William A. Orme, Jr., 'While Mrs. Clinton Looks On, Palestinian Officials Criticize Israel', *N.Y. Times*, 12 Nov. 1999.

[37] Jon Immanuel, 'PA official: Israel lacing gum with aphrodisiac', *Jerus. Post*, 27 May 1997.

[38] PA Information Ministry press release, 10 Dec. 1997, quoted in Jay Bushinsky, 'PA antisemitism documented by GPO', *Jerus. Post*, 17 Dec. 1997.

Hitler's *Mein Kampf*.[39] References to the Nazi regime also take the form of denying the full scope of the Holocaust. The PA's official television station once broadcast a programme asserting that 'the Jews exaggerate what the Nazis did to them [in the Holocaust]. They claim there were 6 million killed, but precise scientific research demonstrates that there were no more than 400,000.'[40]

Some Palestinian propaganda has taken the form of anti-Semitic slurs. Much of this has emanated from Palestinians who are not officials of the PA per se but who none the less have connections to the PA or whose comments have been broadcast in the PA-controlled media. In a Friday prayer sermon in 1997, for example, Mufti Ikrima Sabri, who was appointed by Arafat, called for the destruction of America because it is 'ruled by Zionist Jews' and foresaw vengeance against 'colonialist settlers who are sons of monkeys and pigs'.[41] Some 'independent' Palestinian sources were reportedly 'appalled' by the Mufti's remarks and criticized the Speaker of the Palestinian Legislative Council, Ahmed Qurie, who was present during the sermon, for not leaving in protest.[42] But the PA does not seem to have done much to discourage further outbursts by the Mufti. Indeed, a year later the Mufti denigrated the Western Wall as nothing more than a 'fence belonging to a Moslem holy site' and said that 'If the Jews really want peace, they must absolutely forget about having any rights over the Temple Mount.'[43]

It seems clear that much of this constitutes prohibited 'hostile propaganda' within the meaning of the Interim Agreement. The clearest violations are the inflammatory statements issued directly by the PA or its officials. But even incitement by individual Palestinians, or quasi-official statements like those of the Mufti, are cognizable under the Agreement, for it requires the PA to take steps to 'prevent' such propaganda. Until recently, there was little evidence that the PA had done so.

In defence of the PA, it might be argued that the phrase 'incitement, including hostile propaganda' in Article XXII of the Interim Agreement

[39] Elli Wohlgelernter, 'Learning to See "The Enemy" as Victims', ibid. (quoting Nahid Munir Al-Rayyis, writing in *Al-Quds*, 15 Oct. 1997: 'Just as Hitler's *Mein Kampf* was a warning sign for his future political path which brought disaster on Germany and the world, so Netanyahu's *A Place Among the Nations* explains all of the author's initiatives since he took power in Israel. . . . The racist curses against the enemy and the legendary praises of himself make a noticeable point of similarity between Hitler's and Netanyahu's books').

[40] Ibid., quoting official PA television station, 25 Aug. 1997. The Palestinian media has also suggested that 'cooperation between the Jews and the Nazis during World War II' led to 'forged claims of the Zionists regarding alleged acts of slaughter perpetrated against the Jews during the same period'. Ibid. See also Bushinsky, 'PA antisemitism'.

[41] Jay Bushinsky, 'Arafat-appointed mufti calls settlers "sons of monkeys and pigs" ', *Jerus. Post*, 14 July 1997.

[42] Ibid.

[43] Margot Dudkevitch, 'PM: PA officials disparaging Jewish holy sites', ibid. 27 May 1998.

should be read narrowly, as outlawing only incitement to violence, not insults or anti-Semitic slurs. Indeed, international criminal law, like municipal law, normally couples 'incitement' with a substantive offence, often a violent offence, not with mere insults.[44] But the text of the Interim Agreement makes clear that 'incitement' includes more than direct incitement to violence, for it also includes 'hostile propaganda'. Moreover, what might be merely obnoxious speech in some countries might seem more like incitement to violence in Israel, where many people perceive at least an indirect link between 'fighting words' and the assassination of Prime Minister Rabin.[45]

That said, the anti-propaganda provision in the Interim Agreement probably should be read narrowly. The Interim Agreement itself warns that the parties must prohibit incitement (including propaganda) 'without derogating from the principle of freedom of expression'.[46] But the norms of free expression in human rights law generally permit, indeed encourage, restrictions on incitement. Human rights law *requires* states to refrain from some forms of incitement, including 'propaganda for war' and 'advocacy of . . . hatred', and to prohibit individuals from engaging in similar conduct. In particular, Article 20 of the International Covenant on Civil and Political Rights provides that '[a]ny propaganda for war shall be prohibited by law' and that '[a]ny advocacy of national, racial or religious hatred that constitutes incitement to discrimination, hostility or violence shall be prohibited by law'.[47] This provision not only makes clear that

[44] See, e.g., Statute of the International Tribunal for the Former Yugoslavia, in Report of the Secretary-General, UN Doc. S/25704 (1993), Art. 4(3)(c) (providing for punishment of 'direct and public incitement to commit genocide'); Convention on the Prevention and Punishment of the Crime of Genocide, 9 Dec. 1948, 78 U.N.T.S. 277, Art. 3(c) (similar). Cf. also Henry Campbell Black *et al.*, *Black's Law Dictionary*, 6th edn (St Paul, MN: West Publishing Co., 1990), 762 (defining 'incite' as, among other things, to 'arouse; urge; provoke; encourage; spur on; goad; stir up; instigate; set in motion; as, to "incite" a riot').

[45] See, e.g., Editorial, 'Poisonous Palestinian Rhetoric', *Jerus. Post*, 15 Nov. 1999.

[46] Interim Agreement, Art. XXII(1).

[47] International Covenant on Civil and Political Rights, 16 Dec. 1966, 999 U.N.T.S. 171, Art. 20(1) and (2). The Covenant's requirement that states prohibit incitement is, however, derogable in 'time of public emergency which threatens the life of the nation' provided that such derogation does not involve 'discrimination on the basis of race, color, sex, language, religion or social origin'. Ibid., Art. 4(1).

Some states do take a narrower view of a state's duty to prohibit incitement. The United States is one prominent example. When giving its advice and consent to ratification of the Civil and Political Covenant, the US Senate's first reservation concerned the incitement provision in Article 20. The Senate said that Article 20 'does not authorize or require legislation or other action by the United States that would restrict the right of free speech and association' under the US Constitution. US Senate Resolution of Advice and Consent to Ratification of the International Covenant on Civil and Political Rights, 138 Cong. Rec. S4781 (1991), ¶I(1). See also *Brandenburg v. Ohio*, 395 U.S. 444 (1969) (per curiam) (First Amendment to the US Constitution does not permit a State to forbid 'advocacy of the use of force' except where such advocacy 'is directed to inciting or producing imminent lawless action and is likely to incite or produce such action'). The United States apparently reads its obligations states are duty-bound to refrain themselves from engaging in 'propaganda for war', but are also required to prohibit incitement to 'discrimination' and 'hostility'—not just incitement to violence—by private parties.

Nor can the PA excuse its propagandizing by pointing to similar violations by the Israeli side. While the Israeli government has not exactly been circumspect in its criticisms of Arafat and the PA, it has not made the kind of baseless and prejudiced allegations that have emanated from Palestinian officials and institutions. In particular, the Israeli government has not made racist comments about Palestinians. Moreover, Israel has taken steps to punish individual Israelis who engage in incitement against Palestinians. In December 1997, for example, an Israeli judge imposed a lengthy prison sentence on an Israeli woman who had, among other things, posted pictures in Hebron denigrating the prophet Mohammed.[48] Admittedly, Israel has tolerated some inflammatory statements by anti-Palestinian Israelis, but in general Israel has balanced its anti-incitement obligations against its free-speech obligations much more prudently than has the PA.

In any event, even if Israel has also failed to comply fully with its obligations under the incitement clause—and the Israeli record on this issue is much better than the PA record—that partial non-compliance does not legally justify the PA's clear non-compliance. As we have seen, countermeasures must be proportional to the original breach. More to the point, the PA has not seriously tried to justify incitement as a 'countermeasure' to Israeli incitement—i.e. as a means of deterring or punishing Israeli incitement. The objectionable outbursts by the PA have been directed at Israeli policy and practice, not at Israeli incitement.

Finally, in so far as the incitement provisions have a 'humanitarian' character—the prevention of hateful speech and denigration of religion—then a breach of those provisions by one party cannot justify their suspension by the other. The Vienna Convention provides that 'material breach' never justifies the suspension of 'provisions relating to the protection of the human person contained in treaties of a humanitarian character'.[49] The incitement provisions probably are 'provisions relating to the protection of the human person', since part of their effect is to prevent the spread of hateful or prejudiced propaganda. As we have seen, Article 20 of the International Covenant on Civil and Political Rights does regard

to punish incitement under the Genocide Convention as 'consistent' with the language from *Brandenburg*. See Sen. Comm. on For'n Rels, 'International Covenant on the Prevention and Punishment of the Crime of Genocide', S. Exec. Rep. No. 92–6, 92d Cong., 1st Sess. 1–18 (4 May 1971).

48 Elli Wohlgelernter, 'Susskin convicted of putting up pig flyer in Hebron', *Jerus. Post*, 31 Dec. 1997.

49 Vienna Convention on the Law of Treaties, Art. 60(5).

propaganda as a potential human rights violation, and the anti-propaganda provisions of the Oslo Accords are consistent with those of the Covenant. It is somewhat more doubtful whether the Oslo Accords qualify as 'treaties of a humanitarian character', but it is true that their major purposes are to secure a basic human right for the Palestinians—self-determination—and equally important rights for the Israelis—peace and security. In any event, the important question should be whether the provisions at issue are humanitarian, not whether the broader Accords of which they are part are humanitarian. In other words, the Vienna Convention's special provision on material breach of human rights obligations should be interpreted as covering all treaties that contain reciprocal human rights obligations, not just treaties primarily dedicated to human rights or humanitarian law. One party's material breach of a human rights obligation should never justify the other party in retaliating with further violations of human rights.

There have been recent signs that the PA is taking incitement more seriously. In the 1998 Wye River Memorandum, the PA agreed to adopt a decree 'prohibiting all forms of incitement to violence or terror', and the parties established an anti-incitement committee.[50] The PA has issued the anti-incitement decree.[51] The committee met for the first time in late 1998, and since then has met numerous times; on occasion, it has reported progress.[52] Among other things, the committee has been working to agree on whether incitement should be defined to include direct or indirect incitement to violence.[53] More recently, the chair of the Israeli delegation to the committee deplored Suha Arafat's comments on poisoning.[54]

Finally, both parties are obliged to ensure that their educational systems 'contribute' to peace and avoid unhelpful 'motifs'. Israel has made important steps forward on this score. In 1999 the government approved new textbooks that present a more balanced view of the history of the Arab–Israeli conflict.[55] The Palestinians have been slower to adopt

50 Wye River Memorandum, ¶2(A)(3)(b).

51 See Danna Harman *et al.*, 'Wye redeployment begins today', *Jerus. Post*, 20 Nov. 1998; Danna Harman, *et al.*, 'PNC vote not enough for withdrawal', ibid. 14 Dec. 1998.

52 See, e.g., Hillel Kuttler, 'Gov't: Progress with PA over incitement claims', ibid. 28 Feb. 1999. See also Danna Harman, 'Officials: Wye on hold till after elections', ibid. 17 Dec. 1998.

53 Danna Harman, 'News in brief', ibid. 19 Jan. 1999.

54 Laura King, 'Hillary Clinton ends "difficult" Mideast trip', ibid. 14 Nov. 1999.

55 Ethan Bronner, 'Israel's History Textbooks Replace Myths With Facts', *N.Y. Times*, 14 Aug. 1999. This development parallels the intensifying debate between 'new historians' in Israel and 'traditionalist' or 'Zionist' historians. See Larry Derfner, 'Doing battle over history', *Jerus. Post*, 15 Oct. 1999; Ethan Bronner, 'Israel: The Revised Edition', *N.Y. Times Book Review*, 14 Nov. 1999. Bronner's essay reviews two interesting examples of the new history: Benny Morris, *Righteous Victims: A History of the Zionist–Arab Conflict, 1881–1999* (New York: Knopf, 1999); and Avi Shlaim, *The Iron Wall: Israel and the Arab World Since 1948* (New York: Norton, 1999).

more conciliatory textbooks, only in part because of a lack of resources. The PA adopted old Egyptian and Jordanian books, some of which contained some passages comparing Zionism to Nazism and denying Jewish connections to Jerusalem. The Palestinians say they intend to replace these objectionable texts with new ones, perhaps by Palestinian authors, but they also stress that Palestinian schools face larger problems, such as lack of electricity and other basic resources.[56]

In sum, the obligation in the Interim Agreement is clear: the parties must refrain from incitement, including hostile propaganda, and must take steps to prevent it by private parties. The PA's record on this point falls far short of the mark. Israel's transgressions on this issue have been much less serious, and in any event treaty law does not permit the PA to justify its own serious violations of the incitement clause by pointing to similar violations by Israel. Both parties, but especially the PA, must do more to prevent incitement and hostile propaganda.

Combating terrorist organizations and infrastructure

The Note for the Record accompanying the Hebron Protocol next obliges the PA to '[c]ombat systematically and effectively terrorist organizations and infrastructure'.[57] This obligation grows out of similar commitments in the Interim Agreement. Article XIV(3) of the Interim Agreement provides: 'Except for the Palestinian Police and the Israeli military forces, no other armed forces shall be established or operate in the West Bank and Gaza Strip.' Article XV(1) states more explicitly: 'Both sides shall take all measures necessary in order to prevent acts of terrorism, crime and hostilities directed against each other, against individuals falling under the other's authority and against their property, and shall take legal measures against offenders.' There are similar provisions in the Wye and Sharm el-Sheikh Memoranda. For that matter, there are similar provisions in the Note for the Record itself: the obligation to combat terrorism is obviously closely linked to the more particularized obligation to cooperate in security matters, already discussed in detail above. Since this obligation is similar to that one, the following discussion will be brief.

The PA has a mixed record on fighting terror groups, though it seems to have improved in 1999. On the one hand, the PA has taken steps to arrest and incarcerate some terrorists, and it has on occasion cooperated with Israel in combating terrorism. There is considerable debate, however,

[56] See Ben Lynfield, 'Mapping a Palestinian curriculum', *Jerus. Post*, 27 Aug. 1999; 'Conference deals with antisemitism', ibid. 17 June 1999.

[57] Note for the Record, 'Palestinian Responsibilities', ¶2(c).

over whether the actual rate of terror has dropped since the Oslo Accords. Some observers have argued that the rate of deaths from terrorist attacks has actually increased since the Declaration of Principles, but others say that PA cooperation has helped prevent terror bombings.[58] Moreover, while the PA has taken action against individual terrorists, it has apparently done less to curb the activities of terrorist groups, and in fact senior PA officials have on occasion praised Hamas and spoken of war with Israel. Still, Arafat did step up his efforts to rein in terror groups in 1999. The Palestinian police arrested scores of members of Hamas and other radical groups in 1999—arrests that dismayed human rights activists.

Moreover, it is difficult to document instances in which the PA has condoned, encouraged, or carried out specific terrorist acts. As we have already seen, the most famous allegation is that Arafat gave the 'green light' to terrorist groups to renew acts of terrorism in March 1997, in the wake of Israel's announcement of plans to build Jewish housing at Har Homa and of Netanyahu's proposed pullback from 9 per cent of the West Bank. The Netanyahu government alleged that in early March, Arafat met with leaders of various terrorist groups and made it known that he would not oppose renewed terrorist attacks.[59] The PA, however, hotly disputes that Arafat ever gave a 'green light' or any other form of consent to renewed terrorism. Subsequent events, however, do raise questions. On 21 March 1997, shortly after the supposed 'green light', Hamas did in fact carry out a terrorist bombing in Tel Aviv, causing the death of three Israelis.[60] Israel has also alleged that Palestinian police have actively promoted terror. Israel asserted that an official of the PA police in Nablus has ordered terrorist attacks, and it cites 'strong indications' that Palestinian Police Chief Ghazi Jabali 'is involved'.[61]

It may never be entirely certain whether Arafat gave a 'green light' to terrorism in March 1997, but it is clear that the PA has not stopped all terrorism against Israel. The PA (like Israel) lacks the capacity to stop all violence, but the PA's often inflammatory rhetoric—already discussed in the section on incitement above—is grounds for suspicions that the PA's commitment to stop terrorism is less than complete. Still, the tone of PA and Israeli statements moderated in the second half of 1999, and there is reason to hope that the PA will continue to improve its record on fighting terror groups.

[58] See Greenberg, '3-Way Effort Seems to Slow Bombings By Terrorists'.

[59] See Jon Immanuel, 'Ya'alon: Arafat okayed terror. Army chiefs warn of future attacks', *Jerus. Post*, 24 Mar. 1997.

[60] *N.Y. Times*, 22 Mar. 1997.

[61] Office of the Prime Minister, 'Special Report: PA Has Failed to Fulfill Its Commitments Under the Hebron Accord', 20 July 1997, ¶2c, available at http://www.pmo.gov.il.

Arrest, prosecution, and punishment of terrorists

The Note for the Record calls for the 'apprehension, prosecution and punishment of terrorists',[62] and the Interim Agreement requires both sides to 'take all legal measures against offenders', including terrorists.[63] Annexe I to the Interim Agreement is more specific: 'The Palestinian Police will arrest and prosecute individuals who are suspected of perpetrating acts of violence and terror.'[64] The Wye River and Sharm el-Sheikh Memoranda reaffirm these obligations.[65]

Again, the parties disagree about the extent of PA compliance with these obligations. The PA says it is complying in good faith. Indeed, since the onset of the Oslo process, the PA has arrested, prosecuted, and imprisoned a number of common criminals and terrorists, as well as some PA policemen, for crimes against Israelis.[66] In the spring of 1998 the PA made mass arrests of Hamas members in connection with the death of a Hamas bomb-maker,[67] arrests that were welcomed by Netanyahu.[68] The PA made another round of mass arrests in 1999. The PA position is that this record amounts to substantial compliance.

Israel, however, has complained that there have been relatively few reported prosecutions (as opposed to arrests) of terrorists. Israel has charged that the PA has adopted a 'revolving door' policy of detaining and then releasing known terrorists.[69] If true, this charge would undermine PA

62 Note for the Record, 'Palestinian responsibilities', ¶2(d).

63 Interim Agreement, Art. XV(1).

64 Interim Agreement, Annexe I, Art. II(1)(d). See also ibid., Art. II(1)(b) ('The Palestinian Police will act systematically against *all expressions* of violence and terror') (emphasis added). It is not entirely clear what is meant by an 'expression' of violence and terror. It might be taken literally to mean only 'incitement' to violence, as is already prohibited by Article XXII(1) of the Interim Agreement, or more figuratively to refer to any 'manifestation' of terror or violence.

65 Wye River Memorandum, ¶II(A)(1)(d); Sharm el-Sheikh Memorandum, ¶8(b)(2).

66 See, e.g., Joel Greenberg, 'Arafat Orders the Arrest of Policemen', *N.Y. Times*, 22 July 1997 (reporting that Arafat ordered the arrest of several PA policemen accused of conspiring to attack Jewish settlers in the West Bank); Steve Rodan and Mohammed Najib, 'PA arrests 2 Hamas men', *Jerus. Post*, 5 Sept. 1997; Joel Greenberg, 'Islamic Militants in Gaza Picked Up by Arafat Police', *N.Y. Times*, 10 Sept. 1997; Clyde Haberman, 'Palestinian Police Rounding Up Radicals', ibid. 15 Nov. 1994; Joel Greenberg, 'Palestinians in Gaza Arrest 13 Militants After Attacks on Israelis', ibid. 16 Aug. 1994.

67 See Serge Schmemann, 'Palestinian Police Arrest Suspected Hamas Killer', ibid. 12 Apr. 1998 (reporting that the PA arrested 'dozens' of Hamas members); Cockburn, 'Arafat's battle with Hamas pushes Palestinians to war' (reporting on the mass arrest of at least 60 and perhaps as many as 300 members of Hamas); Steve Rodan and Mohammed Najib, 'Hamas leader Rantisi held by PA', *Jerus. Post*, 10 Apr. 1998 (reporting that the PA arrested Hamas leader Abdel Aziz Rantisi, who had accused the PA of involvement in the death of the Hamas bombmaker).

68 See Jay Bushinsky, 'Netanyahu: Arrests a positive sign', ibid. 7 Apr. 1998.

69 See Office of the PM, 'Special Report', ¶2d (citing the release of 'dozens of terrorists' from detention).

claims of good faith, since quick release of prisoners hardly constitutes 'prosecution' or 'punishment' within the meaning of the Oslo Accords. Israel has also asserted that the PA employs 'numerous' terrorists in its security services, 'including at least 23 wanted for the murder of Israelis', and the PA Police Commander 'has acknowledged that more than 150 members of Hamas and the PFLP are currently in key positions in the Palestinian police'.[70] This allegation, if true, is troubling, but it is not so clearly a violation of the arrest-and-punish provisions of the Accords. That said, the Accords do impose some restrictions on the composition of the Palestinian police force; those restrictions will be considered in the next section.

On balance, the available evidence suggests that the PA has substantially complied with its obligation to 'arrest' criminals but not with its obligation to prosecute and punish them. Indeed, the PA may have gone too far in arresting terrorists and not far enough in actually trying and convicting them. Palestinian human rights groups, however, have bitterly criticized the PA's mass arrests of terror suspects as a violation of human rights and the rule of law.[71] Critics have also noted that the PA arrests not only terror suspects but also opponents of Arafat who do not advocate violence against Israel.[72] According to Amnesty International, the PA arrested more than 1,200 people on security grounds in 1996, and yet detainees 'were rarely charged with any offence or brought before a judge within the legal limits laid down by Palestinian law'.[73] Amnesty reports that torture of detainees by the PA was 'widespread', and at least ten people died at the hands of PA security forces in 1996.[74] The *AI Reports* for more recent years document similar patterns. These practices obviously raise serious questions of human rights law; these are taken up in Chapter 13.

Extradition of criminal suspects to Israel

The Note for the Record provides: 'Requests for transfer of suspects and defendants will be acted upon in accordance with Article II(7)(f) of Annex IV to the Interim Agreement.'[75] Annex IV deals with 'Legal

[70] See Office of the PM, 'Special Report', ¶2d.

[71] See, e.g., John Lancaster, 'Palestinian Authority Wins Few Kudos for Arrest Sweep; U.S. Lauds Show of Anti-Terrorism Commitment, but Israel and Suspects' Relatives Protest', *Wash. Post*, 13 Sept. 1997 (reporting that the director of the Palestinian Center for Human Rights condemned a PA mass arrest as 'an incredible setback for the rule of law').

[72] Ibid.

[73] Amnesty International, *AI Report 1997: Palestinian Authority*, available at http://www.amnesty.org/ailib/aireport/ar97/MDE21.htm.

[74] Ibid.

[75] Note for the Record, 'Palestinian Responsibilities', ¶2(e).

Matters', and Article II(7) of that Annex contains a rather perfunctory extradition agreement.[76] The Wye River Memorandum reiterates these obligations and adds that the US has been asked to report on compliance with them.[77] Israel charges that the PA has violated the extradition agreement by failing to render any of several dozen terror suspects whose extradition has been requested by Israel. Before considering the extent of PA compliance with its extradition obligations, it is worth pausing to examine some of the highly unusual features of the extradition provisions of the Oslo Accords.

One startling aspect of the extradition agreement is its broad scope. Articles II(7)(a) and (b) require each side to transfer to the other fugitives who are 'suspected of, charged with, or convicted of' certain offences. This provision is unusual because it mandates extradition even for fugitives who are merely 'suspected' of a crime, whereas most extradition treaties require that the fugitive either have been charged or convicted. This provision doubtless reflects Israel's wish to interrogate suspected terrorists, but it may also reflect Palestinian preferences as well. Such a provision seems inconsistent with human rights law, which establishes a presumption of innocence and forbids 'arbitrary arrest and detention'.[78] It is conceivable that these are *jus cogens* norms, from which no derogation is permitted.

The evidentiary requirements for extradition, set forth in Articles II(7)(c) and (d) of the Annexe, are somewhat more relaxed than is usual for an international extradition treaty. Under these provisions of the Annexe, the requesting party need only 'specify the grounds' for the request and supply an arrest warrant issued by a competent court. No showing of 'reasonable grounds' is required unless the PA is requesting a non-Palestinian, in which case the PA must also show that the offence is punishable by not less than 7 years imprisonment.[79] By contrast, most extradition treaties require that the requesting state present evidence sufficient to convince a court of the requested state that there is a reasonable basis (in common-law terms, 'probable cause') to hold the fugitive for trial, regardless of the nationality of the defendant. Again, the absence of such a provision from the Oslo Accords could conceivably raise questions of human rights law. As noted above, human rights law forbids 'arbitrary arrest and detention' and provides that anyone detained is entitled to a judicial proceeding to determine the 'lawfulness of his detention'.[80]

[76] These provisions are based on substantially similar extradition obligations set forth in Annexe III to the Gaza–Jericho Agreement of May 1994. Gaza–Jericho Agreement, Annexe III, Arts. I–II.

[77] Wye River Memorandum, ¶II(C)(3).

[78] International Covenant on Civil and Political Rights, Arts. 9(1), 14(2). See also Universal Declaration of Human Rights, 10 Dec. 1948, G.A. Res. 217 (III 1948), Art. 9 ('No one shall be subjected to arbitrary arrest, detention or exile').

[79] Interim Agreement, Annexe IV, Art. II(7)(d)(1)–(2).

[80] International Covenant on Civil and Political Rights, Art. 9(1) and (4).

The provision of the Annexe limiting extradition to crimes punishable by at least 7 years imprisonment is distinctive in three ways. First, most extradition treaties do limit extradition to more serious offences, but those are typically defined as involving imprisonment for at least one year, not seven years.[81] Second, extradition treaties typically require that conduct be criminal in *both* jurisdictions, not just in the requesting state.[82] This is known as the requirement of 'dual criminality'. Finally, most extradition treaties require dual criminality for *all* offenders, not just offenders of a particular nationality. The seven-year minimum for non-Palestinian fugitives reflects concern about subjecting non-Palestinians to the jurisdiction of the nascent Palestinian judicial system. Still, while these provisions may be unusual, they probably do not run afoul of any *jus cogens* norm.

The extradition arrangements are also unusual in how they treat extradition of the requested party's own nationals. As a general matter, Israel is required to extradite only non-Israelis, whereas the PA is obliged to extradite all individuals, including Palestinians.[83] Most extradition treaties either oblige both sides to extradite their nationals or oblige neither side to do so. Thus the extradition arrangements strike Palestinians as one-sided.[84] Even some Israelis concede that it is too much to ask the PA to extradite Palestinians when Israel is not expected to extradite Israelis.[85] Still, there is probably no *jus cogens* norm prohibiting parties from making an agreement by which one agrees to extradite its nationals and the other does not, especially when one of the parties is not yet a state with its own 'nationals'.

The extradition arrangements are unusual in yet another way: they do not contain any exemption for so-called 'political offences'. Almost all international extradition treaties (including those of Israel) provide that

81 See, e.g., Treaty of Extradition, US–UK, 8 June 1972, 28 U.S.T. 227, Art. III(1)(a) (requiring extradition for any offence punishable under the laws of both states by imprisonment for more than one year). But see Convention on Extradition Between the Government of the United States of America and the Government of the State of Israel, 10 Dec. 1962, 14 U.S.T. 1707, Art. II (providing that certain offences are not extraditable unless punishable in both countries by 'imprisonment exceeding three years').

82 See, e.g., Treaty of Extradition, US–UK, Art. III(1)(a).

83 Compare Interim Agreement, Annexe IV, Art. II(7)(a) (providing that the PA may request Israel to extradite a 'non-Israeli') with ibid., Art. II(7)(b) (providing that Israel may request the PA to extradite 'an individual'). Other provisions of Annexe IV make clear that each party is legally bound to act on such requests. See, e.g., ibid., Art. II(7)(f)(1) ('Both sides, upon receipt of a request in accordance with this Article, shall effect the arrest and transfer requested').

84 See, e.g., Mary Curtius, 'Palestinians Thwarting Extraditions, Israel Says', *L.A. Times*, 14 Sept. 1995 (noting that Palestinians regarded the nationality provisions in the Gaza–Jericho extradition agreement as 'unfair').

85 See, e.g., Abraham Ravinovich, 'Poor chemistry, but plenty of complaints', *Jerus. Post*, 16 Jan. 1998 (attributing this view to Ron Pundak, one of the 'architects' of the Oslo Accords, and to Israel's then Internal Security Minister Avigdor Kahalani).

no one shall be extradited for a 'political offense'.[86] Although that phrase has produced at least three varying definitions in international practice,[87] at a minimum it is understood to mean that 'pure' political offences—non-violent political speech, for example—might be exempt from extradition. Thus the exclusion is a bit striking. Still, there is debate over whether terrorist offences qualify as political offences, and because at least some case law suggest that terrorism is 'political',[88] it is not surprising that the political offence exception was omitted altogether from the Oslo Accords.

One open question is whether the political offence exception is none the less an implied term of the Accords, on the theory that the political offence doctrine is a norm of customary international law that applies to any international extradition agreement. The short answer is that one should be quite reluctant to import such an exception into the Oslo Accords, a major purpose of which was, after all, to curb terrorism and other violence. Moreover, the modern multilateral treaties on terrorism treat many 'political' offences as extraditable.[89] It thus is unlikely that the

[86] See, e.g., Convention on Extradition Between the Government of the United States of America and the Government of the State of Israel, 10 Dec. 1962, 14 U.S.T. 1707, Art. VI(4) (providing that extradition shall be denied when 'the offense is regarded by the requested Party as one of a political character or if the person sought proves that the request for his extradition has, in fact, been made with a view to trying or punishing him for an offense of a political character'). Still, the political offence doctrine does not preclude the extradition of terrorists to Israel, for not every politically-motivated crime is a political offence. See, e.g., *In re Extradition of Atta*, 706 F. Supp. 504, 521 (1981) (holding that not all politically-motivated acts are political offences); *Eain v. Wilkes*, 641 F.2d 504 (7th Cir. 1981) (approving extradition to Israel of a bombing suspect).

[87] See In re Castioni, 1 Q.B. 149, 167 (1891) (Anglo-American 'incidence' test); *In re Giovanni Gatti*, 14 Ann. Dig. 145 (Cour d'appel, Grenoble 1947) (French 'political objective' test); *The Pavan Case*, 4 Ann. Dig. 347 (Fed. Trib., Switz. 1928) (Swiss 'predominance' test); cf. *In re Piperno*, No. 1343–79, Cour d'appel de Paris, Chambre d'accusation, 17 Oct. 1979 (adopting the Swiss test).

More ink has been spilled on the political offence exception than on any other topic in extradition law. See, e.g., M. Cherif Bassiouni (ed.), *International Terrorism and Political Crimes* (Springfield, IL: Thomas, 1975); Christine van den Wijngaert, *The Political Offense Exception to Extradition: the Delicate Problem of Balancing the Rights of the Individual and the International Public Order* (Deventer, the Netherlands; Boston: Kluwer, 1980); Miriam E. Sapiro, Note, 'Extradition in an Era of Terrorism: The Need to Abolish the Political Offense Exception', 61 *N.Y.U. L. Rev.* 654 (1986); Geoff S. Gilbert, 'Terrorism and the Political Offense Exemption Reappraised', 34 *Int'l & Comp. L. Q.* 695 (1985); Thomas E. Carbonneau, 'Terrorist Acts—Crimes or Political Infractions?', 3 *Hastings Int'l & Comp. L. Rev.* 265 (1980); Manuel R. Garcia-Mora, 'The Nature of Political Offenses: A Knotty Problem of Extradition Law', 48 *Va. L. Rev.* 1226 (1962).

[88] See, e.g., *In re Doherty*, 599 F. Supp. 270 (S.D.N.Y. 1984) (refusing to extradite IRA operative accused of homicide in Northern Ireland).

[89] See, e.g., Convention for the Suppression of Unlawful Acts Against the Safety of Civil Aviation, 23 Sept. 1971, 10 I.L.M. 1151 (1971), Art. 1, 7–8. Cf. also Supplementary Treaty Concerning the Extradition Treaty, US–UK, 25 June 1985, 24 I.L.M. 1105 (1985), Art. I (providing that certain violent offences do not constitute political offences).

PA can invoke a 'political offence exception' to extradition. In fact, it does not appear to have done so.

The provisions on 'provisional arrest' are also unusual. Most extradition treaties provide that the requesting state can ask the requested state for 'provisional arrest' of a fugitive pending submission of a formal, documented request for extradition. Typically the requesting state has 30 to 60 days after provisional arrest in which to submit a full-scale extradition request.[90] But Annex IV to the Interim Agreement provides for a detention period of only seven days following provisional arrest. This clause is of a piece with the rest of the extradition arrangements: it is designed to promote a speedy and relatively informal system of extradition. In many respects it resembles extradition between states of a federal entity more than it does international extradition. There is no reason to believe that this arrangement violates human rights law; if anything, a shorter provisional-arrest period helps protect human rights.

One provision that *is* increasingly typical of modern extradition treaties is Article II(7)(g), which provides that '[n]o person shall be transferred in respect of an offense punishable by capital punishment unless the requesting side undertakes that capital punishment shall not be imposed in the case'. This provision would seem to allay concerns that a fugitive might be put to death by the requesting side against the wishes of the requested side. Some recent high-profile extradition cases do suggest that assurances have to be ironclad before they will be honoured.[91]

The PA does not have a good record of compliance with its extradition obligations. On 31 March 1997, for example, Israel requested the extradition of some thirty-one terror suspects from the PA.[92] The PA has generally ignored these requests. In only a few cases has the PA actually refused extradition. In most cases, it simply does nothing. According to critics of the PA, it has occasionally given a fugitive a very perfunctory trial, imposed a lengthy sentence, and then released the prisoners within a few months.[93] On occasion the PA has turned over one or two fugitives, as in the spring of 1998, when it extradited the killers of an Israeli Arab.[94] But for the most part the PA has dragged its feet. By early 1999, the number of fugitives sought by Israel had grown to forty-four.[95]

[90] See, e.g., Treaty of Extradition, US–UK, Art. VIII(2) (45 days).

[91] See, e.g., *Soering v. UK*, 161 E.C.H.R. 4 (ser. A, 1989), reprinted in 28 I.L.M. 1063 (1990); *In re Venezia*, 25 June 1996, Sentence No. 223-1996, Const. Ct. Italy, reprinted in 47 *Cath. U. L. Rev.* 591 (1998).

[92] See Office of the PM, 'Special Report', ¶2e.

[93] Evelyn Gordon, 'PA routinely flouts extradition requests for terrorists', *Jerus. Post*, 13 Dec. 1996.

[94] See Aaron Lerner, 'No artful dodging', ibid. 6 Apr. 1998.

[95] See Elli Wohlgelernter's addendum to Hillel Kuttler *et al.*, 'Arafat to ask US to support statehood', ibid. 22 Mar. 1999.

The PA's justifications for its inaction are hardly reassuring. Just before the conclusion of the Interim Agreement in 1995, the head of Palestinian security services openly announced: 'The Palestinian Authority has decided, with Arafat's approval, not to extradite our fellow Palestinians to Israel—even though this is a breach of our [1994 Gaza–Jericho] agreement with Israel. . . . We are not prepared to go down in history as having extradited Palestinians to Israel.'[96] The PA has also suggested that Israel is not 'pressuring' the PA to extradite, but Israel's recent public demands for extradition seem to contradict this assertion.[97]

More recently the PA has adopted a more legalistic tone, contending that its obligation to extradite Palestinians is not absolute. The PA's policy is not to extradite any Palestinians, but instead to prosecute them in PA courts.[98] In the PA's view, in other words, the Oslo Accords give the PA the alternative to prosecute, just as multilateral conventions on terrorism often require states either to extradite their own nationals or submit their cases for prosecution in their own courts.

In fact, however, the PA has only limited authority to prosecute in lieu of extradition. It is true that the Interim Agreement provides that the PA 'shall' investigate and prosecute in the case of crimes committed 'in the areas under the security responsibility of the Council by a non-Israeli against Israel or an Israeli'.[99] But this provision requires prosecution rather than extradition in only a limited number of cases. Similarly, the Interim Agreement permits the PA to prosecute Palestinians for offences outside the PA's jurisdiction, but only if the offences are 'not related to Israel's security interests'.[100] Israel is most interested in extradition for crimes that *do* relate to its security interests; most of its extradition requests fall into that category.

[96] Moshe Zak, 'The importance of alternatives', ibid. 14 Sept. 1995 (quoting Mohammed Dahlan). See also Editorial, 'Extraditions and releases', ibid. 2 July 1995 6 (quoting Lt.-Col. Rashid Abu Shbak, deputy commander of the Palestinian Intelligence Service in Gaza, in remarks to Peace Watch) ('No wanted suspects will be handed over to Israel . . .).

[97] See Editorial, 'Extraditions and releases', ibid. 2 July 1995 6 (quoting deputy commander Abu Shbak) ('Israel itself is not pressuring us to do so').

Indeed, the Rabin government's reaction to the PA's flat refusal to extradite Palestinians was mixed. As one press report put it, Rabin 'shrugg[ed] off' his Justice Minister's condemnation of the PA position. Zak, 'The importance of alternatives'. The Israeli government was criticized for having merely 'gone through the motions' of requesting extradition and keeping the issue 'muted'. Editorial, 'Extraditions and releases'.

[98] See Evelyn Gordon, 'PA refuses to hand over killers', ibid. 30 June 1995 (quoting deputy commander Abu Shbak) ('those suspected of terror attacks after the Oslo Accords were signed would instead be tried by the PA's court in Gaza'). Cf. also Lally Weymouth, 'Netanyahu: Ready to Deal', *Wash. Post*, 23 Apr. 1998 (Op-Ed) (stating that the US 'has asked the Palestinian Authority to extradite nine persons—some for murder of Americans—without success').

[99] Interim Agreement, Annex IV, Art. I(5).

[100] Ibid., Annex IV, Article I(1)(b).

In any event, as we saw in the foregoing section, the PA has done relatively little to prosecute suspects wanted for criminal offences in Israel, and sometimes PA prosecutions seem to have been designed primarily to preclude extradition. In July 1995, for example, a Palestinian court in Jericho sentenced two members of Hamas to twelve years imprisonment for undermining Palestinian security. Israel protested that the conviction came just a day after Israel had requested the extradition of the two individuals. Similarly, in September 1995 a Palestinian court in Jericho convicted two Palestinian cousins, Yussef Ra'ii and Shaher Ra'ii, of 'incitement' and condemned each to seven years of hard labour.[101] Israel protested that each was wanted for the murder of two Israelis, and that a seven-year sentence for murder was too light and designed to foreclose extradition.[102] After the Wye River Memorandum, the PA did undertake to arrest fugitives sought by Israel, but it is not clear to what extent the PA has followed through with prosecutions and convictions.

The PA has also argued that the extradition provisions do not apply to crimes committed before the adoption of the Gaza–Jericho Agreement.[103] There were press reports that Prime Minister Rabin accepted this interpretation despite the 'unanimous opinion' of the Israeli government's legal advisers that the interpretation was incorrect.[104] These reports were quickly denied by the Rabin government, which said that it did not 'accept' the PA's refusal to extradite two Palestinians accused of murdering an Israeli before the adoption of the Gaza–Jericho agreement.[105] None the less, the Rabin government still left open the possibility that the PA's refusal was not a violation of the Gaza–Jericho pact.[106] This point has receded in importance since it flared up in late 1994 and 1995, since most crimes charged hereafter will involve conduct that took place after May 1994. None the less, just as the parties have haggled over release of prisoners whose crimes pre-date

[101] See Curtius, 'Palestinians Thwarting Extraditions, Israel Says'.

[102] Ibid. (quoting an Israeli official) ('What we saw in Jericho was a trial to stop extradition but not a real trial').

[103] See, e.g., Evelyn Gordon, 'Rabin has accepted PA's refusal to extradite murderers', *Jerus. Post*, 20 Jan. 1995 (noting that the PA asserted that the Gaza–Jericho Agreement did not cover the alleged murderers of Uri Megidish because the crime took place before the Agreement was signed).

[104] Ibid. (reporting that Rabin's spokesman believed the Gaza–Jericho Agreement 'exists only from the day it was signed' and therefore that non-extradition 'is not a violation' of the Agreement). The spokesman reportedly repeated his interpretation even after consulting with other members of the government, including a representative of the Attorney-General's office, who disagreed with the interpretation. Ibid.

[105] See Evelyn Gordon, 'Rabin aide: We still want Megidish killers from PA', ibid. 22 Jan. 1995 (reporting that Rabin's spokesman clarified that 'Israel does not in any way accept the PA's refusal to extradite' the two cousins wanted for the murder of Uri Megidish).

[106] Ibid. ('Due to an editing error the report published in Friday's Jerusalem Post said that Rabin had accepted the PA's refusal instead of saying merely that he did not consider the refusal a violation of the Cairo [i.e. Gaza–Jericho] Agreement').

the Oslo process, it is likely that they will disagree over the extradition of prisoners whose crimes also pre-date the process.

On their face, the extradition provisions do not clearly indicate whether they apply retroactively. The 'final clauses' of the Gaza–Jericho Agreement, like those of the Interim Agreement and other Oslo Accords, say nothing of retroactive effect. They provide only that the agreements come into force upon signature.[107] Moreover, the default rule in treaty law is that a treaty does not have retroactive effect unless a 'different intention' can be established.[108]

None the less, a 'different intention' can be established by reference to state practice. When states enter into extradition agreements, they sometimes provide explicitly that the agreement will apply to crimes committed 'before or after' the treaty enters into force, so long as the offence was criminal in both states at all relevant times, thus avoiding any problems with the *ex post facto* doctrine (*nullum crimen sine lege*).[109] But even states that do not write such provisions into their extradition treaties follow them in practice anyway. For example, the 1962 US–Israel extradition treaty makes no mention of retroactive application, but it none the less was invoked as a basis for extradition of John Demjanjuk to Israel for crimes allegedly committed during World War II—committed not only before the entry into force of the extradition treaty, but also before the birth of the requesting state, Israel. The absence of an explicit retroactivity provision did not prevent Demjanjuk's extradition (though other aspects of the case may otherwise limit its relevance as precedent).[110] In sum, state practice strongly suggests that parties to extradition agreements intend their agreement to apply to crimes committed both before and after the agreement enters into force. Thus it may be problematic for the PA to maintain that the extradition arrangements do not apply to fugitives whose crimes pre-date Oslo.

The PA's last line of defence on the extradition question seems to be that Israel has acquiesced in the PA's no-extradition policy and thereby waived any objection Israel might have to that policy. One theme of

[107] See, e.g., Gaza–Jericho Agreement, Art. XXIII(1) ('This Agreement shall enter into force on the date of its signing'); Interim Agreement, Art. XXXI(1) (identical).

[108] Vienna Convention on the Law of Treaties, Art. 28.

[109] See, e.g., Treaty of Extradition, US–UK, Art. XVI(2) ('extradition shall not be granted for an offense committed before this Treaty enters into force which was not an offense under the laws of both Contracting Parties at the time of its commission'). Human rights law permits prosecution for an act so long as it constituted a crime 'at the time when it was committed'. International Covenant on Civil and Political Rights, Art. 15(1).

[110] See *Demjanjuk v. Petrovsky*, 776 F.2d 571 (6th Cir. 1985). Cf. also International Covenant on Civil and Political Rights, Art. 15(2) (notwithstanding the prohibition on retroactive criminal punishment, states may punish persons for 'any act or omission which, at the time when it was committed, was criminal according to the general principles of law recognized by the community of nations').

Palestinian statements on the issue is that Israel has not consistently pressured the PA to extradite fugitives.[111] Even the Netanyahu government was sometimes criticized for not doing enough to secure the rendition of fugitives from the PA.[112]

Treaty law does recognize that subsequent practice of the parties can shed light on the treaty's meaning. Article 31(3)(b) of the Vienna Convention on the Law of Treaties provides that interpretation should take into account 'any subsequent practice in the application of the treaty which establishes the agreement of the parties regarding its interpretation'. Moreover, Article 39 of the Vienna Convention provides that a treaty 'may be amended by agreement of the parties'. And Article 45 of the Convention acknowledges that a state may waive its right to suspend or terminate its treaty obligations. But Israel has clearly not waived its right to complain of the PA's refusal to honour its extradition obligations. At most, the Rabin government may have waived any objections to the PA's view that the extradition agreement is not retroactive. The Netanyahu government, for its part, consistently and repeatedly took the position that the PA was violating its extradition obligations. It can hardly be accused of having waived the extradition obligations. The Barak government has followed the same general policy; the Sharm el-Sheikh Memorandum reflects Israel's insistence that the PA cooperate through all available means to prevent and punish crime and terrorism.

In sum, the PA's blanket refusal to extradite any Palestinians to Israel is not justified by the Oslo Accords. The agreements do permit the PA to prosecute rather than extradite Palestinians, but only if they are not accused of offences involving Israel's security, and most of Israel's extradition requests have been for terrorists whose crimes do implicate Israeli security. Israel has not waived its right to the rendition of fugitives charged with (or suspected of) crimes. Finally, some of the unusual provisions of the extradition arrangements—the obligation to extradite people who have not been charged or convicted, the absence of any requirement that the requesting state establish probable cause—may be inconsistent with human rights law.

Confiscating illegal firearms

Finally, the Note for the Record calls on the PA to confiscate illegal firearms.[113] This obligation is set out in more detail in the Interim

[111] See, e.g., Gordon, 'PA refuses to hand over killers' (quoting a Palestinian officer) ('Israel itself is not pressuring us' to extradite 'security related suspects').

[112] See, e.g., Itim, 'A–G's Office: Politicians must deal with extradition', *Jerus. Post*, 12 Dec. 1997.

[113] Note for the Record, 'Palestinian Responsibilities', ¶2(f).

Agreement and its first Annexe. Article XIV(4) of the Interim Agreement provides that no organization other than the Palestinian Police and the Israeli military forces is permitted to 'manufacture, sell, acquire, possess, import or otherwise introduce into the West Bank or the Gaza Strip any firearms, ammunitions, weapons, explosives, gunpowder or any related equipment . . .'. Annex I to the Interim Agreement sets out the confiscation obligation most clearly: 'The [Palestinian] Council will issue permits in order to legalize the possession and carrying of arms by civilians. Any illegal arms will be confiscated by the Palestinian Police.'[114]

The Wye River Memorandum elaborates on these provisions. It requires the Palestinians to criminalize unlawful acquisition or possession of firearms and to 'establish and vigorously and continuously implement' a programme for 'collection' of firearms. It also provides that the US 'has agreed to assist in carrying out this program'.[115] The Sharm el-Sheikh Memorandum reaffirms these provisions in general terms.[116]

The Netanyahu government repeatedly accused the PA of violating the confiscation obligations in the Interim Agreement and Note for the Record. Israel contended that the PA had made no 'public campaigns' or 'major sweeps' to confiscate illegal weapons, and that the PA had collected almost none of the 'tens of thousands' of weapons in the autonomous areas. Israel added that five 'illegally armed groups' continue to operate in the PA's territories: Hamas, Islamic Jihad, Fatah, the PFLP (Popular Front for the Liberation of Palestine), and the DFLP (Democratic Front for the Liberation of Palestine).[117] The PA did establish a new confiscation programme after the Wye River Memorandum, but the Netanyahu government complained that it had not been implemented effectively. In November 1999 the PA did deliver a list of confiscated weapons to an Israeli negotiator, who welcomed this development but added 'there is no way for Israel to verify what the list represents, in terms of what is still out there'.[118]

The PA says that it has made reasonable efforts to comply but that it lacks the capacity to confiscate tens of thousands of weapons. There is a certain degree of plausibility to this position: even the most technologically advanced states in the world have found it difficult to implement gun control once guns are widely dispersed in the population. But Israel is right that there has been relatively little public evidence of any good-faith effort at mass confiscation, and as usual 'good faith' is the minimum standard

114 Interim Agreement, Annexe I, Art. II(1)(c).

115 Wye River Memorandum, ¶II(A)(2)(a)–(b).

116 Sharm el-Sheikh Memorandum, ¶8(b)(1).

117 See Office of the PM, 'Special Report', ¶2f.

118 Lamia Lahoud, 'PA reports on police, weapons at "intense" interim agreement talks', *Jerus. Post*, 10 Nov. 1999 (quoting Oded Eran).

that applies to the parties' obligations under the Accords. In 1999 there were signs that the PA was taking more active steps in confiscating firearms. Even so, the burden is on the PA to demonstrate a fuller measure of compliance with this obligation.

In sum, the Palestinian Authority has a disappointing record on its obligation to prevent and punish terror and other forms of violence. It has taken some steps to strengthen security cooperation with Israel, but it has permitted (and sometimes engaged in) inflammatory anti-Israeli propaganda that verges on incitement to violence, and it has not done all it could do to combat terrorist organizations or to arrest, prosecute, or extradite terrorists. Nor is there much evidence that it has made a good faith effort to confiscate illegal firearms in the autonomous areas. True, some of the PA's security obligations—notably those on incitement and arrest—are in tension with the PA's human rights obligations under the Accords. But the PA's non-compliance with its security-related obligations seems to stem more from a lack of capacity or will to comply, not from hypersensitivity to human rights concerns.

We turn next to the PA's compliance with the Interim Agreement's provisions restricting the scope of PA activities.

12

Limits on Palestinian Self-Government

The Oslo Accords impose a variety of limits on the size, location, and function of Palestinian governing institutions. The Interim Agreement, for example, limits the size of the Palestinian Police force. Similarly, the Declaration of Principles and subsequent agreements forbid the Palestinian Authority to establish governing institutions in Jerusalem and in certain parts of the West Bank and the Gaza Strip. Likewise, the Oslo Accords place functional restrictions on Palestinian governmental activity, for example by prohibiting the conduct of full-fledged diplomatic relations with foreign countries. This Chapter considers Palestinian compliance with each of these restrictions. It also asks whether the Oslo Accords terminated on 4 May 1999, the end of the five-year interim period, and whether the end of the five-year period implies Palestinian statehood.

The Palestinian Police

The 1993 Declaration of Principles provided that the Palestinians 'will establish a strong police force'.[1] To implement this general command, the 1994 Gaza–Jericho Agreement authorized the Palestinians to deploy a total of 9,000 police.[2] The 1995 Interim Agreement expanded the allowable number of Palestinian Police to a total of 24,000, with an additional 6,000 to be deployed 'according to the phases of the further redeployments or as needed, as agreed upon by the two Parties'.[3] The Interim Agreement permitted recruitment of some Palestinian Police 'from abroad', but it also required the Palestinians to 'notify Israel of any candidate' for recruitment, and it gave Israel a veto over recruitment of any candidate.[4] The Agreement also required the Palestinians to provide Israel with a list of the names of policemen and to maintain a register of weapons held by the police.[5]

[1] Declaration of Principles, Art. VIII. See also Interim Agreement, Art. XIV(1) (similar). This language seems to be borrowed from the Camp David Accords. See Framework for Peace in the Middle East, 17 Sept. 1978, ¶A.1.b, ¶A.1.d (envisioning a 'strong local police force').

[2] Gaza–Jericho Agreement, Annexe I, Art. III(3).

[3] Interim Agreement, Annexe I, Art. IV(3)(a)–(b).

[4] Ibid., Art. IV(4)(a) and (d).

[5] As to lists, see Interim Agreement, Art. XIII(2)(b)(7); ibid., Annexe I, Art. IV(3)(a). As to weapons, see ibid., Art. IV(5)(e).

The later Accords mostly reiterated the obligations in the Interim Agreement. The Note for the Record provided simply: 'Size of the Palestinian Police will be pursuant to the Interim Agreement.'[6] The Wye River Memorandum again called on the PA to provide a list of its policemen to Israel, and it added that the United States would monitor implementation of the police provisions and possibly render technical assistance to the PA.[7] The Sharm el-Sheikh Memorandum yet again reiterated the PA duty to provide a list of policemen, and this time it added a deadline for delivery of the list: 13 September 1999.[8]

Israel contends that the PA has consistently violated these provisions. According to Israel, for example, the PA deployed twice as many police as were permitted by the Gaza–Jericho Agreement. Israel also asserts that the PA later deployed a total of 30,000 police, 6,000 more than the initial deployment permitted by the Interim Agreement. Israel also says that the PA repeatedly ignored its duty to provide a list of police.

The PA has, belatedly, met its obligation to provide a list of police. In November 1999 the PA delivered a list of some 41,000 Palestinian Police to a senior Israeli negotiator, who observed that the number of police exceeded the Oslo limits but none the less welcomed the list as a step forward. The PA, for its part, expressed the hope that Israel would waive its right to insist on a smaller number of police, since it is in Israel's interests for the PA to have a strong police force.[9]

Thus the PA has admitted that it has deployed more police than is called for in the Accords. Until recently, the PA had refused to admit this, and the parties had squabbled over whether the Interim Agreement permitted deployment of 30,000 police (as the PA argued) or just 24,000 (as Israel argued). That argument centred around language in the Interim Agreement providing that the final 6,000 police would be deployed 'according to the phases of the further redeployments or as needed, as agreed upon by the two Parties'.[10]

This provision is not a model of clarity, but it does appear to support Israel's view that the PA was wrong to deploy the extra police without agreement from Israel. It might be argued that the parties had agreed unconditionally to the deployment of the additional 6,000 police at the time of further Israeli pullbacks from the West Bank, and that the condition of mutual agreement merely modified the immediately preceding

[6] Note for the Record, 'Palestinian Responsibilities', ¶3.

[7] Wye River Memorandum, ¶II(C)(1).

[8] Sharm el-Sheikh Memorandum, ¶8(b)(3).

[9] Lamia Lahoud, 'PA reports on police, weapons at "intense" interim agreement talks', *Jerus. Post*, 10 Nov. 1999.

[10] Interim Agreement, Annexe I, Art. IV(3)(a)–(b).

words—'as needed'.[11] In other words, 6,000 police would be deployed during the following phases of withdrawal from the West Bank, or sooner if needed and the parties so agreed. The more natural reading, though, is that the reference to mutual agreement modifies the entire sentence; if it were intended to modify only the as-needed clause, the comma in the sentence would have been placed between the redeployment clause and the as-needed clause. This reading also comports with the constant references to mutual agreement throughout the Accords. Israel therefore appears to be correct that the provision required agreement by both parties before extra police can be added.

Still, the PA might argue that this provision, like the rest of the Oslo Accords, was subject to an implied obligation of good faith, and that Israel's failure to make an adequate redeployment on a timely basis unlawfully prevented the occurrence of the condition precedent to the expansion of the Palestinian Police. That argument would not explain why the PA apparently deployed extra police well before the further redeployment was due. Moreover, even with a further redeployment, the provision appears to contemplate further agreement on just when (and especially where) the extra 6,000 police might be deployed.

The parties have also jousted over just how many Palestinian Police have been deployed. Part of the disagreement stems from the definition of 'police'. The PA has also deployed intelligence agents, plainclothes agents, and security officers, not all of whom would ordinarily be regarded as 'police'. As a result, there is confusion even among Palestinians and inside the Israeli government as to just how many Palestinian Police have been deployed. For example, a Palestinian human rights activist is said to have declared that there are at least 80,000 PA 'policemen', including intelligence agents and security officers.[12] The PA Information Ministry has itself sometimes refused to provide a number, saying only that the information is 'not available'. Even the Israeli government has contradicted itself on this issue. In 1997 Defence Minister Yitzhak Mordechai said that the 'authorized' number of Palestinian Police do not exceed the limits in the Interim Agreement.[13] But thereafter the Netanyahu government steadfastly maintained that the PA has in fact deployed 30,000 police, in excess of the 24,000 cap.[14]

[11] There is arguably analogous precedent for this conclusion in municipal contract law. Courts sometimes treat clauses that seem like conditions merely as suggested timetables for completion of an agreed-upon obligation, rather than an express condition for performance of that obligation. See, e.g., *Peacock Construction Co. v. Modern Air Conditioning, Inc.*, 353 So. 2d 840 (1977). See also *Gulf Construction Co. v. Self*, 676 S.W.2d 624 (Tex. App. 1984).

[12] See letter of Patrick Goodenough to the Editor, *Jerus. Post*, 9 June 1997.

[13] Ibid.

[14] See Office of the Prime Minister, 'Special Report: PA Has Failed to Fulfill Its Commitments Under the Hebron Accord', 20 July 1997, ¶3, found at http:// www.pmo.gov.il.

In any event, it is now clear that the PA has exceeded its allowable quota of police, putting it in violation of the Interim Agreement. To some extent, though, the quota is in tension with another important obligation—that the PA create a 'strong' police force, one that would combat violence, crime, and terrorism and confiscate illegal firearms.[15] Indeed, a somewhat oversized Palestinian Police seems less important than concerns about the effectiveness and composition of that police force. If the Palestinian Police has been as ineffective in combating terrorism and confiscating firearms as Israel suggests, then Israel is entitled to be suspicious about why an overly large police force is so inefficient. And Israel is certainly entitled to be angry when the Palestinian Police open fire on Israeli soldiers and citizens, as took place during the unrest in the West Bank and Gaza in September 1996.[16] The Oslo Accords plainly require the parties to take steps to 'prevent acts of terrorism, crime and hostilities directed against each other [and] against individuals falling under the other's authority'.[17] The Palestinian Police must be an instrument for preserving the peace, not undermining it.

Limits on PA activity

The Interim Agreement established geographic and functional limits on PA activity. On geographic confines of PA activity, the Agreement stated: 'The offices of the Council, and the offices of its Ra'ees and its Executive Authority and other committees, shall be located in areas under Palestinian territorial jurisdiction in the West Bank and the Gaza Strip.'[18] (The reference to the Palestinian 'Council', which the Interim Agreement vested with both legislative and executive authority, is understood to mean the PA.[19]) This language was intended to prohibit the PA from establishing and maintaining 'offices' in Jerusalem, the status of which has been deferred until final status negotiations. The Interim Agreement's functional limits on PA activity are more complex, ranging from restrictions on land-use and construction to communications and the conduct of foreign policy. The Note for the Record reaffirmed all these commitments.[20]

It appears that the PA has violated a number of these limits on self-government. The most clear example is the PA's operation of governmental

[15] See Interim Agreement, Art. XIV(1).

[16] See Steve Rodan, 'Palestinians have 80,000 armed fighters, defense sources say', *Jerus. Post*, 27 Sept. 1996 (describing the 'breakdown in the command of the Palestinian Police' during the disturbances).

[17] Interim Agreement, Art. XV(1).

[18] Ibid., Art. I(7).

[19] Ibid., Art. I(2).

[20] Note for the Record, 'Palestinian Responsibilities', ¶4.

and quasi-governmental offices at Orient House, in East Jerusalem. During its tenure, the Netanyahu government shut down a number of such offices, though a number of them later re-opened.[21] Among other things, the Netanyahu government demanded that the PA must close its 'Ministry of Jerusalem Affairs', which, Netanyahu said, operated out of the Orient House in East Jerusalem 'under cover of the "Arab Affairs Society".'[22] In the same vein, the Mayor of Jerusalem, Ehud Olmert, sought to prevent the PA from using Orient House to receive foreign ministers.[23] Similarly, Netanyahu protested after a member of the Palestinian Legislative Council opened an 'office' in his East Jerusalem home to meet with constituents.[24] Members of the PA's Ministry of Religious and Waqf Affairs seem to have carried out at least some political and quasi-governmental business at informal offices in Jerusalem.[25] The Interim Agreement's restrictions apply most clearly to the operation of 'offices' such as the governmental offices at Orient House.[26]

Now, it might be argued that Israel has waived these restrictions by failing to shut down Orient House altogether. Indeed, a state may effectively waive its right to suspend or terminate its own performance if expressly or 'by reason of its conduct' it acquiesces in 'maintenance in force' of the treaty even after the other party materially breaches it.[27] But Israel has tolerated Orient House not because it wishes to waive the geographic restrictions on PA activity, but only because Israel fears that closing Orient House would generate a fierce political backlash.[28] Indeed, Israel has repeatedly demonstrated its objection to symbols of Palestinian governmental activity in Jerusalem. For example, just before the signing of the Interim Agreement, Israel shut down the Jerusalem branches of

[21] Ben Lynfield and Danna Harman, 'Gov't shuts 3 PA offices in capital', *Jerus. Post*, 30 Mar. 1999.

[22] See Office of the Prime Minister, 'Palestinian Obligations As Per the Note for the Record of the Hebron Protocol of January 15, 1997', ¶4A ('Jerusalem'), 13 Jan. 1998, available at http://www.pmo.gov.il.

[23] Serge Schmemann, 'For Both the Arabs and the Israelis, Jerusalem Is Where the Heart Is', *N.Y. Times*, 27 Oct. 1996. See also Bill Hutman, 'Olmert: PA official liaising with churches', *Jerus. Post*, 28 Nov. 1996.

[24] Joel Greenberg, 'Palestinian's Jerusalem Office Stirs Pot', *N.Y. Times*, 6 Aug. 1996 (reporting on the new East Jerusalem 'office' of Council member Hatem Abdel Qader).

[25] Elli Wohlgelernter, 'PA official violating Oslo', *Jerus. Post*, 12 Mar. 1998.

[26] See Jeffrey Weiss, 'Terminating the Israel–PLO Declaration of Principles: Is It Legal Under International Law?', 18 *Loy. L.A. Int'l & Comp. L.J.* 109, 122 (1995).

[27] Vienna Convention on the Law of Treaties, 23 May 1969, UN Doc. A/CONF. 39/27, Art. 45(a) and (b).

[28] See, e.g., Joseph Berger, 'Israeli Executives Urge Moderation on Netanyahu', *N.Y. Times*, 8 June 1996 (reporting predictions that Netanyahu would 'sidestep' closure of Orient House, since closure would 'inflame the Palestinians needlessly'); Clyde Haberman, 'Arafat's Return: Jericho Wondering When', ibid. 2 June 1994 (noting that the Rabin government had not shut down Orient House because its closure would be a 'political bombshell').

three Palestinian quasi-governmental institutions.[29] And Israeli municipal law, like the Interim Agreement, restricts the conduct of Palestinian governmental activity in areas outside PA-controlled territory.[30] 'As long as the nonbreaching party continues the process of contesting by means of official protest and negotiation, it neither acquiesces in the breach nor waives its rights'[31] to suspend or terminate the treaty. Even if Israel has waived its right to suspend or terminate its own performance under the Accords—which, as we have seen, seems unlikely here—it is not necessarily estopped to complain about Palestinian violations.[32]

Still, it is possible that Israel has waived its objections to Orient House and other PA activity in Jerusalem in another way—namely, by making a unilateral undertaking to permit such activity. In October 1993, just after the signing of the Declaration of Principles, then Foreign Minister Shimon Peres wrote a letter to Norwegian Foreign Minister Johan Jorgen Holst in which Peres said:

> I wish to confirm that the Palestinian institutions of East Jerusalem and the interests and well-being of the Palestinians of East Jerusalem are of great importance and will be preserved. Therefore, all the Palestinian institutions of East Jerusalem, including the economic, social, educational and cultural, and the Christian and Moslem places, are performing an essential task for the Palestinian population.
>
> Needless to say, we will not hamper their activity. On the contrary, the fulfillment of this important mission is to be encouraged.[33]

The letter prompted cries of outrage from Likud politicians and other critics, who charged that the letter had compromised Israel's 'sovereignty' over Jerusalem.[34] But the letter probably does not authorize the PA to

[29] Serge Schmemann, 'Israeli Government Closes 3 Palestinian Offices in Jerusalem', *N.Y. Times*, 28 Aug. 1995 (reporting on the shutdown of Jerusalem offices of the Palestinian Broadcasting Corporation, the Palestinian Health Council, and the Central Bureau of Statistics, but noting that Israel 'conspicuously' failed to shut down Orient House as well).

[30] Joel Greenberg, 'New Israeli Law Limits Area of Palestinian Authority', ibid. 27 Dec. 1994.

[31] Richard L. Doernberg, 'Overriding Tax Treaties: The U.S. Perspective', 9 *Emory Int'l L. Rev.* 71, 127 (1995).

[32] Cf. Shabtai Rosenne, *Breach of Treaty* (Cambridge: Grotius, 1985), 7 (suggesting that a state that waives a particular treaty provision might be estopped to terminate the treaty but not to assert a violation of the underlying substantive obligation contained in the treaty provision). But cf. Herbert W. Briggs, Book Review, 82 *Am. J. Int'l L.* 387 (1988) (reviewing Rosenne's *Breach of Treaty*) (critiquing Rosenne's distinction between the law of the 'treaty-instrument' and the law of the 'treaty-obligation'). For more on waiver in treaty law, see, e.g., Malcolm N. Shaw, *International Law*, 2nd edn (Cambridge: Grotius, 1986), 483.

[33] Letter of 11 Oct. 1993 from Shimon Peres to Johan Jorgen Holst, reprinted in David Makovsky and Dan Izenberg, 'Peres letter in October '93 encouraged Palestinian institutions in capital', *Jerus. Post*, 7 June 1994.

[34] See, e.g., ibid. (quoting Benny Begin, a Likud Member of the Knesset) (calling the government 'stupid' and asserting that '[t]he letter severely impairs Israel's sovereignty over its capital').

conduct governmental activities in East Jerusalem. To begin with, it is not clear that the letter was ever intended to be legally binding. It was addressed to the Norwegian Foreign Minister, not to the Palestinians, and it was in the form of a unilateral statement, not a bilateral agreement. As we saw in Part II, unilateral statements can be binding if made in good faith with intent to be legally bound, particularly if they induce reliance,[35] so it is conceivable that the letter might have some legal effect. But even if the letter was intended to be legally binding, the letter did not expressly endorse activities by Palestinian governmental institutions. Admittedly it did speak of 'all' Palestinian institutions, 'including' (and presumably not limited to) 'the economic, social, educational and cultural'. None the less, if Peres had intended to authorize Palestinian governmental activity in East Jerusalem, presumably he would have said so more explicitly.[36] Moreover, Peres' letter obviously pre-dates the Interim Agreement, with its much more specific and categorical prohibition on Palestinian governmental activities outside PA-controlled territory. The later, more specific instrument presumably supersedes the earlier, more general one,[37] especially when the later instrument is more clearly legally binding than the earlier one. Thus the Interim Agreement's prohibition on PA 'offices' in Jerusalem is probably still in force.

The restriction on offices is not the only geographic limit on PA activity. The Accords confer on the PA jurisdiction only over the territory of Areas A and B, plus functional jurisdiction over a wide variety of matters in Area C—but not over any matters in Jerusalem.[38] Put another way,

[35] See *Frontier Dispute Case* (Burkina Faso v. Mali), 1986 I.C.J. 554, 573–4, ¶¶39–40; *Nuclear Tests* (Aus. v. Fr.; NZ v. Fr.), 1974 I.C.J. 253, 267 (Dec. 20); *Case Concerning the Temple of Preah Vihear* (Cambodia v. Thai.), 1962 I.C.J. 6 (15 June); *Case of Certain Norwegian Loans* (Fr. v. Nor.), 1957 I.C.J. 9 (6 July); *Fisheries Case* (UK v. Nor.), 1951 I.C.J. 116 (18 Dec.); *Legal Status of Eastern Greenland* (Nor. v. Den.), [1933] P.C.I.J. Ser. A/B, No. 53, 71 (5 April).

For analysis and critique of the Court's decisions on unilateral promises and 'international promissory estoppel', see, e.g., Geoffrey R. Watson, 'The Death of Treaty', 55 *Ohio St. L.J.* 781 (1994); Thomas Franck, Editorial Comment, 'Word Made Law: The Decision of the ICJ in the Nuclear Test Cases', 69 *Am. J. Int'l L.* 612, 615 (1975); Alfred P. Rubin, 'The International Legal Effects of Unilateral Declarations', 71 *Am. J. Int'l L.* 1 (1977). For the seminal economic argument for enforcing gratuitous promises in municipal law, see Richard A. Posner, 'Gratuitous Promises in Economics and Law', 6 *J. Legal Stud.* 411 (1977).

[36] Cf. Sir Robert Jennings and Sir Arthur Watts (eds.), *Oppenheim's International Law*, §633, 2:1279 (Harlow, Essex: Longman, 1993) ('The maxim *expressio unius est exclusio alterius* has been followed in the interpretation of treaties by international tribunals in a number of cases').

[37] Ibid. 2:1280 ('*Generalia specialibus non derogant* is a maxim which has sometimes been applied in order to resolve apparent conflicts between' specific and general rules, though it is 'not always easy to determine which of the two rules is the general one and which is the specific') (citing *Rights of Passage over Indian Territory Case*, 1960 I.C.J. 44; *INA Corp. v. Gov't of the Islamic Republic of Iran*, 75 I.L.R. 596, 602 (1983)). 'The maxim is not limited to conflicts between treaty rules.' Ibid. 2:1280 n. 21.

[38] See Interim Agreement, Arts. IX, XVII–XVIII.

Palestinian jurisdiction stops short of permanent status 'issues' such as Jerusalem.[39] The Netanyahu government seemed to take the view that the Interim Agreement thereby prohibits any Palestinian quasi-governmental activity in Jerusalem that is even indirectly linked to the PA. For example, the Netanyahu government complained that the Mufti of Jerusalem, Sheikh Ikrama Sabri, who was appointed by Arafat, was exercising PA governmental functions on the Temple Mount by using his weekly prayer sermon to castigate Israel and the United States. Similarly, the Netanyahu government complained that the PA has conducted matriculation exams and 'imposed its curriculum on Arab schools in Jerusalem', and that the PA has attempted to conduct a census in East Jerusalem.[40] Reports of Palestinian undercover police activity in Jerusalem may be of particular concern to Israel.[41] In so far as such activities are attributable primarily to the PA, then they would indeed seem to be prohibited. But the Interim Agreement permits lawful community-building activities in Jerusalem by private individuals or groups not connected with or acting on behalf of the PA.

The Netanyahu government also complained that the PA exceeded the limits on its authority in Area C. The Interim Agreement does authorize the PA to exercise civil authority over a variety of spheres there, excluding land. As the Interim Agreement puts it, the PA has territorial jurisdiction over Areas A and B and some functional jurisdiction over Area C.[42] Israel has complained that the PA's exercise of its regulatory functions in Area C has sometimes intruded on regulation of land there. For example, the Netanyahu government argued that the PA, through its Ministry of Local Government, in effect 'zoned' parts of Area C for the expansion of villages that are now part of Areas A or B. The Netanyahu government also alleged that the PA issued construction permits in Area C, that it unlawfully undertook construction on roadwork and 'agricultural infrastructure' in some areas, that it is 'active at archaeological sites', and that it 'organized and financed a campaign to plant trees in Area C'. The Netanyahu government also argued that PA land-use policies have led to the flow of uncontrolled sewage and water pollution in the West Bank, that the PA has dumped waste and garbage without concern for the natural environment there, and that the PA has made 'indiscriminate use of Israeli waste removal sites' in Area C.[43] In so far as these PA activities

[39] Interim Agreement, Art. XVII(1)(a).

[40] Elli Wohlgelernter, 'Gov't memo: PA becoming Islamic guardian in Jerusalem', *Jerus. Post*, 29 Sept. 1997.

[41] Cf. Editorial, 'Undermining visit', ibid. 9 Sept. 1996.

[42] Interim Agreement, Art. XVII(2)(a) and (d).

[43] Office of the PM, 'Palestinian Obligations', ¶4B. The Netanyahu government also contended that the PA has made unauthorized television broadcasts from various locations

encroach on Israeli jurisdiction over land in Area C, they are inconsistent with the Interim Agreement.

Finally, Israel contends that the PA has engaged in foreign relations in violation of Article IX(5) of the Interim Agreement, which limits Palestinian foreign relations. As we have already seen in Part II, these restrictions are intended in part to forestall claims of Palestinian statehood. Statehood, it will be recalled, requires both the capacity to engage in foreign relations and governmental control over defined territory and population. The Accords reflect the existence of two Palestinian entities, one (the PLO) with the power to engage in foreign relations but not to control territory, and the other (the PA) with the power to control and govern territory but not to engage in foreign relations.

In particular, the Interim Agreement flatly provides that the PA 'will not have powers and responsibilities in the sphere of foreign relations', broadly defined.[44] The PLO, on the other hand, is empowered to negotiate international agreements on economic, cultural, scientific, and educational matters 'for the benefit' of the PA.[45] The phrase 'for the benefit' was apparently chosen to avoid the suggestion that the PLO is merely the agent, or foreign-policy branch, of the PA, and instead to suggest that the PA is something more like a third-party beneficiary of the agreement between Israel and the PLO. Now, the PA–PLO division of labour would seem to be difficult to enforce, given the overlap between the two organizations. Likewise, it is not surprising that the PLO has interpreted the list of acceptable foreign-policy subjects broadly. Still, a good-faith interpretation would preclude the negotiation or conclusion of agreements, express or implied, that threaten Israel's security, prejudge final-status questions, or otherwise undermine the purposes of the Oslo Accords.

It might be argued that the restrictions on the PA's foreign-policy operations conflict with the inalienable right of the Palestinian people to self-determination. On this view, self-determination includes a right to engage in international relations with other peoples, and this norm is so fundamental that it constitutes *jus cogens*—a peremptory norm that cannot be bargained away by the Oslo Accords.[46] As we saw in Chapter 1, there is

in the West Bank and Gaza, that it has made unauthorized use of certain broadcast frequencies, and that it has 'caused disturbances to transmissions in Israel'. Ibid.

44 Interim Agreement, Art. IX(5)(a).

45 Ibid., Art. IX(5)(b).

46 Cf. Vienna Convention on the Law of Treaties, Art. 53 (on *jus cogens*). For assertions that the right of self-determination is a *jus cogens* norm, see, e.g., Halim Moris, 'Self-Determination: An Affirmative Right Or Mere Rhetoric?', 4 *ILSA J. Int'l & Comp L.* 201, 204 (1997) ('Today, the right to self-determination is considered *jus cogens*') (citing Laurence S. Hanauer, 'The Irrelevance of Self-Determination Law to Ethno-National Conflict: A New Look at the Western Sahara Case', 9 *Emory Int'l L. Rev.* 133, 153 (1995) and Sam Blay, 'Self-Determination: A Reassessment in Post Communist Era', 22 *Denv. J. Int'l L. & Pol'y* 275 (1994)).

unquestionably a right of self-determination, but its content and peremptory nature are uncertain.[47]

Assuming there is a meaningful right of self-determination—a question taken up in more detail in Chapters 1 and 14—that right would seem to be vindicated here, since the Accords do permit the PLO to conduct foreign policy for the 'benefit' of the PA (and the Palestinian people) in a number of important areas. That the PA is a 'beneficiary' of the PLO–Israel agreements is not inconsistent with self-determination; a number of full-fledged states have assigned foreign-affairs decisions to other states. The PLO, with diplomatic missions all around the world, has proven quite capable of representing Palestinian interests overseas.

In fact, these half-restrictions on the conduct of Palestinian foreign policy are quite consistent with the temporary nature of the Oslo Accords. Their main purpose is to lay the foundation for a final settlement to the Palestinian question, a settlement that many believe will result in some form of Palestinian sovereignty. Once there is a Palestinian state, it will of course enjoy the full right to conduct its own foreign policy. In the meantime, the Accords implicitly recognize that the Palestinians have a right to do so—but only through the PLO, and only on certain matters.

Of course, many Palestinians believe that statehood need not await a final status agreement. The next section considers whether the Oslo Accords permit such a declaration of statehood.

Termination of the Accords and Palestinian statehood

In 1998 *Ra'ees* Arafat indicated that he might declare a Palestinian state on 4 May 1999, the date on which the five-year interim period was originally scheduled to expire.[48] The United States and other players in the region persuaded Arafat not to make good on this pledge, but he remains committed to the proposition that a Palestinian state need not await a final status agreement with Israel. Moreover, by pressing (and then waiving) his

[47] Cf. Richard B. Lillich and Hurst Hannum, *International Human Rights*, 3rd edn (Boston: Little, Brown & Co., 1995), 335 (noting that the Human Rights Committee has avoided passing on the merits of a number of self-determination claims). For a sampling of diverse scholarly opinions on self-determination, see W. Michael Reisman, 'Coercion and Self-Determination: Construing Charter Article 2(4)', 78 *Am. J. Int'l L.* 642, 644–5 (1984); Malvina Halberstam, 'Self-Determination in the Arab–Israeli Conflict: Meaning, Myth, and Politics', 21 *N.Y.U.J. Int'l L. & Pol.* 465, 477–80 (1989); S. James Anaya, 'A Contemporary Definition of the International Norm of Self-Determination', 3 *Transnat'l L. & Contemp. Probs.* 131 (1993); Hurst Hannum, 'Rethinking Self-Determination', 34 *Va. J. Int'l L.* 1 (1993); Malvina Halberstam, 'Nationalism and the Right to Self-Determination: The Arab–Israeli Conflict', 26 *N.Y.U. J. Int'l L. & Pol.* 573, 575 (1995).

[48] See, e.g., Mohammed Najib, *et al.*, 'Palestinians reaffirm plan to declare statehood at the UN', *Jerus. Post*, 25 Sept. 1998.

4 May argument, Arafat may have advanced his political goals. As the *Jerusalem Post* intoned on the fateful day itself, 'Arafat's bluff succeeded in endowing his goal of Palestinian statehood with an even greater sense of inevitability'.[49]

In legal terms, Arafat's position rests on the supposedly finite duration of the Oslo Accords themselves. His theory is that the Accords terminated (or at least could have terminated) on 4 May 1999, and that a Palestinian state was supposed to come into existence on that day. But the Accords do not contain an express termination clause, and the Interim Agreement provides that neither side will 'take any step that will change the status of the West Bank and the Gaza Strip pending the outcome of the permanent status negotiations'.[50] Moreover, the parties appear to have acquiesced in their continuation in force.[51] These considerations would seem to support Israel's point of view.

Still, Arafat's argument is not a frivolous one. Ironically enough, Israeli politicians themselves may have inadvertently given it some credence, when in the years before 1999 they stressed the importance of the 4 May 1999 deadline.[52] As the date approached, however, Israeli officials and pro-Israel commentators repeatedly argued that the Accords would not terminate on 4 May.[53] Even now that the date is past, the argument continues to have significance, since it is all too possible that the parties will fail to reach a final status agreement by the autumn of 2000—the target date set by the Sharm el-Sheikh Memorandum. Arafat may then revive his contention that the Accords have expired and have paved the way for declaration of a Palestinian state. Accordingly, the issue will be considered briefly here.

The 1993 Declaration of Principles provided that '[t]he five-year transitional period will begin upon the withdrawal from the Gaza Strip and

[49] Editorial, 'A full peace', ibid. 4 May 1999.

[50] Interim Agreement, Art. XXXI(7).

[51] See generally Herbert Hansell and Nicholas Rostow, *Legal Implications of May 4, 1999* (Washington, DC: The Washington Institute for Near East Policy, 1999). See also Joel Singer, 'Remarks from The Washington Institute's Annual Policy Conference, October 18, 1999', in ibid. 27. For an example of the Palestinian viewpoint, see Nasser al-Kidwa, 'Remarks from The Washington Institute's Annual Policy Conference, October 18, 1999', in ibid. 23.

[52] See, e.g., Yossi Beilin, 'Welcome, Ms. Albright', *Jerus. Post*, 10 Sept. 1997 ('There is even a date for [the Interim Agreement's] implementation: May 4, 1999. Do not forget. This is the most crucial date of the Israeli–Arab conflict . . .'). Cf. also Hillel Kuttler, 'Former negotiator warns PA statehood declaration will trigger violence', ibid. 13 Sept. 1998 (reporting Israeli negotiator Joel Singer's view that while the Accords would not terminate on 4 May, 'There is no way to live even one day [beyond 4 May] without some sort of agreement. The situation will deteriorate into violence . . .').

[53] See, e.g., Joel Singer, 'The ticking clock', ibid. 5 Feb. 1999. See also Marilyn Henry, 'Palestinian sovereignty on UN agenda', ibid. 17 Sept. 1998 (quoting the Israeli delegate to the UN) ('We entirely reject the notion that the Oslo agreements expire at a certain point in time').

Jericho Area'.[54] That withdrawal began with the adoption of the Gaza–Jericho Agreement on 4 May 1994.[55] The Declaration envisioned that permanent status talks would begin by 4 May 1996 and, presumably, that implementation of a final status accord would take place by 4 May 1999.[56]

The PA interprets these provisions to mean that the Oslo Accords expired, at least for some purposes, at the end of the five-year interim period established by the Declaration of Principles. In the PA's view, the end of the five-year interim period marks the beginning of a permanent resolution of the Palestinian question—presumably in favour of a Palestinian state in the areas already under PA control. The PA's view is that it is simply seeking the benefit of its bargain. It pledged to end the *intifada*, to recognize Israel, and to combat terror, in exchange for interim withdrawals from the West Bank followed by a permanent settlement within five years. The PA seems to believe that 'time is of the essence' in this deal.

The decisive argument against the Palestinian position is that there is no termination clause in the Accords. There is no provision that declares the Oslo process dead if the parties do not meet each and every deadline. By contrast, the Accords do contain quite precise provisions on entry into force.[57] The parties' practice under the Accords supports this interpretation: they have missed virtually every important deadline to date, but they have still treated the Accords as controlling. The parties' flexible approach to deadlines thus far belies any assertion that the most unrealistic deadline of all, the five-year deadline for conclusion of permanent status arrangements, is inflexible.[58] Indeed, the five-year deadline presumed that all the other deadlines would be met, and in fact each has been delayed, which in turn makes the five-year deadline all the more difficult to meet. This deadline is better read as a guiding timetable for completion of permanent status talks, not as a rigid condition that must be met to ensure survival of the Oslo process.

[54] Declaration of Principles, Art. V(1).

[55] See David Makovsky, 'Rabin, Arafat sign Gaza/Jericho pact; PLO asks Israel to delay implementation by four weeks', *Jerus. Post*, 5 May 1994 (reporting on adoption of the Gaza–Jericho Agreement).

[56] See Declaration of Principles, Art. V(2) (providing that permanent status negotiations should begin 'not later than' the beginning of the third year of the interim period).

[57] The Declaration of Principles, for example, entered into force 'one month after its signing'. Ibid., Art. XVII(1). The Interim Agreement entered into force 'on the date of its signing'. Interim Agreement, Art. XXXI(1). See Hansell and Rostow, *Legal Implications of May 4, 1999* (emphasizing the absence of a termination clause in the Accords).

[58] The parties' practice under the Accords is of course relevant to interpretation of the Accords. Vienna Convention on the Law of Treaties, Arts. 31(3) and 3(b) ('There shall be taken into account . . . any subsequent practice in the application of the treaty which establishes the agreement of the parties regarding its interpretation').

If there were any doubt on this score, it would seem to have been removed by the parties' mutual agreement to continue the Accords in force after 4 May 1999. In particular, the PA acquiesced in Israel's view that the Accords continued in force after 4 May. Whereas Arafat had once talked of proclaiming 4 May 'independence day', when the moment arrived, the PA treated the date as an 'ordinary' day like any other.[59] Thus even if the PA had a right to terminate the Accords on 4 May, they waived that right.[60]

Thus the Accords remain in force. Indeed, there is no reason that they cannot remain in force for a long while. In the absence of termination clauses, general international law presumes that an international agreement remains in force unless either (1) the parties actually intended to permit denunciation or withdrawal, or (2) a right of denunciation or withdrawal may be 'implied by the nature of the treaty'.[61] It hardly seems that the Oslo Accords were intended to be temporary by either of the men who shook hands on the White House lawn that warm day in September 1993. The Interim Agreement itself—and the parties' public statements—declared unequivocally that the Oslo process was 'irreversible'.[62]

This is not to say that the parties are eternally locked into the Oslo Accords no matter how egregious the violations by one side or the other. Treaty law permits an aggrieved party to suspend or terminate a treaty in response to certain serious ('material') breaches by the other, subject to certain limitations.[63] But even then, termination is merely optional; it is never required by treaty law, which favours continuity in treaty relations. Even in the absence of a breach, the parties may mutually agree at any time to set aside their agreement.

Nor should it be inferred that the five-year 'interim period' can be stretched into an indefinite 'permanent period' of 'interim arrangements'. As with all other obligations under the Accords, the obligation to negotiate on final status is subject to an implied term of good faith.[64] Good faith requires that both parties make a continuing, honest effort to negotiate. Now, it is conceivable that both parties might negotiate in good faith and yet no agreement is ever reached on final status. If that level of deadlock is reached, it might be appropriate for the parties to

[59] Ben Lynfield, 'Erekat: May 4 will be a normal day', *Jerus. Post*, 4 May 1999.

[60] Cf. Vienna Convention on the Law of Treaties, Art. 45 (on waiver).

[61] Ibid., Art. 56(1). Even if a party is permitted to denounce or withdraw from a treaty, it must give 12 months notice of its intention to do so unless the treaty provides some other provision on notice. Ibid., Art. 56(2). Like other procedural requirements in the Vienna Convention, however, the twelve-month notice provision is often disregarded.

[62] Interim Agreement, Preamble, ¶4.

[63] Vienna Convention on the Law of Treaties, Art. 60(3).

[64] Ibid., Art. 26 ('Every treaty in force is binding upon the parties to it and must be performed by them in good faith').

consider modifying the Oslo Accords to make the 'interim' arrangements more permanent.

In any event, the main point is that the arrival of 4 May 1999 did not automatically terminate the Oslo Accords. Nor does it seem likely that either party will take the affirmative step of completely repudiating the Accords. The best evidence for this prediction is experience: although each side claims the other has violated Oslo, neither side has purported to terminate Oslo, and indeed each claims to be abiding by the Accords. The parties have continued with Oslo because it is, ultimately, in their interests to do so.

Even if the Oslo Accords had terminated in May 1999, it is unlikely that the PA would have met the criteria for statehood in international law. As we saw earlier in Part II, the most commonly accepted definition of statehood includes four elements: (1) a defined territory, (2) a permanent population, (3) a government in control of that territory, and (4) the capacity to engage in foreign relations.[65] As of now elements (3) and (4) are both in doubt. As to element (3), the PA does not have unfettered control over any of its territory, even in Area A, since Israel retains responsibility for borders and external security even as to that Area. As to element (4), the PA now plainly lacks the capacity to engage in foreign relations, since the Oslo Accords forbid it to do so except for certain limited purposes.

More to the point, the question of Palestinian statehood is the quintessential 'permanent status' issue. True, the Accords do not explicitly list statehood as a 'permanent status' issue, but the dimensions and capacity of a Palestinian state depend on prior resolution of several issues that *are* on the list: Jerusalem, borders, settlements, security arrangements, relations between the parties, and 'other issues of common interest'.[66] That this list does not mention statehood was hardly intended to imply that the parties had agreed that a Palestinian state should come into existence automatically even before a final status agreement had been reached. On the contrary: it reflects Israel's refusal to concede on this issue prematurely. The surest route to Palestinian statehood lies in 'permanent status' talks.

To summarize this Chapter, the PA appears to have exceeded some of the Accords' restrictions on Palestinian self-government. The size of the Palestinian Police force exceeds that permitted by the Interim Agreement, though it remains to be seen whether Israel will vigorously object to this development, which might help the PA abide by its obligation to maintain

[65] Montevideo Convention on Rights and Duties of States, 26 Dec. 1933, 165 L.N.T.S. 19, Art. I.

[66] Interim Agreement, Art. XXXI(5).

a 'strong' police force. The PA also appears to have exceeded the geographic and functional limits on its governmental activity, in particular at Orient House in East Jerusalem. Again, Israel appears willing to tolerate some such activity, and by doing so it has not prejudiced its position that the status of Jerusalem remains unaltered pending final status negotiations. The Accords remain intact even though the five-year interim period is now more than five years old. Likewise, the question of Palestinian statehood must be resolved in permanent status negotiations.

We now turn to the final major Palestinian undertaking under the Oslo Accords: the obligation to respect human rights.

13

Palestinian Human Rights Obligations

As we saw in Chapter 9 (on Israeli human rights obligations), the Oslo Accords treat human rights in rather general terms. Recall that the Interim Agreement provides simply: 'Israel and the [Palestinian] Council shall exercise their powers and responsibilities pursuant to this Agreement with due regard to internationally-accepted norms and principles of human rights and the rule of law.'[1] Similar provisions were found in the Gaza–Jericho Agreement.[2]

It might be argued that these provisions contain no binding obligations whatsoever. Chapter 9 concluded, however, that the 'due regard' clause imposes some legal obligation on the parties to respect general norms of human rights. This conclusion is especially significant for the PA: without the 'due regard' clause, it would not generally be subject to international human rights law, since it is not a state. Under the 'due regard' clause, the PA (like Israel) is potentially bound by a wide range of norms, the most important of which will be considered here.

In addition, the PLO and the PA have made other undertakings to respect human rights. Some of these reflect an intent to be bound politically and perhaps legally. On 30 October 1993, for example, the PLO issued a decree reaffirming its commitment to observe human rights norms. Arafat and his aides have made similar pledges to non-governmental organizations (NGOs) such as Amnesty International.[3] As we have seen, unilateral declarations by a state can create binding obligations; it is possible that unilateral declarations by a 'subject of international law' like the PLO also creates such obligations. In the same vein, the PLO and other

[1] Interim Agreement, Article XIX. Similarly, Annexe I to the Interim Agreement provides that security personnel of both sides shall exercise their authority with 'due regard' to human rights norms and the rule of law, 'and shall be guided by the need to protect the public, respect human dignity and avoid harassment'. Ibid., Annexe I, Art. XI(1). As to human rights in extradition proceedings, see ibid., Annexe IV, Art. II(7)(h)(1) ('Both sides shall take all necessary measures to ensure that the treatment of the individuals transferred under this article complies with . . . internationally-accepted norms of human rights regarding criminal investigations'). Chapter 11 provides more detail on the human rights problems raised by the extradition provisions of the Accords.

[2] Gaza–Jericho Agreement, Art. XIV (on human rights generally); ibid., Annexe III, Art. II(7)(h) (on human rights in extradition); ibid., Annexe I, Art. VIII(1) (on conduct of security forces).

[3] See Irwin Cotler, 'Palestinian Undertakings to Respect Human Rights—Basic Sources', in *The Palestine Human Rights Monitor*, No. 3, May–June 1997, §§ A and B.

'subjects of international law' may to some extent be bound by the customary international law of human rights.[4]

A significant potential source of Palestinian human rights obligations is the PA's draft Basic Law. The Palestinian Legislative Council approved the Basic Law in October 1997, but Arafat has thus far refused to approve it, reportedly because he objected to the limits it places on his authority and, perhaps, because it raises issues of succession that he would rather not face.[5] The Draft Basic Law contains a number of general and specific articles on human rights. Draft Article 11 states that 'Palestine recognizes and respects the fundamental human rights and freedoms' prescribed in a variety of human rights instruments, including the Universal Declaration and the Civil and Political Covenant. Draft Article 12, modelled after Article 9(1) of the Civil and Political Covenant, outlaws 'arbitrary arrest or detention'. Draft Article 13, modelled in part after Article 7 of the Covenant, prohibits torture and degrading punishment, and it provides that coerced confessions shall be given '[n]o effect'. Draft Article 23 guarantees freedom of the press, subject to certain limits.

At the time of writing, however, the Basic Law is still in draft form.[6] It would thus appear that the primary source of the PA's human rights obligations remains the Oslo Accords, in particular the Interim Agreement and its Annexes, as well as the vast body of international human rights law that the Interim Agreement incorporates by reference. Measured by these standards, the PA's human rights record falls woefully short.

Extrajudicial killings

PA security officials have been responsible for a number of extrajudicial killings. According to Amnesty International, at least ten people were

[4] See ibid., §E.

[5] See Agence France Presse, 'Palestinian council passes Basic Law for self-rule authority', 2 Oct. 1997 ('Council members have said Arafat is reluctant to back the Basic Law because it would limit his powers in the self-rule authority'); Jon Immanuel, 'Palestinian Council spars with Arafat', *Jerus. Post*, 1 Aug. 1996. Cf. Marjorie Miller, 'Arafat's Sickly Appearance Raises Questions About Health, Succession', *L.A. Times*, 18 Nov. 1997 (quoting Khalil Shikaki, director of the Palestine Center for Research and Studies) ('Arafat should ratify the Basic Law. . . . Then he should abandon this Stalinistic system in which one person holds all these positions. He must strengthen institutions'). Cf. also Ben Lynfield, 'Progress report to strengthen PA relations with donor countries', *Jerus. Post*, 29 June 1999 (reporting that donor countries urged the PA to adopt the Basic Law).

[6] For a critical analysis of the PA's Draft Basic Law, see Adrien Katherine Wing, 'Conceptualizing Violence: Present and Future Developments in International Law: Panel III: Sex and Sexuality: Violence and Culture in the New International Order: A Critical Race Feminist Conceptualization of Violence: South African and Palestinian Women', 60 *Alb. L. Rev.* 943 (1997).

killed by Palestinian security forces in 1996. In some cases, the deaths may have been unintended, as when civilians were caught in what Amnesty describes as 'cross-fire between rival branches of the security services'. But Amnesty also reports that PA security forces entered the home of two members of Islamic Jihad in Gaza in February 1996 and killed them, even though there were no signs that they resisted arrest.[7] In 1997 a PA court convicted five PA security officials of negligent homicide of a Palestinian woman after the vehicle in which she was riding failed to obey the officials' order to stop.[8]

In May 1997 the PA Minister of Justice, Freih Abu Middein, declared that any Palestinian who sold land to Jews would be sentenced to death. Later that month, two Palestinian land dealers were found dead. They reportedly had sold land to Jews. The PA denied any involvement in their deaths and arrested two individuals in connection with one of the deaths.[9]

According to the US State Department, PA security officials were responsible for 'several' extrajudicial killings in 1998. Among these were two Palestinians who died in PA custody, at least one of whom had been tortured. The PA executed two other Palestinians by firing squad after cursory trials.[10] Extrajudicial killings, as well as firing-squad executions, continued in 1999.[11]

Many of the intentional killings by PA officials are violations of human rights law. A central tenet of that law, expressed in the Covenant on Civil and Political Rights, is that 'no one shall be arbitrarily deprived of his life'.[12] Even the PA's negligent and unintentional homicides may be cognizable under human rights law. The Civil and Political Covenant speaks of 'arbitrary' deprivation of life, not 'intentional' deprivation of life. Depending on the circumstances, negligent or reckless homicide might still constitute an 'arbitrary' deprivation of life.

Moreover, a party to the Covenant is required 'to respect and to ensure to all individuals within its territory and subject to its jurisdiction' the human rights recognized in the Covenant.[13] Even if the PA was not

[7] See Amnesty International, *AI Report 1997: Palestinian Authority* (London: Amnesty International, 1997).

[8] US Dept. of State, 'Country Report on Human Rights Practices for 1997—the Occupied Territories' (Washington, DC: US Dept. of State, 1998), §1.a.

[9] See Jon Immanuel, 'Jerusalem Arab land dealer found murdered', *Jerus. Post*, 11 May 1997; Liat Collins, 'US, Israel slam Arafat; Blast land death penalty', ibid. 22 May 1997.

[10] US Dept. of State, 'Country Report on Human Rights Practices for 1998—Occupied Territories' (Washington, DC: US Dept. of State, 1999), §1.a.

[11] See, e.g., Joel Greenberg, '2 Teen-Agers Killed at Protest of Gaza Verdict', *N.Y. Times*, 11 Mar. 1999.

[12] International Covenant on Civil and Political Rights, 16 Dec. 1966, 999 U.N.T.S. 171, Art. 6(1). See also Universal Declaration of Human Rights, 10 Dec. 1948, U.N.G.A. Res. 217 (III 1948), Art. 3 ('Everyone has the right to life, liberty and the security of the person').

[13] International Covenant on Civil and Political Rights, Art. 2(1).

directly involved in the murders of Palestinian land dealers, its announcement of a death penalty for selling land to Jews surely increased the risk that private individuals might exact retribution against land dealers, and thus constituted failure to 'ensure' those land dealers their human rights. In any event, the imposition of the death penalty for selling land to Israelis is itself contrary to human rights law, which permits capital punishment 'only for the most serious crimes in accordance with the law in force at the time of the commission of the crime'.[14]

Torture

Some of the PA's extrajudicial killings have involved torture. There have been reports that at least two Palestinians died in PA custody after being tortured in 1996. The autopsy of one of those killed, a Palestinian named Yusif Baba, revealed that his body was marked with cigarette burns, rope burns, and burns caused by an 'electrical instrument'. According to the US State Department, the PA admitted that Baba had been tortured to death but never charged any of the perpetrators with a crime. The State Department reports similar incidents of death following torture in 1997. On 30 June 1997 Nasser Abed Radwan, a Palestinian from the Gaza Strip, died in PA custody after having been tortured by PA officials. The PA's Presidential Security force (Force 17) asserted that Radwan died after banging his head on the wall, but that assertion was contradicted by a PA autopsy. Later a PA court sentenced three of the responsible members of Force 17 to death and three others to various terms of imprisonment. In June 1997 Hakim Qamhawi died in PA custody, and his wife alleged that he had been tortured as well. The State Department reports instances of PA torture in 1998 as well.[15] Credible reports of torture have surfaced again in 1999.[16]

Indeed, Amnesty International alleges that torture by the PA is 'widespread'. PA officials have beat detainees, suspended them from the ceiling by their feet, burned them with cigarettes and other implements, and dropped molten plastic on their bodies. In July 1996 PA officials in a Nablus prison tortured to death Mahmud Jumayel, who had been whipped with cables while strung upside-down from the ceiling. Three members of the PA's naval police were sentenced to varying prison terms in connection with Jumayel's death.[17] Fathi Sobh, a professor at Gaza

[14] Ibid., Art. 6(2).

[15] US Dept. of State, 'Country Reports—The Occupied Territories', for 1997 and 1998, §1.a and §1.c.

[16] See, e.g., Joel Greenberg, 'Host of TV Show Says He Was Tortured by Palestinian Jailers', *N.Y. Times*, 14 Oct. 1999.

[17] See Amnesty International, *AI Report 1997: Palestinian Authority.*

University, has reported that he was detained, shackled, deprived of sleep, and forced to stand up for long periods of time.[18]

Again, torture by the PA is a clear violation of human rights law. The Torture Convention is presumably one of the 'internationally accepted' norms of human rights to which the PA has pledged itself in the Oslo Accords. That Convention requires 'effective legislative, administrative, judicial or other measures to prevent acts of torture', and it provides unequivocally that '[n]o exceptional circumstances whatsoever, whether a state of war or a threat of war, internal political instability or any other public emergency, may be invoked as a justification of torture'.[19] Threats to the 'security' of the PA, whether real or imaginary, never justify torture. If somehow the PA tries to argue that the Torture Convention has not been ratified by enough states to constitute an 'internationally-accepted' norm, then the PA is still bound by the Civil and Political Covenant, perhaps the most widely accepted human rights convention, which clearly provides: 'No one shall be subjected to torture or to cruel, inhuman or degrading treatment or punishment.'[20]

Arbitrary arrest and detention

The PA has also repeatedly engaged in arbitrary arrest and detention of Palestinians. According to Amnesty International, more than 1,200 people were arrested by the PA on security grounds in 1996, and of these only a small fraction were charged with a crime or brought before a PA court.[21] This pattern of mass arrests continued through 1999. In addition, PA security forces have regularly arrested and harassed journalists, human rights activists, and academics who criticize the PA. According to human rights groups, the PA has held dozens of people without charge for long periods of time.[22]

The PA stresses that the Oslo Accords oblige it to arrest and prosecute terrorists, and indeed Israel has repeatedly criticized the PA for failing to do enough to prevent and punish terrorism and other crimes of violence. For example, Annexe I to the Interim Agreement provides: 'The Palestinian Police will arrest and prosecute individuals who are

[18] US Dept. of State, 'Country Report for 1997—The Occupied Territories', §1.c.

[19] Convention Against Torture and Other Cruel, Inhuman, or Degrading Treatment or Punishment, 10 Dec. 1984, 23 I.L.M. 1027 (1984), as modified, 24 I.L.M. 535 (1985), Art. 2(1) and 2(2).

[20] International Covenant on Civil and Political Rights, Art. 7.

[21] See Amnesty International, *AI Report 1997: Palestinian Authority* and subsequent *AI Reports*.

[22] See US Dept. of State, 'Country Reports—The Occupied Territories' for 1997 and 1998, §1.d.

suspected of perpetrating acts of violence and terror.'[23] But the answer is not for the PA to arrest ever greater numbers of people without charge. The answer is for the PA to work harder to identify and prosecute the actual perpetrators of crime, to take a more active role in security cooperation with Israel, to share intelligence with Israeli security officials, and to act on Israeli intelligence when it is provided.

In those relatively unusual cases in which the PA actually brings a detained person to trial, it has regularly violated the defendant's right to a fair, public trial. Human rights organizations have expressed particular concern over the PA's State Security Courts in Gaza and the West Bank, established in 1995 to handle security-related cases. Three military judges preside over these courts, the judgments of which are not appealable except to PA Chairman Arafat.[24] Amnesty International charges that '[a]t least 20 political detainees received unfair trials' before the security courts in 1996.[25] This pattern continued through 1999. Often defendants have little or no notice of the charges against them.

Defendants are typically assigned court-appointed counsel. None the less, the US State Department reports, 'Court sessions often take place on short notice in the middle of the night and without lawyers present. In some instances, security courts try cases, issue verdicts, and impose sentences in a single session lasting several hours.'[26]

These practices are clear violations of human rights law. The Civil and Political Covenant states categorically that a defendant is entitled to be 'informed promptly and in detail' of the 'nature and cause of the charge against him'.[27] There is supposed to be a presumption of innocence. The defendant is entitled to have 'adequate time' to prepare a defence and adequate opportunity to consult with a lawyer. Any trial is required to be public unless closure is dictated by morals, public order, national security, or the privacy of the parties. As with free expression, the exceptions for public order and national security were intended to be construed narrowly. The defendant is entitled to have counsel appear at any hearing or trial, to cross-examine witnesses, and to have any conviction reviewed by a 'higher tribunal according to law'.[28] It is doubtful that the Covenant

[23] Interim Agreement, Annexe I, Art. II(1)(d). See also ibid., Art. II(1)(b) ('The Palestinian Police will act systematically against *all expressions* of violence and terror') (emphasis added).

[24] See US Dept. of State, 'Country Reports—The Occupied Territories' for 1997 and 1998, §1.d and §1.e.

[25] See Amnesty International, *AI Report 1997: Palestinian Authority*, and subsequent *AI Reports*.

[26] US Dept. of State, 'Country Report for 1998—The Occupied Territories', §1.e.

[27] International Covenant on Civil and Political Rights, Art. 14(3)(a).

[28] Ibid., Art. 14(2) (presumption of innocence); ibid., Art. 14(3)(b) (adequate time); ibid., Art. 13(d) (legal representation); ibid., Art. 13(e) (cross-examination); ibid., Art. 14(5) (appeal).

intended that the only 'higher tribunal' would be a court of one: the Chairman of the PA.

Freedom of expression

The PA also has a fairly dismal record on free expression. It has arrested Palestinians and others for criticizing the PA's corruption and human rights abuses. In May 1996, for example, the PA arrested Dr Iyad al-Sarraj, Commissioner-General of the Palestinian Independent Commission for Citizens' Rights, because he had criticized the PA's human rights record.[29] In January 1996 a fieldworker for the Israeli human rights group B'Tselem was detained by the PA for 24 hours.[30] In July 1997 the PA arrested and tortured a Palestinian professor because he had asked his students, in a final exam question, how they would handle PA corruption.[31]

The PA has also harassed journalists. In May 1997 the PA detained a Palestinian–American journalist for broadcasting a Palestinian Legislative Council session in which legislators were discussing corruption in the PA. He was held for more than a week. The PA has also closed opposition newspapers. According to the US State Department, this pattern continued through 1998,[32] and there are no indications it has changed materially since.

The PA has, however, been relatively tolerant of demonstrations and public assembly, in part because anti-Israel demonstrations sometimes serve the PA's interests. According to the State Department, 'The PA does not impose restrictions on freedom of assembly, although it does require permits for rallies, demonstrations, and large cultural events. These permits are rarely denied. In Gaza police approval is required for "political" meetings at several specific large meeting halls. . . .'[33]

The PA cannot justify its arrests of journalists and human rights activists on the grounds that the Interim Agreement obliges the PA to prevent 'incitement, including hostile propaganda'.[34] This obligation is limited to the prevention of incitement 'against each other'—for example, Palestinian incitement of violence against Israel, or Israeli incitement of

[29] See Amnesty International, *AI Report 1997: Palestinian Authority*.

[30] Ibid. Another example is the arrest in 1996 of Muhammad Dahlan, Director of *al-Damir* (Conscience), a human rights group, on charges that his organization published a false report that a detainee had died in PA custody. Ibid.

[31] US Dept. of State, 'Country Report for 1997—The Occupied Territories', §2.a.

[32] US Dept. of State, 'Country Report for 1998—The Occupied Territories', §2.a.

[33] Ibid., §2.b. The right of freedom of association is recognized in Article 22(1) of the International Covenant on Civil and Political Rights, which provides in pertinent part that everyone 'shall have the right to freedom of association with others . . .'.

[34] Interim Agreement, Art. XXII(1).

violence against the PA—not non-violent criticism of the PA by Palestinians, journalists or professors. Moreover, the incitement clause of the Interim Agreement makes clear that if the PA takes 'legal measures' against incitement it must do so 'without derogating from the principle of freedom of expression'.[35]

Admittedly, the principle of free expression is not absolute in either human rights law (or, for that matter, in the PA's draft Basic Law). The Civil and Political Covenant recognizes a 'right to freedom of expression', but it can be subject to 'certain restrictions' to protect national security, public order, public health or morals, or the 'rights or reputations' of others.[36] Moreover, the Covenant provides that 'Any propaganda for war shall be prohibited by law', as shall any 'advocacy of national, racial or religious hatred that constitutes incitement to discrimination, hostility or violence'.[37] These provisions do permit the PA to take steps to curb violent or anti-Semitic rhetoric by militant Palestinians—but only if it is so inflammatory that it amounts to advocacy of 'hatred' that constitutes 'incitement' to 'hostility or violence'. But the Covenant does not authorize the PA to arrest anyone who criticizes it. The exceptions for 'national security' and 'public order' should be construed narrowly; otherwise the Covenant's protections would be emptied of content.

Women's rights; non-discrimination; other rights

The PA's record on women's rights is mixed. There is violence against women in Palestinian society, and women's groups assert that there are few Palestinian institutions or resources available to aid victims of such violence. Most cases of spousal abuse are dealt with informally, through the family structure, rather than through the legal system.[38] Oddly, the leading treaty on women's rights, the Convention on the Elimination of All Forms of Discrimination Against Women (CEDAW), has little to say about a party's obligation to safeguard women from rape and domestic violence or to provide shelters or other resources for battered women. As its title implies, the text of CEDAW is instead preoccupied with discrimination against women.[39] Still, the committee charged with implementing CEDAW regards violence against women as a 'form of discrimination'

[35] Ibid.

[36] International Covenant on Civil and Political Rights, Art. 19(2), 19(3)(a) and (b).

[37] Ibid., Art. 20(1), 20(2).

[38] US Dept. of State, 'Country Report for 1998—The Occupied Territories', §5.

[39] See Convention on the Elimination of All Forms of Discrimination Against Women, Art. 2(b) (calling on states parties to adopt legislation combating discrimination); ibid., Art. 2(f) (calling on states parties to abolish discriminatory laws); ibid., Art. 7 (calling on states parties to abolish discrimination in elections).

against women, and thus within the ambit of the Convention.[40] In any event, other sources of human rights law clearly impose on the PA a duty to take steps to prevent violence against women. The Civil and Political Covenant, for example, guarantees the 'right to liberty and security of person' and the right not to be subjected to 'cruel, inhuman or degrading treatment'.[41] And a party to the Covenant is obliged to 'respect and to ensure to all individuals within its territory and subject to its jurisdiction' these rights.[42]

Palestinian women are permitted to work outside the home, and they make up an increasing percentage of the workforce. None the less, there are persistent complaints of discrimination against women in the workplace, and Palestinian women remain vastly under-represented in most professions.[43] The CEDAW contains a wide variety of provisions obliging parties to pass and enforce laws prohibiting discrimination against women. The PA, like most governments, falls short. The PA can, however, point to the failure of most other states to eliminate discrimination against women as evidence that the CEDAW does not reflect the 'internationally recognized norms' incorporated into the Oslo Accords. Even if the CEDAW is such a norm, the PA can argue that the CEDAW generally requires only a good-faith effort to eliminate discrimination, not actual success. Article 2(e) of the CEDAW, for example, obliges states to 'take all appropriate measures' to eliminate discrimination against women in the workplace. Still, at the very least the CEDAW requires that parties adopt anti-discrimination laws: Article 2(b) calls on states to 'adopt appropriate legislative measures . . . prohibiting all discrimination against women'. The PA has not fully complied with this obligation.

The PA also has an uneven record on worker rights. Palestinians are free to create and join trade unions.[44] Most West Bank unions belong to the Palestinian General Federation of Trade Unions, the largest Palestinian labour coalition.[45] The PGFTU has upwards of 86,000 dues-

[40] 'Violence against women', UN Committee on the Elimination of Discrimination Against Women, 11th Sess., General Recommendation No. 19, at 1, UN Doc. CEDAW/C. 1992/L.1/Add. 15 (1992). See generally Pamela Goldberg and Nancy Kelly, 'Recent Developments: International Human Rights and Violence against Women', 6 *Harv. Hum. Rts. J.* 195 (1993).

[41] International Covenant on Civil and Political Rights, Art. 9(1), Art. 7.

[42] Ibid., Art. 2(1).

[43] US Dept. of State, 'Country Report for 1998—The Occupied Territories', §5.

[44] International law provides that everyone has 'the right to form and join trade unions for the protection of his interests'. International Covenant on Civil and Political Rights, Art. 22(1). See also International Covenant on Economic, Social and Cultural Rights, 16 Dec. 1966, 993 U.N.T.S. 3, Art. 8(1)(a) (recognizing a 'right of everyone to form trade unions and join the trade union of his choice').

[45] The Economic and Social Covenant recognizes a 'right of trade unions to establish national federations or confederations' and a right of such federations to join 'international

paying members, or about 30 per cent of Palestinian workers. But Palestinian unions are not entitled to strike unless they first agree to arbitration by the PA Ministry of Labour, and if the union rejects the result of arbitration, the Ministry retains the right to impose sanctions on the union for striking. According to the US State Department's annual report on human rights, there are few if any protections for striking workers. In March 1997, for example, the PA arrested twenty-five members of a teacher's union who had gone on strike to protest low wages. They remained in jail for forty days.[46]

Conditions of work are less than ideal. At the time of writing, the PA has not established a minimum wage for the West Bank or Gaza Strip, and wages for Palestinian workers are in fact quite low.[47] It is not clear, however, that failing to establish a minimum wage is itself a human rights violation. The Economic and Social Covenant says only that the states parties 'recognize the right of everyone to the enjoyment of just and favourable conditions of work, which ensure, in particular . . . a decent living . . .'.[48] As for low wages, the PA can again argue quite plausibly that low wages, not the 'decent living' standard of the Economic and Social Covenant, are the only relevant 'internationally accepted norm' for the purposes of the Oslo Accords. The same might be said of the long work weeks that are common among Palestinian workers. Although the Economic and Social Covenant speaks of a right to 'reasonable limitation of working hours',[49] the 'internationally accepted norm' is that long work weeks are common.

The minimum working age for Palestinians is 14,[50] a limit that nominally complies with human rights law. The International Covenant on Economic and Social Rights simply obliges states to 'set age limits below which the paid employment of child labour should be prohibited and punishable by law'.[51] There is an International Labour Organization convention on minimum age, but it does not flatly prohibit work by 14 year olds.[52] That convention does, however, look unfavourably on labour by children under age 12, and many Palestinian children under that age 'are engaged in some work activities'.[53]

trade-union organizations'. International Covenant on Economic, Social and Cultural Rights, Art. 8(1)(b).

46 US Dept. of State, 'Country Report for 1997—The Occupied Territories', §6.

47 Ibid.

48 International Covenant on Economic, Social and Cultural Rights, Art. 7 and 7(a)(ii).

49 Ibid., Art. 7(d).

50 US Dept. of State, 'Country Report for 1998—The Occupied Territories', §6.d.

51 International Covenant on Economic and Social Rights, Art. 10(3).

52 ILO Convention (No. 138) Concerning Minimum Age for Admission to Employment, 26 June 1973, 1015 U.N.T.S. 297. See generally Janelle M. Diller and David A. Levy, 'Child Labor, Trade and Investment: Toward the Harmonization of International Law', 91 *Am. J. Int'l L.* 663 (1997).

53 US Dept. of State, 'Country Report for 1998—The Occupied Territories', §6.d.

In sum, the PA has a discouraging record on human rights. It cannot justify its human rights violations by pointing to similar (or dissimilar) violations by Israel. As we saw in Chapter 11, Article 60(5) of the Vienna Convention on the Law of Treaties does not permit one party to a treaty of a 'humanitarian character' to suspend its own human rights obligations simply because another party has violated its obligations. This prohibition on retaliation surely extends to human rights obligations in all international agreements, including those (like the Oslo Accords) whose primary 'character' is not necessarily 'humanitarian'. The PA cannot justify its human rights violations by pointing to similar violations by Israel or anyone else.

This brings us to the end of Part IV, on Palestinian compliance with the Oslo Accords. During the Netanyahu era, the PA violated or at least neglected many of its important obligations, including its obligations to cooperate in security matters, to combat terrorism, to amend its Charter, to observe the geographical and functional limits on its governmental activity, and to respect human rights. It justified many of these violations on grounds of reciprocity, but the PA too often resorted to disproportionate countermeasures, and too often disregarded its own implied obligation to interpret and perform the Accords in good faith.

Since the Wye River Memorandum, however, the PA's record of compliance has improved notably, to the point where it may well be in substantial compliance with its obligations on the whole. The PA has (belatedly) complied with its obligation to amend its Charter. Even Israel acknowledges that the PA has played an important role in foiling individual terror attacks, even if it has not done all it can to attack the infrastructure of terror groups. And the PA managed to restrain itself from recklessly declaring 'independence' on 4 May 1999, instead opting to continue in force the Oslo Accords and to pursue final status negotiations. In some areas, notably human rights, PA performance has hardly improved at all. But the PA's overall record now approaches substantial compliance.

As of now, then, it appears that neither party has a basis for termination of the Accords. More to the point, each party continues to regard the Accords as in force. Thus even if one or the other party has grounds for suspension or termination, they have declined to exercise it, at least for now.[54] In November 1999 they initiated a series of permanent status talks,

[54] Whether the parties' acquiescence constitutes a waiver or an estoppel is a separate question. See Vienna Convention on the Law of Treaties, Art. 45(a) and (b) (on waiver); F. A. Mann, 'Note and Comment: Foreign Investment in the International Court of Justice: The ELSI Case', 86 *Am. J. Int'l L.* 92, 101–2 (1992) (arguing that silence does not ordinarily imply

and while the parties appeared as far apart as ever on the ultimate issues, they did pledge to continue meeting and to negotiate in good faith.[55] Those negotiations are, after all, the ultimate point of the Oslo Accords. The final Part of this book considers some of the many legal questions that loom over the final status talks.

waiver or estoppel). See generally J. G. Merrills, *The Development of International Law by the European Court of Human Rights*, 2nd edn (Manchester: Manchester University Press, 1993), 177–98.

[55] See Ben Lynfield, 'Final-status talks open without signs of flexibility', *Jerus. Post*, 9 Nov. 1999. According to one account, the 'real diplomatic show' opened in Paris, where Barak met with Arafat and Egyptian President Hosni Mubarak in early November. Michel Zlotowski and Danna Harman, 'Barak to meet Arafat, Mubarak in Paris today. PA leader: Barak must respect UN Resolution 242', ibid. 9 Nov. 1999.

PART V

After Oslo

The goal of the Oslo Accords, of course, is a comprehensive settlement of the Israeli–Palestinian conflict. To this end, the Accords list a number of 'issues' to be resolved in 'permanent status negotiations'. Article V of the 1993 Declaration of Principles provided: 'It is understood that these negotiations shall cover remaining issues, including: Jerusalem, refugees, settlements, security arrangements, borders, relations and cooperation with other neighbors, and other issues of common interest.' (Interestingly, 'Palestinian statehood' and 'water' were not mentioned explicitly.) It further provided that such negotiations 'will commence as soon as possible, but not later than' the beginning of the third year of the interim period—4 May 1996, two years after Israel's withdrawal from Gaza and the Jericho Area.

Article XXXI of the Interim Agreement contained an identical list of issues, and a substantially identical timetable: 'Permanent status negotiations will commence as soon as possible, but not later than May 4, 1996, between the Parties.' But May 1996 came and went without any serious negotiations. The Hebron Protocol of 15 January 1997 committed the parties to begin negotiations on permanent status within two months—another deadline that went unmet. The Wye River Memorandum of 1998 likewise set a timetable for the start of serious negotiations; that timetable too went by the board.

None the less, the Barak government and the Palestinian leadership seem genuinely interested in pursuing permanent status negotiations. The Sharm el-Sheikh Memorandum of September 1999 expressed the hope that the parties would reach a framework agreement by early 2000 and a final settlement by the end of 2000. To this end, the parties commenced final status talks in November 1999.

The enormity of the task cannot be underestimated. Not only is each final status issue controversial, but each issue bears on several other issues, making it difficult to make progress on one issue without addressing many thorny issues at once. For example, the resolution of the Jerusalem question might influence the status of Jewish settlements around the eastern half of Jerusalem. The resolution of the settlement issue has implications not only for Jerusalem but also for the boundaries of Israel and a Palestinian entity, and for the resettlement of Palestinian and Jewish refugees. The delimitation of boundaries in turn will influence the allocation of water rights, the disposition of settlements, and so on.

As the parties negotiate, they will of course base their negotiating strategies primarily on political considerations, but legal considerations will also affect each party's positions, if only because the parties will be anxious not to undermine their own traditional legal positions. Thus international law will have at least some relevance to the final status talks. Accordingly, it is appropriate to ask what legal questions might arise in permanent status issues, and how international law might shape a final settlement. This Part takes up each issue in turn, beginning with Jerusalem.

The permanent status issues raise countless legal questions. A complete analysis of all these issues would be another book in itself. None the less, some consideration of these issues is essential here. The Oslo Accords cannot be understood without some reference to their ultimate objective, and a review of the most salient legal issues might prove useful to negotiators and commentators as final status negotiations move forward. Accordingly, the final part of this book takes up these issues in the hope that the parties themselves will follow suit.

14

International Law and the 'Permanent Status' Issues

The Oslo Accords list seven 'permanent status' issues, in this order: (1) Jerusalem, (2) refugees, (3) settlements, (4) security arrangements, (5) borders, (6) relations and cooperation with other neighbours, and (7) other issues of common interest. We consider them in that order.

A. Jerusalem

What is the status of Jerusalem, and who is entitled to territorial sovereignty there? There are few questions in international law that evoke a stronger emotional response than this one. If the negotiators wish to make any progress, they will not answer it. Still, the negotiators should and will be influenced by legal considerations, and their goal should be to supplant the existing arguments about Jerusalem with a new legal regime that is binding on, and generally acceptable to, all parties. Thus, while the important task is to create new law, current law can and should play a role in the birth of the new.

Unfortunately, there is no shortage of disagreement about the legal status of Jerusalem. A full critique of the large volume of scholarship on this question is beyond the scope of this book,[1] but a brief summary and some tentative conclusions can at least add perspective to the options that follow. (For a map of Jerusalem, see Map 6, p. 50.)

[1] For a sampling of the large body of legal literature on Jerusalem, see, e.g., Ruth Lapidoth, 'Jerusalem—Some Jurisprudential Aspects', 45 *Catholic U. L. Rev.* 661, 671–3 (1996); Silvio Ferrari, 'The Religious Significance of Jerusalem in the Middle East Peace Process: Some Legal Implications', ibid. 733 (1996); John Quigley, 'Sovereignty in Jerusalem', ibid. 765 (1996); Moshe Hirsch *et al.*, *Whither Jerusalem? Proposals and Positions Concerning the Future of Jerusalem* (The Hague; Boston: Martinus Nijhoff, 1995); Ruth Lapidoth, 'Jerusalem and the Peace Process', 28 *Israel L. Rev.* 402 (1994); Julius Stone, *Israel and Palestine: Assault on the Law of Nations* (Baltimore, MD: Johns Hopkins University Press, 1981); Henry Cattan, *Jerusalem* (New York: St Martin's Press, 1981); Yehuda Z. Blum, 'The Missing Reversioner: Reflections on the Status of Judea and Samaria', 3 *Israel L. Rev.* 279, 294 (1968); Elihu Lauterpacht, *Jerusalem and the Holy Places* (London: Anglo-Israel Association, 1968). See also *Temple Mount Faithful—Amutah et al. v. Attorney-General*, 23 Sept. 1993 (H. Ct. Justice, Isr.), reprinted in 45 *Catholic U. L. Rev.* 861 (1996).

For a collection of legal documents on Jerusalem, see Ruth Lapidoth and Moshe Hirsch (eds.), *The Jerusalem Question and its Resolution: Selected Documents* (Dordrecht; Boston: Martinus Nijhoff, 1994).

As to West Jerusalem, there is a wide range of scholarly opinion. It includes the view that Israel acquired sovereignty there in 1948; the view that sovereignty over Jerusalem is suspended pending a final settlement; the view that Jerusalem is still governed by the Partition Resolution of 1947, which called for a *corpus separatum*; and the view that the Palestinian Arab people have full legal sovereignty over all of Jerusalem.

As to East Jerusalem, opinion ranges from the view that Israel occupied East Jerusalem in self-defence in 1967 and is now entitled to fill a vacuum in sovereignty that had existed there earlier; that Israel has the strongest relative title to East Jerusalem, since Jordan was never a legitimate sovereign; the view that sovereignty is in suspension, awaiting final settlement; the view that the Partition Resolution still governs; and the view that the Palestinians have legal sovereignty over East Jerusalem.[2] Obviously Israel and the Palestinians traditionally have adopted the views that favour their respective claims to the city.

No arbitral tribunal will ever resolve this dispute, so in one sense an assessment of the competing claims is pointless: plainly the only way out of the logjam is some negotiated compromise. Still, the contours of that compromise should be shaped by the underlying legal and political equities.

The most reasonable assessment of the conflicting legal claims is that neither party's maximal solution is compelled by law. As to West Jerusalem, Israel's claim is very strong. West Jerusalem has been a part of the State of Israel since its inception; it has had a Jewish majority since the nineteenth century; and states have *de facto* acquiesced in Israeli sovereignty over West Jerusalem. It is true that many states still decline to locate their embassies there, but this posture reflects concern over recognizing Israeli sovereignty over East Jerusalem, not West Jerusalem. As for the United Nations, Resolution 242 implicitly acknowledges Israel's sovereignty over West Jerusalem, since it calls only for withdrawal from 'territories occupied' in the 1967 War. Even the PLO does not vigorously press a claim to the western sector of the city.

Israel's claim to East Jerusalem, however, is weaker. East Jerusalem was not part of the State of Israel at its inception; though it now houses a Jewish majority, its demographic history is much more Arab than is the case in the western sector; and while it was acquired in a war of self-defence, conquest even in self-defence does not necessarily confer territorial sovereignty. Arab states and the United Nations have repeatedly made known their view that East Jerusalem is occupied territory, as well as their view that the Palestinian Arab people have a right to self-determination.

[2] For a useful recent summary of these theories, see Lapidoth, 'Jerusalem—Some Jurisprudential Aspects', 671–3.

On the other hand, the Palestinian claim to East Jerusalem also has its weaknesses. Even if East Jerusalem is occupied territory, that does not necessarily imply any ultimate conclusion about territorial sovereignty. The mixed demographic make-up of East Jerusalem suggests that Jews as well as Arabs have rights of self-determination there. Moreover, there has never been a Palestinian state there (or anywhere else). Even the UN Partition Plan did not call for Palestinian sovereignty over East Jerusalem, but rather a *corpus separatum*. Likewise, Resolution 242 called for Israeli withdrawal from 'territories' occupied in the 1967 War, but it apparently did not call for withdrawal from *all* territories.[3]

The weaknesses in each party's claim to East Jerusalem lend support to the intermediate theories of sovereignty over East Jerusalem, such as the theory that sovereignty there is suspended pending a final settlement. This conclusion only bolsters the conviction that a final settlement must involve some negotiated compromise between the parties. Given the depth of the parties' attachments to their respective claims, how can they fashion a workable compromise on Jerusalem, one that comports with legal and political constraints?

There is agreement on at least one point: Arabs and Jews alike say they do not want the city to be physically re-divided.[4] Beyond that, a number of competing options present themselves, some more realistic than others. These range from full Palestinian sovereignty over East Jerusalem to full Israeli sovereignty, with intermediate options in between. The discussion that follows argues that international law affords the parties fairly wide latitude to negotiate an agreement resembling any one of the options, but that international law does set some constraints, albeit loose ones. The options are presented with Israeli preferences first, but this ordering is not intended to endorse any one solution over another.

1. *Full Israeli sovereignty over West and East Jerusalem, with Palestinian extraterritorial rights and a Palestinian capital in a Jerusalem suburb*

This type of solution obviously faces enormous political obstacles: it is unacceptable to most Palestinians, who see East Jerusalem as an Arab city. This outcome also raises a host of legal issues. These include whether and how the Palestinians could exercise 'extraterritorial rights' in the Old City

[3] It will be recalled from Ch. 1 that the French and Spanish texts could be read as calling for total withdrawal. The important point, however, is that the English text was the basis for negotiations over Resolution 242. See Sydney D. Bailey, *The Making of Resolution 242* (Dordrecht: Martinus Nijhoff, 1985), 152–3.

[4] See, e.g., Adnan Abu Odeh, 'Religious Inclusion, Political Inclusion: Jerusalem as an Undivided Capital', 45 *Catholic U. L. Rev.* 687, 694 (1996); Lapidoth, 'Jerusalem—Some Jurisprudential Aspects', 686.

or East Jerusalem; more fundamentally, whether an agreement recognizing Israeli sovereignty over both East and West Jerusalem would violate Palestinian rights of self-determination; whether such an arrangement would be void or voidable for duress; and whether the 1947 Partition Resolution forbids any agreement to confer exclusive sovereignty on one party or the other.

The extraterritoriality question can be dealt with briefly here, since its more difficult dimensions relate to Israeli settlements, to be discussed later in this Chapter. For now, it can be said that modern international law would permit a wide array of arrangements by which Palestinians could administer and worship at Holy Sites in the Old City without being subject to the full range of Israeli civil and criminal jurisdiction. Likewise, international law would permit an agreement between Israel and the Palestinians providing for wide powers of Palestinian regulation over future Palestinian nationals living in East Jerusalem. That regulation could take the form of exclusive Palestinian criminal or civil jurisdiction, or it could take the form of concurrent Palestinian and Israeli jurisdiction, perhaps with a Palestinian 'right of first refusal'. Enforcement of extraterritorial Palestinian criminal law would presumably be handled by extradition of Palestinians to the new State of Palestine; enforcement of extraterritorial Palestinian civil law would presumably be handled by a system of mutual enforcement of civil judgments.

The question of self-determination is much more difficult. It goes to the heart of the parties' dispute over Jerusalem. (It should be noted, however, that this dispute centres around East Jerusalem and the Old City; Palestinian leaders do not seriously press a claim to West Jerusalem.) Some pro-Palestinian commentators have argued that any resolution that awards East Jerusalem and the Old City to Israel, no matter how generous the extraterritorial arrangements, would violate the Palestinian inhabitants' fundamental right to self-determination. That right, they argue, is a *jus cogens* norm—one that cannot be dispensed with by agreement.[5] This amounts to an argument that the Palestinian leadership is not free to agree to Israeli sovereignty over East Jerusalem. The argument parallels the traditional Palestinian view that the Balfour Declaration, the British Mandate, and the Partition Resolution all violated Palestinian rights of self-determination.

The problem with this argument is that the content of the right of self-determination is indeterminate.[6] In particular, there is little consensus on

[5] Some commentators go further, suggesting that the Oslo Accords themselves violate Palestinian rights of self-determination. See, e.g., Edward W. Said, *Peace and its Discontents: Essays on Palestine in the Middle East Peace Process* (New York: Vintage Books, 1995).

[6] See Ian Brownlie, *Principles of Public International Law*, 4th edn (Oxford: Clarendon Press; New York: Oxford University Press, 1990), 513. For examples of enunciation of the

what, if any, remedy exists for impingement on a people's right of self-determination. For example, there is no consensus on whether there is a general right of secession. Some UN General Assembly resolutions endorse some right to secede from states with unrepresentative or racist governments,[7] but some precedents and a number of prominent scholars take a more sceptical view.[8] Likewise, the Namibia and Western Sahara cases suggest that some claims can be vindicated by plebiscite or other democratic self-expression,[9] but other recent practice—in Northern Ireland, for example—suggests that in some circumstances, self-determination can be achieved only through peaceful negotiation and agreement. This variegated practice might lead one to conclude that there is no meaningful right of self-determination at all.

right in conventional law, see UN Charter, 26 June 1945, T.S. No. 993, Arts. 1(2) and 55; International Covenant on Civil and Political Rights, 16 Dec. 1966, 999 U.N.T.S. 171, Art. 1(1). For an example of scepticism about the reach of such a right, see Boutros Boutros-Ghali, 'An Agenda for Peace', UN Doc. S/24111, ¶17 (1992), 31 I.L.M. 948, 953 (1992) (noting that statehood for every ethnic group would result in 'no limit to fragmentation' of states).

The Oslo Accords themselves avoid the term 'self-determination', speaking instead of the 'legitimate rights' of the Palestinian people. See, e.g., Declaration of Principles, Art. 3(3). See also John Strawson, 'Palestine's Basic Law: Constituting New Identities Through Liberating Legal Culture', 20 *Loy. L.A. Int'l & Comp. L.J.* 411, 424 (1998) ('the Oslo Accord talks coyly of "legitimate rights" ' rather than self-determination).

7 See, e.g., Declaration on Principles of International Law concerning Friendly Relations and Co-operation among States in accordance with the Charter of the United Nations, Annexe to GA Res. 2625, UN GAOR, 25th Sess., Supp. No. 28, at 121, UN Doc. A/8028 (1970), reprinted in 9 I.L.M. 1292 (1970).

8 See, e.g., Inter-American Commission on Human Rights, 'Report on the Situation of Human Rights of a Segment of the Nicaraguan Population of Miskito Origin', OAS Doc. OEA/Ser.L/V/II.62, Doc. 10, rev. 3 (1983); 'Report of the Commission of Rapporteurs presented to the League of Nations Council', League of Nations Doc. B.7.21/68/106 (1921) (maintaining that a right of secession would 'destroy order and stability within States' and 'inaugurate anarchy in international life'). These and other examples are quoted in Frederic L. Kirgis, Jr., 'The Degrees of Self-Determination in the United Nations Era', 88 *Am. J. Int'l L.* 304, 304 (1994), a thoughtful comment on the different flavours of 'self-determination'. For scholarly scepticism about a right of secession, see, e.g., Hurst Hannum, *Autonomy, Sovereignty, and Self-Determination: The Accommodation of Conflicting Rights* (Philadelphia: University of Pennsylvania Press, 1990), 30; Thomas Franck, 'Postmodern Tribalism and the Right to Secession', in Catherine Brölmann, René Lefeber, and Marjoleine Zieck (eds.), *Peoples and Minorities in International Law* (Dordrecht; Boston: M. Nijhoff, 1993), 3, 13–14.

It is doubtful that there is a 'general principle of law' endorsing secession. States have resisted recognizing such a right in their municipal law. For example, some of the most famous political rhetoric in American history deals with the question of secession. See, e.g., Abraham Lincoln, First Inaugural Address (1861), in Michael Les Benedict, *Sources in American Constitutional History* (Lexington, MA: D. C. Heath & Co., 1993), 108–9 ('no State upon its mere motion can lawfully get out of the Union'); Daniel Webster, 'Reply to Hayne' (1830), in Benedict, *Sources*, 81–3; cf. Abraham Lincoln, The Gettysburg Address (1863), in Benedict, *Sources*, 114 (implying that government is of 'the people' as a whole, not individual states, and vowing that 'government of the people, by the people, for the people, shall not perish from the earth').

9 See generally Antonio Cassese, *Self-Determination of Peoples: A Legal Reappraisal* (Cambridge; New York: Cambridge University Press, 1995).

Still, there are some definable contours to the right of self-determination. It has expressed itself in a number of forms, ranging from full sovereignty to limited autonomy a right to decide democratically *not* to pursue independence or autonomy.[10] As Professor Kirgis puts it, the right of self-determination is a 'variable' one. In particular, Kirgis suggests, the scope of self-determination is a function of two important variables: 'the degree of destabilization in any given claim, taking into account all the circumstances surrounding it, and the degree to which the responding government represents the people belonging to the territory.'[11]

Applying these standards to East Jerusalem, it would appear that the law of self-determination does not demand any one particular solution. It gives Palestinian and Israeli negotiators alike considerable room in which to manoeuvre. East Jerusalem includes both a substantial Arab and a substantial Jewish population, and the Old City obviously houses Holy Places of enormous importance to both sides. Self-determination might take the form of full Palestinian sovereignty in East Jerusalem (an option to be discussed momentarily), but it might not have to take that form. The parties might conceivably agree that such a solution would be too 'destabilizing', in that it would presumably result in a city divided the way Jerusalem was divided from 1948 to 1967. Or they might conclude that self-determination can be vindicated by ensuring that Israel is a sufficiently representative home for the Palestinian residents of East Jerusalem—that it affords them full rights of citizens, including the right to vote, to own property, to have access to public resources, and the like. As we have seen, Israel has often fallen short of its human rights obligations to the Palestinians; an agreement that offered stricter guarantees for Palestinian rights would more likely be regarded as consistent with norms of self-determination. Alternatively, the negotiators might conclude that self-determination can be effectuated by a mix of Israeli sovereignty and Palestinian extraterritorial jurisdiction as to certain classes of crimes and civil matters. The point is that self-determination is not a fixed norm that points to only one solution.

Palestinians may also argue that any permanent status agreement that does not secure sovereignty over East Jerusalem would be void or voidable for coercion or duress. If Palestinian leaders do sign such an agreement, they should not count on claims of duress to allow them to undo it later. As a practical matter, such a strategy would be self-defeating because it would invite Israel to disown its own obligations under the

[10] See generally Frederic L. Kirgis, Jr., 'The Degrees of Self-Determination in the United Nations Era', 88 *Am. J. Int'l L.* 304 (1994).

[11] Ibid. 310.

agreement. Beyond that, however, it should be recalled that coercion is a very narrow ground for invalidation of an international agreement.

As for coercion of a state party to an agreement, Article 52 of the Vienna Convention on the Law of Treaties holds a treaty 'void' only if it was 'procured by the threat or use of force'. Peace treaties are routinely sustained even when they result from the massive use of force, and in any event Israel is not likely to threaten or use force to obtain a permanent status agreement. And the negotiating history of the Convention suggests that 'force' means armed force, not economic or political pressure.[12] The Vienna Convention also provides that coercion of a state's 'representative' can deprive that state's consent of its 'legal effect,' but again this norm is rarely invoked in practice, and only in cases resembling extortion, such as one case involving a 'threat to ruin the career of a representative by exposing a private indiscretion as well as a threat to injure a member of his family'.[13] Israel will not resort to such tactics.

A final issue is whether the General Assembly Partition Resolution of 1947 prevents the parties from agreeing to confer sovereignty over East Jerusalem to either party. The most sensible answer is that the Resolution does not stand in the way of such an arrangement. It is true that the Resolution called for a *corpus separatum* in Jerusalem—though it should also be remembered that the Resolution envisioned that the status of Jerusalem would be revisited after a period of time. In any event, as we saw in Chapter 1, the Partition Resolution is not legally binding now. It might have been binding when adopted, but it quickly fell into desuetude, and its terms were implicitly rejected by Security Council Resolution 242.

In sum, a final status agreement conferring upon Israel sovereignty over East Jerusalem would not deprive Palestinians there of their self-determination, so long as the agreement was freely negotiated and so long as the agreement fully protected the civil and political rights of Palestinians there. A concomitant regime of extraterritoriality would likewise be lawful. It is quite improbable that such an agreement would be invalid for coercion or duress.

2. *Shared sovereignty*

There are a variety of proposals for shared sovereignty over East Jerusalem and the Old City. The most famous of these is the unpublished plan for joint administration advanced by Israeli politician Yossi Beilin

[12] See Sir Ian Sinclair, *The Vienna Convention on the Law of Treaties*, 2nd edn (Manchester; Dover, NH: Manchester University Press, 1984), 15–17.

[13] Louis Henkin *et al.*, *International Law: Cases and Materials*, 3rd edn (St Paul, MN: West Publishing, 1993), 492.

and Palestinian negotiator Abu Mazen.[14] This plan would establish a Palestinian capital at the East Jerusalem suburb of Abu Dis, which would be renamed *Al-Quds* (the Arabic term for Jerusalem). It would also provide for some Palestinian role in the day-to-day governance of East Jerusalem, while leaving control of the city as a whole to Israel. Beilin and Abu Mazen were apparently unable to agree on *de jure* sovereignty over East Jerusalem; their plan apparently would have finessed that issue, leaving it for another day.[15] Other shared-sovereignty plans include proposals for a 'condominium', proposals for 'functional' sovereignty, and proposals to govern the city through local councils, boroughs, or *arrondissements*.[16]

There are significant differences among these plans, but they all have in common some form of joint administration of the city. Many of them also envision a larger Jerusalem, one that might accommodate the aspirations and institutions of both societies. A larger Jerusalem might also have advantages for the more mundane aspects of city management.[17]

International law plainly permits subjects of international law to share sovereignty over the same territory. One prominent example is the condominium, an arrangement in which two or more states jointly exercise sovereignty over a single territory.[18] Austria and Prussia governed Schleswig-Holstein and Lauenburg as a condominium from 1864 to 1866; Britain and Egypt governed the Sudan as a condominium from 1898 to 1955; and Britain and France governed the New Hebrides (now the state of Vanuatu) as a condominium from 1914 to 1980.[19] The joint administration of Berlin may not have been a condominium, and it might not be the best model for governing Jerusalem, but it is further evidence that states can share control over territory. For that matter, federal states, customs unions, the European Union, and other arrangements exemplify the flexibility with which international law regards shared 'sovereignty' over territory. The Mandate and Trusteeship systems themselves were examples of divided sovereignty, though obviously not examples to which Jerusalem should return. It has even been suggested that 'leases' of territory—such

[14] See Ze'ev Schiff, 'Beilin and Abu Mazen Drafted a Document on Final Status; Agreed to Establish a Palestinian State', *Ha'aretz*, 22 Feb. 1996.

[15] See Marshall J. Breger and Thomas A. Idinopulos, *Jerusalem's Holy Places and the Peace Process* (Washington, DC: Washington Institute for Near East Policy, Policy Papers Ser. No. 46, 1998), 67.

[16] See Marshall J. Breger, 'The Future of Jerusalem: A Symposium—An Introduction', 45 *Catholic U. L. Rev.* 653, 656–7 (1996).

[17] See Lapidoth, 'Jerusalem—Some Jurisprudential Aspects', 678.

[18] *Oppenheim's International Law*, 9th edn, §170, 2:565. There has traditionally been disagreement about the precise definition of a condominium and the precise status of the condominial territory. See D. P. O'Connell, 'The Condominium of the New Hebrides', 43 *Brit. Yb. Int'l L.* 71, 77–84 (1968–9).

[19] See *Oppenheim's International Law*, 9th edn, §170, 2:565–6.

as China's lease of Hong Kong to Britain—are a sort of shared sovereignty, though again not the best model for Jerusalem.[20]

In sum, international law permits a wide range of arrangements involving shared sovereignty. In Jerusalem, shared sovereignty raises two further issues: what law would govern in Jerusalem, and how the Holy Places would be managed.

As to choice of law, a number of options present themselves. One possible approach is 'territorial'. Under this approach, Israeli law might apply to boroughs or *arrondissements* with large majorities of Jews, or it might apply only in West Jerusalem, while Palestinian law might apply in Palestinian boroughs or throughout most or all of East Jerusalem. A second approach would be 'personal'. That is, Israelis would always be governed by Israeli law, and Palestinians would likewise be governed by Palestinian law, regardless of where they are. A third possibility is a combination of the first two: Israeli law might apply exclusively in the western sector of the city, Palestinian law in the eastern sector, and the law of the person might apply in the Old City and other areas. A fourth possibility is concurrent jurisdiction, with one side or the other exercising 'primary' jurisdiction in certain territories or in respect of their own nationals. A fifth possibility would be a 'flexible system' in which the governing law 'would depend on the subject matter, the parties involved, and the municipal district in which the issue or dispute arises'.[21]

Each option has its strengths and weaknesses. A territory-based system has the virtue of simplicity and clear notice to the public. But it ignores the nationality of the parties, which means that each side will have jurisdiction over some 'foreign' transactions in which it has little interest. A personality-based system ensures that each side will retain jurisdiction over its own nationals, but it is more complex than a territorial system. For example, who would have jurisdiction over a crime by a Palestinian against an Israeli? The more widely accepted 'active personality' theory would favour a Palestinian court; the more controversial 'passive personality' theory would favour an Israeli court.[22]

A mixed territory-personality system shares the virtues and vices of each of its components. A system of concurrent jurisdiction, with one side presumptively exercising jurisdiction in certain cases, has the advantage of ensuring that one side's courts can act in the event that the other side's courts are delinquent, but it has the disadvantage of inviting conflicts

[20] Leases and the other examples cited are discussed in ibid. 567–72.

[21] John V. Whitbeck, 'The Road to Peace Starts in Jerusalem: The "Condominium" Solution', 45 *Catholic U. L. Rev.* 781, 790 (1996).

[22] Compare Geoffrey R. Watson, 'Offenders Abroad: The Case for Nationality-Based Criminal Jurisdiction', 17 *Yale J. Int'l L.* 41 (1992) with Geoffrey R. Watson, 'The Passive Personality Principle', 28 *Texas Int'l L. J.* 1 (1993).

over jurisdiction. The 'flexible' approach has precedent in extradition treaties, which often call on the requested state to evaluate all jurisdictional factors before choosing which of two competing extradition requests to honour.[23] This approach best accounts for all the jurisdictional circumstances, but it also introduces the most complexity—and the most potential for conflict between courts of each side.

The parties would be well-advised to favour the clarity and simplicity of territory-based rules. Conflicts of law is one corner of jurisprudence that is best served by bright lines. A territory-based system is the easiest system to administer: the evidence and witnesses are already in the court's territory. Such a system also provides the clearest notice to individuals of what law governs. Signs and other cues can physically indicate to people precisely what law governs where. In personality-based systems, by contrast, the law wanders the streets with each individual, creating uncertainty about what law governs where. Personality-based systems can also bog down in arguments over whether the individual is or is not a national of the state seeking to exercise jurisdiction. Such systems also permit trials to take place far away from the site of the transaction, thus complicating the collection of evidence and the appearance of witnesses.

None the less, the parties appear committed to at least some form of personality-based jurisdiction. The Oslo Accords themselves provide that either side can exercise personality-based jurisdiction in some circumstances.[24] Thus the parties will have to fashion some system that accounts for both personality and territory. Some 'flexibility' in administering such a system will therefore be essential.

The final question about shared sovereignty relates to the Holy Places in Jerusalem. Even if the parties do not agree to share sovereignty over secular aspects of life in Jerusalem, they almost certainly will choose to share responsibility for the Holy Places. Actually, the term 'sovereignty' is inappropriate for joint administration of the Holy Places, since it seems likely that such administration would be in the hands of private religious groups or committees, not states. As King Hussein put it: 'My religious faith demands that sovereignty over the Holy Places in Jerusalem reside with God and God alone.'[25]

There are various proposals to accomplish this objective. One would vest control over the Holy Places to an interfaith committee of some sort.[26] Another would entrust power over the sites to the interested religious

[23] See, e.g., Treaty of Extradition, 8 June 1972, US–UK, 28 U.S.T. 227, Art. X.

[24] See, e.g., Interim Agreement, Annex I, Art. 1(1)(b) (permitting the PA to prosecute Palestinians for certain offences outside PA jurisdiction).

[25] Cf. HRH King Hussein, speech before the US Congress, reprinted in 140 Cong. Rec. H6204, H6205 (daily edn. 26 July 1994).

[26] See Breger and Idinopulos, *Jerusalem and the Holy Places*, 61 and n. 5.

confessions. Moslem Holy Sites would be governed by a Moslem committee, Christian Sites by a Christian committee, and Jewish Sites by either a Jewish committee or the State of Israel itself.[27] Any such solution obviously must confront the reality of intramural disagreements among different denominations of a particular faith. Still another option might grant certain Holy Places, such as the Temple Mount and Haram, semi-autonomous status like that of Mount Athos in Greece.[28] Yet another might be a Vatican-like solution, in which the Holy Sites of the Old City are fully sovereign, with power to tax, police, issue passports, regulate immigration, and so forth. Still another might involve some measure of UN sponsorship.[29]

These options raise several common issues of international law. One is whether any such arrangement would comport with existing norms of human rights law, in particular the law relating to religious freedom. The law of human rights contains only relatively general norms on religious freedom; states have not been able to agree on whether there is a right of international religious pilgrimage, and there is continued uncertainty about the scope of a right to proselytize.[30] But human rights law does contain strong if general norms protecting religious expression. It would be unlawful for any of the above arrangements to impinge on existing religious rights unless necessary to 'protect public safety, order, health, or morals or the fundamental rights and freedoms of others'.[31]

In addition, any of the above options for the Holy Places would have to comply with Israel's international obligations to 'maintain and respect' the historical 'status quo' in certain Holy Places. The 'status quo' grew out of nineteenth-century Ottoman *firmans* designed to determine the rights of various denominations in various Holy Places. It has since been memorialized in a variety of international instruments that continue to bind Israel, including the Holy See–Israel Fundamental Agreement of 1993, which reaffirmed Israel's commitment to the historical 'status quo'.[32] Israel's municipal law also obliges it to respect existing religious rights in

[27] See Elihu Lauterpacht, *Jerusalem and the Holy Places* (London: Anglo-Israel Association, 1968), 58–9.

[28] See Breger and Idinopulos, *Jerusalem and the Holy Places*, 63–6.

[29] Ibid. 21–2, 66.

[30] See Moshe Hirsch, 'The Freedom of Proselytism Under the Fundamental Agreement and International Law', 47 *Catholic U. L. Rev.* 407 (1998); Geoffrey R. Watson, 'Progress for Pilgrims? An Analysis of the Holy See–Israel Fundamental Agreement', ibid. 497, 506–27 (1998).

[31] International Covenant on Civil and Political Rights, Art. 18(3).

[32] Fundamental Agreement Between the Holy See and the State of Israel, 30 Dec. 1993, Art. 4(1), reprinted in 33 I.L.M. 153 (1994) and 47 *Catholic U. L. Rev.* 529 (1998). For more on the 'status quo', see generally L. G. A. Cust, *The Status Quo in the Holy Places* (Jerusalem: Ariel Pub. House, 1980); Walter Zander, *Israel and the Holy Places of Christendom* (New York: Praeger, 1971).

the Holy Places.[33] Likewise, Israel is obliged to respect the applicable multilateral conventions on protection of cultural property.[34]

Finally, any agreement Israel makes in respect of the Holy Places must presumably conform with Israel's own bilateral commitments. The most controversial of these is the provision of the Israel–Jordan peace treaty providing that Israel would respect the 'special role' of the Hashemite Kingdom in the Moslem Holy Sites in Jerusalem, and that Israel would give 'high priority' to Jordan's 'historic role' in those shrines.[35] The Palestinians angrily denounced these terms, accusing Israel of violating its earlier obligations under the Declaration of Principles.[36]

It is true that the Declaration provides that the outcome of permanent status talks 'should not be prejudiced or preempted by agreements reached for the interim period', but the Declaration also calls on the parties to cooperate with Jordan on matters of 'common concern'.[37] The peace treaty would seem to give effect to this latter obligation without directly stripping the PA of any concrete rights in the Holy Places. Indeed, the Interim Agreement of 1995 contained a number of specific provisions designed to protect Palestinian rights respecting the Holy Places, including the transfer of responsibility for some Holy Places to the PA.[38]

In sum, shared sovereignty over East Jerusalem and the Old City is permissible under international law. The parties should seek to share jurisdiction along territorial lines where possible, though political reality may demand that nationality-based jurisdiction play some role as well. Shared administration of the Holy Places must be carried out in accordance with the 'status quo' and general human rights law.

3. *Full Palestinian sovereignty over East Jerusalem, including the Old City, with Israeli extraterritorial rights in the Old City*

For most Palestinians, this is the best of the options. It will almost certainly never come to pass. Absent some radical shift in Israeli politics and demographics, no Israeli government could withstand the political earthquake that would result. Actually, this option does not represent the maximal Palestinian position—sovereignty over West *and* East

[33] See generally Ruth Lapidoth, 'Freedom of Religion and of Conscience in Israel', 47 *Catholic U. L. Rev.* 441, 449–55 (1998).

[34] See, e.g., Convention for the Protection of World Cultural and Natural Heritage, 14 May 1954, 249 U.N.T.S. 215.

[35] Treaty of Peace between Israel and Jordan, 26 Oct. 1994, Isr.–Jordan, 34 I.L.M. 43, 46. This language grew out of similar language in the Washington Declaration of 25 July 1994. See Menachem Klein, 'The Islamic Holy Places as a Political Bargaining Card (1993–1995)', 47 *Catholic U. L. Rev.* 745, 747 (1996).

[36] Ibid. 750–1.

[37] Declaration of Principles, Art. V(4), XII.

[38] See Interim Agreement, Annex 3 (Civil Matters), Art. 32.

Jerusalem—but (unlike some radical Palestinians and academics) the Palestinian leadership itself does not seriously propose Palestinian sovereignty over West Jerusalem.[39]

The PLO does, however, advocate Palestinian sovereignty over all of East Jerusalem, which the PLO has claimed as the capital of a coming Palestinian state. And yet almost half the city's Jews live in East Jerusalem.[40] If, against all expectations, an Israeli government somehow agreed to these terms, would such an agreement comply with international law? In particular, would such an agreement violate Jewish rights of self-determination in East Jerusalem?

The most sensible answer is that Israel is free to agree to full Palestinian sovereignty in East Jerusalem. Admittedly, such a solution raises questions about both of Kirgis's standards. It would be 'destabilizing' in that it would create a tense, divided city, in the mould of the Jerusalem that was carved in half with barbed wire from 1948 to 1967. It would also destabilize internal Israeli politics, perhaps radically. One might also question whether a Palestinian government over East Jerusalem and the Old City would in any way 'represent' Jews who live or work there, to say nothing of Jews who wish to pray at the Holy Places in the Old City. Israelis still have bitter memories of Jordanian management of the Holy Places in the years after 1948.

Still, in the unlikely event that an Israeli government is willing to accept these risks, it is not forbidden to do so. Destabilization in Israeli politics might at least be offset by some stabilization in Palestinian politics. And extraterritorial arrangements could help protect the rights of Jews living, working, or praying in East Jerusalem or the Old City. Again, this is not necessarily to suggest that this is the best solution, only that it is a lawful one.

4. *Deferred resolution or implementation*

Finally, it should be noted that the parties need not reach agreement on each and every aspect of the Jerusalem question. The parties may have a duty to bargain in good faith over the issues, but they do not necessarily have a duty to reach a final agreement on each issue. Some issues, such as the precise legal status of East Jerusalem, may best be postponed indefinitely in favour of an ambiguous solution under which both parties can claim victory. Others, such as the location of a Palestinian capital, probably will require resolution relatively soon. The point is that constructive

39 Cf. Quigley, 'Sovereignty in Jerusalem', 779 (asserting that the Palestinians have the better claim to 'both sectors' of Jerusalem).

40 Abraham Rabinovich, 'On capitals and compromise', *Jerus. Post*, 18 June 1999.

ambiguity need not be limited to the Oslo Accords themselves: it can also have a place in a final status agreement.

B. Refugees

One of the most emotionally charged 'final status' issues is the problem of refugees[41] and displaced persons. Between 600,000 and 750,000 Palestinian refugees 'left, ran away, or were expelled'[42] from the territory of the new State of Israel in the 1948 War. These Palestinians and their descendants now live mostly in Jordan, the occupied territories, and in the territory of other neighbouring Arab states. Estimates of those displaced by the 1967 War vary from 100,000 to 400,000 or more Palestinians.[43]

Again, there are various possibilities for a final status agreement on refugees. Again, some possibilities are more realistic than others. This

[41] Some analysts prefer the term 'displaced Palestinian' to 'refugee' because a refugee is traditionally defined as someone who does *not* wish to return home because of a fear of persecution. See John Quigley, 'Displaced Palestinians and a Right of Return', 39 *Harv. Int'l L.J.* 171, 171 n. 4 (1998), citing Vojin Dimitrijevic, 'Legal Position of Palestine Refugees', *19 Rev. Int'l Aff.* 427 (1968). Indeed, there is some doubt about whether all Palestinians outside Israel qualify as 'refugees' within the traditional meaning of the term. See Convention on the Status of Refugees, 28 July 1951, 189 U.N.T.S. 137, Art. 1(A)(2) (defining a refugee as a person who has a 'well-founded fear of being persecuted for reasons of race, religion, nationality, membership of a particular social group or political opinion').

The Middle East peace agreements themselves, however, have adopted the convention of describing those fleeing the 1948 War as 'refugees' and those dislocated by the 1967 War as 'displaced persons'. See, e.g., Treaty of Peace, Isr.–Jor., Art. 8(2). The apparent theory behind this distinction is that the 1948 War sent Palestinians abroad, whereas the 1967 War merely resulted in their relocation within the occupied territories. Some analysts have also adopted this convention. See Salim Tamari, *Palestinian Refugee Negotiations: From Madrid to Oslo II* (Washington, DC: Institute for Palestine Studies, 1996), 21–2, 59, 61. For the sake of convenience, and because international law may draw some distinctions between the two, that convention is adopted here.

[42] Benvenisti and Zamir, 'Private Claims to Property Rights', 297 (asserting that 600,000–700,000 Palestinians left).

The number of refugees, and especially the cause of their flight, is a matter of intense disagreement to this day. For examples of differing numerical estimates, see Benny Morris, *The Birth of the Palestinian Refugee Problem, 1947–49* (Cambridge: Cambridge University Press, 1987), App. I, pp. 297–8 ('loose' estimate of between 600,000 and 760,000 refugees); Shlomo Gazit, *The Palestinian Refugee Problem* 3 (1995) (putting the number at about 604,000); Janet Abu-Lughod, 'The Demographic Transformation of Palestine', in Ibrahim Abu-Lughod (ed.), *The Transformation of Palestine: Essays on the Origin and Development of the Arab–Israeli Conflict* (Evanston: Northwestern University Press, 1971), 139, 160 (asserting that after the first Israeli census, only 120,000 Arabs remained of 900,000 present before the war).

For a sampling of the passionate arguments on both sides of the causes of the Palestinian exodus, compare Justus Weiner, 'The Palestinian Refugees' "Right to Return" and the Peace Process', 20 *B.C. Int'l & Comp. L. Rev.* 1, 21–6 (1997) with Quigley, 'Displaced Palestinians', 173–82.

[43] See Benvenisti and Zamir, 'Private Claims to Property Rights', 18; Quigley, 'Displaced Palestinians', 181; Sydney D. Bailey, *The Making of Resolution 242* (Dordrecht: Martinus Nijhoff, 1985), 172.

section groups the various possibilities into two major options: (1) a general Palestinian right of return to Israel and a concomitant right to repossess property there; and its more likely alternative, (2) a Palestinian right to compensation and to return to a Palestinian entity, with only a limited provision for Palestinians to immigrate to Israel.

1. *A Palestinian right to return to Israel and to repossess property there*

The maximal Palestinian position is a final status agreement recognizing a Palestinian right of return to Israel and a correlative right to repossess lost property. The traditional Palestinian view is that this outcome is required by international law. The traditional Israeli view is that there is no such right, and that any resolution of the refugee problem should take place in the context of comprehensive peace negotiations. As with the status of Jerusalem, a thorough analysis of these legal issues is beyond the scope of this book. As with Jerusalem, however, assessment of the parties' respective positions requires at least some attention to the underlying legal equities. Accordingly, a brief look at the parties' conflicting positions on refugees is in order.

The Palestinian claim to a right of return begins with UN General Assembly Resolution 194 of 1948, in which the Assembly resolved that

> the refugees wishing to return to their homes and live at peace with their neighbors should be permitted to do so at the earliest practicable date, and that compensation should be paid for the property of those choosing not to return and for loss of or damage to property which, under principles of international law or in equity, should be made good by the Governments or authorities responsible.[44]

At first blush, this provision would seem to support both a right of return and a right of repossession; after all, it speaks of 'return to *their homes*', not just return to Israel.

But there are a number of holes in Resolution 194. It is not cast in mandatory language; it says 'should', not 'shall'.[45] It is true that a number of delegates to the General Assembly explained that they were endorsing a 'right' of Arab refugees to return to their homes.[46] But international law

[44] G.A. Res. 194, UN GAOR, 3rd Sess., ¶11, UN Doc. A/810 (1948).

[45] See Ruth Lapidoth, 'The Right of Return in International Law, with Special Reference to the Palestinian Refugees', 16 *Isr. YB. Hum. Rts.* 103, 116 (1986); Kurt René Radley, 'The Palestinian Refugees: the Right to Return in International Law', 72 *Am. J. Int'l L.* 586, 601 (1978).

[46] See Quigley, 'Displaced Palestinians', 189 and n. 110 (citing examples).

Professor Quigley attaches significance to the statement of the resolution's drafter, the United Kingdom, that the provision was a 'precise directive'. Ibid. 189, quoting UN GAOR, 3rd Sess., 184th mtg. at 948, UN Doc. A/PV.184 (1948) (Mr McNeil, UK). According to Quigley, this characterization 'makes sense only if it is a call for repatriation'. Ibid.

ordinarily looks to the plain meaning of an instrument,[47] and the term 'should' is clear on its face: it is hortatory, not obligatory. Indeed, the word 'right' does not appear in the operative paragraph. Moreover, the Resolution states that refugees should be 'permitted' to return—language which the Palestinian Arab delegation to the Assembly later characterized as inconsistent with a right of return.[48] Finally, the instrument is a resolution of the General Assembly, and as such is not legally binding.[49]

It is true that General Assembly resolutions of the 1970s and 1980s declared a Palestinian 'right' of return, and later resolutions may have some bearing on interpretation of earlier ones,[50] but none of those later resolutions were any more binding than Resolution 194. Moreover, not every Assembly resolution after 194 squarely endorses a right of return: General Assembly Resolution 513,[51] adopted in 1951, called on Arab states to resettle displaced Palestinians in their own territory, implying that displaced Palestinians had as much a right to resettle in Arab states as to return to Israel. Nor has the practice of the Security Council (whose resolutions can bind all states) squarely endorsed a right of return. Security Council Resolution 237 did call on Israel to 'facilitate' the return of Palestinians displaced by the 1967 War, but it did not announce a 'right of return' on the part of all Palestinian refugees.[52] And Security Council Resolution 242 stops short of declaring a right of return, calling instead for a 'just settlement' of the refugee problem.[53]

It is true that human rights law emphatically proclaims the right of an individual to return home. The Universal Declaration of Human Rights

[47] See Vienna Convention on the Law of Treaties, 23 May 1969, UN Doc. A/CONF. 39/27, Art. 31(1); cf. ibid., Art. 32(a) and (b).

[48] 21 GAOR, Special Political Committee (501st mtg.) 23, UN Doc. A/SPC/SR. 501 (1966) (statement of Mr Al-Ghouri, chairman of the Palestine Arab Delegation) ('That right [to return] could never be a matter of option or permission').

[49] See UN Charter, Art. 10.

There are other, less persuasive objections to the claim that General Assembly Resolution 194 established a right of return and repossession as a matter of international law. It has been said, for example, that because the Resolution is limited to Palestinians 'wishing to . . . live at peace with their neighbors', it confers on Israel discretion to determine which refugees might return peacefully. See Yoav Tadmor, 'Comment: The Palestinian Refugees of 1948: The Right to Compensation and Return', 8 *Temple Int'l & Comp. L.J.* 434 (1994). But the provision says nothing about vesting such determinations in Israel; it could plausibly be read simply to suggest that displaced Palestinians may choose between returning to Israel or remaining abroad. See Quigley, *supra*, at 187. Moreover, as Quigley points out, subsequent Assembly resolutions eliminated the phrase 'wishing to live at peace'. Ibid.

[50] Cf. Vienna Convention on the Law of Treaties, Art. 31(3) (providing that treaty interpretation shall consider subsequent practice).

[51] G.A. Res. 513, UN GAOR, 6th Sess., Supp. No. 20, at 12, UN Doc. A/2119 (1951).

[52] S.C. Res. 237, UN SCOR, 22nd Sess., at 5, UN Doc. S/INF/22/Rev. 2 (1967). The General Assembly also called for the return of Palestinians displaced by the 1967 War. See G.A. Res. 2452A, UN GAOR, 23rd Sess., Supp. No. 18, at 22, UN Doc. A/7218 (1968).

[53] See S.C. Res. 242, UN SCOR, 22nd Sess., at 8, UN Doc. S/INF/22/Rev. 2 (1967).

states flatly: 'Everyone has the right to leave any country, including his own, *and to return to his country*.'[54] Likewise, Article 12(4) of the Civil and Political Covenant provides: 'No one shall be arbitrarily deprived of the right to enter his own country.' There has been interesting scholarly argument over whether the Palestinian refugee problem involves 'arbitrary' deprivations.[55] It also has been suggested that the Covenant covers only individuals, not groups.[56] This interpretation does not seem to be required by the plain text of the instrument, and as a policy matter it is unappealing: it implies that one's right to return is somehow less compelling if others share the same predicament.

The strongest argument against applicability of the Covenant is that the displaced Palestinians are not seeking return to their 'own' country, since they are not Israeli nationals.[57] Most Palestinian refugees probably do not consider themselves Israeli nationals. Israel surely does not. Israel conferred Israeli nationality on Palestinian Arabs who remained (and still remain) in the territory of Israel after the 1948 War, but it did not grant citizenship to Palestinians who were present when Israel was declared a state but shortly thereafter fled Israeli territory.[58] Because the International Covenant's reference to one's 'own' country apparently means one's country of nationality,[59] Israel argues that non-nationals—including displaced Palestinians and Palestinian refugees—have no absolute right to enter or reside in Israel.

This argument might be difficult to accept if there were no Palestinian entity on the horizon, since it would leave large numbers of Palestinians with no 'home' to which to return. But the argument does imply that Palestinians will have a right of return to a new Palestinian entity, if and when it is constituted at the close of final status talks.

Other relevant treaties lend only ambiguous support to the Palestinian

[54] Universal Declaration of Human Rights, 10 Dec. 1948, G.A. Res. 217 (III 1948).

[55] For argument over the meaning of the term 'arbitrary', and about whether Israel has given proper notice of derogation from this obligation, compare Lapidoth, 'The Right of Return', 110, 115, with Quigley, 'Displaced Palestinians', 203–4.

[56] See, e.g., Lapidoth, 'The Right of Return', 108–9; cf. Hurst Hannum, *The Right to Leave and Return in International Law and Practice* (Dordrecht; Boston: Martinus Nijhoff, 1987), 71; Stig Jagerskiold, 'The Freedom of Movement', in Louis Henkin, ed., *The International Bill of Rights* (New York: Columbia University Press, 1981), 180.

[57] See, e.g., Radley, 'The Palestinian Refugees', 613–14; Lapidoth, 'The Right of Return', 114 ('The Palestinian Arab refugees have never been nationals or permanent residents of Israel').

[58] See Nationality Law, art. 3, in 6 L.S.I. 50 (1952).

[59] One problem with this argument is that the text of the Covenant does not, strictly speaking, limit the right of return to nationals. It speaks instead of a right to return to one's 'own country'. For the view that the right to return is none the less limited to nationals, see Inglés, 'Study of Discrimination in Respect of the Right of Everyone to Leave Any Country, Including his Own, and to Return to his Country', at 5, 18, 56, 66 (1963), UN Doc. E/CN.4/Sub.2/229/Rev. 1; Lapidoth, 'The Right of Return', 107–8. For the view that permanent residents also enjoy a right of return, see ibid. 108 and nn. 25–6.

claim of an absolute legal right to return to Israel. The Refugee Convention does not speak to the issue directly; its focus is on refugees who fear persecution at home and thus seek asylum abroad, not those who actually wish to return.[60] Nor do treaties on the law of war clearly vindicate the Palestinian claim.[61] The Camp David Accords did not confer on the Palestinians a right of return.[62] The Madrid peace talks ushered in multilateral negotiations on refugees in Moscow in 1992, talks that continued after adoption of the Oslo Accords, but these multilateral negotiations have not produced any resolution of the problem, at least not publicly.[63]

The 1993 Declaration of Principles and the succeeding Oslo Accords called for final status negotiations to cover 'remaining issues', including 'refugees'.[64] The Declaration also called for a Continuing Committee, modelled on a similar provision in the Camp David Accords, to decide on 'the modalities of admission of persons displaced from the West Bank and Gaza Strip in 1967, together with necessary measures to prevent disruption and disorder'.[65] And, citing the 'spirit of the peace process', the Interim Agreement did grant the Palestinians some role in admitting Palestinians for family reunification.[66] But the Oslo Accords did not establish a right of return or repossession, or even specify whether the question

[60] See Refugee Convention, Art. 3 (providing that the state of refuge should not discriminate against the refugee); ibid., Art. 21 (requiring favourable housing); ibid., Art. 22 (education); ibid., Art. 23 (public relief); ibid., Art. 33 (restricting *refoulement*).

[61] For example, the Hague Convention and its accompanying Regulations require respect for 'public order and safety' (*'l'ordre et la vie public'*) in occupied territory, but they do not contain a specific obligation of repatriation. Convention Respecting the Laws and Customs of War on Land, 18 Oct. 1907, Annexe: Regulations Respecting the Laws and Customs of War on Land, T.S. 539, Art. 43. As to whether the English text is an inaccurate translation of the French, see Yoram Dinstein, 'The Israel Supreme Court and the Law of Belligerent Occupation: Deportations', 23 *Isr. Yb. Hum. Rts.* 1, 19–20 (1993); Edmund Schwenk, 'Legislative Power of the Military Occupant under Article 43, Hague Regulations', 54 *Yale L.J.* 393, 398 (1945); Quigley, 'Displaced Palestinians', 198 and n. 154.

[62] The Camp David Accords provided that Egypt and Israel would work together and with 'other interested parties' to 'establish agreed procedures for a prompt, just and permanent implementation of the resolution of the refugee problem'. A Framework for Peace in the Middle East Agreed at Camp David, Art. A(4), reprinted in Lapidoth and Hirsch, *The Arab–Israeli Conflict*, 195.

[63] See generally Salim Tamari, *Palestinian Refugee Negotiations: From Madrid to Oslo II* (Washington, DC: Institute for Palestine Studies, 1996).

[64] Declaration of Principles, Art. V(3); see also Interim Agreement, Art. XXXI(5) (identical language); Wye River Memorandum, ¶IV.

[65] Declaration of Principles, Art. XII; see also Gaza–Jericho Agreement, Art. XVI; Interim Agreement, Art. XXVII. Pursuant to these provisions, Egypt, Israel, Jordan, and the Palestinians did create a Quadripartite Committee for Displaced Persons. For more on the work of the Committee, see Tamari, *Palestinian Refugee Negotiations*, 21–2.

[66] See Interim Agreement, Annex III, Appendix 1, Art. 28(11) and (12); ibid., Annexe II, Art. II(1)(g)(2). The Interim Agreement also establishes a joint committee to deal with reissuance of identity cards to 'those residents who have lost their identity cards'. Ibid., Annexe III, Appendix I, Art. 28(3). For more on these changes, see generally Tamari, *Palestinian Refugee Negotiations*, 24–6, 63–6.

of refugees covers displaced Jews as well as displaced Palestinians. The 1994 Israel–Jordan peace treaty likewise called for bilateral negotiations to deal with refugees and displaced persons, but again stopped short of announcing a right of return or repossession.[67]

In sum, the relevant sources of international law—UN materials, human rights law, humanitarian law, the Refugee Convention, the Middle East peace agreements, and customary law—do not impose an absolute obligation on Israel to admit all displaced Palestinians and Palestinian refugees. Obviously this conclusion also implies that there is no general right of repossession of property—though, as we shall see, there is an Israeli duty to compensate Palestinians for lost property. Even the Palestinians' most ardent supporters concede that 'a perfect restoration of the *status quo* is not possible'.[68]

That said, there is nothing in international law that *forbids* Israel to agree to permit significant numbers of Palestinians to return to Israel. Israel has in the past offered to accept as many as 100,000 Palestinian refugees,[69] and Israel has long permitted small amounts of Palestinian immigration for family reunification. Likewise, nothing prevents Israel from agreeing to permit Palestinians to repossess property located in Israel. In so far as that property is now in the hands of Israelis, such an arrangement would require compensation for current possessors, as would be the case if Israel evicted any Israeli settlers.

Still, practical considerations have stood in the way of return and repossession in other similar cases. As Benvenisti and Zamir put it, 'history shows that in no case of massive relocation—either in accordance with an agreed plan or as a result of the horrors of war—have the refugees regained the property they left behind'.[70] It is unlikely that this historical pattern will be altered in this instance. The forced, massive displacement of hundreds of thousands of Israelis by returning Palestinians would in all likelihood lead to unmanageable social unrest or worse.

Again, it is to be hoped that Israel does agree to permit some Palestinian immigration, perhaps along the lines of Ben-Gurion's proposal to permit the return of 100,000 Palestinians. But Israel is not likely to agree to large-scale return of Palestinian refugees, or to large-scale repossession of land. Accordingly, the parties will probably have to

[67] Treaty of Peace, Isr.–Jor., Art. 8(2).

[68] Quigley, 'Displaced Palestinians', 226. See also 'Progress Report of the U.N. Conciliation Commission for Palestine', UN GAOR, 6th Sess., Supp. No. 18, at 5, UN Doc. A/1985 (1951) ('The areas from which the refugees came are no longer vacant, and any movement of return would have to be carefully worked out and executed with the active co-operation of the Government of Israel').

[69] See Yossi Beilin, *Touching Peace: From the Oslo Accord to a Final Agreement*, trans. Philip Simpson (London: Weidenfeld & Nicolson, 1999), 187.

[70] Benvenisti and Zamir, 'Private Claims to Property Rights', 324.

supplement a limited right of Palestinian return with other options. Most of these will probably involve a combination of compensation to Palestinians and recognition of a Palestinian right to return to a new Palestinian entity. We turn to these options next.

2. No general right of return to Israel or repossession, but a right of compensation and a right of Palestinian immigration to a Palestinian entity

Just as Israel is not likely to agree to a final settlement that requires large-scale Palestinian repatriation to Israel, the Palestinians are not likely to agree to a final settlement that foregoes significant compensation for dispossessed Palestinian refugees and their families. This option is considerably more likely to be acceptable to Israel than the first option. Some Israeli politicians do recognize that compensation is appropriate, though they do not necessarily concede that it must come from Israel.[71]

This option raises a series of legal issues. The first is whether there is an Israeli duty to compensate. Assuming there is some such duty, the second legal issue is the proper quantum of compensation. A third issue is what form compensation may take, what procedures are appropriate, and whether it might include claims by and against third-party Arab states (which may have borne the expense for housing refugees, but which may also be responsible to Israel for dispossession and displacement of Jews). A final issue is whether international law requires an unlimited right of Palestinian immigration to a new Palestinian entity.

The first issue, the duty to compensate, is relatively straightforward. It is generally agreed that states have a duty to compensate for expropriation of the property of an alien, though the precise measure of compensation is a matter of continuing debate.[72] More generally, international law obliges states causing injury to an alien to make reparations to the state of which the alien is a national.[73] The requirement of compensation would plainly cover the expropriation of property of a non-national, and as we have seen Israel regards displaced Palestinians and Palestinian refugees

[71] Cf. Beilin, *Touching Peace*, 187 (Palestinian refugees 'will be entitled to compensation from the international organisation that is to be established to replace the existing aid and development agencies . . .').

[72] See Patrick M. Norton, 'A Law of the Future or a Law of the Past? Modern Tribunals and the International Law of Expropriation', 85 *Am. J. Int'l L.* 474, 479–88 (1991); Oscar Schachter, 'Compensation for Expropriation', 78 *Am. J. Int'l L.* 121 (1984); G.A. Res. 1803 (XVII), 14 Dec. 1962 (87–2, with 12 abstentions) (requiring 'appropriate compensation'); *Texaco Overseas Petroleum et al. v. Libyan Arab Republic*, Int'l Arb. Award, 19 Jan. 1977, 17 I.L.M. 1 (1978), ¶87 (holding that Resolution 1803 'seems to this Tribunal to reflect the state of customary law'); Charter of Economic Rights and Duties of States, G.A. Res. 3281 (XXIX), 12 Dec. 1974, Art. 2(2)(c) ('appropriate compensation').

[73] See *Case Concerning the Factory at Chorzów (Merits)*, P.C.I.J. Ser. A, No. 17, at 28 (1928).

as non-nationals. Israel cannot have it both ways: if Palestinians are Israeli nationals, then human rights law entitles them to return 'home' to Israel; if they are aliens, then they are entitled to compensation for expropriation and other injuries. Even if the Palestinians are somehow treated as Israeli nationals for the purposes of compensation but not return, it may well be that the right of compensation for expropriation now extends to a national of the state who flees from that state.[74]

To its credit, Israel did not immediately expropriate all of the refugees' property, implicitly acknowledging that they might retain some reversionary interest. A number of laws, most notably the Absentees' Property Law, 1950, provided for public administration of the refugees' property in their absence, under terms permitting the government to enter into long-term leases for it but not to sell it, and generally (though not always) precluding return of the property to the original owner.[75] Until the enactment of the Absentees' Property (Compensation) Law, 1973,[76] however, these laws did not provide for a right of compensation, and for a variety of reasons compensation has not often been paid since. In any event, these aspects of Israeli municipal law suggest that Israel is not unalterably opposed to making some compensation.

The second issue—the appropriate amount of compensation—is more complex. Even for ordinary expropriations of alien property, the precise standard of compensation is a matter of intense disagreement.[77] There is even less consensus on the proper standard of compensation for expropriation of refugees' property, in large part because there is relatively little state practice on which to draw.[78]

Benvenisti and Zamir suggest a standard of 'adequate compensation' for refugees, as opposed to 'full compensation'. Among other things, they argue that full compensation is inappropriate because supervening investments by third parties might have changed the value of the property, whose original value at the time of dispossession could be difficult to assess. They also contend that full compensation could 'drain the resources of the state' and 'create instability during a delicate transitional

[74] See Luke T. Lee, 'The Right to Compensation: Refugees and Countries of Asylum', 80 *Am. J. Int'l L.* 532 (1986).

[75] 4 L.S.I. 68. This regime is described more fully in Benvenisti and Zamir, 'Private Claims to Property Rights', 300–1. See also Sabri Jiryis, 'Settlers' Law: Seizure of Palestinian Lands', 2 *Palestine Y.B. Int'l L.* 17 (1985); David Kretzmer, *The Legal Status of the Arabs in Israel* (Boulder, CO: Westview Press, 1990), 60–6.

[76] 27 L.S.I. 176. As to the Jordanian administration of Israeli property in the West Bank from 1948 to 1967, see Benvenisti and Zamir, 'Private Claims to Property Rights', 301–4. As to Egyptian administration of Israeli property in Gaza, see ibid. 304–5. As to Israeli practice in the occupied territories since 1967, see ibid. 305–16.

[77] See generally Norton, 'A Law of the Future'; Schachter, 'Compensation for Expropriation'.

[78] See Benvenisti and Zamir, 'Private Claims to Property Rights', 330–1 and n. 207.

period'. Like a regime of equitable compensation, a regime of 'adequate' compensation might mean that some refugees obtain less than full market value; in other cases, 'when the rehabilitation of refugees requires more funds than the value of their abandoned property', it might mean greater than full market value.[79]

Not all the reasons advanced for this proposal are persuasive. It is not clear why, as a matter of principle, difficulties of valuation should affect the choice of legal rule; such difficulties will exist regardless of the choice of standard. Likewise, if 'full compensation' unduly strained Israel's fisc, the parties could agree on a system of instalment payments, or perhaps on arrangements for contribution from international organizations or Israeli allies. But there is considerable merit to the notion that the precise quantum of compensation might depend on more factors than just the original value of property lost fifty years ago, but might also include other equitable factors, such as the current needs of the refugee or the refugee's community. The phrase 'equitable compensation' would none the less seem to capture this notion better than 'adequate compensation'.

The third issue, the form and procedure of compensation, also raises complicated logistical questions. At least three alternatives present themselves: (1) an international Claims Tribunal to adjudicate individual Palestinian claims on a case-by-case basis, along the lines of the US–Iran Claims Tribunal in the Hague; (2) a UN Compensation Commission along the lines of that established in connection with the Iraq–Kuwait crisis; and (3) a lump-sum settlement.

Of these, a lump-sum settlement seems most appropriate. A claims tribunal is a programme for long-term, festering disagreement between the parties, or at least between individual Palestinians and Israel. Adjudication is not the most amicable means of resolving disputes, nor is it the most efficient or speedy. A claims tribunal would inevitably be bogged down for years and decades in case-by-case arbitration. Some deserving plaintiffs will inevitably fail to file. The US–Iran tribunal, a relatively successful example, is a case in point.[80] The chief advantage of such an arrangement is that it permits the most individualized justice, but valuation problems and the cost and slow pace of adjudication easily outweigh this advantage.

Similarly, a compensation commission invites further argument and disagreement, when what is needed is an end to retrospective combat and a beginning of prospective problem-solving. Such a commission would collect each government's claim for compensation (including, perhaps,

[79] Benvenisti and Zamir, 'Private Claims to Property Rights', 331.

[80] Ibid. 331–3.

claims by Arab states, and claims by Israel against Arab states relating to displaced Jews). A compensation commission does have one advantage over a lump-sum settlement: it would provide some reassurance to both parties that a disinterested international organization would distribute the funds, minimizing the possibility of corruption. But, like arbitration, this solution would be time-consuming, bureaucratic, and costly, and it would require the parties to submit to the fact-finding of an international organization.

A lump-sum settlement would allow the parties to dispose of the compensation question quickly, once and for all. It would be nowhere near as costly or time-consuming as the two other alternatives. Perhaps more important, it would eliminate the prospect of continued argument over compensation well into the twenty-first century. Like the compensation commission, it could take the form of a multilateral agreement so as to account for claims by and against third-party states. For many of these reasons, the UN Conciliation Commission for Palestine proposed just such a solution in 1951.[81]

The chief disadvantage of a lump-sum arrangement is that it does not immediately transfer compensation to the hands of deserving individuals or to improvement of conditions at existing refugee camps. Benvenisti and Zamir suggest establishing a multilateral institution to supervise allocation of funds to and among all interested parties.[82] This suggestion is sensible. Unlike a compensation commission, such an institution would not pass on the merits of compensation disputes, but simply administer the remedy already agreed upon by all parties.

With such an arrangement, a lump-sum settlement seems like the most appropriate solution for the parties. There is no question that it is consistent with international law: of all the three options, it plainly has the most precedent in state practice. As Lillich and Weston have concluded, 'this procedural device has become, without doubt, the paramount vehicle for settling international claims'.[83]

The option under consideration—compensation plus a right of return to a Palestinian entity—obviously raises one final issue: what is the scope of a Palestinian right of return to Palestinian territory? Many Israelis are uncomfortable with the prospect of unlimited immigration to a new Palestinian entity in the West Bank and Gaza Strip. In September 1999,

[81] Progress Report of the UN Conciliation Commission for Palestine, UN GAOR, 6th Sess., Supp. No. 18, UN Doc. A/1985 (1951).

[82] Benvenisti and Zamir, 'Private Claims to Property Rights', 339–40.

[83] Richard B. Lillich and Burns H. Weston, 'Lump Sum Agreements: Their Continuing Contribution to the Law of International Claims', 82 *Am. J. Int'l L.* 69, 70 (1988). See generally Richard B. Lillich and Burns H. Weston, *International Claims: Their Settlement by Lump Sum Agreements*, 2 vols (Charlottesville: University of Virginia Press, 1975).

for example, Israel's Minister of Immigrant Absorption, Yuli Tamir, was criticized for instructing her Ministry to give advice to the PA on how to absorb Palestinian immigrants.

Other Israelis, however, are relatively unconcerned about the prospect of large-scale Palestinian immigration into a new Palestinian entity. Labour's Yossi Beilin believes it 'impossible to impose immigration quotas' on any new Palestinian state, and he adds that 'even if there comes a stage where the Palestinian population increases substantially as a result of immigration, I still don't see this as a threat to Israel'.[84]

If the peace process does result in a Palestinian state, then nationals of that state will have a right to return home. As we have seen, human rights instruments provide that people may not be 'arbitrarily' deprived of this right. Some restrictions on Palestinian immigration might not be arbitrary. But the emphasis on non-discrimination in the human rights treaties implies that discriminatory exclusion would be arbitrary. In addition, the arbitrariness test probably also requires that the proponent of exclusion be able to point to some reasonable basis for it.

For example, it would not be arbitrary for the parties to agree that the Palestinians should place some initial limits on annual immigration in order to avoid chaos at the Palestinian borders and to ensure that new residents can be properly housed. It would, however, seem arbitrary for the parties to agree in advance to prohibit some Palestinians from ever returning. Such an agreement would rest on the untested premise that a Palestinian state can absorb only a limited number of people—a premise that rankles some Israelis who recall 'ludicrous predictions' made about the 'absorption potential' of the Jewish state.[85] The parties are not free to strip Palestinians of their right to return to a Palestinian homeland, but they are free to impose reasonable regulations on Palestinian immigration to ensure an orderly transition.

In sum, international law permits a settlement whereby the parties agree to compensation for Palestinian refugees. Indeed, international law probably requires some form of compensation. The precise form and procedure for compensation is within the parties' discretion, but the most workable choice would be a lump-sum agreement. No agreement between the parties may lawfully strip Palestinians of their eventual right to return to a Palestinian entity, but the parties may agree to reasonable regulations designed to facilitate safe and orderly repatriation.

[84] Beilin, *Touching Peace*, 187.

[85] Ibid.

C. Settlements

Negotiators are most likely to make progress on settlements if they avoid rehashing decades-old arguments on the lawfulness of Israeli settlements in the West Bank and East Jerusalem. As we saw in Chapter 7, the better view is that such settlements are inconsistent with the Fourth Geneva Convention and other relevant sources of humanitarian law, but Israel's arguments are not nearly as frivolous as Israel's critics would suggest. In any event, these issues can and should be mooted by a final settlement. If the Palestinians freely agree to permit some settlements to remain, perhaps with some under Israeli sovereignty and others under Palestinian sovereignty, then the old arguments about occupation law would seem no longer relevant. If a final agreement ends Israel's occupation, then of course occupation law will be inapplicable.

A final disposition of the settlement problem might take a number of forms, each raising legal issues. (For relevant maps, see Maps 5, 6, and 7 on pp. 35, 50, and 108.)

1. *Extraterritoriality*

It is not likely that the Palestinians will agree to any arrangement for extraterritorial Israeli jurisdiction over settlements in the territory of a new Palestinian state. Even some supporters of Israel acknowledge that in such circumstances, 'the new state of Palestine would consist of little more than a series of patches, enclaves and roads, and Palestinian police and courts would have no legal jurisdiction over the foreigners (that is, Israelis) who would travel through' these enclaves.[86] Moreover, extraterritoriality smacks of legal imperialism. It harks back to the consular jurisdiction of the nineteenth century, in which citizens of Western states were subject only to the jurisdiction of their own consuls when travelling in developing countries, on the theory that there was no reliable local law.[87]

Still, Israeli officials in the past have indicated support for some form of extraterritoriality for settlements.[88] It is therefore worth asking whether international law permits this type of arrangement. The law of nations of the nineteenth century embraced consular jurisdiction.[89] In fact, as late as

[86] See Ze'ev Schiff, *Israeli Preconditions for Palestinian Statehood* (Washington, DC: Washington Institute for Near East Policy, 1999), 32.

[87] See Watson, 'Offenders Abroad', 50.

[88] See Abraham Rabinovich, 'West Bank Pullout Could Isolate Settlers; Netanyahu Plan Faces Flak in Cabinet', *Wash. Times*, 17 Dec. 1997, at A1 (reporting on then-Defence Minister Mordechai's plan for Israeli extraterritoriality over 42 out of the 144 settlements on the West Bank).

[89] Cf. *Daienese v. Hall*, 91 U.S. 13, 15 (1875) (stating that treaties could lawfully establish consular jurisdiction, at least in 'Pagan and Mahometan countries').

1952 the International Court of Justice was willing to enforce US consular jurisdiction in Morocco, at least in so far as it was clearly established by treaty.[90] But by the mid-twentieth century, this form of extraterritoriality was quickly vanishing. In Palestine itself, the UN Partition Resolution 'invited' Western states 'to renounce any right pertaining to the re-establishment' of consular jurisdiction.[91] Is it fair to conclude that modern international law no longer permits extraterritorial arrangements?

The disappearance of extraterritoriality might suggest that customary law now rejects such arrangements. The practice of the United Nations lends support to this argument. The UN Charter stresses the 'principle of sovereign equality of all its Members', and the General Assembly Declaration on Friendly Relations defines 'sovereign equality' as including the proposition that 'States are judicially equal'.[92] Likewise, the Montevideo Convention on Rights and Duties of States (to which neither Israel nor the PLO is a party) provides that a state's jurisdiction 'applies to all the inhabitants' and that 'foreigners may not claim rights other or more extensive than those of nationals'.[93] These provisions alone might not be dispositive, since states may generally enter into agreements that 'vary or even dispense altogether with most rules of international law'.[94] But international agreements cannot dispense with Charter norms or with peremptory norms of international law (*jus cogens*).[95] There is, moreover, some evidence that the principle of 'sovereign equality' is a peremptory norm.[96]

Still, the foregoing norms of 'sovereign equality', even if they are peremptory norms, do not rule out all forms of extraterritoriality. To begin with, the norms are vague; to say that all states are 'judicially equal' might just mean that states are equally free to decline to exercise jurisdiction within their own territory if they see fit. If Israel is free to permit Palestinian extraterritorial rights over the Haram, then Palestine should be equally free to permit Israeli extraterritorial rights over settlements.

[90] *Case Concerning Rights of Nationals of the United States of America in Morocco* (Fr. v. US), 1952 I.C.J. 176, 188. The United States relinquished its consular jurisdiction in Morocco in 1956. See Marjorie M. Whiteman, *Digest of International Law* (Washington, DC: US Dept. of State, 1968), 6:315.

[91] Partition Resolution, U.N.G.A. Res. 181(II), 29 Nov. 1947, part IV.

[92] See UN Charter, Art. 2(1); Declaration on Friendly Relations and Co-operation Among States in Accordance with the Charter of the United Nations, G.A. Res. 2625 (XXXV), 24 Oct. 1970, 25 GAOR, Supp. (No. 28) 121, 9 I.L.M. 1292 (1970).

[93] Convention on Rights and Duties of States, 26 Dec. 1933, 165 L.N.T.S. 19, T.S. 881, Art. 9.

[94] Sir Robert Jennings and Sir Arthur Watts (eds.), *Oppenheim's International Law*, 9th edn (Harlow, Essex: Longman, 1993), 1:7.

[95] See UN Charter, Art. 103; Vienna Convention on the Law of Treaties, Art. 53.

[96] See 1966 *Y.B. Int'l L. Comm'n*, ii:247–9, cited in *Oppenheim's International Law*, 9th edn, 1:8 and n. 4.

Moreover, state practice plainly endorses the notion that some extraterritoriality is acceptable. States often acquiesce in other states' exercise of extraterritorial jurisdiction in both civil and criminal matters. Consider the Status of Forces Agreements between the United States and states hosting US armed forces: these typically provide that the United States will exercise jurisdiction over minor crimes by US personnel posted in the host state.[97] Extraterritorial jurisdiction over settlements may be a bad idea from a policy standpoint, but if the Palestinians freely agreed to it in exchange for concessions on other points, the resulting agreement would not violate international law.

2. *Forcible eviction of settlers*

It is highly unlikely Israel will ever agree to destruction of existing settlements or forcible eviction of current settlers.[98] Israel did agree to dismantle settlements in the Sinai Peninsula in order to implement the Egypt–Israel peace treaty.[99] But those settlements were tiny compared to the existing settlements in the West Bank and Gaza Strip, whose population exceeds 160,000 people.[100] The option none the less deserves brief consideration here not only because of the Sinai precedent, but also because the United Nations and the Palestinians have repeatedly called on Israel to remove the settlements.

However unpalatable such an option might be to Israel, it probably would not violate international law so long as fair compensation were paid to settlers whose property was taken or destroyed. To be sure, states do not have unfettered discretion to seize the property of their own nationals. Article 17(2) of the Universal Declaration of Human Rights provides that no one shall be 'arbitrarily deprived of his property'. The property provisions of other general human rights instruments suggest that 'arbitrary' deprivations would include discriminatory takings of property.[101] But it would not be 'discriminatory' or 'arbitrary' for the government of Israel to facilitate peace by trading settlements for other

[97] See, e.g., North Atlantic Treaty: Status of Forces, 19 June 1951, 199 U.N.T.S. 67, 4 U.S.T. 1792, Art. VII.

[98] See Beilin, *Touching Peace*, 186 ('We have no use for a solution whereby 140,000 people are evicted from their homes').

[99] See Treaty of Peace Between the State of Israel and the Arab Republic of Egypt, 26 Mar. 1979, Art. I(2), in Ruth Lapidoth and Moshe Hirsch (eds.), *The Arab–Israel Conflict and its Resolution: Selected Documents* (Dordrecht: Martinus Nijhoff, 1992), 218. See also Martin Gilbert, *Israel: A History* (New York: William Morrow and Co., 1998), 492, 499–500. For a photograph of the Yamit settlement in the Sinai, and a photograph of its destruction, see ibid. after p. 496 (plates 58–9).

[100] See Schiff, *Israeli Preconditions*, 27, 31.

[101] See, e.g., International Covenant on Civil and Political Rights, Art. 26.

concessions. The Sinai precedent itself suggests that the dismantling of settlements is not inconsistent with international law.

Palestinians and the UN Security Council have gone further and asserted that Israel is *required* to destroy existing settlements.[102] Even if one assumes that the Fourth Geneva Convention and other sources of humanitarian law are applicable, and further that Israel's settlements violate humanitarian law, it does not appear that humanitarian law requires destruction of such settlements. On the contrary: the Fourth Geneva Convention envisions war-crimes prosecutions, not the forcible evacuation of civilian settlers.[103]

In the unlikely event that Israel does dismantle some settlements, international law probably requires it to pay compensation to dispossessed Israeli settlers. There is some authority for the proposition that 'the international law standard of compensation does not apply to the taking by a state of its own nationals' property'.[104] The better view, however, is that nationals are entitled to compensation for property taken by their government. This rule does not appear in many of the leading human rights treaties, but it is a common feature of municipal law, suggesting that it may rise to the level of a 'general principle' of law.[105] In any event, Israel's own internal law and practice suggests that dispossessed settlers would have a right of compensation enforceable in the Israeli courts.[106]

The precise quantum of compensation required is another matter. The proper level of compensation for expropriation of aliens' property is one of the most controversial subjects in international law. The appropriate level of compensation for expropriation of citizens' property is likewise uncertain. There is state practice to suggest that states feel free to compensate their own nationals less generously than they compensate foreign nationals. Whatever the precise standard, it is safe to say that Israel would satisfy its international obligations if it supplied dispossessed settlers with prompt, adequate, and effective compensation.[107]

In sum, it is unlikely that Israel will forcibly remove any significant number of settlers from the West Bank or the Gaza Strip. If it did agree to do so, that agreement would be lawful provided that Israel paid some

[102] See, e.g., S.C. Res. 465, 1 Mar. 1980, ¶6 (calling on Israel 'to dismantle the existing settlements').

[103] See Jennifer S. Berman, 'No Place Like Home: Anti-Vietnamese Discrimination and Nationality in Cambodia', 84 *Calif. L. Rev.* 817, 843 (1996).

[104] *Oppenheim's International Law*, §407, 1:918 n. 26, citing *Lithgow and Others*, 75 I.L.R. 439, 482 (1986).

[105] See Brice M. Clagett, 'The Cuban Liberty and Democratic Solidarity (Libertad) Act: Title III of the Helms–Burton Act is Consistent with International Law', 90 *Am. J. Int'l L.* 436, 439 (1996).

[106] See generally Benvenisti and Zamir, 'Private Claims to Property Rights', 310–16.

[107] See *Oppenheim's International Law*, §407, 1:921–2.

measure of compensation to the settlers. Moreover, nothing in international law prevents Israel from attempting to induce settlers to leave voluntarily, perhaps by offering them compensation and new housing in Israel proper.

3. *Israeli sovereignty over settlements*

A third option is full Israeli sovereignty over some or all of the settlements. This solution is obviously popular with Israelis and unpopular with Palestinians. Full Israeli sovereignty over all existing settlements would leave only a highly splintered chequerboard of land remaining for a new Palestinian entity. This arrangement might simplify Israeli municipal law,[108] but it would raise troubling questions of international law.

To begin with, Palestinians and human rights activists argue that such a disposition would violate the Palestinian right of self-determination.[109] As we have already seen, however, the right of self-determination leaves the parties wide discretion to fashion a final settlement. In the unlikely event that the PLO freely agreed to full Israeli sovereignty—presumably in exchange for other concessions—the PLO's consent would represent a form of Palestinian self-determination.

In addition to self-determination, there remains the question of whether a future Palestinian state can lawfully consist of large numbers of disconnected islands of land, separated by pockets of Israeli sovereignty. (See Map 7, p. 108.) There is apparently no general requirement in international law that a state enjoy unbroken sovereignty over contiguous territory. That is not to say that contiguity is entirely irrelevant to claims of territorial sovereignty. There was a time when international law placed great emphasis on contiguity. In the nineteenth century European states in particular asserted that their geographic proximity to supposedly 'empty' territory (*terra nullius*) might itself form a basis for sovereignty, even in the absence of effective control of that territory.[110] But this doctrine was repudiated in the twentieth century, when international law adopted the view that effective control, not geographical contour, was the most important component of a claim to sovereignty.[111] The doctrine still has some relevance to the law

[108] See Beilin, *Touching Peace*, 187–8.

[109] See Samira Shah, 'On the Road to Apartheid: The Bypass Road Network in the West Bank', 29 *Colum. Human Rts. L. Rev.* 221, 224 (1997).

[110] For an excellent discussion of the history of the contiguity doctrine, see generally Thomas D. Grant, 'Defining Statehood: The Montevideo Convention and its Discontents', 37 *Colum. J. Transnat'l L.* 403, 420–33 (1999).

[111] See Humphrey M. Waldock, 'Disputed Sovereignty on the Falkland Islands Dependencies', 25 *Brit. Y.B. Int'l L.* 331, 341–2 (1948). One of the most famous examples of the demise of contiguity doctrine is in *Island of Palmas* (*Neth. v. U.S.*), 2 R.I.A.A. 829 (Perm. Ct. Arb. 1928) (asserting that the 'title of contiguity, understood as a basis of territorial

of the sea, which defines the continental shelf and continental margin in terms of the natural 'prolongation' of a coastal state's land mass.[112] But the Montevideo Convention of 1933, which contains the most generally accepted definition of a state, omits any requirement of contiguity.[113] It thus appears there is no general legal requirement that a state have contiguous boundaries.

That said, there are of course important political and practical reasons to ensure that a state does have reasonably contiguous boundaries. It is not in anyone's interest to require travellers to stop repeatedly at passport-control stations just to make their way across the West Bank. The free flow of people, goods, and information is hardly enhanced by such an arrangement. It is to be hoped that the parties can come to some agreement, perhaps involving a mix of all the options listed here, to minimize the geographical splintering of any future Palestinian entity.

4. Palestinian sovereignty over Israeli settlements

Most Israeli settlers vigorously reject any suggestion that their lands and homes be placed under Palestinian sovereignty. None the less, not all Israelis are unalterably opposed to such a solution for at least some settlements.[114] It is unlikely, moreover, that such an arrangement would violate international law. Again, it may be that Israel would be required to pay compensation to settlers who refuse to live under Palestinian sovereignty but are unable to sell their property for full market value. Again, past Israeli practice suggests that Israel would make compensation in such circumstances. Of course any Palestinian entity would be obliged to respect the human rights of Israeli nationals in its territory.

There is also a question of whether Israeli settlers placed under the sovereignty of a Palestinian state would be treated as double nationals—i.e. as Palestinian as well as Israeli nationals. (There seems little reason to fear that settlers would become stateless; it is exceedingly unlikely that Israel would deprive them of their Israeli nationality.) Dual nationality is not an unalloyed benefit. A double national will normally wish to avoid being subject to the tax and military-service requirements of both states.

sovereignty, has no foundation in international law'). For the view that the *Palmas* arbitration should not be read as a wholesale rejection of contiguity doctrine, see Sir Hersch Lauterpacht, 'Sovereignty Over Submarine Areas', 1950 *Brit. Y. B. Int'l L.* 376, 428–9.

[112] See UN Convention on the Law of the Sea, 10 Dec. 1982, U.N. Doc. A/CONF. 62/122, 21 I.L.M. 1261 (1982), Art. 76(1), 76(3).

[113] See Convention on the Rights and Duties of States, 26 Dec. 1933, Art. I, 165 L.N.T.S. 19, reprinted in 28 *Am. J. Int'l L.* (Supp.) 75 (1934). For a recent critique of the Convention, see Grant, 'Defining Statehood', 433–57.

[114] See, e.g., Beilin, *Touching Peace*, 188 ('I don't subscribe to the view that living under another sovereignty spells perpetual danger').

Likewise, dual Israeli–Palestinian nationals living in a Palestinian state might wish to ensure that their Palestinian nationality did not preclude Israel from asserting diplomatic protection on their behalf.[115] These concerns can presumably be put to rest in a final status agreement.

5. *Deferred or delayed resolution*

As with Jerusalem, it may be best to leave some settlement issues unresolved. The parties might agree to leave some settlements under Israeli sovereignty for now without foreclosing the possibility of a change in status later. Alternatively, the parties might agree to change the status of some settlements but also agree to delay or at least phase in implementation, as was done with the reversion of Hong Kong to Chinese sovereignty. Gradual implementation, over years or decades, could help minimize disruption to the lives of existing settlers.

In sum, there is no solution to the settlement issue that will completely satisfy each side. As with the other final status issues, agreement will require significant compromise by both parties. International law permits any of the foregoing options, subject to the limitations discussed. Most likely an agreement will involve a mix of several options: some Israeli sovereignty over settlements; some Palestinian sovereignty; perhaps some limited extraterritoriality; some voluntary relocation of settlers; deferred resolution of some issues; delayed implementation of some agreements; and, least likely of all, the forcible removal of settlers.

D. Security arrangements

Israel is likely to attempt to place restrictions on the powers of any new Palestinian state. In particular, Israel will seek to ensure that a Palestinian state is not a military threat to Israel. It will likely press for a demilitarized Palestinian state and for limits on that state's capacity to enter into military alliances. This section briefly considers whether such restrictions would be consistent with international law.

1. *Military pacts and alliances*

Israel may seek to prohibit the Palestinian state from 'entering into, or participating in, any military pact or alliance' and from hosting diplomatic missions from any country at war with Israel.[116] This possibility

[115] Cf. generally *Oppenheim's International Law*, §395, 1:884–6.
[116] See Schiff, *Israeli Preconditions*, 42–3.

raises a question of international law: may a new state lawfully agree to such limitations?

The answer appears to be yes. It seems generally acknowledged that 'associated states', such as the Federated States of Micronesia, can delegate authority to decide on alliances to other states.[117] Even states that do not bear this special status sometimes delegate defence and foreign-affairs decisions to other states. Liechtenstein relies on Switzerland to carry out much of its foreign affairs, and the state of Monaco (which was recently admitted to the United Nations) cedes much of its foreign-policy decisions to France.[118] Moreover, every state is subject to some limits on its powers to make alliances. The UN Charter norm against the use of force probably has the character of *jus cogens*, implying that states may not enter into alliances for offensive military purposes.[119] Such prohibitions are, of course, quite common in the municipal law of federal states.[120]

Palestinian 'delegation' of alliance-making capacity to Israel would be different from that of Monaco or Liechtenstein in that Palestinian interests are more likely to conflict with those of Israel. But this difference seems more a difference in degree than in kind. Even the most cosy relationship between protecting and protected states is likely to give rise to friction now and then. In any event, this concern could be mitigated by establishing a multilateral regional security regime including Israel, the Palestinian state, Jordan, and perhaps even Egypt.[121]

2. *Diplomatic relations*

If the parties are free to agree to limits on Palestinian alliances, they are probably also free to agree to limit Palestinian diplomatic relations, for example by prohibiting a Palestinian state from receiving diplomats from states at war with Israel. Israel may in fact be more concerned about foreign representation in a Palestinian state than Palestinian representation abroad, since hostile states might conceivably use embassies within the Palestinian state to carry out espionage against Israel or to smuggle in

[117] Hurst Hannum and Richard B. Lillich, 'The Concept of Autonomy in International Law', 74 *Am. J. Int'l L.* 858, 860 n. 13 (1980).

[118] See generally Jorri C. Duursma, *Fragmentation and the International Relations of Micro-States* (Cambridge, Melbourne, New York: Cambridge University Press, 1996); Gregory H. Fox, Book Review, 92 *Am. J. Int'l L.* 359, 361 (1998). Cf. also Michael J. Kelly, 'Political Downsizing: The Re-Emergence of Self-Determination, and the Movement Toward Smaller, Ethnically Homogenous States', 47 *Drake L. Rev.* 209, 224–5 (1999). But see Thomas D. Grant, 'Review Article: Between Diversity and Disorder', 12 *Am. U.J. Int'l L. & Pol'y* 629, 666–7 (1997) (arguing that Monaco's delegation of its foreign-affairs powers undermines its claim to statehood).

[119] See UN Charter Art. 2(4), 103.

[120] See, e.g., 1848 Switzerland Constitution, Art. 9; US Constitution, Art. I, §10, cl. 1.

[121] See Schiff, *Israeli Preconditions*, 43.

heavy weapons for the Palestinians. In any event, the Palestinians are free to delegate some or all of their decisions on diplomatic activity to Israel, or alternatively to agree to some trilateral arrangement (with Jordan) for management of Palestinian diplomatic relations. International law does not forbid (or require) such a delegation of authority.

3. *Demilitarization*

For similar reasons, the parties are free to conclude an agreement providing that any new Palestinian state will be demilitarized. In particular, the parties may lawfully agree that the Palestinian state cannot raise or deploy a standing army, cannot equip its police with anything other than light weapons, cannot deploy an air force or navy, and cannot permit the deployment of foreign troops on its soil. Likewise, the parties are free to agree to some Israeli, American, or UN military presence in the West Bank. So long as such agreements are not coerced—and, as we have seen, coercion is a narrow basis for invalidity of treaties in international law—they would be valid. International law neither forbids nor requires the Palestinians to delegate defence policy to Israel, Jordan, the United States, or the United Nations.

4. *Counter-terrorism, extradition, and other security arrangements*

Obviously Israel will remain intensely interested in obtaining Palestinian cooperation on fighting terrorism and maintaining security. Fortunately, the Oslo Accords, including the Wye River and Sharm el-Sheikh Memoranda, have already created an elaborate legal infrastructure for cooperation on terrorism and security. A final status agreement will likely build on these foundations to establish continuing (rather than merely interim) obligations to cooperate on security matters.

E. Borders

The physical shape of a new state of Palestine will depend in large part on what agreements the parties reach on several of the issues already discussed, such as Jerusalem and settlements. As we saw during the discussion of settlements, international law does not require that a Palestinian state be contiguous, but there are none the less compelling reasons of policy to maximize the contiguity of such a state. Likewise, international law permits a variety of creative solutions to the boundaries of Jerusalem, including solutions that would expand the city's boundaries to help accommodate both parties' claims. The resolution of the parties' differences on water also has obvious implications for the borders of a Palestinian state.[122]

As a general matter, then, the delimitation and demarcation of an eventual Israeli–Palestinian border is inextricably intertwined with resolution of other final-status issues. The resolution of these issues depends less on law than on a mutual commitment to negotiate seriously and in good faith.

F. Relations and cooperation with other neighbours

The Oslo Accords also envision final-status negotiations over 'relations and cooperation with other neighbors'. Again, this issue is closely linked to a number of final-status issues, including Jerusalem, refugees, security arrangements, and water. Jerusalem is a subject of intense interest not only to Jordan, which has historically maintained that it has a role in management of the Holy Places there, but also to individuals, states, and religious organizations around the world. A final-status agreement on Jerusalem will have to account for all these interests. Likewise, any resolution of the refugee question will have to involve Arab states that currently house significant numbers of Palestinian refugees.

Similarly, we have already noted that Israel will press for restrictions on Palestinian diplomatic and military relations with other states. But the parties may also turn to third states to help implement their security commitments, much as they sought to rely on the CIA for assistance in implementing the Wye River Memorandum. Finally, a number of states in the region—for example, Jordan, Syria, Lebanon, and Turkey—have a strong interest in the water question. All these issues will require some measure of multilateral negotiation along the lines of the talks begun in Madrid.

G. Other issues of common interest: Palestinian statehood and water

Finally, the parties committed themselves to resolve 'other issues of common interest'. As has already been observed, it might seem a bit odd that the parties did not enumerate one or two of the largest remaining issues: the question of Palestinian statehood, and the allocation of water.

The parties could hardly be expected to enumerate all the issues that remain, for countless 'interim' arrangements in the Oslo Accords will eventually need to become permanent arrangements. For example, the

[122] Cf. Schiff, *Israeli Preconditions*, 26.

parties may need to revisit their rather intricate mutual extradition arrangements by negotiating a full-fledge bilateral extradition treaty. None the less, it is unlikely the parties will regularize all of their 'interim' arrangements right away. As was said at the outset of this book, even if the parties reach a final-status agreement on the largest issues, the Oslo Accords will probably continue to furnish the legal basis for the day-to-day relations of the parties.

In any event, the two remaining large issues would seem to be Palestinian statehood and water. Statehood has already been discussed in Chapter 12, which rejected the argument that a Palestinian state came into being on 4 May 1999. That leaves the question of water. Again, a full treatment of this issue is beyond the scope of this book, but a brief discussion is in order.

Water has been a serious source of tension in the Middle East for decades. Disputes over water have contributed to armed conflict between Israel and its neighbours.[123] If the issue is not resolved on a regional level—not just on a bilateral basis between Israel and Jordan or Israel and the Palestinians—there is the possibility that disputes over water might again lead to war. There have been efforts to reach a regional solution to the water question, including the plan developed by American mediator Eric Johnston in the 1950s, but until recently these efforts have languished.[124]

On water, as on so many other issues, Israelis and Palestinians see things very differently. The Palestinian view is that Israel uses much more than its share of available water, and that a substantial volume of water should be reallocated for Palestinian use.[125] Some also argue that water should be apportioned in accordance with the amount of rain that falls in each party's territory.[126] Israel acknowledges that the Palestinians need more water.[127] Many Israelis argue, however, that Israel should not be penalized for having invested in the technology necessary to procure and

[123] See Aaron Wolf and John Ross, 'The Impact of Scarce Water Resources on the Arab–Israeli Conflict', 32 *Nat. Res. J.* 919, 920 (1992).

[124] See ibid. 932–5; Miriam R. Lowi, *Water and Power: the Politics of a Scarce Resource in the Jordan River Basin* (Cambridge: Cambridge University Press, 1993), 79–114.

[125] See, e.g., Sharif S. Elmusa, *The Water Issue and the Palestinian–Israeli Conflict* (1993), 2; Sharif S. Elmusa, 'Dividing Common Water Resources According to International Water Law: The Case of the Palestinian–Israeli Waters', 35 *Nat. Res. J.* 223 (1995); Gemal Abouali, 'Natural Resources under Occupation: The Status of Palestinian Water under International Law', 10 *Pace Int'l L. Rev.* 411, 417 (1998).

[126] See, e.g., Jeffrey D. Dillman, 'Water Rights in the Occupied Territories', *J. Palestine Studies* (Autumn 1989), 46, 57; Joseph W. Dellapenna, 'Water in the Jordan Valley: The Potential and Limits of Law', 5 *Palestine Yb. Int'l L.* 15, 35 (1989).

[127] Cf. Interim Agreement, Annexe III, Art. 40, ¶¶6–7 (acknowledging the 'future' and 'immediate' water needs of the Palestinians in the West Bank); see also Schiff, *Israeli Preconditions*, 24.

use water efficiently, that allocation of water should give a higher priority to existing uses than topographical considerations, and that the emphasis should be on developing new resources to satisfy everyone's needs.[128] And yet, despite these differences, it is often said that water presents an opportunity for cooperation between the parties, since joint efforts to manage the water supply can benefit all parties.[129]

The factual setting of the problem is complex. That said, some things are fairly clear. The overriding fact is that there is not now enough fresh water for all the parties in the region.[130] Likewise, it is clear that Israel uses much more water than the Palestinians. According to one assessment by a pair of Israeli scholars, 'Palestinian average per capita consumption is less than one-third of average per capita consumption in Israel'.[131] Palestinians in the Gaza Strip have a particularly dire need for more water.[132] Other facts are less easy to ascertain. For example, it is difficult to assess how much water naturally 'belongs' to each side's 'territory'. In the Middle East as elsewhere, freshwater sources do not necessarily follow international boundaries. In particular, aquifers and other groundwater flow without regard to political circumstances. There are a variety of measures of how much water is 'part' of each side's 'territory'. These include the amount of rainfall that falls in feeding areas, the volume of storage areas under each party's territory, or some combination of the two.[133] And, as we shall see in a moment, there is disagreement over whether existing levels of use are more important than the natural hydrological characteristics of the region. There is hope that new sources will be developed in the future, and that agriculture—the sector that uses the most water—will become more efficient. But those processes will take a long time.

The Oslo process has led to some progress on water disputes in the region, and not just between Israel and the Palestinians. The most significant achievement is the 1994 Israel–Jordan peace treaty, which established detailed rules on allocation, storage, protection, and quality of water, and created a Joint Water Committee to help implement these provisions.[134] The Oslo Accords have not achieved this level of success, but they do reflect some agreement on general principles. An annexe to the 1993 Declaration of Principles contained one paragraph endorsing the norm of 'equitable utilization' but refraining from any detailed consideration of the water question.[135] The 1995 Interim Agreement addressed water in somewhat

[128] See, e.g., Eyal Benvenisti and Haim Gvirtzman, 'Harnessing International Law to Determine Israeli–Palestinian Water Rights: The Mountain Aquifer', 33 *Nat. Res. J.* 543, 547–50 (1993); Schiff, *Israeli Preconditions*, 24–5.

[129] See, e.g., Wolf and Ross, 'The Impact of Scarce Water Resources', 921.

[130] Ibid. 920 ('water consumption has routinely exceeded annual supply . . .').

[131] Benvenisti and Gvirtzman, 'The Mountain Aquifer', 561.

[132] Ibid.

[133] See ibid. 556–7.

[134] Treaty of Peace, Isr.–Jor., Art. 6 and Annexe II.

[135] Declaration of Principles, Annexe III, ¶1.

greater detail. In Annex III, Israel recognized 'Palestinian water rights in the West Bank'[136]—a concession of considerable importance to the Palestinians. Israel also agreed to make more water available to the Palestinians, and the parties further agreed to establish a Joint Water Committee along the lines of the Israel–Jordan model. None the less, the Interim Agreement stopped short of any longer-term resolution on allocation, protection, or storage of water. It is hoped that a final-status agreement will resolve these issues.

International law provides only the most general guidance for the parties, in part because the law in this area has been slow to develop. A century ago, many states apparently took the view that a state had absolute territorial sovereignty over waters running through its territory, regardless of the interests of downstream riparians.[137] In the past few decades, however, international law has gradually embraced a more communitarian principle of 'equitable utilization' of waters flowing through more than one state. This principle was enshrined in the Helsinki Rules on the Uses of the Waters of International Rivers, promulgated by the International Law Association in 1966.[138] Recently it has also been adopted in the municipal law of federal states.[139] This doctrinal shift reflects a growing consensus that there is a human right to an adequate supply of water.[140] The major human rights instruments do not refer explicitly to a right to water, but such a right can be readily inferred from other enumerated rights, such as the rights to food and life.[141] Humanitarian law also speaks to water rights.[142]

136 Interim Agreement, Annexe III, Art. 40, ¶1.

137 See, e.g., the 'Harmon Doctrine,' enunciated in 21 Op. Att'y Gen. 274, 280–3 (1895) (opinion of US Attorney General Judson Harmon). See generally Stephen C. McCaffrey, 'The Harmon Doctrine One Hundred Years Later: Buried, Not Praised', 36 *Nat. Res. J.* 549 (1997). The United States has since abandoned the Harmon Doctrine, but some states apparently still adhere to it. See Kevin P. Scanlan, Note, 'The International Law Commission's First Ten Draft Articles on the Law of the Non-Navigational Uses of International Watercourses: Do They Adequately Address All the Major Issues of Water Usage in the Middle East?', 19 *Fordham Int'l L.J.* 2180, 2207 (1996).

138 20 Aug. 1966, 52 I.L.A. 484 (1967), Ch. 2.

139 See, e.g., *Colorado v. New Mexico*, 459 U.S. 176 (1982); see also A. Dan Tarlock, 'The Law of Equitable Apportionment Revisited, Updated, and Restated', 56 *U. Colo. L. Rev.* 381 (1985).

140 See generally Stephen C. McCaffrey, 'A Human Right to Water: Domestic and International Implications', 5 *Geo. Int'l Envtl. L. Rev.* 1 (1992); Eyal Benvenisti, 'Collective Action in the Utilization of Shared Freshwater: The Challenges of International Water Resources Law', 90 *Am. J. Int'l L.* 384, 406–8 (1996); Abouali, 'Natural Resources under Occupation', 411.

141 See, e.g., International Covenant on Economic, Social and Cultural Rights, 16 Dec. 1966, 993 U.N.T.S. 3, Art. 11(1) ('adequate food'); International Covenant on Civil and Political Rights, Art. 6 ('life'). See generally Philip Alston and Katarina Tomaševski (eds.), *The Right to Food* (Boston, MA: Martinus Nijhoff, 1984).

142 See generally Harold Dichter, 'The Legal Status of Israel's Water Policies in the Occupied Territories', 35 *Harv. Int'l L. J.* 565 (1994); Abouali, 'Natural Resources under Occupation', 461–95; Dillman, 'Water Rights in the Occupied Territories'.

But while the Helsinki Rules have weight as an authoritative attempt at codification by a prestigious non-governmental organization, they do not constitute a treaty or other binding instrument.[143] The International Law Commission laboured for many years to fill this gap,[144] and at last in 1997 the UN General Assembly adopted the ILC's proposed Convention on the Law of the non-Navigational Uses of International Watercourses.[145] It is not yet clear whether the Convention will enter into force; the Convention requires thirty-five ratifications to enter into force, and despite the lopsided vote in favour of the Convention in the General Assembly, there is some doubt about how soon thirty-five states will actually ratify it. Indeed, even if it does come into force, it may never have enough support to qualify as an authoritative codification of customary law.[146] Moreover, parties may by agreement depart from the norms established by the Convention.[147] None the less, the Convention is a significant development in the law of transboundary watercourses.[148]

Like the Helsinki Rules, the Convention endorses the principle of 'equitable utilization' of shared watercourses. Article 6 of the Convention enumerates the factors relevant to equitable utilization, and thereby supplies ammunition to both Israeli and Palestinian negotiators. On the one hand, Article 6 lends support to Israel's contention that international law protects existing uses. It provides that utilization should take into account 'all relevant factors and circumstances', including '[e]xisting and potential uses of the watercourse', the 'social and economic needs' of each party, the 'population dependent' on the water, and the 'effects of the use or uses of the watercourse in one watercourse State on other watercourse States'. Israel's investments in water technology might be protected by yet another factor: 'Conservation, protection, development, and economy of use' of water and 'costs of measures taken to that effect'.[149]

143 Niva Telerant, 'Riparian Rights under International Law: A Study of the Israeli–Jordanian Peace Treaty', 18 *Loy. L.A. Int'l & Comp. L.J.* 175, 189–90 (1995).

144 For earlier ILC drafts on watercourses, see, e.g., Report of the International Law Commission on the work of its forty-sixth session, UN GAOR, 49th Sess., Supp. No. 10, at 195, UN Doc. A/49/10 (1994); Report of the International Law Commission on the work of its forty-third session, UN GAOR, 46th Sess., UN Doc. A/46/405, 30 I.L.M. 1563 (1991).

145 Convention on the Law of the Non-Navigational Uses of International Watercourses, GA Res. 51/229, annexe (21 May 1997), 36 I.L.M. 700 (1997).

146 See Aaron Schwabach, 'The United Nations Convention on the Law of Non-navigational Uses of International Watercourses, Customary International Law, and the Interests of Developing Upper Riparians', 33 *Tex. Int'l L. J.* 257, 258 (1998).

147 Stephen C. McCaffrey and Mpazi Sinjela, 'The 1997 United Nations Convention on International Watercourses', 92 *Am. J. Int'l L.* 97, 98 (1998).

148 Another important development is the International Court's decision in the *Case Concerning the Gabcikovo-Nagymaros Project* (Slovakia v. Hungary), 1997 I.C.J. 3 (1997), 37 I.L.M. 162 (1998), ¶85 (citing the Convention as evidence that international law requires 'equitable' sharing of watercourses).

149 Convention on International Watercourses, Art. 6(1).

Article 7 of the Convention also seems to protect existing use. It obliges watercourse states that use watercourses to 'take all appropriate measures to prevent the causing of significant harm to other watercourse States'. Paragraph 2 of the same article—the most controversial provision in the entire text—provides that where harm is caused, the state causing harm shall 'take all appropriate measures' to 'eliminate or mitigate' the harm and, where appropriate, to 'discuss' compensation with the injured state. As one study has put it, this provision 'has all the hallmarks of a hard-won compromise: it is rather awkward, somewhat ambiguous and probably not satisfying to anyone, but something most delegations could live with'.[150] The Oslo Accords are not the only instruments that contain constructive ambiguity. In any event, Israel can argue plausibly that Articles 6 and 7 together protect its existing use.

On the other hand, the Palestinians can point to other provisions of Article 6 that favour Palestinian interests. The very first factors listed in Article 6 arguably vindicate Palestinian claims to more water. These factors are: 'Geographic, hydrographic, hydrological, climatic, ecological and other factors of a natural character.'[151] Prior to the adoption of this provision of the Convention, some Israeli commentators argued vigorously that international law established a hierarchy of factors, and that 'natural characteristics' were distinctly less important than existing use.[152] There is some municipal law to support this view,[153] though there is also some municipal authority that seems more ambiguous.[154] The Convention, in any event, seems to have rejected it. It treats all factors equally, and even lists natural characteristics before existing use. If natural characteristics are as important as existing use, then the Israelis' current level of use—including any profligate or wasteful uses—must be balanced against 'natural' considerations, such as the fact that aquifers in the West Bank help supply Israel with water. Again, it may be that the Convention's attention to natural considerations is greater than that found in customary international law, but there is relatively little state practice in this area, so the Convention's position at least has a certain amount of persuasive authority.

Other factors in Article 6 also might bolster the Palestinian position in negotiations. One such factor is the 'potential' use of water. Again, the

[150] McCaffrey and Sinjela, 'The 1997 Convention', 101.

[151] Convention on International Watercourses, Art. 6(1)(a).

[152] See Benvenisti and Gvirtzman, 'The Mountain Aquifer', 547–50.

[153] See *Arizona v. California*, 373 U.S. 546 (1963) (majority opinion); but cf. ibid. 627 (Douglas, J., dissenting) (arguing that apportionment can turn in part on the size of the basin within each competing state). See G. Sherk, 'Equitable Apportionment After Vermejo: The Demise of a Doctrine', 29 *Nat. Res. J.* 656, 577 n. 65 (1989).

[154] See, e.g., American Law Institute, Restatement (2nd) of Torts, §858(1).

Convention treats this factor as being on a par with 'existing' uses, but there is municipal law suggesting that the state arguing that water is necessary for a 'potential' use must do so with clear and convincing evidence.[155] It would seem appropriate that a party seeking water for future uses would bear the burden of proving a future need for that water. Some of the other factors in Article 6 might bolster both Palestinian and Israeli claims. The 'social and economic needs' of Israel can be balanced against the 'social and economic needs' of Gazans, whose low water supply is approaching emergency levels.

Even if one disregards the Convention and treats 'existing use' as the most important factor, the Palestinians still have room to argue for a greater allocation of water. The law surely does not (or at least should not) favour existing wasteful or profligate uses. As one commentator puts it, it is not 'sustainable' for Israeli settlers 'to enjoy three or four times more water than their Palestinian neighbors, with Jewish children playing in swimming pools while nearby Arab children lack enough water to bathe'.[156] Moreover, any assessment of 'existing use' must account for the realities of Israeli occupation, through which Israel has exercised control over Palestinian decisions on water use.

In sum, the international law on equitable allocation of water is still in its formative stages. There is relatively little state practice or conventional law on which to draw, and the new ILC Convention on the subject does not bind the parties to any one particular set of rules. Still, the Convention does offer useful guidelines on the general shape of an Israeli–Palestinian agreement on water. In particular, it suggests that Israel has a legitimate right to protect its existing uses, so long as those uses are not unduly profligate or wasteful, and that the Palestinians have a legitimate right to seek a greater allocation of water that meets their social and economic needs.

Any such agreement will be most stable if it also takes account of the interests of other states in the region. Indeed, the ideal settlement would be a multilateral regional agreement on water, but of course a multilateral agreement might also be more difficult to achieve. Among other things, it would probably require revisiting the Israel–Jordan understandings, and it would have to overcome not only traditional differences between Israel and its Arab neighbours, but disagreements among the Arab states. But even if a multilateral agreement is not feasible, a bilateral Israeli–Palestinian agreement is still essential. The parties need to come to some agreement to address the increasingly dire situation of Palestinians in Gaza and to address the problem of over-pumping in the area generally. And, of course, if there is to be an independent Palestinian state, there

155 See, e.g., *Colorado v. New Mexico*, 467 U.S. 310 (1984).
156 Schiff, *Israeli Preconditions*, 24.

should be some rules governing how it shares water with its Israeli neighbour. Otherwise the water issue might make peace in the Middle East only temporary.

In sum, international law offers general guidance on how the parties might resolve most of the final-status issues, including Jerusalem, refugees, settlements, security, borders, regional relations, and water. Of course, the main part of the task ahead is political, not legal. The law will not dictate any particular outcome. But law can draw baselines for the parties. It can set limits. It can help advance negotiations by providing a common language for discussion. If it can do these things, the law will have served its purpose.

15

Conclusion

Like other momentous documents, the Oslo Accords have been more discussed than read. In part this is because the Accords are not easy reading. They are long, detailed legal instruments, not broad statements of policy or political theory. That is not to say that legal documents can never achieve stylistic distinction; consider the US Declaration of Independence, with its pronouncement that 'All men are created equal', or the Preamble of the UN Charter, which speaks movingly of the 'scourge of war'. The Oslo Accords do contain an occasional literary flourish; the Declaration of Principles, for example, declares that 'it is time to put an end to decades of confrontation and conflict'. By and large, however, the Oslo Accords will not be remembered as great works of political theory or literature. In this respect the Accords also illustrate the time-honoured proposition that peace makes for less compelling reading than war.[1]

For most people, media reports contain more than enough detail about the content of the Oslo Accords. Moreover, even those people who are interested in more details on the Accords may have trouble finding them. This is part of a more general problem with international and comparative law. To paraphrase a scholar of Chinese law, the most difficult thing about international law is finding it.[2] Accordingly, the main texts of the Accords are reproduced in the Appendices to this book. For reasons of space the Annexes to the Accords had to be omitted.

A close reading of the Oslo Accords is important to a full understanding of the Middle East peace process. This book's analysis of the Accords yields several conclusions. First, the Accords are legally binding instruments, not simply political undertakings. They create legal and not just moral obligations. Even sceptics about international law may concede that there is a difference between legal and political obligations, that states and international organizations expect a higher degree of fidelity to the former than the latter.

Second, neither party has fully complied with the Accords, but each is now in substantial compliance. The road to substantial performance,

[1] 'My argument is that War makes rattling good history; but Peace is poor reading.' Thomas Hardy, *The Dynasts*, part I, act II, scene v (Spirit Sinister). The Spirit adds: 'So I back Bonaparte for the reason that he will give pleasure to posterity.'

[2] Cf. Note, 'Concepts of Law in the Chinese Anti-Crime Campaign', 98 *Harv. L. Rev.* 1890, 1890 (1985) ('The chief problem for students of modern Chinese law has often been one of finding it').

however, has been unnecessarily rocky. Neither side has fully acknowledged that each of its obligations must be interpreted and performed in good faith. And each side has been too quick to seize on non-performance by the other as a basis for suspension of its own obligations. In particular, neither side has fully acknowledged that even when countermeasures are appropriate, they should be proportionate to the original breach.

Third, the Oslo Accords remain in force. They did not automatically terminate on 4 May 1999, and neither party has invoked the other's breach as a basis for terminating the Accords outright. Indeed, the parties have acquiesced in the continuation in force of the Accords as they have moved into final-status negotiations.

Finally, the Accords themselves offer little guidance on the shape of a final settlement, but general international law does supply some general parameters within which negotiations may proceed. For the most part the two sides have wide latitude to fashion a negotiated compromise. But the Oslo Accords oblige each side to negotiate, and this obligation carries with it an implied obligation to negotiate in good faith.

The Oslo Accords also teach broader lessons about the peaceful settlement of disputes. One lesson is the value of vagueness and ambiguity. The deliberate ambiguity in phrases like 'specified military locations' allowed the parties to focus on those matters on which they could readily agree and to defer those on which they could not. To be sure, the Israelis and Palestinians are hardly the first negotiators to recognize the 'virtues of ambiguity'.[3] Constitutions and other organic instruments are often better served by general rather than specific commands. Of course, ambiguity has its limits, but the Oslo Accords demonstrate that it can be a useful tool for isolating and defusing deal-breakers.

A second, related lesson—again, hardly a new one—is the value of gradualism. One puzzle-solving heuristic is to solve the easy part of the puzzle first; once that part is solved, the harder parts of the puzzle may seem easier. The final-status issues are still enormously difficult puzzles, but they do seem a bit easier to solve now than they did ten years ago.

A third lesson taught by the Accords is the importance of reciprocity. Reciprocal agreements are generally more stable than unilateral promises. A party is more likely to perform if its performance is a condition of the other party's performance. A condition, like an ambiguity, can promote stable relations. As Shakespeare put it, 'Your If is the only peacemaker; much virtue in If'.[4] That said, reciprocity is one area in which ambiguity is *not* necessarily a virtue. The parties have gradually come to realize this, and their more recent agreements reflect greater attention to reciprocity.

[3] See Lee Bollinger, *The Tolerant Society* (New York: Oxford University Press, 1986), 175.
[4] *As You Like It*, V. iv.

Thus the detailed timetable for mutual performance in the Wye River Memorandum resembles a train schedule as much as a treaty.

Unfortunately, international law has not fully accounted for the importance of reciprocity. The treaty on treaties, the Vienna Convention on the Law of Treaties, is preoccupied with major or 'material' breaches, and yet parties to international agreements are often more concerned with lesser breaches, as to which the Convention is silent. International law needs to clarify whether and to what extent a party may respond to a minor breach by the other. The guiding principles surely must be good faith and proportionality.

A final lesson is that not every regional conflict requires mediation. The most electrifying of all the Oslo Accords was the 1993 Declaration of Principles, which was sprung on the world by surprise. The parties reached this historic agreement without the presence of an arm-twisting third party like the United States. This achievement suggests that mediation is not always the best procedure for dispute resolution, particularly when the parties fear that leaks might spoil an impending deal. True, the United States did play an effective role as a mediator in the Wye River Memorandum, but in large part the Memorandum reaffirms and refines understandings already carved out by the parties themselves.

As Israel and the Palestinians attempt to move from interim to permanent agreements, it is not too early to ask whether the Oslo Accords have been a success. At the time of writing, the answer has to be yes. True, the peace process has repeatedly broken down, and the parties are still a long way from a final settlement. But the parties have also made significant progress towards a peaceful resolution of the Palestinian question. They have managed to establish a measure of Palestinian autonomy without jeopardizing Israel's fundamental security. The Palestinians have recognized Israel, changed their Charter, and taken steps to cooperate with Israel on security matters. Israel has withdrawn from significant portions of the West Bank and Gaza Strip, recognized the PLO as the representative of the Palestinian people, and committed itself to negotiate in good faith on Jerusalem, settlements, and other hot-button issues. In doing these things, both parties have opted for peaceful coexistence over violent confrontation. The goal of the Oslo Accords, of course, is a 'just and lasting peace'. Ultimately, the success of the Accords will be measured against that goal. But even now the Accords stand as an impressive and historic achievement.

The Accords are also an important achievement for international law. They vindicate the principle that people should resolve their disputes peacefully, through law. The Accords demonstrate that whether or not international law is really 'law', it affects the behaviour of international actors: Israel and the Palestinians now routinely cast their political arguments in legal terms, by reference to the text of the Accords. Further, the Accords remind us that international law is not static. By making international agreements, international actors can create new law, law that is optimized for their circumstances.

Finally, the Accords are both an example and a challenge to the rest of the world. If mortal enemies such as Yitzhak Rabin and Yasser Arafat can shake hands—if men such as Rabin and Anwar el-Sadat can give their lives for peace—then anyone should be able to make peace. There are too many monuments to war. The Oslo Accords are a monument to peace. They are a monument to the capacity of human beings to awaken, to grow, and to astonish.

APPENDICES

The Oslo Accords and Related Documents

Appendix A

Arafat–Rabin–Holst Letters [9 September 1993]

September 9, 1993

Yitzhak Rabin
Prime Minister of Israel

Mr. Prime Minister,

The signing of the Declaration of Principles marks a new era in the history of the Middle East. In firm conviction thereof, I would like to confirm the following PLO commitments:

The PLO recognizes the right of the State of Israel to exist in peace and security.

The PLO accepts United Nations Security Council Resolutions 242 and 338.

The PLO commits itself to the Middle East peace process, and to a peaceful resolution of the conflict between the two sides and declares that all outstanding issues relating to permanent status will be resolved through negotiations.

The PLO considers that the signing of the Declaration of Principles constitutes a historic event, inaugurating a new epoch of peaceful coexistence, free from violence and all other acts which endanger peace and stability. Accordingly, the PLO renounces the use of terrorism and other acts of violence and will assume responsibility over all PLO elements and personnel in order to assure their compliance, prevent violations and discipline violators.

In view of the promise of a new era and the signing of the Declaration of Principles and based on Palestinian acceptance of Security Council Resolutions 242 and 338, the PLO affirms that those articles of the Palestinian Covenant which deny Israel's right to exist, and the provisions of the Covenant which are inconsistent with the commitments of this letter are now inoperative and no longer valid. Consequently, the PLO undertakes to submit to the Palestinian National Council for formal approval the necessary changes in regard to the Palestinian Covenant.

Sincerely,

Yasser Arafat
Chairman
The Palestine Liberation Organization

September 9, 1993

His Excellency
Johan Jorgen Holst
Foreign Minister of Norway

Dear Minister Holst,

I would like to confirm to you that, upon the signing of the Declaration of Principles, I will include the following positions in my public statements:

In light of the new era marked by the signing of the Declaration of Principles, the PLO encourages and calls upon the Palestinian people in the West Bank and Gaza Strip to take part in the steps leading to the normalization of life, rejecting violence and terrorism, contributing to peace and stability and participating actively in shaping reconstruction, economic development and cooperation.

Sincerely,

Yasser Arafat
Chairman
The Palestine Liberation Organization

September 9, 1993

Yasser Arafat
Chairman
The Palestinian Liberation Organization

Mr. Chairman,

In response to your letter of September 9, 1993, I wish to confirm to you that, in light of the PLO commitments included in your letter, the Government of Israel has decided to recognize the PLO as the representative of the Palestinian people and commence negotiations with the PLO within the Middle East peace process.

Sincerely,

Yitzhak Rabin
Prime Minister of Israel

Appendix B

Declaration of Principles on Interim Self-Government Arrangements [13 September 1993]

The Government of the State of Israel and the P.L.O. team (in the Jordanian–Palestinian delegation to the Middle East Peace Conference) (the "Palestinian Delegation"), representing the Palestinian people, agree that it is time to put an end to decades of confrontation and conflict, recognize their mutual legitimate and political rights, and strive to live in peaceful coexistence and mutual dignity and security and achieve a just, lasting and comprehensive peace settlement and historic reconciliation through the agreed political process. Accordingly, the two sides agree to the following principles:

Article I

AIM OF THE NEGOTIATIONS

The aim of the Israeli–Palestinian negotiations within the current Middle East peace process is, among other things, to establish a Palestinian Interim Self-Government Authority, the elected Council (the "Council"), for the Palestinian people in the West Bank and the Gaza Strip, for a transitional period not exceeding five years, leading to a permanent settlement based on Security Council Resolutions 242 and 338.

It is understood that the interim arrangements are an integral part of the whole peace process and that the negotiations on the permanent status will lead to the implementation of Security Council Resolutions 242 and 338.

Article II

FRAMEWORK FOR THE INTERIM PERIOD

The agreed framework for the interim period is set forth in this Declaration of Principles.

Article III

ELECTIONS

1. In order that the Palestinian people in the West Bank and Gaza Strip may govern themselves according to democratic principles, direct, free and general political elections will be held for the Council under agreed supervision and international observation, while the Palestinian police will ensure public order.

2. An agreement will be concluded on the exact mode and conditions of the elections in accordance with the protocol attached as Annex I, with the goal of holding the elections not later than nine months after the entry into force of this Declaration of Principles.
3. These elections will constitute a significant interim preparatory step toward the realization of the legitimate rights of the Palestinian people and their just requirements.

Article IV

JURISDICTION

Jurisdiction of the Council will cover West Bank and Gaza Strip territory, except for issues that will be negotiated in the permanent status negotiations. The two sides view the West Bank and the Gaza Strip as a single territorial unit, whose integrity will be preserved during the interim period.

Article V

TRANSITIONAL PERIOD AND PERMANENT STATUS NEGOTIATIONS

1. The five-year transitional period will begin upon the withdrawal from the Gaza Strip and Jericho area.
2. Permanent status negotiations will commence as soon as possible, but not later than the beginning of the third year of the interim period, between the Government of Israel and the Palestinian people representatives.
3. It is understood that these negotiations shall cover remaining issues, including: Jerusalem, refugees, settlements, security arrangements, borders, relations and cooperation with other neighbors, and other issues of common interest.
4. The two parties agree that the outcome of the permanent status negotiations should not be prejudiced or preempted by agreements reached for the interim period.

Article VI

PREPARATORY TRANSFER OF POWERS AND RESPONSIBILITIES

1. Upon the entry into force of this Declaration of Principles and the withdrawal from the Gaza Strip and the Jericho area, a transfer of authority from the Israeli military government and its Civil Administration to the authorised Palestinians for this task, as detailed herein, will commence. This transfer of authority will be of a preparatory nature until the inauguration of the Council.
2. Immediately after the entry into force of this Declaration of Principles and the withdrawal from the Gaza Strip and Jericho area, with the view to promoting economic development in the West Bank and Gaza Strip, authority will be transferred to the Palestinians on the following spheres: education and culture,

health, social welfare, direct taxation, and tourism. The Palestinian side will commence in building the Palestinian police force, as agreed upon. Pending the inauguration of the Council, the two parties may negotiate the transfer of additional powers and responsibilities, as agreed upon.

Article VII

INTERIM AGREEMENT

1. The Israeli and Palestinian delegations will negotiate an agreement on the interim period (the "Interim Agreement").
2. The Interim Agreement shall specify, among other things, the structure of the Council, the number of its members, and the transfer of powers and responsibilities from the Israeli military government and its Civil Administration to the Council. The Interim Agreement shall also specify the Council's executive authority, legislative authority in accordance with Article IX below, and the independent Palestinian judicial organs.
3. The Interim Agreement shall include arrangements, to be implemented upon the inauguration of the Council, for the assumption by the Council of all of the powers and responsibilities transferred previously in accordance with Article VI above.
4. In order to enable the Council to promote economic growth, upon its inauguration, the Council will establish, among other things, a Palestinian Electricity Authority, a Gaza Sea Port Authority, a Palestinian Development Bank, a Palestinian Export Promotion Board, a Palestinian Environmental Authority, a Palestinian Land Authority and a Palestinian Water Administration Authority, and any other Authorities agreed upon, in accordance with the Interim Agreement that will specify their powers and responsibilities.
5. After the inauguration of the Council, the Civil Administration will be dissolved, and the Israeli military government will be withdrawn.

Article VIII

PUBLIC ORDER AND SECURITY

In order to guarantee public order and internal security for the Palestinians of the West Bank and the Gaza Strip, the Council will establish a strong police force, while Israel will continue to carry the responsibility for defending against external threats, as well as the responsibility for overall security of Israelis for the purpose of safeguarding their internal security and public order.

Article IX

LAWS AND MILITARY ORDERS

1. The Council will be empowered to legislate, in accordance with the Interim Agreement, within all authorities transferred to it.

2. Both parties will review jointly laws and military orders presently in force in remaining spheres.

Article X

JOINT ISRAELI–PALESTINIAN LIAISON COMMITTEE

In order to provide for a smooth implementation of this Declaration of Principles and any subsequent agreements pertaining to the interim period, upon the entry into force of this Declaration of Principles, a Joint Israeli–Palestinian Liaison Committee will be established in order to deal with issues requiring coordination, other issues of common interest, and disputes.

Article XI

ISRAELI–PALESTINIAN COOPERATION IN ECONOMIC FIELDS

Recognizing the mutual benefit of cooperation in promoting the development of the West Bank, the Gaza Strip and Israel, upon the entry into force of this Declaration of Principles, an Israeli–Palestinian Economic Cooperation Committee will be established in order to develop and implement in a cooperative manner the programs identified in the protocols attached as Annex III and Annex IV.

Article XII

LIAISON AND COOPERATION WITH JORDAN AND EGYPT

The two parties will invite the Governments of Jordan and Egypt to participate in establishing further liaison and cooperation arrangements between the Government of Israel and the Palestinian representatives, on the one hand, and the Governments of Jordan and Egypt, on the other hand, to promote cooperation between them. These arrangements will include the constitution of a Continuing Committee that will decide by agreement on the modalities of admission of persons displaced from the West Bank and Gaza Strip in 1967, together with necessary measures to prevent disruption and disorder. Other matters of common concern will be dealt with by this Committee.

Article XIII

REDEPLOYMENT OF ISRAELI FORCES

1. After the entry into force of this Declaration of Principles, and not later than the eve of elections for the Council, a redeployment of Israeli military forces in the West Bank and the Gaza Strip will take place, in addition to withdrawal of Israeli forces carried out in accordance with Article XIV.

2. In redeploying its military forces, Israel will be guided by the principle that its military forces should be redeployed outside populated areas.
3. Further redeployments to specified locations will be gradually implemented commensurate with the assumption of responsibility for public order and internal security by the Palestinian police force pursuant to Article VIII above.

Article XIV

ISRAELI WITHDRAWAL FROM THE GAZA STRIP AND JERICHO AREA

Israel will withdraw from the Gaza Strip and Jericho area, as detailed in the protocol attached as Annex II.

Article XV

RESOLUTION OF DISPUTES

1. Disputes arising out of the application or interpretation of this Declaration of Principles, or any subsequent agreements pertaining to the interim period, shall be resolved by negotiations through the Joint Liaison Committee to be established pursuant to Article X above.
2. Disputes which cannot be settled by negotiations may be resolved by a mechanism of conciliation to be agreed upon by the parties.
3. The parties may agree to submit to arbitration disputes relating to the interim period, which cannot be settled through conciliation. To this end, upon the agreement of both parties, the parties will establish an Arbitration Committee.

Article XVI

ISRAELI–PALESTINIAN COOPERATION CONCERNING REGIONAL PROGRAMS

Both parties view the multilateral working groups as an appropriate instrument for promoting a "Marshall Plan", the regional programs and other programs, including special programs for the West Bank and Gaza Strip, as indicated in the protocol attached as Annex IV.

Article XVII

MISCELLANEOUS PROVISIONS

1. This Declaration of Principles will enter into force one month after its signing.
2. All protocols annexed to this Declaration of Principles and Agreed Minutes pertaining thereto shall be regarded as an integral part hereof.

Done at Washington, D.C., this thirteenth day of September, 1993.

For the Government of Israel: For the P.L.O.:

Witnessed By:

The United States of America The Russian Federation

Annex I

PROTOCOL ON THE MODE AND CONDITIONS OF ELECTIONS

1. Palestinians of Jerusalem who live there will have the right to participate in the election process, according to an agreement between the two sides.
2. In addition, the election agreement should cover, among other things, the following issues:
   a. the system of elections;
   b. the mode of the agreed supervision and international observation and their personal composition; and
   c. rules and regulations regarding election campaign, including agreed arrangements for the organizing of mass media, and the possibility of licensing a broadcasting and TV station.
3. The future status of displaced Palestinians who were registered on 4th June 1967 will not be prejudiced because they are unable to participate in the election process due to practical reasons.

Annex II

PROTOCOL ON WITHDRAWAL OF ISRAELI FORCES FROM THE GAZA STRIP AND JERICHO AREA

1. The two sides will conclude and sign within two months from the date of entry into force of this Declaration of Principles, an agreement on the withdrawal of Israeli military forces from the Gaza Strip and Jericho area. This agreement will include comprehensive arrangements to apply in the Gaza Strip and the Jericho area subsequent to the Israeli withdrawal.
2. Israel will implement an accelerated and scheduled withdrawal of Israeli military forces from the Gaza Strip and Jericho area, beginning immediately with the signing of the agreement on the Gaza Strip and Jericho area and to be completed within a period not exceeding four months after the signing of this agreement.
3. The above agreement will include, among other things:
   a. Arrangements for a smooth and peaceful transfer of authority from the Israeli military government and its Civil Administration to the Palestinian representatives.
   b. Structure, powers and responsibilities of the Palestinian authority in these areas, except: external security, settlements, Israelis, foreign relations, and other mutually agreed matters.

c. Arrangements for the assumption of internal security and public order by the Palestinian police force consisting of police officers recruited locally and from abroad (holding Jordanian passports and Palestinian documents issued by Egypt). Those who will participate in the Palestinian police force coming from abroad should be trained as police and police officers.
d. A temporary international or foreign presence, as agreed upon.
e. Establishment of a joint Palestinian–Israeli Coordination and Cooperation Committee for mutual security purposes.
f. An economic development and stabilization program, including the establishment of an Emergency Fund, to encourage foreign investment, and financial and economic support. Both sides will coordinate and cooperate jointly and unilaterally with regional and international parties to support these aims.
g. Arrangements for a safe passage for persons and transportation between the Gaza Strip and Jericho area.

4. The above agreement will include arrangements for coordination between both parties regarding passages:

   a. Gaza–Egypt; and
   b. Jericho–Jordan.

5. The offices responsible for carrying out the powers and responsibilities of the Palestinian authority under this Annex II and Article VI of the Declaration of Principles will be located in the Gaza Strip and in the Jericho area pending the inauguration of the Council.
6. Other than these agreed arrangements, the status of the Gaza Strip and Jericho area will continue to be an integral part of the West Bank and Gaza Strip, and will not be changed in the interim period.

Annex III

PROTOCOL ON ISRAELI–PALESTINIAN COOPERATION IN ECONOMIC AND DEVELOPMENT PROGRAMS

The two sides agree to establish an Israeli–Palestinian Continuing Committee for Economic Cooperation, focusing, among other things, on the following:

1. Cooperation in the field of water, including a Water Development Program prepared by experts from both sides, which will also specify the mode of cooperation in the management of water resources in the West Bank and Gaza Strip, and will include proposals for studies and plans on water rights of each party, as well as on the equitable utilization of joint water resources for implementation in and beyond the interim period.
2. Cooperation in the field of electricity, including an Electricity Development Program, which will also specify the mode of cooperation for the production, maintenance, purchase and sale of electricity resources.
3. Cooperation in the field of energy, including an Energy Development Program, which will provide for the exploitation of oil and gas for industrial purposes, particularly in the Gaza Strip and in the Negev, and will encourage

further joint exploitation of other energy resources. This Program may also provide for the construction of a Petrochemical industrial complex in the Gaza Strip and the construction of oil and gas pipelines.

4. Cooperation in the field of finance, including a Financial Development and Action Program for the encouragement of international investment in the West Bank and the Gaza Strip, and in Israel, as well as the establishment of a Palestinian Development Bank.
5. Cooperation in the field of transport and communications, including a Program, which will define guidelines for the establishment of a Gaza Sea Port Area, and will provide for the establishing of transport and communications lines to and from the West Bank and the Gaza Strip to Israel and to other countries. In addition, this Program will provide for carrying out the necessary construction of roads, railways, communications lines, etc.
6. Cooperation in the field of trade, including studies, and Trade Promotion Programs, which will encourage local, regional and inter-regional trade, as well as a feasibility study of creating free trade zones in the Gaza Strip and in Israel, mutual access to these zones, and cooperation in other areas related to trade and commerce.
7. Cooperation in the field of industry, including Industrial Development Programs, which will provide for the establishment of joint Israeli–Palestinian Industrial Research and Development Centers, will promote Palestinian–Israeli joint ventures, and provide guidelines for cooperation in the textile, food, pharmaceutical, electronics, diamonds, computer and science-based industries.
8. A program for cooperation in, and regulation of, labor relations and cooperation in social welfare issues.
9. A Human Resources Development and Cooperation Plan, providing for joint Israeli–Palestinian workshops and seminars, and for the establishment of joint vocational training centers, research institutes and data banks.
10. An Environmental Protection Plan, providing for joint and/or coordinated measures in this sphere.
11. A program for developing coordination and cooperation in the field of communication and media.
12. Any other programs of mutual interest.

Annex IV

PROTOCOL ON ISRAELI–PALESTINIAN COOPERATION CONCERNING REGIONAL DEVELOPMENT PROGRAMS

1. The two sides will cooperate in the context of the multilateral peace efforts in promoting a Development Program for the region, including the West Bank and the Gaza Strip, to be initiated by the G-7. The parties will request the G-7 to seek the participation in this program of other interested states, such as members of the Organisation for Economic Cooperation and Development, regional Arab states and institutions, as well as members of the private sector.
2. The Development Program will consist of two elements:

a. an Economic Development Program for the West Bank and the Gaza Strip.
b. a Regional Economic Development Program.

A. The Economic Development Program for the West Bank and the Gaza strip will consist of the following elements:
1. A Social Rehabilitation Program, including a Housing and Construction Program.
2. A Small and Medium Business Development Plan.
3. An Infrastructure Development Program (water, electricity, transportation and communications, etc.)
4. A Human Resources Plan.
5. Other programs.

B. The Regional Economic Development Program may consist of the following elements:
1. The establishment of a Middle East Development Fund, as a first step, and a Middle East Development Bank, as a second step.
2. The development of a joint Israeli–Palestinian–Jordanian Plan for coordinated exploitation of the Dead Sea area.
3. The Mediterranean Sea (Gaza)—Dead Sea Canal.
4. Regional Desalinization and other water development projects.
5. A regional plan for agricultural development, including a coordinated regional effort for the prevention of desertification.
6. Interconnection of electricity grids.
7. Regional cooperation for the transfer, distribution and industrial exploitation of gas, oil and other energy resources.
8. A Regional Tourism, Transportation and Telecommunications Development Plan.
9. Regional cooperation in other spheres.

3. The two sides will encourage the multilateral working groups, and will coordinate towards their success. The two parties will encourage intersessional activities, as well as pre-feasibility and feasibility studies, within the various multilateral working groups.

AGREED MINUTES TO THE DECLARATION OF PRINCIPLES ON INTERIM SELF-GOVERNMENT ARRANGEMENTS

A. GENERAL UNDERSTANDINGS AND AGREEMENTS

Any powers and responsibilities transferred to the Palestinians pursuant to the Declaration of Principles prior to the inauguration of the Council will be subject to the same principles pertaining to Article IV, as set out in these Agreed Minutes below.

B. SPECIFIC UNDERSTANDINGS AND AGREEMENTS

Article IV

It is understood that:
1. Jurisdiction of the Council will cover West Bank and Gaza Strip territory,

except for issues that will be negotiated in the permanent status negotiations: Jerusalem, settlements, military locations, and Israelis.

2. The Council's jurisdiction will apply with regard to the agreed powers, responsibilities, spheres and authorities transferred to it.

Article VI (2)

It is agreed that the transfer of authority will be as follows:

1. The Palestinian side will inform the Israeli side of the names of the authorised Palestinians who will assume the powers, authorities and responsibilities that will be transferred to the Palestinians according to the Declaration of Principles in the following fields: education and culture, health, social welfare, direct taxation, tourism, and any other authorities agreed upon.
2. It is understood that the rights and obligations of these offices will not be affected.
3. Each of the spheres described above will continue to enjoy existing budgetary allocations in accordance with arrangements to be mutually agreed upon. These arrangements also will provide for the necessary adjustments required in order to take into account the taxes collected by the direct taxation office.
4. Upon the execution of the Declaration of Principles, the Israeli and Palestinian delegations will immediately commence negotiations on a detailed plan for the transfer of authority on the above offices in accordance with the above understandings.

Article VII (2)

The Interim Agreement will also include arrangements for coordination and cooperation.

Article VII (5)

The withdrawal of the military government will not prevent Israel from exercising the powers and responsibilities not transferred to the Council.

Article VIII

It is understood that the Interim Agreement will include arrangements for cooperation and coordination between the two parties in this regard. It is also agreed that the transfer of powers and responsibilities to the Palestinian police will be accomplished in a phased manner, as agreed in the Interim Agreement.

Article X

It is agreed that, upon the entry into force of the Declaration of Principles, the Israeli and Palestinian delegations will exchange the names of the individuals designated by them as members of the Joint Israeli–Palestinian Liaison Committee.

It is further agreed that each side will have an equal number of members in the Joint Committee. The Joint Committee will reach decisions by agreement. The Joint Committee may add other technicians and experts, as necessary. The Joint Committee will decide on the frequency and place or places of its meetings.

Annex II

It is understood that, subsequent to the Israeli withdrawal, Israel will continue to be responsible for external security, and for internal security and public order of settlements and Israelis. Israeli military forces and civilians may continue to use roads freely within the Gaza Strip and the Jericho area.

DONE at Washington, D.C., this thirteenth day of September, 1993.

For the Government of Israel:	For the P.L.O.:

Witnessed By:

The United States of America	The Russian Federation

Appendix C

Agreement on the Gaza Strip and the Jericho Area
[4 May 1994]

The Government of the State of Israel and the Palestine Liberation Organization (hereinafter "the PLO"), the representative of the Palestinian people;

PREAMBLE

WITHIN the framework of the Middle East peace process initiated at Madrid in October 1991;

REAFFIRMING their determination to live in peaceful coexistence, mutual dignity and security, while recognizing their mutual legitimate and political rights;

REAFFIRMING their desire to achieve a just, lasting and comprehensive peace settlement through the agreed political process;

REAFFIRMING their adherence to the mutual recognition and commitments expressed in the letters dated September 9, 1993, signed by and exchanged between the Prime Minister of Israel and the Chairman of the PLO;

REAFFIRMING their understanding that the interim self-government arrangements, including the arrangements to apply in the Gaza Strip and the Jericho Area contained in this Agreement, are an integral part of the whole peace process and that the negotiations on the permanent status will lead to the implementation of Security Council Resolutions 242 and 338;

DESIROUS of putting into effect the Declaration of Principles on Interim Self-Government Arrangements signed at Washington, D.C. on September 13, 1993, and the Agreed Minutes thereto (hereinafter "the Declaration of Principles"), and in particular the Protocol on withdrawal of Israeli forces from the Gaza Strip and the Jericho Area;

HEREBY AGREE to the following arrangements regarding the Gaza Strip and the Jericho Area:

Article 1

DEFINITIONS

For the purpose of this Agreement:

a. the Gaza Strip and the Jericho Area are delineated on map No. 1 and map No. 2 attached to this Agreement;
b. "the Settlements" means the Gush Katif and Erez settlement areas, as well as the other settlements in the Gaza Strip, as shown on attached map No. 1;
c. "the Military Installation Area" means the Israeli military installation area along the Egyptian border in the Gaza Strip, as shown on map No. 1; and

d. the term "Israelis" shall also include Israeli statutory agencies and corporations registered in Israel.

Article II

SCHEDULED WITHDRAWAL OF ISRAELI MILITARY FORCES

1. Israel shall implement an accelerated and scheduled withdrawal of Israeli military forces from the Gaza Strip and from the Jericho Area to begin immediately with the signing of this Agreement. Israel shall complete such withdrawal within three weeks from this date.
2. Subject to the arrangements included in the Protocol Concerning Withdrawal of Israeli Military Forces and Security Arrangements attached as Annex I, the Israeli withdrawal shall include evacuating all military bases and other fixed installations to be handed over to the Palestinian Police, to be established pursuant to Article IX below (hereinafter "the Palestinian Police").
3. In order to carry out Israel's responsibility for external security and for internal security and public order of Settlements and Israelis, Israel shall, concurrently with the withdrawal, redeploy its remaining military forces to the Settlements and the Military Installation Area, in accordance with the provisions of this Agreement. Subject to the provisions of this Agreement, this redeployment shall constitute full implementation of Article XIII of the Declaration of Principles with regard to the Gaza Strip and the Jericho Area only.
4. For the purposes of this Agreement, "Israeli military forces" may include Israel police and other Israeli security forces.
5. Israelis, including Israeli military forces, may continue to use roads freely within the Gaza Strip and the Jericho Area. Palestinians may use public roads crossing the Settlements freely, as provided for in Annex I.
6. The Palestinian Police shall be deployed and shall assume responsibility for public order and internal security of Palestinians in accordance with this Agreement and Annex I.

Article III

TRANSFER OF AUTHORITY

1. Israel shall transfer authority as specified in this Agreement from the Israeli military government and its Civil Administration to the Palestinian Authority, hereby established, in accordance with Article V of this Agreement, except for the authority that Israel shall continue to exercise as specified in this Agreement.
2. As regards the transfer and assumption of authority in civil spheres, powers and responsibilities shall be transferred and assumed as set out in the Protocol Concerning Civil Affairs attached as Annex II.
3. Arrangements for a smooth and peaceful transfer of the agreed powers and responsibilities are set out in Annex II.

4. Upon the completion of the Israeli withdrawal and the transfer of powers and responsibilities as detailed in paragraphs 1 and 2 above and in Annex II, the Civil Administration in the Gaza Strip and the Jericho Area will be dissolved and the Israeli military government will be withdrawn. The withdrawal of the military government shall not prevent it from continuing to exercise the powers and responsibilities specified in this Agreement.
5. A Joint Civil Affairs Coordination and Cooperation Committee (hereinafter "the CAC") and two Joint Regional Civil Affairs Subcommittees for the Gaza Strip and the Jericho Area respectively shall be established in order to provide for coordination and cooperation in civil affairs between the Palestinian Authority and Israel, as detailed in Annex II.
6. The offices of the Palestinian Authority shall be located in the Gaza Strip and the Jericho Area pending the inauguration of the Council to be elected pursuant to the Declaration of Principles.

Article IV

STRUCTURE AND COMPOSITION OF THE PALESTINIAN AUTHORITY

1. The Palestinian Authority will consist of one body of 24 members which shall carry out and be responsible for all the legislative and executive powers and responsibilities transferred to it under this Agreement, in accordance with this Article, and shall be responsible for the exercise of judicial functions in accordance with Article VI, subparagraph 1.b. of this Agreement.
2. The Palestinian Authority shall administer the departments transferred to it and may establish, within its jurisdiction, other departments and subordinate administrative units as necessary for the fulfillment of its responsibilities. It shall determine its own internal procedures.
3. The PLO shall inform the Government of Israel of the names of the members of the Palestinian Authority and any change of members. Changes in the membership of the Palestinian Authority will take effect upon an exchange of letters between the PLO and the Government of Israel.
4. Each member of the Palestinian Authority shall enter into office upon undertaking to act in accordance with this Agreement.

Article V

JURISDICTION

1. The authority of the Palestinian Authority encompasses all matters that fall within its territorial, functional and personal jurisdiction, as follows:
   a. The territorial jurisdiction covers the Gaza Strip and the Jericho Area territory, as defined in Article I, except for Settlements and the Military Installation Area. Territorial jurisdiction shall include land, subsoil and territorial waters, in accordance with the provisions of this Agreement.
   b. The functional jurisdiction encompasses all powers and responsibilities as

specified in this Agreement. This jurisdiction does not include foreign relations, internal security and public order of Settlements and the Military Installation Area and Israelis, and external security.

c. The personal jurisdiction extends to all persons within the territorial jurisdiction referred to above, except for Israelis, unless otherwise provided in this Agreement.

2. The Palestinian Authority has, within its authority, legislative, executive and judicial powers and responsibilities, as provided for in this Agreement.

3. a. Israel has authority over the Settlements, the Military Installation Area, Israelis, external security, internal security and public order of Settlements, the Military Installation Area and Israelis, and those agreed powers and responsibilities specified in this Agreement.

 b. Israel shall exercise its authority through its military government, which, for that end, shall continue to have the necessary legislative, judicial and executive powers and responsibilities, in accordance with international law. This provision shall not derogate from Israel's applicable legislation over Israelis in personam.

4. The exercise of authority with regard to the electromagnetic sphere and airspace shall be in accordance with the provisions of this Agreement.

5. The provisions of this Article are subject to the specific legal arrangements detailed in the Protocol Concerning Legal Matters attached as Annex III. Israel and the Palestinian Authority may negotiate further legal arrangements.

6. Israel and the Palestinian Authority shall cooperate on matters of legal assistance in criminal and civil matters through the legal subcommittee of the CAC.

Article VI

POWERS AND RESPONSIBILITIES OF THE PALESTINIAN AUTHORITY

1. Subject to the provisions of this Agreement, the Palestinian Authority, within its jurisdiction:

 a. has legislative powers as set out in Article VII of this Agreement, as well as executive powers;

 b. will administer justice through an independent judiciary;

 c. will have, inter alia, power to formulate policies, supervise their implementation, employ staff, establish departments, authorities and institutions, sue and be sued and conclude contracts; and

 d. will have, inter alia, the power to keep and administer registers and records of the population, and issue certificates, licenses and documents.

2.

 a. In accordance with the Declaration of Principles, the Palestinian Authority will not have powers and responsibilities in the sphere of foreign relations, which sphere includes the establishment abroad of embassies, consulates or other types of foreign missions and posts or permitting their establishment in the Gaza Strip or the Jericho Area, the appointment of or admission of diplomatic and consular staff, and the exercise of diplomatic functions.

b. Notwithstanding the provisions of this paragraph, the PLO may conduct negotiations and sign agreements with states or international organizations for the benefit of the Palestinian Authority in the following cases only:
   1. economic agreements, as specifically provided in Annex IV of this Agreement;
   2. agreements with donor countries for the purpose of implementing arrangements for the provision of assistance to the Palestinian Authority;
   3. agreements for the purpose of implementing the regional development plans detailed in Annex IV of the Declaration of Principles or in agreements entered into in the framework of the multilateral negotiations; and
   4. cultural, scientific and educational agreements.

c. Dealings between the Palestinian Authority and representatives of foreign states and international organizations, as well as the establishment in the Gaza Strip and the Jericho Area of representative offices other than those described in subparagraph 2.a. above, for the purpose of implementing the agreements referred to in subparagraph 2.b. above, shall not be considered foreign relations.

Article VII

LEGISLATIVE POWERS OF THE PALESTINIAN AUTHORITY

1. The Palestinian Authority will have the power, within its jurisdiction, to promulgate legislation, including basic laws, laws, regulations and other legislative acts.
2. Legislation promulgated by the Palestinian Authority shall be consistent with the provisions of this Agreement.
3. Legislation promulgated by the Palestinian Authority shall be communicated to a legislation subcommittee to be established by the CAC (hereinafter "the Legislation Subcommittee"). During a period of 30 days from the communication of the legislation, Israel may request that the Legislation Subcommittee decide whether such legislation exceeds the jurisdiction of the Palestinian Authority or is otherwise inconsistent with the provisions of this Agreement.
4. Upon receipt of the Israeli request, the Legislation Subcommittee shall decide, as an initial matter, on the entry into force of the legislation pending its decision on the merits of the matter.
5. If the Legislation Subcommittee is unable to reach a decision with regard to the entry into force of the legislation within 15 days, this issue will be referred to a board of review. This board of review shall be comprised of two judges, retired judges or senior jurists (hereinafter "Judges"), one from each side, to be appointed from a compiled list of three Judges proposed by each. In order to expedite the proceedings before this board of review, the two most senior Judges, one from each side, shall develop written informal rules of procedure.
6. Legislation referred to the board of review shall enter into force only if the board of review decides that it does not deal with a security issue which falls under Israel's responsibility, that it does not seriously threaten other significant Israeli interests protected by this Agreement and that the entry into force of the legislation could not cause irreparable damage or harm.

7. The Legislation Subcommittee shall attempt to reach a decision on the merits of the matter within 30 days from the date of the Israeli request. If this Subcommittee is unable to reach such a decision within this period of 30 days, the matter shall be referred to the Joint Israeli–Palestinian Liaison Committee referred to in Article XV below (hereinafter "the Liaison Committee"). This Liaison Committee will deal with the matter immediately and will attempt to settle it within 30 days.
8. Where the legislation has not entered into force pursuant to paragraphs 5 or 7 above, this situation shall be maintained pending the decision of the Liaison Committee on the merits of the matter, unless it has decided otherwise.
9. Laws and military orders in effect in the Gaza Strip or the Jericho Area prior to the signing of this Agreement shall remain in force, unless amended or abrogated in accordance with this Agreement.

Article VIII

ARRANGEMENTS FOR SECURITY AND PUBLIC ORDER

1. In order to guarantee public order and internal security for the Palestinians of the Gaza Strip and the Jericho Area, the Palestinian Authority shall establish a strong police force, as set out in Article IX below. Israel shall continue to carry the responsibility for defense against external threats, including the responsibility for protecting the Egyptian border and the Jordanian line, and for defense against external threats from the sea and from the air, as well as the responsibility for overall security of Israelis and Settlements, for the purpose of safeguarding their internal security and public order, and will have all the powers to take the steps necessary to meet this responsibility.
2. Agreed security arrangements and coordination mechanisms are specified in Annex I.
3. A joint Coordination and Cooperation Committee for mutual security purposes (hereinafter "the JSC"), as well as three joint District Coordination and Cooperation Offices for the Gaza district, the Khan Yunis district and the Jericho district respectively (hereinafter "the DCOs") are hereby established as provided for in Annex I.
4. The security arrangements provided for in this Agreement and in Annex I may be reviewed at the request of either Party and may be amended by mutual agreement of the Parties. Specific review arrangements are included in Annex I.

Article IX

THE PALESTINIAN DIRECTORATE OF POLICE FORCE

1. The Palestinian Authority shall establish a strong police force, the Palestinian Directorate of Police Force (hereinafter "the Palestinian Police"). The duties, functions, structure, deployment and composition of the Palestinian Police, together with provisions regarding its equipment and operation, are set out in

Annex I, Article III. Rules of conduct governing the activities of the Palestinian Police are set out in Annex I, Article VIII.

2. Except for the Palestinian Police referred to in this Article and the Israeli military forces, no other armed forces shall be established or operate in the Gaza Strip or the Jericho Area.
3. Except for the arms, ammunition and equipment of the Palestinian Police described in Annex I, Article III, and those of the Israeli military forces, no organization or individual in the Gaza Strip and the Jericho Area shall manufacture, sell, acquire, possess, import or otherwise introduce into the Gaza Strip or the Jericho Area any firearms, ammunition, weapons, explosives, gunpowder or any related equipment, unless otherwise provided for in Annex I.

Article X

PASSAGES

Arrangements for coordination between Israel and the Palestinian Authority regarding the Gaza–Egypt and Jericho–Jordan passages, as well as any other agreed international crossings, are set out in Annex I, Article X.

Article XI

SAFE PASSAGE BETWEEN THE GAZA STRIP AND THE JERICHO AREA

Arrangements for safe passage of persons and transportation between the Gaza Strip and the Jericho Area are set out in Annex I, Article IX.

Article XII

RELATIONS BETWEEN ISRAEL AND THE PALESTINIAN AUTHORITY

1. Israel and the Palestinian Authority shall seek to foster mutual understanding and tolerance and shall accordingly abstain from incitement, including hostile propaganda, against each other and, without derogating from the principle of freedom of expression, shall take legal measures to prevent such incitement by any organizations, groups or individuals within their jurisdiction.
2. Without derogating from the other provisions of this Agreement, Israel and the Palestinian Authority shall cooperate in combatting criminal activity which may affect both sides, including offenses related to trafficking in illegal drugs and psychotropic substances, smuggling, and offenses against property, including offenses related to vehicles.

Article XIII

ECONOMIC RELATIONS

The economic relations between the two sides are set out in the Protocol on Economic Relations signed in Paris on April 29, 1994 and the Appendices thereto, certified copies of which are attached as Annex IV, and will be governed by the relevant provisions of this Agreement and its Annexes.

Article XIV

HUMAN RIGHTS AND THE RULE OF LAW

Israel and the Palestinian Authority shall exercise their powers and responsibilities pursuant to this Agreement with due regard to internationally-accepted norms and principles of human rights and the rule of law.

Article XV

THE JOINT ISRAELI–PALESTINIAN LIAISON COMMITTEE

1. The Liaison Committee established pursuant to Article X of the Declaration of Principles shall ensure the smooth implementation of this Agreement. It shall deal with issues requiring coordination, other issues of common interest and disputes.
2. The Liaison Committee shall be composed of an equal number of members from each Party. It may add other technicians and experts as necessary.
3. The Liaison Committee shall adopt its rules of procedure, including the frequency and place or places of its meetings.
4. The Liaison Committee shall reach its decisions by Agreement.

Article XVI

LIAISON AND COOPERATION WITH JORDAN AND EGYPT

1. Pursuant to Article XII of the Declaration of Principles, the two Parties shall invite the Governments of Jordan and Egypt to participate in establishing further liaison and cooperation arrangements between the Government of Israel and the Palestinian representatives on the one hand, and the Governments of Jordan and Egypt on the other hand, to promote cooperation between them. These arrangements shall include the constitution of a Continuing Committee.
2. The Continuing Committee shall decide by agreement on the modalities of admission of persons displaced from the West Bank and the Gaza Strip in 1967, together with necessary measures to prevent disruption and disorder.
3. The Continuing Committee shall deal with other matters of common concern.

Article XVII

SETTLEMENT OF DIFFERENCES AND DISPUTES

Any difference relating to the application of this Agreement shall be referred to the appropriate coordination and cooperation mechanism established under this

Agreement. The provisions of Article XV of the Declaration of Principles shall apply to any such difference which is not settled through the appropriate coordination and cooperation mechanism, namely:

1. Disputes arising out of the application or interpretation of this Agreement or any subsequent agreements pertaining to the interim period shall be settled by negotiations through the Liaison Committee.
2. Disputes which cannot be settled by negotiations may be settled by a mechanism of conciliation to be agreed between the Parties.
3. The Parties may agree to submit to arbitration disputes relating to the interim period, which cannot be settled through conciliation. To this end, upon the agreement of both Parties, the Parties will establish an Arbitration Committee.

Article XVIII

PREVENTION OF HOSTILE ACTS

Both sides shall take all measures necessary in order to prevent acts of terrorism, crime and hostilities directed against each other, against individuals falling under the other's authority and against their property, and shall take legal measures against offenders. In addition, the Palestinian side shall take all measures necessary to prevent such hostile acts directed against the Settlements, the infrastructure serving them and the Military Installation Area, and the Israeli side shall take all measures necessary to prevent such hostile acts emanating from the Settlements and directed against Palestinians.

Article XIX

MISSING PERSONS

The Palestinian Authority shall cooperate with Israel by providing all necessary assistance in the conduct of searches by Israel within the Gaza Strip and the Jericho Area for missing Israelis, as well as by providing information about missing Israelis. Israel shall cooperate with the Palestinian Authority in searching for, and providing necessary information about, missing Palestinians.

Article XX

CONFIDENCE BUILDING MEASURES

With a view to creating a positive and supportive public atmosphere to accompany the implementation of this Agreement, and to establish a solid basis of mutual trust and good faith, both Parties agree to carry out confidence building measures as detailed herewith:

1. Upon the signing of this Agreement, Israel will release, or turn over, to the Palestinian Authority within a period of 5 weeks, about 5,000 Palestinian detainees and prisoners, residents of the West Bank and the Gaza Strip. Those

released will be free to return to their homes anywhere in the West Bank or the Gaza Strip. Prisoners turned over to the Palestinian Authority shall be obliged to remain in the Gaza Strip or the Jericho Area for the remainder of their sentence.

2. After the signing of this Agreement, the two Parties shall continue to negotiate the release of additional Palestinian prisoners and detainees, building on agreed principles.
3. The implementation of the above measures will be subject to the fulfillment of the procedures determined by Israeli law for the release and transfer of detainees and prisoners.
4. With the assumption of Palestinian authority, the Palestinian side commits itself to solving the problem of those Palestinians who were in contact with the Israeli authorities. Until an agreed solution is found, the Palestinian side undertakes not to prosecute these Palestinians or to harm them in any way.
5. Palestinians from abroad whose entry into the Gaza Strip and the Jericho Area is approved pursuant to this Agreement, and to whom the provisions of this Article are applicable, will not be prosecuted for offenses committed prior to September 13, 1993.

Article XXI

TEMPORARY INTERNATIONAL PRESENCE

1. The Parties agree to a temporary international or foreign presence in the Gaza Strip and the Jericho Area (hereinafter "the TIP"), in accordance with the provisions of this Article.
2. The TIP shall consist of 400 qualified personnel, including observers, instructors and other experts, from 5 or 6 of the donor countries.
3. The two Parties shall request the donor countries to establish a special fund to provide finance for the TIP.
4. The TIP will function for a period of 6 months. The TIP may extend this period, or change the scope of its operation, with the agreement of the two Parties.
5. The TIP shall be stationed and operate within the following cities and villages: Gaza, Khan Yunis, Rafah, Deir El Ballah, Jabaliya, Absan, Beit Hanun and Jericho.
6. Israel and the Palestinian Authority shall agree on a special Protocol to implement this Article, with the goal of concluding negotiations with the donor countries contributing personnel within two months.

Article XXII

RIGHTS, LIABILITIES AND OBLIGATIONS

1.
    a. The transfer of all powers and responsibilities to the Palestinian Authority, as detailed in Annex II, includes all related rights, liabilities and obligations arising with regard to acts or omissions which occurred prior to the transfer.

Israel will cease to bear any financial responsibility regarding such acts or omissions and the Palestinian Authority will bear all financial responsibility for these and for its own functioning.

b. Any financial claim made in this regard against Israel will be referred to the Palestinian Authority.

c. Israel shall provide the Palestinian Authority with the information it has regarding pending and anticipated claims brought before any court or tribunal against Israel in this regard.

d. Where legal proceedings are brought in respect of such a claim, Israel will notify the Palestinian Authority and enable it to participate in defending the claim and raise any arguments on its behalf.

e. In the event that an award is made against Israel by any court or tribunal in respect of such a claim, the Palestinian Authority shall reimburse Israel the full amount of the award.

f. Without prejudice to the above, where a court or tribunal hearing such a claim finds that liability rests solely with an employee or agent who acted beyond the scope of the powers assigned to him or her, unlawfully or with willful malfeasance, the Palestinian Authority shall not bear financial responsibility.

2. The transfer of authority in itself shall not affect rights, liabilities and obligations of any person or legal entity, in existence at the date of signing of this Agreement.

Article XXIII

FINAL CLAUSES

1. This Agreement shall enter into force on the date of its signing.
2. The arrangements established by this Agreement shall remain in force until and to the extent superseded by the Interim Agreement referred to in the Declaration of Principles or any other agreement between the Parties.
3. The five-year interim period referred to in the Declaration of Principles commences on the date of the signing of this Agreement.
4. The Parties agree that, as long as this Agreement is in force, the security fence erected by Israel around the Gaza Strip shall remain in place and that the line demarcated by the fence, as shown on attached map No. 1, shall be authoritative only for the purpose of this Agreement.
5. Nothing in this Agreement shall prejudice or preempt the outcome of the negotiations on the interim agreement or on the permanent status to be conducted pursuant to the Declaration of Principles. Neither Party shall be deemed, by virtue of having entered into this Agreement, to have renounced or waived any of its existing rights, claims or positions.
6. The two Parties view the West Bank and the Gaza Strip as a single territorial unit, the integrity of which will be preserved during the interim period.
7. The Gaza Strip and the Jericho Area shall continue to be an integral part of the West Bank and the Gaza Strip, and their status shall not be changed for the

period of this Agreement. Nothing in this Agreement shall be considered to change this status.

8. The Preamble to this Agreement, and all Annexes, Appendices and maps attached hereto, shall constitute an integral part hereof.

Done in Cairo this fourth day of May, 1994.

For the Government of the State of Israel	For the PLO

Witnessed By:

The United States of America	The Russian Federation

The Arab Republic of Egypt

[Annexes omitted]

Appendix D

Agreement on Preparatory Transfer of Powers and Responsibilities [29 August 1994]

The Government of the State of Israel and the Palestine Liberation Organization (hereinafter "the PLO"), the representative of the Palestinian people;

PREAMBLE

WITHIN the framework of the Middle East peace process initiated at Madrid in October 1991;

REAFFIRMING their determination to live in peaceful coexistence, mutual dignity and security, while recognizing their mutual legitimate and political rights;

REAFFIRMING their desire to achieve a just, lasting and comprehensive peace settlement through the agreed political process;

REAFFIRMING their adherence to the mutual recognition and commitments expressed in the letters dated September 9, 1993, signed by and exchanged between the Prime Minister of Israel and the Chairman of the PLO;

REAFFIRMING their understanding that the interim self-government arrangements, including the preparatory arrangements to apply in the West Bank contained in this Agreement, are an integral part of the whole peace process and that the negotiations on the permanent status will lead to the implementation of Security Council Resolutions 242 and 338;

FOLLOWING the Agreement on the Gaza Strip and the Jericho Area as signed at Cairo on May 4, 1994 (hereinafter "the Gaza–Jericho Agreement");

DESIROUS of putting into effect the Declaration of Principles on Interim Self-Government Arrangements as signed at Washington, D.C. on September 13, 1993 (hereinafter "the Declaration of Principles"), and in particular Article VI regarding preparatory transfer of powers and responsibilities and the Agreed Minutes thereto;

HEREBY AGREE to the following arrangements regarding the preparatory transfer of powers and responsibilities in the West Bank:

Article I

DEFINITIONS

For the purpose of this Agreement, unless otherwise indicated in the attached Protocols:

a. the term "the Palestinian Authority" means the Palestinian Authority established in accordance with the Gaza–Jericho Agreement;

b. the term "Joint Liaison Committee" means the Joint Israeli–Palestinian Liaison Committee established pursuant to Article X of the Declaration of Principles;
c. the term "Interim Agreement" means the interim agreement referred to in Article VII of the Declaration of Principles; and
d. the term "Israelis" also includes Israeli statutory agencies and corporations registered in Israel.

Article II

PREPARATORY TRANSFER OF POWERS AND RESPONSIBILITIES

1. Israel shall transfer and the Palestinian Authority shall assume powers and responsibilities from the Israeli military government and its Civil Administration in the West Bank in the following spheres: education and culture, health, social welfare, tourism, direct taxation and Value Added Tax on local production (hereinafter "VAT"), as specified in this Agreement (hereinafter "the Spheres").
2. For the purposes of this Agreement, the Palestinian Authority shall constitute the authorized Palestinians referred to in Article VI of the Declaration of Principles.
3. The Parties will explore the possible expansion of the transfer of powers and responsibilities to additional spheres.

Article III

SCOPE OF THE TRANSFERRED POWERS AND RESPONSIBILITIES

1. The scope of the powers and responsibilities transferred in each Sphere, as well as specific arrangements regarding the exercise of such powers and responsibilities, are set out in the Protocols attached as Annexes I through VI.
2. In accordance with the Declaration of Principles, the jurisdiction of the Palestinian Authority with regard to the powers and responsibilities transferred by this Agreement will not apply to Jerusalem, settlements, military locations and, unless otherwise provided in this Agreement, Israelis.
3. The transfer of powers and responsibilities under this Agreement does not include powers and responsibilities in the sphere of foreign relations, except as indicated in Article VI(2)(b) of the Gaza–Jericho Agreement.

Article IV

MODALITIES OF TRANSFER

1. The transfer of powers and responsibilities in the sphere of education and culture pursuant to this Agreement will be implemented on August 29, 1994. The transfer of powers and responsibilities in the remaining Spheres will be implemented in accordance with Article XI below.

2. The transfer of powers and responsibilities shall be coordinated through the Civil Affairs Coordination and Cooperation Committee referred to in Article X below and shall be implemented in accordance with the arrangements set out in this Agreement in a smooth, peaceful and orderly manner.
3. Upon the signing of this Agreement, the Israeli side shall provide the Palestinian side with, or enable free access to, all information that is necessary for an effective and smooth transfer.
4. On the date of the transfer of powers and responsibilities, Israel shall also transfer all movable and immovable property which exclusively serves the offices of the Civil Administration in the Spheres, including premises, whether government-owned or rented, equipment, registers, files and computer programs. The treatment of property which serves the offices transferred to the Palestinian Authority as well as offices which are not so transferred will be as mutually agreed between the two sides, such as on the basis of sharing or exchange.
5. The coordination of the transfer of powers and responsibilities pursuant to this Article shall also include a joint review of the Civil Administration contracts the duration of which extends beyond the date of the transfer with a view to deciding which contracts will remain in force and which will be terminated.

Article V

ADMINISTRATION OF THE TRANSFERRED OFFICES

1. The Palestinian Authority shall be fully responsible for the proper functioning of the offices included in the Spheres and for the management of their personnel in all aspects, including employment and placement of employees, payment of their salaries and pensions and ensuring other employee rights.
2. The Palestinian Authority will continue to employ Palestinian Civil Administration employees currently employed in the offices included in each Sphere and shall maintain their rights.
3. The main office of each of the Spheres will be situated in the Jericho Area or in the Gaza Strip. The Palestinian Authority will operate the existing subordinate offices in the West Bank. The two sides may agree on the establishment of additional subordinate offices in the West Bank, if necessary, in such locations as mutually agreed.
4. The Palestinian Authority has the right to coordinate its activities in each of the Spheres with other Spheres in which it is empowered.

Article VI

RELATIONS BETWEEN THE TWO SIDES

1. With regard to each Sphere, the Palestinian Authority shall coordinate with the Civil Administration on issues relating to other spheres in which the Palestinian Authority is not empowered.
2. The military government and its Civil Administration shall assist and support the Palestinian Authority in promoting the effective exercise of its powers and

responsibilities. In addition, the military government and its Civil Administration shall, in exercising their own powers and responsibilities, take into account the interests of the Palestinian Authority and do their utmost to remove obstacles to the effective exercise of powers and responsibilities by the Palestinian Authority.

3. The Palestinian Authority shall prevent any activities with a military orientation within each of the Spheres and will do its utmost to maintain decorum and discipline and to avoid disruption in the institutions under its responsibility.
4. The Palestinian Authority will notify the military government and its Civil Administration and will coordinate with them regarding any planned public large-scale events and mass gatherings within the Spheres.
5. Nothing in this Agreement shall affect the continued authority of the military government and its Civil Administration to exercise their powers and responsibilities with regard to security and public order, as well as with regard to other spheres not transferred.

Article VII

LEGISLATIVE POWERS OF THE PALESTINIAN AUTHORITY

1. The Palestinian Authority may promulgate secondary legislation regarding the powers and responsibilities transferred to it. Such legislation includes amendments and changes to the existing laws, regulations and military orders specified in Appendix A to each Annex.
2. Legislation promulgated by the Palestinian Authority shall be consistent with the provisions of this Agreement.
3. Legislation promulgated by the Palestinian Authority shall be communicated to Israel which may, within a period of thirty (30) days, notify the Palestinian Authority that it opposes such legislation for any of the following reasons:
   a. it exceeds the powers and responsibilities transferred to the Palestinian Authority;
   b. it is inconsistent with the provisions of this Agreement; or
   c. it otherwise affects legislation or powers and responsibilities which were not transferred to the Palestinian Authority.
4. Where Israel opposes proposed legislation, it shall specify the reason for the opposition.
5. If Israel has no reservations concerning the proposed legislation, it shall accordingly notify the Palestinian Authority at the earliest opportunity. If at the end of the thirty-day period Israel has not communicated any opposition concerning the proposed legislation, such legislation shall enter into force.
6. The Palestinian Authority may, in the event of opposition to the proposed draft legislation, submit a new draft or request a review by the Legislation Subcommittee established under the Gaza–Jericho Agreement.
7. The Legislation Subcommittee shall attempt to reach a decision on the merits of the matter within thirty days. If the Legislation Subcommittee is unable to reach a decision within this period, the Palestinian Authority shall be entitled to refer the matter to the Joint Liaison Committee. The Joint Liaison Committee

shall consider the matter immediately and will attempt to settle it within thirty days.

8. Where, upon communicating to Israel proposed legislation consisting of detailed technical regulations, the Palestinian Authority states that such regulations fulfill the requirements of paragraph 3 above and requests a speedy review, Israel shall immediately respond to such a request.
9. Legislation regarding the West Bank shall be published as a separate part of any publication of legislation regarding the Gaza Strip and the Jericho Area issued by the Palestinian Authority.

Article VIII

LAW ENFORCEMENT

1. The Palestinian Authority may bring disciplinary proceedings concerning persons it employs in the West Bank before disciplinary tribunals operating in the Gaza Strip or the Jericho Area.
2. The Palestinian Authority may, within each of the Spheres, authorize employees to act as civilian inspectors to monitor compliance with laws and regulations in that Sphere, within the powers and responsibilities transferred to the Palestinian Authority. Such inspectors shall operate in each Sphere separately and shall not be organized into a central unit. These inspectors shall not wear uniforms or carry arms, and shall not in any other way have the nature of a police force. They shall be required to carry the identification documentation referred to in paragraph 3 below. The number of employees to be authorized as civilian inspectors shall be agreed upon by both sides. The names of these employees shall be notified to Israel and, where these employees enjoy privileges pursuant to subparagraph 3 below, shall be agreed upon by both sides.
3. The Palestinian Authority shall issue the civilian inspectors in the West Bank with identification documentation specifying the office in which they are employed. Such documentation shall be used for identification and will not grant privileges, except those agreed in the Civil Affairs Coordination and Cooperation Committee referred to in Article X below, or immunities. This committee shall determine the format of the identification documentation.
4. Except as specifically provided in this Agreement, all powers and responsibilities regarding law enforcement, including investigation, judicial proceedings and imprisonment, will continue to be under the responsibility of the existing authorities in the West Bank.

Article IX

RIGHTS, LIABILITIES AND OBLIGATIONS

1.
   a. The transfer of powers and responsibilities to the Palestinian Authority under this Agreement will include all related rights, liabilities and obligations arising with regard to acts or omissions which occurred prior to the transfer. Israel and the Civil Administration will cease to bear any financial responsibility

regarding such acts or omissions and the Palestinian Authority will bear all financial responsibility for these and for its own functioning.

b. Any financial claim made in this regard against Israel or the Civil Administration will be referred to the Palestinian Authority.

c. Israel shall provide the Palestinian Authority with the information it has regarding pending and anticipated claims brought before any court or tribunal against Israel or the Civil Administration in this regard.

d. Where legal proceedings are brought in respect of such a claim, Israel will notify the Palestinian Authority and enable it to participate in defending the claim and raise any arguments on its behalf.

e. In the event that an award is made against Israel or the Civil Administration by any court or tribunal in respect of such a claim, the Palestinian Authority shall, once the award has been paid by Israel, reimburse Israel the full amount of the award.

f. Without prejudice to the above, where a court or tribunal hearing such a claim finds that liability rests solely with an employee or agent who acted beyond the scope of the powers assigned to him or her, unlawfully or with willful malfeasance, the Palestinian Authority shall not bear financial responsibility.

g. Notwithstanding subparagraphs 1.d through 1.f above, Israel may, pursuant to agreement within the Legal Subcommittee of the CAC established under the Gaza–Jericho Agreement, request an Israeli court or tribunal to dismiss a claim brought before it and, with regard to a pending claim, dismiss the claim and transfer the proceedings to a local court or tribunal.

h. Where a claim has been so transferred or where a new claim has been brought in a local court or tribunal subsequent to the dismissal of the claim pursuant to subparagraph 1.g above, the Palestinian Authority shall defend it and, in accordance with subparagraph 1.a above, in the event that an award is made for the plaintiff, shall pay the amount of the award.

i. The Legal Subcommittee referred to in subparagraph 1.g above shall agree on arrangements for the transfer of proceedings from Israeli courts or tribunals pursuant to subparagraph 1.g above and, where necessary, for the provision of legal assistance by Israel to the Palestinian Authority in defending such claims.

2. In accordance with paragraph 1 above:

a. The Palestinian Authority may bring legal proceedings in respect of any acts or omissions relating to powers and responsibilities transferred under this Agreement which occurred prior to the date of the transfer. Israel shall provide the Palestinian Authority with the legal assistance necessary to bring such proceedings.

b. The Palestinian Authority may collect any taxes due under Annexes V and VI on the date of the transfer of powers and responsibilities in respect of these taxes, and shall assume responsibility for the payment of any rebates or refunds.

3. Subject to the provisions of this Article, the transfer of powers and responsibilities in itself shall not affect rights, liabilities and obligations of any person or legal entity, in existence at the date of signing of this Agreement.

Article X

LIAISON AND COORDINATION

1. The Joint Civil Affairs Coordination and Cooperation Committee established in accordance with the Gaza–Jericho Agreement, (hereinafter "the CAC"), will deal with all issues of mutual concern regarding this Agreement.
2. The operation of the CAC shall not impede daily contacts between representatives of the Civil Administration and the Palestinian Authority in all matters of mutual concern.

Article XI

BUDGETARY ISSUES

1. The military government and its Civil Administration shall provide the Palestinian Authority with full information concerning the budget of each Sphere.
2. The Palestinian Authority shall immediately employ personnel who will promptly begin the process of becoming acquainted with the current budget issues. On the date of the transfer of powers and responsibilities in each of the Spheres, these personnel will assume responsibility for all accounts, assets and records on behalf of the Palestinian Authority.
3. Israel shall continue to provide the services of Israeli experts currently employed in the fields of income tax and VAT to ensure a smooth transition and efficient establishment of the taxation system of the Palestinian Authority. The terms of their employment shall be agreed upon by the two sides.
4. The Palestinian Authority will do its utmost to establish its revenue collection system immediately with the intent of collecting direct taxes and VAT.
5. The two sides will jointly approach the donor countries during the upcoming meetings of the Consultative Group and of the Ad Hoc Liaison Committee, scheduled for September 8 through 10, 1994 in Paris, with a request to finance the shortfall that may be created in the collection of the direct taxes and the VAT during the initial period while the Palestinian Authority establishes its own revenue collection system.
6. The two sides will meet no later than three days after the conclusion of these meetings in order to decide on the date of transfer of powers and responsibilities in the remaining Spheres, based, among other things, on the response of the donor countries to the joint request.
7. The CAC will provide the donor countries, when necessary, with information to help adjust the allocation of contributions as a result of variations in tax collection.
8. The Palestinian Authority shall also assume full responsibility for any additional expenditures beyond the agreed budget which is attached as Schedule 1, as well as for any shortfall in tax collection that is not actually covered by the donor countries.

9. If actual revenues from the Spheres, including the donor contributions, exceed the budgeted revenues, the excess shall be applied to development of the Spheres.
10. The inclusion of the sphere of VAT in the spheres to be transferred to the Palestinian Authority shall constitute the adjustment referred to in paragraph (3) of the Agreed Minute to Article VI(2) of the Declaration of Principles, and no further adjustment shall be required.

Article XII

MUTUAL CONTRIBUTION TO PEACE AND RECONCILIATION

With regard to each of the Spheres, Israel and the Palestinian Authority will ensure that their respective systems contribute to the peace between the Israeli and Palestinian peoples and to peace in the entire region, and will refrain from the introduction of any motifs that could adversely affect the process of reconciliation.

Article XIII

FINAL CLAUSES

1. This Agreement shall enter into force on the date of its signing.
2. The arrangements established by this Agreement are preparatory measures and shall remain in force until and to the extent superseded by the Interim Agreement or by any other agreement between the Parties.
3. Nothing in this Agreement shall prejudice or preempt the outcome of the negotiations on the Interim Agreement or on the permanent status to be conducted pursuant to the Declaration of Principles. Neither Party shall be deemed, by virtue of having entered into this Agreement, to have renounced or waived any of its existing rights, claims or positions.
4. The two Parties view the West Bank and the Gaza Strip as a single territorial unit, the integrity of which will be preserved during the interim period.
5. The Gaza Strip and the Jericho Area shall continue to be an integral part of the West Bank and the Gaza Strip. The status of the West Bank shall not be changed for the period of this Agreement. Nothing in this Agreement shall be considered to change this status.
6. The Preamble to this Agreement and the Annexes, Appendices and Schedules attached hereto, shall constitute an integral part hereof.

Done at Erez this twenty-ninth day of August 1994.

For the Government of the State of Israel	For the PLO

List of Annexes:

Schedule 1—Six-month Budget for the Spheres

Annex I—Protocol Concerning Preparatory Transfer of Powers and Responsibilities in the Sphere of Education and Culture

Annex II—Protocol Concerning Preparatory Transfer of Powers and Responsibilities in the Sphere of Health

Annex III—Protocol Concerning Preparatory Transfer of Powers and Responsibilities in the Sphere of Social Welfare

Annex IV—Protocol Concerning Preparatory Transfer of Powers and Responsibilities in the Sphere of Tourism

Annex V—Protocol Concerning Preparatory Transfer of Powers and Responsibilities in the Sphere of Direct Taxation

Annex VI—Protocol Concerning Preparatory Transfer of Powers and Responsibilities in the Sphere of VAT on Local Production

[Annexes omitted]

Appendix E

Israeli–Palestinian Interim Agreement on the West Bank and the Gaza Strip [28 September 1995]

The Government of the State of Israel and the Palestine Liberation Organization (hereinafter "the PLO"), the representative of the Palestinian people;

PREAMBLE

WITHIN the framework of the Middle East peace process initiated at Madrid in October 1991;

REAFFIRMING their determination to put an end to decades of confrontation and to live in peaceful coexistence, mutual dignity and security, while recognizing their mutual legitimate and political rights;

REAFFIRMING their desire to achieve a just, lasting and comprehensive peace settlement and historic reconciliation through the agreed political process;

RECOGNIZING that the peace process and the new era that it has created, as well as the new relationship established between the two Parties as described above, are irreversible, and the determination of the two Parties to maintain, sustain and continue the peace process;

RECOGNIZING that the aim of the Israeli–Palestinian negotiations within the current Middle East peace process is, among other things, to establish a Palestinian Interim Self-Government Authority, i.e. the elected Council (hereinafter "the Council" or "the Palestinian Council"), and the elected Ra'ees of the Executive Authority, for the Palestinian people in the West Bank and the Gaza Strip, for a transitional period not exceeding five years from the date of signing the Agreement on the Gaza Strip and the Jericho Area (hereinafter "the Gaza–Jericho Agreement") on May 4, 1994, leading to a permanent settlement based on Security Council Resolutions 242 and 338;

REAFFIRMING their understanding that the interim self-government arrangements contained in this Agreement are an integral part of the whole peace process, that the negotiations on the permanent status, that will start as soon as possible but not later than May 4, 1996, will lead to the implementation of Security Council Resolutions 242 and 338, and that the Interim Agreement shall settle all the issues of the interim period and that no such issues will be deferred to the agenda of the permanent status negotiations;

REAFFIRMING their adherence to the mutual recognition and commitments expressed in the letters dated September 9, 1993, signed by and exchanged between the Prime Minister of Israel and the Chairman of the PLO;

DESIROUS of putting into effect the Declaration of Principles on Interim Self-Government Arrangements signed at Washington, D.C. on September 13, 1993, and the Agreed Minutes thereto (hereinafter "the DOP") and in particular Article

III and Annex I concerning the holding of direct, free and general political elections for the Council and the Ra'ees of the Executive Authority in order that the Palestinian people in the West Bank, Jerusalem and the Gaza Strip may democratically elect accountable representatives;

RECOGNIZING that these elections will constitute a significant interim preparatory step toward the realization of the legitimate rights of the Palestinian people and their just requirements and will provide a democratic basis for the establishment of Palestinian institutions;

REAFFIRMING their mutual commitment to act, in accordance with this Agreement, immediately, efficiently and effectively against acts or threats of terrorism, violence or incitement, whether committed by Palestinians or Israelis;

FOLLOWING the Gaza–Jericho Agreement; the Agreement on Preparatory Transfer of Powers and Responsibilities signed at Erez on August 29, 1994 (hereinafter "the Preparatory Transfer Agreement"); and the Protocol on Further Transfer of Powers and Responsibilities signed at Cairo on August 27, 1995 (hereinafter "the Further Transfer Protocol"); which three agreements will be superseded by this Agreement;

HEREBY AGREE as follows:

Chapter I—The Council

Article I

TRANSFER OF AUTHORITY

1. Israel shall transfer powers and responsibilities as specified in this Agreement from the Israeli military government and its Civil Administration to the Council in accordance with this Agreement. Israel shall continue to exercise powers and responsibilities not so transferred.
2. Pending the inauguration of the Council, the powers and responsibilities transferred to the Council shall be exercised by the Palestinian Authority established in accordance with the Gaza–Jericho Agreement, which shall also have all the rights, liabilities and obligations to be assumed by the Council in this regard. Accordingly, the term "Council" throughout this Agreement shall, pending the inauguration of the Council, be construed as meaning the Palestinian Authority.
3. The transfer of powers and responsibilities to the police force established by the Palestinian Council in accordance with Article XIV below (hereinafter "the Palestinian Police") shall be accomplished in a phased manner, as detailed in this Agreement and in the Protocol concerning Redeployment and Security Arrangements attached as Annex I to this Agreement (hereinafter "Annex I").
4. As regards the transfer and assumption of authority in civil spheres, powers and responsibilities shall be transferred and assumed as set out in the Protocol Concerning Civil Affairs attached as Annex III to this Agreement (hereinafter "Annex III").

5. After the inauguration of the Council, the Civil Administration in the West Bank will be dissolved, and the Israeli military government shall be withdrawn. The withdrawal of the military government shall not prevent it from exercising the powers and responsibilities not transferred to the Council.
6. A Joint Civil Affairs Coordination and Cooperation Committee (hereinafter "the CAC"), Joint Regional Civil Affairs Subcommittees, one for the Gaza Strip and the other for the West Bank, and District Civil Liaison Offices in the West Bank shall be established in order to provide for coordination and cooperation in civil affairs between the Council and Israel, as detailed in Annex III.
7. The offices of the Council, and the offices of its Ra'ees and its Executive Authority and other committees, shall be located in areas under Palestinian territorial jurisdiction in the West Bank and the Gaza Strip.

Article II

ELECTIONS

1. In order that the Palestinian people of the West Bank and the Gaza Strip may govern themselves according to democratic principles, direct, free and general political elections will be held for the Council and the Ra'ees of the Executive Authority of the Council in accordance with the provisions set out in the Protocol concerning Elections attached as Annex II to this Agreement (hereinafter "Annex II").
2. These elections will constitute a significant interim preparatory step towards the realization of the legitimate rights of the Palestinian people and their just requirements and will provide a democratic basis for the establishment of Palestinian institutions.
3. Palestinians of Jerusalem who live there may participate in the election process in accordance with the provisions contained in this Article and in Article VI of Annex II (Election Arrangements concerning Jerusalem).
4. The elections shall be called by the Chairman of the Palestinian Authority immediately following the signing of this Agreement to take place at the earliest practicable date following the redeployment of Israeli forces in accordance with Annex I, and consistent with the requirements of the election timetable as provided in Annex II, the Election Law and the Election Regulations, as defined in Article I of Annex II.

Article III

STRUCTURE OF THE PALESTINIAN COUNCIL

1. The Palestinian Council and the Ra'ees of the Executive Authority of the Council constitute the Palestinian Interim Self-Government Authority, which will be elected by the Palestinian people of the West Bank, Jerusalem and the Gaza Strip for the transitional period agreed in Article I of the DOP.
2. The Council shall possess both legislative power and executive power, in

accordance with Articles VII and IX of the DOP. The Council shall carry out and be responsible for all the legislative and executive powers and responsibilities transferred to it under this Agreement. The exercise of legislative powers shall be in accordance with Article XVIII of this Agreement (Legislative Powers of the Council).

3. The Council and the Ra'ees of the Executive Authority of the Council shall be directly and simultaneously elected by the Palestinian people of the West Bank, Jerusalem and the Gaza Strip, in accordance with the provisions of this Agreement and the Election Law and Regulations, which shall not be contrary to the provisions of this Agreement.
4. The Council and the Ra'ees of the Executive Authority of the Council shall be elected for a transitional period not exceeding five years from the signing of the Gaza–Jericho Agreement on May 4, 1994.
5. Immediately upon its inauguration, the Council will elect from among its members a Speaker. The Speaker will preside over the meetings of the Council, administer the Council and its committees, decide on the agenda of each meeting, and lay before the Council proposals for voting and declare their results.
6. The jurisdiction of the Council shall be as determined in Article XVII of this Agreement (Jurisdiction).
7. The organization, structure and functioning of the Council shall be in accordance with this Agreement and the Basic Law for the Palestinian Interim Self-Government Authority, which Law shall be adopted by the Council. The Basic Law and any regulations made under it shall not be contrary to the provisions of this Agreement.
8. The Council shall be responsible under its executive powers for the offices, services and departments transferred to it and may establish, within its jurisdiction, ministries and subordinate bodies, as necessary for the fulfillment of its responsibilities.
9. The Speaker will present for the Council's approval proposed internal procedures that will regulate, among other things, the decision-making processes of the Council.

Article IV

SIZE OF THE COUNCIL

The Palestinian Council shall be composed of 82 representatives and the Ra'ees of the Executive Authority, who will be directly and simultaneously elected by the Palestinian people of the West Bank, Jerusalem and the Gaza Strip.

Article V

THE EXECUTIVE AUTHORITY OF THE COUNCIL

1. The Council will have a committee that will exercise the executive authority of the Council, formed in accordance with paragraph 4 below (hereinafter "the Executive Authority").

2. The Executive Authority shall be bestowed with the executive authority of the Council and will exercise it on behalf of the Council. It shall determine its own internal procedures and decision-making processes.
3. The Council will publish the names of the members of the Executive Authority immediately upon their initial appointment and subsequent to any changes.
4. a. The Ra'ees of the Executive Authority shall be an ex officio member of the Executive Authority.
   b. All of the other members of the Executive Authority, except as provided in subparagraph c. below, shall be members of the Council, chosen and proposed to the Council by the Ra'ees of the Executive Authority and approved by the Council.
   c. The Ra'ees of the Executive Authority shall have the right to appoint some persons, in number not exceeding twenty percent of the total membership of the Executive Authority, who are not members of the Council, to exercise executive authority and participate in government tasks. Such appointed members may not vote in meetings of the Council.
   d. Non-elected members of the Executive Authority must have a valid address in an area under the jurisdiction of the Council.

Article VI

OTHER COMMITTEES OF THE COUNCIL

1. The Council may form small committees to simplify the proceedings of the Council and to assist in controlling the activity of its Executive Authority.
2. Each committee shall establish its own decision-making processes within the general framework of the organization and structure of the Council.

Article VII

OPEN GOVERNMENT

1. All meetings of the Council and of its committees, other than the Executive Authority, shall be open to the public, except upon a resolution of the Council or the relevant committee on the grounds of security, or commercial or personal confidentiality.
2. Participation in the deliberations of the Council, its committees and the Executive Authority shall be limited to their respective members only. Experts may be invited to such meetings to address specific issues on an ad hoc basis.

Article VIII

JUDICIAL REVIEW

Any person or organization affected by any act or decision of the Ra'ees of the Executive Authority of the Council or of any member of the Executive Authority, who believes that such act or decision exceeds the authority of the Ra'ees or of such member, or is otherwise incorrect in law or procedure, may apply to the relevant Palestinian Court of Justice for a review of such activity or decision.

Article IX

POWERS AND RESPONSIBILITIES OF THE COUNCIL

1. Subject to the provisions of this Agreement, the Council will, within its jurisdiction, have legislative powers as set out in Article XVIII of this Agreement, as well as executive powers.
2. The executive power of the Palestinian Council shall extend to all matters within its jurisdiction under this Agreement or any future agreement that may be reached between the two Parties during the interim period. It shall include the power to formulate and conduct Palestinian policies and to supervise their implementation, to issue any rule or regulation under powers given in approved legislation and administrative decisions necessary for the realization of Palestinian self-government, the power to employ staff, sue and be sued and conclude contracts, and the power to keep and administer registers and records of the population, and issue certificates, licenses and documents.
3. The Palestinian Council's executive decisions and acts shall be consistent with the provisions of this Agreement.
4. The Palestinian Council may adopt all necessary measures in order to enforce the law and any of its decisions, and bring proceedings before the Palestinian courts and tribunals.
5. a. In accordance with the DOP, the Council will not have powers and responsibilities in the sphere of foreign relations, which sphere includes the establishment abroad of embassies, consulates or other types of foreign missions and posts or permitting their establishment in the West Bank or the Gaza Strip, the appointment of or admission of diplomatic and consular staff, and the exercise of diplomatic functions.
   b. Notwithstanding the provisions of this paragraph, the PLO may conduct negotiations and sign agreements with states or international organizations for the benefit of the Council in the following cases only:
      (1) economic agreements, as specifically provided in Annex V of this Agreement;
      (2) agreements with donor countries for the purpose of implementing arrangements for the provision of assistance to the Council;
      (3) agreements for the purpose of implementing the regional development plans detailed in Annex IV of the DOP or in agreements entered into in the framework of the multilateral negotiations; and
      (4) cultural, scientific and educational agreements.
   c. Dealings between the Council and representatives of foreign states and international organizations, as well as the establishment in the West Bank and the Gaza Strip of representative offices other than those described in subparagraph 5.a above, for the purpose of implementing the agreements referred to in subparagraph 5.b above, shall not be considered foreign relations.

6. Subject to the provisions of this Agreement, the Council shall, within its jurisdiction, have an independent judicial system composed of independent Palestinian courts and tribunals.

Chapter 2—Redeployment and Security Arrangements

Article X

REDEPLOYMENT OF ISRAELI MILITARY FORCES

1. The first phase of the Israeli military forces redeployment will cover populated areas in the West Bank—cities, towns, villages, refugee camps and hamlets—as set out in Annex I, and will be completed prior to the eve of the Palestinian elections, i e., 22 days before the day of the elections.
2. Further redeployments of Israeli military forces to specified military locations will commence after the inauguration of the Council and will be gradually implemented commensurate with the assumption of responsibility for public order and internal security by the Palestinian Police, to be completed within 18 months from the date of the inauguration of the Council as detailed in Articles XI (Land) and XIII (Security), below and in Annex I.
3. The Palestinian Police shall be deployed and shall assume responsibility for public order and internal security for Palestinians in a phased manner in accordance with XIII (Security) below and Annex I.
4. Israel shall continue to carry the responsibility for external security, as well as the responsibility for overall security of Israelis for the purpose of safeguarding their internal security and public order.
5. For the purpose of this Agreement, "Israeli military forces" includes Israel Police and other Israeli security forces.

Article XI

LAND

1. The two sides view the West Bank and the Gaza Strip as a single territorial unit, the integrity and status of which will be preserved during the interim period.
2. The two sides agree that West Bank and Gaza Strip territory, except for issues that will be negotiated in the permanent status negotiations, will come under the jurisdiction of the Palestinian Council in a phased manner, to be completed within 18 months from the date of the inauguration of the Council, as specified below:
   a. Land in populated areas (Areas A and B), including government and Al Waqf land, will come under the jurisdiction of the Council during the first phase of redeployment.
   b. All civil powers and responsibilities, including planning and zoning, in Areas A and B, set out in Annex III, will be transferred to and assumed by the Council during the first phase of redeployment.

c. In Area C, during the first phase of redeployment Israel will transfer to the Council civil powers and responsibilities not relating to territory, as set out in Annex III.
d. The further redeployments of Israeli military forces to specified military locations will be gradually implemented in accordance with the DOP in three phases, each to take place after an interval of six months, after the inauguration of the Council, to be completed within 18 months from the date of the inauguration of the Council.
e. During the further redeployment phases to be completed within 18 months from the date of the inauguration of the Council, powers and responsibilities relating to territory will be transferred gradually to Palestinian jurisdiction that will cover West Bank and Gaza Strip territory, except for the issues that will be negotiated in the permanent status negotiations.
f. The specified military locations referred to in Article X, paragraph 2 above will be determined in the further redeployment phases, within the specified time-frame ending not later than 18 months from the date of the inauguration of the Council, and will be negotiated in the permanent status negotiations.

3. For the purpose of this Agreement and until the completion of the first phase of the further redeployments:
   a. "Area A" means the populated areas delineated by a red line and shaded in brown on attached map No. 1;
   b. "Area B" means the populated areas delineated by a red line and shaded in yellow on attached map No. 1, and the built-up area of the hamlets listed in Appendix 6 to Annex I; and
   c. "Area C" means areas of the West Bank outside Areas A and B, which, except for the issues that will be negotiated in the permanent status negotiations, will be gradually transferred to Palestinian jurisdiction in accordance with this Agreement.

Article XII

ARRANGEMENTS FOR SECURITY AND PUBLIC ORDER

1. In order to guarantee public order and internal security for the Palestinians of the West Bank and the Gaza Strip, the Council shall establish a strong police force as set out in Article XIV below. Israel shall continue to carry the responsibility for defense against external threats, including the responsibility for protecting the Egyptian and Jordanian borders, and for defense against external threats from the sea and from the air, as well as the responsibility for overall security of Israelis and Settlements, for the purpose of safeguarding their internal security and public order, and will have all the powers to take the steps necessary to meet this responsibility.
2. Agreed security arrangements and coordination mechanisms are specified in Annex I.
3. A Joint Coordination and Cooperation Committee for Mutual Security Purposes (hereinafter "the JSC"), as well as Joint Regional Security Committees

(hereinafter "RSCs") and Joint District Coordination Offices (hereinafter "DCOs"), are hereby established as provided for in Annex I.

4. The security arrangements provided for in this Agreement and in Annex I may be reviewed at the request of either Party and may be amended by mutual agreement of the Parties. Specific review arrangements are included in Annex I.
5. For the purpose of this Agreement, "the Settlements" means, in the West Bank the settlements in Area C; and in the Gaza Strip—the Gush Katif and Erez settlement areas, as well as the other settlements in the Gaza Strip, as shown on attached map No. 2.

Article XIII

SECURITY

1. The Council will, upon completion of the redeployment of Israeli military forces in each district, as set out in Appendix 1 to Annex I, assume the powers and responsibilities for internal security and public order in Area A in that district.
2. a. There will be a complete redeployment of Israeli military forces from Area B. Israel will transfer to the Council and the Council will assume responsibility for public order for Palestinians. Israel shall have the overriding responsibility for security for the purpose of protecting Israelis and confronting the threat of terrorism.
   b. In Area B the Palestinian Police shall assume the responsibility for public order for Palestinians and shall be deployed in order to accommodate the Palestinian needs and requirements in the following manner:
      (1) The Palestinian Police shall establish 25 police stations and posts in towns, villages, and other places listed in Appendix 2 to Annex I and as delineated on map No. 3. The West Bank RSC may agree on the establishment of additional police stations and posts, if required.
      (2) The Palestinian Police shall be responsible for handling public order incidents in which only Palestinians are involved.
      (3) The Palestinian Police shall operate freely in populated places where police stations and posts are located, as set out in paragraph b(1) above.
      (4) While the movement of uniformed Palestinian policemen in Area B outside places where there is a Palestinian police station or post will be carried out after coordination and confirmation through the relevant DCO, three months after the completion of redeployment from Area B, the DCOs may decide that movement of Palestinian policemen from the police stations in Area B to Palestinian towns and villages in Area B on roads that are used only by Palestinian traffic will take place after notifying the DCO.
      (5) The coordination of such planned movement prior to confirmation through the relevant DCO shall include a scheduled plan, including the number of policemen, as well as the type and number of weapons and vehicles intended to take part. It shall also include details of arrangements for ensuring continued coordination through appropriate

communication links, the exact schedule of movement to the area of the planned operation, including the destination and routes thereto, its proposed duration and the schedule for returning to the police station or post. The Israeli side of the DCO will provide the Palestinian side with its response, following a request for movement of policemen in accordance with this paragraph, in normal or routine cases within one day and in emergency cases no later than 2 hours.

(6) The Palestinian Police and the Israeli military forces will conduct joint security activities on the main roads as set out in Annex I.

(7) The Palestinian Police will notify the West Bank RSC of the names of the policemen, number plates of police vehicles and serial numbers of weapons, with respect to each police station and post in Area B.

(8) Further redeployments from Area C and transfer of internal security responsibility to the Palestinian Police in Areas B and C will be carried out in three phases, each to take place after an interval of six months, to be completed 18 months after the inauguration of the Council, except for the issues of permanent status negotiations and of Israel's overall responsibility for Israelis and borders.

(9) The procedures detailed in this paragraph will be reviewed within six months of the completion of the first phase of redeployment.

Article XIV

THE PALESTINIAN POLICE

1. The Council shall establish a strong police force. The duties, functions, structure, deployment and composition of the Palestinian Police, together with provisions regarding its equipment and operation, as well as rules of conduct, are set out in Annex I.
2. The Palestinian police force established under the Gaza–Jericho Agreement will be fully integrated into the Palestinian Police and will be subject to the provisions of this Agreement.
3. Except for the Palestinian Police and the Israeli military forces, no other armed forces shall be established or operate in the West Bank and the Gaza Strip.
4. Except for the arms, ammunition and equipment of the Palestinian Police described in Annex I, and those of the Israeli military forces, no organization, group or individual in the West Bank and the Gaza Strip shall manufacture, sell, acquire, possess, import or otherwise introduce into the West Bank or the Gaza Strip any firearms, ammunition, weapons, explosives, gunpowder or any related equipment, unless otherwise provided for in Annex I.

Article XV

PREVENTION OF HOSTILE ACTS

1. Both sides shall take all measures necessary in order to prevent acts of terrorism, crime and hostilities directed against each other, against individuals

falling under the other's authority and against their property and shall take legal measures against offenders.

2. Specific provisions for the implementation of this Article are set out in Annex I.

Article XVI

CONFIDENCE BUILDING MEASURES

With a view to fostering a positive and supportive public atmosphere to accompany the implementation of this Agreement, to establish a solid basis of mutual trust and good faith, and in order to facilitate the anticipated cooperation and new relations between the two peoples, both Parties agree to carry out confidence building measures as detailed herewith:

1. Israel will release or turn over to the Palestinian side, Palestinian detainees and prisoners, residents of the West Bank and the Gaza Strip. The first stage of release of these prisoners and detainees will take place on the signing of this Agreement and the second stage will take place prior to the date of the elections. There will be a third stage of release of detainees and prisoners. Detainees and prisoners will be released from among categories detailed in Annex VII (Release of Palestinian Prisoners and Detainees). Those released will be free to return to their homes in the West Bank and the Gaza Strip.
2. Palestinians who have maintained contact with the Israeli authorities will not be subjected to acts of harassment, violence, retribution or prosecution. Appropriate ongoing measures will be taken, in coordination with Israel, in order to ensure their protection.
3. Palestinians from abroad whose entry into the West Bank and the Gaza Strip is approved pursuant to this Agreement, and to whom the provisions of this Article are applicable, will not be prosecuted for offenses committed prior to September 13, 1993.

Chapter 3—Legal Affairs

Article XVII

JURISDICTION

1. In accordance with the DOP, the jurisdiction of the Council will cover West Bank and Gaza Strip territory as a single territorial unit, except for:
   a. issues that will be negotiated in the permanent status negotiations: Jerusalem, settlements, specified military locations, Palestinian refugees, borders, foreign relations and Israelis; and
   b. powers and responsibilities not transferred to the Council.
2. Accordingly, the authority of the Council encompasses all matters that fall within its territorial, functional and personal jurisdiction, as follows:

a. The territorial jurisdiction of the Council shall encompass Gaza Strip territory, except for the Settlements and the Military Installation Area shown on map No. 2, and West Bank territory, except for Area C which, except for the issues that will be negotiated in the permanent status negotiations, will be gradually transferred to Palestinian jurisdiction in three phases, each to take place after an interval of six months, to be completed 18 months after the inauguration of the Council. At this time, the jurisdiction of the Council will cover West Bank and Gaza Strip territory, except for the issues that will be negotiated in the permanent status negotiations. Territorial jurisdiction includes land, subsoil and territorial waters, in accordance with the provisions of this Agreement.

b. The functional jurisdiction of the Council extends to all powers and responsibilities transferred to the Council, as specified in this Agreement or in any future agreements that may be reached between the Parties during the interim period.

c. The territorial and functional jurisdiction of the Council will apply to all persons, except for Israelis, unless otherwise provided in this Agreement.

d. Notwithstanding subparagraph a. above, the Council shall have functional jurisdiction in Area C, as detailed in Article IV of Annex III.

3. The Council has, within its authority, legislative, executive and judicial powers and responsibilities, as provided for in this Agreement.

4. a. Israel, through its military government, has the authority over areas that are not under the territorial jurisdiction of the Council, powers and responsibilities not transferred to the Council and Israelis.

   b. To this end, the Israeli military government shall retain the necessary legislative, judicial and executive powers and responsibilities, in accordance with international law. This provision shall not derogate from Israel's applicable legislation over Israelis in personam.

5. The exercise of authority with regard to the electromagnetic sphere and air space shall be in accordance with the provisions of this Agreement.

6. Without derogating from the provisions of this Article, legal arrangements detailed in the Protocol Concerning Legal Matters attached as Annex IV to this Agreement (hereinafter "Annex IV") shall be observed. Israel and the Council may negotiate further legal arrangements.

7. Israel and the Council shall cooperate on matters of legal assistance in criminal and civil matters through a legal committee (hereinafter "the Legal Committee"), hereby established.

8. The Council's jurisdiction will extend gradually to cover West Bank and Gaza Strip territory, except for the issues to be negotiated in the permanent status negotiations, through a series of redeployments of the Israeli military forces. The first phase of the redeployment of Israeli military forces will cover populated areas in the West Bank—cities, towns, refugee camps and hamlets, as set out in Annex I—and will be completed prior to the eve of the Palestinian elections, i.e. 22 days before the day of the elections. Further redeployments of Israeli military forces to specified military locations will commence immediately upon the inauguration of the Council and will be effected in three phases, each to take place after an interval of six months, to be concluded no later than eighteen months from the date of the inauguration of the Council.

Article XVIII

LEGISLATIVE POWERS OF THE COUNCIL

1. For the purposes of this Article, legislation shall mean any primary and secondary legislation, including basic laws, laws, regulations and other legislative acts.
2. The Council has the power, within its jurisdiction as defined in Article XVII of this Agreement, to adopt legislation.
3. While the primary legislative power shall lie in the hands of the Council as a whole, the Ra'ees of the Executive Authority of the Council shall have the following legislative powers:
   a. the power to initiate legislation or to present proposed legislation to the Council;
   b. the power to promulgate legislation adopted by the Council; and
   c. the power to issue secondary legislation, including regulations, relating to any matters specified and within the scope laid down in any primary legislation adopted by the Council.
4. a. Legislation, including legislation which amends or abrogates existing laws or military orders, which exceeds the jurisdiction of the Council or which is otherwise inconsistent with the provisions of the DOP, this Agreement, or of any other agreement that may be reached between the two sides during the interim period, shall have no effect and shall be void ab initio.
   b. The Ra'ees of the Executive Authority of the Council shall not promulgate legislation adopted by the Council if such legislation falls under the provisions of this paragraph.
5. All legislation shall be communicated to the Israeli side of the Legal Committee.
6. Without derogating from the provisions of paragraph 4 above, the Israeli side of the Legal Committee may refer for the attention of the Committee any legislation regarding which Israel considers the provisions of paragraph 4 apply, in order to discuss issues arising from such legislation. The Legal Committee will consider the legislation referred to it at the earliest opportunity.

Article XIX

HUMAN RIGHTS AND THE RULE OF LAW

Israel and the Council shall exercise their powers and responsibilities pursuant to this Agreement with due regard to internationally-accepted norms and principles of human rights and the rule of law.

Article XX

RIGHTS, LIABILITIES AND OBLIGATIONS

1. a. The transfer of powers and responsibilities from the Israeli military government and its civil administration to the Council, as detailed in Annex III,

includes all related rights, liabilities and obligations arising with regard to acts or omissions which occurred prior to such transfer. Israel will cease to bear any financial responsibility regarding such acts or omissions and the Council will bear all financial responsibility for these and for its own functioning.

b. Any financial claim made in this regard against Israel will be referred to the Council.

c. Israel shall provide the Council with the information it has regarding pending and anticipated claims brought before any court or tribunal against Israel in this regard.

d. Where legal proceedings are brought in respect of such a claim, Israel will notify the Council and enable it to participate in defending the claim and raise any arguments on its behalf.

e. In the event that an award is made against Israel by any court or tribunal in respect of such a claim, the Council shall immediately reimburse Israel the full amount of the award.

f. Without prejudice to the above, where a court or tribunal hearing such a claim finds that liability rests solely with an employee or agent who acted beyond the scope of the powers assigned to him or her, unlawfully or with willful malfeasance, the Council shall not bear financial responsibility.

2. a. Notwithstanding the provisions of paragraphs l.d through l.f above, each side may take the necessary measures, including promulgation of legislation, in order to ensure that such claims by Palestinians including pending claims in which the hearing of evidence has not yet begun, are brought only before Palestinian courts or tribunals in the West Bank and the Gaza Strip, and are not brought before or heard by Israeli courts or tribunals.

b. Where a new claim has been brought before a Palestinian court or tribunal subsequent to the dismissal of the claim pursuant to subparagraph a. above, the Council shall defend it and, in accordance with subparagraph l.a above, in the event that an award is made for the plaintiff, shall pay the amount of the award.

c. The Legal Committee shall agree on arrangements for the transfer of all materials and information needed to enable the Palestinian courts or tribunals to hear such claims as referred to in subparagraph b. above, and, when necessary, for the provision of legal assistance by Israel to the Council in defending such claims.

3. The transfer of authority in itself shall not affect rights, liabilities and obligations of any person or legal entity, in existence at the date of signing of this Agreement.
4. The Council, upon its inauguration, will assume all the rights, liabilities and obligations of the Palestinian Authority.
5. For the purpose of this Agreement, "Israelis" also includes Israeli statutory agencies and corporations registered in Israel.

Article XXI

SETTLEMENT OF DIFFERENCES AND DISPUTES

Any difference relating to the application of this Agreement shall be referred to the appropriate coordination and cooperation mechanism established under this Agreement. The provisions of Article XV of the DOP shall apply to any such difference which is not settled through the appropriate coordination and cooperation mechanism, namely:

1. Disputes arising out of the application or interpretation of this Agreement or any related agreements pertaining to the interim period shall be settled through the Liaison Committee.
2. Disputes which cannot be settled by negotiations may be settled by a mechanism of conciliation to be agreed between the Parties.
3. The Parties may agree to submit to arbitration disputes relating to the interim period, which cannot be settled through conciliation. To this end, upon the agreement of both Parties, the Parties will establish an Arbitration Committee.

Chapter 4—Cooperation

Article XXII

RELATIONS BETWEEN ISRAEL AND THE COUNCIL

1. Israel and the Council shall seek to foster mutual understanding and tolerance and shall accordingly abstain from incitement, including hostile propaganda, against each other and, without derogating from the principle of freedom of expression, shall take legal measures to prevent such incitement by any organizations, groups or individuals within their jurisdiction.
2. Israel and the Council will ensure that their respective educational systems contribute to the peace between the Israeli and Palestinian peoples and to peace in the entire region, and will refrain from the introduction of any motifs that could adversely affect the process of reconciliation.
3. Without derogating from the other provisions of this Agreement, Israel and the Council shall cooperate in combating criminal activity which may affect both sides, including offenses related to trafficking in illegal drugs and psychotropic substances, smuggling, and offenses against property, including offenses related to vehicles.

Article XXIII

COOPERATION WITH REGARD TO TRANSFER OF POWERS AND RESPONSIBILITIES

In order to ensure a smooth, peaceful and orderly transfer of powers and responsibilities, the two sides will cooperate with regard to the transfer of security powers and responsibilities in accordance with the provisions of Annex I, and the transfer of civil powers and responsibilities in accordance with the provisions of Annex III.

Article XXIV

ECONOMIC RELATIONS

The economic relations between the two sides are set out in the Protocol on Economic Relations signed in Paris on April 29, 1994, and the Appendices thereto, and the Supplement to the Protocol on Economic Relations all attached as Annex V, and will be governed by the relevant provisions of this Agreement and its Annexes.

Article XXV

COOPERATION PROGRAMS

1. The Parties agree to establish a mechanism to develop programs of cooperation between them. Details of such cooperation are set out in Annex VI.
2. A Standing Cooperation Committee to deal with issues arising in the context of this cooperation is hereby established as provided for in Annex VI.

Article XXVI

THE JOINT ISRAELI–PALESTINIAN LIAISON COMMITTEE

1. The Liaison Committee established pursuant to Article X of the DOP shall ensure the smooth implementation of this Agreement. It shall deal with issues requiring coordination, other issues of common interest and disputes.
2. The Liaison Committee shall be composed of an equal number of members from each Party. It may add other technicians and experts as necessary.
3. The Liaison Committee shall adopt its rules of procedures, including the frequency and place or places of its meetings.
4. The Liaison Committee shall reach its decisions by agreement.
5. The Liaison Committee shall establish a subcommittee that will monitor and steer the implementation of this Agreement (hereinafter "the Monitoring and Steering Committee"). It will function as follows:
   a. The Monitoring and Steering Committee will, on an ongoing basis, monitor the implementation of this Agreement, with a view to enhancing the co-operation and fostering the peaceful relations between the two sides.
   b. The Monitoring and Steering Committee will steer the activities of the various joint committees established in this Agreement (the JSC, the CAC, the Legal Committee, the Joint Economic Committee and the Standing Cooperation Committee) concerning the ongoing implementation of the Agreement, and will report to the Liaison Committee.

c. The Monitoring and Steering Committee will be composed of the heads of the various committees mentioned above.
d. The two heads of the Monitoring and Steering Committee will establish its rules of procedures, including the frequency and places of its meetings.

Article XXVII

LIAISON AND COOPERATION WITH JORDAN AND EGYPT

1. Pursuant to Article XII of the DOP, the two Parties have invited the Governments of Jordan and Egypt to participate in establishing further liaison and cooperation arrangements between the Government of Israel and the Palestinian representatives on the one hand, and the Governments of Jordan and Egypt on the other hand, to promote cooperation between them. As part of these arrangements a Continuing Committee has been constituted and has commenced its deliberations.
2. The Continuing Committee shall decide by agreement on the modalities of admission of persons displaced from the West Bank and the Gaza Strip in 1967, together with necessary measures to prevent disruption and disorder.
3. The Continuing Committee shall also deal with other matters of common concern.

Article XXVIII

MISSING PERSONS

1. Israel and the Council shall cooperate by providing each other with all necessary assistance in the conduct of searches for missing persons and bodies of persons which have not been recovered, as well as by providing information about missing persons.
2. The PLO undertakes to cooperate with Israel and to assist it in its efforts to locate and to return to Israel Israeli soldiers who are missing in action and the bodies of soldiers which have not been recovered.

Chapter 5—Miscellaneous Provisions

Article XXIX

SAFE PASSAGE BETWEEN THE WEST BANK AND THE GAZA STRIP

Arrangements for safe passage of persons and transportation between the West Bank and the Gaza Strip are set out in Annex I.

Article XXX

PASSAGES

Arrangements for coordination between Israel and the Council regarding passage to and from Egypt and Jordan, as well as any other agreed international crossings, are set out in Annex I.

Article XXXI

FINAL CLAUSES

1. This Agreement shall enter into force on the date of its signing.
2. The Gaza–Jericho Agreement, except for Article XX (Confidence-Building Measures), the Preparatory Transfer Agreement and the Further Transfer Protocol will be superseded by this Agreement.
3. The Council, upon its inauguration, shall replace the Palestinian Authority and shall assume all the undertakings and obligations of the Palestinian Authority under the Gaza–Jericho Agreement, the Preparatory Transfer Agreement, and the Further Transfer Protocol.
4. The two sides shall pass all necessary legislation to implement this Agreement.
5. Permanent status negotiations will commence as soon as possible, but not later than May 4, 1996, between the Parties. It is understood that these negotiations shall cover remaining issues, including: Jerusalem, refugees, settlements, security arrangements, borders, relations and cooperation with other neighbors, and other issues of common interest.
6. Nothing in this Agreement shall prejudice or preempt the outcome of the negotiations on the permanent status to be conducted pursuant to the DOP. Neither Party shall be deemed, by virtue of having entered into this Agreement, to have renounced or waived any of its existing rights, claims or positions.
7. Neither side shall initiate or take any step that will change the status of the West Bank and the Gaza Strip pending the outcome of the permanent status negotiations.
8. The two Parties view the West Bank and the Gaza Strip as a single territorial unit, the integrity and status of which will be preserved during the interim period.
9. The PLO undertakes that, within two months of the date of the inauguration of the Council, the Palestinian National Council will convene and formally approve the necessary changes in regard to the Palestinian Covenant, as undertaken in the letters signed by the Chairman of the PLO and addressed to the Prime Minister of Israel, dated September 9, 1993 and May 4, 1994.
10. Pursuant to Annex I, Article IX of this Agreement, Israel confirms that the permanent checkpoints on the roads leading to and from the Jericho Area (except those related to the access road leading from Mousa Alami to the

Allenby Bridge) will be removed upon the completion of the first phase of redeployment.

11. Prisoners who, pursuant to the Gaza–Jericho Agreement, were turned over to the Palestinian Authority on the condition that they remain in the Jericho Area for the remainder of their sentence, will be free to return to their homes in the West Bank and the Gaza Strip upon the completion of the first phase of redeployment.
12. As regards relations between Israel and the PLO, and without derogating from the commitments contained in the letters signed by and exchanged between the Prime Minister of Israel and the Chairman of the PLO, dated September 9, 1993 and May 4, 1994, the two sides will apply between them the provisions contained in Article XXII, paragraph 1, with the necessary changes.
13.
    a. The Preamble to this Agreement, and all Annexes, Appendices and maps attached hereto, shall constitute an integral part hereof.
    b. The Parties agree that the maps attached to the Gaza–Jericho Agreement as:
        a. map No. 1 (The Gaza Strip), an exact copy of which is attached to this Agreement as map No. 2 (in this Agreement "map No. 2");
        b. map No. 4 (Deployment of Palestinian Police in the Gaza Strip), an exact copy of which is attached to this Agreement as map No. 5 (in this Agreement "map No. 5"); and
        c. map No. 6 (Maritime Activity Zones), an exact copy of which is attached to this Agreement as map No. 8 (in this Agreement "map No. 8");

    are an integral part hereof and will remain in effect for the duration of this Agreement.
14. While the Jeftlik area will come under the functional and personal jurisdiction of the Council in the first phase of redeployment, the area's transfer to the territorial jurisdiction of the Council will be considered by the Israeli side in the first phase of the further redeployment phases.

Done at Washington DC, this 28th day of September, 1995.

For the Government of the State of Israel	For the PLO

Witnessed by:

____

The United States of America

____

The Russian Federation

____

The Arab Republic of Egypt

The Hashemite Kingdom of Jordan

The Kingdom of Norway

The European Union

List of Annexes and Maps:
- Annex 1—Redeployment and Security Arrangements
- Annex 2—Elections Protocol
- Annex 3—Civil Affairs
- Annex 4—Legal Matters
- Annex 5—Economic Relations
- Annex 6—Israeli–Palestinian Cooperation
- Annex 7—Release of Palestinian Prisoners
- Map No. 1—First Phase of Redeployment (A & B)
- Map No. 2—Security Arrangements in the Gaza Strip
- Map No. 5—Palestinian Police Deployment—Gaza
- Map No. 6—Safe Passage Routes
- Map No. 8—Maritime Activity Zones
- Map No. 9—Hebron

[Annexes and maps omitted]

Appendix F

Protocol Concerning the Redeployment in Hebron [15 January 1997]

In accordance with the provisions of the Interim Agreement and in particular of Article VII of Annex I to the Interim Agreement, both Parties have agreed on this Protocol for the implementation of the redeployment in Hebron.

Security arrangements regarding redeployment in Hebron

1. Redeployment in Hebron

   The redeployment of Israeli Military Forces in Hebron will be carried out in accordance with the Interim Agreement and this Protocol. This redeployment will be completed not later than ten days from the signing of this Protocol. During these ten days both sides will exert every possible effort to prevent friction and any action that would prevent the redeployment. This redeployment shall constitute full implementation of the provisions of the Interim Agreement with regard to the City of Hebron unless otherwise provided for in Article VII of Annex I to the Interim Agreement.

2. Security Powers and Responsibilities

   a.
      1. The Palestinian Police will assume responsibilities in Area H-1 similar to those in other cities in the West Bank; and
      2. Israel will retain all powers and responsibilities for internal security and public order in Area H-2. In addition, Israel will continue to carry the responsibility for overall security of Israelis.

   b. In this context—both sides reaffirm their commitment to honor the relevant security provisions of the Interim Agreement, including the provisions regarding—Arrangements for Security and Public Order (Article XII of the Interim Agreement); Prevention of Hostile Acts (Article XV of the Interim Agreement); Security Policy for the Prevention of Terrorism and Violence (Article II of Annex I to the Interim Agreement); Guidelines for Hebron (Article VII of Annex I to the Interim Agreement); and Rules of Conduct in Mutual Security Matters (Article XI of Annex I to the Interim Agreement).

3. Agreed Security Arrangements

   a. With a view to ensuring mutual security and stability in the City of Hebron, special security arrangements will apply adjacent to the areas under the security responsibility of Israel, in Area H-1, in the area between the Palestinian Police checkpoints delineated on the map attached to this Protocol as Appendix 1 (hereinafter referred to as "the attached map") and the areas under the security responsibility of Israel.

b. The purpose of the abovementioned checkpoints will be to enable the Palestinian Police, exercising their responsibilities under the Interim Agreement, to prevent entry of armed persons and demonstrators or other people threatening security and public order, into the abovementioned area.

4. Joint Security Measures

a. The DCO will establish a sub-office in the City of Hebron as indicated on the attached map.

b. JMU will operate in Area H-2 to handle incidents that involve Palestinians only. The JMU movement will be detailed on the attached map. The DCO will coordinate the JMU movement and activity.

c. As part of the security arrangements in the area adjacent to the areas under the security responsibility of Israel, as defined above, Joint Mobile Units will be operating in this area, with special focus on the following places:
   1. Abu Sneinah
   2. Harat A-Sheikh
   3. Sha'aba
   4. The high ground overlooking new Route No. 35.

d. Two Joint Patrols will function in Area H-1:
   1. a Joint Patrol which will operate on the road from Ras e-Jura to the north of the Dura junction via E-Salaam Road, as indicated on the attached map; and
   2. a Joint Patrol which will operate on existing Route No. 35, including the eastern part of existing Route No. 35, as indicated on the attached map.

e. The Palestinian and Israeli side of the Joint Mobile Units in the City of Hebron will be armed with equivalent types of weapons (Mini-Ingraham submachine guns for the Palestinian side and short M16s for the Israeli side).

f. With a view to dealing with the special security situation in the City of Hebron, a Joint Coordination Center (hereinafter the "JCC") headed by senior officers of both sides, will be established in the DCO at Har Manoah/Jabel Manoah. The purpose of the JCC will be to coordinate the joint security measures in the City of Hebron. The JCC will be guided by all the relevant provisions of the Interim Agreement, including Annex I and this Protocol. In this context, each side will notify the JCC of demonstrations and actions taken in respect of such demonstrations, and of any security activity, close to the areas under the responsibility of the other side, including in the area defined in Article 3(a) above. The JCC shall be informed of activities in accordance with Article 5(d)(3) of this Protocol.

5. The Palestinian Police

a. Palestinian police stations or posts will be established in Area H-1, manned by a total of up to 400 policemen, equipped with 20 vehicles and armed with 200 pistols, and 100 rifles for the protection of the police stations.
b. Four designated Rapid Response Teams (RRTs) will be established and stationed in Area H-1, one in each of the police stations, as delineated on the attached map. The main task of the RRTs will be to handle special security cases. Each RRT shall be comprised of up to 16 members.
c. The abovementioned rifles will be designated for the exclusive use of the RRTs, to handle special cases.
d.
   1. The Palestinian Police shall operate freely in Area H-1.
   2. Activities of the RRTs armed with rifles in the Agreed Adjacent Area, as defined in Appendix 2, shall require the agreement of the JCC.
   3. The RRTs will use the rifles in the rest of Area H-1 to fulfill their abovementioned tasks.
e. The Palestinian Police will ensure that all Palestinian policemen, prior to their deployment in the City of Hebron, will pass a security check in order to verify their suitability for service, taking into account the sensitivity of the area.

6. Holy Sites

a. Paragraphs 2 and 3(a) of Article 32 of Appendix 1 to Annex III of the Interim Agreement will be applicable to the following Holy Sites in Area H-1:
   1. The Cave of Othniel Ben Knaz/El-Khalil;
   2. Elonei Mamre/Haram Er-Rameh;
   3. Eshel Avraham/Balotat Ibrahim; and
   4. Maayan Sarah/Ein Sarah.
b. The Palestinian Police will be responsible for the protection of the above Jewish Holy Sites. Without derogating from the above responsibility of the Palestinian Police, visits to the above Holy Sites by worshippers or other visitors shall be accompanied by a Joint Mobile Unit, which will ensure free, unimpeded and secure access to the Holy Sites, as well as their peaceful use.

7. Normalization of Life in the Old City

a. Both sides reiterate their commitment to maintain normal life throughout the City of Hebron and to prevent any provocation or friction that may affect the normal life in the city.
b. In this context, both sides are committed to take all steps and measures necessary for the normalization of life in Hebron, including:
   1. The wholesale market—Hasbahe—will be opened as a retail market in

which goods will be sold directly to consumers from within the existing shops.

2. The movement of vehicles on the Shuhada Road will be gradually returned, within 4 months, to the same situation which existed prior to February 1994.

8. The Imara

The Imara will be turned over to the Palestinian side upon the completion of the redeployment and will become the headquarters of the Palestinian Police in the City of Hebron.

9. City of Hebron

Both sides reiterate their commitment to the unity of the City of Hebron, and their understanding that the division of security responsibility will not divide the city. In this context, and without derogating from the security powers and responsibilities of either side, both sides share the mutual goal that movement of people, goods and vehicles within and in and out of the city will be smooth and normal, without obstacles or barriers.

Civil Arrangements Regarding the Redeployment in Hebron

10. Transfer of Civil Powers and Responsibilities

a. The transfer of civil powers and responsibilities that have yet to be transferred to the Palestinian side in the city of Hebron (12 spheres) in accordance with Article VII of Annex I to the Interim Agreement shall be conducted concurrently with the beginning of the redeployment of Israeli military forces in Hebron.

b. In Area H-2, the civil powers and responsibilities will be transferred to the Palestinian side, except for those relating to Israelis and their property, which shall continue to be exercised by the Israeli Military Government.

11. Planning, Zoning and Building

a. The two parties are equally committed to preserve and protect the historic character of the city in a way which does not harm or change that character in any part of the city.

b. The Palestinian side has informed the Israeli side that in exercising its powers and responsibilities, taking into account the existing municipal regulations, it has undertaken to implement the following provisions:

1. Proposed construction of buildings above two floors (6 meters) within 50 meters of the external boundaries of the locations specified in the list attached to this Protocol as Appendix 3 (hereinafter referred to as "the attached list") will be coordinated through the DCL.

2. Proposed construction of buildings above three floors (9 meters) between 50 and 100 meters of the external boundaries of the locations specified in the attached list will be coordinated through the DCL.
3. Proposed construction of non-residential, non-commercial buildings within 100 meters of the external boundaries of the locations specified in the attached list that are designed for uses that may adversely affect the environment (such as industrial factories) or buildings and institutions in which more that 50 persons are expected to gather together will be coordinated through the DCL.
4. Proposed construction of buildings above two floors (6 meters) within 50 meters from each side of the road specified in the attached list will be coordinated through the DCL.
5. The necessary enforcement measures will be taken to ensure compliance on the ground with the preceding provisions.
6. This Article does not apply to existing buildings or to new construction or renovation for which fully approved permits were issued by the Municipality prior to January 15th, 1997.

12. Infrastructure

a. The Palestinian side shall inform the Israeli side, through the DCL, 48 hours in advance of any anticipated activity regarding infrastructure which may disturb the regular flow of traffic on roads in Area H-2 or which may affect infrastructure (such as water, sewage, electricity and communications) serving Area H-2.
b. The Israeli side may request, through the DCL, that the Municipality carry out works regarding the roads or other infrastructure required for the well being of the Israelis in Area H-2. If the Israeli side offers to cover the costs of these works, the Palestinian side will ensure that these works are carried out as a top priority.
c. The above does not prejudice the provisions of the Interim Agreement regarding the access to infrastructure, facilities and installations located in the city of Hebron, such as the electricity grid.

13. Transportation

The Palestinian side shall have the power to determine bus stops, traffic arrangements and traffic signalization in the city of Hebron. Traffic signalization, traffic arrangements and the location of bus stops in Area H-2 will remain as they are on the date of the redeployment in Hebron. Any subsequent change in these arrangements in Area H-2 will be done in cooperation between the two sides in the transportation sub-committee.

14. Municipal Inspectors

a. In accordance with paragraph 4.c of Article VII of Annex I of the Interim Agreement, plainclothes unarmed municipal inspectors will operate in Area H-2. The number of these inspectors shall not exceed 50.

b. The inspectors shall carry official identification cards with a photograph issued by the Municipality.
c. The Palestinian side may request the assistance of the Israel Police, through the DCL of Hebron, in order to carry out its enforcement activities in Area H-2.

15. Location of Offices of the Palestinian Council

The Palestinian side, when operating new offices in Area H-2, will take into consideration the need to avoid provocation and friction. Where establishing such offices might affect public order or security the two sides will cooperate to find a suitable solution.

16. Municipal Services

In accordance with paragraph 5 of Article VII of Annex I of the Interim Agreement, municipal services shall be provided regularly and continuously to all parts of the city of Hebron, at the same quality and cost. The cost shall be determined by the Palestinian side with respect to work done and materials consumed, without discrimination.

Miscellaneous

17. Temporary International Presence

There will be a Temporary International Presence in Hebron (TIPH). Both sides will agree on the modalities of the TIPH, including the number of its members and its area of operation.

18. Annex I

Nothing in this Protocol will derogate from the security powers and responsibilities of either side in accordance with Annex I to the Interim Agreement.

19. Attached Appendices

The appendices attached to this Protocol shall constitute an integral part hereof.

Done at Jerusalem, this 17th day of January 1997.

D. Shomrom	S. Erakat
For the Government of the State of Israel	For the PLO

Appendix G

Note for the Record
[15 January 1997]

The two leaders met on January 15, 1997, in the presence of the U.S. Special Middle East Coordinator. They requested him to prepare this Note for the Record to summarize what they agreed upon at their meeting.

Mutual Undertakings

The two leaders agreed that the Oslo peace process must move forward to succeed. Both parties to the Interim Agreement have concerns and obligations. Accordingly, the two leaders reaffirmed their commitment to implement the Interim Agreement on the basis of reciprocity and, in this context, conveyed the following undertakings to each other:

Israeli Responsibilities

The Israeli side reaffirms its commitments to the following measures and principles in accordance with the Interim Agreement:

Issues for Implementation

1. Further Redeployment Phases

The first phase of further redeployments will be carried out during the first week of March.

2. Prisoner Release Issues

Prisoner release issues will be dealt with in accordance with the Interim Agreement's provisions and procedures, including Annex VII.

Issues for Negotiation

3. Outstanding Interim Agreement Issues

Negotiations on the following outstanding issues from the Interim Agreement will be immediately resumed. Negotiations on these issues will be conducted in parallel:

a. Safe Passage
b. Gaza Airport
c. Gaza port
d. Passages
e. Economic, financial, civilian and security issues
f. People-to-people

4. Permanent Status Negotiations

Permanent status negotiations will be resumed within two months after implementation of the Hebron Protocol.

Palestinian Responsibilities

The Palestinian side reaffirms its commitments to the following measures and principles in accordance with the Interim Agreement:

1. Complete the process of revising the Palestinian National Charter
2. Fighting terror and preventing violence
   a. Strengthening security cooperation
   b. Preventing incitement and hostile propaganda, as specified in Article XXII of the Interim Agreement
   c. Combat systematically and effectively terrorist organizations and infrastructure
   d. Apprehension, prosecution and punishment of terrorists
   e. Requests for transfer of suspects and defendants will be acted upon in accordance with Article II(7)(f) of Annex IV to the Interim Agreement
   f. Confiscation of illegal firearms
3. Size of Palestinian Police will be pursuant to the Interim Agreement.
4. Exercise of Palestinian governmental activity, and location of Palestinian governmental offices, will be as specified in the Interim Agreement.

The aforementioned commitments will be dealt with immediately and in parallel.

Other Issues

Either party is free to raise other issues not specified above related to implementation of the Interim Agreement and obligations of both sides arising from the Interim Agreement.

Prepared by Ambassador Dennis Ross at the request of Prime Minister Benjamin Netanyahu and Ra'ees Yasser Arafat

Appendix H

The Wye River Memorandum
[23 October 1998]

The following are steps to facilitate implementation of the Interim Agreement on the West Bank and Gaza Strip of September 28, 1995 (the "Interim Agreement") and other related agreements including the Note for the Record of January 17, 1997 (hereinafter referred to as "the prior agreements") so that the Israeli and Palestinian sides can more effectively carry out their reciprocal responsibilities, including those relating to further redeployments and security respectively. These steps are to be carried out in a parallel phased approach in accordance with this Memorandum and the attached time line. They are subject to the relevant terms and conditions of the prior agreements and do not supersede their other requirements.

I. Further Redevelopments

A. Phase One and Two Further Redeployments

1. Pursuant to the Interim Agreement and subsequent agreements, the Israeli side's implementation of the first and second F.R.D. will consist of the transfer to the Palestinian side of 13% from Area C as follows:

1% to Area (A)

12% to Area (B)

The Palestinian side has informed that it will allocate an area/areas amounting to 3% from the above Area (B) to be designated as Green Areas and/or Nature Reserves. The Palestinian side has further informed that they will act according to the established scientific standards, and that therefore there will be no changes in the status of these areas, without prejudice to the rights of the existing inhabitants in these areas including Bedouins; while these standards do not allow new construction in these areas, existing roads and buildings may be maintained.

The Israeli side will retain in these Green Areas/Nature Reserves the overriding security responsibility for the purpose of protecting Israelis and confronting the threat of terrorism. Activities and movements of the Palestinian Police forces may be carried out after coordination and confirmation; the Israeli side will respond to such requests expeditiously.

2. As part of the foregoing implementation of the first and second F.R.D., 14.2% from Area (B) will become Area (A).

B. Third Phase of Further Redeployments

With regard to the terms of the Interim Agreement and of Secretary Christopher's letters to the two sides of January 17, 1997 relating to the further redeployment process, there will be a committee to address this question. The United States will be briefed regularly.

II. Security

In the provisions on security arrangements of the Interim Agreement, the Palestinian side agreed to take all measures necessary in order to prevent acts of terrorism, crime and hostilities directed against the Israeli side, against individuals falling under the Israeli side's authority and against their property, just as the Israeli side agreed to take all measures necessary in order to prevent acts of terrorism, crime and hostilities directed against the Palestinian side, against individuals falling under the Palestinian side's authority and against their property. The two sides also agreed to take legal measures against offenders within their jurisdiction and to prevent incitement against each other by any organizations, groups or individuals within their jurisdiction.

Both sides recognize that it is in their vital interests to combat terrorism and fight violence in accordance with Annex I of the Interim Agreement and the Note for the Record. They also recognize that the struggle against terror and violence must be comprehensive in that it deals with terrorists, the terror support structure, and the environment conducive to the support of terror. It must be continuous and constant over a long-term, in that there can be no pauses in the work against terrorists and their structure. It must be cooperative in that no effort can be fully effective without Israeli–Palestinian cooperation and the continuous exchange of information, concepts, and actions.

Pursuant to the prior agreements, the Palestinian side's implementation of its responsibilities for security, security cooperation, and other issues will be as detailed below during the time periods specified in the attached time line:

A. Security Actions

1. Outlawing and Combating Terrorist Organizations
   - (a) The Palestinian side will make known its policy of zero tolerance for terror and violence against both sides.
   - (b) A work plan developed by the Palestinian side will be shared with the U.S. and thereafter implementation will begin immediately to ensure the systematic and effective combat of terrorist organizations and their infrastructure.
   - (c) In addition to the bilateral Israeli–Palestinian security cooperation, a U.S.–Palestinian committee will meet biweekly to review the steps being taken to eliminate terrorist cells and the support structure that plans, finances, supplies and abets terror. In these meetings, the Palestinian side will inform the U.S. fully of the actions it has taken to outlaw all organizations (or wings of organizations, as appropriate) of a military, terrorist or violent character and their support structure and to prevent them from operating in areas under its jurisdiction.
   - (d) The Palestinian side will apprehend the specific individuals suspected of perpetrating acts of violence and terror for the purpose of further investigation, and prosecution and punishment of all persons involved in acts of violence and terror.
   - (e) A U.S.–Palestinian committee will meet to review and evaluate information pertinent to the decisions on prosecution, punishment or other

legal measures which affect the status of individuals suspected of abetting or perpetrating acts of violence and terror.

2. Prohibiting Illegal Weapons
   (a) The Palestinian side will ensure an effective legal framework is in place to criminalize, in conformity with the prior agreements, any importation, manufacturing or unlicensed sale, acquisition or possession of firearms, ammunition or weapons in areas under Palestinian jurisdiction.
   (b) In addition, the Palestinian side will establish and vigorously and continuously implement a systematic program for the collection and appropriate handling of all such illegal items in accordance with the prior agreements. The U.S. has agreed to assist in carrying out this program.
   (c) A U.S.–Palestinian–Israeli committee will be established to assist and enhance cooperation in preventing the smuggling or other unauthorized introduction of weapons or explosive materials into areas under Palestinian jurisdiction.

3. Preventing Incitement
   (a) Drawing on relevant international practice and pursuant to Article XXII (1) of the Interim Agreement and the Note for the Record, the Palestinian side will issue a decree prohibiting all forms of incitement to violence or terror, and establishing mechanisms for acting systematically against all expressions or threats of violence or terror. This decree will be comparable to the existing Israeli legislation which deals with the same subject.
   (b) A U.S.–Palestinian–Israeli committee will meet on a regular basis to monitor cases of possible incitement to violence or terror and to make recommendations and reports on how to prevent such incitement. The Israeli, Palestinian and U.S. sides will each appoint a media specialist, a law enforcement representative, an educational specialist and a current or former elected official to the committee.

B. Security Cooperation

The two sides agree that their security cooperation will be based on a spirit of partnership and will include, among other things, the following steps:

1. Bilateral Cooperation
   There will be full bilateral security cooperation between the two sides which will be continuous, intensive and comprehensive.
2. Forensic Cooperation
   There will be an exchange of forensic expertise, training, and other assistance.
3. Trilateral Committee
   In addition to the bilateral Israeli–Palestinian security cooperation, a

high-ranking U.S.–Palestinian–Israeli committee will meet as required and not less than biweekly to assess current threats, deal with any impediments to effective security cooperation and coordination and address the steps being taken to combat terror and terrorist organizations. The committee will also serve as a forum to address the issue of external support for terror. In these meetings, the Palestinian side will fully inform the members of the committee of the results of its investigations concerning terrorist suspects already in custody and the participants will exchange additional relevant information. The committee will report regularly to the leaders of the two sides on the status of cooperation, the results of the meetings and its recommendations.

C. *Other Issues*

1. Palestinian Police Force
   (a) The Palestinian side will provide a list of its policemen to the Israeli side in conformity with the prior agreements.
   (b) Should the Palestinian side request technical assistance, the U.S. has indicated its willingness to help meet these needs in cooperation with other donors.
   (c) The Monitoring and Steering Committee will, as part of its functions, monitor the implementation of this provision and brief the U.S.
2. PLO Charter
   The Executive Committee of the Palestine Liberation Organization and the Palestinian Central Council will reaffirm the letter of 22 January 1998 from PLO Chairman Yasir Arafat to President Clinton concerning the nullification of the Palestinian National Charter provisions that are inconsistent with the letters exchanged between the PLO and the Government of Israel on 9/10 September 1993. PLO Chairman Arafat, the Speaker of the Palestine National Council, and the Speaker of the Palestinian Council will invite the members of the PNC, as well as the members of the Central Council, the Council, and the Palestinian Heads of Ministries to a meeting to be addressed by President Clinton to reaffirm their support for the peace process and the aforementioned decisions of the Executive Committee and the Central Council.
3. Legal Assistance in Criminal Matters
   Among other forms of legal assistance in criminal matters, the requests for arrest and transfer of suspects and defendants pursuant to Article II (7) of Annex IV of the Interim Agreement will be submitted (or resubmitted) through the mechanism of the Joint Israeli–Palestinian Legal Committee and will be responded to in conformity with Article II (7) (f) of Annex IV of the Interim Agreement within the twelve week period. Requests submitted after the eighth week will be responded to in conformity with Article II (7) (f) within four weeks of their submission. The U.S. has been requested by the sides to report on a regular basis on the steps being taken to respond to the above requests.

4. Human Rights and the Rule of Law
   Pursuant to Article XI (1) of Annex I of the Interim Agreement, and without derogating from the above, the Palestinian Police will exercise powers and responsibilities to implement this Memorandum with due regard to internationally accepted norms of human rights and the rule of law, and will be guided by the need to protect the public, respect human dignity, and avoid harassment.

III. Interim Committees and Economic Issues

1. The Israeli and Palestinian sides reaffirm their commitment to enhancing their relationship and agree on the need actively to promote economic development in the West Bank and Gaza. In this regard, the parties agree to continue or to reactivate all standing committees established by the Interim Agreement, including the Monitoring and Steering Committee, the Joint Economic Committee (JEC), the Civil Affairs Committee (CAC), the Legal Committee, and the Standing Cooperation Committee.

2. The Israeli and Palestinian sides have agreed on arrangements which will permit the timely opening of the Gaza Industrial Estate. They also have concluded a "Protocol Regarding the Establishment and Operation of the International Airport in the Gaza Strip During the Interim Period."

3. Both sides will renew negotiations on Safe Passage immediately. As regards the southern route, the sides will make best efforts to conclude the agreement within a week of the entry into force of this Memorandum. Operation of the southern route will start as soon as possible thereafter. As regards the northern route, negotiations will continue with the goal of reaching agreement as soon as possible. Implementation will take place expeditiously thereafter.

4. The Israeli and Palestinian sides acknowledge the great importance of the Port of Gaza for the development of the Palestinian economy, and the expansion of Palestinian trade. They commit themselves to proceeding without delay to conclude an agreement to allow the construction and operation of the port in accordance with the prior agreements. The Israeli–Palestinian Committee will reactivate its work immediately with a goal of concluding the protocol within sixty days, which will allow commencement of the construction of the port.

5. The two sides recognize that unresolved legal issues adversely affect the relationship between the two peoples. They therefore will accelerate efforts through the Legal Committee to address outstanding legal issues and to implement solutions to these issues in the shortest possible period. The Palestinian side will provide to the Israeli side copies of all of its laws in effect.

6. The Israeli and Palestinian sides also will launch a strategic economic dialogue to enhance their economic relationship. They will establish within the framework of the JEC an Ad Hoc Committee for this purpose. The committee will review the following four issues: (1) Israeli purchase taxes; (2) cooperation in combating vehicle theft; (3) dealing with unpaid Palestinian debts; and (4) the impact of Israeli standards as barriers to trade and the expansion of the A1 and A2 lists. The committee will submit an interim report within three weeks of the entry

into force of this Memorandum, and within six weeks will submit its conclusions and recommendations to be implemented.

7. The two sides agree on the importance of continued international donor assistance to facilitate implementation by both sides of agreements reached. They also recognize the need for enhanced donor support for economic development in the West Bank and Gaza. They agree to jointly approach the donor community to organize a Ministerial Conference before the end of 1998 to seek pledges for enhanced levels of assistance.

IV. Permanent Status Negotiations

The two sides will immediately resume permanent status negotiations on an accelerated basis and will make a determined effort to achieve the mutual goal of reaching an agreement by May 4, 1999. The negotiations will be continuous and without interruption. The United States has expressed its willingness to facilitate these negotiations.

V. Unilateral Actions

Recognizing the necessity to create a positive environment for the negotiations, neither side shall initiate or take any step that will change the status of the West Bank and the Gaza Strip in accordance with the Interim Agreement.

ATTACHMENT: Time Line

This Memorandum will enter into force ten days from the date of signature.

Done at Washington, D.C. this 23d day of October 1998.

For the Government of the State of Israel: Benjamin Netanyahu	For the PLO: Yassir Arafat

Witnessed by:
William J. Clinton
The United States of America

Time Line

Note: Parenthetical references below are to paragraphs in "The Wye River Memorandum" to which this time line is an integral attachment. Topics not included in the time line follow the schedule provided for in the text of the Memorandum.

1. Upon Entry into Force of the Memorandum:
   —Third further redeployment committee starts (I(B))
   —Palestinian security work plan shared with the U.S. (II(A)(1)(b))
   —Full bilateral security cooperation (II(B)(1))
   —Trilateral security cooperation committee starts (II(B)(3))
   —Interim committees resume and continue; Ad Hoc Economic Committee starts (III)
   —Accelerated permanent status negotiations start (IV)

2. Entry into Force—Week 2:
   —Security work plan implementation begins (II(A)(1)(b)); (II(A)(1)(c)) committee starts
   —Illegal weapons framework in place (II(A)(2)a));
   —Palestinian implementation report (II(A)(2)(b))
   —Anti-incitement committee starts (II(A)(3)(b)); decree issued (II(A)(3)(a))
   —PLO Executive Committee reaffirms Charter letter (II(C)(2))
   —Stage 1 of F.R.D. implementation: 2% C to B, 7.1% B to A. Israeli officials acquaint their Palestinian counterparts as required with areas; F.R.D. carried out; report on F.R.D. implementation (I(A))

3. Week 2–6:
   —Palestinian Central Council reaffirms Charter letter (weeks two to four) (II(C)(2))
   —PNC and other PLO organizations reaffirm Charter letter (weeks four to six) (II(C)(2))
   —Establishment of weapons collection program (II(A)(2)(b)) and collection stage (II(A)(2)(c)); committee starts and reports on activities.
   —Anti-incitement committee report (II(A)(3)(b))
   —Ad Hoc Economic Committee: interim report at week three; final report at week six (III)
   —Policemen list (II(C)(1)(a)); Monitoring and Steering Committee review starts (II(C)(1)(c)

   Stage 2 of F.R.D. implementation: 5% C to B. Israeli officials acquaint their Palestinian counterparts as required with areas; F.R.D. carried out; report on F.R.D. implementation (I(A))

4. Week 6–12:
   —Weapons collection stage (II(A)(2)(b)); (II(A)(2)(c)) committee report on its activities.
   —Anti-incitement committee report (II(A)(3)(b))
   —Monitoring and Steering Committee briefs U.S. on policemen list (II(C)(1)(c))
   —Stage 3 of F.R.D. implementation: 5% C to B, 1% C to A, 7.1% B to A. Israeli officials acquaint Palestinian counterparts as required with areas; F.R.D. carried out; report on F.R.D. implementation (I (A))

5. After Week 12:

Activities described in the Memorandum continue as appropriate and if necessary, including:

—Trilateral security cooperation committee (II(B)(3))
—(II(A)(1)(c)) committee
—(II(A)(1)(e)) committee
—Anti-incitement committee (II(A)(3)(b))
—Third Phase F.R.D. Committee (I(B))
—Interim Committees (III)
—Accelerated permanent status negotiations (IV)

Appendix I

The Sharm el-Sheikh Memorandum on Implementation Timeline of Outstanding Commitments of Agreements Signed and the Resumption of Permanent Status Negotiations [4 September 1999]

The Government of the State of Israel ("GOI") and the Palestine Liberation Organization ("PLO") commit themselves to full and mutual implementation of the Interim Agreement and all other agreements concluded between them since September 1993 (hereinafter "the prior agreements"), and all outstanding commitments emanating from the prior agreements. Without derogating from the other requirements of the prior agreements, the two Sides have agreed as follows:

1. Permanent Status Negotiations:
   a. In the context of the implementation of the prior agreements, the two Sides will resume the Permanent Status negotiations in an accelerated manner and will make a determined effort to achieve their mutual goal of reaching a Permanent Status Agreement based on the agreed agenda, i.e. the specific issues reserved for Permanent Status negotiators and other issues of common interest.
   b. The two Sides reaffirm their understanding that the negotiations on the Permanent Status will lead to the implementation of Security Council Resolutions 242 and 338;
   c. The two Sides will make a determined effort to conclude a Framework Agreement on all Permanent Status issues in five months from the resumption of the Permanent Status negotiations;
   d. The two Sides will conclude a comprehensive agreement on all Permanent Status issues within one year from the resumption of the Permanent Status negotiations;
   e. Permanent Status negotiations will resume after the implementation of the first stage of release of prisoners and the second stage of the First and Second Further Redeployments and not later than September 13, 1999. In the Wye River Memorandum, the United States has expressed its willingness to facilitate these negotiations.

2. Phase One and Phase Two of the Further Redeployments

The Israeli Side undertakes the following with regard to Phase One and Phase Two of the Further Redeployments:

   a. On September 5, 1999, to transfer 7% from Area C to Area B;
   b. On November 15, 1999, to transfer 2% from Area B to Area A and 3% from Area C to Area B;

c. On January 20, 2000, to transfer 1% from Area C to Area A, and 5.1% from Area B to Area A.

3. Release of Prisoners
   a. The two Sides shall establish a joint committee that shall follow-up on matters related to release of Palestinian prisoners.
   b. The Government of Israel shall release Palestinian and other prisoners who committed their offences prior to September 13, 1993, and were arrested prior to May 4, 1994. The Joint Committee shall agree on the names of those who will be released in the first two stages. Those lists shall be recommended to the relevant Authorities through the Monitoring and Steering Committee;
   c. The first stage of release of prisoners shall be carried out on September 5, 1999 and shall consist of 200 prisoners. The second stage of release of prisoners shall be carried out on October 8, 1999 and shall consist of 150 prisoners;
   d. The joint committee shall recommend further lists of names to be released to the relevant Authorities through the Monitoring and Steering Committee;
   e. The Israeli side will aim to release Palestinian prisoners before next Ramadan.

4. Committees
   a. The Third Further Redeployment Committee shall commence its activities not later than September 13, 1999;
   b. The Monitoring and Steering Committee, all Interim Committees (i.e. CAC, JEC, JSC, legal committee, people to people), as well as Wye River Memorandum committees shall resume and/or continue their activity, as the case may be, not later than September 13, 1999. The Monitoring and Steering Committee will have on its agenda, inter alia, the Year 2000, Donor/PA projects in Area C, and the issue of industrial estates;
   c. The Continuing Committee on displaced persons shall resume its activity on October 1, 1999 (Article XXVII, Interim Agreement);
   d. Not later than October 30, 1999, the two sides will implement the recommendations of the Ad-hoc Economic Committee (article III–6, WRM).

5. Safe Passage
   a. The operation of the Southern Route of the Safe Passage for the movement of persons, vehicles, and goods will start on October 1, 1999 (Annex I, Article X, Interim Agreement) in accordance with the details of operation, which will be provided for in the Safe Passage Protocol that will be concluded by the two Sides not later than September 30, 1999;
   b. The two Sides will agree on the specific location of the crossing point of the Northern Route of the Safe Passage as specified in Annex I, Article X, provision c-4, in the Interim Agreement not later than October 5, 1999;
   c. The Safe Passage Protocol applied to the Southern Route of the Safe

Passage shall apply to the Northern Route of the Safe Passage with relevant agreed modifications;

d. Upon the agreement on the location of the crossing point of the Northern Route of the Safe Passage, construction of the needed facilities and related procedures shall commence and shall be ongoing. At the same time, temporary facilities will be established for the operation of the Northern Route not later than four months from the agreement on the specific location of the crossing point;

e. In between the operation of the Southern crossing point of the Safe Passage and the Northern crossing point of the Safe Passage, Israel will facilitate arrangements for the movement between the West Bank and the Gaza Strip, using non-Safe Passage routes other than the Southern Route of the Safe Passage;

f. The location of the crossing points shall be without prejudice to the Permanent Status negotiations (Annex I, Article X, provision e, Interim Agreement).

6. Gaza Sea Port

The two Sides have agreed on the following principles to facilitate and enable the construction works of the Gaza Sea Port. The principles shall not prejudice or preempt the outcome of negotiations on the Permanent Status:

a. The Israeli Side agrees that the Palestinian Side shall commence construction works in and related to the Gaza Sea Port on October 1, 1999;

b. The two Sides agree that the Gaza Sea Port will not be operated in any way before reaching a joint Sea Port protocol on all aspects of operating the Port, including security;

c. The Gaza Sea Port is a special case, like the Gaza Airport, being situated in an area under the responsibility of the Palestinian Side and serving as an international passage. Therefore, with the conclusion of a joint Sea Port Protocol, all activities and arrangements relating to the construction of the Port shall be in accordance with the provisions of the Interim Agreement, especially those relating to international passages, as adapted in the Gaza Airport Protocol;

d. The construction shall ensure adequate provision for effective security and customs inspection of people and goods, as well as the establishment of a designated checking area in the Port;

e. In this context, the Israeli side will facilitate on an on-going basis the works related to the construction of the Gaza Sea Port, including the movement in and out of the Port of vessels, equipment, resources, and material required for the construction of the Port;

f. The two Sides will coordinate such works, including the designs and movement, through a joint mechanism.

7. Hebron Issues

a. The Shuhada Road in Hebron shall be opened for the movement of Palestinian vehicles in two phases. The first phase has been carried out, and the second shall be carried out not later than October 30, 1999;

b. The wholesale market-Hasbahe will be opened not later than November 1, 1999, in accordance with arrangements which will be agreed upon by the two Sides;
c. A high level Joint Liaison Committee will convene not later than September 13, 1999 to review the situation in the Tomb of the Patriarchs / Al Haram Al Ibrahimi (Annex I, Article VII, Interim Agreement and as per the January 15, 1998 US Minute of Discussion).

8. Security
   a. The two Sides will, in accordance with the prior agreements, act to ensure the immediate, efficient and effective handling of any incident involving a threat or act of terrorism, violence or incitement, whether committed by Palestinians or Israelis. To this end, they will cooperate in the exchange of information and coordinate policies and activities. Each side shall immediately and effectively respond to the occurrence or anticipated occurrence of an act of terrorism, violence or incitement and shall take all necessary measures to prevent such an occurrence;
   b. Pursuant to the prior agreements, the Palestinian side undertakes to implement its responsibilities for security, security cooperation, on-going obligations and other issues emanating from the prior agreements, including, in particular, the following obligations emanating from the Wye River Memorandum:
      1. continuation of the program for the collection of the illegal weapons, including reports;
      2. apprehension of suspects, including reports;
      3. forwarding of the list of Palestinian policemen to the Israeli Side not later than September 13, 1999;
      4. beginning of the review of the list by the Monitoring and Steering Committee not later than October 15, 1999.
9. The two sides call upon the international donor community to enhance its commitment and financial support to the Palestinian economic development and the Israeli–Palestinian peace process.
10. Recognizing the necessity to create a positive environment for the negotiations, neither side shall initiate or take any step that will change the status of the West Bank and the Gaza Strip in accordance with the Interim Agreement.
11. Obligations pertaining to dates, which occur on holidays or Saturdays, shall be carried out on the first subsequent working day.

This memorandum will enter into force one week from the date of its signature.[1]

[1] It is understood that, for technical reasons, implementation of Article 2-a and the first stage mentioned in Article 3-c will be carried out within a week from the signing of this Memorandum.

Made and signed in Sharm el-Sheikh, this fourth day of September 1999.

For the Government of the State of Israel	For the PLO

Witnessed by

For the Arab Republic of Egypt

For the United States of America

For the Hashemite Kingdom of Jordan

Bibliography

Abbas, Mahmoud [Abu Mazen], *Through Secret Channels* (Reading: Garnet Publishing, 1995).

Abouali, Gamal, 'Natural Resources under Occupation: The Status of Palestinian Water under International Law', 10 *Pace Int'l L. Rev.* 411 (1998).

Abu-Lughod, Janet, 'The Demographic Transformation of Palestine', in Ibrahim Abu-Lughod (ed.), *The Transformation of Palestine: Essays on the Origin and Development of the Arab–Israeli Conflict* (Evanston: Northwestern University Press, 1971).

Abu Odeh, Adnan, 'Religious Inclusion, Political Inclusion: Jerusalem as an Undivided Capital', 45 *Catholic U. L. Rev.* 687 (1996).

Ackerman, Bruce A., *We The People: Foundations* (Cambridge, MA: Belknap Press of Harvard University Press, 1991).

Al-Haq, *A Human Rights Assessment of the Declaration of Principles on Interim Self-Government Arrangements for Palestinians* (1993).

Allott, Philip, 'Power Sharing in the Law of the Sea,' 77 *Am. J. Int'l L.* 1 (1983).

Alston, Philip and Katarina Tomaševski (eds.), *The Right to Food* (Boston, MA: Martinus Nijhoff, 1984).

American Law Institute, *Restatement of the Law (2nd), Contracts* (1979).

—— *Restatement (3rd) of the Foreign Relations Law of the United States* (1987).

Amnesty International, *AI Report* (London: Amnesty International, published periodically).

Anaya, S. James, 'The Rights of Indigenous Peoples and International Law and Contemporary Perspective', in *1989 Harvard Indian Law Symposium* (1990).

—— 'A Contemporary Definition of the International Norm of Self-Determination', 3 *Transnat'l L. & Contemp. Probs.* 131 (1993).

Bacchi, Roberto, *The Population of Israel* (Jerusalem: Scientific Translations International, 1974).

Bailey, Sydney D., *The Making of Resolution 242* (Dordrecht: Martinus Nijhoff, 1985).

—— and Sam Daws, *The Procedure of the UN Security Council* (Oxford: Clarendon Press, 1998).

Barberis, Julio A., 'Nouvelles questions concernant la personalité juridique internationale', 179 *Rec. des Cours* 145 (1983–I).

Barkey, Karen, *Bandits and Bureaucrats: The Ottoman Route to State Centralization* (Ithaca, NY: Cornell University Press, 1997).

Baron, Salo W., *A Social and Religious History of the Jews*, 2nd edn., 15 vols (New York: Columbia University Press, 1952).

Bassiouni, M. Cherif (ed.), *International Terrorism and Political Crimes* (Springfield, IL: Thomas, 1975).

—— *International Criminal Law—A Draft International Criminal Code* (Dordrecht; Boston: Martinus Nijhoff, 1980).

—— 'Protection of Diplomats Under Islamic Law', 74 *Am. J. Int'l L.* 609 (1980).

Bauer, Yehuda, *The Holocaust in Historical Perspective* (Seattle: University of Washington Press, 1978).

Bauer, Yehuda with Nili Keren, *A History of the Holocaust* (New York: F. Watts, 1982).

Bayefsky, Anne F., 'Cultural Sovereignty, Relativism, and International Human Rights: New Excuses for Old Strategies', 9 *Ratio Juris* 42 (1996).

Beilin, Yossi, *Touching Peace: From the Oslo Accord to a Final Agreement*, translated by Philip Simpson (London: Weidenfeld & Nicolson, 1999).

Benedict, Michael Les, *Sources in American Constitutional History* (Lexington, MA: D. C. Heath, 1993).

Benvenisti, Eyal, *The International Law of Occupation* (Princeton, NJ: Princeton University Press, 1993).

—— 'The Israeli–Palestinian Declaration of Principles: A Framework for Future Settlement', 4 *Eur. J. Int'l L.* 542 (1993).

—— 'Collective Action in the Utilization of Shared Freshwater: The Challenges of International Water Resources Law', 90 *Am. J. Int'l L.* 384 (1996).

—— and Haim Gvirtzman, 'Harnessing International Law to Determine Israeli–Palestinian Water Rights: The Mountain Aquifer', 33 *Nat. Res. J.* 543 (1993).

—— and Eyal Zamir, 'Private Claims to Property Rights in the Future Israeli–Palestinian Settlement', 89 *Am. J. Int'l L.* 295 (1995).

Beres, Louis Rene, 'Opposing the "Peace Process": Israel, Civil Disobedience and the Principle of a Higher Law', 13 *Ariz. J. Int'l & Comp. Law* 117 (1996).

—— 'Response to John Quigley', 12 *Am. U.J. Int'l L. & Pol'y* 509 (1997).

—— 'Why the Oslo Accords Should Be Abrogated by Israel', 12 *Am. U. J. Int'l L. & Pol'y* 267 (1997).

—— and Zalman Shoval, 'On Demilitarizing a Palestinian "Entity" and the Golan Heights: An International Law Perspective', 28 *Vand. J. Transnat'l L.* 959 (1995).

—— —— 'Why a Demilitarized Palestinian State Would Not Remain Demilitarized: A View Under International Law', 11 *Temp. Int'l & Comp. L. J.* 347 (1997).

Berkovitz, Shmuel, 'The Holy Places in Jerusalem: Legal Aspects (Part One)', 11 *Justice* 4 (1996).

Berman, Jennifer S., 'No Place Like Home: Anti-Vietnamese Discrimination and Nationality in Cambodia', 84 *Calif. L. Rev.* 817 (1996).

Berman, Nathaniel, 'Sovereignty in Abeyance: Self-Determination and International Law', 7 *Wis. Int'l L.J.* 51 (1988).

Bethmann, Erich W. (ed.), *Decisive Years in Palestine, 1918–1948* (New York: American Friends of the Middle East, 1957).

Bin-Nun, Ariel, *The Law of the State of Israel: An Introduction*, 2nd edn. (translated from the German by Menachem Eichelberg; edited by Daniel C. Furman) (Jerusalem: Rubin Mass, 1992).

Bisharat, George E., 'Land, Law, and Legitimacy in Israel and the Occupied Territories', 43 *Am. U. L. Rev.* 467 (1994).

Bittker, Boris I. and Lawrence Lokken, *Fundamentals of International Taxation* (Boston; New York: Warren, Gorham & Lamont, 1991).

Black, Henry Campbell, Joseph R. Nolan, and Jacqueline M. Nolan-Haley, *Black's Law Dictionary*, 6th edn (St Paul, MN: West Publishing Co., 1990).

Blay, Sam, 'Self-Determination: A Reassessment in Post Communist Era', 22 *Denv. J. Int'l L. & Pol'y* 275 (1994).

Blum, Yehuda, 'The Missing Reversioner: Reflections on the Status of Judea and Samaria', 3 *Israel L. Rev.* 279 (1968).

Bollinger, Lee, *The Tolerant Society* (New York: Oxford University Press, 1986).

Bonell, M. J., 'Interpretation of Convention', in *Commentary On The International Sales Law: The 1980 Vienna Sales Convention* (Dott. A. Guiffre ed., 1987).

Bossuyt, Marc J., *Guide to the 'Travaux Préparatories' of the International Covenant on Civil and Political Rights* (Dordrecht; Boston: Martinus Nijhoff, 1987).

Boutros-Ghali, Boutros, 'La Ligue des Etats arabes', 137 *Rec. des Cours* 37 (1972–III).

—— 'An Agenda for Peace: Preventive diplomacy, peacemaking and peacekeeping: Report of the Secretary-General pursuant to the Statement adopted by the Summit Meeting of the Security Council on 31 January 1992', UN Doc. A/47/277-S/24111 (1992), 31 I.L.M 953 (1992).

Bower, Dennis, Note, 'An Evaluation of the Proposed Fair Trade in Financial Services Act', 27 *Case W. Res. J. Int'l L.* 407 (1995).

Boyd, S. M., Symposium, 'The applicability of international law to the occupied territories', 1 *Isr. Yb. Hum. Rts.* 367 (1971).

Boyle, Francis A., 'The Creation of the State of Palestine', 1 *Eur. J. Int'l L.* 301 (1990).

Brandon, Michael, 'Analysis of the Terms "Treaty" and "International Agreement" for Purposes of Registration Under Article 102 of the United Nations Charter', 47 *Am. J. Int'l L.* 49 (1953).

Breger, Marshall J., 'The Future of Jerusalem: A Symposium—An Introduction', 45 *Catholic U. L. Rev.* 653 (1996).

—— and Thomas A. Idinopulos, *Jerusalem's Holy Places and the Peace Process* (Washington, DC: Washington Institute for Near East Policy, Policy Papers Ser. No. 46, 1998).

Briggs, Herbert W., Book Review, 82 *Am. J. Int'l L.* 387 (1988).

Bright, John, *A History of Israel* (Philadelphia, PA: Westminster Press, 1959).

Brownlie, Ian, *Principles of Public International Law*, 4th edn (Oxford: Clarendon Press; New York: Oxford University Press, 1990).

—— *Treaties and Indigenous Peoples* (Oxford: Clarendon Press; New York: Oxford University Press, 1992).

Bruha, Thomas, 'Security Council', in Rüdiger Wolfrum (ed.), *United Nations: Law, Policies and Practice* (Dordrecht: Martinus Nijhoff, 1995), vol. 2.

Burris, Christopher C., Comment, 'Re-examining the Prisoner of War Status of the PLO Fedayeen', 22 *N.C. J. Int'l L. & Com. Reg.* 943 (1997).

Carbonneau, Thomas E., 'Terrorist Acts—Crimes or Political Infractions?', 3 *Hastings Int'l & Comp. L. Rev.* 265 (1980).

Carlson, Jonathan, 'Hunger, Agricultural Trade Liberalization, and Soft International Law: Addressing the Legal Dimensions of a Political Problem', 70 *Iowa L. Rev.* 1187 (1985).

Carlson-Whitley, Angela K., Note, 'Dowry Death: A Violation of the Right to Life Under Article Six of the International Covenant on Civil and Political Rights', 17 *U. Puget Sound L. Rev.* 637 (1994).

Cassese, Antonio, 'The Israel–PLO Agreement and Self-Determination', 4 *Eur. J. Int'l L.* 564 (1993).

—— *Self-Determination of Peoples: A Legal Reappraisal* (Cambridge; New York: Cambridge University Press, 1995).

Cattan, Henry, *Palestine, The Arabs and Israel: The Search for Justice* (London: Longmans, 1969).

—— *Palestine and International Law: the Legal Aspects of the Arab–Israeli Conflict* (London: Longman, 1973).

—— *Jerusalem* (New York: St Martin's Press, 1981).

Chayes, Abram and Antonia H. Chayes, *The New Sovereignty: Compliance with International Regulatory Agreements* (Cambridge, MA: Harvard University Press, 1995).

Cheng, Bin, *General Principles of Law as Applied by International Courts and Tribunals* (London: Stevens, 1953).

Churchill, Randolph S. and Winston S. Churchill, *The Six-Day War* (Boston, MA: Houghton Mifflin, 1967).

Clagett, Brice M., 'The Cuban Liberty and Democratic Solidarity (Libertad) Act: Title III of the Helms–Burton Act is Consistent with International Law', 90 *Am. J. Int'l L.* 436 (1996).

Clark, Roger S., 'The United Nations and Religious Freedom', 11 *N.Y.U. J. Int'l L. & Pol.* 197 (1978).

Cohen, Esther R., *Human Rights in the Israeli-Occupied Territories 1967–1982* (Manchester: Manchester University Press 1985).

Cohen, Nili, 'Good Faith in Bargaining and Principles of Contract Law', 9 *Tel Aviv Univ. Studies in Law* 249 (1989).

—— 'Status, Freedom and Contract', 10 *Tel Aviv Univ. Studies in Law* 213 (1990).

—— 'Political Agreements', 26 *Israel L. Rev.* 499 (1992).

Cotran, Eugene, Chibli Mallat, and David Stott (eds), *The Arab–Israeli Accords: Legal Perspectives* (London: Kluwer Law International, 1996).

Crawford, James, *The Creation of States in International Law* (Oxford: Clarendon Press, 1979).

—— 'The Creation of the State of Palestine: Too Much Too Soon?', 1 *Eur. J. Int'l L.* 307 (1990).

Cust, L. G. A., *The Status Quo in the Holy Places* (Jerusalem: Ariel Pub. House, 1980, reprint of London: Printed for the Government of Palestine by His Majesty's Stationery Office, 1929).

Dajani, Omar M., 'Stalled Between Seasons: The International Legal Status of Palestine During the Interim Period', 26 *Denv. J. Int'l L. & Pol'y* 27 (1997).

Damrosch, Lori Fisler, 'Retaliation or Arbitration—or Both? The 1978 United States–France Aviation Dispute', 74 *Am. J. Int'l L.* 785 (1980).

Danilenko, Gennady M., 'International Jus Cogens', 2 *Eur. J. Int'l L.* 42 (1991).

Dawidowicz, Lucy S., *The War Against the Jews, 1933–1945* (New York: Holt, Rinehart, and Winston, 1975).

Dawson, John P., 'Unconscionable Coercion: The German Version', 89 *Harv. L. Rev.* 1041 (1976).

de Aréchaga, Jiménez, 'International Law in the Past Third of a Century', 159 *Rec. des Cours* 1 (1978–I).

Dellapenna, Joseph W., 'Water in the Jordan Valley: The Potential and Limits of Law', 5 *Palestine Yb. Int'l L.* 15 (1989).

Dershowitz, Alan M., 'Is it Necessary to Apply "Physical Pressure" to Terrorists—And to Lie About it?', 23 *Israel L. Rev.* 193 (1989).

Developing the Occupied Territories: An Investment in Peace (The World Bank, Washington, D.C., Sept. 1993), vol. 2, *The Economy*.

Dichter, Harold, 'The Legal Status of Israel's Water Policies in the Occupied Territories', 35 *Harv. Int'l L. J.* 565 (1994).

Diller, Janelle M. and David A. Levy, 'Child Labor, Trade and Investment: Toward the Harmonization of International Law', 91 *Am. J. Int'l L.* 663 (1997).

Dillman, Jeffrey D., 'Water Rights in the Occupied Territories', *J. Palestine Studies* (Autumn 1989).

Dimitrijevic, Vojin, 'Legal Position of Palestine Refugees', 19 *Rev. Int'l Aff.* 427 (1968).

Dinstein, Yoram, 'The Legal Issues of "Para-War" and Peace in the Middle East', 44 *St. John's L. Rev.* 466 (1970).

—— 'The International Law of Belligerent Occupation and Human Rights', 8 *Isr. Yb. Hum. Rts.* 104 (1978).

—— 'Settlements and deportations in the occupied territories', 7 *Tel Aviv Univ. L. Rev.* 188 (1979) (in Hebrew).

—— 'The Israel Supreme Court and the Law of Belligerent Occupation: Deportations', 23 *Isr. Yb. Hum. Rts.* 1 (1993).

Divine, Donna Robinson, *Politics and Society in Ottoman Palestine: The Arab Struggle for Survival and Power* (Boulder, CO; London: Lynne Rienner Publishers, 1994).

Doernberg, Richard L., 'Overriding Tax Treaties: The U.S. Perspective', 9 *Emory Int'l L. Rev.* 71 (1995).

Dumper, Michael, *Islam and Israel: Muslim Religious Endowments and the Jewish State* (Washington, DC: Institute for Palestine Studies, 1994).

Durham, W. Cole, Jr., Lauren B. Homer, Pieter van Dijk, and John Witte, Jr., 'The Future of Religious Liberty in Russia: Report of the De Burght Conference on Pending Russian Legislation Concerning Religious Liberty', 8 *Emory Int'l L. Rev.* 1 (1994).

Duursma, Jorri C., *Fragmentation and the International Relations of Micro-States* (Cambridge, Melbourne, New York: Cambridge University Press, 1996).

Eban, Abba, *Voice of Israel* (New York, Horizon Press, 1957).

Eisner, Michael, 'Jerusalem: An Analysis of Legal Claims and Political Realities', 12 *Wis. Int'l L.J.* 221 (1994).

Elagab, Omer Yousif, *The Legality of Non-Forcible Counter-Measures in International Law* (Oxford: Clarendon Press; New York: Oxford University Press, 1988).

ElBaradei, Mohamed, 'The Egyptian–Israeli Peace Treaty and Access to the Gulf of Aqaba: A New Legal Regime', 76 *Am. J. Int'l L.* 532 (1982).

Elias, T. O., 'The Doctrine of Intertemporal Law', 74 *Am. J. Int'l L.* 285 (1980).

Elmusa, Sharif S., *The Water Issue and the Palestinian–Israeli Conflict* (1993).

—— 'Dividing Common Water Resources According to International Water Law: The Case of the Palestinian–Israeli Waters', 35 *Nat. Res. J.* 223 (1995).

—— and Mahmud El-Jaafari, 'Power and Trade: The Israeli–Palestinian Economic

Protocol', in Eugene Cotran, Chibli Mallat, and David Stott (eds.), *The Arab–Israeli Accords: Legal Perspectives* (London: Kluwer Law International, 1996).

Englard, Izhak, 'The Legal Status of the Holy Places in Jerusalem', 28 *Isr. L. Rev.* 589 (1994).

Esposito, John L. (ed.), *Oxford Encyclopedia of the Modern Islamic World* (New York: Oxford University Press, 1995).

Ettinger, S., 'The Modern Period', in *A History of the Jewish People*, edited by H. H. Ben-Sasson (Cambridge, MA: Harvard University Press, 1976).

Falk, Richard A. and Burns H. Weston, 'The Relevance of International Law to Palestinian Rights in the West Bank and Gaza: In Legal Defense of the Intifada', 32 *Harv. Int'l L.J.* 129 (1991).

Farnsworth, E. Allan, *Contracts*, 2nd edn (Boston: Little, Brown & Co., 1990).

—— 'The Eason–Weinmann Colloquium on International and Comparative Law: Duties of Good Faith and Fair Dealing under the UNIDROIT Principles, Relevant International Conventions, and National Laws', 3 *Tul. J. Int'l & Comp. L.* 47 (1995).

—— and William F. Young, *Contracts*, 5th edn (Foundation Press, 1995).

Farrior, Stephanie, 'Molding the Matrix: The Historical and Theoretical Foundations of International Law Concerning Hate Speech', 14 *Berk. J. Int'l L.* 3 (1996).

Faulkner, Elizabeth A., 'The Right to Habeas Corpus: Only in the Other Americas', 9 *Am. U.J. Int'l L. & Pol'y* 653 (1994).

Feith, Douglas J., 'Protocol I: Moving Humanitarian Law Backwards', 19 *Akron L. Rev.* 531 (1986).

Ferrari, Silvio, 'The Fundamental Agreement Between the Holy See and Israel and the Conventions Between States and the Church Since the Vatican II Council', 47 *Cath. L. Rev.* 385 (1998).

—— 'The Religious Significance of Jerusalem in the Middle East Peace Process: Some Legal Implications', 45 *Catholic U. L. Rev.* 733 (1996).

Feuer, Guy, 'Les accords passés par les Gouvernements de Jordanie et du Liban avec les organisations palestiniennes', 1970 *Ann. Français de Droit Int'l* 177.

Fidler, David P., 'Foreign Private Investment in Palestine: An Analysis of the Law on the Encouragement of Investment in Palestine', 19 *Fordham Int'l L.J.* 529 (1995).

—— 'Peace Through Trade? Developments in Palestinian Trade Law During the Peace Process', 38 *Va. J. Int'l L.* 155 (1998).

FitzHerbert, Margaret, *The Man Who Was Greenmantle: A Biography of Aubrey Herbert* (London: John Murray, 1983).

Fitzmaurice, Sir Gerald, 'The Future of Public International Law', in *Livre du Centenaire, Ann. Inst. de Droit Int'l* (1973), 233.

Fletcher, George, *Basic Concepts of Criminal Law* (New York; Oxford: Oxford University Press, 1998).

Flory, Maurice, 'Naissance d'un Etat Palestinien', 93 *Revue Generale de Droit Int'l Public* 385 (1989).

Fox, Gregory H., Book Review, 92 *Am. J. Int'l L.* 359 (1998).

Franck, Thomas M., 'Who Killed Article 2:4?', 64 *Am. J. Int'l L.* 804 (1970).

—— Editorial Comment, 'Word Made Law: The Decision of the ICJ in the Nuclear Test Cases', 69 *Am. J. Int'l L.* 612 (1975).

—— *The Power of Legitimacy Among Nations* (New York: Oxford University Press, 1990).

—— 'Postmodern Tribalism and the Right to Secession', in Catherine Brölmann, René Lefeber and Marjoleine Zieck (eds), *Peoples And Minorities in International Law* (Dordrecht; Boston: M. Nijhoff, 1993).

Freudenschuss, Helmut, 'Article 39 of the UN Charter Revisited: Threats to the Peace and the Recent Practice of the UN Security Council', 46 *Austrian J. Pub. & Int'l L.* 33–4 (1993).

Friedlander, Saul, *Memory, History, and the Extermination of the Jews of Europe* (Bloomington: Indiana University Press, 1993).

—— *Nazi Germany and the Jews* (New York: HarperCollins 1997).

Friedman, Thomas, *From Beirut to Jerusalem* (New York: Farrar, Straus & Giroux, 1989).

Fromkin, David, *A Peace to End All Peace: The Fall of the Ottoman Empire and the Creation of the Modern Middle East* (New York: Henry Holt, 1989).

Fuller, Lon L., 'The Case of the Speluncean Explorers', 62 *Harv. L. Rev.* 616 (1949).

Gabor, Francis A., 'Reflections on the Freedom of Movement in Light of the Dismantled "Iron Curtain" ', 65 *Tul. L. Rev.* 849 (1991).

Garcia-Mora, Manuel R., 'The Nature of Political Offenses: A Knotty Problem of Extradition Law', 48 *Va. L. Rev.* 1226 (1962).

Gardner, Richard, 'Commentary on the Law of Self-Defense', in Laurie Fisler Damrosch and David J. Scheffer (eds), *Law and Force in the New International Order* (Boulder: Westview Press, 1991).

Garvey, Jack I., 'Regional Free Trade Dispute Resolution as Means for Securing the Middle East Peace Process', 47 *Am. J. Comp. L.* 147 (1999).

Gaudiosi, Monica M., Comment, 'The Influence of The Islamic Law of Waqf on the Development of the Trust in England: The Case of Merton College', 136 *U. Pa. L. Rev.* 1231 (1988).

Gerson, Allan, 'Trustee-Occupant: the Legal Status of Israel's Presence in the West Bank', 14 *Harv. Int'l L. J.* 1 (1973).

—— *Israel, the West Bank and International Law* (London; Totowa, NJ: Frank Cass, 1978).

—— Book Review, 77 *Am. J. Int'l L.* 918 (1983).

—— Review of Pogany, *The Security Council and the Arab–Israeli Conflict*, 79 *Am. J. Int'l L.* 801 (1985).

Gilbert, Geoff S., 'Terrorism and the Political Offense Exemption Reappraisal', 34 *Int'l & Comp. L. Q.* 695 (1985).

Gilbert, Martin, *Sir Horace Rumbold: Portrait of a Diplomat 1869–1941* (London: Heinemann, 1973).

—— *Israel: A History* (New York: William Morrow, 1998).

Goldberg, Pamela and Nancy Kelly, 'Recent Developments: International Human Rights and Violence against Women', 6 *Harv. Hum. Rts. J.* 195 (1993).

Goodrich, Leland M., Edvard Hambro, and Anne Patricia Simons, *Charter of the United Nations: Commentary and Documents*, 3rd edn (New York: Columbia University Press, 1969).

Gottheil, Fred M., 'Arab Immigration into Pre-state Israel', in *Palestine and Israel in the 19th and 20th Centuries*, edited by Elie Kedourie and Sylvia C. Haim (London, Totowa, NJ: Frank Cass, 1982).

Gottlieb, Gidon, 'Global Bargaining: The Legal and Diplomatic Framework', in Nicholas G. Onuf (ed.), *Law-making in the Global Community* (Durham, NC: Carolina Academic Press, 1982).

—— 'Legal Theory for a Relational Society', 50 *U. Chi. L. Rev.* 567 (1983).

Grant, Thomas D., 'Review Article: Between Diversity and Disorder', 12 *Am. U.J. Int'l L. & Pol'y* 629 (1997).

Grant, Thomas D., 'Defining Statehood: The Montevideo Convention and its Discontents', 37 *Colum. J. Transnat'l L.* 403 (1999).

Greig, D. W., 'Reciprocity, Proportionality, and the Law of Treaties', 34 *Va. J. Int'l L.* 295 (1994).

Grotius, Hugo, *De Jure Belli ac Pacis* (1624).

Guelke, Adrian, *The Age of Terrorism and the International Political System* (London: Tauris Academic Studies, I.B. Tauris Publishers, 1995).

Gunn, T. Jeremy, Book Review, 90 *Am. J. Int'l L.* 707, 708 (1996) (reviewing Bahiyyih G. Tahzib, *Freedom of Religion or Belief: Ensuring Effective International Legal Protection* (The Hague, Boston, London: Martinus Nijhoff, 1996)).

Habermas, Jurgen, 'The European State: Its Achievements and Its Limitations: On the Past and Future of Sovereignty and Citizenship', 9 *Ratio Juris* 125 (1996).

Habib, John L., 'Israeli Deportations of Palestinians Under International Law', 4 *Emory Int'l L. Rev.* 133 (1990).

Halberstam, Malvina, 'Self-Determination in the Arab–Israeli Conflict: Meaning, Myth, and Politics', 21 *N.Y.U.J. Int'l L. & Pol.* 465 (1989).

—— 'Nationalism and the Right to Self-Determination: The Arab–Israeli Conflict', 26 *N.Y.U. J. Int'l L. & Pol.* 573 (1995).

Hall, William Edward, *A Treatise on International Law*, 8th edn, edited by A. Pearce Higgins (Oxford: Clarendon Press, 1924).

Han, Henry H. (ed.), *Terrorism & Political Violence: Limits & Possibilities of Legal Control* (New York: Oceana, 1993).

Hanauer, Laurence S., 'The Irrelevance of Self-Determination Law to Ethno-National Conflict: A New Look at the Western Sahara Case', 9 *Emory Int'l L. Rev.* 133 (1995).

Hannum, Hurst, *The Right to Leave and Return in International Law and Practice* (Dordrecht; Boston: Martinus Nijhoff, 1987).

—— *Autonomy, Sovereignty, and Self-Determination: The Accommodation of Conflicting Rights* (Philadelphia, PA: University of Pennsylvania Press, 1990).

—— 'Rethinking Self-Determination', 34 *Va. J. Int'l L.* 1 (1993).

—— and Richard B. Lillich, 'The Concept of Autonomy in International Law', 74 *Am. J. Int'l L.* 858 (1980).

Hansell, Herbert and Nicholas Rostow, *Legal Implications of May 4, 1999* (Washington, DC: The Washington Institute for Near East Policy, 1999).

Hartkamp, Arthur S., 'Judicial Discretion Under the New Civil Code of the Netherlands', 40 *Am. J. Comp. L.* (1992).

Henkin, Louis, *How Nations Behave: Law and Foreign Policy*, 2nd edn (New York: Columbia University Press, 1979).

—— 'International Human Rights as "Rights" ', 1 *Cardozo L. Rev.* 446 (1979).

—— 'International Law: Politics, Values and Functions', 216 *Rec. des Cours* 58 (1989–IV).

—— Richard Crawford Pugh, Oscar Schachter, and Hans Smit, *International Law: Cases and Materials*, 3rd edn (St Paul, MN: West Publishing, 1993).

Higgins, Rosalyn, 'Derogations Under Human Rights Treaties', 48 *Brit. Y.B. Int'l L.* 281 (1975–6).

—— Review of Gerson, *Israel, the West Bank and International Law*, 74 *Am. J. Int'l L.* 704, 705 (1980).

—— *United Nations Peacekeeping 1946–1967: Documents and Commentary*, vol. 1 (London, New York: Oxford University Press, 1969–81).

Hilberg, Raul, *The Destruction of the European Jews* (New York: Holmes & Meier, 1985).

Hinsley, F. H., *Sovereignty* (Cambridge: Cambridge University Press, 2nd edn 1986).

Hirsch, Moshe, 'The Freedom of Proselytism Under the Fundamental Agreement and International Law', 47 *Catholic U. L. Rev.* 407 (1998).

—— Deborah Housen-Couriel, and Ruth Lapidoth, *Whither Jerusalem? Proposals and Positions Concerning the Future of Jerusalem* (The Hague; Boston: Martinus Nijhoff, 1995).

Hofman, Rainer, *Die Ausreisefreiheit nach Volkerrecht und staatlichem Recht* (Berlin; New York: Springer, 1988).

Honnold, John O., *Uniform Law for International Sales under the 1980 United Nations Convention* (Deventer, Netherlands; Boston: Kluwer Law and Taxation Publishers, 1982).

Hopenfeld, James E., Book Review, 89 *Mich. L. Rev.* 1800 (1991).

Hudson, Manley O., *World Court Reports: A Collection of the Judgments, Orders, and Opinions of the Permanent Court of International Justice* (Washington: Carnegie Endowment for International Peace, 1934–43).

Humphrey, 'The International Bill of Rights: Scope and Implementation', 17 *Wm. & Mary L. Rev.* 527 (1976).

Hurewitz, J. C., *The Struggle for Palestine* (New York: Norton, 1950).

International Committee of the Red Cross, 'Geneva Conventions of 12 August 1949 and Additional Protocols of 8 June 1977: Ratifications, accessions and successions as at 31 December 1994', 304 *Int'l Rev. Red Cross* 111 (1995).

Jaeger, Fr. David-Maria A., 'The Fundamental Agreement Between the Holy See and the State of Israel: A New Legal Régime of Church–State Relations', 47 *Cath. L. Rev.* 427 (1998).

Jagerskiold, Stig, 'The Freedom of Movement', in Louis Henkin (ed.), *The International Bill of Rights: the Covenant on Civil and Political Rights* (New York: Columbia University Press, 1981).

Jean, Patrice, 'Le Contenu de la Liberté de Circulation', in Maurice Flory, Rosalyn Higgins, and Claude J. Berr (eds), *Liberté de Circulation des Personnes en Droit International* (Paris: Economica, 1988).

Jefferson, Thomas, 'Opinion on the French Treaties', in *Thomas Jefferson: Writings* (Merrill D. Peterson (ed.), New York, NY: Viking Press, 1984).

Jennings, Sir Robert, 'The Identification of International Law', in Bin Cheng (ed.), *International Law, Teaching and Practice* (London: Stevens, 1982).

Jennings, Sir Robert, and Sir Arthur Watts (eds.), *Oppenheim's International Law*, 9th edn (Harlow, Essex: Longman, 1993).
Jessup, Phillip, 'The Palmas Island Arbitration', 22 *Am. J. Int'l L.* 735 (1928).
—— *A Modern Law of Nations: An Introduction* (New York: Macmillan, 1948).
Jewish Agency for Palestine, 'The Influence of Jewish Colonization on Arab Development in Palestine', 3 *Palestine Y.B.* 185 (1947–8).
Jiryis, Sabri, 'Settlers' Law: Seizure of Palestinian Lands', 2 *Palestine Y.B. Int'l L.* 17 (1985).
Johnson, Paul, *A History of the Jews* (New York: Harper & Row, 1987).
Kafadar, Cemal, *Between Two Worlds: The Construction of the Ottoman State* (Berkeley, CA: University of California Press, 1995).
Kawakami, Shoji, 'Precontractual Liability: Japan', reprinted in Merryman, *The Civil Law Tradition* (Charlottesville: Michie, 1994), 1227–30.
Kedourie, Elie, *England and the Middle East: The Destruction of the Ottoman Empire 1914–1921* (London: Bowes & Bowes, 1956; reprint, Hassocks, Sussex: The Harvester Press, 1978).
—— *In the Anglo–Arab Labyrinth: The McMahon–Husayn Correspondence and its Interpreters 1914–1939* (Cambridge: Cambridge University Press, 1976).
Kelly, Michael J., 'Political Downsizing: The Re-Emergence of Self-Determination, and the Movement Toward Smaller Ethnically Homogenous States', 47 *Drake L. Rev.* 209 (1999).
Kelsen, Hans, *The Law of the United Nations: A Critical Analysis of Its Fundamental Problems* (London: Stevens & Sons, 1954).
Khadduri, Majid, and Herbert J. Liebesny (eds.), *Law in the Middle East: Origin and Development of Islamic Law* (vol. 1) (Washington, DC: Middle East Institute, 1955).
Khalidi, Rashid, *Under Siege: PLO Decision-making During the 1982 War* (New York: Columbia University Press, 1986).
Khoury, Amir H., 'An American Bank in the Palestinian Authority: Investing in the Peace', 24 *Brooklyn J. Int'l L.* 739 (1999).
—— 'International Trade and Commerce: A Bridge for the Israeli–Palestinian Peace', 7 *Cardozo J. Int'l & Comp. L.* 11 (1999).
Kirgis, Frederic L., Jr., 'Some Lingering Questions about Article 60 of the Vienna Convention on the Law of Treaties', 22 *Cornell Int'l L.J.* 549 (1989).
—— 'Admission of "Palestine" as a Member of a Specialized Agency and Withholding the Payment of Assessments in Response', 84 *Am. J. Int'l L.* 218 (1990).
—— 'The Degrees of Self-Determination in the United Nations Era', 88 *Am. J. Int'l L.* 304 (1994).
Klein, Claude, 'French Administrative Law as a Paradigm: Some Remarks Concerning Its Use by the Supreme Court of Israel', 11 *Tel Aviv Univ. Studies in Law* 111 (1992).
Klein, Menachem, 'The Islamic Holy Places as a Political Bargaining Card (1993–1995)', 47 *Catholic U. L. Rev.* 745 (1996).
Klieman, Aharon, *Approaching the Finish Line: The United States in Post-Oslo Peace Making* (Ramat Gan, Israel: Begin–Sadat Center of Bar-Ilan University, 1995).
Koh, Harold Hongju, Review of *The New Sovereignty* by Abram Chayes and Antonia H. Chayes, 91 *Am. J. Int'l L.* 389 (1997).

Koplow, David A., 'Parsing Good Faith: Has the United States Violated Article VI of the Nuclear Non-Proliferation Treaty?', 1993 *Wisc. L. Rev*. 301.

Kretzmer, David, *The Legal Status of the Arabs in Israel* (Boulder, CO: Westview Press, 1990).

—— 'Political Agreements—A Critical Introduction', 26 *Israel L. Rev*. 407 (1992).

Kushner, David (ed.), *Palestine in the Late Ottoman Period: Political, Social, and Economic Transformation* (Oxford: Oxford University Press, 1986; Jerusalem: Yad Izhak Ben-Zvi, 1986).

Lapidoth, Ruth, 'The Right of Return in International Law, with Special Reference to the Palestinian Refugees', 16 *Isr. YB. Hum. Rts*. 103 (1986).

—— 'International Law Within the Israeli Legal System', 24 *Isr. L. Rev*. 451 (1990).

—— 'Jerusalem and the Peace Process', 28 *Israel L. Rev*. 402 (1994).

—— 'International Law', in *The Law of Israel: General Surveys* (Itzhak Zamir & Sylvanie Colombo eds, 1995).

—— 'Jerusalem—Some Jurisprudential Aspects', 45 *Catholic U. L. Rev*. 661 (1996).

—— 'Freedom of Religion and of Conscience in Israel', 47 *Catholic U. L. Rev*. 441 (1998).

—— and N. K. Calvo-Goller, 'Les Elements Constitutifs de L'Etat et la Declaration du Conseil National Palestinien du 15 Novembre 1988', 96 *Revue Generale de Droit Int'l Public* 777 (1992).

—— and Moshe Hirsch (eds), *The Arab–Israel Conflict and Its Resolution: Selected Documents* (Dordrecht, Boston: Martinus Nijhoff, 1992).

—— —— *The Jerusalem Question and its Resolution: Selected Documents* (Dordrecht; Boston: Martinus Nijhoff, 1994).

Laqueur, Walter, *The Road to War, 1967: The Origins of the Arab–Israeli Conflict*, 2nd edn (London: Weidenfeld & Nicolson, 1969).

—— (ed.), *The Israel–Arab Reader: A Documentary History of the Middle East Conflict* 15 (New York: Bantam, 1970).

Lauterpacht, Elihu, *Recognition in International Law* (Cambridge: Cambridge University Press, 1948).

—— 'Sovereignty Over Submarine Areas', 1950 *Brit. Y. B. Int'l L*. 376.

—— 'The Contemporary Practice of the United Kingdom in the Field of International Law—Survey and Comment, IX', 10 *Int'l & Comp. L. Q*. 548 (1961).

—— *Jerusalem and the Holy Places* (London: Anglo-Israel Association, 1968).

Lee, Luke T., 'The Right to Compensation: Refugees and Countries of Asylum', 80 *Am. J. Int'l L*. 532 (1986).

Leigh, Monroe, Comment, 81 *Am. J. Int'l L*. 220 (1987).

LeStrange, Guy, *Palestine Under the Moslems: A Description of Syria and the Holy Land from* AD *650 to 1500* (London: 1890; Beirut: 1975).

Levie, Howard S., 'Prisoners of War Under the 1977 Protocol I', 23 *Akron L. Rev*. 55 (1989).

Levine, Mel, 'Palestinian Economic Progress Under the Oslo Agreements', 19 *Fordham Int'l L. J*. 1393 (1996).

Lillich, Richard B. and Hurst Hannum, *International Human Rights: Problems of Law, Policy, and Practice*, 3rd edn (Boston: Little, Brown & Co., 1995).

—— and Burns H. Weston, *International Claims: Their Settlement by Lump Sum Agreements*, 2 vols (Charlottesville: University of Virginia Press, 1975).

Lillich, Richard B. and Hurst Hannum, 'Lump Sum Agreements: Their Continuing Contribution to the Law of International Claims', 82 *Am. J. Int'l L.* 69 (1988).

Lipson, Charles, 'Why Are Some International Agreements Informal?', 45 *Int'l Org.* 495 (1991).

Lissitzyn, Oliver, 'Territorial Entities Other Than States in the Law of Treaties', 125 *Rec. des Cours* 5 (1983–III).

Long, David E., *The Anatomy of Terrorism* (New York: Free Press; Toronto: Collier Macmillan Canada; New York: Maxwell Macmillan International, 1990).

Lorch, Nathan, 'The Applicability of the Fourth Geneva Convention to the Territories Administered by Israel', 1 *Isr. Yb. Hum. Rts.* 366 (1971).

Lowi, Miriam R., *Water and Power: the Politics of a Scarce Resource in the Jordan River Basin* (Cambridge: Cambridge University Press, 1993).

Lustick, Ian S., 'Ending Protracted Conflicts: The Oslo Peace Process Between Political Partnership and Legality', 30 *Cornell Int'l L.J.* 741 (1997).

McCaffrey, Stephen C., 'A Human Right to Water: Domestic and International Implications', 5 *Geo. Int'l Envtl. L. Rev.* 1 (1992).

—— 'The Harmon Doctrine One Hundred Years Later: Buried, Not Praised', 36 *Nat. Res. J.* 549 (1997).

—— and Mpazi Sinjela, 'The 1997 United Nations Convention on International Watercourses', 92 *Am. J. Int'l L.* 97 (1998).

McCarthy, Justin, *The Population of Palestine: Population History and Statistics of the Late Ottoman Period and the Mandate* (New York: Columbia University Press, 1990).

McCormack, Timothy L. H., *Self-Defense in International Law: The Israeli Raid on the Iraqi Nuclear Reactor* (New York: St Martin's Press; Jerusalem: The Magnes Press, The Hebrew University, 1996).

McDowall, David, *The Palestinians: The Road to Nationhood* (London: Minority Rights Group, 1994).

McNair, Baron Arnold Duncan, *The Law of Treaties* (New York: Columbia University Press, 1938, and Oxford: Clarendon Press, 1961).

McWhinney, Edward, *United Nations Law Making: Cultural and Ideological Relativism and International Law Making for an Era of Transition* (New York: Holmes & Meier Publishers, 1984).

Makovsky, David, *Making Peace with the PLO: The Rabin Government's Road to the Oslo Accord* (Boulder, CO: Westview Press, 1996).

Mallison, W. Thomas and Sally V. Mallison, 'The Juridical Status of Irregular Combatants under the International Humanitarian Law of Armed Conflict', 9 *Case W. J. Int'l L.* 39 (1977).

Mann, F. A., 'Note and Comment: Foreign Investment in the International Court of Justice: The ELSI Case', 86 *Am. J. Int'l L.* 92 (1992).

Margolis, Max L., and Marx, Alexander, *A History of the Jewish People* (New York: Atheneum, 1969) (reprint of Philadelphia, PA: Jewish Publication Society of America, 1927).

Martens, Georg Friedrich de, *Nouveau Recueil Général de Traités et Autres Actes Relatifs aux Rapports de Droit International*, 3 sér.

Meron, Theodor, 'The Meaning and Reach of the International Convention on the Elimination of All Forms of Racial Discrimination', 79 *Am. J. Int'l L.* 283 (1985).

Merrills, J. G., *The Development of International Law by the European Court of Human Rights*, 2nd edn (Manchester: Manchester University Press, 1993).

Merryman, John Henry, David S. Clark, John O. Haley, *The Civil Law Tradition: Europe, Latin America, and East Asia* (Charlottesville, VA: Michie, 1994).

Metz, Helen C., *Israel: A Country Study*, 3rd edn (Washington: Library of Congress, 1990).

Molkner, Keith C., 'Legal and Structural Hurdles to Achieving Political Stability and Economic Development in the Palestinian Territories', 19 *Fordham Int'l L.J.* 1419 (1996).

Moore, John Norton (ed.), *The Arab–Israeli Conflict*, 4 vols. (Princeton, NJ: Princeton University Press, 1974).

—— 'The Regime of Straits and the Third United Nations Conference on the Law of the Sea', 74 *Am. J. Int'l L.* 77 (1980).

Moris, Halim, 'Self-Determination: An Affirmative Right Or Mere Rhetoric?', 4 *ILSA J. Int'l & Comp L.* 201 (1997).

Morris, Benny, *The Birth of the Palestinian Refugee Problem 1947–49* (New York: Cambridge University Press, 1987).

—— *Righteous Victims: A History of the Zionist–Arab Conflict, 1881–1999* (New York: Knopf, 1999).

Mosler, Hermann, 'The International Society as a Legal Community', 140 *Rec. des Cours* 1 (1974–IV).

Murphy, John F., *Punishing International Terrorists: The Legal Framework for Policy Initiatives* (Totowa, NJ: Rowman & Allanheld, 1985).

—— 'The Future of Multilateralism and Efforts to Combat International Terrorism', 25 *Colum. J. Trans. L.* 35 (1986).

—— 'Civil Liability for the Commission of International Crimes as an Alternative to Criminal Prosecution', 12 *Harv. Hum. Rts. J.* 1 (1999).

Murphy, Sean D., 'Developments in International Criminal Law: Progress and Jurisprudence of the International Criminal Tribunal for the Former Yugoslavia', 93 *Am. J. Int'l L.* 57 (1999).

Muslih, Muhammad Y., *The Origins of Palestinian Nationalism* (New York: Columbia University Press, 1988).

Nafziger, James A. R., 'The General Admission of Aliens Under International Law', 77 *Am. J. Int'l L.* 804 (1983).

Nanda, Ved, 'Self-Determination: The Case of Palestine', 82 *Am. Soc'y Int'l L. Proc.* 334 (1988).

Noone, Michael F. and Yonah Alexander (eds), *Cases and Materials on Terrorism: Three Nations' Response* (The Hague: Kluwer Law International, 1997).

Norton, Patrick M., 'A Law of the Future or a Law of the Past? Modern Tribunals and the International Law of Expropriation', 85 *Am. J. Int'l L.* 474 (1991).

Note, 'The Israel–PLO Declaration of Principles: Prelude to a Peace?', 34 *Va. J. Int'l L.* 435 (1994).

Nowak, Manfred, *U.N. Covenant on Civil and Political Rights: CCPR Commentary* (Kehl, Germany; Arlington, VA: N. P. Engel, 1993).

O'Brien, Conor Cruise, *The Siege: The Saga of Israel and Zionism* (New York: Simon and Schuster, 1986).

O'Connell, D. P., 'The Condominium of the New Hebrides', 43 *Brit. Yb. Int'l L.* 71 (1968–9).

O'Connor, J. F., *Good Faith in International Law* (Aldershot, Hants; Brookfield, VT: Dartmouth, 1991).

O'Kane, Rosemary H. T., *Terror, Force, and States: The Path from Modernity* (Cheltenham, UK; Brookfield, US: Edward Elgar, 1996).

Olson, Wendy, 'UN Security Council Resolutions Regarding Deportations From Israeli Administered Territories: The Applicability of the Fourth Geneva Convention Relative to the Protection of Civilian Persons in Time of War', 24 *Stan. J. Int'l L.* 611 (1988).

Oppenheim, Lassa Francis Lawrence, *International Law*, 3rd edn, edited by Ronald F. Roxburgh (London: Longmans, Green and Co., 1920).

Paust, Jordan J., *et al.*, *International Criminal Law: Cases and Materials* (Durham, NC: Carolina Academic Press, 1996).

Peres, Shimon, *Battling for Peace: A Memoir*, edited by David Landau (New York: Random House, 1995).

Perez, Antonio F., 'Survival of Rights Under the Nuclear Non-Proliferation Treaty: Withdrawal and the Continuing Right of International Atomic Energy Agency Safeguards', 34 *Va. J. Int'l L.* 749 (1994).

—— 'Who Killed Sovereignty? Or: Changing Norms Concerning Sovereignty in International Law', 14 *Wis. Int'l L.J.* 463 (1996).

Pictet, Jean S. (ed.), *The Geneva conventions of 12 August 1949* (Geneva: International Committee of the Red Cross, 1958), 4 volumes, translated from the French.

Pogany, Istvan S., *The Security Council and the Arab–Israeli Conflict* (New York: St Martin's Press, 1984).

Pomerance, Michla, 'The United States and Self-Determination: Perspectives on the Wilsonian Conception', 70 *Am. J. Int'l L.* 1 (1976).

Porath, Yehoshua, *The Emergence of the Palestinian–Arab National Movement, 1918–1929* (London: Frank Cass, 1974).

—— *The Palestinian Arab National Movement: From Riots to Rebellion* (London: Frank Cass, 1977).

Posner, Richard A., 'Gratuitous Promises in Economics and Law', 6 *J. Legal Stud.* 411 (1977).

Quandt, William B., *The Palestinian Arab National Movement: From Riots to Rebellion* (London: Frank Cass, 1977).

—— *Camp David: Peacemaking and Politics* (Washington: Brookings Institution, 1986).

Quigley, John, *Politics, Law, and Society: Palestine and Israel: A Challenge to Justice* (Durham, NC: Duke University Press, 1990).

—— 'The Israel–PLO Agreements versus the Geneva Civilians Convention', 7 *Palestine Yb. Int'l L.* 45 (1992/4).

—— 'Sovereignty in Jerusalem', 47 *Catholic U. L. Rev.* 765 (1996).

—— 'The Israel–PLO Interim Agreements: Are They Treaties?', 30 *Cornell Int'l L. J.* 717 (1997).

—— 'The Oslo Accords: More than Israel Deserves', 12 *Am. U. Int'l L. & Pol'y* 285 (1997).

—— 'Displaced Palestinians and a Right of Return', 39 *Harv. Int'l L.J.* 171 (1998).

Radley, Kurt René, 'The Palestinian Refugees: the Right to Return in International Law', 72 *Am. J. Int'l L.* 586 (1978).

Ramcharan, B. G., 'The Concept and Dimensions of the Right to Life', in B. G. Ramcharan (ed.), *The Right to Life in International Law* (Dordrecht; Boston: Martinus Nijhoff, 1985).

—— 'The Drafting History of Treaty Provisions on the Right to Life: The Drafting History of Article 6 of the International Covenant on Civil and Political Rights', in B. G. Ramcharan (ed.), *The Right to Life in International Law* (Dordrecht; Boston: Martinus Nijhoff, 1985).

Reich, Bernard, *Quest for Peace: United States–Israel Relations and the Arab–Israeli Conflict* (New Brunswick, NJ: Transaction Books [Rutgers University], 1977).

Reisman, W. Michael, 'Coercion and Self-Determination: Construing Charter Article 2(4)', 78 *Am. J. Int'l L.* 642 (1984).

'Research in International Law Under the Auspices of the Faculty of the Harvard Law School, Part III', 29 *Supp. Am. J. Int'l L.* 981 (1935).

Robinson, Glenn E., *Building a Palestinian State: The Incomplete Revolution* (Bloomington, IN: Indiana University Press, 1997).

Rogoff, Martin A., 'Interpretation of International Agreements by Domestic Courts and the Politics of International Treaty Relations: Reflections On Some Recent Decisions Of The United States Supreme Court', 11 *Am. U.J. Int'l L. & Pol'y* 559 (1996).

Rosenne, Shabtai, 'On multi-lingual interpretation', 6 *Israel L. Rev.* 360 (1971).

—— 'The Settlement of Treaty Disputes under the Vienna Convention of 1969', 32 *Zeitschrift für Ausländisches Öffentliches Recht und Völkerrecht* 1 (1971).

—— *Breach of Treaty* (Cambridge: Grotius, 1985).

Rostow, Eugene V., 'Legal Aspects of the Search for Peace in the Middle East', 64 *Proc. of the Am. Soc. of Int'l L.* 64 (1970).

—— ' "Palestinian Self-Determination": Possible Futures for the Unallocated Territories of the Palestine Mandate', 5 *Yale Stud. in World Pub. Order* 147 (1979).

Rozakis, Christos L., *The Concept of* Jus Cogens *in the Law of Treaties* (Amsterdam; New York: North-Holland Pub. Co., 1976).

Rubin, Alfred P., 'The International Legal Effects of Unilateral Declarations', 71 *Am. J. Int'l L.* 1 (1977).

Rubin, Benjamin, 'PLO Violence and Legitimate Combatancy: A Response to Professor Green', 19 *Isr. Y.B. Hum. Rts.* 167 (1989).

Rubinstein, Amnon, 'The Changing Status of the "Territories" (West Bank and Gaza): From Escrow to Legal Mongrel', 8 *Tel-Aviv U. Studies in Law* 59 (1988).

Sachar, Howard M., *A History of Israel: From the Rise of Zionism to Our Time* (New York: Knopf, 1981).

Said, Edward W., *Peace and its Discontents: Essays on Palestine in the Middle East Peace Process* (New York: Vintage Books, 1995).

Sapiro, Miriam E., Note, 'Extradition in an Era of Terrorism: The Need to Abolish the Political Offense Exception', 61 *N.Y.U. L. Rev.* 654 (1986).

Scanlan, Kevin P., Note, 'The International Law Commission's First Ten Draft

Articles on the Law of the Non-Navigational Uses of International Watercourses: Do They Adequately Address All the Major Issues of Water Usage in the Middle East?', 19 *Fordham Int'l L.J.* 2180 (1996).
Schachter, Oscar, 'The Charter and the Constitution: The Human Rights Provisions in American Law', 4 *Vand. L. Rev.* 643 (1951).
—— 'International Law in Theory and Practice', 178 *Rec. des Cours* 111 (1982–V).
—— 'The Right of States to Use Armed Force', 82 *Mich L. Rev.* 1620 (1982).
—— 'Compensation for Expropriation', 78 *Am. J. Int'l L.* 121 (1984).
—— 'United Nations Law', 88 *Am. J. Int'l L.* 1 (1994).
Schiff, Ze'ev, *Israeli Preconditions for Palestinian Statehood* (Washington, DC: Washington Institute for Near East Policy, 1999).
Schmidt, Alex P., *Political Terrorism: A Research Guide To Concepts, Theories, Data Bases and Literature* (New Brunswick, NJ: Transaction Press, 1994).
Schwabach, Aaron, 'The United Nations Convention on the Law of Non-navigational Uses of International Watercourses, Customary International Law, and the Interests of Developing Upper Riparians', 33 *Tex. Int'l L. J.* 257 (1998).
Schwebel, Stephen M., 'What Weight to Conquest?', 64 *Am. J. Int'l L.* 344 (1970).
Schwelb, Egon, 'Some Aspects of International *Jus Cogens* as Formulated by the International Law Commission', 61 *Am. J. Int'l L.* 946 (1967).
Schwenk, Edmund, 'Legislative Power of the Military Occupant under Article 43, Hague Regulations', 54 *Yale L.J.* 393 (1945).
Segev, Samuel, *Crossing the Jordan* (New York: St Martin's Press, 1998).
Selth, Andrew, *Against Every Human Law: the Terrorist Threat to Diplomacy* (Rushcutters Bay, NSW, Australia; Elmsford, NY: Australian National University Press, 1988).
Setear, John K., 'Responses to Breach of a Treaty and Rationalist International Relations Theory: The Rules of Release and Remediation in the Law of Treaties and the Law of State Responsibility', 83 *Va. L. Rev.* 1 (1997).
Shah, Samira, 'On the Road to Apartheid: The Bypass Road Network in the West Bank', 29 *Colum. Human Rights L. Rev.* 221 (1997).
Shalev, Gabriela, 'Political Agreements', 16 *Iyunei Mishpat* 215 (1991).
—— 'Contract Law', in Itzhak Zamir and Sylvanie Colombo (eds), *The Law of Israel: General Surveys* (Jerusalem: Sacher Institute, 1995).
Shamgar, Meir, 'The Observance of International Law in the Administered Territories', 1 *Isr. Yb. Hum. Rts.* 262 (1971).
Shaw, Malcolm N., *International Law*, 4th edn (Cambridge: Grotius Publications, 1997).
Shaw, Stanford, *History of the Ottoman Empire and Modern Turkey* (Cambridge: Cambridge University Press, 1976).
Shehadeh, Raja, 'Can the Declaration of Principles Bring About a "Just and Lasting Peace"?', 4 *Eur. J. Int'l L.* 555 (1993).
—— *From Occupation to Interim Accords: Israel and the Palestinian Territories* (London: Kluwer Law International, 1997).
Shlaim, Avi, *The Iron Wall: Israel and the Arab World Since 1948* (New York: Norton, 1999).
Shoham, Uri, 'The Principle of Legality and the Israeli Military Government in the Territories', 153 *Mil. L. Rev.* 245 (1996).

Silverberg, Sanford R., 'Diplomatic Recognition of States in Statu Nascendi: The Case of Palestine', 6 *Tulsa J. Comp. & Int'l L.* 21 (1998).

Simma, Bruno (ed.), *The Charter of the United Nations: A Commentary* (New York: Oxford University Press, 1994).

Simon, Dan, 'The Demolition of Homes in the Israeli Occupied Territories', 19 *Yale J. Int'l L.* 1 (1994).

Sinclair, Sir Ian, *The Vienna Convention on the Law of Treaties*, 2nd edn (Manchester; Dover, NH: Manchester University Press, 1984).

Singer, Joel, 'Aspects of Foreign Relations Under the Israeli–Palestinian Agreements on Interim Self-Government Arrangements for the West Bank and Gaza', 28 *Israel L. Rev.* 268 (1994).

—— 'The Declaration of Principles on Interim Self-Government Arrangements', in *Justice*, Feb. 1994, No. 1.

—— 'The West Bank and Gaza Strip: Phase Two', in *Justice*, Dec. 1995, at 3.

Slonim, Shlomo, 'The United States and the Status of Jerusalem 1947–1984', 19 *Israel L. Rev.* 179 (1984).

Smith, Charles D., *Palestine and the Arab–Israeli Conflict*, 3rd edn (New York: St Martin's Press, 1996).

Smith, Edwin M., 'Understanding Dynamic Obligations: Arms Control Agreements', 64 *S. Cal. L. Rev.* 1549 (1991).

Sohn, Louis, 'The Human Rights Law of the Charter', 12 *Tex. Int'l L.J.* 129 (1977).

Spiro, Peter J., 'New Players on the International Stage', 2 *Hofstra L. & Pol'y Symp.* 19 (1997).

Stein, Leonard, *The Balfour Declaration* (New York: Simon & Schuster, 1961).

Stone, Julius, *Israel and Palestine: Assault on the Law of Nations* (Baltimore, MD: Johns Hopkins University Press, 1981).

Strawson, John, 'Palestine's Basic Law: Constituting New Identities Through Liberating Legal Culture', 20 *Loy. L.A. Int'l & Comp. L.J.* 411 (1998).

Sussman, Yoel, 'A Forecast of Problems in the Law of Contracts', 2 *Tel Aviv Studies in Law* 17 (1976).

Sztucki, Jerzy, Jus Cogens *and the Vienna Convention on the Law of Treaties: A Critical Appraisal* (Vienna, New York: Springer-Verlag, 1974).

Tadmor, Yoav, 'The Palestinian Refugees of 1948: The Right to Compensation and Return', 8 *Temp. Int'l & Comp. L.J.* 403 (1994).

Tamari, Salim, *Palestinian Refugee Negotiations: From Madrid to Oslo II* (Washington, DC: Institute for Palestine Studies, 1996).

Tanter, Raymond, *Rogue Regimes: Terrorism and Proliferation* (New York: St Martin's Press, 1998).

Tarlock, A. Dan, 'The Law of Equitable Apportionment Revisited, Updated, and Restated', 56 *U. Colo. L. Rev.* 381 (1985).

Telerant, Niva, 'Riparian Rights under International Law: A Study of the Israeli–Jordanian Peace Treaty', 18 *Loy. L.A. Int'l & Comp. L.J.* 175 (1995).

Tessler, Mark, *A History of the Israeli–Palestinian Conflict* (Bloomington, IN: Indiana University Press, 1994).

Tribe, Laurence H., *American Constitutional Law*, 2nd edn (Mineola, New York: Foundation Press, 1988).

Tuchman, Barbara W., *Bible and Sword: England and Palestine from the Bronze Age to Balfour* (New York: Funk & Wagnalls, 1956).

United Nations, *The Origins and Evolution of the Palestine Problem: 1917–1988* (New York: United Nations, 1990).

United Nations Office of the Special Coordination in the Occupied Territories, *Economic and Social Conditions in the West Bank and Gaza Strip* (published quarterly).

United Nations Secretariat, *Multilateral Treaties Deposited with the Secretary-General*, ST/LEG/SER. E/—(published periodically).

United States Department of State, *Country Reports on Human Rights Practices* (Washington, DC: published annually).

Usher, Graham, *Palestine in Crisis: the Struggle for Peace and Political Independence after Oslo* (London; East Haven, CT: Pluto Press, 1995).

Vagts, Detlev F., 'The Proposed Expatriation Tax—A Human Rights Violation?', 89 *Am. J. Int'l L.* 578 (1995).

van den Wijngaert, Christine, *The Political Offense Exception to Extradition: the Delicate Problem of Balancing the Rights of the Individual and the International Public Order* (Deventer, the Netherlands; Boston: Kluwer, 1980).

Vattel, Emmerich de, *Le Droit des Gens, ou Principes de la Loi Naturelle* (1758).

Verdross, Alfred and Bruno Simma, *Universelles Völkerrecht* (Berlin: Duncker und Humblot, 1976).

Vincent, R. J., *Nonintervention and International Order* (Princeton, NJ: Princeton University Press, 1974).

Virally, Michel, 'Good Faith in Public International Law', 77 *Am. J. Int'l L.* 130 (1983).

Vitoria, Francisco de, *De Indis et de Ivre Belli Relectiones* (1532), translated by John Pawley Bate (Washington: Carnegie Institution, 1917).

von Glahn, Gerhard, *Law Among Nations: An Introduction to Public International Law*, 2nd edn (New York: Macmillan, 1970).

von Mehren, Arthur Taylor, and James Russell Gordley, *The Civil Law System: An Introduction to the Comparative Study of Law*, 2nd edn (Boston: Little, Brown & Co., 1977).

Waldock, Humphrey M., 'Disputed Sovereignty on the Falkland Islands Dependencies', 25 *Brit. Y.B. Int'l L.* 331 (1948).

Walker, George K., 'Anticipatory Collective Self-Defense in the Charter Era: What the Treaties Have Said', 31 *Cornell Int'l L.J.* 321 (1998).

Wasserstein, Bernard, *The British in Palestine: The Mandatory Government and the Arab–Jewish Conflict 1917–1929*, 2nd edn (Oxford: Basil Blackwell, 1991).

Watson, Geoffrey R., 'Offenders Abroad: The Case for Nationality-Based Criminal Jurisdiction', 17 *Yale J. Int'l L.* 41 (1992).

—— 'Constitutionalism, Judicial Review, and the World Court', 34 *Harv. Int'l L.J.* 1 (1993).

—— 'The Passive Personality Principle', 28 *Texas Int'l L.J.* 1 (1993).

—— 'The Death of Treaty', 55 *Ohio St. L.J.* 781 (1994).

—— 'The Law of State Succession', in *Contemporary Practice of Public International Law* (Dobbs Ferry, New York: Oceana, 1997).

—— 'Progress for Pilgrims? An Analysis of the Holy See–Israel Fundamental

Agreement', 47 *Catholic U. L. Rev.* 497 (1998).

Weil, Prosper, 'Towards Relative Normativity in International Law', 77 *Am. J. Int'l L.* 413 (1983).

Weiner, Justus R., 'Hard Facts Meet Soft Law—The Israel–PLO Declaration of Principles and the Prospects for Peace: A Response to Katherine W. Meighan', 35 *Va. J. Int'l L.* 931 (1995).

—— 'An Analysis of the Oslo II Agreement in Light of the Expectations of Shimon Peres and Mahmoud Abbas', 17 *Mich J. Int'l L.* 667 (1996) (book review).

—— 'The Palestinian Refugees' "Right of Return" and the Peace Process', 20 *B.C. Int'l & Comp. L. Rev.* 1 (1997).

Weiss, Jeffrey, 'Terminating the Israel–PLO Declaration of Principles: Is It Legal Under International Law?', 18 *Loy. L.A. Int'l & Comp. L.J.* 109 (1995).

Wellens, Karel C. (ed.), *Resolutions and Statements of the United Nations Security Council (1946–1992)*, 2nd edn (Dordrecht; Boston; London: Martinus Nijhoff, 1993).

Westlake, John, *Chapters on the Principles of International Law* (Cambridge: Cambridge University Press, 1894).

Whitbeck, John V., 'The Road to Peace Starts in Jerusalem: The "Condominium" Solution', 45 *Catholic U. L. Rev.* 781 (1996).

White, Phillip Allen, 'The Tribal Exhaustion Doctrine: "Just Stay on the Good Roads, and You've Got Nothing to Worry About" ', 22 *Am. Indian L. Rev.* 65 (1997).

Whiteman, Marjorie M., *Digest of International Law* (Washington, DC: US Dept. of State, 1968).

Wilner, Richard, Comment, 'Nationalist Movements And The Middle East Peace Process: Exercises In Self-Determination', 1 *U.C. Davis J. Int'l L. & Pol'y* 297 (1995).

Wing, Adrien Katherine, 'Conceptualizing Violence: Present and Future Developments in International Law: Panel III: Sex and Sexuality: Violence and Culture in the New International Order: A Critical Race Feminist Conceptualization of Violence: South African and Palestinian Women', 60 *Alb. L. Rev.* 943 (1997).

Wolf, Aaron and John Ross, 'The Impact of Scarce Water Resources on the Arab–Israeli Conflict', 32 *Nat. Res. J.* 919 (1992).

Wright, Quincy, *Mandates Under the League of Nations* (Chicago, IL: University of Chicago Press, 1930).

Zamir, Itzhak, 'Political Contracts', 26 *Israel L. Rev.* 461 (1992).

Zander, Walter, *Israel and the Holy Places of Christendom* (New York: Praeger, 1971).

Zoller, Elisabeth, *La Bonne Foi en Droit International Public* (Paris: A. Pedone, 1977).

Index

Index compiled by the author